RRB NTPC

23 Solved Papers (2016-2017)

Stage I & II

- **Corporate Office :** 45, 2nd Floor, Maharishi Dayanand Marg, Corner Market, Malviya Nagar, New Delhi-110017

  Tel. : 011-49842349 / 49842350

Typeset by Disha DTP Team

Printed at : Repro Knowledgecast Limited, Thane

DISHA PUBLICATION

ALL RIGHTS RESERVED

For further information about the books from DISHA,

Log on to www.dishapublication.com or email to info@dishapublication.com

CONTENTS

RRB NTPC STAGE – II SOLVED PAPERS (2016-2017)

RRB NTPC STAGE-I SOLVED PAPER-1
Held On 28th March 2016 (Shift-1)

1. The dance form Kuchipudi originated from which part of India?
   (a) Tamil Nadu   (b) Maharashtra
   (c) Andhra Pradesh   (d) Odisha

2. The number of bicycles sold by a shopkeeper in a particular week is shown below. How many bicycles were sold from Thursday to Sunday?

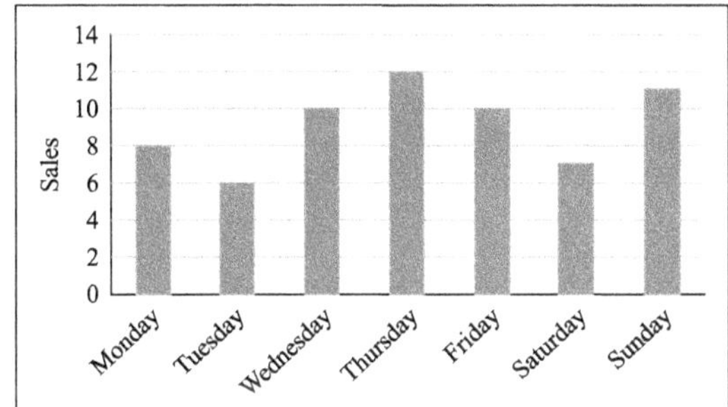

   (a) 39   (b) 38
   (c) 40   (d) 36

3. Which river used to be called the 'Sorrow of Bengal'?
   (a) Brahmaputra   (b) Hooghly
   (c) Bhagirathi   (d) Damcdar

4. How many moons does the planet Mars have?
   (a) 1   (b) 2
   (c) 3   (d) 4

5. The distance between two places, A and B, is 300 km. Two riders, on scooters start simultaneously from A and B towards each other. The distance between them after 2.5 hrs is 25 km. If the speed of one scooter is 10 km/hr more than the other, find the speed of each scooter in km/hr
   (a) 50 and 60   (b) 30 and 40
   (c) 40 and 50   (d) 60 and 70

6. If $(a^2 - b^2) \div (a + b) = 25$, find $a - b$.
   (a) 15   (d) 18
   (c) 25   (d) 30

7. What is the shape of the Earth?
   (a) Perfect hemisphere
   (b) Mostly flat
   (c) Perfect Sphere
   (d) Oblate Sphere

8. Who gave the slogan 'Do or Die' during India's freedom struggle?
   (a) Veer Savarkar
   (b) Nethaji Subhas Chandra Bose
   (c) Mahatma Gandhi
   (d) Subramanya Bharati

9. Calculate the amount on ₹ 37,500 @ 8% p.a compounded half yearly for $1\frac{1}{2}$ years.
   (a) ₹ 42,182.40   (b) ₹ 42,000
   (c) ₹ 42,120   (d) ₹ 42,812.40

10. When did Vasco da Gama land m India?
    (a) 1492   (b) 1498
    (c) 1948   (d) 1857

11. In 2014, the _________ Lok Sabha was elected.
    (a) 16th   (b) 19th
    (c) 14th   (d) 23rd

12. Arteries carry blood, that is filled with
    (a) Oxygen   (b) Carbon dioxide
    (c) Toxins   (d) Lipids

13. Pick the odd one out:
    28, 44, 68, 80, 92
    (a) 28   (b) 44
    (c) 80   (d) 92

14. Find the product of square root of 16 and square of 4?
    (a) 8   (b) 64
    (c) 16   (d) 256

15. In a company 10 employees get a salary of ₹ 36,200 each and 15 employees get a salary of ₹ 33,550 each. What is the average salary per employee?
    (a) 34,875   (b) 34,610
    (c) 27,900   (d) 36,410

16. Find the odd one out.
    1, 8, 27, 36, 125, 216
    (a) 1   (b) 8
    (c) 36   (d) 216

17. What is the desert adjoining the Thar desert called in Pakistan?
    (a) Gobi   (b) Cholistan
    (c) Sukkur   (d) Mirpur

18. Mohan is taller than Rohan but shorter than Farhan Kannan is shorter than Mohan hut taller than Rohan Shankar is taller than Rohan and Farhan. Who is the tallest?
    (a) Mohan   (b) Farhan
    (c) Shankar   (d) Kannan

19. Which of the following is true?
    (a) 1 Gigabyte = 1024 MB
    (b) 1 Gigabyte = 1,000,000 Kilobytes
    (c) 1 Gigabyte = 10,000 MB
    (d) 1 Gigabyte = 100,000 KB

20. If **COW=41**, **GOAT=43**, then **DOG=?**
    (a) 47   (b) 38
    (c) 25   (d) 26

DIRECTIONS (Qs. 21-23): *Read the following information and answer the following questions.*

Five girls are sitting in front, facing each other.
Ruhi and Manali respectively are sitting to the right and left of Urja.
Dhwani is sitting between Manali and Tanya.

21. How many girls are there between Dhwani and Ruhi?
    (a) 1   (b) 2
    (c) 3   (d) 4

22. Who is sitting in the middle?
    (a) Dhwani   (b) Urja
    (c) Manali   (d) Tanya

23. Who is sitting to the right of Tanya?
    (a) Ruhi   (b) Manali
    (c) Dhwani   (d) Urja

24. Which among the below choices can cause a Tsunami (also known as harbor wave)
    (a) Under sea earthquakes
    (b) Typhoon
    (c) Volcanic eruptions on land
    (d) Drought

25. In the following number series, one missing term is shown by '?' choose the missing term from the options below.
    6, 12, 20, 30, ?, 56, 72

    (a) 40   (b) 42
    (c) 44   (d) 48

26. Raj scored 67, 69, 78, and 88 in 4 of his subjects. What should be his score in the 5th subject so that his average equals 80?
    (a) 88   (b) 90
    (c) 96   (d) 98

27. Aruna Asaf Ali is remembered for hoisting the Indian National Congress Flag at
    (a) Non-cooperation Movement.
    (b) Civil Disobedience Movement
    (c) Self-rule Movement
    (d) Quit India Movement

28. A man buys 144 oranges for ₹360 and sells them at a gam of 10%. At what rate per dozen does he sell them?
    (a) 25   (b) 30
    (c) 33   (d) 36

29. Three bells ring at intervals of 15, 20 and 30 minutes respectively If they all ring at 11:00 a m together at what time will they next ring together?
    (a) 11:30 a.m.   (b) 12 noon
    (c) 12.30 p.m.   (d) 1.00 p.m.

30. Aman and Ajay can build a wall in 9 days and 12 days respectively. In how many days can they finish the work if they work together?
    (a) $5\dfrac{1}{7}$ (b) $11\dfrac{1}{2}$
    (c) 2   (d) 7

31. Which of the following is also called Marsh Gas?
    (a) Propane   (b) Ethane
    (c) Methane   (d) Butane

32. Five students Priyanka, Mary, Sunil, Asha and Ryan are standing in a line Priyanka and Sunil are standing ahead of Ryan Sunil is standing between Rvan and Asha. Between Sunil and Mary, Ryan is standing. Who is the first in the line?
    (a) Asha   (b) Sunil
    (c) Ryan   (d) Priyanka

33. What should be subtracted from 107.03 to get 96.4?
    (a) 1.63   (b) 10.63
    (c) 10.53   (d) 9 63

34. Julia started walking towards North direction from her house. After a while she turned left and later on turned right. She further turned right. Which direction is she facing now?
    (a) East   (b) West
    (c) North   (d) South

35. How much is one decalitre?
    (a) 10 kilolitre (b) 10 litre
    (c) 100 litre   (d) 10 centilitre

36. Anil bought 100 eggs at ₹ 6 per egg. He sold 25 eggs at 10% profit another 25 eggs at 25% loss and the balance 50 eggs at 20% profit. Find the overall profit or loss percent Anil made?
    (a) 6.25% loss   (b) 6.25% profit
    (c) 8% profit   (d) 12% loss

37. Who is thought to have invented the thermo-scope?
    (a) Galileo Galilei (b) Copernicus
    (c) Isaac Newton   (d) J. Kepler

38. In a running race, if you overtake the last but one contestant, which position are you in?
    (a) L ast   (b) Second from last
    (c) Third from last   (d) Fourth from last

39. Find the odd one out : **External Hard drive, Keyboard, Digital camera, Compact Disc**
    (a) External Hard drive
    (b) Keyboard
    (c) Digital camera
    (d) Compact Disc

40. Meena took a car loan for ₹ 275,000 from the bank. She paid an interest @ 8% p.a. and settled the account after 3 years. At the tune of settlement she gave her old scooter to the bank plus ₹335,000. What price did the scooter fetch?
    (a) 60.000   (b) 6,000
    (c) 66,000   (d) 6,600

41. A Lank can be filled by two taps X and Y in 5 hrs and 10 hrs respectively while another tap Z empties the Lank in 20 hrs. In bow many hours can the tank be filled if all 3 taps are kept open?
    (a) 5   (b) 4
    (c) 7   (d) 8

42. A man travelling by bus finds that the bus crosses 35 electric poles in 1 minute and the distance between 2 poles is 50 metres. Find the speed of the bus.
    (a) 112 km/hr.   (b) 102 km/hr.
    (c) 110 km/hr.   (d) 120 km/hr.

43. **Blunt: Sharp** as **Sow :**
    (a) Reap   (b) Seeds
    (c) Farmer   (d) Crop

44. If $\text{Cot A} = \dfrac{12}{5}$ then $(\text{Sin A} + \text{Cos A}) \therefore \text{Cosec A}$ is?
    (a) 12/5   (b) 17/5
    (c) 11/5   (d) 2

45. As the frequency of a wave increases, what happens to its wavelength?
    (a) It increases
    (b) It remains same
    (c) It decreases
    (d) There is no connection between the two

46. A seven-sided polygon is called
    (a) Nonagon   (b) Hexagon
    (c) Heptagon   (d) Octagon

47. In BRICS, which country is denoted by 'B'?
    (a) Bangladesh   (b) Belgium
    (c) Brazil   (d) Bahrain

48. **Circle: Circumference** as **Square:**
    (a) Sides   (b) Area
    (c) Perimeter   (d) Diagonal

49. Which is the capital of Cyprus?
    (a) Nicosia   (b) Polls
    (c) Lamaca   (d) Araddipou

50. If **AMERICA=1734651, INDIA=68961,** how will you write **CANADA**?
    (a) 719181   (b) 518191
    (c) 519581   (d) 715148

51. World Tuberculosis (TB) day is observed on?
    (a) 28th March   (b) 24th March
    (c) 24th May   (d) 28th May

52. A's height is 5/8th of B's height. What is the ratio of B's height to A's height?
    (a) 5:8   (b) 3:8
    (c) 5:3   (d) 8:5

53. The product of 2 numbers is 35828 and their HCF is 26. Find their LCM.
    (a) 931788   (b) 689
    (c) 1378   (d) 3583

54. Which number will be in the middle if the following numbers are arranged in descending order?

4456, 4465, 4655, 4665, 4565

(a) 4456   (b) 4465
(c) 4565   (d) 4655

55. In which State is Karla, famous for its Buddhist caves, located?

(a) Maharashtra   (b) Uttar Pradesh
(c) Uttarakhand   (d) Madhya Pradesh

56. Two-thirds of children are in the age group 1-12 years of this, if three-fourths are in the age group of 1-8 years, find the fraction of children in the age group of 9-12 years?

(a) 1/3   (b) 1/4
(c) 1/6   (d) 1/2

57. The Rowlatt Act was passed in which year?

(a) 1919   (b) 1921
(c) 1923   (d) 1916

58. Read statements 1 and 2. Also read the conclusions 3 and 4 drawn from the statements.

Statement:

1. Some birds are Donkeys.
2. All donkeys are stupid.

Conclusions:

3. All birds are stupid.
4. Some birds are stupid.

Choose which of the conclusions are right.

(a) Only 3 is correct
(b) Only 4 is correct
(c) Both 3 and 4 are correct
(d) Neither 3 nor 4 is correct

59. Which boxer is nicknamed The Real Deal'?

(a) Mike Tyson   (b) Mohammed Ali
(c) Evander Holyfield(d) Joe Louis

60. Arrange the following word in alphabetical order and find the third word?

Singer, Single, Sinister, Simple.

(a) Single   (b) Singer
(c) Sinister   (d) Simple

61. A man sells a table for ₹ 4200 at 25% loss. At what price must he sell to get a profit of 25%?

(a) 1,400   (b) 8,400
(c) 7,000   (d) 5,600

62. Who is a hacker?

(a) A person who sells goods in the street.
(b) A person who uses computers to gam un-authorized access to data.
(c) A person who only sells computers online.
(d) A person who records phone calls.

63. If your father were your mother, your mother your brother, your brother your sister and your sister your father, how would you call your sister?

(a) Father   (b) Mother
(c) Brother   (d) Sister

64. Which of the following

(a) Angles totalling 180°
(b) Angles totalling 135°
(c) Angles totalling 75°
(d) Angles totalling 90°

65. What is the measure of the two equal angles of a right isosceles triangle?

(a) 30°   (b) 45°
(c) 60°   (d) 90°

66. What percent of 1 hour is 1 minute and 12 seconds?

(a) 2%   (b) 12%
(c) 11%   (d) 1.2%

67. Mrinalini Sarabhai passed away recently. Who was she?

(a) Film Actress   (b) Scientist
(c) Classical Dancer (d) Playback Singer

68. Unscramble the letter 'CCITRKE' to from an English word and find the fifth letter of the unscrambled word?

(a) C   (b) K
(c) E   (d) I

69. What was the name of Maharana Pratap's horse?

(a) Bulbul   (b) Chetak
(c) Hayagriva   (d) Badai

70. The function of the lens in our eyes is to

(a) Cover the eyes
(b) Send messages of images to the brain
(c) Change the focal distance of the eye
(d) Protects eyes from injury.

71. In India who is the executive head of the state?
    (a) Prime Minister
    (b) The President
    (c) The Chief justice of Supreme Court
    (d) The Governor

72. Who is believed to have built the Konark Temple?
    (a) Raja Kulothunga (b) Narasimha Deva I
    (c) Vishnugopa (d) Malnpala

73. Who invented Penicillin?
    (a) Ian Fleming
    (b) Alexander Fleming
    (c) Stephen Hawking
    (d) Alexander Graham Bell

74. If **TEACHER : BOOKS, DOCTOR : ?**
    (a) Chalk (b) Cycle
    (c) Stethoscope (d) Apron

75. Which was the first satellite to orbit our Moon?
    (a) Luna 2 (b) Luna 10
    (c) Apollo 10 (d) Apollo 11

76. Find the odd one out:
    Ostrich, Crow, Pigeon, Sparrow.
    (a) Ostrich (b) Pigeon
    (c) Crow (d) Sparrow

77. Science of the study of preserved remains or traces of animals, plants, and other organisms from the remote past is called
    (a) Anthropology (b) Archaeology
    (c) Paleontology (d) Pharmacology

78. With which sport is Karnam Malleswari associated?
    (a) Tennis (b) Swimming
    (c) Athletics (d) Weightlifting

79. How many prime numbers are there between 50 and 100?
    (a) 6 (b) 10
    (c) 13 (d) 5

80. If Christmas was on Sunday in 2011, what day will it be in 2012?.
    (a) Monday (b) Tuesday
    (c) Wednesday (d) Thursday

81. Emperor Ashoka was the successor of?
    (a) Chandragupta Maurya
    (b) Bindusara
    (c) Susima
    (d) Dasharatha

DIRECTIONS (Qs. 82-84): *Amar, Babu, Cera and Diya were asked to solve a question paper with 4 multiple choice questions with choices 1,2,3,4. The answer sheet as marked by them is reproduced here.*

	Amar	Babu	Cera	Diva
Q1	2	1	1	3
Q2	4	3	2	4
Q3	3	4	3	1
Q4	3	2	2	4

Babu got all answers wrong. Amar's first two answers were definitely wrong. Diva got two answers right but her fourth answer was definitely wrong. Amar and Cera each have got only one correct answer.

82. Which of Cera's question is correct?
    (a) Q1 (b) Q2
    (c) Q3 (d) Q4

83. Whose answer to Q4 is correct?
    (a) Amar (b) Babu
    (c) Diya (d) None

84. Which two answers of Diva is correct?
    (a) Q1 and Q2 (b) Q1 and Q3
    (c) Q2 and Q3 (d) Q3 and Q4

85. If 'A' is the son of 'B' and is the father of 'C', how is 'B' related to 'C'?
    (a) Father (b) Son
    (c) Grandparent (d) Grandchild

86. Simplify $\sqrt{(1-\sin^2\theta) \div (1-\cos^2\theta)}$
    (a) Cot θ (b) Tan θ
    (c) Sec θ (d) Cosec θ

87. Atomic weight of an element is compared with which of the following to get the atomic weight of that element?
    (a) Oxygen (b) Carbon
    (c) Hydrogen (d) Nitrogen

DIRECTIONS (Qs. 88-90): *Read the following information and answer the following questions.*

In a class of 40 students, 28 can speak Tamil and 30 can speak Telugu.

All students can speak at least one of the two languages.

88. Find the number of persons who can speak only Telugu?
    (a) 8 (b) 10
    (c) 12 (d) 14

89. Find the minimum number of students who can speak both Tamil and Telugu.
(a)   12   (b)   15
(c)   18   (d)   22

90. Find the number of students who can speak only Tamil.
(a)   8   (b)   10
(c)   12   (d)   14

91. Rajiv said pointing to a girl, "She is the only daughter of the father of my sister's brother". If so how is the girl related to Rajiv?
(a)   Mother   (b)   Aunt
(c)   Sister   (d)   Sister-in-law.

92. Ram is 4 times his son's age today. Five years hence, Ram will be thrice his son's age. Find their current ages?
(a)   60,15   (b)   40,10
(c)   20,5   (d)   32,8

93. Where can you find the Golden Temple of Dambulla?
(a)   Amritsar   (b)   Sri Lanka
(c)   Indonesia   (d)   Malaysia

94. From the following which is an example of a single-celled organism?
(a)   Protozoa   (b)   Anthropods
(c)   Echinoderms   (d)   Annelids

95. Which two teams played the firs
(a)   England and Australia
(b)   England and West Indies
(c)   USA and Canada
(d)   Australia and India

96. Which of this is not a memorial to a dead person?
(a)   Bibi ka Maqbara
(b)   Taj Mahal
(c)   Charminar
(d)   Itmad Ud Daulah

97. XCVI denotes
(a)   116   (b)   496
(c)   96   (d)   84

98. When was the Indian Constitution amended for the first time?
(a)   1949   (b)   1951
(c)   1952   (d)   1953

99. Find two consecutive numbers where thrice the first number is more than twice the second number by 5.
(a)   5 and 6   (b)   6 and 7
(c)   7 and 8   (d)   9 and 10

100. Which is the smallest continent?
(a)   Australia   (b)   Antarctica
(c)   Africa   (d)   South America

HINTS & EXPLANATIONS

1. **(c)**

2. **(c)** No. of bicycles sold on :

   Thursday = 12

   Friday = 10

   Saturday = 7

   Sunday = 11

   $\therefore$ bicycles sold from Thursday to Sunday

   = 12 + 10 + 7 + 11 = 40

3. **(d)**   4.   **(b)**

5. **(a)** Let the speed of one scooter = x km/hr

   then the speed of other scooter = (x + 10) km/hr

   ATQ

   2.5 x + 2.5 $(x + 10)$ = 275

   2.5 x + 2.5 x + 25 = 275

   5 x = 250 $\Rightarrow x$ = 50 km/hr, x + 10 = 60 km/hr

   $\therefore$ The speed of each scooter is 50 km/hr and 60 km/hr

6. **(c)**

7. **(d)** The average shape of the earth is not perfect sphere, but slightly flattened out. Due to its rotation, this shape is called an oblate spheroid.

8. **(c)**

9. **(a)** As it is said that interest is compound half yearly. So, the rate of interest will be halved and time will be doubled.

   $$A = 37500\left[1 + \frac{4}{100}\right]^3$$

   $= 37500[1.04]^3 = ₹\ 42{,}182.40$

10. **(b)** Vasco da Gama, a portuguese sailor, was the first European to land in India on 17th May, 1498.

11. **(a)**   12.   **(a)**

13. **(c)** $8 \times 3 + 4 = 28$

    $8 \times 5 + 4 = 44$

    $8 \times 8 + 4 = 68$

    $8 \times 9 + 8 = 80$

$8 \times 11 + 4 = 92$

So, no. 80 is the odd one.

14. **(b)** $\sqrt{16}$ = 4 and $(4)^2$ = 16

    $\therefore$ $4 \times 16 = 64$

15. **(b)** Average salary per employee

    $$= \frac{36200 \times 10 + 33550 \times 15}{25}$$

    = 34610

16. **(c)** 1, 8, 27, 36, 125, 216
    $1^3\ 2^3\ 3^3\ \times\ 5^3\ 6^3$

    No. 36 is the odd one.

17. **(b)** Cholistan Desert is locally known as Rohi and covers the area of Bhawalpur, Punjab. It adjoins the Thar Desert extending over to Sindh and into India.

18. **(c)**

19. **(a)**

20. **(d)** COW = (3 + 15 + 23) = 41

    GOAT = (7 + 15 + 1 + 20) = 43

    $\therefore$ DOG = (4 + 15 + 7) = 26

Sol. (21-23):

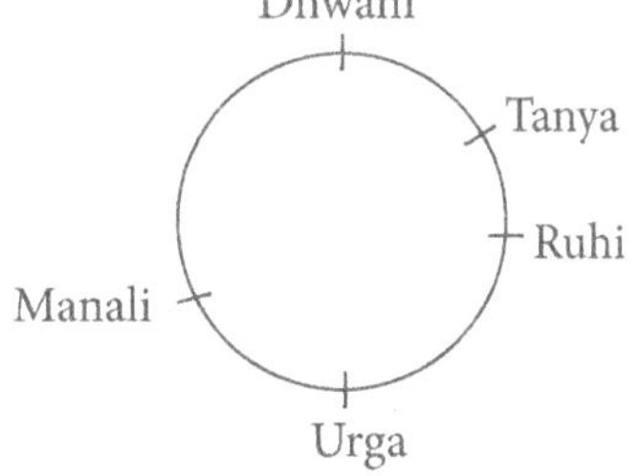

The sitting arrangement of five girls are as:

Tanya Dhwani Manali Urga Ruhi

21. **(b)** Two girls are sitting between Dhwani and Ruhi

22. **(c)** Manali is sitting in the middle

23. **(c)** Dhwani is sitting to the right of Tanya

24. **(a)**

25. **(b)** 6 12 20 30 42 56 72
    +6 +8 +10 +12 +14 +16

    $\therefore$ missing term = 42

26. (d) Let x be the score of 5th subject.
Then according to question,

$$\frac{67+69+78+88+x}{5}=80$$

$$\Rightarrow 302+x=400 \Rightarrow x=98$$

27. (d) Aruna Asaf Ali was an Indian Independence activist. She is widely remembered for hoisting the Indian National flag at Gowalia Tank Maidan in Bombay during the Quit India Movement in 1942.

28. (c) At 10% gain price of 144 orange

$$=\frac{360\times110}{100}=396$$

$$\therefore \text{ rate per dozen } =\frac{396}{12}=33$$

29. (b) The time when the bells will ring together can be calculated by taking LCM of 15, 20 and 30 = 60 minutes
$\therefore$ they will ring at 12 noon.

30. (a) Let x be the no. of days in which Aman and Ajay can build a wall together
Aman's one day's work = 1/9
Ajay's one day's work = 1/12

$$\therefore \frac{x}{9}+\frac{x}{12}=1 \Rightarrow \frac{7x}{36}=1 \Rightarrow x=\frac{36}{7}=5\frac{1}{7}$$

31. (c)

32. (d) The order in which the students are standing in a line is:
Priyanka
Asha
Sunil
Ryan
Mary

33. (b) $107.03 - 96.4 = 10.63$

34. (a)

Julia is facing East now.

35. (b)

36. (b) Initial cost of 100 eggs = 600

$$25 \text{ eggs at 10\% profit } =\frac{150\times110}{100}=165$$

$$25 \text{ eggs at 25\% loss } =\frac{150\times75}{100}=112.5$$

50 eggs at 20% profit

$$=\frac{300\times120}{100}=360$$

Total cost = 165 + 112.5 + 360 = 637.5
$\therefore$ percentage profit

$$=\frac{637.5-600}{600}\times100=6.25\%$$

37. (a)

38. (b) On overtaking the last but one contestant we occupy the same place i.e., second from last.

39. (b)

40. (b) Amount after 3 year

$$=\frac{275000\times8\times3}{100}+275000$$

$$= 66000 + 275000 = 341000$$

$\therefore$ price of scooter = 341000 – 335000
$= 6000$

41. (b) Let x be the hours in which the tank is failed then

$$\frac{x}{5}+\frac{x}{10}-\frac{x}{20}=1 \Rightarrow \frac{3x}{10}-\frac{x}{20}=1$$

$$\Rightarrow 5x=20 \Rightarrow x=4$$

42. (b) Total distance between 35 poles = 34 × 50 metres
Time = 1 min

$$\therefore \text{ speed } =\frac{34\times50}{60}=\frac{85}{3}\text{m/s}$$

$$\Rightarrow \text{ speed } =\frac{85}{3}\times\frac{18}{5}=102\text{ km/hr}$$

43. (a)

44. (b) $(\sin A + \cos A) \times \operatorname{cosec} A = \dfrac{\sin A + \cos A}{\sin A}$

$$=(1+\cot A)=\left(1+\frac{12}{5}\right)=\frac{17}{5}$$

45. (c)

46. (c) A seven-sided polygon is called Heptagon.

47. (c)

48. (c) Circle : Circumference {Perimeter of circle}
$\therefore$ Square : Perimeter

49. **(a)**

50. **(b)** AMERICA = 1734651

INDIA = 68961

Comparing the values in above examples

CANADA = 518191

51. **(b)**

52. **(d)** ATQ $A : B = 5 : 8$

$\therefore$ $B : A = 8 : 5$

53. **(c)** The product of two numbers is equal to the product of the their LCM and HCF

$\therefore$ $LCM = \dfrac{35828}{26} = 1378$

54. **(c)** After arranging the numbers in descending order

4665, 4655, 4565, 4465, 4456

$\therefore$ the no. in the middle is 4565.

55. **(a)**

56. **(c)** Fraction of age group of 1-8 $= \dfrac{2}{3} \times \dfrac{3}{4} = \dfrac{1}{2}$

$\therefore$ Fraction of age group of 9-12

$= \dfrac{2}{3} - \dfrac{1}{2} = \dfrac{1}{6}$

57. **(a)**   **58.** **(b)**   **59.** **(c)**

60. **(a)** Simple, Singer, Single, Sinister

Hence the third word is Single.

61. **(c)** Actual price of table $= 4200 \times \dfrac{100}{75} = 5600$

For 25% profit price of table

$= 5600 \times \dfrac{125}{100} = 7000$

62. **(b)**

63. **(a)** Father, As sister = father

64. **(a)**

65. **(b)** Since the triangle is right isosceles triagle

$\therefore$ one angle is 90° and other two angle are equal.

Hence, measure of two equal angles

$= \dfrac{90}{2} = 45$ each

66. **(a)** Required percentage $= \dfrac{72}{3600} \times 100 = 2\%$

67. **(c)**

68. **(b)** The word formed is CRICKET

$\therefore$ fifth letter is K.

69. **(b)**

70. **(c)**

71. **(a)** The prime minister acts as the head of the executive and is responsible for running the Union Government.

72. **(b)** Konark Sun Temple is believed to have been built in the 13th century C.E. The temple was believed to be built by the King Narasimha Deva I from the Eastern Ganga Dynasty between 1238-1250 C.E.

73. **(b)**   **74.** **(c)**   **75.** **(b)**   **76.** **(a)**   **77.** **(c)**

78. **(d)**

79. **(b)** No. of prime numbers between 50-100 is 10.

80. **(b)**

81. **(b)**

Sol. (82-84):

	Amar	Babu	Cera	Diva
Q_1	×	×	×	✓
Q_2	×	×	✓	×
Q_3	×	×	×	✓
Q_4	✓	×	×	×

82. **(b)**   **83.** **(a)**   **84.** **(b)**

85. **(c)** B (Grand parent)

|

A (Father)

|

C (Son)

86. **(a)** $\sqrt{(1 - \sin^2 \theta) \div (1 - \cos^2 \theta)} = \sqrt{\cos^2 \theta \div \sin^2 \theta}$

$= \sqrt{\cot^2 \theta} = \cot \theta$

87. **(c)**

Sol. (88-90):

Let n (Tam) = 28

n (Tel) = 30

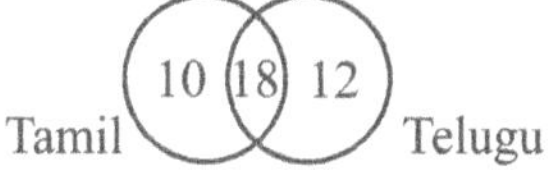

Now $n(\text{Tam} \cup \text{Tel}) = 28 + 30 - n(\text{Tam} \cap \text{Tel})$

$40 = 28 + 30 - n(\text{Tam} \cap \text{Tel})$

$\Rightarrow \quad n(\text{Tam} \cap \text{Tel}) = 58 - 40 = 18$

88. (c)

89. (c)

90. (b) $28 - 18 = 10$

91. (c) The girl is the sister of Rajiv.

92. (b) Let x be Ram's age

and y be his son's age

Now, ATQ

$$x = 4y \qquad ....(1)$$
$$x + 5 = 3(y + 5) \qquad ....(2)$$

From (1) and (2)

$$y = 10$$
$$x = 4(10) = 40$$

93. (b) Dambulla Cave temple, also known as the Golden Temple of Dambulla, is a world heritage site in Sri Lanka. It is the largest best preserved cave temple complex in Sri Lanka.

94. (a)

95. (c)

96. (c)

97. (c) $X = 10$

$C = 100$

$V = 5$

$I = 1$

$\therefore \; X\,C\,V\,I = 96$

98. (b)

99. (c) Let the two consecutive no.s be x and $(x + 1)$

ATQ

$$3x = 2(x + 1) + 5$$
$$3x = 2x + 7$$
$$x = 7$$

$\therefore \;$ the no.s are 7, 8

100.(a)

1. Which Indian king used naval power to conquer parts of East Asia?
   (a) Akbar
   (b) Krishna deva Raya
   (c) Rajendra Chola
   (d) Shivaji

2. Pollination by wind is called?
   (a) Hydrophily
   (b) Pollinophily
   (c) Anemophily
   (d) Herbophily

3. Simplify $\sqrt{50} + \sqrt{18} - \sqrt{8}$
   (a) $8\sqrt{2}$
   (b) $7\sqrt{2}$
   (c) $6\sqrt{2}$
   (d) $5\sqrt{2}$

4. If $a = \times$, $b = \div$ and $c = +$, find the value of $[7a5c1]b6$
   (a) 4
   (b) 6
   (c) 5/3
   (d) 7

5. Which revolutionary took his own life?
   (a) Khudiram Bose
   (b) Rash Behari Bose
   (c) Bhagat Singh
   (d) Chandrashekhar Azad

6. After allowing a discount of 20% on Marked price Kishore makes a profit of 12%. What percentage is the Marked price above the Cost price?
   (a) 40%
   (b) 32%
   (c) 25%
   (d) 8%

7. Punched card is also called
   (a) Hollerith card
   (b) Video card
   (c) Sound card
   (d) Accelerator card

8. What smallest number should be added to the sum of squares of 15 and 14, so that the resulting number is a perfect square?
   (a) 17
   (b) 20
   (c) 11
   (d) 9

9. The ratio between the weights of gold and silver in an alloy is 17:3. If the weight of silver in the alloy is 2.7gm, find the weight of | gold in the alloy?
   (a) 12.6 gm
   (b) 15.3 gm
   (c) 18 gm
   (d) 21.2 gm

10. where was paper invented?
    (a) China
    (b) India
    (c) Zambia
    (d) Germany

11. Where is the Island of Seychelles located?
    (a) Indian Ocean
    (b) Pacific Ocean
    (c) Atlantic Ocean
    (d) The Southern Ocean

12. Find the odd one out: **Chicken pox, Rubella, Flu, Meningitis**
    (a) Chicken pox
    (b) Rubella
    (c) Flu
    (d) Meningitis

13. Find the value of:
$$\frac{(0.0112 - 0.0012) \text{ of } 0.14 + 0.25 \times 0.2}{0.02 \times 0.01}$$
    (a) 257
    (b) 25.7
    (c) 2.57
    (d) 0.0257

14. A points to B and says to a lady C "His mother is the only daughter of your father". If so, how is C related to B?
    (a) Mother
    (b) Daughter
    (c) Grandmother
    (d) Son

15. From where was Mangalyaan launched?
    (a) Chennai
    (b) Sriharikota
    (c) Trombay
    (d) Gopalpur, on sea

16. The sum of two digits of a number is 10. If the digits are interchanged, then its value increases by 18. Find the number.
    (a) 46
    (b) 64
    (c) 19
    (d) 28

17. In a certain code language. North = West, South-East. East-North, which direction does the sun rise?
    - (a) East
    - (b) West
    - (c) North
    - (d) South

18. **CAT : MOUSE as SNAKE :**
    - (a) Reptile
    - (b) Mongoose
    - (c) Hole
    - (d) Poison

19. If $\triangle O = 52$, $\square\# = 43$ what is $\#\triangle\square$?
    - (a) 523
    - (b) 245
    - (c) 432
    - (d) 354

20. Name the official language of Brazil?
    - (a) Portuguese
    - (b) German
    - (c) Italian
    - (d) Brazilian

21. Which number will fit both the series of numbers?
    Series A: 1, 4, 9... Series B: 1, 8, 27...
    - (a) 42
    - (b) 36
    - (c) 64
    - (d) 25

22. Which of the following is the name of a medieval Indian book on mathematics?
    - (a) Vastushastra
    - (b) Leelavati
    - (c) Panchadashi
    - (d) Roopmati

23. Din-i-llahi was promoted by
    - (a) Babur
    - (b) Bahadur Shah
    - (c) Akbar
    - (d) Humayun

24. If 1/4th of the wall is painted blue, 1/2 is painted yellow and remaining 3 m is painted white, what is the length of the wall?
    - (a) 10
    - (b) 8
    - (c) 16
    - (d) 12

25. The runs scored by two batsmen over 7 matches are given below. Which batsman's average was better?

Batsman 1	42	51	09	78	63	20	12
Batsman 2	30	22	91	76	84	11	07

   - (a) Batsman 1 - 39.3
   - (b) Batsman 1 - 45.9
   - (c) Batsman 1 - 43.2
   - (d) Batsman 2 - 45.9

26. In which year was RBI nationalized?
    - (a) 1969
    - (b) 1947
    - (c) 1949
    - (d) 1974

27. Which is the only organ in the human body that can regrow/regenerate?
    - (a) Spleen
    - (b) Brain
    - (c) Liver
    - (d) Pancreas

28. which is the largest non-polar desert in the World?
    - (a) Kalahari
    - (b) Gobi
    - (c) Sahara
    - (d) Great Australian

29. Who wrote the National song of India?
    - (a) Rabindranath Tagore
    - (b) Bankim Chandra Chatterjee
    - (c) Mohammed Iqbal
    - (d) Chitragupta

30. If **3:27:: 5:?**
    - (a) 25
    - (b) 125
    - (c) 250
    - (d) 625

31. Find the value of $\sin^2 30\cos^2 45 + 4\tan^2 30 + (1/2)\sin^2 90 - 2\cos^2 90 + 1/24$
    - (a) 3
    - (b) 4
    - (c) 2
    - (d) 1

32. Where in the human body can you find the islets of Langerhans?
    - (a) Small intestine
    - (b) Pancreas
    - (c) Stomach
    - (d) Heart

33. where can you find the Kunchikal waterfalls?
    - (a) Kerala
    - (b) Karnataka
    - (c) Andhra Pradesh
    - (d) Telangana

34. Which single discount will be equal to two successive discounts of 12% and 5%?
    - (a) 17%
    - (b) 8.5%
    - (c) 16.4%
    - (d) 15.2%

35. Which of the following gases are responsible for the greenhouse gas effect on Earth?
    - (a) Water Vapour and Carbon dioxide
    - (b) Carbon dioxide and Nitrogen
    - (c) Carbon dioxide and Methane
    - (d) Ozone and Methane

36. If **ALPHA = 36, BETA = 26**, then **DELTA = ?**
    - (a) 38
    - (b) 31
    - (c) 40
    - (d) 36

37. What is the technology used in a compact disc?
    - (a) Electrical
    - (b) Laser
    - (c) Electro magnetic
    - (d) Aeronautical

38. In a camp 180 students had ration for 20 days. How many students should leave the camp if the ration should last for 25 days?
    - (a) 36
    - (b) 24
    - (c) 28
    - (d) 40

39. Fill in the blanks: $\sin A = \underline{\quad} \times \cos A$
  (a) sin A
  (b) tan A
  (c) cot A
  (d) cos A

40. If x is a prime number, LCM of x and its successive number would be
  (a) x
  (b) $x + 1$
  (c) $x(x + 1)$
  (d) $\dfrac{x}{x+1}$

41. Jimmy Wales and Larry Sanger are associated with?
  (a) Wikipedia
  (b) Google
  (c) Whatsapp
  (d) Facebook

42. The average age of 27 students of a class is 22. If the age of the teacher is also added to their ages, then the average increases by one. Find the age of the teacher.
  (a) 42
  (b) 48
  (c) 50
  (d) 52

43. Which is the brightest star in our night sky?
  (a) Canopus
  (b) Sirius A
  (c) Vega
  (d) Spica

44. Madhubani painting style is native to which state?
  (a) Orissa
  (b) Andhra Pradesh
  (c) Bihar
  (d) Madhya Pradesh

45. A certain sum when invested at 5% interest compounded annually for 3 years yields an interest of ₹ 2,522. Find the Principal?
  (a) ₹ 12,522
  (b) ₹ 15,200
  (c) ₹ 16,000
  (d) ₹ 17,200

46. if **SUN=108, MOON=114** what is **STAR=?**
  (a) 120
  (b) 116
  (c) 122
  (d) 128

47. If **1 = 2, 3 = 6, 4 = 8,** and **+ = –,** what would be the value of **41 + 34 + 13 =?**
  (a) –88
  (b) 88
  (c) 12
  (d) –12

48. Which of the following is always present in organic compounds?
  (a) Carbon
  (b) Nitrogen
  (c) Sulphur
  (d) Potassium

49. In an equilateral triangle ABC, D, E, F are the mid points of AB, BC and AC respectively. The quadrilateral BEFD is a
  (a) Square
  (b) Rectangle
  (c) Parallelogram
  (d) Rhombus

DIRECTIONS (Qs. 50-52): *The below table gives rice production in each year. Read and answer the following questions.*

Year	Production in tons
2005	325
2006	438
2007	429
2008	258
2009	495

50. What was the decline in production in year 2008 compared to 2007?
  (a) 40%
  (b) 51%
  (c) 67%
  (d) 45%

51. What is the increased percentage of production in 2009 compared to year 2005?
  (a) 38.1%
  (b) 29.2%
  (c) 52.3%
  (d) 46.3%

52. What was the average production of rice in the period 2005-2009?
  (a) 378
  (b) 389
  (c) 399
  (d) 412

53. Below are given statements followed by some conclusions. You have to take the given statements to be true even if they seem to be at variance with the commonly known facts.
Statements:
1. Health insurance in India eaters only to rich.
2. Health insurance sector should be regulated.
Conclusion
I. Health insurance sector should be nationalized
II. Health insurance is not required for the poor.
Decide which of the given conclusions logically follow(s) from the given statements.
  (a) Neither I nor II follow
  (b) Only conclusion I follows
  (c) Either I or II follow
  (d) Only conclusion II follow's

54. If Reena sold 12 mobile phones for ₹ 188,160 which cost ₹ 14,056 per phone, what was the total profit made by her?
  (a) ₹ 19,488
  (b) ₹ 17,621
  (c) ₹ 21,014
  (d) ₹ 18,958

55. Sita told her friend Gita "I am leaving today and will reach Mumbai tomorrow for my exams starting the day after tomorrow, which is Friday". What day is tomorrow in this conversation?
  (a) Wednesday   (b) Thursday
  (c) Tuesday   (d) Saturday

56. The perimeter of a rectangle is 28cm. If the length is 5/2 times its breadth, find the length and breadth of the rectangle.
  (a) 9 & 5   (b) 10 & 4
  (c) 6 & 7   (d) 11 & 3

57. What comes next in the series?
  B, D, H, N?
  (a) V   (b) P
  (c) S   (d) W

58. Which country has won maximum number of World cup titles in football?
  (a) Italy   (b) Argentina
  (c) Brazil   (d) France

59. Who was the first to score a perfect 10 in Olympics in gymnastics?
  (a) Nadia Comaneci
  (b) Daniela Silivas
  (c) Alexander Dityatin
  (d) Mary Lou Retton

60. Below are given statements followed by some conclusions. You have to take the given statements to be true even if they seen to be at variance with the commonly known facts.
  Statements:
  (1) Because of motor vehicles like cars, pollution has increased manifold.
  (2) Respiratory diseases are increasing due to pollution.
  Conclusions:
  I.   If cars are were not there pollution would be nil.
  II. Doctors earn a lot due to pollution.
  Decide which of the given conclusions logically follow(s) from the given statements.
  (a) Either I or II follow
  (b) Neither I nor II follow
  (c) Only conclusion I follows
  (d) Only conclusion II follows

DIRECTIONS (Qs. 61-63): *Read the following information and answer the following questions below.*

In a class of 90 students, 80 students like burger or pizza. 62 like burger and 56 like pizza.

61. How many don't like burger?
  (a) 18   (b) 28
  (c) 38   (d) 48

62. How many like neither burger nor pizza?
  (a) 10   (b) 28
  (c) 16   (d) 14

63. How many like both burger and pizza?
  (a) 24   (b) 38
  (c) 32   (d) 18

64. If **COW÷CW = 13**, what might be the value of **COW**?
  (a) 272   (b) 195
  (c) 323   (d) 387

65. Find the mean of the first 6 prime numbers?
  (a) 14/3   (b) 3
  (c) 41/6   (d) 13/2

66. Which is the largest fresh water lake in the World?
  (a) Lake Victoria   (b) Lake Erie
  (c) Lake Superior   (d) Lake Ontario

67. Which of the following is called Aurum?
  (a) Bronze   (b) Gold
  (c) Silver   (d) Copper

68. If A's sister's husband is B's mother-in-law's son-in-law, how is A related to B?
  (a) Father   (b) Father-in-law
  (c) Brother-in-law   (d) Husband

69. Simplify: $\left[2\dfrac{1}{3}-1\dfrac{1}{2}\right]$ of $\dfrac{3}{5}+1\dfrac{2}{5}\div 2\dfrac{1}{3}$
  (a) $\dfrac{1}{10}$ (b) $\dfrac{3}{10}$
  (c) $1\dfrac{1}{10}$ (d) 1

70. 'Queensberry rules' is the code followed in which sport?
  (a) Tennis   (b) Cricket
  (c) Boxing   (d) Equestrian

71. World environment day is observed on
(a) February 28   (b) May 16
(c) June 05   (d) September 12

72. 'E' is related to 'BH' in the same way as 'N' is related to?
(a) IP   (b) KQ
(c) LP   (d) DE

73. If angles of a quadrilateral are in the ratio 3:5:9:13, find the largest angle?
(a) 165   (b) 180
(c) 156   (d) 190

74. Headquarters of UNESCO is located at
(a) Moscow   (b) New York
(c) London   (d) Paris

75. who was the last Mughal Emperor?
(a) Babur   (b) Jehangir
(c) Akbar   (d) Bahadur Shah

DIRECTIONS (Qs. 76-78): *Read the following information and answer the following questions below.*

Bindu is standing exactly in the middle of a line of girls. Asha is 6th to the left of Bindu and Ritu is 16th to Bindu's right.

76. What is Bindu's position in the line?
(a) 11   (b) 14
(c) 16   (d) 17

77. What should be the minimum number of girls in the line?
(a) 22   (b) 28
(c) 33   (d) 32

78. What is Asha's position in the line?
(a) 22   (b) 12
(c) 18   (d) 11

79. At a telephone exchange, three phones ring at intervals of 20 sec, 24 sec and 30 seconds. If they ring together at 11:25 a.m, when will they next ring together?
(a) 11:29 a m.   (b) 11:27 a.m.
(c) 11:51 am.   (d) 12:29 p.m.

80. The diagonal of a rhombus is 8m and 6m respectively. Find its area.
(a) 48 sq.m.   (b) 24 sq.m.
(c) 12 sq.m.   (d) 96 sq.m.

81. With which sport is the term 'Tee' connected?
(a) Hockey   (b) Polo
(c) Golf   (d) Badminton

82. Which of the following is reared for its fleece/fiber?
(a) Alpaca   (b) Alabama
(c) Apache   (d) Alluvial

83. Below are given statements followed by some conclusions. You have to take the given statements to be true even if they seem to be at variance with the commonly known facts.

Statements:
(1) Some kids are clever.
(2) Some kids are players.

Conclusion:
I. Some players are clever
II. Some clever kids are players.

Decide which of the given conclusions logically follow (s) from the given statements.
(a) Only conclusion I follows
(b) Only conclusion II follows
(c) Both conclusion I and II follows
(d) Neither conclusion I nor II follows

84. If cost price of 5 cars is equal to selling price of 4 cars. Find the percentage of profit or loss
(a) 10% Profit   (b) 10% Loss
(c) 25% Profit   (d) 25% Loss

85. Divide 13,680 in three parts such that 1st part is 3/5th of the third part and the ratio between 2nd and 3rd part is 4:7. How much is the first part?
(a) 3780   (b) 6300
(c) 3600   (d) 4800

86. Geetha weighs 11.235 kg. Her sister weighs 1.4 times her weight. Find their combined weight?
(a) 15.729 kg.   (b) 25.964 kg.
(c) 26.964 kg.   (d) 26.946 kg.

87. Granite is an example of
(a) Metamorphic rock   (b) Sedimentary rock
(c) Igneous rock   (d) Artificial stone

88. Which of the following is the currency of Thailand?
(a) Rupee   (b) Ringgit
(c) Baht   (d) Yuan

89. Simplify $\dfrac{81x^2 - 49y^2}{9x + 7y}$
(a) $9x + 7y$ (b) $9x - 7y$
(c) $9x$ (d) $7y$

90. Which of the following is a land locked country?

(a) Azerbaijan

(b) Kazakhstan

(c) Pakistan

(d) Bangladesh

91. If ! = ÷, # = +, ^ = ×, the calculate the value of **32!4^7#5**

(a) 58   (b) 61

(c) 64   (d) 55

92. Smita can finish a work in 12 days and Sam can finish the same work in 9 days. After working together for 4 days they both leave the job. What is the fraction of unfinished work?

(a) 1/2   (b) 7/9

(c) 2/9   (d) 1/4

93. what did Edward Jenner pioneer?

(a) Vaccination

(b) Electrocution

(c) Dialysis

(d) Open heart surgery

94. Who is called the Frontier Gandhi?

(a) Muhammad All Jinnah

(b) Mahatma Gandhi

(c) Khan Abdul Ghaffar Khan

(d) Bal Gangadhar Tilak

95. What is the minimum age for getting elected to the Lok Sabha?

(a) 18   (b) 21

(c) 16   (d) 25

96. Azhar can complete a journey in 10 hours. He travels the first half of the journey at a speed of 21km/hr. and the balance at 24km/hr. Find the total distance in km?

(a) 234   (b) 225

(c) 224   (d) 232

97. A deep crack in a glacier is called

(a) A crevice   (b) A crevasse

(c) A crack   (d) A cleft

98. Which number will fit in '?' place in the following series? **2, ?, 12, 20, 30, 42**

(a) 2   (b) 4

(c) 6   (d) 8

99. Where is the headquarters of Interpol located?

(a) Paris   (b) London

(c) Lyon   (d) Brussels

100. Ram and Rahim standing at a distance of 680m run towards each other at a speed of 8m/sec and 9m/sec respectively. After how long will they meet?

(a) 17 sec   (b) 24 sec

(c) 40 sec   (d) 36 sec

HINTS & EXPLANATIONS

1. (c) Rajendra Chola was considered as one of the greatest emperors of India. During his reign, he extended the influence of the Chola empire to the banks of the river Ganga in North India and across the Indian ocean to the West and South East Asia, making the Chola Empire one of the most powerful empires of India.

2. (c)

3. (c) $\sqrt{50} + \sqrt{18} - \sqrt{8} = 5\sqrt{2} + 3\sqrt{2} - 2\sqrt{2}$
$= 6\sqrt{2}$

4. (b) $[7 \times 5 + 1] \div 6$
$36 \div 6 = 6$

5. (d) Chandrashekhar Azad was a fearless freedom fighter and a daring revolutionary who took his own life by shooting himself after being left with the last bullet in an encounter against the British.

6. (a) Let marked price = 100

After 20% discount $100 \times \dfrac{80}{100} = 80$

For profit of 12% cost price $= 80 \times \dfrac{100}{112} = 71$

$\therefore$ Percentage of marked price above cost price

$= \dfrac{100 - 71}{71} = 40\%$

7. (a)

8. (b) Sum of squares of 15 and 14 $= 225 + 196 = 421$
Nearest perfect square to 421 is 441
$\therefore 441 - 421 = 20$ is the required number

9. (b) Let the weight of gold in the alloy be $= x$

Then ATQ, $\dfrac{x}{2.7} = \dfrac{17}{3}$

$\Rightarrow 3x = 45.9$
$\Rightarrow x = 15.3$ gm

10. (a)

11. (a) Seychelles, an archipelago country, is located in the Indian Ocean to the northeast of Madagascar and about 1,600 km east of Kenya.

12. (d)

13. (a) $\dfrac{.01 \times .14 + .25 \times .2}{.02 \times .01} = \dfrac{\dfrac{14}{10000} + \dfrac{500}{10000}}{\dfrac{2}{10000}}$

$= \dfrac{514}{2} = 257$

14. (a) B's mother is the only daughter of C's father means C is the mother of B.

15. (b)

16. (a) Let the two digits be x (ten's place) and y (units place)
ATQ $x + y = 10$ ...(1)
Also $10y + x - 10x - y = 18$
$\Rightarrow 9y - 9x = 18$
$\Rightarrow y - x = 2$ ...(2)
From (1) and (2)
$x = 4$ and $y = 6$
$\therefore$ The required no. is 46

17. (c) Sun rises in North as East = North

18. (b)

19. (d)

$$\begin{array}{cccc} \Delta & O \ \Box & & \# \\ \uparrow & \uparrow \ \uparrow & & \uparrow \\ 5 & 2 \ \ 4 & & 3 \end{array}$$

$\therefore \# \ \Delta \ \Box = 354$

20. (a)

21. (c) Series A = 1, 4, 9, 16, 25, 36, 49, 64 ...
Series B = 1, 8, 27, 64 .....
Both the series have 64 in common

22. (b) Written in 1150, the Leelavati is Indian mathematician Bhaskara II's treatise on mathematics. It is the first volume of his main work, the *Siddhanta Shiromani*, alongside the *Bijaganita*, the *Grahaganita* and the *Goladhyaya*. His book on arithmetic is the source of interesting legends that assert that it was written for his daughter, Lilavati.

23. (c)

24. (d) Let the length of the wall $= x$ mts.
The remaining part of the wall

$$= x - \left(\frac{x}{4} + \frac{x}{2} \right)$$

$$= \frac{x}{4}$$

$$\Rightarrow \quad \frac{x}{4} = 3\text{m} \Rightarrow x = 12 \text{ m}$$

25. (d) Average of Batsman 1

$$= \frac{42 + 51 + 9 + 78 + 63 + 20 + 12}{7} = 39.2$$

Average of Batsman 2

$$= \frac{30 + 22 + 91 + 76 + 84 + 11 + 7}{7} = 45.8$$

Clearly average of Batsman 2 is better.

26. (c) The Reserve Bank of India was founded on 1st April, 1935 to respond to economic troubles after the First World War. But it was nationalized with effect from 1st January, 1949 on the basis of the Reserve Bank of India Act, 1948. After being nationalized, all shares in the capital were deemed transferred to the Central Government on payment of a suitable compensation.

27. (c) **28. (c)** **29. (b)**

30. (b) $3 : 27 :: 5 : 125$

      $\uparrow$ $\uparrow$

     $(3)^3$ $(5)^3$

31. (c) $\sin^2 30 \cos^2 45 + 4 \tan^2 30 + \left(\frac{1}{2} \right) \sin^2 90$

$$- 2 \cos^2 90 + \frac{1}{24}$$

$$= \frac{1}{4} \times \frac{1}{2} + 4 \left(\frac{1}{3} \right) + \frac{1}{2}(1) - 2(0) + \frac{1}{24}$$

$$= \frac{1}{8} + \frac{4}{3} + \frac{1}{2} + \frac{1}{24} = \frac{48}{24} = 2$$

32. (b) **33. (b)**

34. (c) Let 100 be the no. on which the discount is applied

On first discount we get $100 \times \dfrac{88}{100} = 88$

On second discount $88 \times \dfrac{95}{100} = 83.6$

$\therefore$ the single discount $= 100 - 83.6 = 16.4\%$

35. (*) Greenhouse gasses are CO_2, CH_4, water vapor, nitrous oxide, chlorofluro carbons (CFC) Hydrofluro carbons (HFCs) & sulfur hexafluro-ride (SF_6).

36. (c)   ALPHA $= (1 + 12 + 16 + 8 + 1) - 2 = 36$

           BETA $= (2 + 5 + 20 + 1) - 2 = 26$

    $\therefore$ DELTA $= (4 + 5 + 12 + 20 + 1) - 2 = 40$

37. (b)

38. (a) Let x be the no. of students who remain in the camp.

Then $180 \times 20 = x \times 25 \Rightarrow x = 144$

$\therefore$ no. of students who left $= 180 - 144 = 36$

39. (b) $\sin A = \tan A \times \cos A$

$$= \frac{\sin A}{\cos A} \times \cos A = \sin A$$

40. (c) LCM of any two numbers when one being the prime no. is the product of those numbers.

$\therefore$ LCM of x and $(x + 1) = x(x + 1)$

41. (a) Jimmy Wales and Larry Sanger are said to be founder of Wikipedia. Jimmy Wales along with Larry Sanger launched Wikipedia—a free, open content encyclopedia on January 15, 2001.

42. (c) Total age of students $= 27 \times 22 = 594$

On adding age of teacher total age $= 28 \times 23 = 644$

$\therefore$ age of teacher $= 644 - 594 = 50$

43. (b) **44. (c)**

45. (c)   CI $= P \left[1 + \dfrac{r}{100} \right]^n - P$

$$2522 = P \left(\left[1 + \frac{5}{100} \right]^3 - 1 \right)$$

$$2522 = P(1.157 - 1)$$

$$\Rightarrow \quad P = \frac{2522}{157} \simeq ₹16000$$

46. (b) SUN $= (19 + 21 + 14) \times 2 = 108$

MOON $= (13 + 15 + 15 + 14) \times 2 = 114$

$\Rightarrow$ STAR $= (19 + 20 + 1 + 18) \times 2 = 116$

47. (d) $41 + 34 + 13 = ?$

On equating the value the equation becomes

$82 - 68 - 26 = -12$

48. (a) **49. (c)**

50. **(a)** Decline in production $= \dfrac{429-258}{429}\times100$

$= 39.86 \approx 40\%$

51. **(c)** Required percentage $= \dfrac{495-325}{325}\times100$

$= 52.3\%$

52. **(b)** Average production of rice

$= \dfrac{325+438+429+258+495}{5}$

$= \dfrac{1945}{5} = 389$

53. **(a)**

54. **(a)** SP of 12 phones $= ₹\ 188160$

CP of 12 phones $= 14056 \times 12 = ₹\ 168672$

$\therefore$ total profit $= 188160 - 168672 = ₹\ 19488$

55. **(b)** Day after tomorrow is Friday

$\Rightarrow$ Tomorrow is Thursday

56. **(b)** Let the length of breadth be 'x'

Length then breadth $= \dfrac{5x}{2}$

ATQ $2\left(x+\dfrac{5x}{24}\right)=28$

$14x = 56 \Rightarrow x = 4$

$\therefore$ breadth $= 4$ and length $= \dfrac{5\times4}{2} = 10$

57. **(a)** $\underset{+1}{B}\ \underset{+3}{D}\ \underset{+5}{H}\ \underset{+7}{N}\ \underline{V}$

58. **(c)**

59. **(a)** At age 14, Romanian gymnast Nadia Comaneci became the first woman to score a perfect 10 in an Olympic gymnastics event at the 1976 Olympic Games. Her performance at the 1976 Olympics redefined both her sport and audiences' expectations of female athletes.

60. **(b)**

Sol. (61-63):

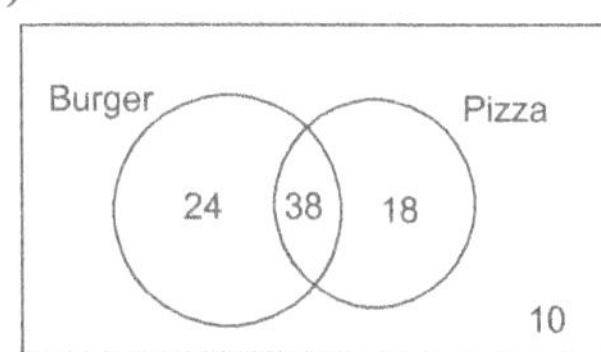

$n(B) = 62$ {Who like burger}

$n(P) = 56$ {who like pizza}

$n(B \cap P) = 118 - 80 = 38$

61. **(b)** $18 + 10 = 28$

62. **(a)** 10

63. **(b)** 38

64. **(b)** Among the options given only 195 is divisible by 13

$\therefore$ COW $= 195$

65. **(c)** Mean of first 6 prime numbers

$= \dfrac{2+3+5+7+11+13}{6} = \dfrac{41}{6}$

66. **(c)**   **67.** **(b)**

68. **(d)** Let X be A's sister

Y be X's husband

and Z be Y's mother

Then

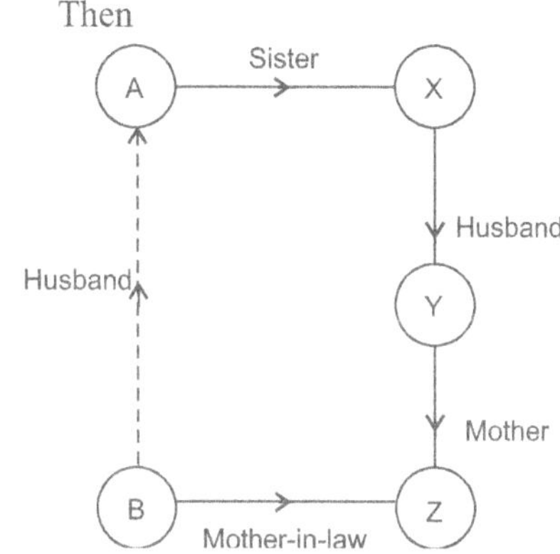

69. **(c)** $\left[\dfrac{7}{3}-\dfrac{3}{2}\right]\times\dfrac{3}{5}+\dfrac{7}{5}\div\dfrac{7}{3}$

$= \dfrac{5}{6}\times\dfrac{3}{5}+\dfrac{7}{5}\times\dfrac{3}{7}$

$= \dfrac{1}{2}+\dfrac{3}{5} = \dfrac{11}{10} = 1\dfrac{1}{10}$

70. **(c)**   **71.** **(c)**   **72.** **(b)**

73. **(c)** Let the angles be $3x$, $5x$, $9x$ and $13x$

$\Rightarrow\ 3x + 5x + 9x + 13x = 360$

[Sum of angles of quadrilateral]

$\Rightarrow 30x = 360$

$\Rightarrow x = 12$

$\therefore$ largest angle $= 13x = 13 \times 12 = 156$

74. **(d)**   **75.** **(d)**

Sol. (76-78):

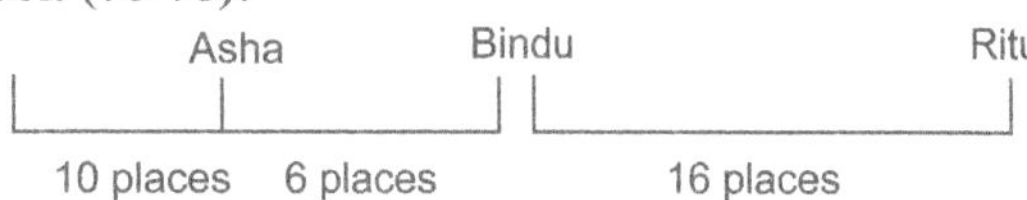

76. (d) Bindu's position in the line is $16 + 1 = 17$

77. (c) Minimum no. of girls $= 16 + 16 + 1 = 33$

78. (d) Asha's position in the line is $10 + 1 = 11$

79. (b) The time interval for the next ring will be equal to the LCM of 20, 24, 30, $= 120$ Seconds.

$= 2$ min.

$\therefore$ next ring will be at 11:27 am.

80. (b) Area of rhombus

$$= \frac{1}{2}(\text{product of diagonals})$$

$$= \frac{1}{2}(8 \times 6) = \frac{48}{2} = 24 \text{ sq.m.}$$

81. (c) 82. (a)   83. (c)

84. (c) Let $CP = x$

then $SP = x + a$ {where a is profit/loss}

Since $5x = 4(x + a)$

$\Rightarrow 5x = 4x + 4a \Rightarrow a = \dfrac{x}{4}$

Let 100 be the CP of each car

$\therefore$ profit $\% = \dfrac{100}{4} = 25\%$

85. (a) Let x be the third part

Then first part $= \dfrac{3x}{5}$ and 2nd part $= \dfrac{4x}{7}$

Now $x + \dfrac{3x}{5} + \dfrac{4x}{7} = 13680$

$\Rightarrow \dfrac{76x}{35} = 13680 \Rightarrow x = 6300$

$\therefore$ first part $= 3780$

86. (c) Geetha's weight $= 11.235$ kg

Her sister's weight $= 1.4 \times 11.235$

$= .15.729$ kg

$\therefore$ their combined weight $= 11.235 + 15.729$

$= 26.964$ kg

87. (c) 88. (c)

89. (b) $\dfrac{81x^2 - 49y^2}{9x + 7y} = \dfrac{(9x)^2 - (7y)^2}{9x + 7y}$

$= \dfrac{(9x + 7y)(9x - 7y)}{9x + 7y}$

$= 9x - 7y$

90. (b) A landlocked state or landlocked country is a sovereign state entirely enclosed by land, or whose only coastlines lie on closed seas. Kazakhstan is a landlocked country situated in eastern Asia. The large country is bordered by four countries; Russia, Turkmenistan, Kyrgyzstan, and Uzbekistan.

91. (b) On substituting the values

$32!4^7\#5 = 32 \div 4 \times 7 + 5$

$= 8 \times 7 + 5$

$= 56 + 5 = 61$

92. (c) Smita's one day's work $= \dfrac{1}{12}$

Sam's one day's work $= \dfrac{1}{9}$

Smita's and Sam's four days work

$= 4\left(\dfrac{1}{12} + \dfrac{1}{9}\right) = 4 \times \dfrac{7}{36} = \dfrac{7}{9}$

Fraction of work unfinished

$= 1 - \dfrac{7}{9} = \dfrac{2}{9}$

93. (a) 94. (c)   95. (d)

96. (c) Let $V_1 = 21$ km/hr

$V_2 = 24$ Km/hr

Then average speed $= \dfrac{2V_1 V_2}{V_1 + V_2}$

$= \dfrac{2 \times 21 \times 24}{45} = \dfrac{112}{5}$

$\therefore$ total distance $=$ average speed $\times$ time

$= \dfrac{112}{5} \times 10 = 224$ km

97. (b)

98. (c) 2, 6, 12, 20, 30, 42

$\underbrace{\quad}_{+4} \underbrace{\quad}_{+6} \underbrace{\quad}_{+8} \underbrace{\quad}_{+10} \underbrace{\quad}_{+12}$

99. (c)

100. (c) Relative speed of Ram and Rahim $= 8 + 9$

$= 17$ m/sec

$\therefore$ time required to meet $= \dfrac{680}{17} = 40 \sec$

RRB NTPC STAGE-1 SOLVED PAPER-3
Held On 30th March 2016 (Shift-3)

1. Find the factors of $(x^2 - x - 132)$
   - (a) $(x - 11)(x - 12)$
   - (b) $(x + 12)(x - 11)$
   - (c) $(x + 11)(x + 12)$
   - (d) $(x - 12)(x + 11)$

2. A college council is auditioning students for a cultural festival. They must satisfy the following criteria -
   1. Student must know at least one dance form.
   2. Student must know' to play at least one musical instrument.
   3. Student must have good acting skills.

   Which one of the following will the council definitely select?
   - (a) Z is a Bharat Natyam dancer, a violinist but does not have any acting skills.
   - (b) P plays football, guitar, has acted in road shows and is a classical dancer.
   - (c) J is a contemporary dancer, a great actor and is planning to learn flute.
   - (d) A plays sitar, is a hip-hop dancer and does not have any acting skills.

3. If **RESEARCH** is $\$\#!\#\%\$\&@$ then **SCARE** is
   - (a) !&%\$#
   - (b) !@%\$#
   - (c) !\$%#<&
   - (d) !@%#\$

DIRECTIONS (Qs. 4-6): *The likes and professions of five friends Rosy, Mary, Lily, Andy and Daisy are given. Consider the following information and answer questions based on it.*

1. Rosy likes Yellow and is a Student.
2. The Librarian likes Green.
3. Mary and Andy like Purple and Blue respectively and neither of them is a Teacher.
4. Lily likes Brown and the Inspector likes Blue.
5. One of the five is a Principal.

4. Which colour does the Teacher like?
   - (a) Blue
   - (b) Brown
   - (c) Purple
   - (d) Green

5. Who is the Principal?
   - (a) Daisy
   - (b) Andy
   - (c) Mary
   - (d) Lily

6. Which among the following is the wrong pair?
   - (a) Andy – Inspector
   - (b) Purple – Principal
   - (c) Daisy – Green
   - (d) Rosy – Teacher

7. $1.123 + 11.23 + 112.3 = ?$
   - (a) 123.453
   - (b) 132.343
   - (c) 124.643
   - (d) 134.643

8. The standard deviation of the set {10, 10, 10, 10, 10} is
   - (a) 0
   - (b) 1
   - (c) 5
   - (d) 10

9. Karan purchased one dozen pens for ₹ 120/- and sold a pack of 3 pens for ₹ 35/- each. What is his gain?
   - (a) 16.67%
   - (b) 20%
   - (c) 15%
   - (d) 33.33%

10. If **Deplete : Exhaust** then **Replenish :**
    - (a) Exhale
    - (b) Inhale
    - (c) Reuse
    - (d) Restore

11. What is the noise level of normal conversation?
    - (a) About 60 dB
    - (b) About 70 dB
    - (c) About 80 dB
    - (d) About 90 dB

12. Statements followed by some conclusions are given below.

    Statements:
    1. X is 7 meters tall, Y is half as high and Z is 3 times the height of X,
    2. P is taller than Z but shorter than A and B.

Conclusions:

I.   B is the tallest of all.

II. The average height of X, Y and Z is less than 10 meters.

Find which of the given conclusions logically follows from the given statements.

(a) Only conclusion I follows.

(b) Only conclusion II follows.

(c) Both I and II follow.

(d) Neither I nor II follows.

13. G is twice as fast as S in doing work. If G can do a work in 30 days less than S, how many days will they take to complete the work together?

(a) 25   (b) 20

(c) 22   (d) 15

14. What is the ratio of simple interest earned on certain amount at the rate of 12% p. a. for 9 years and that for 12 years?

(a) 1:2   (b) 2:3

(c) 3:4   (d) 4:5

15. 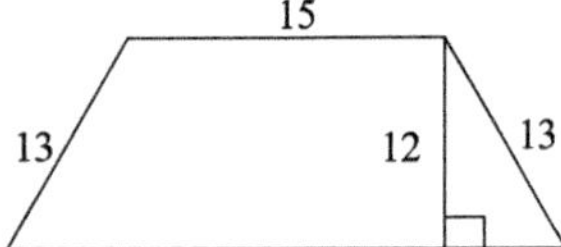

What is the area of this trapezoidal garden? (All measurements are in cm)

(a) 60 sq. cm

(b) 180 sq. cm

(c) 210 sq. cm

(d) 240 sq. cm

16. Select the alternative that shows a similar relationship as the given pair — **Mandatory : Compulsory**

(a) Philosophy : Idealism

(b) Thesis : Proposition

(c) Generosity : Narrow-mindedness

(d) Hypothesis : Supposition

17. For how many months is a cheque valid from the date of issue?

(a) 1 month   (b) 2 months

(c) 3 months   (d) 6 months

18. 'Ganga Action Plan' initiated

(a) Streamlining the flow of Ganga river.

(b) Reduction of pollution on Ganga river.

(c) Efficient use of Ganga water for irrigation.

(d) Using Ganga river for generating hydel energy.

19. Find the range and mode of the data 17, 18, 28, 19, 16, 18, 17, 29, 18

(a) 12 and 18   (b) 13 and 18

(c) 12 and 17   (d) 11 and 17

20. The percentage of nitrogen in the air is about

(a) 74%   (b) 76%

(c) 78%   (d) 80%

21. K purchased a table for ₹ 11,000 and sold it for ₹ 13,500. What is his gain in percentage?

(a) 19.8%   (b) 20.6%

(c) 22.7%   (d) 22%

22. Shimla Agreement 1972 between India & Pakistan was signed in

(a) Bame's Court

(b) Ellerslie Building

(c) Viceregal Lodge

(d) Gorton Castle

23. The value of $(\sin\theta + \cos\theta)^2 =$

(a) $1 + \sin^2\theta$

(b) $\sin^2\theta + \cos^2\theta$

(c) $1 + 2\cos\theta\sin\theta$

(d) $\cos^2\theta + 1$

24. The instrument used to regulate temperature to a particular degree is called

(a) Thermostat

(b) Thermometer

(c) Pyrometer

(d) Thermocouple

25. Pressure is measured in terms of

(a) Mass & Density

(b) Work done

(c) Force and Area

(d) Force and Distance

26. How many times does the number 3 occur in unit's place for numbers ranging from 1 to 100?
    (a) 20   (b) 11
    (c) 10   (d) 19

27. Between small and large human intestine which one is longer?
    (a) Small intestine
    (b) Large intestine
    (c) Both are equal in length
    (d) Depends on male or female

28. To conduct detailed study into disease causing organism in livestock, Biosafety Laboratory has been setup in India at
    (a) Ludhiana
    (b) Bengaluru
    (c) Anand
    (d) Allahabad

29. A pole is taller than a Giraffe which is taller than a tree. A signal is shorter than a pole but taller than a building which is taller than a Giraffe. Who is the shortest?
    (a) Signal   (b) Giraffe
    (c) Tree   (d) Building

30. Find the missing (?) in the series
    NA, PC, RE, TG, ?, XK, ZM
    (a) JV   (b) VI
    (c) VII   (d) VJ

31. Rearrange the jumbled letters to make a meaningful word and then select the one which is different.
    (a) DNHA   (b) EDAH
    (c) THEA   (d) IRHA

32. Sunil has a son Kama and a sister Sangeeta who is the mother of Jagdish and Vijay. Hamish is Jagdish's maternal uncle. How is Harnish related to Kama?
    (a) Brother
    (b) Father
    (c) Nephew
    (d) Paternal Uncle

33. International Maritime Organisation is concerned with
    (a) Air pollution.   (b) Sea pollution.
    (c) Adulteration in food.   (d) Deforestation.

34. Find the G.C.F. & L.C.M. of 20 and 28.
    (a) 20.280   (b) 5.280
    (c) 10.140   (d) 4,140

35. Astrosat is India's first
    (a) Reconnaissance satellite
    (b) Remote sensing satellite
    (c) Space observatory
    (d) Communication satellite

36. Ali travels a distance of 300 m in 2 minutes and 30 seconds. What is his speed in kmph?
    (a) 6.9   (b) 7.1
    (c) 7.2   (d) 7.3

37. Four pairs of words are given. Find the odd one out.
    (a) Chalk : Slate
    (b) Pencil : Notebook
    (c) Pen : Ink
    (d) Sketch Pen : Drawing Book

38. The Gandhi-Irwin pact was signed in the year
    (a) 1930   (b) 1931
    (c) 1932   (d) 1933

39. Twice the difference between two numbers is equal to their sum. If one number is 15, find the other number,
    (a) 15   (b) 10
    (c) 5   (d) 20

40. The sum of three consecutive numbers is 126. Find the highest number.
    (a) 41   (b) 42
    (c) 43   (d) 44

41. Surya is 25 years older than his son. In 5 years, he will be twice as old as his son. What will be Surya's age after 3 years?
    (a) 20   (b) 23
    (c) 45   (d) 48

42. The name of the first bank established in India was
   (a) Bank of Hindustan
   (b) Reserve Bank of India
   (c) Imperial Bank
   (d) State Bank of India

43. If **M = 14, TANK = 61**, then **STARDOM =**
   (a) 79   (b) 89
   (c) 99   (d) 109

44. what is the 4th proportional of 3, 8, 12, ?
   (a) 36   (b) 26
   (c) 32   (d) 16

45. Which of the following is a Space-Based Augmentation System?
   (a) INSAT   (b) GAGAN
   (c) GSAT   (d) SARAL

46. An assertion (A) and a reason (R) are given below.

   Assertion (A): Forest cover in the country has gradually decreased.

   Reason (R): Encroachment by humans is one of the concerns for the forest department.

   Choose the correct option.
   (a) Both A and R are true and R is the correct explanation of A
   (b) Both A and R are true, but R is not the correct explanation of A
   (c) A is true, but R is false
   (d) A is false, but R is true

47. If the interior angle of a polygon is 108°, then it is a
   (a) Octagon
   (b) Hexagon
   (c) Pentagon
   (d) Tetragon

48. Rupee sign '₹' is a
   (a) Devanagari letter
   (b) Roman letter
   (c) Sanskrit Script
   (d) A combination of Roman & Devanagari letters

49. Which of the following does not belong to the group?
   (a) Lakshadweep   (b) Puducherry
   (c) Nicobar   (d) Andaman

50. The headquarters of ISRO is located at
   (a) Bengaluru   (b) New Delhi
   (c) Pune   (d) Mumbai

51. Which of the following will appear third, if they are arranged according to a dictionary?
   (a) Autumn   (b) Austere
   (c) Assert   (d) Auspicious

52. If $\sin\theta = 1/\sqrt{2}$ then $(\tan\theta + \cos\theta) =$
   (a) $1/\sqrt{2}$ (b) $2/\sqrt{2}$
   (c) $3/\sqrt{2}$ (d) $(1 + \sqrt{2})/\sqrt{2}$

53. The mean and median of 7, 5, 5, 2, 7, 6, 5, 3, 7, 6
   (a) 5.3 and 5   (b) 5 and 6
   (c) 5 and 5.5   (d) 5.3 and 5.5

54. Find the similarity in the following:

   Olive Oil, Coconut Oil, Cod liver Oil, Sunflower Oil
   (a) All of them are vegetable oils.
   (b) All of them are rich in Vitamin A.
   (c) All of them are rich in Vitamin
   (d) All of them are oils.

55. Human nails are made of
   (a) Pigment   (b) Elastin
   (c) Albumin   (d) Keratin

56. Eastern boundary of Kashmir is
   (a) LOC
   (b) Jammu
   (c) POK
   (d) Ladakh region

57. The medicine paracetamol is
   (a) An analgesic
   (b) An antipyretic
   (c) An analgesic and antipyretic
   (d) A nonsteroidal anti-inflammatory drug

58. Sachin Tendulkar made his test debut in 1989 at

(a) Karachi, Pakistan

(b) Mumbai, India

(c) Kolkata, India

(d) Melbourne, Australia

59. Which key on a windows keyboard sets to full screen mode in most browsers?

(a) FI   (b) F10

(c) F11   (d) F12

60. The test for diagnosing HIV is

(a) Pap Smear   (b) ELISA

(c) DNA   (d) Mantoux

61. B has 32 pens, 24 pencils and 16 erasers. How many sets of these three items can B make without any left over?

(a) 6   (b) 7

(c) 8   (d) 9

62. Air Quality Index is

(a) A measuring instrument of air pollution.

(b) A number.

(c) For measuring humidity level.

(d) For forecasting rain.

63. Who served as the first Deputy Prime Minister of independent India?

(a) K. Kamaraj

(b) Morarji Desai

(c) Sardar Vallabhbhai Patel

(d) C. Rajagopalachari

64. Gopal covers 100 km. He travels at a speed of 60 kmph for the first 40 km and the rest of the distance at 60 kmph. What is his average speed in kmph?

(a) 44.20   (b) 45.20

(c) 46.20   (d) 47.20

65. Secularism means

(a) Not practicing any religion.

(b) Practicing multiple religions.

(c) Freedom to join any satsang.

(d) Freedom of religion and worship.

66. A farmer purchased a piece of land for ₹ 18 lakh and spent ₹ 5 lakh for fencing it. He sold it for ₹ 24.57 lakh. Find his profit in percentage?

(a) 15%   (b) 14.15%

(c) 16.5%   (d) 6.82%

67. National Science Day falls on

(a) 26th February   (b) 27th February

(c) 28th February   (d) 29th February

DIRECTIONS (Qs. 68-70): *Study the following diagram and answer questions based on it.*

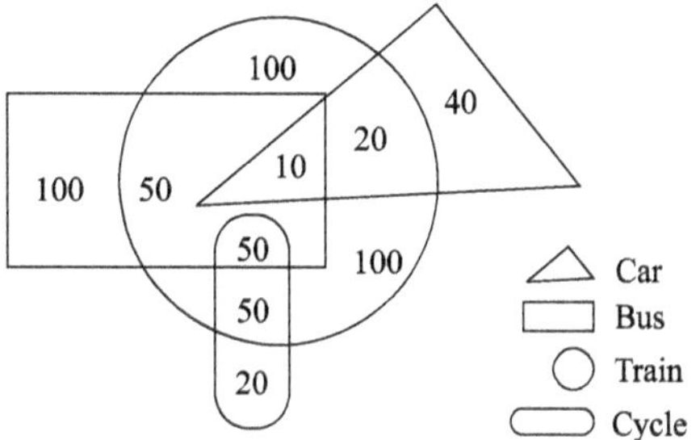

68. The ratio of total number of train traveliers to the people who do not travel by train is

(a) 27/16   (b) 28/16

(c) 37/16   (d) 38/16

69. How many people who travel by train also travel by car or bus but not cycle?

(a) 50   (b) 70

(c) 80   (d) 100

70. Which two modes of transport used by people are mutually exclusive?

(a) Car – Bus

(b) Car – Cycle

(c) Bus - Cycle

(d) Cannot be determined

71. Find the missing (?) in the series 14, 28, 42, 56, ?, 84, 98

(a) 68   (b) 70

(c) 72   (d) 74

72. After 9/11 tragedy, the rebuilt World Trade Center complex in New York is called

(a) New World Trade Center

(b) Empire State Building

(c) One World Trade Center

(d) World Trade Complex

73. The famous Nek Chand's Rock Garden is located in
    - (a) Srinagar
    - (b) Jammu
    - (c) Chandigarh
    - (d) Shimla

74. Expand: $(w - 9)^2$
    - (a) $(w^2 - 9w + 81)$
    - (b) $(w^2 - 9w + 18)$
    - (c) $(w^2 - 18w + 81)$
    - (d) $(w^2 - 18w - 81)$

75. On a certain principal, simple interest amounts to ₹ 1.000 in 1 year at the rate of 10% p.a. What will be the effective rate of interest if the same is compounded on half yearly basis?
    - (a) 10.10
    - (b) 10.15
    - (c) 10.20
    - (d) 10.25

76. In a certain code language if **41095** is **READY** and **840327** is **FRAILS** then **83145 419** is
    - (a) FEARY RED
    - (b) FIERY RED
    - (c) FAIRY RED
    - (d) FIREY RED

77. Which one of the following does not belong to the group?
    - (a) Monitor
    - (b) Keyboard
    - (c) Webcam
    - (d) Mouse

78. If **RATIONAL** is **CLETZYLW** then **EXPERIENCE** is
    - (a) OIZOCTOYMO
    - (b) QJBDUQZOQ
    - (c) OHZBSOXMO
    - (d) PIAPCTPYNP

79. 1\$ = ₹ 67.89. Money changer adds a margin of ₹ 1.11. What will be the cost of \$150?
    - (a) ₹ 10,183
    - (b) ₹ 10,350
    - (c) ₹ 10,330
    - (d) ₹ 10,450

80. If the area of a circle is 9π sq. cm then its circumference is
    - (a) 9 cm
    - (b) 6π cm
    - (c) 3π cm
    - (d) 6 cm

81. 'Maharatna' refers to a group of
    - (a) Emerging small and medium enterprises.
    - (b) Central public sector enterprises.
    - (c) Leading private sector enterprises.
    - (d) Leading multi-national companies.

DIRECTIONS (Qs. 82-84): *The bar chart represents number of fiction and non-fiction books in four libraries L1, L2, L3 and L4. Consider the bar chart and answer questions based on it.*

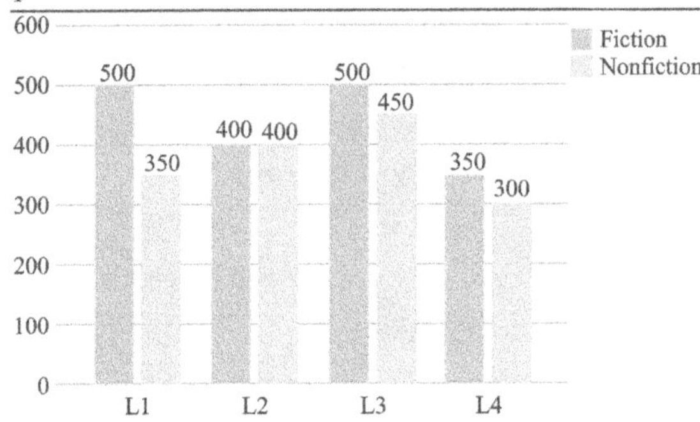

82. What is the percentage difference of total number of Fiction books in libraries L3 and L4 to the Non Fiction books in L3 and L4?
    - (a) 13.34%
    - (b) 11.76%
    - (c) 6.67%
    - (d) It is the same

83. The ratio of total books of libraries L1 and L3 to L2 and L4 is
    - (a) 29/36
    - (b) 33/32
    - (c) 36/29
    - (d) 32/33

84. The ratio of total number of Non Fiction to Fiction books in all libraries is 4
    - (a) 7/6
    - (b) 6/7
    - (c) 15/17
    - (d) 17/15

85. Which of the following statements is true with respect to ASCII?
    - (a) A programming language
    - (b) ASCII chart is not for decimals
    - (c) American security code for information interchange
    - (d) A character encoding scheme

86. The first Olympics games was held in
    - (a) U.K.
    - (b) U. S. A.
    - (c) Greece
    - (d) Italy

87. A person carries ₹ 165/- in the form of currency notes of denominations ₹ 5, ₹ 10 & ₹ 20 in the ratio of 3:2:1. What is the value of currency notes of ₹ 20 denomination?
    - (a) ₹ 60
    - (b) ₹ 100
    - (c) ₹ 40
    - (d) ₹ 80

88. which of the following fractions is the highest of all?

(a) 5/4   (b) 4/3

(c) 3/2   (d) 6/5

89. Name the Indian who became the CEO of Google in 2015.

(a) Satya Nadella   (b) Cyrus Mistry

(c) Sundar Pichai   (d) Vishal Sikka

90. The periodicity of the Commonwealth games is

(a) No fixed interval   (b) 4 years

(c) 5 years   (d) 6 years

91. Cricket World Cup 2023 is scheduled to be hosted by

(a) India   (b) Pakistan

(c) Sri Lanka   (d) West Indies

92. Which country launched its first commercial satellite on 24th November 2015 as a part of its National Space Program?

(a) Russia   (b) India

(c) Japan   (d) China

93. Which of the following is not a Union Territory?

(a) Puducherry   (b) Chandigarh

(c) Lakshadweep   (d) Sikkim

94. If '+' and '÷'; '×' and '−' are interchanged in the equation: $17 ÷ 7 − 27 + 7 × 37$, then its value will be

(a) 7   (b) 17

(c) 27   (d) 37

95. If the mathematical operator '+' means division, '−' means multiplication, '×' means subtraction and '÷' means addition, then the value of

$1 × 7 + 21 × 2 ÷ 2 + 3 − 4$ **is**

(a) 8/3   (b) 4/3

(c) −4/3   (d) −8/3

96. 10 people can do a work in 30 days. In how many days, can 15 people complete double the work?

(a) 20   (b) 25

(c) 40   (d) 45

97. Look carefully at the sequence of symbols to find the pattern.

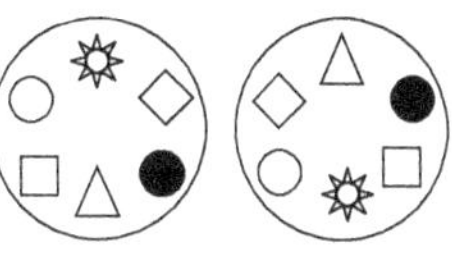 

Which of the following will replace the (?) in the sequence?

(a) 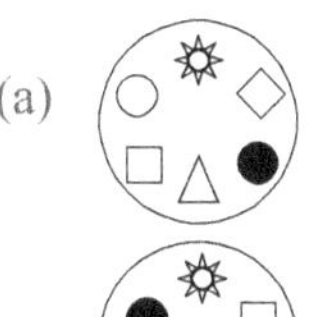   (b) 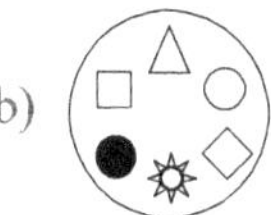

(c) 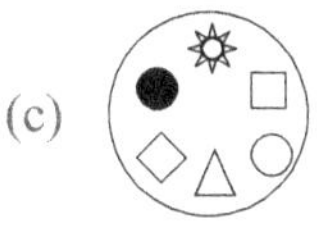   (d) 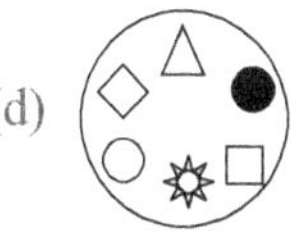

98. Statements followed by some conclusions are given below.

Statements:

1. Most people have orange scooters while some have red ones.

2. People like bright coloured scooters.

Conclusions:

I. People cannot afford bright coloured cars.

II. Most people prefer orange over other bright colours.

Find which of the given conclusions logically follows from the given statements.

(a) Only conclusion I follows.

(b) Only conclusion II follows.

(c) Both I and II follows.

(d) Neither I nor II follows.

99. Which of the following is not a bleaching agent?

(a) Sodium hypochlorite

(b) Calcium hypochlorite

(c) Hydrogen peroxide

(d) Hydrogen sulphide

100. Which movement was called off following the violence at 'Chauri Chaura' incident?

(a) Khilafat Movement

(b) Quit India Movement

(c) Non co-operation Movement

(d) Home Rule Movement

HINTS & EXPLANATIONS

1. **(d)** $(x^2 - x - 132)$
$$x^2 - (12 - 11)\,x - 132$$
$$(x^2 - 12x) + (11x - 132)$$
$$x(x - 12) + 11\,(x - 12)$$
$$(x - 12)(x + 11)$$

2. **(b)**   **3.** **(a)**

Sol. (4-6):

Rosy	Daisy	Mary	Andy	Lily
↓	↓	↓	↓	↓
Yellow	Green	Purple	Blue	Brown
↓	↓	↓	↓	↓
Student	Librarian	Principal	Inspector	Teacher

4. **(b)** Lily is a teacher and likes brown.

5. **(c)** Mary is the Principal.

6. **(d)** Rosy is a student.

7. **(*)**
```
     1.123
    11.230
 +112.300
 --------
  124.653
```
(None of the options)

8. **(a)**

x	$\bar{x}$	$(x-\bar{x})^2$
10	10	$(10-10)^2 = 0$
10	10	$(10-10)^2 = 0$
10	10	$(10-10)^2 = 0$
10	10	$(10-10)^2 = 0$
10	10	$(10-10)^2 = 0$
		$\Sigma(x-\bar{x})^2 = 0$

$\therefore$ Standard deviation $= \sqrt{\dfrac{\Sigma(x-\bar{x})^2}{N-1}}$

$$= \sqrt{\dfrac{0}{5-1}} = 0$$

9. **(a)** CP of 12 pens = ₹120

CP of 1 pen = ₹120 ÷ 12 = ₹10

SP of 3 pens = ₹35

SP of 1 pen = ₹$\dfrac{35}{3}$

Gain % $= \left(\dfrac{SP - CP}{CP} \times 100\right)\%$

$$= \left(\dfrac{\left(\dfrac{35}{3} - 10\right)}{10} \times 100\right)\% = \left(\dfrac{5}{3 \times 10} \times 100\right)\%$$

$$= \dfrac{50}{3}\% = 16.67\%$$

10. **(d)**   **11.** **(a)**   **12.** **(d)**

13. **(b)** Since G is twice as first as S

also if G can do a work in 30 days less than S.

Then, S takes 60 days to complete the work and G takes 30 days to complete the work

Let x be the no. of days the work together then

$$\dfrac{x}{30} + \dfrac{x}{60} = 1 \Rightarrow \dfrac{2x + x}{60} = 1$$

$$3x = 60 \Rightarrow x = 20$$

14. **(c)** S.I. for 9 years $= \dfrac{P \times R \times T}{100} = ₹\left(\dfrac{P \times 12 \times 9}{100}\right)$

S.I. for 12 years $= \dfrac{P \times R \times T}{100} = ₹\left(\dfrac{P \times 12 \times 12}{100}\right)$

$\therefore$ Required ratio

$$= \dfrac{\dfrac{P \times 12 \times 9}{100}}{\dfrac{P \times 12 \times 12}{100}} = \left(\dfrac{P \times 12 \times 9}{P \times 12 \times 12}\right)$$

$$= \dfrac{3}{4} = 3:4$$

15. **(d)**

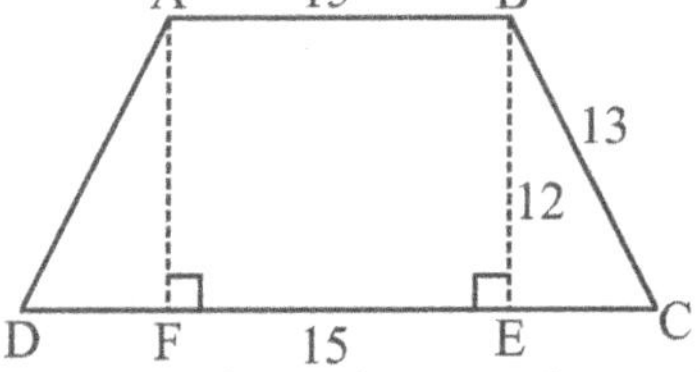

A   15   B — 13 — 12 — D F 15 E C

In $\triangle BEC$ (by Pythagoras theorem)

$$H^2 = B^2 + P^2$$

$\Rightarrow \quad (BC)^2 = (BE)^2 + (CE)^2$

$\Rightarrow \quad (13)^2 = (12)^2 + (CE)^2$

$\Rightarrow \quad \sqrt{169 - 144} = (CE)^2$

$\Rightarrow \quad CE = 5$ cm

or $\quad DF = CE = 5$ cm

$CD = DF + EF + CE = 5$ cm $+ 15$ cm $+ 5$ cm

$= 25$ cm

$\therefore$ Area of trapezoid $= \dfrac{1}{2}(AB + CD) \times BE$

$= \dfrac{1}{2} \times (15 + 25) \times 12$

$= \dfrac{1}{2} \times 40 \times 12 = 240$ cm^2

16. (*)   17. (c)   18. (b)

19. (b) Arranging in ascending order

16, 17, 17, 18, 18, 18, 19, 28, 29

Mode = 18 (as 18 occurs maximum times)

and Range = Highest value – lowest value

$= 29 - 16 = 13$

20. (c)

21. (c) CP of table = ₹ 11000

SP of table = ₹ 13500

Gain = SP – CP

$= ₹ 13500 - ₹ 11000 = ₹ 2500$

Gain% $= \left(\dfrac{2500}{11000} \times 100 \right)\% = \dfrac{250}{11}\%$

$= 22.7\%$

22. (a)

23. (c) $(\sin\theta + \cos\theta)^2 = \sin^2\theta + \cos^2\theta + 2\sin\theta.\cos\theta$

$= (1 + 2\sin\theta.\cos\theta)$

24. (a)   25. (c)

26. (c) The numbers having 3 at unit's place are

3. 13, 23, 33, 43, 53, 63, 73, 83, 93

$\therefore$ 10 numbers has digit 3 at unit's place.

27. (a)   28. (b)

29. (c) According to the question

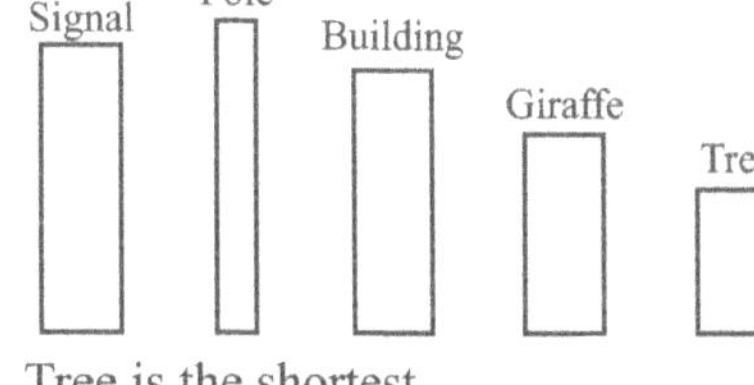

Tree is the shortest.

30. (b)

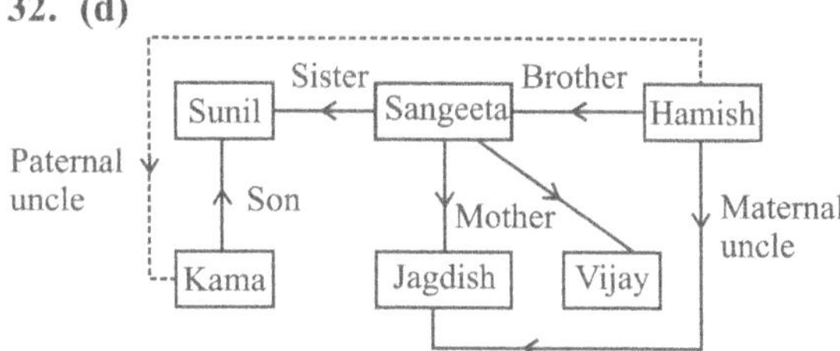

$\therefore$ VI is the missing term.

31. (c)

32. (d)

Sunil ← Sister ← Sangeeta ← Brother ← Hamish

Paternal uncle

Son

Mother

Maternal uncle

Kama   Jagdish   Vijay

33. (b)

34. (d) 20, 28

$20 = 2 \times 2 \times 5$

$28 = 2 \times 2 \times 7$

LCM $= 2 \times 2 \times 5 \times 7 = 140$

GCF $= 2 \times 2 = 4$

35. (c)

36. (c) Distance = 300 m $= \dfrac{300}{1000} = \dfrac{3}{10}$ km

Time = 2 min 30 sec

$= 150$ sec $= \dfrac{150}{3600}$ hr $= \dfrac{1}{24}$ hr

$\therefore$ Speed $= \dfrac{D}{T} = \dfrac{3}{10} \div \dfrac{1}{24} = \dfrac{3}{10} \times 24$

$= 7.2$ kmph

37. (c)   38. (b)

39. (c) Let the other no. be x

ATQ

$2(15 - x) = (15 + x)$

$30 - 2x = 15 + x$

$15 = 3x$

$x = 5$

$\therefore$ other number = 5

40. (c) Let three consecutive numbers are

x, (x + 1), (x + 2) respectively.

$\therefore$ Sum of numbers = 126

$x + (x + 1) + (x + 2) = 126$

$3x + 3 = 126$

$3x = 123$

$x = 41$

$\therefore$ Highest number $= x + 2 = 43$

41. (d) Let Surya's son's present age $= x$ yrs.

and Surya's age $= (x + 25)$ yrs.

5 yrs. later,

Surya's age $= (x + 25 + 5) = (x + 30)$ yrs.

His son's age $= (x + 5)$ yrs.

According to the question

$(x + 30) = 2(x + 5)$

$x + 30 = 2x + 10$

$x = 20$

$\therefore$ Surya's age after 3 yrs. $= (x + 25 + 3)$

$= (20 + 28)$ yrs.

$= 48$ yrs.

and son's age after 3 yrs. $= (x + 3)$

$= (20 + 3)$

$= 23$ yrs

42. (a) 43. (*)

44. (c) 3, 8, 12, x

Product of means = Product of extremes

$3 \times x = 12 \times 8$

$x = 32$

45. (b) 46. (a)

47. (c) Since interior angle $= 108°$

exterior angle $= 180° - 108° = 72°$

Sum of exterior angles of a polygon $= 360°$

$\Rightarrow 72 \times$ no. of sides $= 360°$

$\Rightarrow$ no. of sides $= \dfrac{360°}{72} = 5$

Thus, pentogon is the required polygon.

48. (d) The new rupee sign is a combination of the Devanagari letter "र" and the Latin capital letter "R" .The parallel lines at the top (with white space between them) are said to make an allusion to the tricolor Indian flag and depict an equality sign that symbolizes the nation's desire to reduce economic disparity.

49. (b) 50. (a) 51. (b)

52. (d) $\sin\theta = \dfrac{1}{\sqrt{2}} \Rightarrow \sin\theta = \sin 45° \Rightarrow \theta = 45°$

$\therefore \tan\theta + \cos\theta = \tan 45° + \cos 45°$

$$= 1 + \dfrac{1}{\sqrt{2}} = \dfrac{1 + \sqrt{2}}{\sqrt{2}}$$

53. (d) Arranging in increasing order

2, 3, 5, 5, 5, 6, 6, 7, 7, 7

Here, n = 10

Mean

$$= \dfrac{2+3+5+5+5+6+6+7+7+7}{10} = \dfrac{53}{10} = 5.3$$

$$\text{Median} = \dfrac{\left(\dfrac{n}{2}\right)^{th} \text{term} + \left(\dfrac{n}{2} + 1\right)^{th} \text{term}}{2}$$

For even no. of terms

$$= \dfrac{5^{th} \text{ term} + 6^{th} \text{ term}}{2}$$

$$= \dfrac{5 + 6}{2} = \dfrac{11}{2} = 5.5$$

54. (d) 55. (d) 56. (d) 57. (c)

58. (a) Sachin Tendulkar made his test debut in November 1989 against Pakistan in Karachi. He was just sixteen years old when he became to be known to the international cricket fraternity.

59. (c) 60. (b)

61. (c) HCF of 32, 24, 16 = 8

$\therefore$ B can make 8 sets of these three items without any leftover.

62. (b)

63. (c) The first Deputy Prime Minister of independent India was Sardar Vallabhbhai Patel, who was served as the home minister in Jawaharlal Nehru's cabinet. He took the charge on 15th August, 1947 and served till 15th December, 1950.

64. (*) Here speed for the first 40 km is 60 kmph

and for next 60 km is 60 kmph

since, there is no change in speed

$\therefore$ Average speed will remain same, i.e., 60 kmph.

65. (d) Secularism in India means equal treatment of all the religions by the state. It simply means that the government should remain neutral on the matter of religion, hence giving the citizens freedom to practice one's faith or belief without harming others, or to change it or not have one, according to one's own conscience.

66. (d) CP of land = ₹ 18 lakh

Money spent on fencing = ₹ 5 lakh

∴ Total CP = ₹ (18 + 5) lakh

= ₹ 23 lakh

SP of land = = ₹ 24.57 lakh

∴ Proft = SP – CP

= ₹ (24.57 – 23) lakh

= ₹ 1.57 lakh

Profit %

$$= \left(\frac{P}{CP} \times 100 \right)\% = \left(\frac{1.57 \text{ lakh}}{23 \text{ lakh}} \times 100 \right)\% = 6.82\%$$

67. (c)

68. (d) Total no. of train travellers

= 100 + 10 + 20 + 50 + 50 + 50 + 100

= 380

No. of people who do not travel by train

= 100 + 40 + 20 = 160

∴ Required ratio $= \dfrac{380}{160} = 38 : 16$

69. (c) Let t – train

c – car

b – bus

From venn diagram

n(t ∩ c) = 30 {People who travel by train or car}

n(t ∩ b) = 60 {People who travel by train or bus}

n(t ∩ b ∩ c) = 10 {People travelling by train, car or bus}

People who travel by train also by car or bus but not by cycle

= n[(t ∩ c) ∪ (t ∩ b)] = 30 + 60 – 10 = 80

70. (b) From venn diagram cycle and car have nothing in common, hence being mutually exclusive.

71. (b) 14 × 1 = 14

14 × 2 = 28

14 × 3 = 42

14 × 4 = 56

14 × 5 = 70

72. (c) 73. (c)

74. (c) (W – 9)² = (W)² + (9)² – 2(9)(W)

= (W² + 81 – 18W)

75. (d)

76. (b)

```
4  ①  0  ⑨  ⑤      ⑧  ④  0  ③  2  7
↓  ↓  ↓  ↓  ↓      ↓  ↓  ↓  ↓  ↓  ↓
R  Ⓔ  A  Ⓓ  Ⓨ      Ⓕ  Ⓡ  A  Ⓘ  L  S

8  3  1  4  5      4  1  9
↓  ↓  ↓  ↓  ↓      ↓  ↓  ↓
F  I  E  R  Y      R  E  D
```

77. (a)

78. (d)

```
      R    A    T    I    O    N    A    L
+11↓ +11↓ +11↓ +11↓ +11↓ +11↓ +11↓ +11↓
      C    L    E    T    Z    Y    L    W

E    X    P    E    R    I    E    N    C    E
+11↓ +11↓ +11↓ +11↓ +11↓ +11↓ +11↓ +11↓ +11↓ +11↓
P    I    A    P    C    T    P    Y    N    P
```

79. (b) 1$ = ₹67.89

Since money changer adds a margin of ₹1.11

∴ Total cost of 1$ = ₹ 67.89 + ₹1.11

= ₹ 69.

cost of $150 = 150 × ₹ 69

= ₹ 10350.

80. (b) Area of circle = 9π sq. cm.

⇒ πr² = 9π

⇒ r = 3 cm

∴ circumference = 2πr

= 2 × π × 3

= 6π cm.

81. (b) "Maharatna" refers to a group of Central Public Sector Enterprises who have the potential to become Indian Multinational Companies (MNCs). It was felt that these CPSEs are at the higher end of the Navratna category, and thus, can be recognized as a separate class, i.e., 'Maharatna'.

82. **(*)** Total fiction books in libraries L3 and L4
= 500 + 350 = 850
Total non-fiction books in libraries = L3 and L4
= 450 + 300 = 750
% Fiction books in L3 & L4 = $\dfrac{850}{1750} \times 100$

= 48.57

% Non-fiction books L3 & L4

$= \dfrac{750}{1500} \times 100 = 50\%$

∴ Percentage difference

50 – 48.57

=   1.43%

83. **(c)** Books in libraries L1 and L3
= 500 + 350 + 500 + 450
= 1800
Total books in libraries L2 and L4 = 400 + 400
+ 350 + 300 = 1450

∴ Ratio $= \dfrac{1800}{1450} = \dfrac{36}{29}$

84. **(b)** Total number of non-fiction books = 350 + 400
+ 450 + 300   = 1500

Total number of fiction books = 500 + 400
+ 500 + 350   = 1750

∴ Required ratio $= \dfrac{1500}{1750} = \dfrac{6}{7}$

85. **(d)** **86.** **(c)**

87. **(a)** Let the no. of ₹20 notes = x
no. of ₹10 not-es = 2x
no. of ₹20 notes = 3x
According to question
Total currency = ₹165

⇒   20(x) + 10 (2x) + 5(3x) = 165
⇒   20 x + 20x + 15x = 165
⇒   55 x = 165

⇒ $x = \dfrac{165}{55} = 3$

Hence, value of ₹ 20 denominations = ₹20 × x
= ₹ 20 × 3 = ₹ 60

88. **(c)** $\dfrac{5}{4} = 1.25,\ \dfrac{4}{3} = 1.33$

$\dfrac{3}{2} = 1.50,\ \dfrac{6}{5} = 1.20$

∴ $\dfrac{3}{2}$ is the highest of all fraction.

89. **(c)** Sundar Pichai, an Indian-American Tamil business executive, became the CEO of Google in 2015. He was formerly the Product Chief of Google. His current role was announced on August 10, 2015 and he undertook the position on October 02, 2015.

90. **(b)** The periodicity of the Commonwealth Games if 4 years. Commonwealth Games are an international multi-sport event that was first held in 1930, and has taken place every four years since then.

91. **(a)** **92.** **(c)**   **93.** **(d)**

94. **(a)** $17 \div 7 - 27 + 7 \times 37$

New expression $= 17 + 7 \times 27 \div 7 - 37$

$= 17 + \left(7 \times \dfrac{27}{7}\right) - 37$

$= 17 + 27 - 37 = 7$

95. **(b)** $1 \times 7 + 21 \times 2 \div 2 + 3 - 4$

New expression $= 1 - 7 \div 21 - 2 + 2 \div 3 \times 4$

$= 1 - \dfrac{1}{3} - 2 + \left(\dfrac{2}{3} \times 4\right)$

$= 1 - \dfrac{1}{3} - 2 + \dfrac{8}{3}$

$= -1 + \dfrac{7}{3} = \dfrac{4}{3}$

96. **(c)** 10 people can do a work in 30 days
1 man can do it in (30 × 10) = 300 days

15 people can do this work in $\dfrac{300}{15} = 20$ days

∴ 15 people will complete double the work in (20×2) = 40 days

97. **(c)** Observing the pattern we see that the elements * and Δ at the top and bottom interchange their places, and the rest of the elements rotate anticlock wise.

98. **(b)**

99. **(d)**

100.(c) The Chauri Chaura incident, which took place on February 5, 1922, in the Gorakhpur district of British India, is considered as one of the most prominent incidents of pre-independent India. It was during this incident that led Mahatma Gandhi to call off the Non-Cooperation Movement in February 1922.

RRB NTPC STAGE-I SOLVED PAPER-4
Held On 2ʳᵈ April 2016 (Shift 3)

Rahul and Kusum are good in Hindi and Maths. Sameer and Rahul are good in Hindi and Biology. Gita and Kusum are good in Marathi and Maths. Sameer, Gita and Mihir are good in History and Biology.

1. Who is good in both Biology and Marathi?
   (a) Gita
   (b) Kusum
   (c) Sameer
   (d) Mihir

2. Who is good in only Hindi, Marathi and Maths?
   (a) Sameer
   (b) Rahul
   (c) Kusum
   (d) Gita

3. Who is good in Maths, Biology and Hindi?
   (a) Gita
   (b) Rahul
   (c) Sameer
   (d) Mihir

4. Given below is a statement followed by some conclusions. You have to take the given statement to be true even if it seems to be at variance with the commonly known facts and then decide which of the given conclusions logically follow(s) from the given statement

   Statement: Hrthik, in spite of his busy schedule, finds time to rest.

   Conclusions:

   I. Hrthik is an organized person.

   II. Rest is the most important thing for a busy person.

   Decide the right option from below.
   (a) Only conclusion I follows
   (b) Only conclusion II follows
   (c) Both I and II follow
   (d) Neither of them follows

5. Which among the following is true for the given numbers?
   (a) $13/33 < 32/47 < 20/47 < 25/27$
   (b) $13/33 < 20/47 < 25/27 < 32/47$
   (c) $13/33 < 20/47 < 32/47 < 25/27$
   (d) $20/47 < 13/33 < 32/47 < 25/27$

6. The colour of solid Iodine is -
   (a) White
   (b) Colorless
   (c) Purplish Grey to Black
   (d) Reddish Brown

7. Find the LCM of 25/7, 15/28, 20/21.
   (a) 300/7
   (b) 300
   (c) 320/23
   (d) 320

8. Who was the last emperor of the Mauryan Dynasty?
   (a) Chandragupta
   (b) Ashoka
   (c) Brihadratha
   (d) Shatadhanvan

9. X is 5 ft tall and he notices that he casts a shadow that's 3 ft long. He then measures that the shadow cast by his school building is 30 ft long. How tall is the building?
   (a) 50 ft
   (b) 18 ft
   (c) 90 ft
   (d) 150 ft

10. 3 chairs and 2 tables cost ₹ 700 and 5 chairs and 3 tables cost ₹ 1100. What is the cost of 1 chair and 2 tables?
    (a) ₹ 350
    (b) ₹ 400
    (c) ₹ 500
    (d) ₹ 550

11. The LCM of two numbers is 210. If their HCF is 35 and one of the numbers is 105, find the other number.
    (a) 35
    (b) 70
    (c) 105
    (d) 140

12. Working alone, A can do a job in 15 days and B can do the same job in 12 days. In how many days will the job be completed if both work together?
    (a) 20/3 days
    (b) 36/5 days
    (c) 5/36 days
    (d) 15 days

13. In 2015, ___________, a new species of the genus Homo was discovered in the Dinaledi Chamber of the Rising Star cave system. Cradle of Humankind, South Africa.
    (a) Homo naledi
    (b) Homo erectus
    (c) Homo habilis
    (d) Homo rudolfensis

14. Given below is a statement followed by some conclusions. You have to take the given statement to be true even if it seems to be at variance with the commonly known facts and then decide which of the given conclusions logically follow(s) from the given statement.

    Statement: All hard-working people are successful.

    Conclusions:

    I. All successful people are hard-working.

    II. Only hard work can guarantee success in life.

    Decide the right option from below.

    (a)   Only conclusion I follows

    (b)   Only conclusion II follows

    (c)   Both I and II follow

    (d)   Neither of them follows

15. In a web browser, which of the following is used to save frequently visited websites?

    (a)   History   (b)   Task Manager

    (c)   Favorites   (d)   Save as

16. Tbe Khajuraho Group of Monuments is a UNESCO World Heritage Site located in

    (a)   Madhya Pradesh   (b)   Uttar Pradesh

    (c)   Uttarakhand   (d)   Chattisgarhi.

17. '+' means '×', '−' means '÷', '×' means '+' and '÷' means '−'; compute the value of the expression: $45 - 9 + 4 \times 5$

    (a)   21   (b)   25

    (c)   26   (d)   23

18. On which lake is the Golden Temple located?

    (a)   Amrit Sarovar Lake

    (b)   Golden Lake

    (c)   Harike Lake

    (d)   Sukhna Lake

19. If three numbers are in the ratio of 1:3:5 and their sum is 10,800. Find the largest of the three numbers.

    (a)   1200   (b)   3600

    (c)   6000   (d)   5400

20. If A = 1 and PAT = 37, then PART =

    (a)   55   (b)   52

    (c)   51   (d)   54

21. A positive number exceed its positive square root by 30. Find the number.

22. A car travels at the speed of 50 km/hr for the first half of the journey and at the speed of 60 km/hr for the second half of the journey. What is the average speed of the car for the entire journey?

    (a)   54.54 km/hr   (b)   36.36 km/hr

    (c)   50.5 km/hr   (d)   45.45 km/hr

23. In 2016, who has partnered with ISRO to use space technology for 'predictive policing'?

    (a)   Delhi Police

    (b)   Mumbai Police

    (c)   Chennai Metropolitan Police

    (d)   Kolkata Police

24. Which of the following technological inventions came first?

    (a)   Telegraph   (b)   Telescope

    (c)   Telephone   (d)   Teletype

25. Rita introduced Seema as her mother's father's only son's daughter. How is Rita related to Seema?

    (a)   Cousin   (b)   Paternal Aunt

    (c)   Niece   (d)   Maternal Aunt

26. Which art form was Mrinalini Sarabhai associated with?

    (a)   Pattachitra

    (b)   Tanjore Painting

    (c)   Bharatnatyam

    (d)   Madhubani Painting

27. Choose the pair which is related in the same way as the words in the first pair from the given choices.

    INDIA : TIGER :: USA : __________

    (a)   UNICORN   (b)   BALD EAGLE

    (c)   TURUL   (d)   DRUK

28. The dimensions of a luggage box are 80 cm, 60 cm and 40 cm. How many sq. cm of cloth is required to cover the box?

    (a)   10400 sq. cm   (b)   20800 sq. cm

    (c)   20400 sq. cm   (d)   10200 sq. cm

29. The sum of digits of a two-digit number is 10. When the digits are reversed, the number decreases by 54. Find the changed number.

    (a)   73   (b)   28

    (c)   82   (d)   37

30. The incomes of A and B are in the ratio of 3:2 and their expenditures are ₹ 14,000 and ₹ 10,000 respectively. If A saves ₹ 4000, then B's savings will be:
    (a) ₹ 4000   (b) ₹ 2000
    (c) ₹ 3000   (d) ₹ 5000

31. Ganesh said, "Anjali is my paternal grandfather's only daughter-in-law's only granddaughter". Ganesh is single and has only one sibling, i.e., an elder sister. How is Ganesh related to Anjali?
    (a) Maternal Uncle   (b) Paternal Uncle
    (c) Cousin   (d) Nephew

32. Which of the following type of rays does NOT penetrate Earth's atmosphere?
    (a) Visible Light   (b) X-Rays
    (c) Ultraviolet Rays   (d) Radio Waves

33. Simplify: $(2/9 + 3/5) \div (2/9 + 2/5)$
    (a) 47/48   (b) 47/43
    (c) 43/47   (d) 41/47

34. The first captain of the Indian Cricket team for One Day International was -
    (a) Ajit Wadekar   (b) Sunil Gavaskar
    (c) Kapil Dev   (d) C K Nayudu

35. The principle of regarding the beliefs, values, and practices of a culture from the viewpoint of that culture itself is called -
    (a) Cultural Functionalism
    (b) Cultural Relativism
    (c) Cultural Independence
    (d) Cultural Interdependence

36. Rearrange the following jumbled sentences to make a meaningful one:
    P: are inhibiting progress
    Q: they look for creative
    R: rather than the conventional solution of outsourcing
    S: solutions to problems that
    The proper sequence should be:
    (a) SRQP   (b) QSPR
    (c) PQRS   (d) QRPS

37. P is twice as efficient as Q. Q takes 12 days to complete a job. If both of them work together, how much time will they take to complete the job?
    (a) 6 days   (b) 5 days
    (c) 4 days   (d) 3 days

38. In January 2016, Indian Defence Minister hoisted the world's largest tri-colour on the tallest flag-post at -
    (a) New Delhi   (b) Jaipur
    (c) Ranchi   (d) Leh

39. What is the median of the following list of numbers: 5,3, 6, 9, 11, 19, and 1?.
    (a) 5   (b) 6
    (c) 9   (d) 11

40. A sold a toy to B at a profit of 15%. Later on. B sold it back to A at a profit of 20%, thereby gaining ₹ 552. How much did A pay for the toy originally?
    (a) ₹ 2400   (b) ₹ 2560
    (c) ₹ 2760   (d) ₹ 2800

41. Which of the following is NOT a Greenhouse Gas?
    (a) Nitrous Oxide
    (b) Methane
    (c) Sulphur Hexafluoride
    (d) Copper Dioxide

42. On which festival did the Jallianwala Baug Massacre take place?
    (a) Baisakhi
    (b) Guru Nanak Jayanti
    (c) Diwali
    (d) Holi

43. The 2016 World Economic Forum Annual Meeting took place in -
    (a) Germany   (b) Switzerland
    (c) France   (d) United Kingdom

44. Which of the following is NOT a computer virus?
    (a) AIDS
    (b) Anna Kournikova
    (c) Brain
    (d) Don

45. In the Republic of India, the administrative head of a Union Territory is -
    (a) Lieutenant Governor
    (b) Governor
    (c) President
    (d) Prime Minister

46. The Jayakwadi Project, which is one of the largest irrigation projects is on the river -
  (a) Godavari   (b) Narmada
  (c) Krishna   (d) Tapi

47. Which of the following is the largest glacier in India?
  (a) Gangotri Glacier
  (b) Drang Drung Glacier
  (c) Siachen Glacier
  (d) Shafat Glacier

48. Which was the first women's sport to be introduced in the Olympics?
  (a) Gymnastics   (b) Volleyball
  (c) Golf   (d) Badminton

49. A wire when bent in the form of a square encloses an area of 484 sq. cm. If the same wire is bent in the form of a circle, what is the area enclosed by it?
  (a) 264 sq. cm   (b) 616 sq. cm
  (c) 488 sq. cm   (d) 492 sq. cm

50. What will ₹ 40.000 amount in 2 years at the rate of 20% p.a., if interest is compounded yearly?
  (a) ₹ 48,620   (b) ₹ 58,564
  (c) ₹ 57,600   (d) ₹ 60,000

51. How long will a sum of money take to double, if it is invested at 9.09% p.a. simple interest?
  (a) 12 years   (b) 14 years
  (c) 11 years   (d) 13 years

52. From 1337 to 1453. who were the main combatants in the Hundred Year's War?
  (a) Kingdom of Germany and Kingdom of France
  (b) Kingdom of Germany and Kingdom of Italy
  (c) Kingdom of France and Kingdom of Spain
  (d) Kingdom of England and Kingdom of France

53. A train crosses a stationary object in 10 seconds. What is the length of the train if the speed of the train is 25 m/s?
  (a) 300 m   (b) 250 m
  (c) 320 m   (d) 200 m

54. Google; in partnership with the Railway's telecom wing RailTel, introduced the first public Wi-Fi service at the _______________ railway station.

  (a) Trivandrum Central
  (b) Mumbai Central
  (c) Howrah Station
  (d) Kanpur Central

55. It the pH value of a substance is lower than 7, it would be considered as -
  (a) Neutral   (b) Base
  (c) Acid   (d) Ion

56. In 2013, the first human liver was grown from stem cells in -
  (a) Japan   (b) USA
  (c) Germany   (d) France

57. Two poles of the height 12 m and 17 m stand vertically upright on a plane ground. If the distance between their feet is 12 m, find the distance between their tops.
  (a) 11 m   (b) 12 m
  (c) 13 m   (d) 14 m

58. In which state is the World Heritage Site 'Basilica of Bom Jesus' located?
  (a) Goa   (b) Andhra Pradesh
  (c) Tamil Nadu   (d) Kerala

59. If PLUTO = QKVSP, then SATURN =
  (a) TZUTSM   (b) TATUTM
  (c) TZUTRO   (d) RZUTSO

60. If P713 is divisible by 11, find the value of the smallest natural number P?
  (a) 5   (b) 6
  (c) 7   (d) 9

61. If '+' means ×, '−' means '÷' '×' means '+' and '÷' means '−'; compute the value of the expression:

  15 + 9 × 10 ÷ 5
  (a) 140   (b) 190
  (c) 145   (d) 130

62. Which of the following is NOT a rich source of Calcium?
  (a) Cheese   (b) Collard Greens
  (c) Figs   (d) Carrots

63. Pointing at a photograph, Ramesh said, "He is Rahul, my brother's son's only paternal uncle's wife's brother". How is Rahul related to Ramesh?
  (a) Brother-in-law   (b) Brother
  (c) Cousin   (d) Son

64. Who was the first Indian to become a Nobel
    (a) Rabindranath Tagore
    (b) Mahatma Gandhi
    (c) C. V. Raman
    (d) Mother Teresa

65. Choose the pair which is related in the same way as the words in the first pair from the given choices.
    OPTHALMOLOGIST : EYE ::
    NEPHROLOGIST : ______
    (a) NERVOUS SYSTEM
    (b) LIVER
    (c) KIDNEY
    (d) STOMACH

66. Indian born Shiva Ayyadurai is associated with the invention of -
    (a) Email   (b) Internet
    (c) Keyboard   (d) Mouse

67. Below are given statements followed by some conclusions. You have to take the given statements to be true even if they seem to be at variance with the commonly known facts and then decide which of the given conclusions logically foliow(s) from the given statements.
    Statements:
    (A) All boys are monkeys.
    (B) Some plants are monkeys.
    Conclusions:
    I.   Some monkeys are boys.
    II. All plants are boys.
    Decide which of the below conclusions logically follows from the given statements.
    (a) Only conclusion I follows
    (b) Only conclusion II follows
    (c) Both I and II follow
    (d) Neither of them follows

68. The average of 11 results is 50. The average of the first 6 results is 49 and that of the last 6 results is 52. What is the 6th result?
    (a) 48   (b) 51
    (c) 56   (d) 49

69. $5.36 \times 3.6 =$
    (a) 19.296   (b) 18.946
    (c) 21.996   (d) 20.26

70. Compute: $(18 + 2 \times 3.3) \div 0.003$
    (a) 11200   (b) 5100
    (c) 1120   (c) 1610

71. A ladder 10 m long is leaning against a vertical wall. It makes an angle of 60° with the ground. How far is the foot of the ladder from the wall?
    (a) 5 m   (b) 8.66 m
    (c) 17.32 m   (d) 15 m

72. Given below is a statement followed by some conclusions. You have to take the given statement to be true even if it seems to be at variance with the commonly known facts and then decide which of the given conclusions logically follow(s) from the given statement.
    Statement: Sachin Tendulkar was the greatest batsman in Indian Cricket.
    Conclusions:
    I.   There will be no other batsman greater than Sachin Tendulkar in Indian Cricket.
    II. Sachin Tendulkar is the greatest batsman in the world.
    Choose the right option from below.
    (a) Only conclusion I follows
    (b) Only conclusion II follows
    (c) Both I and II follow
    (d) Neither of them follows

73. In January 2016, the Union Cabinet approved the proposal of the Ministry of Power for amendments in the Tariff Policy with the focus on 4 Es. Which of the following is NOT a part of the 4 Es?
    (a) Electricity for all
    (b) Environment for sustainable future
    (c) Ease of doing business to attract investments
    (d) Ensuring affordable electrical goods to all

74. Choose the pair which is related in the same way as the words in the first pair from the given choices.
    CRICKET : PITCH :: SKATING : ______
    (a) RINK   (b) GROUND
    (c) COURT   (d) RING

75. Below are two statements. You have to take the given statements to be true even if they seem to be at variance with the commonly known facts.
    Statements:
    I.   Some trees are buildings.
    II. All buildings are parrots.

Decide which of the below conclusions logically follows from the given statements.

(a) All parrots are trees

(b) All parrots are buildings

(c) Some parrots are buildings

(d) No parrot is a tree

76. Re-location of endangered or rare species from their natural habitat to protected areas equipped for their protection and preservation is called -

(a) Ex situ conservation

(b) In situ conservation

(c) Exiie conservation

(d) Escaped conservation

77. From which country is the 'Fundamental Duties of the Indian Constitution borrowed?

(a) UK   (b) USA

(c) USSR   (d) Australia

78. In India, the highest cricket ground above sea level lies in which state?

(a) Himachal Pradesh

(b) Sikkim

(c) Uttar Pradesh

(d) Assam

DIRECTIONS (Qs. 79-81): *Study the following table and answer the questions based on it.*

Given below is the list of expenditures (in lakh rupees) per annum of Company Z over the years.

Year	Expenditure Items for Company Z				
	Salary	Fuel & Transport	Bonus	Interest on Loans	Taxes
2011	412	227	15	133.4	98
2012	557	233	16.5	142.5	138
2013	656	245	17.3	151.6	174
2014	680	260	17.9	166.4	188
2015	720	284	18.5	179.4	198

79. What is the average amount of Bonus per year?

(a) ₹ 17.04 Lakhs   (b) ₹ 17 Lakhs

(c) ₹ 17.4 Lakhs   (d) ₹ 16.8 Lakhs

80. What is the total expenditure of Company Z in the year 2011?

(a) ₹ 897.2 Lakhs   (b) ₹ 827.5 Lakhs

(c) ₹ 885.4 Lakhs   (d) ₹ 727.1 Lakhs

81. What is the expenditure on Fuel and Transport as a percentage of expenditure on Salary for the year 2012?

(a) 41.8%   (b) 40.1%

(c) 43.1%   (d) 44.2%

82. The cost of 2 pencils, 4 pens and 8 erasers is ₹ 12 and the cost of 8 pens, 10 pencils and 4 erasers is ₹ 36. How much will 3 pencils, 3 pens and 3 erasers cost?

(a) ₹ 10   (b) ₹ 15

(c) ₹ 12   (d) ₹ 18

83. If BEAR = YVZI, then BUILDING =

(a) ATHKCHMF

(b) YFROWRMT

(c) YFSWOSMR

(d) ATHKCHMT

84. What is Geotropism?

(a) Growth of plants in response to Gravity

(b) Growth of plants in response to Sunlight

(c) Growth of plants in response to Nutrients

(d) Growth of plants in response to Water

85. If the cost price of 120 articles is equal to the selling price of 80 articles, find the profit percent.

(a) 33.33%   (b) 40%

(c) 50%   (d) 60%

86. In 2016, ISRO conducted 1st satellite-based warning system trial for Indian Railways in -

(a) Mumbai   (b) Ahmedabad

(c) Kolkata   (d) Delhi

87. In 1831, electricity became viable for use in technology when created the electric dynamo.

(a) Benjamin Franklin (b) Alessandro Volta

(c) Michael Faraday (d) Thomas Edison

88. If **RAILWAY** is coded as **24-7-15-18-29-7-31** then how will you code **STATION**?

(a) 25-24-7-24-15-21-19

(b) 25-26-7-26-15-21-20

(c) 25-24-8-24-15-21-19

(d) 25-26-8-26-15-21-20

89. Select the correct set of symbols:

64 4 5 8 = 88

(a) ×, −, ÷   (b) +, ÷, −

(c) +, −, ÷   (d) ÷, ×, +

DIRECTIONS Qs. (90-92): *Study the diagram given below and answer the questions based on it.*

△ represents Students who have chosen Arts course

◯ represents Students who have chosen Science course

▢ represents Students who have chosen Dance course

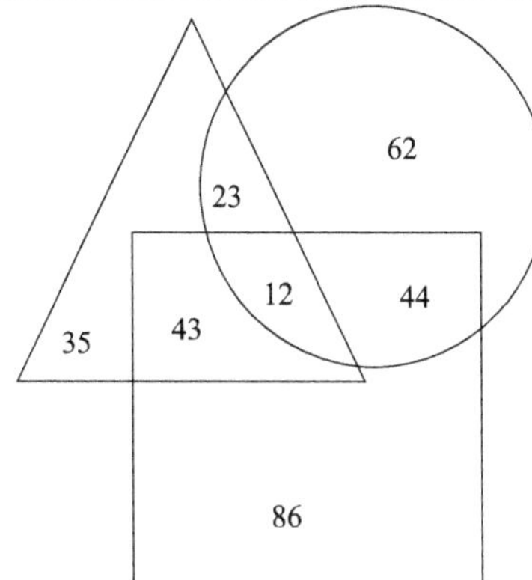

90. How many students have chosen the Science course?

(a) 141   (b) 185

(c) 113   (d) 145

91. How many students have chosen Dance course and Science course but not the Arts course?

(a) 43   (b) 44

(c) 12   (d) 23

92. How many students have chosen Arts course and Science course but not the Dance course?

(a) 23   (b) 12

(c) 35   (d) 44

93. When an object thrown straight upwards gets to the top of its path, its

(a) Velocity is zero and its acceleration is zero

(b) Velocity is zero and its acceleration is about 10 m/s^2

(c) Velocity is 10 m/s and its acceleration is zero

(d) Velocity is 10 m/s and its acceleration is about 10 m/s^2

94. Select the correct set of symbols:

21 9 13 7 = 195

(a) ×, −, ÷   (b) +, ÷, −

(c) +, −, ÷   (d) ÷, +, −

95. Which of the following gases in air is responsible for the discoloration of Brass?

(a) Hydrogen Sulphide

(b) Carbon Dioxide

(c) Nitrogen

(d) Carbon Monoxide

96. Choose the one which is different or odd from the following.

(a) Dal Lake   (b) Sambhar Lake

(c) Vembanad Lake   (d) Wular Lake

97. What is the mode of the following list of numbers: 2, 4, 5, 6, 5, 4, 3, 5, 3, 1, and 7?

(a) 3   (b) 4

(c) 5   (d) 2

98. India's national motto, Satyameva Jayate (lit. "Truth alone triumphs"), is a mantra from the ancient Indian scripture -

(a) Rigveda

(b) Mundaka Upanishad

(c) Bhagavad Gita

(d) MatsyaPurana

99. P bought an article for ₹ 400 and sold it at a profit of 10%. What would have been the increase in the profit percent if it was sold for ₹460?

(a) 5%   (b) 10%

(c) 12%   (d) 15%

100. In 2016, ISRO successfully launched its fifth navigation satellite called -

(a) IRNSS ID   (b) IRNSS IE

(c) VELOX-C1   (d) TeLEOS-1

HINTS & EXPLANATION

Sol. (1-3):

Rahul & Kusum	Sameer & Rahul	Gita & Kusum	Sameer & Gita & Mihir
↓	↓	↓	↓
Hindi & Maths	Hindi & Biology	Marathi & Maths	History & Biology

1. **(a)** Gita is good in Biology and Marathi.

2. **(c)** Kusum is good in Hindi, Marathi and Maths.

3. **(b)** Rahul is good in Maths, Biology and Hindi.

4. **(d)**

5. **(c)** $\dfrac{13}{33} = 0.39$; $\dfrac{32}{47} = 0.68$

$\dfrac{20}{47} = 0.42$; $\dfrac{25}{27} = 0.92$

$\dfrac{13}{33} < \dfrac{20}{47} < \dfrac{32}{47} < \dfrac{25}{27}$

6. **(c)**

7. **(a)** $\dfrac{25}{7}, \dfrac{15}{28}, \dfrac{20}{21}$

LCM of fractions

$$= \dfrac{\text{LCM of numerators}}{\text{HCF of denominators}}$$

$$= \dfrac{\text{LCM of } (25, 15 \text{ and } 20)}{\text{HCF of } (7, 28, 21)}$$

$$= \dfrac{300}{7}$$

8. **(c)**

9. **(a)** This is a case of direct proportion.

$$\dfrac{\text{Height of X}}{\text{Length of X's shadow}}$$

$$= \dfrac{\text{Height of building}}{\text{Length of buildings shadow}}$$

$$\Rightarrow \dfrac{5}{3} = \dfrac{\text{Height of building}}{30}$$

$$\Rightarrow \text{Height of building} = \dfrac{5}{3} \times 30 = 50 \text{ ft.}$$

10. **(c)** Let the cost of 1 chair = ₹ x

Cost of 1 table = ₹ y

According to question :

$$3x + 2y = 700 \qquad \text{...(i)}$$

$$5x + 3y = 1100 \qquad \text{...(ii)}$$

On solving (i) and (ii), we get

$x = 100$ and $y = 200$

Hence, cost of 1 chair and 2 tables

$$= x + 2y$$

$$= (100 + 2 \times 200) = ₹ 500$$

11. **(b)** LCM × HCF = Product of the number

$$\Rightarrow \text{Other number} = \dfrac{35 \times 210}{105} = 70$$

12. **(a)** **13.** **(a)** **14.** **(d)** **15.** **(c)**

16. **(a)** The Khajuraho Group of Monuments is a group of Hindu Temples in Chhatarpur, Madhya Pradesh. They are one of the UNESCO World Heritage sites in India. These temples are famous for their nagara style architectural symbolism and their erotic sculptures.

17. **(b)** $45 - 9 + 4 \times 5$

New expression

$$= 45 \div 9 \times 4 + 5$$

$$= 5 \times 4 + 5$$

$$= 20 + 5 = 25$$

18. **(a)** The temple is located on Amrit Sarovar lake. 'Amrit' means the 'nector' of immortality and 'sar' or 'sarovar' means 'pond'. This sarovar was created by the fourth Guru of the Sikh religion.

19. **(c)** Let the numbers be $x, 3x, 5x$ respectively.

Sum of numbers = 10800

$\Rightarrow \quad x + 3x + 5x = 10800$

$\Rightarrow \quad 9x = 10800$

$\Rightarrow \quad x = 1200$

Largest number $= 5x = 5 \times 1200 = 6000$

20. (a) A = 1, first letter of alphabets

P is 16th and T is 20th.

Which shows PAT $= \text{P} + \text{A} + \text{T}$

$= 16 + 1 + 20 = 37$

PART $= \text{P} + \text{A} + \text{R} + \text{T}$

$= 16 + 1 + 18 + 20 = 55$

21. (b) $x - \sqrt{x} = 30$

$\Rightarrow (\sqrt{x})^2 - \sqrt{x} = 30$

$\Rightarrow (\sqrt{x})^2 - \sqrt{x} - 30 = 0$

$\Rightarrow (\sqrt{x} - 6)(\sqrt{x} + 5) = 0$

$\sqrt{x} = 6$

$\Rightarrow x = 36$

and $\sqrt{x} = (-5)$ which is not applicable

22. (a)

23. (a) Delhi police partnered with ISRO in 2015 to develop space technology to map crime live and predictive policing.

24. (b)

25. (a) Rita's mother's father in her Grandfather.

Her Grandfather's son is her maternal uncle.

Her maternal uncle's daughter is her cousin.

26. (c) Mrinalini Sarabhai was an Indian dancer and choreographer. She was a Bharatnatyam and Kathakali dancer. She founded Darpana Academy of Performing Arts in Ahmedabad.

27. (b) National animal of India is tiger.

National animal of USA is Bald eagle.

28. (b) Surface area of box

$= 2(lb + bh + hl)$

$= 2 (80 \times 60 + 60 \times 40 + 40 \times 80)$

$= 2 (4800 + 2400 + 3200)$

$= 2 \times 10400$

$= 20800 \text{ cm}^2$

or Area of cloth required $= 20800 \text{ cm}^2$.

29. (b) Let unit's digit and ten's digit are x and $(10 - x)$ respectively.

Original number $= 10(10 - x) + x$

$= (100 - 9x)$

andNumber obtained on reversing the digits

$= 10x + (10 - x)$

$= 9x + 10$

According to question :

$(9x + 10) = (100 - 9x) - 54$

$\Rightarrow \quad 9x + 10 + 9x = 46$

$\Rightarrow \quad 18x = 36$

$\Rightarrow \quad x = 2$

Changed number $= 9x + 10 = 28$

30. (b) Let income of A and B are ₹ $3x$ and ₹ $2x$ respectively.

A's saves $= ₹ 4000$

or ₹ $3x - 14000 = ₹ 4000$

$\Rightarrow \quad x = \dfrac{18000}{3} = 6000$

B's income $= ₹ 2x = ₹ 12000$

and B's savings $= ₹ 12000 - ₹ 10000 = ₹ 2000$

31. (a)

32. (b)

33. (a) $\left(\dfrac{2}{9} + \dfrac{3}{5}\right) \div \left(\dfrac{2}{9} + \dfrac{2}{5}\right)$

$= \left(\dfrac{10 + 27}{45}\right) \div \left(\dfrac{10 + 18}{45}\right)$

$= \dfrac{37}{45} \times \dfrac{45}{28} = \dfrac{37}{28}$

34. (a) Ajit Wadekar became India's inaugurated ODI captain in 1974 against England.

35. (b) 36. (b)

37. (c) Q takes 12 days to complete a job.

P takes 6 days to complete a job.

In 1 day, P and Q will complete $\left(\dfrac{1}{P}+\dfrac{1}{Q}\right)$ work together.

$$= \left(\dfrac{1}{6}+\dfrac{1}{12}\right) \text{ work}$$

$$= \dfrac{2+1}{12} = \dfrac{3}{12} = \dfrac{1}{4} \text{ work}$$

Hence, P and Q together will complete the work in 4 days.

38. (c)

39. (b) 1, 3, 5, 6, 9, 11, 19

Here $n = 7$

$$\text{Median} = \left(\dfrac{n+1}{2}\right)^{\text{th}} \text{ term}$$

$$= \left(\dfrac{7+1}{2}\right)^{\text{th}} \text{ term}$$

$$= 4^{\text{th}} \text{ term} = 6$$

40. (a) A's case :

Let CP of toy = ₹ x

Gain = 15%

$$\text{SP of toy} = \left(\dfrac{100+G\%}{100}\right) \times CP$$

$$= \dfrac{(100+15)}{100} \times x$$

$$= \dfrac{115}{100}x = ₹ \dfrac{23}{20}x$$

B's case :

CP of toy = ₹ $\dfrac{23}{20}x$

$$\text{Profit} = \dfrac{20}{100} \times \dfrac{23}{20}x$$

or $552 = \dfrac{20}{100} \times \dfrac{23}{20}x$

$$\Rightarrow \dfrac{55200}{23} = x$$

$$\Rightarrow x = ₹ 2400$$

or   CP of toy for A = ₹ 2400

41. (d) 42. (a)

43. (b) The 2016 World Economic Forum Annual Meeting took place in Davos, Switzerland, IT is an international organization for Public-Private Cooperation.

44. (d) 45. (a)

46. (a) The Jayakwadi Project is one of the largest irrigation projects in India. It is located on Godavari River at the site of Jayakwadi village in Paithan. Jayakwadi is one of the largest earthen dams in Asia.

47. (c) 48. (c)

49. (b) Area of square = (side)²

$484 = $ (side)²

side = 22 cm

Perimeter of square = Circumference of circle

$$\Rightarrow 4 \times \text{side} = 2 r$$

$$\Rightarrow 4 \times 22 = 2 \times \dfrac{22}{7} \times r$$

$$\Rightarrow r = 2 \times 7 = 14 \text{ cm}$$

$$\text{Area of circle} = r^2 = \dfrac{22}{7} \times (14)^2 = 616 \text{ cm}^2$$

50. (c) $A = P\left(1+\dfrac{R}{100}\right)^n$

$$= 40000\left(1+\dfrac{20}{100}\right)^n$$

$$= 40000 \times \left(\dfrac{6}{5}\right)^2$$

$$= 40000 \times \dfrac{36}{25} = ₹ 57600$$

51. (c) 52. (d)

53. (b) Here, time = 10 secs

Speed of train = 25 m/s

Since, object is stationary,

Distance = Speed × Time

$= (25 \times 10)$ m

$= 250$ m

54. (b) 55. (c) 56. (a) 57. (c)

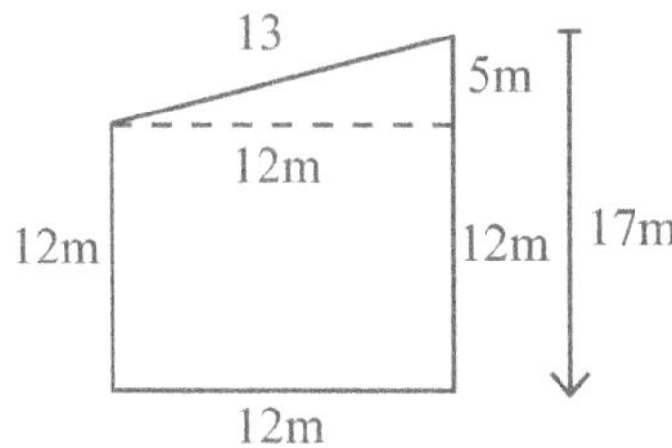

$$\Rightarrow \sqrt{12^2 + 5^2} = 13$$

58. (a) 59. (a)

60. (d) A number is divisible by 11, if sum of digits at odds places

= Sum of digits at even places

$\Rightarrow$ P + 1 = 7 + 3

$\Rightarrow$ P = 9

61. (a) New expression = $15 \times 9 + 10 - 5$

$= 135 + 10 - 5 = 140$

62. (d) 63. (a) 64. (a) 65. (c) 66. (a)

67. (a)

68. (c) Average of 11 numbers = 50

Sum of 11 numbers = 50 × 11 = 550

Sum of first 6 results = 49 × 6 = 294

Sum of last 6 results = 52 × 6 = 312

6th result = (294 + 312) – 550 = 56

69. (a) $5.36 \times 3.6 = 19.296$

70. (*) $(18 + 2 \times 3.3) \div 0.003$

$$= \frac{18 + 2 \times 3.3}{0.003} = \frac{24.6}{0.003}$$

$= 8200$

71. (a)

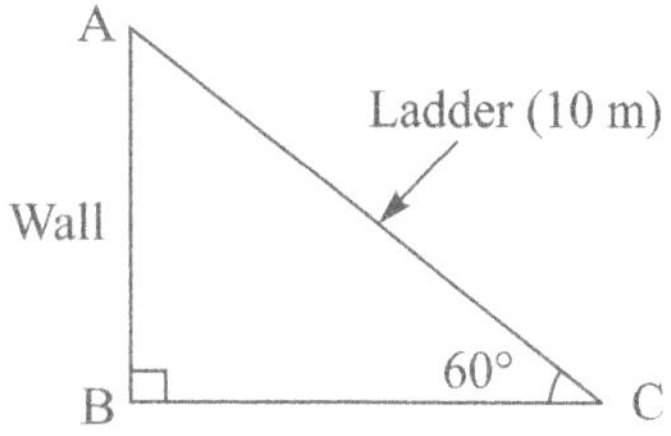

$$\cos 60° = \frac{\text{Base}}{\text{Hypotense}}$$

$$\frac{1}{2} = \frac{BC}{AC} = \frac{BC}{10}$$

BC = 5 m

Foot of the ladder is 5 m away from the wall.

72. (d) 73. (d) 74. (a) 75. (c) 76. (a) 77. (c)

78. (a)

79. (a) Average amount of bonus

$$= \frac{15 + 16.5 + 17.3 + 17.9 + 18.5}{5}$$

$$= \frac{85.2}{5} = ₹\ 17.04 \text{ lakhs}$$

80. (c) Total expenditure of company Z in year 2011

= ₹ (412 + 227 + 15 + 133.4 + 98) lakhs

= ₹ 885.4 lakhs

81. (a) Required percentage

$$= \frac{233}{557} \times 100$$

$= 41.8\ \%$

82. (c) Let cost of one pencil = ₹ x

Cost of 1 pen = ₹ y

Cost of 1 eraser = ₹ z

$2x + 4y + 8z = ₹\ 12$ ...(i)

and $10x + 8y + 4z = ₹\ 36$ ...(ii)

Adding (i) and (ii),

$12x + 12y + 12z = ₹\ 48$

$$\frac{1}{4}(12x + 12y + 12z) = ₹\ 48 \times \frac{1}{4}$$

$3x + 3y + 3z = ₹\ 12$

or Cost of 3 pens, 3 pencils and 3 erasers is ₹ 12.

83. (b) 84. (a)

85. (c) Let CP for 1 article = ₹ 1

CP of 120 articles = ₹ 120

Also, SP of 80 articles = ₹ 120

$$\text{SP of 1 article} = ₹ \frac{120}{80} = ₹ 1.50$$

$$\text{Profit \%} = \left(\frac{SP - CP}{CP} \times 100\right)\%$$

$$= \left(\frac{1.50 - 1}{1}\right) \times 100 = 50\%$$

86. (b) 87. (c)

88. (b) From the given information, we observe

$A \rightarrow 7$

$B \rightarrow 8$

$C \rightarrow 9$

$D \rightarrow 10$

$E \rightarrow 11$

$F \rightarrow 12$ and so on.

Code for STATION is

$25 - 26 - 7 - 26 - 15 - 21 - 20$

89. (d) $64 \div 4 \times 5 + 8 = 16 \times 5 + 8$

$$= 80 + 8 = 88$$

90. (a) No. of students chosen the science course

$$= 23 + 62 + 12 + 44$$

$$= 141$$

91. (b) Only 44 students have chosen Dance and Science course, but not the Arts course.

92. (a) Only 23 students have chosen Arts and Science course, but not the Dance course.

93. (b)

94. (d) $21 \times 9 + 13 - 7 = 189 + 13 - 7$

$$= 202 - 7 = 195$$

95. (a) 96. (b)

97. (c) $1, 2, 3, 3, 4, 4, 5, 5, 5, 6, 7$

Since, 5 occurs maximum times, i.e. 3 times

Mode = 5

98. (b)

99. (a) CP of article = ₹ 400

New SP of article = ₹ 460

$$\text{New profit \%} = \left(\frac{₹(460 - 400)}{₹400} \times 100\right)\%$$

$$= 15\%$$

Old profit = 10%

There will be an increase of 5% profit.

100.(b)

RRB NTPC STAGE-I SOLVED PAPER 5
Held On 2ⁿᵈ April 2016 (Shift 2)

1. P bought an article for ₹1600 and sold it at a profit of 10%. What would have been the increase in the profit percent if it was sold for ₹1840?
   (a) 5%
   (b) 10%
   (c) 12%
   (d) 15%

2. Which of the following is the most common kidney stone-forming compound?
   (a) Calcium oxalate
   (b) Magnesium oxide
   (c) Sodium bicarbonate
   (d) Magnesium citrate

3. Divide 3740 in three parts in such a way that half of the first part, one-third of the second part and one- sixth of the third part are equal.
   (a) 700, 1000. 2040
   (b) 340, 1360, 2040
   (c) 680, 1020, 2040
   (d) 500, 1200, 2040

4. Given below is a statement followed by some conclusions. You have to take the given statement to be true even if it seems to be at variance with the commonly known facts and then decide which of the given conclusions logically follow(s) from the given statement.

Statement: Success cannot be achieved without hard work.

Conclusions:
I. Every hardworking person is successful.
II. Every successful person is hardworking.
   (a) Only conclusion I follows
   (b) Only conclusion II follows
   (c) Both I and II follow
   (d) Neither of them follows

DIRECTIONS (Qs. 5-7): *Study the following table and Answer the questions based on it.*

Below is the Household Expenditure (in Thousand Rupees) per annum.

Year	Household Expenditure				
	Grocery	Rent	Leisure	EMI	Taxes
2010	32	12	5	3.4	9
2011	37	13	6.5	4.5	13
2012	46	14	7.3	5.6	17
2013	43	16	7.9	6.4	18
2014	52	18	8.5	7.4	19

5. What is the average spending on Leisure per annum?
   (a) ₹7,040
   (b) ₹ 6,500
   (c) ₹7,100
   (d) ₹7,400

6. What is the total Household Expenditure for the year 2012?
   (a) ₹89,900
   (b) ₹87,120
   (c) ₹89,100
   (d) ₹88,200

7. Expenditure on EMI forms what percentage of expenditure on Grocery for the year 2014?
   (a) 11.34 %
   (b) 14.23 %
   (c) 13.22%
   (d) 15.55 %

8. Choose the one which is different or odd from the following.
   (a) Aluminum
   (b) Iron
   (c) Copper
   (d) Brass

DIRECTIONS (Qs. 9-11): *Use the following passage for the questions based on it.*

There are six flats on a floor in two rows. Out of these, three are north facing and the other three are south facing flats. The flats are to be allotted amongst Arun, Biswajyot, Chitra, Derek. Evan and Fatima. Biswajyot gets a north facing flat and is not next to Derek. Derek and Fatima get diagonally opposite flats. Chitra is next to Fatima, and gets a south facing flat. Evan gets a north facing flat.

9. Except Derek and Fatima, which other pair is diagonally opposite to each other?
   (a) Arun and Biswajyot
   (b) Arun and Chitra
   (c) Evan and Derek
   (d) Evan and Chitra

10. Which of the following combination gets south facing flats?
   (a) Arun, Chitra and Fatima
   (b) Chitra, Biswajyot and Derek
   (c) Evan, Arun and Fatima
   (d) Derek, Arun and Biswajyot

11. Which of the following pairs is exactly opposite to each other?
    (a) Derek and Evan   (b) Fatima and Chitra
    (c) Evan and Chitra   (d) Evan and Arun
12. The filament of a light bulb is made up of -
    (a) Platinum   (b) Tantalum
    (c) Tungsten   (d) Antimony
13. The oldest oil field in Asia is located in -
    (a) Gujarat
    (b) Assam
    (c) Arunachal Pradesh
    (d) Nagaland
14. Which of the following is false?
    Sound waves are _________________ waves.
    (a) Pressure   (b) Longitudinal
    (c) Electromagnetic   (d) Mechanical
15. Which astronomer was placed under house arrest for his support of heliocentrism?
    (a) Nicolaus Copernicus (b) Galileo Galilei
    (c) Johannes Kepler   (d) Friedrich Bessel
16. The operating system UNIX is the trademark of -
    (a) Microsoft   (b) Bell Laboratories
    (c) Apple   (d) Motorola
17. A piece of cloth costs ₹35. If the piece were 4 m longer and each meter were to cost ₹1 lesser, then the total cost would remain unchanged. How long is the piece of cloth?
    (a) 10 m   (b) 14 m
    (c) 12 m   (d) 8 m
18. There are 90 coins, comprising of 5 and 10 paisa coins. The value of all the coins is ₹7. How many 5 paisa coins are there?
    (a) 50   (b) 45
    (c) 40   (d) 35
19. Who was the first President of the Indian National Congress?
    (a) Womesh Chunder Bonneijee
    (b) Bal Gangadhar Tilak
    (c) Allan Octavian Hume
    (d) Dadabhai Naoroji
20. Which of the following is not an example of a Word Processor?
    (a) IBM Lotus Symphony
    (b) Microsoft Word
    (c) Google Docs
    (d) Microsoft Excel
21. A closed wooden rectangular box made of 1 cm thick wood has the following outer dimensions: length 22 cm, breadth 17 cm, and height 12 cm. It is filled to capacity with cement. What is the volume of the cement in the box?
    (a) 1488 cu. cm   (b) 3000 cu. cm
    (c) 4488 cu. cm   (d) 2880 cu. cm
22. A shopkeeper marks the price of an article at ₹320. Find the cost price if after allowing a discount of 10%, he still gains 20% on the cost price.
    (a) ₹240   (b) ₹280
    (c) ₹300   (d) ₹264
23. The simple interest on a certain sum of money invested at a certain rate for 2 years amounts to ₹1200. The compound interest on the same sum of money invested at the same rate of interest for 2 years amounts to ₹1290. What was the principal?
    (a) ₹12000   (b) ₹16000
    (c) ₹6000   (d) ₹4000
24. Given below is a statement followed by some conclusions. You have to take the given statement to be true even if it seems to be at variance with the commonly known facts and then decide which of the given conclusions logically follow(s) from the given statement.

Statement: According to a recent health survey, people who exercise for at least half an hour every day are less prone to lifestyle diseases.

Conclusions:
I.   Moderate exercise is essential to lead a healthy life.
II. Everyone with no exercise on their routine suffer from lifestyle diseases.
    (a) Only conclusion I follows
    (b) Only conclusion II follows
    (c) Both I and II follow
    (d) Neither of them follows
25. Choose the pair which is related in the same way as the words in the first pair from the given choices. SOLDIERS : ARMY :: MUSICIANS : ______________
    (a) FLOCK   (b) GANG
    (c) COLONY   (d) BAND
26. Below are given statements followed by some conclusions. You have to take the given statements to be true even if they seem to be at variance with the commonly known facts and then decide which of the given conclusions logically follow(s) from the given statements.

Statements:
A. Some fruits are vegetables.
B. All vegetables are plants.
Conclusions:
I. Some plants are vegetables.
II. Some fruits are plants.
(a) Only conclusion I follows
(b) Only conclusion II follows
(c) Both I and II follow
(d) Neither of them follows

27. Maanch is a folk dance from -
(a) Haryana   (b) Kerala
(c) Assam   (d) Madhya Pradesh

28. Which Indian won the 2014 Nobel Prize for Peace?
(a) Kailash Satyarthi (b) Malala Yosufzai
(c) Sanjiv Chaturvedi (d) Anshu Gupta

29. The Mughal empire was founded by -
(a) Babur   (b) Humayun
(c) Akbar   (d) Shah Jahan

30. In Tennis, hard court is the type of court whose surface is made of -
(a) Concrete   (b) Clay
(c) Grass   (d) Carpet

31. $5.16 \times 3.2 =$
(a) 15.502   (b) 16.512
(c) 17.772   (d) 17.52

32. Who among the following became the first tourist to space by spending $20 million for 8 days in orbit?
(a) Greg Olsen   (b) Charles Simonyi
(c) Dennis Tito   (d) Mark Shuttleworth

33. If three numbers are in the ratio 2:3:5 and the twice their sum is 100. Find the square of the largest of the three numbers.
(a) 225   (b) 625
(c) 25   (d) 100

34. Below are given statements. You have to take the given statements to be true even if they seem to be at variance with the commonly known facts and then decide which of the given conclusions logically follows from the given statements.
Statements:
I. All rats are hills.
II. All hills are rivers.
(a) Some rivers are rats
(b) No river is a hill
(c) All hills are rats
(d) No river is a rat

35. The upstream speed of the boat is 40 km/hr and the speed of the boat in still water is 55 km/hr. What is the downstream speed of the boat?
(a) 75 km/hr   (b) 70 km/hr
(c) 60 km/hr   (d) 65 km/hr

36. If MENTOR = NVMGLI then PROFESSOR =
(a) QSPGFTTPS   (b) KILUVHHLI
(c) KSLGVTHMI   (d) KILGFHHLI

37. How many bones does a new bom human baby have?
(a) 350   (b) 206
(c) 211   (d) 411

38. Choose the pair which is related in the same way as the words in the first pair from the given choices. DOG : KENNEL :: BEE :
____
(a) HIVE   (b) BARN
(c) HOLE   (d) NEST

39. Working together, P, Q and R reap a field in 6 days. If P can do it alone in 10 days and Q in 24 days, in how many days will R alone be able to reap the field?
(a) 32 days   (b) 40 days
(c) 45 days   (d) 60 days

40. What is $C_{12}H_{22}O_{11}$ also known as -
(a) Sand   (b) Sugar
(c) Salt   (d) Clay

41. On an average, how many taste buds are present in a human tongue?
(a) 2000 to 8000
(b) 50000 to 100000
(c) 1 million to 10 million
(d) More than 10 million

42. In 2013, the first woman to be elected as the President of South Korea is -
(a) Park Young-sun   (b) Yuk Young-soo
(c) ParkGeun-hye   (d) Sim Sang-jung

43. The national song of India was composed by -
(a) Rabindranath Tagore
(b) Bankim Chandra Chatterjee
(c) Pydimarri Venkata Subba Rao
(d) Pingali Venkayya

44. Find the LCM of 15, 25 and 29.
(a) 2335   (b) 3337
(c) 2175   (d) 2375

45. In 2015, which auto manufacturer manipulated emissions testing data leading to the resignation of its CEO Martin Winterkom?
(a) Volkswagen   (b) Ford
(c) Toyota   (d) General Motors

46. A ladder 20 m long is leaning against a vertical wall. It makes an angle of 30° with the ground. How high on the wall does the ladder reach?
(a) 10 m
(b) 17.32 m
(c) 34.64 m
(d) 30 m

47. Which of the following organisms does NOT reproduce by budding?
(a) Coral   (b) Hydra
(c) Sponges   (d) Annelido

48. Compute: $(50 + 0.5 \times 20) \div 0.7$
(a) 8.571   (b) 857.1
(c) 85.71   (d) 72.85

49. How high is the badminton net at the center?
(a) 5 feet   (b) 5.1 feet
(c) 5.5 feet   (d) 4.8 feet

50. Choose the pair which is related in the same way as the words in the first pair from the given choices. TENNIS : COURT :: BOXING:
____
(a) STADIUM   (b) RING
(c) PITCH   (d) GROUND

51. The earliest hominoids to be classified as homo sapiens were the -
(a) Ergaster line
(b) Cro-magnon
(c) Neanderthal
(d) Proconsul

52. Which of the following Acts under the Indian Constitution is described by Article 21A?
(a) Right to Education
(b) Right to Information
(c) Representation of the People
(d) Right to Freedom of Religion

53. What is the compound interest on ₹48,000 for 2 years at 20 % p.a., if interest is compounded annually?
(a) ₹69,120   (b) ₹21,120
(c) ₹76,800   (d) ₹72,000

54. The only non-metal which is liquid at room temperature is -
(a) Mercury   (b) Bromine
(c) Chlorine   (d) Gallium

55. A triangle has a perimeter of 200. If two of its sides are equal and the third side is 20 more than the equal sides, what is the length of the third side?
(a) 60   (b) 50
(c) 80   (d) 70

56. In 1981, ISRO launched India's first geostationary satellite called -
(a) Aryabhata   (b) APPLE
(c) Bhaskara II   (d) INSAT IB

57. If '+' means ×, '−' means ÷, '×' means + and '÷' means −; compute the value of the expression:
$36 - 4 + 7 \times 8$
(a) 72   (b) 71
(c) 74   (d) 75

58. The process when the computer is switched on and the operating system gets loaded from hard disk to main memory is called -
(a) Booting
(b) Fetching
(c) Processing
(d) Multi-Processing

59. Given below is a statement followed by some conclusions. You have to take the given statement to be true even if it seems to be at variance with the commonly known facts and then decide which of the giver conclusions logically follow(s) from the given statement.
Statement: In some tier 2 cities in India, transportation is one of the major problems.
Conclusions:
I.   All tier 2 cities are not well connected.
II. Lack of transportation facilities is the only problem in Indian metros.
(a) Only conclusion I follows
(b) Only conclusion II follows
(c) Both I and II follow
(d) Neither of them follows

60. How is Sameer related to Akbar if Sameer introduced Akbar as his maternal grandmother's only son's son?
(a) Brother   (b) Son
(c) Maternal Uncle (d) Cousin

61. The first large scale electrical air conditioning was invented and used in 1902 by -
(a) Willis Carrier (b) John Gome
(c) Stuart Cramer (d) H. H. Schultz

62. Simplify: $(2/7 + 3/5) \div (2/5 + 2/7)$
(a) 31/24
(b) 24/31
(c) 26/25
(d) 12/13

63. If P travelled the first half of a journey at 40 km/hr and the remaining distance at 50 km/hr. what is the average speed of his travel?

(a) 44.44 km/hr
(b) 53.33 km/hr
(c) 45 km/hr
(d) 60 km/hr

64. What is the median of the following list of numbers: 55, 53, 56, 59, 61, 69, and 31?
(a) 55 (b) 56
(c) 59 (d) 61

65. Rearrange the following jumbled sentences to make a meaningful one:
P: weather conditions across a vast geographic
Q: the climate of India
R: scale and varied topography
S: comprises of a wide range of The proper sequence should be:
(a) SRQP
(b) QSPR
(c) PQRS
(d) QRPS

66. Which leader adopted Orthodox Christianity as the official religion of Russia?
(a) Vladimir the Great
(b) Michael Romanov
(c) Ivan IV
(d) Boris Godunov

67. Which chess piece moves straight ahead but captures diagonally?
(a) Knight
(b) Rook
(c) Bishop
(d) Pawn

68. Which of the following coloured light has the lowest frequency?
(a) Green (b) Blue
(c) Red (d) Violet

69. The area of a triangle ABC is 63 sq. units. Two parallel lines DE, FG, are drawn such that they divide the line segments AB and AC into three equal parts. What is the area of the quadrilateral DEGF?
(a) 28 sq. units
(b) 35 sq. units
(c) 21 sq. units
(d) 48 sq. units

70. The sum of digits of a two-digit number is 9. When the digits are reversed, the number decreases by 45. Find the changed number.

(a) 45
(b) 72
(c) 63
(d) 27

71. Ram said, "Sita is my paternal great grandfathers only son's only daughter-in-law". How is Sita related to Ram?
(a) Maternal Aunt (b) Paternal Aunt
(c) Mother (d) Sister

72. Which among the following is true for the given numbers?
(a) $3/8 < 19/73 < 29/47 < 17/39$
(b) $19/73 < 3/8 < 17/39 < 29/47$
(c) $19/73 < 3/8 < 29/47 < 17/39$
(d) $19/73 < 29/47 < 3/8 < 17/39$

73. In which of the following states of India is the White Desert located?
(a) Gujarat
(b) Tamil Nadu
(c) Jammu and Kashmir
(d) Sikkim

74. In 2015, underground glaciers of frozen water were discovered on -
(a) Mars (b) Venus
(c) Jupiter (d) Saturn

75. Which of the following insecticides' harmful effects came under media attention when health issues in Kerala were publicized?
(a) Endosulfan (b) Lethal
(c) Thimet (d) Monocil

76. Malini said, "Rohit is my maternal aunt's mother's only son's son". How is Malini related to Rohit?
(a) Cousin (b) Mother
(c) Sister (d) Daughter

77. If **RUN = 182114** and **BIN = 2914**, then **BRING =**
(a) 2189147
(b) 1178136
(c) 31910158
(d) 21910158

78. 30 men working 5 hours a day can do a task in 16 days. In how many days will 40 men working 6 hours a day do the same task?
(a) 12 days
(b) 10 days
(c) 15 days
(d) 18 days

DIRECTIONS (Qs. 79-81): *Study the diagram given below and answer the questions based on it.*

△ represents Persons who like Reading

○ represents Persons who like Cycling

☐ represents Persons who like Trekking

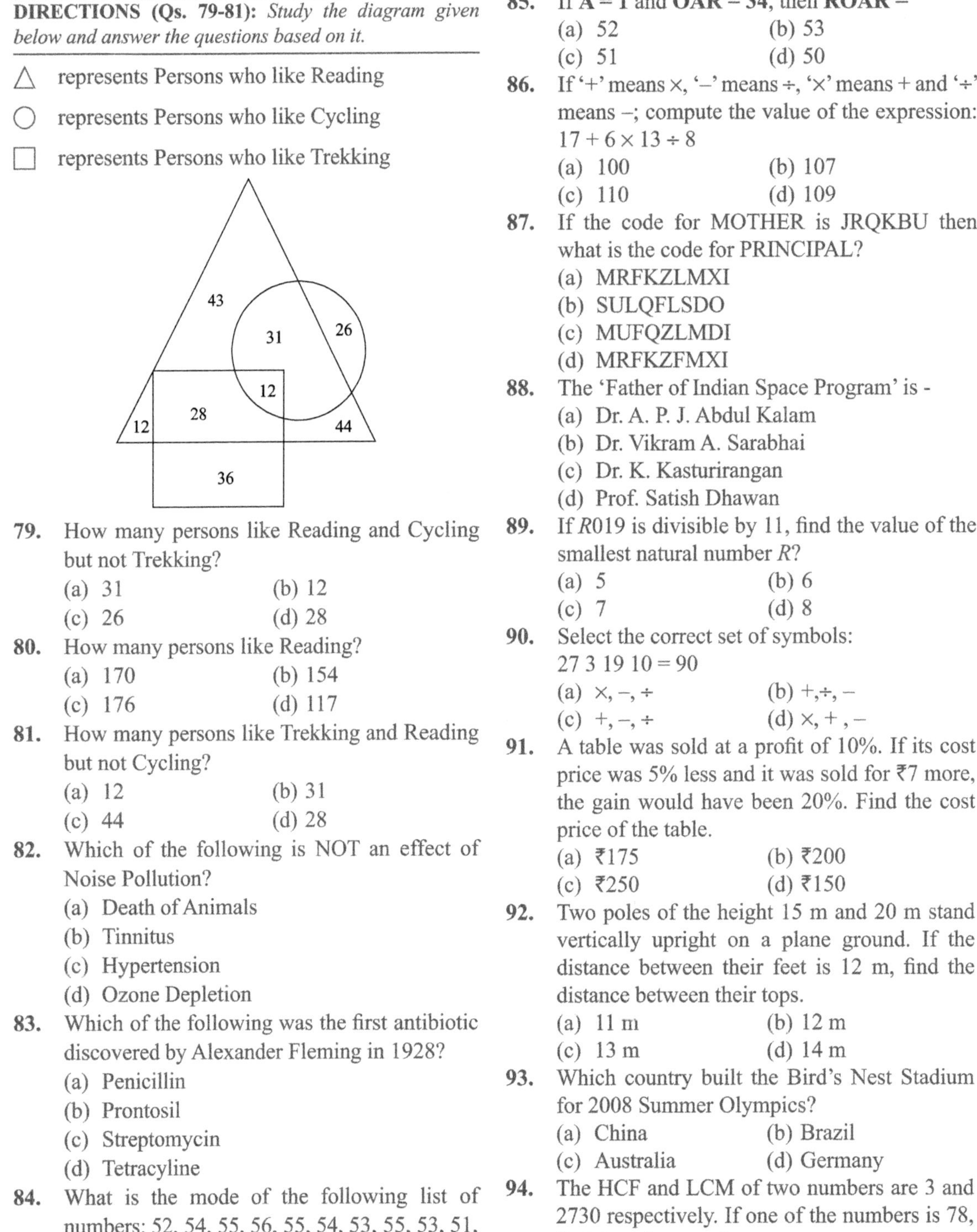

79. How many persons like Reading and Cycling but not Trekking?
    (a) 31   (b) 12
    (c) 26   (d) 28

80. How many persons like Reading?
    (a) 170   (b) 154
    (c) 176   (d) 117

81. How many persons like Trekking and Reading but not Cycling?
    (a) 12   (b) 31
    (c) 44   (d) 28

82. Which of the following is NOT an effect of Noise Pollution?
    (a) Death of Animals
    (b) Tinnitus
    (c) Hypertension
    (d) Ozone Depletion

83. Which of the following was the first antibiotic discovered by Alexander Fleming in 1928?
    (a) Penicillin
    (b) Prontosil
    (c) Streptomycin
    (d) Tetracyline

84. What is the mode of the following list of numbers: 52, 54, 55, 56, 55, 54, 53, 55, 53, 51, and 57?
    (a) 53   (b) 54
    (c) 55   (d) 52

85. If **A = 1** and **OAR = 34**, then **ROAR =**
    (a) 52   (b) 53
    (c) 51   (d) 50

86. If '+' means ×, '−' means ÷, '×' means + and '÷' means −; compute the value of the expression:
    $17 + 6 \times 13 \div 8$
    (a) 100   (b) 107
    (c) 110   (d) 109

87. If the code for MOTHER is JRQKBU then what is the code for PRINCIPAL?
    (a) MRFKZLMXI
    (b) SULQFLSDO
    (c) MUFQZLMDI
    (d) MRFKZFMXI

88. The 'Father of Indian Space Program' is -
    (a) Dr. A. P. J. Abdul Kalam
    (b) Dr. Vikram A. Sarabhai
    (c) Dr. K. Kasturirangan
    (d) Prof. Satish Dhawan

89. If $R019$ is divisible by 11, find the value of the smallest natural number R?
    (a) 5   (b) 6
    (c) 7   (d) 8

90. Select the correct set of symbols:
    27 3 19 10 = 90
    (a) ×, −, ÷   (b) +, ÷, −
    (c) +, −, ÷   (d) ×, + , −

91. A table was sold at a profit of 10%. If its cost price was 5% less and it was sold for ₹7 more, the gain would have been 20%. Find the cost price of the table.
    (a) ₹175   (b) ₹200
    (c) ₹250   (d) ₹150

92. Two poles of the height 15 m and 20 m stand vertically upright on a plane ground. If the distance between their feet is 12 m, find the distance between their tops.
    (a) 11 m   (b) 12 m
    (c) 13 m   (d) 14 m

93. Which country built the Bird's Nest Stadium for 2008 Summer Olympics?
    (a) China   (b) Brazil
    (c) Australia   (d) Germany

94. The HCF and LCM of two numbers are 3 and 2730 respectively. If one of the numbers is 78, find the other number.
    (a) 107   (b) 103
    (c) 105   (d) 102

95. According to the Constitution, the ratio between the length and breadth of the national tricolor should be -
    (a) 3 : 2   (b) 3 : 1
    (c) 2 : 1   (d) 4 : 3

96. Which of the following monuments built by Muhammad Quli Qutb Shah is said to be built to commemorate the eradication of plague?
    (a) Alai Minar   (b) Charminar
    (c) Fateh Burj   (d) Qutub Minar

97. Select the correct set of symbols:
    44 4 7 5 = 82
    (a) ×, −, ÷   (b) +, ÷, −
    (c) +, −, ÷   (d) ÷, ×, +

98. The average of first 20 multiples of 12 is:
    (a) 124   (b) 120
    (c) 126   (d) 130

99. Which of the following popular tourist destinations of India were built in 1911 to commemorate the visit of King George V and Queen Mary?
    (a) India Gate
    (b) Gateway of India
    (c) The Prince of Wales Museum
    (d) Victoria Terminus

100. Six years ago, the ratio of the ages of the two persons P and Q was 3:2. Four years hence the ratio of then ages will be 8:7. What is P's age?
    (a) 10 years   (b) 12 years
    (c) 14 years   (d) 8 years

HINTS & EXPLANATIONS

1. (a) CP of article $= ₹\,1600$
New SP of article $= ₹\,1840$

New profit $\% = \left(\dfrac{\text{SP} - \text{CP}}{\text{CP}} \times 100\right)\%$

$= \left(\dfrac{1840 - 1600}{1600} \times 100\right)\%$

$= 15\%$

Old profit $= 10\%$
$\therefore (15\% - 10\%) = 5\%$ profit would have been increased.

2. (a)

3. (c)

$\dfrac{1}{2}\left(1^{st}\text{ part}\right) = \dfrac{1}{3}\left(2^{nd}\text{ part}\right) = \dfrac{1}{6}\left(3^{rd}\text{ part}\right) = k(\text{say})$

$\Rightarrow$ 1st part $= 2k$
2nd part $= 3k$
3rd part $= 6k$

Now, $2k + 3k + 6k = 3740$

$\Rightarrow$ $11k = 3740 \Rightarrow k = \dfrac{3740}{11} = 340$

$\therefore$ 1st part $= 2k = 2 \times 340 = 680$
2nd part $= 3k = 3 \times 340 = 1020$
3rd part $= 4k = 4 \times 340 = 1360$

4. (b)

5. (a) Average of amount spent on leisure

$= \left(\dfrac{5 + 6.5 + 7.3 + 7.9 + 8.5}{5}\right) \times 100$

$= \dfrac{35}{5} \times 100 = ₹\,7040$

6. (a) Total household expenditure in 2012 :
$= ₹\,(46 + 14 + 7.3 + 5.6 + 17) \times 1000$
$= ₹\,89{,}900$

7. (b) Required percentage

$= \left[\dfrac{(7.4 \times 1000)}{(52 \times 1000)} \times 100\right]\%$

$= \left(\dfrac{7.4 \times 100}{52}\right)\%$

$= 14.23\%$

8. (d)

Sol. (9–11):

Arun Chitra Fatima
←South facing flates
← North facing flates
Derek Evan Biswajyot

9. (a) Arun and Biswajyot got diagonally opposite to each other.

10. (a) Arun, Chitra and Fatima got South facing flates.

11. (c) Evan and Chitra are opposite to each other.

12. (c)   13. (b)   14. (c)   15. (b)

16. (b)

17. (a) Let the length of piece of cloth is x meter.

cost of 1m. of cloth $= ₹\,\dfrac{35}{x}$
According to question,

$(x + 4)\left(\dfrac{35}{x} - 1\right) = 35$

$\Rightarrow (x + 4)\,\dfrac{(35 - x)}{x} = 35$

$\Rightarrow (x + 4)(35 - x) = 35x$

$\Rightarrow 35x - x^2 + 140 - 4x - 35x = 0$

$\Rightarrow x^2 - 140 + 4x = 0$

$(x + 14)(x - 10) = 0$

$\therefore$ $x = 10$

or length of cloth $= 10m$

18. (c) Let the number of 5 paisa coins and 10 paisa coins is x and $(90 - x)$ respectively.
According to the question
Total value of coins $= ₹\,7$

$\Rightarrow \dfrac{5}{100}(x) + \dfrac{10}{100}(90 - x) = 7$

$\Rightarrow \dfrac{x}{20} + \dfrac{90 - x}{10} = 7$

$\Rightarrow x + 2(90 - x) = 140$

$\Rightarrow -x + 180 = 140$

$\Rightarrow x = 40$

$\therefore$ Number of 5 paisa coins $= 40$

19. (a) Womesh Chandra Bonnerjee presided over the first session of Indian National Congress held at Bombay in 1885.

20. (d)

21. (b) Outer dimension of box :–
length = 22 cm, Breadth = 17 cm;
Height = 12cm
Thickness = 1 cm
Inner dimensions of box :–
Length = 22 cm – 1 cm – 1 cm = 20 cm
Breadth = 17 cm – 1 cm – 1 cm = 15 cm
Height = 12 cm – 1 cm – 1 cm = 10 cm
∴ Volume of cement = Inner capacity of box
= l × b × h
= (20 × 15 × 10) cm^3
= 3000 cm^3

22. (a) SP = Marked price – discount

$$= ₹\ 320 - \left(\frac{10}{100} \times 320\right)$$

$$= ₹\ (320 - 32)$$

$$= ₹\ 288$$

$$CP = \frac{100}{(100 + G\%)} \times SP$$

$$= \left(\frac{100}{100 + 20} \times 288\right)$$

$$= ₹ \left(\frac{100}{120} \times 288\right) = ₹\ 240$$

23. (d) Let the principle is ₹ P and rate of interest is r % then rate of interest

$$(r) = \frac{S.I. \times 100}{P \times t}$$

$$= \frac{1200 \times 100}{P \times 2}$$

$$r = \frac{60000}{P} \quad ....(i)$$

Compound interest (C.I.)

$$1290 = P\left[\left(1 + \frac{r}{100}\right)^2 - 1\right]$$

$$1290 = P\left[\frac{r}{50} + \frac{r^2}{10000}\right]$$

Putting $r = \dfrac{60000}{P}$

$$1290 = P\left[\frac{60000}{50P} + \frac{360000}{P^2}\right]$$

$$1290 = \left[1200 + \frac{360000}{P}\right]$$

$$1290 - 1200 = \frac{360000}{P}$$

$$P = \frac{360000}{90}$$

$$= ₹\ 4000$$

24. (a) 25. (d)   26.   (c)

27. (d) Maanch is performed in Madhya Pradesh. It is a distinct folk performed at any place. It is a lyrical folk drama and a form of operatic ballet.

28. (a) 29. (a)

30. (a) A hard court is the surface on the floor on which a sport is played, most usually in reference to tennis court. They are made of rigid materials such as concrete or asphalt.

31. (b) $5.16 \times 3.2 = 16.512$

32. (c)

33. (b) Let three numbers be $2x$, $3x$ and $5x$ respectively.

Now, $2(2x + 3x + 5x) = 100$

$\Rightarrow \qquad 20x = 100$

$\Rightarrow \qquad x = 5$

∴ Square of largest number = $(5x)^2$

$= (5 \times 5)^2$

$= 625$

34. (a)

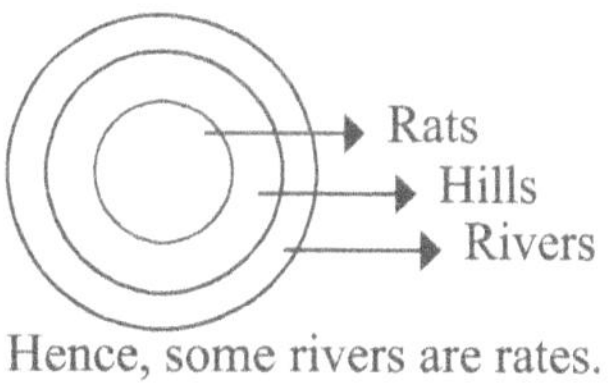

Rats
Hills
Rivers

Hence, some rivers are rates.

35. (b) Upstream speed = speed of boat is still water – speed of stream

⇒ 40 km/hr = 55 km/hr – speed of stream

⇒ Speed of stream = 15 km/hr

Again, Downstream speed

= speed of boat in still water + speed of stream

= 15km/hr + 55km/hr

= 70 km/hr

36. (b)

A	B	C	D		E	F	G	H	I
↓	↓	↓	↓		↓	↓	↓	↓	↓
W	X	Y	Z		R	S	T	U	V

(Letters position in reverse order)

∴ PROFESSOR = KILUVHHLI

37. (a) 38. (a)

39. (b) P does a work in 10 days.

P can do a piece of work in $\dfrac{1}{10}$ days

Q does a work in 24 days.

Q does a piece of work in $\dfrac{1}{24}$ days

Similarly, R will do a piece of work in $\dfrac{1}{R}$ days.

Now, P, Q, R together reap a field in 6 days.

$\therefore \qquad \dfrac{1}{10}+\dfrac{1}{24}+\dfrac{1}{R}=\dfrac{1}{6}$

$\Rightarrow \qquad \dfrac{1}{R}=\dfrac{1}{6}-\dfrac{1}{10}-\dfrac{1}{24}$

$\Rightarrow \qquad \dfrac{1}{R}=\dfrac{20-12-5}{120}$

$\Rightarrow \qquad R=40$

Hence, R alone will take 40 days to reap the field.

40. (b)   41.   (a)   42.(c)   43. (b)

44. (c)

$$\begin{array}{r|rrr}
3 & 15, & 25, & 29 \\ \hline
5 & 5, & 25, & 29 \\ \hline
5 & 1, & 5, & 29 \\ \hline
29 & 1, & 1, & 29 \\ \hline
& 1, & 1, & 1, \\
\end{array}$$

$\therefore \ \mathrm{LCM} = 3 \times 5 \times 5 \times 29$

$\qquad\qquad = 2175$

45. (a)

46. (a)

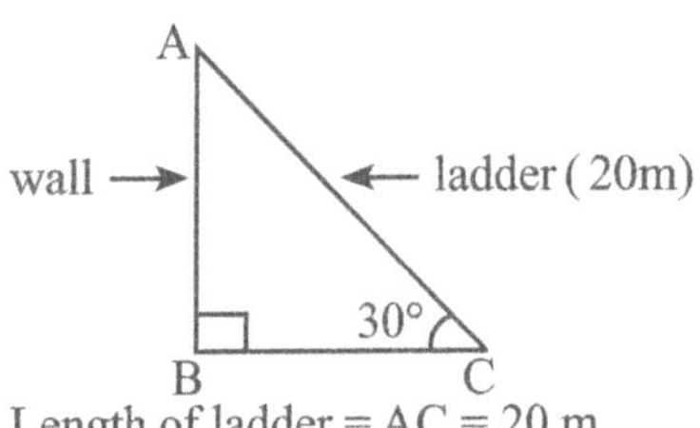

Length of ladder = AC = 20 m

In $\triangle$ ABC,

$\sin 30° = \dfrac{AB}{AC}$

$\Rightarrow \quad \dfrac{1}{2}=\dfrac{AB}{AC} \qquad \Rightarrow \quad \dfrac{1}{2}=\dfrac{AB}{20}$

$\Rightarrow \quad AB = 10m$

47. (d)

48. (c) $\qquad (50 + 0.5 \times 20) \div 0.7$

$\qquad = (50 + 10) \div 0.7$

$\qquad = 60 \div 0.7 = \dfrac{60}{0.7} = 85.71$

49. (a)   50. (b)   51.   (b)

52. (a) The Right to Education Act is an act of the parliament of India enacted on 4th August, 2009. The act describes the modalities of free and compulsory education for children between the ages of 6 to 14 years in India under article 21A.

53. (b) P $= ₹ 48000$, R $= 20\%$ p.a, T $= 2$ years

$\mathrm{CI} = P\left[\left(1+\dfrac{R}{100}\right)^{2}-1\right]$

$\qquad = 48000\left[\left(1+\dfrac{20}{100}\right)^{2}-1\right]$

$\qquad = 48000\left[\left(\dfrac{6}{5}\right)^{2}-1\right]=48000\left(\dfrac{36}{25}-1\right)$

$\qquad = 48000\left(\dfrac{36-25}{25}\right)$

$\qquad = 48000 \times \dfrac{11}{25} = ₹ 21120$

54. (b)

55. (c) Let the three sides of a triangle are x, x round $(x + 20)$ respectively.

$\qquad$ Now, Perimeter $= 200$

$\Rightarrow \qquad x + x + (x + 20) = 200$

$\Rightarrow \qquad\qquad 3x + 20 = 200$

$\Rightarrow \qquad\qquad\qquad x = 60$

$\qquad$ Hence, third side $= x + 20 = 80$

56. (b)

57. (b) New expression

$\qquad\qquad 36 \div 4 \times 7 + 8 = 9 \times 7 + 8$

$\qquad\qquad\qquad\qquad\qquad = 63 + = 71$

58. (a)   59.   (d)   60.(d)   61. (a)

62. (a) $\left(\dfrac{2}{7}+\dfrac{3}{5}\right)\div\left(\dfrac{2}{5}+\dfrac{2}{7}\right)$

$\qquad = \left(\dfrac{10+21}{35}\right)\div\left(\dfrac{14+10}{35}\right)$

$\qquad = \dfrac{31}{35}\times\dfrac{35}{24}=\dfrac{31}{24}$

63. (a)

64. (b) Arranging number in ascending order :

31, 53, 55, 56, 59, 61, 69

$\qquad$ Here $n = 7$

$\therefore \qquad$ Median $=\left(\dfrac{n+1}{2}\right)^{\text{th}}$ term

$$= \left(\frac{7+1}{2}\right)^{th} \text{term}$$
$$= 4^{th} \text{ term}$$
$$= 56$$

65. (b)

66. (a) Vladimir, the Great adopted Orthodox Christianity as the official religion of Russia.

67. (d) 68. (d)   69.(c)

70. (d) Let digit at one's and ten's place be x and $(9-x)$ respectively

$$\therefore \text{ Original number} = 10(9-x) + x$$
$$= 90 - 10x + x$$
$$= 90 - 9x$$

Also, new changed number $= 10x + (9-x)$
$$= 10x + 9 - x$$
$$= 9x + 9$$

Now, $\qquad (9x+9) = (90 - 9x) - 45$
$$\Rightarrow \qquad 9x + 9x = 90 - 45 - 9$$
$$\Rightarrow \qquad\qquad 18x = 36$$
$$\Rightarrow \qquad\qquad x = 2$$
$$\therefore \text{ Changed number} = 9x + 9$$
$$= 9(2) + 9 = 27$$

71. (c)

72. (b) $\dfrac{3}{8} = 0.375$; $\quad \dfrac{19}{73} = 0.26$

$\dfrac{29}{47} = 0.61$; $\quad \dfrac{17}{39} = 0.43$

Arranging in descending order,

$$\frac{19}{73} < \frac{3}{8} < \frac{17}{39} < \frac{29}{47}$$

73. (a) In 2015, underground water of frozen water was discovered on Mars.

74. (a) 75. (a)   76.(a)

77. (a) R U N $\longrightarrow$ 18   21   14
       B I N $\longrightarrow$ 2   9   14

Here, each letter shows its position in English alphabets i.e. R is 18th letters, U is 21st letter, B is 2nd letter and so on,

$\therefore$ B   R   I   N   G
$\longrightarrow$ 2   18   9   14   7

78. (b) Let 40 men will take x days to do the same task.

$\therefore$ Total working hours by 30 men
$=$ Total working hours by 40 men

$$\Rightarrow 30 \times 5 \times 16 = 40 \times x \times 6$$
$$\Rightarrow \qquad x = \frac{30 \times 5 \times 16}{40 \times 6} = 10$$

Hence, 40 men will take 10 days to do the same task

79. (a) Only 31 persons like Reading and Cycling but not Trekking.

80. (a) Number of persons like Reading
$= 43 + 31 + 12 + 28 + 12 + 44 = 170$

81. (d) Only 28 persons like Trekking and Reading but not Cycling.

82. (d) 83.   (a)

84. (c) Number in ascending order :
51, 52, 53, 53, 54, 54, 55, 55, 55, 56, 57
Mode = 55, as it occurs maximum times.

85. (a) A = 1
OAR = 34 = 15 + 1 + 18
Since each letter shows its position in the alphabets
$\therefore$ ROAR = 18 + 15 + 1 + 18 = 52

86. (b) New expression
$= 17 \times 6 + 13 - 8$
$= 102 + 13 - 8$
$= 107$

87. (c) 88.   (b)

89. (d) Sum of digits at old places = R + 1
Sum of digits at even places = 0 + 9 = 9
$\therefore$ Difference = (R + 1) – (9)
$=$ (R – 8), which must be equal to zero
$\therefore$ R – 8 = 0 $\Rightarrow$ R = 8

90. (d) $27 \times 3 + 19 - 10$
$= 81 + 19 - 10$
$= 100 - 10 = 90$

91. (a) Let CP $= ₹ x$

$$SP = ₹ x + \frac{10}{100} x = ₹ 1.1x$$

Now new C.P $= ₹ \left(x - \frac{5}{100} x\right) = ₹ 0.95x$

New SP $= ₹ (1.1x + 7)$
Profit $=$ SP – CP $= ₹ (1.1x + 7) - 0.95x$
$= 0.15x + 7$

$$\text{Profit \%} = \frac{0.15x + 7}{0.95x} \times 100 \Rightarrow \frac{20}{100} = \frac{0.15x + 7}{0.95x}$$

$\Rightarrow 0.95x = 0.75x + 35 \Rightarrow x = \dfrac{3500}{20} = 175$

Cost price of the table = ₹ 175.

92. (c)

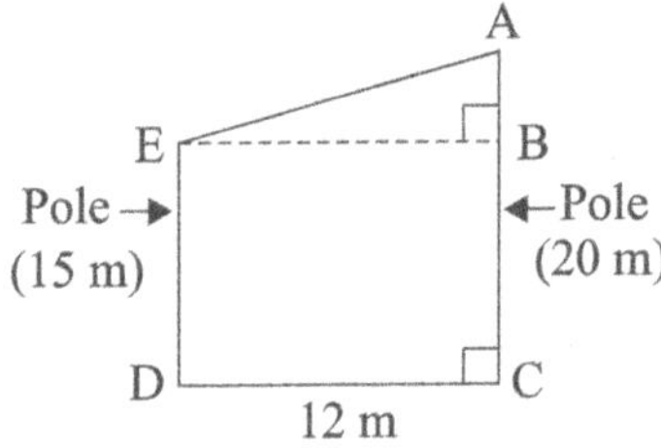

Here DC = EB = 12m and ED = BC = 15m

∴   AB = AC – BC = 20m –15m = 5m

Now, In $\triangle$ ABE, (by Pythogoras theorem)

$H^2 = B^2 + P^2$

$\Rightarrow (AE)^2 = (DC)^2 + (AB)^2$

$\Rightarrow (AE)^2 = (12)^2 + (5)^2$

$\Rightarrow \qquad = 144 + 25$

$AE = 13m$

Distance between their tops.

93. (a)

94. (c) HCF × LCM =Product of two numbers

$\Rightarrow 3 \times 2730 = 78 \times$ other number

$\Rightarrow$ Other no. $= \dfrac{2730 \times 3}{78} = 105$

95. (a) The ratio between the length and breadth of the national tricolor should be 3:2.

96. (b) Charminar is the monument built by Muhammad Quli Qutub Shah in 1591 to commemorate the end of the plague in the city.

97. (d) $44 \div 4 \times 7 + 5 = 11 \times 7 + 5$

$\qquad\qquad = 77 + 5 = 82$

98. (c) First 20 multiples of 12 are: 12, 24, 36, 48, 60, 72, 84, 96, 108, 120, 132, 144, 156, 168, 180, 192, 204, 216, 228, 240,

Sum of multiples = 2520

∴   Average $= \dfrac{2520}{20} = 126$

99. (b) The Gateway of India was built in 1911 as a triumphed arch to commemorate the visit of King George V and Queen Mary. It was built at Apollo Bunder, a popular meeting place.

100. (b) Let the present ages of P and Q are x and y respectively.

Six yrs. ago

P's age $= (x - 6)$ yrs.

Q's age $= (y - 6)$ yrs.

∴ $\dfrac{x-6}{y-6} = \dfrac{3}{2}$

$\Rightarrow 2x - 12 = 3y - 18$

$\Rightarrow 2x - 3y = -18 + 12 = -6$

$\Rightarrow 2x - 3y = -6$

$\Rightarrow 2x = -6 + 3y$

$\qquad x = \dfrac{-6 + 3y}{2}$ \hfill (i)

Four years hence

P's age $= (x + 4)$ yrs

Q's age $= (y + 4)$ yrs

∴ $\dfrac{x+4}{y+4} = \dfrac{8}{7}$

$\Rightarrow 7x + 28 = 8y + 32$

$\Rightarrow 7x - 8y = 4$

$\Rightarrow 7\left(\dfrac{-6 + 3y}{2}\right) - 8y = 4$

$\Rightarrow 7(-6 + 3y) - 16y = 8$

$\Rightarrow 21y - 16y = 8 + 42$

$\Rightarrow 5y = 50 \quad \Rightarrow y = 10$

∴   P's age $= \dfrac{-6 + 3y}{2}$

$\qquad\qquad = \dfrac{-6 + 30}{2} = 12$ yrs.

1. The Make In India Logo is made up of what?
   (a) Lion made of Cogs
   (b) Eagle Made of Steel
   (c) Chakra Made of Cotton
   (d) Tiger Made of Khadi

2. The median of the following numbers arranged in ascending order is 2.5, if so find x?
   0, 0, 1, 1, 2, 2, x, 3, 3, 4, 5, 7
   (a) 2   (b) 3   (c) 4   (d) 0

3. How do Indians celebrate Holi?
   (a) By playing pranks on each other
   (b) By throwing coloured powder and water on each other
   (c) By Lighting Lamps
   (d) By setting pigeons free

4. X is the only daughter of Y's grandfather's only son. Y's grandfather has only child. How is X related to Y?
   (a) Mother   (b) Sister
   (c) Paternal Aunt   (d) Grandmother

5. In Indian sport what does HIL stand for?
   (a) Himachal Indian Lions
   (b) Haryana Indus League
   (c) Hockey India League
   (d) Hyderabad India League

DIRECTIONS (Qs.6-8): *Study the following diagram and answer questions based on it. The diagram represents the likes of children in a society.*

The diagram represents the likes of children in a society.

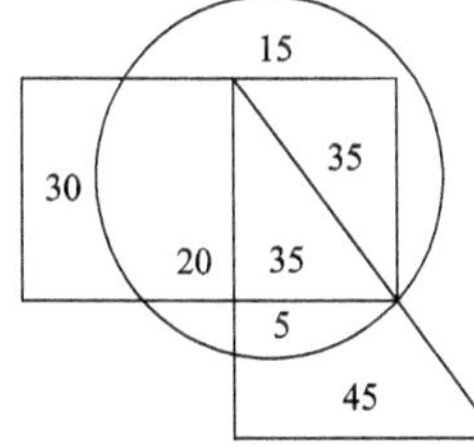

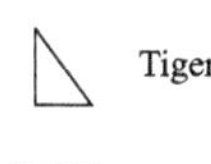

6. The difference between children who like leopard to those who like tiger is
   (a) 50   (b) 35
   (c) 30   (d) 5

7. How many children like both lion and leopard?
   (a) 35   (b) 55
   (c) 90   (d) 95

8. How many children who like lion, also like the tiger?
   (a) 5   (b) 15
   (c) 35   (d) 40

9. Find the missing (?) in the series
   50, 49.5, ?, 45.5, 42, 37.5, ...
   (a) 49   (b) 48
   (c) 47.5   (d) 46

10. Malgudi Days is based on the works of which Indian Writer?
    (a) Shankar Nag
    (b) R.K. Lakshman
    (c) R.K. Narayan
    (d) Girish Karnad

11. Statements followed by some conclusions are given below.
    Statements:
    1. Employees are well paid.
    2. Rajan earns well.
    Conclusions:
    I. Rajan is an employee.
    II. Rajan is self-employed.
    Find which of the given conclusions logically follows from the given statements
    (a) Only conclusion I follows.
    (b) Only conclusion II follows.
    (c) Both I and II follow.
    (d) Neither I nor II follows.

12. At what time did India Gain Independence of 15th August 1947?
    (a) Morning   (b) Midevening
    (c) Midnight   (d) Noon

13. A train having a length of 500 m passes through a tunnel of 1000 m in 1 minute. What is the speed of the train in Km/hr?

(a) 75 Km/hr   (b) 90 Km/hr

(c) 87 Km/hr   (d) 96 Km/hr

14. What is the science or art of designing and accelerating projectiles so as to achieve a desired performance called?

(a) Ballistics

(b) Catapulting

(c) Ejection

(d) Rocket Science

15. Find the similarity in the following: Orange, Peach, Olive, Chrome

(a) All of them are fruits.

(b) All of them are names of seasons.

(c) All of them are colour₹

(d) All of them are shades of orange.

16. What does WLAN stand for?

(a) Wireless Local Area Network

(b) Wide Local Area Network

(c) Wind Light Atmospheric Nature

(d) Wireless Local Area Node

17. What does "Bicameral Legislature" mean?

(a) Legislators are divided into 4 separate assemblies

(b) Legislators are grouped as 1 assembly

(c) Legislators are divided into 2 separate assemblies

(d) Legislators are divided into 8 separate assemblies

18. Find the missing (?) in the series

........, HG, IJ, LK, MN, ?,........

(a) OP   (b) PO

(c) QP   (d) PQ

19. A small shop owner keeps inventory satisfying the following criteria —

1. Shampoo sachets that are priced between ₹4 and ₹ 10 per sachet.

2. Chocolates in the price range of ₹ 1 and ₹ 60 per piece.

3. Dry fruits priced more than ₹ 125 per 100 grams.

4. Milk packets in the price range of ₹ 21 and ₹ 29 per litre.

Which list among the following will definitely NOT be found in his shop?

(a) Shampoo A at ₹4 per sachet, chocolate B at ₹ 1.5 per piece and dry fruit C, at ₹250 per 125 gram.

(b) Shampoo P at ₹5 per sachet, milk packet Q at ₹23 per litre and dry fruit R at ₹ 150 per 100 gram.

(c) Shampoo X at ₹5 per sachet, chocolate Y at ₹ 1 per piece and dry fruit Z at ₹ 100 per 100 gram.

(d) Shampoo L at ₹ 4 per sachet, milk packet M at ₹ 24.5 per packet, and chocolate N at ₹35 per piece and dry fruit O at ₹ 350 per 200 gram.

20. Which is the most abundant combustible natural gas?

(a) Propane   (b) Methane

(c) Ethane   (d) Butane

21. Which among the following is the Largest Freshwater Lake in India?

(a) Dal Lake   (b) Thol Lake

(c) Pushkar Lake   (d) Wular Lake

22. Manu sold a dozen watches for ₹ 1454.64 per watch and made a profit of 16%. Find the cost price of the watches?

(a) 1254.00   (b) 1362.36

(c) 15048.00   (d) 16348.32

23. The famous camel trading event is a part of this annual fair.

(a) Udaipur Mela   (b) Thar Mela

(c) Kumbh Mela   (d) Pushkar Mela

24. What is the rate of change of position of an object with respect to a frame of reference, which is a function of time called?

(a) Mechanics   (b) Vector

(c) Velocity   (d) Magnitude

25. If DELHI is QRYUV, then BOMBAY is

(a) OBZNOL   (b) OZBNOL

(c) OZBONL   (d) OBZONL

26. If GOING IS 38253 and CASUAL is 409106, then LOGICAL is

(a) 6034286   (b) 6834206

(c) 6032486   (d) 6832406

27. Manju takes 16 days to complete a work. If she works with her friend Jenny they complete it in 12 days. How many days will it take for Jenny to complete the work alone?

    (a) 48   (b) 32

    (c) 36   (d) 24

28. Solve: $109 \times 102 \div 103$

    (a) 108   (b) 106

    (c) 102   (d) 105

29. If the circumference of a circle is 22 cm, find the area of the semicircle.

    (a) 38.5 sq.cm   (b) 19.25 sq.cm

    (c) 44 sq.cm   (d) 77 sq.cm

30. Find the interest on ₹ 25000 at 12% p.a. compounded annually for 3 years.

    (a) 9,000   (b) 9,833.40

    (c) 10,123.20   (d) 10,678.90

31. The LCM and HCF of 2 numbers are 168 and 6 respectively. If one of the numbers is 24. find the other.

    (a) 36   (b) 38

    (c) 40   (d) 42

32. Seeta said. "Ram's only brother is the father of my son's father". How is Ram's brother related to Seeta's son?

    (a) Father

    (b) Grandfather

    (c) Maternal Uncle

    (d) Paternal Uncle

33. 78 books, 114 crayons and 141 notebooks were distributed to school children equally. It was found that 6 were left undistributed in each. What was the total number of children?

    (a) 9   (b) 8

    (c) 13   (d) 12

34. What are Vivipara?

    (a) Vertebrates that are bom live

    (b) Type of cactus

    (c) Type of algae

    (d) A mollusk

DIRECTIONS (Qs. 35-37): *The bar chart represents percentage marks scored by four students U, V, W and X in History and Geography. Consider the bar chart and answer questions based on it.*

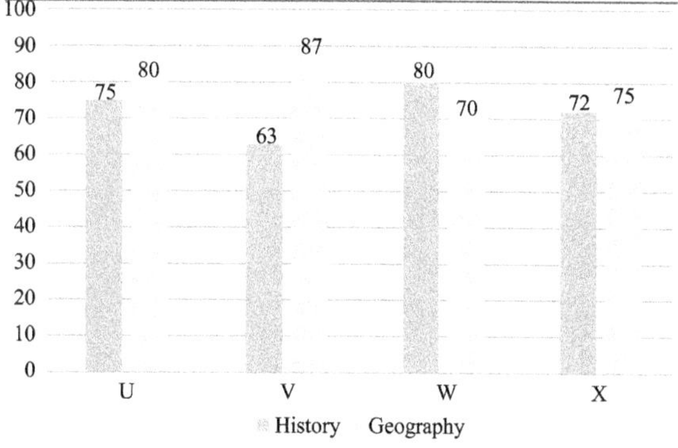

35. Who scored the highest percentage in both the subjects combined?

    (a) Both V and W   (b) V

    (c) W   (d) U

36. What is the percentage difference in the total marks obtained in Geography and History?

    (a) 7.58%   (b) 7%

    (c) 4.13%   (d) 5%

37. What is the average percentage marks obtained in History by all students?

    (a) 78%   (b) 75%

    (c) 72.5%   (d) 70%

38. If $a^{x+y} = a^6$ and x>y by 2 find x.

    (a) 1   (b) 2

    (c) 3   (d) 4

39. What is a Limerick?

    (a) A Type of Lime Stone

    (b) A form of poetry mostly in five-lines

    (c) A type of Theatre Play

    (d) A type of Word game

40. If Annual : One year, then Quinquennial : __________

    (a) Five years

    (b) Ten years

    (c) Hundred years

    (d) Thousand years

41. Andromeda is a

    (a) Galaxy neighboring the Milky way

    (b) Planet

    (c) Name of a black hole

    (d) Comet

42. Whose quote is "In practice of tolerance, one's enemy is the best teacher"?
(a) Gautama Buddha
(b) Mahatma Gandhi
(c) Barack Obama
(d) The Dalai Lama

43. What is Shigmo?
(a) A Goan Spring Festival
(b) The tallest peak in Nilgiris
(c) A type of Rangoli
(d) One of the Names of Lord Shiva

44. In computers, what does Yosemite, Mavericks, Mountain Lion, Lion, Snow Leopard, Leopard, Tiger, Panther, Jaguar, Puma and Cheetah stand for?
(a) Versions of Mac OS X
(b) Types of Storage Servers
(c) Macintosh Clones
(d) Power Books

45. Rearrange the jumbled letters to make a meaningful word and then select the one which is different.
(a) ENNI   (b) NEO
(c) EPPI   (d) REETH

46. Solve: $\dfrac{12}{13} \times \dfrac{285}{96} \div \dfrac{171}{169} = ?$
(a) $3\dfrac{2}{3}$ (b) $2\dfrac{17}{24}$
(c) $\dfrac{7}{8}$ (d) $\dfrac{11}{24}$

47. LIGO, Laser Interferometer Observatory was recently in the news. Why?
(a) Discovery of water in Mars
(b) Discovery of a diamond-filled star
(c) Detection of Gravitational waves
(d) Proving Big Bang theory as wrong

48. In which century did Portuguese merchants first land in Goa?
(a) 14th   (b) 15th
(c) 16th   (d) 17th

49. In 1999 who was the Prime Minister of Pakistan who was overthrown by a Military coupled by General Pervez Musharraf?
(a) Zulifiqar Ali Bhutto
(b) Zia ul-Haq
(c) Nawaz Sharif
(d) Yusuf Raza Gilani

50. What is C_6H_6?
(a) Hydro Carbon
(b) Hydro Cliloric Acid
(c) Benzene
(d) Toluene

51. What is Oneirology, the study of?
(a) Gods   (b) Dreams
(c) Sleep   (d) Colour

52. Which was the host city of the first modem summer Olympic games held in 1896?
(a) Athens   (b) Paris
(c) London   (d) Amsterdam

53. I take a book from a library containing 378 pages to be returned in a week's time. If I can read 14 pages an hour for three hours daily, for how long should it be renewed so that the book can be fully read?
(a) 1 day   (b) 3 days
(c) 4 days   (d) 2 days

54. Carl Sagan was
(a) An American astronomer
(b) British Physicist
(c) French Astronaut
(d) American President

55. Eggs sold by a shopkeeper over a week is given in the table below.

Eggs sold in dozens

Day	Sales in dozen
Sunday	12
Monday	8
Tuesday	11
Wednesday	5
Thursday	9
Friday	10
Saturday	10

If the price of one egg was ₹2.50, how much more did he earn on Friday than on Monday?
(a) 25 rupees   (b) 2.50 rupees
(c) 5.00 rupees   (d) 3.25 rupees.

56. The mean of the marks scored by 12 students of a class is 67.4. If the mean of another class consisting of 15 students is 72.3, find their combined mean?
(a) 70.12   (b) 69.85
(c) 71.23   (d) 68.94

57. If **GUITAR** = **HTJSBQ**, then **VIOLIN** = ________
(a) WHPKHM (b) WHPKJM
(c) WHKPHM (d) WHKPJM

58. A man walks at a certain speed and reaches his destination which is 6 km in 1 hr 40 minutes. If he runs the same distance in 1 hour 20 minutes what is the difference in speed?
(a) 1 km/hr (b) 0.9 km/hr
(c) 1.5 km/hr (d) 1.9 km/hr

59. What is "Binary Electronic Sequence Calculator" (BESK), created in 1953?
(a) Electronic computer
(b) Analogous Computer
(c) Digital Computer
(d) A Banker's Calculator

60. Find $\sin(90° - \theta)$
(a) $\cos 90°$ (b) $1/2$
(c) 1 (d) $\cos \theta$

61. What is India's famous comic series started by Anant Pai called?
(a) Raj Comics
(b) Amar Chitra Katha
(c) Tinkle
(d) Chandamama

62. Find $(x + y)^2 - (x - y)^2$?
(a) $2x^2y^2$ (b) $4xy$
(c) $2x^2 + 2y^2$ (d) $x^2 - y^2 + 2xy$

63. The area of a rectangle is 42sq.cm and its length is 7cm. Find its perimeter.
(a) 14 cm (b) 21cm
(c) 26 cm (d) 24 cm

64. If by selling 20 cycles Vinay incurs a loss equal to the selling price of 2 cycles, find his loss percentage.
(a) 10% (b) 11%
(c) $13\frac{1}{3}\%$ (d) $9\frac{1}{11}\%$

65. Read the following and answer the question based on it.

Proteins are used by the body for energy, metabolism, gene growth and maintenance. 10 to 35 percent of the daily caloric intake should ideally consist of proteins. They are found in all cells of the body. Hair and nail are made up of a protein called keratin, having sulphur bonds. Curlier hair has more sulphur links. Too much intake of proteins can sometimes lea to body weight.

Proteins ________
(a) Are not used by the body for any of its functions.
(b) Are required by the body in adequate quantities.
(c) Makes hair shiny, lengthy and black.
(d) Do not cause weight gain.

Comprehension: Five pickles - mango, lime, tomato, gooseberry and garlic are kept in five jars, in a row, in a random order, from left to right.
1. Gooseberry is not on either extremes.
2. There is one jar between mango and garlic.
3. Tomato is placed on the left side of lime.
4. The second jar from the left contains garlic.

66. There are two jars between which of the following -
(a) Lime and Gooseberry
(b) Gooseberry and Tomato
(c) Mango and Lime
(d) Tomato and Mango

DIRECTIONS (Qs. 67-68): *Consider the following information and answer questions based on it. Five pickles-mango, lime, tomato, gooseberry and garlic are kept in five jars, in a row, in a random order, from left to right.*

---

1. Gooseberry is not on either extremes.
2. There is one jar between mango and garlic.
3. Tomato is placed on the left side of lime.
4. The second jar from the left contains garlic.

67. Lime is in the ________ jar from left.
(a) Fifth (b) Fourth
(c) Third (d) First

68. The middle jar contains
(a) Mango (b) Tomato
(c) Gooseberry (d) Lime

69. What is an interstellar cloud of dust hydrogen, helium and other ionized gases called?
(a) Galaxy (b) Supernova
(c) Nebula (d) Black Hole

70. Where is the mosque, Adhai din ka Jhonpra located?
(a) Agra (b) Ajmer
(c) Ahmedabad (d) Mt.Abu

71. What is the official language in Bhutan?
(a) English (b) Hindi
(c) Dzongkha (d) Khmer

72. If the mathematical operator '+' means '×', '÷' means '–', '–' means '+' and '×' means '÷', find the value of $1 \times 2 + 6 - 2 \div 7$
(a) 2
(b) –2
(c) 3
(d) –1

73. When did Sikkim become a state of India?
(a) 1975
(b) 1973
(c) 1972
(d) 1950

74. What does PNR stand for?
(a) Public Number in Railway
(b) Passenger Name Record
(c) Passenger Number Reservation
(d) Priority Number in Reservation

75. A politician distributed 285 kg of sugar among the people of a village counting 1487. Find out how much sugar does each person get.
(a) 1.91 kg
(b) 191 kg
(c) 0.191 kg
(d) 19.1 kg

76. A sum borrowed at 6% p.a. earns an interest which is 1/3rd or its principal in x year. Find x.
(a) $5\dfrac{5}{9}$
(b) $4\dfrac{2}{9}$
(c) $6\dfrac{3}{7}$
(d) $5\dfrac{3}{4}$

77. +91 is the country calling code for which nation?
(a) Canada
(b) U.S.A
(c) India
(d) China

78. What plant has the scientific name *Solamon Tuberosum*?
(a) Potato
(b) Tomato
(c) Pumpkin
(d) Onion

79. Which signs should be interchanged if the equation below needs to be true?
$2 \div 16 - 2 + 6 \times 1 = 0$
(a) × and –
(b) – and +
(c) – and ÷
(d) + and ×

80. Who is called India's Child surgeon?
(a) Akrit Pran Jaswal
(b) Tathagat Avtar Tulsi
(c) Nischal Narayanain
(d) Sudhina Verma

81. Yash sells vegetables at 40 per kg and incurs a loss of 10%. If the total loss incurred is 144, what is the weight of vegetables sold? (Rounded off)
(a) 36 kg
(b) 32.40 kg
(c) 35 kg
(d) 39.2 kg

82. Name the inter-governmental organization to promote international co-operation?
(a) NATO
(b) UN
(c) WHO
(d) IGO

83. 1.08 tonne = ? kg
(a) 10800
(b) 108
(c) 1080
(d) 1.08

84. Looking at a photo, Anand said, "This man is the eldest son of my father's mother-in-law". How is Anand's mother related to this man?
(a) Mother
(b) Daughter
(c) Maternal Aunt
(d) Sister

85. An assertion (A) and a reason (R) are given below.
Assertion (A): Leaves are green in colour.
Reason (R): Chlorophyll, a green pigment is present in leaves.
Choose the correct option.
(a) Both A and R are true and R is the correct explanation of A
(b) Both A and R are true, but R is not the correct explanation of A
(c) A is true, but R is false
(d) A is false, but R is true

86. What is the opposite of Dharma?
(a) Adharma
(b) Karma
(c) Moksha
(d) Maya

87. A statement followed by some conclusions are given below.
Statement: The price of pulses has increased steeply.
Conclusions:
I. People cannot buy pulses.
II. Pulses have become a rare commodity.
Find which of the given conclusions logically follow from the given statement.
(a) Only conclusion I follows.
(b) Only conclusion II follows.
(c) Both I and II follows
(d) Neither I nor II follows.

88. Who has never been a Vice President of India?
(a) Mohammad Hamid Ansari
(b) A P J Abdul Kalam
(c) Ramaswamy Venkataraman
(d) Shankar Dayal Sharrna

89. Solve: $1 + \tan^2\theta = ?$
(a) $\cos^2\theta$
(b) $\sec^2\theta$
(c) $\tan^2\theta$
(d) 2

90. If x is an even number, what is the consecutive odd number?
   (a) x – 1   (b) x + 1
   (c) x + 2   (d) x – 2

91. Select the alternative that shows a similar relationship as the given pair -
Truthful : Honest
   (a) Notwithstanding : Nevertheless
   (b) Including : Excluding
   (c) Winning : Losing
   (d) Procuring : Disposing

92. Four pairs of words are given. Find the odd one out.
   (a) Ear : Hearing
   (b) Tongue : Taste
   (c) Mouth : Speech
   (d) Light : Vision

93. If **INSECT** = @&* !#\$ and **OR** = %?, then
CISTERN = _______________________
   (a) #@ *\$!%&   (b) #@*\$?!&
   (c) #@*\$!?&   (d) #@*\$%!&

94. How many litres of water can be stored in a tank of 1m length, 1/2 m breadth, and 1/2 m tall?
   (a) 25,000   (b) 250
   (c) 25   (d) 2,500

95 What was recently discovered hidden under ice in Antarctica?
   (a) A massive mountain range
   (b) A lost Kingdom
   (c) A massive canyon system and lake
   (d) A huge Dinosaur Skeleton

96. Jane won a lottery and gets 1/3rd of the winning amount and donates ₹6000 which is 1/6th, find how much the lottery was worth.
   (a) 36000   (b) 18000
   (c) 54000   (d) 108000

97. Find the difference between the place value and face value of the digit 9 in the number 229301?
   (a) 9292   (b) 8991
   (c) 0   (d) 220

98. The sum of two numbers is 437 and their product is 21982. Find the numbers
   (a) 399 and 38   (b) 295 and 142
   (c) 58 and 379   (d) 323 and 114

99. What is the gravitational force exerted on a mass called?
   (a) Stress   (b) Inertia
   (c) Weight   (d) Work

100. A bank agrees to lend a loan to Arvind of ₹2,38,75,697 which falls short by 17% for starting his business. How much more loan would he need?
   (a) 4058868   (b) 4375303
   (c) 5700108   (d) 5125533

HINTS & EXPLANATIONS

1. (a) Make-in-India logo is the silhouette of a lion on the prowl which is entirely made of cogs, symbolising manufacturing, strength and national pride. As disclosed by the RTI, the lion was designed by the Indian branch of a foreign company.

2. (b) Since median = 2.5

$$\Rightarrow \frac{2+x}{2} = 2.5 \Rightarrow x = 5 - 2$$
$$= 3$$

3. (b)

4. (b)

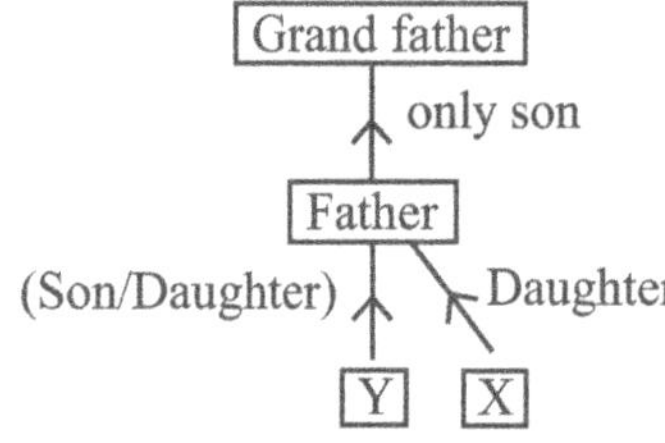

Hence X is the sister of Y.

5. (c) HIL stands for Hockey India League which is also known as the Coal India Hockey India League for sponsorship reasons. The league is organized by Hockey India, the governing body for the sport in India. It consists of six teams, with the regular season lasting two months from January to February.

6. (b) From diagram : children who like leopard = 120

Children who like tiger = 85

∴ difference = 120 – 85 = 35.

7. (c) Childrens who like both lion and leopard is represented by the common area between circle and rectangle = 90.

8. (d) Childrens who like both lion and tiger is represented by the common area between circle and triangle = 40

9. (b)

50, 49.5, <u>48</u>, 45.5, 42, 37.5
   –.5   –1.5   –2.5 –3.5 –4.5

10. (c) 11. (d) 12. (c)

13. (b) Length of train = 500 m

Length of tunnel = 1000 m

⇒ Total distance = 1500 m

Time = 60 sec.

$$\therefore \text{ Speed of train } = \frac{1500}{60} = 25\,\text{m/s}$$

$$= 25 \times \frac{18}{5} = 90\,\text{km/hr}$$

14. (a) 15. (c) 16. (a)

17. (c) A bicameral legislature is the lawmaking body of a system of government that consists of two legislative houses or chambers. The main purpose behind bicameral legislature is to provide for representation for both the citizens of a country, as well as the state legislatures on the federal level or in the central government of a country.

18. (b)

....H G I, J L K M N P O.....
  –1   +1   –1   +1   –1

19. (c) 20. (d) 21. (d)

22. (c) SP of 12 watches = 1454.64 × 12
$$= 17455.68$$
Profit = 16%

$$\therefore \text{CP} = \frac{17455.68 \times 100}{116} = ₹15048$$

23. (d) The Pushkar Fair (Mela) or the Pushkar Camel Fair is an annual muti-day annual camel and livestock fair, held in the town of Pushkar between the months of October and November. It is one of India's largest camel, horse and cattle fairs. This wonderful event also has a religious significance.

24. **(c)**

25. **(d)**

$$D \xrightarrow{+13} Q \qquad B \xrightarrow{+13} O$$

$$E \xrightarrow{+13} R \qquad O \xrightarrow{+13} B$$

$$L \xrightarrow{+13} Y \qquad M \xrightarrow{+13} Z$$

$$H \xrightarrow{+13} U \qquad B \xrightarrow{+13} O$$

$$I \xrightarrow{+13} V \qquad A \xrightarrow{+13} N$$

$$Y \xrightarrow{+13} L$$

26. **(d)**

$$
\begin{array}{ccccc}
G & O & I & N & G \\
\uparrow & \uparrow & \uparrow & \uparrow & \uparrow \\
3 & 8 & 2 & 5 & 3
\end{array}
$$

$$
\begin{array}{cccccc}
C & A & S & U & A & L \\
\uparrow & \uparrow & \uparrow & \uparrow & \uparrow & \uparrow \\
4 & 0 & 9 & 1 & 0 & 6
\end{array}
$$

On Comparing the above values

$$
\begin{array}{ccccccc}
L & O & G & I & C & A & L \\
\uparrow & \uparrow & \uparrow & \uparrow & \uparrow & \uparrow & \uparrow \\
6 & 8 & 3 & 2 & 4 & 0 & 6
\end{array}
$$

27. **(a)** Manju's 1 days work $= \dfrac{1}{16}$

Let x be the number of days Jenny takes to complete the work.

$\Rightarrow$ Jenny's 1 days work $= \dfrac{1}{x}$

Now, ATQ

$$\frac{12}{16} + \frac{12}{x} = 1 \Rightarrow 12x + 192 = 16x$$

$$\Rightarrow 4x = 192 \Rightarrow x = 48 \text{ days.}$$

28. **(a)** $\dfrac{109 \times 102}{103} = \dfrac{11118}{103} = 107.94 \approx 108$

29. **(b)** $2\pi r = 22$ cm

$$\Rightarrow r = \frac{22}{2\pi} = \frac{11}{\pi}$$

$\therefore$ Area of Semicircle

$$= \frac{\pi r^2}{2} = \frac{\pi \times 11 \times 11}{2 \times \pi \times \pi} = \frac{121 \times 7}{44}$$

$$= 19.25 \text{ sq. cm}$$

30. **(c)** $CI = 25000 \left[1 + \dfrac{12}{100} \right]^3 - 25000$

$$= 25000 \, [1.12]^3 - 25000$$
$$= 35123.2 - 25000$$
$$= 10,123.20$$

31. **(d)** Product of two numbers is equal to product of HCF and LCM of the given two numbers. Let the other no. be x.

$$\therefore \ 168 \times 6 = 24 \times x \Rightarrow x = \frac{168 \times 6}{24} = 42$$

32. **(b)** ATQ, Ram's brother is the father of seeta's son's father

$\Rightarrow$ Ram's brother is Grandfather of seeta's son.

33. **(a)** No. of books = 78
No. of crayons = 114
No. of Notebooks = 141
Since 6 are left undistributed in each

$\therefore$ We subtract 6 from each and find the HCF of resultant numbers.

$\Rightarrow$ HCF of 72, 108 and 135
$72 = 3 \times 3 \times 2 \times 2 \times 2$
$108 = 3 \times 3 \times 3 \times 2 \times 2$
$135 = 3 \times 3 \times 3 \times 5$

$\therefore$ HCF = 9

$\Rightarrow$ total number of children = 9.

34. **(a)**

35. **(d)** From the bar graph it is quit clear that student U scored the highest percentage in both subjects combined

36. **(*)** Percentage of total marks in Geography

$$= \frac{75 + 63 + 80 + 72}{400} = \frac{290}{400} = 72.5\%$$

Percentage of total marks in History

$$= \frac{80 + 87 + 70 + 75}{400}$$

$$= \frac{312}{400} = 78\%$$

$\therefore$ Percentage difference $= 78 - 72.5 = 5.5\%$

Answer not applicable

37. **(c)** Average percentage marks in history

$$= \frac{75 + 63 + 80 + 72}{400}$$

$$= 72.5 \, \%$$

38. (d) $a^{x+y} = a^6$

Comparing the coefficients

$x + y = 6$ ...... (1)

also $x > y$ by 2

$\Rightarrow x = y + 2$ ...... (2)

from (1) and (2)

$x = 4$

39. (a) A limerick is a form of verse consisting of five lines. It is a humorous poem with a strict rhyme scheme of AABBA, in which, the first, second, and fifth lines must have seven to ten syllables while the third and fourth lines only have to have five to seven syllables.

40. (a)

41. (a) The Andromeda Galaxy is a spiral galaxy approximately 780 kiloparsecs (2.5 million light-years) from Earth, and the nearest major galaxy to the Milky Way. Its name stems from the area of the Earth's sky. Also known as M31, this galaxy appears as a smudge of light larger than a full moon.

42. (d)

43. (a) Shigmo or Shishirotsava is a spring festival in Goa celebrated by the Konkani diaspora with a lot of pompous and splendour. This festival takes place in the Phalguna month, around the month of March every year. The word "Shigmo" is a Konkani term, which has been coined from Prakrit word 'Suggimaho' and the Sanskrit word, Sugrishmaka.

44. (a) 45. (c)

46. (b) $\dfrac{12}{13} \times \dfrac{285}{96} \div \dfrac{171}{169} = \dfrac{12}{13} \times \dfrac{3 \times 5 \times 19}{3 \times 4 \times 8} \times \dfrac{13 \times 13}{9 \times 19}$

$= \dfrac{5 \times 13}{3 \times 8} = \dfrac{65}{24} = 2\dfrac{17}{24}$

47. (c) 48. (c) 49. (c) 50. (*) 51. (b)

52. (a)

53. (d) No. of pages read in an hour = 14

No. of pages read in 3 hours = $3 \times 14 = 42$

$\therefore$ No. of days required to complete the book

$= \dfrac{378}{42} = 9 \, \text{day's}$ [1 day = 3 hours reading]

Hence number of days required = $9 - 7 = 2$ days.

54. (a)

55. (*) No. of eggs sold on Friday = $10 \times 12 = 120$

Price of 120 eggs = $120 \times 2.50 = ` 300$

No. of eggs sold on Monday = $8 \times 12 = 96$

Price of 96 eggs = $96 \times 2.50 = ₹240$

difference = $300 - 240 = ₹60$

Answer not applicable

56. (a) Total marks of 12 students = 12×67.4

$= 808.8$

Total marks of other 15 students = 15×72.3

$= 1084.5$

$\therefore$ Combined mean

$= \dfrac{1084.5 + 808.8}{15 + 12} = \dfrac{1893.3}{27} = 70.12$

57. (b) 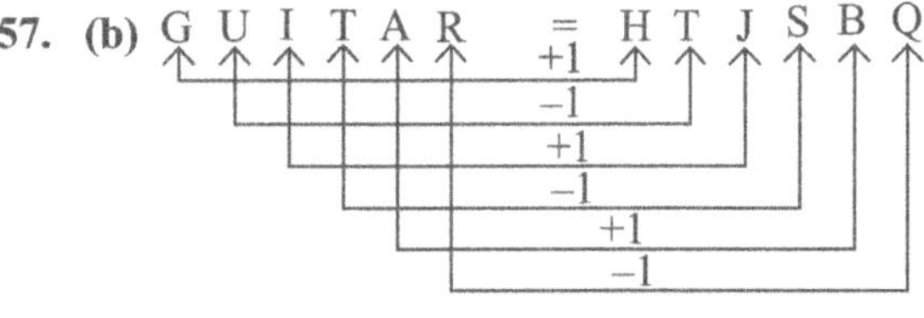

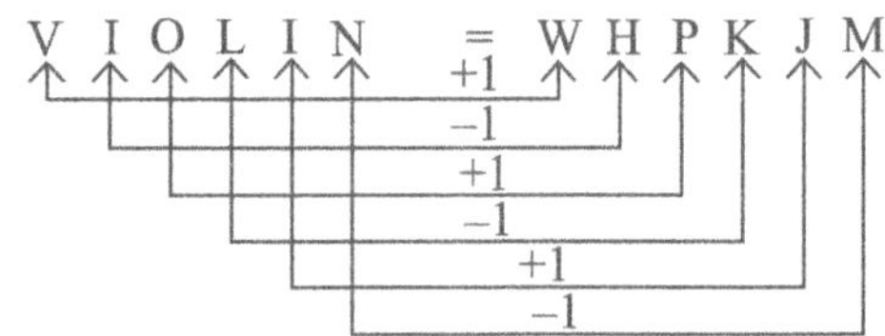

58. (b) Speed while walking $= \dfrac{6 \times 3}{5} = 3.6 \, \text{km/hr}$

Speed while running $= \dfrac{6 \times 3}{4} = 4.5 \, \text{km/hr}$

$\therefore$ difference in speed = $4.5 - 3.6 = .9 \, \text{km/hr}$

59. (a)

60. (d) $\text{Sin}(90° - \theta) = \cos\theta$

61. (b)

62. (b) $(x + y)^2 - (x - y^2) = x^2 + y^2 + 2xy - x^2 - y^2 + 2xy$

$= 4xy$

63. (c) Let L and B be the length and breadth of rectangle respectively.

ATQ, $L \times B = 42$

$7 \times B = 42 \Rightarrow B = 6$

$\therefore$ perimeter = $2(L + B) = 2(7 + 6) = 2(13)$

$= 26 \, \text{cm}$

64. (d) Let the selling price of 1 cycle is x

$\Rightarrow$ SP of 20 cycles = 20x

Since loss = 2x

Also loss = CP – SP

$\Rightarrow$ CP = Loss + SP

$= 2x + 20x = 22x$

$$\therefore \ \%\,loss = \frac{loss}{CP}\times 100$$

$$= \frac{2x}{22x}\times 100 = \frac{100}{11} = 9\frac{1}{11}$$

65. (b)

Sol. (66 - 68):

The sequence of pickle jars would be as follows

Tomato Garlic Gooseberry Mango Lime

66. (d) Tomato and Mango

67. (a) Fifth

68. (c) Gooseberry

69. (c) 70. (b) 71. (c)

72. (b) After changing the sign's

$$1\times 2 + 6 - 2 \div 7 = 1 \div 2 \times 6 + 2 - 7$$

$$= .5\times 6 + 2 - 7$$

$$= 3 + 2 - 7 = 5 - 7 = -2$$

73. (a) 74. (b)

75. (c) Quantity of sugar = 285 kg

Number of people = 1487

$\therefore$ Quantity of sugar each person gets

$$= \frac{285}{1487} = 0.191\,kg$$

76. (a) If principle = p

then S.I = P/3

$$\Rightarrow \quad \frac{p}{3} = \frac{P\times 6\times x}{100}$$

{rate = 6%, time = x year}

$$\Rightarrow \ 100\,P = 18px \Rightarrow x = \frac{100P}{18P} = \frac{50}{9} = 5\frac{5}{9}$$

77. (c) 78. (a)

79. (c) $2 \div 16 - 2 + 6 \times 1 = 0$

Checking each option

(A) $\ 2 \div 16 \times 2 + 6 - 1 \Rightarrow \dfrac{1}{4} + 6 - 1 \neq 0$

(B) $\ 2 \div 16 + 2 - 6 \times 1 \Rightarrow \dfrac{1}{8} + 2 - 6 \neq 0$

(C) $\ 2 - 16 \div 2 + 6 \times 1 = 0 \Rightarrow 2 - 8 + 6 = 0$

$\therefore$ option (c) is the answer.

80. (a)

81. (b) Let x be the total price of vegetables

then $\ x\times \dfrac{10}{100} = 144 \Rightarrow x = 1440$

Price per kg = ₹ 40

$\therefore$ Total weight $= \dfrac{1440}{40} = 36\,kgs.$

82. (b)

83. (c) 1.08 tonne = 1.08 × 1000 = 1080 kg

84. (d) Son of father's mother-in-low = maternal uncle

$\Rightarrow$ Anand's mother is the sister of the man in the photo.

85. (a) 86. (a) 87. (d) 88. (b)

89. (b) $1 + \tan^2\theta = 1 + \dfrac{\sin^2\theta}{\cos^2\theta}$

$$= \frac{\cos^2\theta + \sin^2\theta}{\cos^2\theta}$$

$$= \frac{1}{\cos^2\theta} = \sec^2\theta$$

90. (b) If x is an even number then the consecutive odd number will be the successor.

$\Rightarrow x + 1$ is the consecutive odd number.

91. (a) 92. (d)

93. (c)

I	N	S	E	C	T		O	R
↑	↑	↑	↑	↑	↑		↑	↑
@	&	*	!	#	$		%	?

Comparing above values

C	I	S	T	E	R	N
↑	↑	↑	↑	↑	↑	↑
#	@	*	$	!	?	&

94. (b) The tank is in the shape of cube

Length = 1 m, Breadth = 1/2 m & Height = 1/2 m

Volume = L × B × H

$= 1 \times \frac{1}{2} \times \frac{1}{2} = \frac{1}{4}\ m^3$

$1\,m^3 = 1000$ litres

$\therefore \ \frac{1}{4}\ m^3 = \dfrac{1000}{4} = 250\,lts.$

95. (c) Scientists have discovered three vast canyons hidden below hundreds of feet of ice in the Antarctic. The three canyons are Foundation Trough, Patuxent Trough and Offset Rift Basin which slice through the mountain ranges and divide the two major regions of the frozen continent. The biggest of the canyons is called Foundation Trough. It is over 350 km long and 35 km wide. Scientists have predicted that these canyons could play a crucial role in the continent's shifting future.

96. (d) Let amount of lottery is ₹x.

Amount Jane sets $= \dfrac{1}{3}x$

Amount donated $= \dfrac{1}{6}\left(\dfrac{1}{3}x\right)$

$\Rightarrow \quad 6000 = \dfrac{1}{18}x$

$\Rightarrow \quad x = ₹108000$

97. (b) Place value of digit 9 = 9000
Face value of 9 = 9
$\therefore$ Difference = 9000 – 9 = 8991

98. (c) x + y = 437 and xy = 21982
x = (437 – y)
$\therefore$ xy = 21982 $\Rightarrow$ (437 – y)y = 21982
$\Rightarrow$ 0 = y^2 – 437y + 21982
$\Rightarrow$ 0 = (y – 58) (y –379)
$\Rightarrow$ y = 58 or 379
$\therefore$ x = 58
and y = 379

99. (c)

100. (a) Total amount of loan = ₹ 23875697
Percentage of loan that fell short

$= \dfrac{23875697 \times 17}{100}$

= ₹ 4058868

$\therefore$ Amount of loan need more = ₹ 4058868

1. What among the following is FALSE about the Richter scale?
   (a) It was developed by Charles Richter and Gutenberg in 1935.
   (b) It is a logarithmic scale
   (c) It can be measured using a seismometer
   (d) Magnitude of 8-9 on a Richter scale means it is a micro earthquake.

2. The following graph represent marks obtain in mathematics out of 10 of five students.

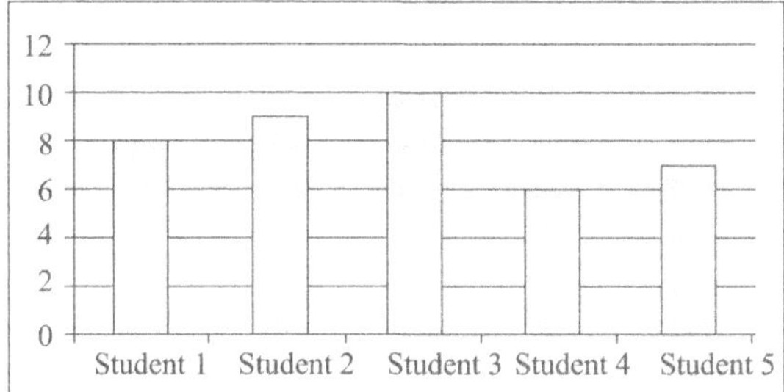

   Student 3 and 5 get how many more marks than student 4 and 1
   (a) 2 (b) 1
   (c) 3 (d) 4

3. Which device use to convert digital signal to analog.
   (a) WiFi (b) Modem
   (c) Port (d) USB

4. If N:38::3:57, Find N.
   (a) 2/3 (b) 1/3
   (c) 3 (d) 2

5. The distance between two points A and B is covered in 5 1/2 hours at a speed of 50 km/hr. If the speed is increased by 5 km/hr. how much time would be saved?
   (a) 5 minutes (b) 15 minutes
   (c) 50 minutes (d) 30 minutes

6. If $x = 7 - 4\sqrt{3}$ find the value of $\sqrt{x} + \dfrac{1}{\sqrt{x}}$
   (a) 0 (b) 1
   (c) 4 (d) –4

7. Which is India's longest river that does not flow into the sea?
   (a) Ganga (b) Jamuna
   (c) Tapti (d) Kaveri

8. What is the most cultivated crop in India?
   (a) Ragi (b) Wheat
   (c) Cora (d) Rice

9. In which city is the value of Gold determined?
   (a) California (b) Sydney
   (c) Rome (d) London

10. Find the similarity in the following:
    Elephant, Camel, Buffalo, Giraffe
    (a) The milk produced by all of them cannot be consumed by people.
    (b) All of them have horns.
    (c) None of them are mammals,
    (d) The young ones of all of them are called calf.

11. If $y = \dfrac{2x-1}{x+3}$ find x when $y = 1$
    (a) 4 (b) –4
    (c) 3/2 (d) 4/3

12. Which vitamin among the following is crucial for blood clotting?
    (a) Vitamin B12 (b) Vitamin D
    (c) Vitamin A (d) Vitamin E

13. If the mathematical operators, '+' and '×' are interchanged, what will he the value of the equation $9 \div 5 + 10 - 23 \times 2$
    (a) 3 (b) 2
    (c) –3 (d) –5

14. A wire is in the shape of a rectangle. Its length is 42.7m and breadth is 21.8m. If the same wire is re-bent in the shape of a square, what will be the measure of the side of the square?
    (a) 16.125 (b) 32.25
    (c) 11.35 (d) 22.70

15. Accordig to the Swachh Bharat 2015 survey, which is the cleanest city in India?
    (a) Chennai (b) Delhi
    (c) Ahmedabad (d) Mysore

16. Which is the most peaceful country according to the 2015 Global Peace Index?
    (a) Iceland   (b) Bhutan
    (c) Austria   (d) New Zealand

17. Where did the Chipko movement begin?
    (a) Rajasthan   (b) Assam
    (c) Arunachal Pradesh   (d) Mizoram

18. Rearrange the jumbled letters to make a meaningful word and then select the one which is different.
    (a) ORIN   (b) NADS
    (c) POPCER   (d) DLOG

DIRECTIONS (Qs. 19-21): *Study the following diagram and answer questions based on it. The diagram represents the likes of kids of a class.*

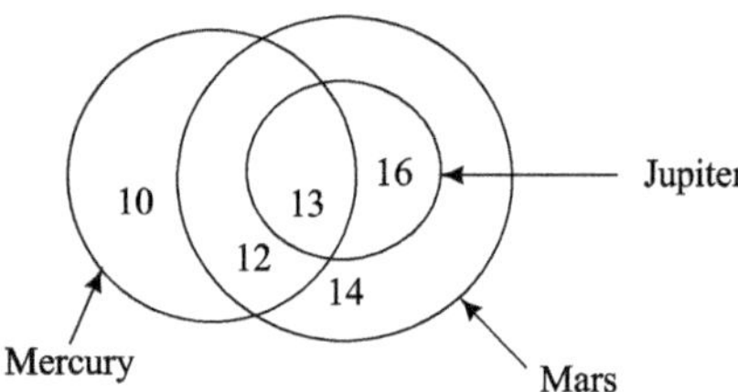

19. The ratio of kids who like only Mars to those who like all the three
    (a) 7/5   (b) 7/8
    (c) 7/6   (d) 14/13

20. What is the difference between the kids who like Mercury and Jupiter?
    (a) 6   (b) 8
    (c) 10   (d) 12

21. How many people who Like Mars like Jupiter also?
    (a) 45   (b) 29
    (c) 26   (d) 13

22. Name the capital of Uganda?
    (a) Mogadishu   (b) Kampala
    (c) Lusaka   (d) Bulenga

23. What is Madhubani art?
    (a) The art of Storytelling
    (b) The art of Gujarat
    (c) A folk art practiced in Bihar
    (d) The art of honey extraction

24. What is 'Planet Nine'?
    (a) A planet in the Comet Galaxy
    (b) A planet in Andromeda Galaxy
    (c) A planet where the 'Star Wars' series took place
    (d) A large icy planet proposed in the outer Solar System

25. Which is NOT an Operating System?
    (a) OS X   (b) Windows 7
    (c) DOS   (d) C++

26. What is the smallest number of 5 digits which is exactly divisible by 12, 24, 48, 60 and 96?
    (a) 10000   (b) 10024
    (c) 10160   (d) 10080

27. Find the cost in rupees for carpeting a room 65dm × 30dm at Rs.45 per sq.m
    (a) 877.50   (b) 87750
    (c) 87.75   (d) 8775

28. What is most common treatment for bacterial infections in humans?
    (a) Aspirin   (b) Antibodies
    (c) Antibiotics   (d) Antigen

29. The ratio of ages of Jai and Joy is 5:2. The sum of their ages is 63. After 9 years what will be the ratio of their ages?
    (a) 5:2   (b) 2:1
    (c) 3:2   (d) 4:3

30. By selling 90 chocolates for ₹160, a chocolate trader loses 20%. How many chocolates should he sell for Rs.96 to make a profit of 20%?
    (a) 45   (b) 36
    (c) 54   (d) 28

31. What is an archipelago?
    (a) Group, chain, cluster or collection of Islands
    (b) The meeting of Land and Sea
    (c) An Architect's paradise
    (d) A type of Church

DIRECTIONS (Qs. 32-34): *Six animals - horse, cow, pig, dog. donkey and goat are tied to a pole each, in a circle, facing each other, in random order. Consider the following information and answer the questions based on it.*

---

1. Goat is to the immediate right of pig.

2. Cow is not tied next to either donkey or dog.

3. If the animals mark the vertices of a hexagon, then the horse is diagonally opposite to the pig.

32. The cow is tied to the immediate left of
    (a) Goat   (b) Pig
    (c) Horse   (d) Dos

33. Which pair is tied next to each other?
    (a) Horse and Goat
    (b) Pig and Cow
    (c) Goat and Dog
    (d) Donkey and Dog

34. Which animal is tied to the immediate left of pig?
(a) Goat
(b) Donkey
(c) Dog
(d) Cannot be determined

35. Who is Sabari Karthik?
(a) Famous Indian Karate Champion
(b) Rugby Player
(c) Cricket Player
(d) Kabaddi Champion

36. Which among the following is popularly called Laughin Gas?
(a) Nitric oxide
(b) Nitrogen dioxide
(c) Nitrous oxide
(d) Nitrogen peroxide

37. Four pairs of words are given. Find the odd one out.
(a) 65th anniversary : Diamond Jubilee
(b) 50th anniversary : Golden Jubilee
(c) 40th anniversary : Ruby Jubilee
(d) 25th anniversary : Silver Jubilee

38. A lady wants to buy the following items in the given price range -
1. Tomato between ₹ 40 and ₹45 per kg.
2. Grapes in the price range of ₹80 and ₹90 per kg.
3. Milk packets at Rs, 23 per litre.
In which shop from the following will she definitely get all her items?
(a) Shop S sells tomato at ₹22.5 per half kg, grapes at ₹82 per kg and milk at ₹24 per litre.
(b) Shop H sells grapes at ₹21 per quarter kg. milk at 12.5 per half litre and tomato at ₹22 per half kg.
(c) Shop O sells milk at ₹11.5 per half litre, tomato at 21 per half kg and grapes at ₹43 per half kg.
(d) Shop P sells tomato at ₹23.5 per half kg, grapes at ₹85 per kg and milk at ₹23 per litre.

39. What did M. S. Swaminathan an Indian geneticist, play a leading role in?
(a) Yellow Revolution
(b) White Revolution
(c) Green Revolution
(d) Black Revolution

40. What is the mean of the marks scored by students in a science exam? 41, 39, 52, 48, 54, 62, 46, 52, 40, 96, 42, 40, 98, 60, 52
(a) 54.8
(b) 58.4
(c) 53.4
(d) 53.8

41. Simplify: $(-4.6) \times (-4.6) \div (-4.6 + 0.6)$
(a) −5.29
(b) −0.529
(c) −4.06
(d) 5.01

42. Indian currency notes. are printed in which place?
(a) New Delhi
(b) Bombay
(c) Nashik
(d) Agra

43. The price of 4 1/2 m of cloth is ₹60 3/4. Find the cost per meter
(a) 15 1/2
(b) 13 1/2
(c) 14 3/4
(d) 13 3/4

44. What is the number of Galilean moons of Jupiter discovered by Galileo Galilei in January 1610?
(a) 2
(b) 3
(c) 4
(d) 5

45. Mica is available abundantly in which state?
(a) West Bengal
(b) Madhya Pradesh
(c) Bihar
(d) Rajasthan

46. If X = 24 and BE = 7, then RING =?
(a) 41
(b) 47
(c) 48
(d) 49

47. The product of two consecutive odd numbers is 399. Find the lower of them
(a) 17
(b) 19
(c) 21
(d) 23

48. Between which stations does India's longest train run?
(a) Kanyakumari - Baramulla
(b) Dibrugarh - Naliya
(c) Dibrugarh - Kanyakumari
(d) Thiruvanathapuram - New Delhi

49. With reference to classification of fundamental rights, which of the following is true?
1. Right to exploitation
2. Right against equality
3. Cultural and economic rights

Select the correct statements from the following codes

(a) Only 1 (b) Only 1 and 2

(c) 1, 2 and 3 (d) None of these

50. What is The Siberian ibex?
(a) Mountain Lions
(b) Large and heavily built goats
(c) Mountain Deer
(d) A Type of Horse

51. Cost price of 25 chairs equals the selling price of 20 chairs. Find the profit %.
(a) 20% (b) 33%
(c) 25% (d) 12.5%

52. A trader marks his goods at 20% above cost price. If he allows a discount of 5% what is his final profit?
(a) 12% (b) 14%
(c) 15% (d) 18%

53. What is Swadeshi?
(a) Made in India, from materials that have also been produced in India
(b) Made in Foreign Lands from materials that are foreign
(c) A Charkha that is used to spin cotton wool
(d) A Country Flag that is made of Cotton

54. Which among the following happens in an oxidation reaction
(a) Electrons are gained
(b) Electrons are lost
(c) Protons are gained
(d) Protons are lost

55. Where is the Masai Mara National Reserve?
(a) Mali (b) Kenya
(c) Gabon (d) Zambia

56. Find the compound interest to the nearest rupee on ₹ 7500 for 2 years 4 months at 12% p.a. reckoned annually?
(a) 2284 (b) 2176
(c) 2097 (d) 2235

DIRECTIONS (Qs. 57-59) : *The following table represents the percentage marks of four students in six subjects. Consider the table and answer questions based on it.*

Student	Maths	Science	History	Geography	English	Hindi
Shamita	75	80	65	68	72	65
Smita	80	85	75	65	70	70
Shilpa	82	88	70	69	71	70
Sheela	78	87	65	70	75	74

57. The average marks obtained by the students in Geography and History are
(a) 68.75 and 68 (b) 70.5 and 69
(c) 68 and 68.75 (d) 68.75 and 68.5

58. Average marks obtained in Science is higher than that of Maths by
(a) 15 (b) 20
(c) 25 (d) 40

59. Who has the highest total marks?
(a) Shamita (b) Smita
(c) Shilpa (d) Sheela

60. If $\cos\theta + \sin\theta = m$, $\sec\theta + \csc\theta = n$, what is m/n
(a) 1 (b) $\sin\theta \cos\theta$
(c) $\sec\theta \csc\theta$ (d) $\cot\theta \tan\theta$

61. M is the son of N. O is the father of N. P is the father of M. How is N related to P?
(a) Wife (b) Husband
(c) Father (d) Mother

62. What is Sepak Takraw?
(a) A Bird
(b) An ancient hunting team in Malaysia
(c) Kick Volleyball
(d) A Type of Combat Flight

63. X, Y and Z take 18 days to complete a piece of work. If X works alone he finishes the work in 36 days and if Y works alone he finishes it in 60 days. How long will it take Z to complete the work alone?
(a) 78 days (b) 90 days
(c) 96 days (d) 14 days

64. Which is the capital of Sri Lanka?
(a) Colombo
(b) Kandy
(c) Jayawardenepura Kotte
(d) Anuradhapura

65. Solve: $\dfrac{\sin\theta}{1+\cos\theta}+\dfrac{1+\cos\theta}{\sin\theta}=?$
   (a) $\tan\theta$
   (b) $\cot\theta$
   (c) $\dfrac{2}{\sin\theta}$
   (d) $\dfrac{2}{\cos\theta}$

66. The panchatantra fables are thought to be composed by
   (a) Mullah Nasruddin
   (b) Vishnu Sharma
   (c) King Sudharshan
   (d) Tenali Raman

67. What was the code name of the nuclear tests conducted by India in Pokhran in 1998
   (a) Operation Desert Storm
   (b) Operation Vijay
   (c) Operation Shakti
   (d) Operation Kaboom

68. An assertion (A) and a reason (R) are given below.
   Assertion (A): Penguins are birds, found in the hottest regions of the earth.
   Reason (R): Birds in hot regions do not have wings.
   Choose the correct option.
   (a) Both A and R are true and R is the correct explanation of A
   (b) Both A and R are true, but R is not the correct explanation of A
   (c) A is true, but R is false
   (d) Both A and R are false

69. Who is Anjolie Ela Menon?
   (a) An Indian politician
   (b) Bharatanatyam dancer
   (c) A popular musician
   (d) Indian Female Artist

70. The sum of the digits of a 2 digit number is 9. When 27 is added to the number, the digits get interchanged. Find the number.
   (a) 45
   (b) 36
   (c) 18
   (d) 27

71. Find the missing (?) in the series
   13, 14, 18, 27, ?, 68, 104 ....
   (a) 36
   (b) 41
   (c) 43
   (d) 54

72. Kitty said, "Uthara is one of the two daughters of my mother's brother's wife". How is Kitty's mother related to Uthara's sister?
   (a) Maternal Aunt
   (b) Mother
   (c) Grandmother
   (d) Sister

73. One angle of a triangle is 55°. If the other two angles are in the ratio 9:16, find the angles-
   (a) 65 and 115
   (b) 90 and 160
   (c) 55 and 165
   (d) 45 and 80

74. Which contemporary painter made a series of paintings on Mahatma Gandhi?
   (a) Amrita Shergill
   (b) Ram Kinkar
   (c) M.F. Hussain
   (d) Atul Dodiya

75. The income of a person is represented by the pie-chart below. If his total income is ₹ 360,000 then find his income of the second week.

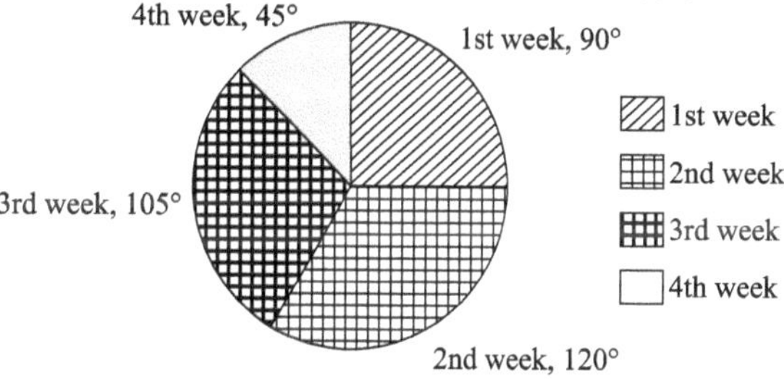

   (a) ₹ 90,000
   (b) ₹ 120,000
   (c) ₹ 46,000
   (d) ₹ 105,000

76. If **HOUSES = GNAYDR**, then **DIARY =**
   (a) CHGXZ
   (b) CHEWZ
   (c) CHGXX
   (d) CHEWX

77. What does "Satyameva Jayate" mean?
   (a) "Truth alone triumphs"
   (b) "True Faith is Rare"
   (c) "Truth is Divine"
   (d) "Truth is a Treasure"

78. Malé is the capital of which Country?
   (a) Mauritius
   (b) Lakshadweep
   (c) Maldives
   (d) Malaysia

79. Select the alternative that does not have a similar relationship as the given pair -
   Forward : Backward
   (a) Hope : Despair
   (b) Love : Hate
   (c) Anger : Wrath
   (d) Light : Dark

80. A statement followed by some conclusions are given below.

Statement: Religions teach the guiding principles for leading one's life.

Conclusions:

I. Religion is a way of life.

II. Religion is a teacher.

Find which of the given conclusions logically follow from the given statement.

    (a) Only conclusion I follows.

    (b) Only conclusion II follow's.

    (c) Both I and II follow.

    (d) Neither I nor II follows.

81. If H_2O : **Hydrogen**, than **KOH** : ________

    (a) Cobalt   (b) Phosphorous

    (c) Potassium   (d) Krypton

82. Simplify: $\dfrac{9}{13} \div \dfrac{18}{26} \div \dfrac{90}{52}$

    (a) 45/26   (b) 13/45

    (c) 26/45   (d) 45/13

83. Zero degree centigrade is equal to what degree Fahrenheit?

    (a) 100°F   (b) 30°F

    (c) 34°F   (d) 32°F

84. If **SHFIF** is **FUSVS**, then **ZEBRA** is

    (a) NRMEO   (b) MRNEO

    (c) NROEM   (d) MROEN

85. What is the normal resting heart rate range for adults (beats/min)?

    (a) 60 to 100   (b) 50 to 80

    (c) 120 to 180   (d) 75 to 120

86. Q's father is B's son-in-law. C is Q's sister and the daughter of P. P is the maternal aunt of D. How is P related to B?

    (a) Son   (b) Daughter

    (c) Grandson   (d) Granddaughter

87. Who was the first woman to reach summit of Mt. Everest?

    (a) Bachendri Pal

    (b) Junko Tabei

    (c) Aruniina Sinha

    (d) Premlata Agarwal

88. 6 carpenters make 96 windows in 6 days. If 8 carpenters work for 4 days how many windows will they make?

    (a) 16   (b) 28

    (c) 36   (d) 32

89. A factory produced 18,58,509 cassettes in the month of January, 7623 more cassettes in the month of February and owing to short supply of electricity produced 25,838 less cassettes in March than in February. Find the total production in all?

    (a) 55,57,312   (b) 59,83,245

    (c) 55,64,935   (d) 56,08,988

90. What is Makar Sankranti?

    (a) Lunar Eclipse

    (b) Harvesting Festival

    (c) Kite Festival

    (d) Puppet Show

91. Statements followed by some conclusions are given below.

Statements:

(a) Confusion causes mental tension.

(b) Mental tension causes anxiety.

Conclusions:

I. Anxiety is a disease.

II. Confusion leads to anxiety.

Find which of the given conclusions logically follow from the given statements.

    (a) Only conclusion I follow's.

    (b) Only conclusion II follows.

    (c) Both I and II follow.

    (d) Neither I nor II follows.

92. If 'Mango, lemon and melon are fruits' is written as 439516; 'Mango and lemon are yellow' is 04396 and 'Melon is green' is 857, which digit represents 'melon'?

    (a) 5

    (b) 8

    (c) 7

    (d) Cannot be determined

93. Find the missing (?) in the series

AIQ, BJR, CKS, DLT, ?, ...

    (a) ENU   (b) EMV

    (c) ENV   (d) EMU

94. Sanjay and Jacob start running in opposite directions from the same point at speeds of 7m/s and 5m/s. After 42 minutes, how far would they be from each other?

    (a) 30.24 km   (b) 504 km

    (c) 8.4 km   (d) 69.5 km

95. In 2015, which country joined the world trade organisation as the 44th member?
(a) Philippines   (b) Liberia
(c) Jordan   (d) Afghanistan

96 Find the difference between compound interest and simple interest on 5000 for 2 years at 8% p.a payable annually.
(a) 45   (b) 32
(c) 57   (d) 84

97. Solve: $12 - [26 - \{2 + 5 \times (6 - 3)\}]$
(a) 2   (b) 3
(c) 7   (d) 8

98. Abdul prepared 42 litres of medicine and filled it in bottles of 280 ml each. Find how many bottles would be required?
(a) 15   (b) 1500
(c) 150   (d) 300

99. The LCM of two consecutive even numbers is 144, find the numbers
(a) 16 and 18   (b) 14 and 16
(c) 18 and 20   (d) 22 and 24

100. The Dibru-Saikhowa, Nameri and Orang National Park are all found in which State?
(a) Andhra Pradesh   (b) Assam
(c) Arunachal Pradesh   (d) Uttarakhand

HINTS & EXPLANATIONS

1. **(d)** The largest known shocks have had magnitudes in the 8.8 to 8.9 range. A magnitude between 8 to 9 range can cause severe damage to life and property.

2. **(c)** Difference $= (10 + 7) - (6 + 8)$
$$= 17 - 14 = 3$$

3. **(b)**

4. **(d)** $N : 38 :: 3 : 57$
Product of extremes $=$ Product of means
$$\Rightarrow N \times 57 = 38 \times 3$$
$$\Rightarrow N = \frac{3 \times 38}{57} = 2$$

5. **(d)** Let distance between A and B $= x$ km
$$\Rightarrow \frac{x}{50} = \frac{11}{2} \Rightarrow = x = \frac{550}{2} = 275 \text{ km}$$
New speed $= 50 + 5 = 55$ km
$$\therefore \text{ time taken} = \frac{275}{55} = 5 \text{ hours}$$
Hence, time saved $= \frac{11}{2} - 5 = \frac{1}{2}$ hours
$= 30$ minutes

6. **(c)** $x = 7 - 4\sqrt{3}$
$$= 4 + 3 - 4\sqrt{3}$$
$$= (2)^2 + \left(\sqrt{3}\right)^2 - 2(2)\left(\sqrt{3}\right)$$
$$x = \left(2 - \sqrt{3}\right)^2$$

$$\sqrt{x} = 2 - \sqrt{3}, \frac{1}{\sqrt{x}} = 2 + \sqrt{3}$$
$$\therefore \sqrt{x} + \frac{1}{x}$$
$$= 2 + \sqrt{3} + 2 - \sqrt{3}$$
$$= 4$$

7. **(b)**   **8.** **(d)**   **9.** **(d)**

10. **(d)** The young ones of all the one mentioned are called calf.

11. **(a)** $y = \dfrac{2x - 1}{x + 3}$
$$\Rightarrow 1 = \frac{2x - 1}{x + 3} \Rightarrow x + 3 = 2x - 1$$
$$\Rightarrow 1 + 3 = x$$
$$\Rightarrow x = 4$$

12. **(a)**

13. **(c)** New expression
$$9 \div 5 \times 10 - 23 + 2 = \frac{9}{5} \times 10 - 23 + 2$$
$$= 18 - 23 + 2 = (-3)$$

14. **(b)** Perimeter of rectangle $=$ Perimeter of square
$$\Rightarrow 2 \times (l + b) = 4 \times \text{side}$$
$$\Rightarrow \text{side} = \frac{2 \times 64.5}{4} = 32.25$$

15. **(d)**

16. **(a)** The Global Peace Index is an index which comprises of 23 qualitative and quantitative indicators that gauge the level of peace in 162 countries. According to the 2015 Global Peace Index, Iceland was the most peaceful country in the world with an index value of 1.148.

17. **(a)**   **18.** **(b)**

19. **(d)** No. of kids like only Mars = 14
No. of kids like all three planets = 13
$$\therefore \text{Ratio} = \frac{14}{13}$$

20. **(a)** Kids like Mercury = 10 + 13 + 12 = 35
Kids like Jupiter = 13 + 16 = 29
$\therefore$ Difference = 35 – 29 = 6

21. **(b)** People like Mars and Jupiter
= 13 + 16 = 29

22. **(b)**

23. **(c)** Madhubani painting is one of the famous Indian art forms. As it is practiced in the Mithila region of Bihar and Nepal, it is also called Mithila or Madhubani art. These paintings are traditionally based on mythological, folk themes and pastoral symbols.

24. **(d)** Planet Nine is a large icy planet in the outer region of the Solar System. This hypothetical Neptune-sized planet orbits our Sun in a highly elongated orbit far beyond Pluto. This undiscovered planet could have a predicted mass of ten times of the Earth and orbit about 20 times farther from the Sun on average than Neptune.

25. **(d)**

26. **(d)** Smallest no. of 5 digits = 10000
LCM of 12, 24, 48, 60, 96 = 480

$$480\overline{)10000}(20$$
$$\underline{9600}$$
$$\underline{400}$$

$\therefore$ Smallest no. of 5 digits which is exactly divisible by 12, 24, 48, 60 and 96
= 10000 + 480 – 400
= 10080

27. **(a)** Area of room $= l \times b = \left(\dfrac{65}{10} \times \dfrac{30}{10}\right) \text{m}^2$
$= 19.5 \text{ m}^2$

$\therefore$ Cost of carpeting = ₹ 45 × 19.5
= ₹ 877.50

28. **(c)**

29. **(b)** Let the ages of Jai and Joy are $5x$ and $2x$ years respectively.
Sum of ages = 63
$\Rightarrow 5x + 2x = 63$
$\Rightarrow x = \dfrac{63}{7} = 9$
After 9 years.
Jai's age $= (5x + 9)$
$= 5(9) + 9 = 54$ years.
Joy's age $= (2x + 9) = 2(9) + 9 = 27$ years
$\therefore$ Ratio $= \dfrac{54}{27} = \dfrac{6}{3} = \dfrac{2}{1} = 2 : 1$

30. **(b)** SP of 90 chocolates = ₹ 160
Loss = 20%

CP of 90 chocolates $= \dfrac{160 \times 100}{100 - 20} = 200$

CP of 1 chocolate $= \dfrac{200}{90} = ₹ \dfrac{20}{9}$

Let x chocolates should be sold to make again of 20%

CP of x chocolates $= ₹ \dfrac{96 \times 100}{120} = ₹ 80$

CP of 1 chocolate $= ₹ \dfrac{80}{x}$
$\Rightarrow \dfrac{20}{9} = \dfrac{80}{x} \Rightarrow x = 36$ chocolates

31. **(a)**

Sol. (32–34):

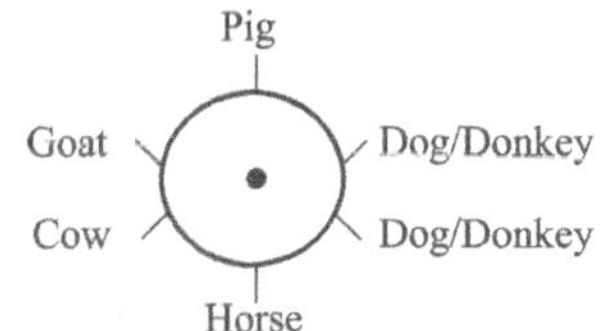

32. **(c)** Cow is tied to the immediate left of Horse.

33. **(d)** Donkey and Dog are tied next to each other.

34. **(d)** The animal tied to the left of Pig can be either dog or donkey. Hence cannot be determined.

35. **(a)**   **36.** **(c)**   **37.** **(a)**

38. **(c)** Price range of tomato = ₹ 40 to ₹ 45 per kg.
Price range of grapes = ₹ 80 to ₹ 90 per kg.

Price range of milk $= ₹ 23$ per litre.

Shop O sells:

Milk at ₹ 11.5 per ½ litre

$\Rightarrow$ 1 litre of milk $= ₹ 23$

Tomato at ₹ 21 per ½ kg

$\Rightarrow$ 1 kg of tomato $= ₹ 42$

Grapes at ₹ 43 per ½ kg

$\Rightarrow$ 1 kg of grapes $= ₹ 86$

$\therefore$ The lady will get all her items at shop O.

39. (c) Mankombu Sambasivan Swaminathan or M.S. Swaminathan is Indian geneticist and international administrator who renowned for his leading role in India's Green Revolution, a program under which high-yield varieties of wheat and rice seedlings were planted in the fields of poor farmers. He is also known as the "Father of the Green Revolution" for his commendable contribution in developing high-yielding varieties of wheat in India.

40. (a) Sum of observations

$= 41 + 39 + 52 + 48 + 54 + 62$
$+ 46 + 52 + 40 + 96 + 42$
$+ 40 + 98 + 60 + 52$
$= 822$

No. of observations $= 15$

$\therefore$ Mean marks $= \dfrac{\text{sum of observations}}{\text{No. of observations}}$

$= \dfrac{822}{15} = 54.8$

41. (a) $(- 4.6) \times (- 4.6) \div (- 4.6 + 0.6)$

$= (- 4.6) \times (- 4.6) \div (- 4)$

$= (- 4.6) \times \left(\dfrac{-4.6}{-4}\right)$

$= \left(\dfrac{- 21.16}{4}\right) = (-5.29)$

42. (c)

43. (b) Cost of $4\dfrac{1}{2}$ m of cloth $= ₹ 60\dfrac{3}{4}$

Cost of 1m of cloth $= ₹ 60\dfrac{3}{4} \div 4\dfrac{1}{2}$

$= \dfrac{243}{4} \div \dfrac{9}{2} = \dfrac{243}{4} \times \dfrac{2}{9}$

$= \dfrac{27 \times 2}{4} = \dfrac{27}{2} = = ₹ 13\dfrac{1}{2}$

44. (c) 45. (c)

46. (c) $X = 24$

$BE = 7 = 2 + 5$

Letters here show their positions in alphabets

$\therefore$ RING $= 18 + 9 + 14 + 7 = 48$

47. (b) 48. (c) 49. (d)

50. (b) The Siberian ibex (Capra sibirica) is a type of wild goat. It can be found in the North and Central Asia. It is considered as the longest and heaviest member of genus Capra. Males are between 88 and 110 cm (35 and 43 in) in shoulder height, and weigh between 60 and 130 kg (130 and 290 lb), whereas females are noticeably smaller with heights between 67 and 92 cm (26 and 36 in), and weights between 34 and 56 kg (75 and 123 lb).

51. (c) Let CP of 1 chair $= ₹ 1$

CP of 25 chairs $= ₹ 25$

and CP of 20 chairs $= ₹ 20$

Also, SP of 20 chairs $=$ CP of 25 chairs

$= ₹ 25$

$\therefore$ Profit $=$ SP of 20 chairs $-$ CP of 20 chairs

$= ₹ 25 - ₹ 20$

$= ₹ 5$

Profit % $= \dfrac{5}{20} \times 100 = 25\%$

52. (b) Let CP $= ₹ 100$

MP $= 20\%$ above cost price

$= \left(\dfrac{20}{100} \times 100\right) + 100 = ₹ 120$

Discount $= 5\%$ of MP

$= \dfrac{5}{100} \times 120 = ₹ 6$

$\therefore$ SP $=$ MP $-$ discount

$= ₹ 120 - ₹ 6 = ₹ 114$

$\therefore$ Profit % $= \dfrac{114 - 100}{100} \times 100 = 14\%$

53. (a) 54. (b) 55. (b)

56. (a) C.I. $= 7500 \left[1 + \dfrac{12}{100}\right]^{7/3} - 7500$

$= 7500 \left[1.12\right]^{7/3} - 7500$

$= 7500 \left[2.21\right]^{1/3} - 7500$

$$= 9770 - 7500 = 2270 \simeq 2284$$

57. (c) Sum of marks obtained in Geography

$$= 68 + 65 + 69 + 70 = 272$$

$$\therefore \text{ Average marks in Geography} = \frac{272}{4}$$
$$= 68$$

Sum of marks obtained in History
$$= 65 + 75 + 70 + 65 = 275$$
$$\therefore \text{ Average marks in History}$$
$$= \frac{275}{4} = 68.75$$

58. (*) Average marks in Science
$$= \frac{80 + 85 + 88 + 87}{4}$$
$$= \frac{340}{4} = 85$$

Average marks in Maths
$$= \frac{75 + 80 + 82 + 78}{4}$$
$$= \frac{315}{4} = 78.75$$
$$\therefore \text{ Difference} = 85 - 78.75 = 6.25$$

59. (c) Shamita's total marks
$$= 75 + 80 + 65 + 68 + 72 + 65$$
$$= 425$$

Smita's total marks
$$= 80 + 85 + 75 + 65 + 70 + 70$$
$$= 445$$

Shilpa's total marks
$$= 82 + 88 + 70 + 69 + 71 + 70$$
$$= 450$$

Sheela's total marks
$$= 78 + 87 + 65 + 70 + 75 + 74$$
$$= 449$$

$\therefore$ Shilpa's has the highest total marks.

60. (b) $\cos\theta + \sin\theta = m$

$\sec\theta + \text{cosec}\theta = n$

$$\Rightarrow \quad \frac{1}{\cos\theta} + \frac{1}{\sin\theta} = n$$

$$\Rightarrow \frac{\sin\theta + \cos\theta}{\sin\theta \cos\theta} = n$$

$$\therefore \quad \frac{m}{n} = \frac{\cos\theta + \sin\theta}{\dfrac{\cos\theta + \sin\theta}{\sin\theta \cos\theta}} = \sec\theta \cos\theta$$

61. (a)

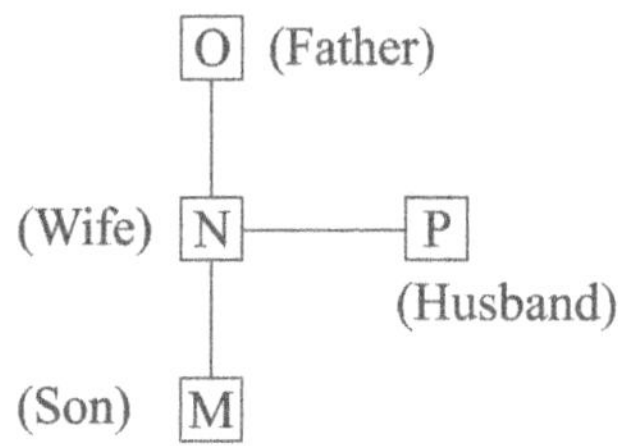

From Fig. P is the father of M

N is the mother of M

$\therefore$ N is the wife of P

62. (c)

63. (b) X will complete a piece of work in $\dfrac{1}{36}$ days.

Y will finish a piece of work in $\dfrac{1}{60}$ days.

Since X, Y and Z take 18 days to complete to work,

$$\frac{1}{Z} = \frac{1}{18} - \left(\frac{1}{36} + \frac{1}{60}\right)$$

$$\Rightarrow \frac{1}{Z} = \frac{1}{18} - \left(\frac{5+3}{180}\right) = \frac{1}{18} - \frac{8}{180}$$

$$\Rightarrow \frac{1}{Z} = \frac{10-8}{180} = \frac{2}{180} = \frac{1}{90}$$

$$\Rightarrow Z = 90 \text{ days}$$

64. (c)

65. (c) $\dfrac{\sin\theta}{1 + \cos\theta} + \dfrac{1 + \cos\theta}{\sin\theta}$

$$= \frac{\sin^2\theta + (1 + \cos\theta)^2}{\sin\theta (1 + \cos\theta)}$$

$$= \frac{\sin^2\theta + 1 + \cos^2\theta + 2\cos\theta}{\sin\theta (1 + \cos\theta)}$$

$$= \frac{2 + 2\cos\theta}{\sin\theta (1 + \cos\theta)} = \frac{2(1 + \cos\theta)}{\sin\theta (1 + \cos\theta)}$$

$$= \frac{2}{\sin\theta}$$

66. (b)

67. (c) The Pokhran-II tests were a series of five nuclear bomb test explosions conducted by India in May 1998. The tests were initiated under the assigned code name

'Operation Shakti', with the detonation of one fusion and two fission bombs.

68. (d)   69.   (d)

70. (b) Let the digits at unit's and tens place be x and $(9 - x)$ respectively.

∴ Original no. $= 10(9 - x) + x$

$= 90 - 10x + x = 90 - 9x$

Now $(90 - 9x) + 27 = 10(x) + (9 - x)$

⟹ $90 + 27 - 9 = 9x + 10x - x$

⟹ $108 = 18x$

⟹ $x = 6$

∴ Number $= 90 - 9x = 90 - 9(6)$

$= 90 - 54 = 36$

71. (c)

$$13,\ 14,\ 18,\ 27,\ ?,\ 68,\ 104$$

Difference 1   4   9

1^2 2^2 3^2

Missing term $= 27 + (4)^2 = 27 + 16 = 43$

72. (a) Kitty's mother is Uthara's maternal aunt.

73. (d) Let the two angles be $9x$ and $16x$

Now, sum of the angles $= 180°$

⟹ $9x + 16x + 55° = 180°$

⟹ $25x + 55° = 180°$

⟹ $25x = 180° - 55° = 125$

⟹ $x = 5$

∴ Required angles are $(5 \times 9) = 45°$ and $(16 \times 5) = 80°$.

74. (d) Atul Dodiya is one of the finest and most celebrated Indian artists of the present generation. He is known for his water colour paintings which are centered on the life of Mahatma Gandhi.

75. (b)

76. (c)

H O U S E S = G N A Y D R

–1

–1

+6

+6

–1

–1

Using the given pattern, we get

DIARY = CHGXX

77. (a) Satyameva Jayate is an ancient Sanskrit saying which means "truth alone truimps". After the independence of India, it was adopted as the national motto of India. It is also inscribed in script at the base of the national emblem.

78. (c)   79.   (c)

80. (a) Religions teach the guiding principles for leading one's life implies that religion is a way of life.

Hence, Conclusion I follows.

81. (c)

82. (c)

$$\frac{9}{13} \sqrt{\frac{18}{26}} \sqrt{\frac{90}{52}}$$

$$= \frac{9}{13} \times \frac{26}{18} \div \frac{90}{52}$$

$$= 1 \div \frac{90}{52} = \frac{52}{90} = \frac{26}{45}$$

83. (d)

84. (d) If SHFIF is written as FUSVS

					Z	E	B	R	A
S	H	F	I	F	↓	↓	↓	↓	↓
+13	+13	+13	+13	+13	+13	+13	+13	+13	+13
F	U	S	V	S	M	R	O	E	N

85. (a)

86. (b)

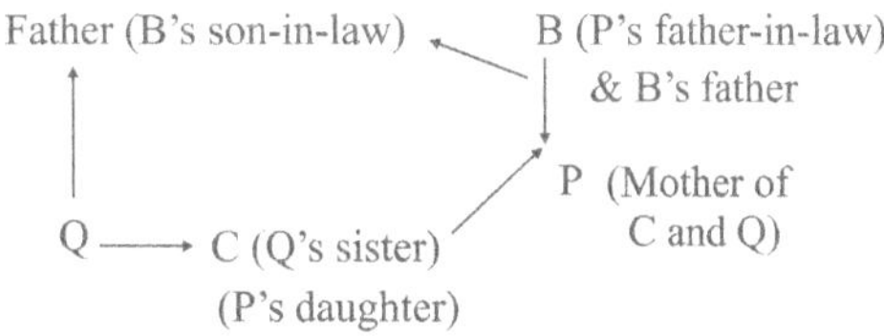

Hence, P ; is the daughter of (B)

87. (b)

88. (d) 6 Carpenter works for 6 days to make 96 windows

8 Carpenter works for 6 days to make 96 windows

$$= \frac{96}{6} \times 8$$

$= 128$ windows.

When 8 carpenter works 4 days, then number of windows

$$= \frac{128}{4} = 32 \text{ windows.}$$

89. (c) Cassettes produced in January

$= 18, 58, 509$

Cassettes produced in February

$= 18, 58, 509 + 7623 = 1866132$

     Cassettes produced in March

     = 1866132 – 25838 = 1840294

∴   Total Cassettes produced

     = 1858509 + 1866132 + 1840294

     = 5564935

90. (*)   **91. (b)**

92. (a) Mango, Lemon and Melon are fruits

     = 439516   ... (1)

     Mango and Lemon are yellow

     = 04396   ... (2)

     Melon is green = 857   ... (3)

     From equation (1) and (3)

     Melon = 5

93. (d) EMU is the missing term in the given pattern.

94. (a) Sanjay and Jacob cover distance in 1 sec

     = 7 m + 5 m = 12 meter

     Total distance covered in 1 minute

     = (12 × 60s) = 720 meter

     Total distance covered in 42 minutes

     = 42 × 720 m = 30240 m

     = 30.24 km

95. (d)

96. (b) $CI = \dfrac{P \times R \times T}{100} = \dfrac{5000 \times 8 \times 2}{100} = ₹\,800$

$$CI = P\left[\left(1 + \frac{R}{100}\right)^n - 1\right]$$

$$= 5000\left[\left(1 + \frac{8}{100}\right)^2 - 1\right]$$

$$= 5000\left[\left(1 + \frac{2}{25}\right)^2 - 1\right]$$

$$= 5000\left(\frac{729}{625} - 1\right) = 5000 \times \frac{104}{625}$$

     = ₹ 832

∴ Difference = CI – SI

     = ₹ 832 – ₹ 800

     = ₹ 32

97. (b) $12 - [26 - \{2 + 5 \times (6 - 3)\}]$

     $= 12 - [26 - \{2 + 5 \times 3\}]$

     $= 12 - [26 - 17] = 12 - 9 = 3$

98. (c) Number of bottles $= \dfrac{42\,l}{280\,ml}$

     $= \dfrac{42000}{280}$ ml $(\because 1\,l = 1000$ ml$)$

     = 150

99. (a) Let two even numbers be $2x$ and $(2x + 2)$ respectively.

     HCF of numbers = 2

     LCM of numbers = 144

     Now, HCF × LCM = Product of two nos.

     ⇒ $2 \times 144 = 2x\,(2x + 2)$

     ⇒ $144 = 2x\,(x + 1)$

     ⇒ $72 = x^2 + x$

     ⇒ $x^2 + x - 72 = 0$

     ⇒ $(x + 9)\,(x - 8) = 0$

     ⇒ $x = 8$

∴ Numbers are 16 and 18.

100. (b)

1. Tashkent Declaration followed Indo-Pak war of
   (a) 1947   (b) 1965
   (c) 1971   (d) 1999

2. Which river does not flow into the Arabian Sea?
   (a) Narmada   (b) Tapti
   (c) Periyar   (d) Mahanadi

3. What will happen to a person's weight when he is in a moving elevator?
   (a) Increase
   (b) Decrease
   (c) Weight will not change
   (d) May increase or decrease

4. E is the daughter of P who is the husband of the only daughter-in-law of K? How is E related to K?
   (a) Daughter   (b) Granddaughter
   (c) Grandmother   (d) Mother

5. If the mathematical operator '+' means '×', '+' means '−', '×' means '+' and '−' means '÷' then $25 + 18 - 3 \times 7 \div 3 = ?$
   (a) 25   (b) 21
   (c) 19   (d) 40

6. Stainless steel is
   (a) A compound.   (b) A mixture.
   (c) An element.   (d) An alloy.

7. $99 \times 99 = ?$
   (a) 9791   (b) 9801
   (c) 9881   (d) 9901

8. Find a pair similar to 'Arrow : Bow' from the following.
   (a) Football : Hand   (b) Salad : Knife
   (c) Bullet : Rifle   (d) Smoke : Water

9. Verification of log-in name and password is for
   (a) Authenticating the user.
   (b) Re-confirming the user.
   (c) Providing formal access to the user.
   (d) Completing the formality of login-in.

10. If the length (L cm) and breadth (B cm) of a rectangle are increased by 25%, find the difference between the areas of the old and new rectangles.
    (a) 3LB/2 sq.cm   (b) 24LB/9 sq.cm
    (c) 9LB/16 sq.cm   (d) 16LB/9 sq.cm

11. NGT stands for
    (a) National Geographic Television
    (b) National Green Transport
    (c) National Green Trust
    (d) National Green Tribunal

12. Project Loon is a search engine project by ______________ for providing internet access to rural and remote areas using high-altitude helium-filled balloons.
    (a) Google   (b) Microsoft
    (c) Apple   (d) Yahoo

13. The product of two numbers is 24 and the sum of their squares is 52. Find their sum.
    (a) 5   (b) 10
    (c) 15   (d) 20

14. India came directly under the rule of the British Crown in the year ________.
    (a) 1857   (b) 1858
    (c) 1859   (d) 1856

15. If **'god is great'** = **'cp an bo'**, **'great help done'** = **'er cp fs'** and **'he is great'** = **'bo cp dq'**, then what represents 'he is god'?
    (a) cp er bo   (b) an bo cp
    (c) dq bo cp   (d) an bo dq

16. What number should be deducted from 1265 to make it divisible by 29 exactly?
    (a) 15   (b) 16
    (c) 18   (d) 17

17. Which one is considered as India's first supercomputer?

   (a) Aditya (b) Vikram-100

   (c) Param 8000 (d) Shastra T

18. The sum of the ages of 4 children born at the intervals of 4 years is 48. Find the age of the youngest child.

   (a) 4 years (b) 5 years

   (c) 6 years (d) 7 years

19. Banaras Hindu University which completed 100 years in February 2016 was founded by

   (a) Gulzari Lal Nanda

   (b) Madan Mohan Malaviya

   (c) Jay Prakash Narayan

   (d) Sarvepalli Radhakrishnan

20. At what percentage simple interest per annum a certain sum will double in 10 years?

   (a) 7% (b) 8%

   (c) 9% (d) 10%

21. Contemporary : Historic : : _________ : Ancient

   (a) Past (b) Classic

   (c) Modern (d) Future

22. A man who had no brother or sister, pointed out to a photo and said "this boy is my father's son". Who was on the photo?

   (a) The man's son

   (b) The man's father

   (c) Himself

   (d) The man's grandfather

23. Rajya Sabha is also known as

   (a) Legislative Council

   (b) Senior House

   (c) Upper House

   (d) Lower House

24. The price of 12 kg of sugar is equal to that of 6 kg of rice. The price of 10 kg of sugar and 8 kg of rice ₹ 1040. Find the price 1 kg of sugar.

   (a) ₹ 80 (b) ₹ 70

   (c) ₹ 60 (d) ₹ 40

25. The historic Conference of Parties (COP 21) 2015, on climate change was held in

   (a) Geneva (b) Davos

   (c) Paris (d) Bonn

26. INSAT-3D the meteorological Satellite with advanced weather monitoring payloads was launched in

   (a) 2012 (b) 2013

   (c) 2014 (d) 2015

27. If $\cot 52° = b$, $\tan 38° =$?

   (a) $\div\sqrt{b}$ (b) $\sqrt{b}/2$

   (c) $-b$ (d) b

28. Statements followed by some conclusions are given below.

   Statement:

   1. God has distributed time equally to mankind but not money.

   2. But God has compensated by giving commonsense.

   Conclusions:

   I. God has not done justice to mankind in distributing money.

   II. One has to use commonsense to manage money wisely.

   Find which of the given conclusions logically follows from the given statements.

   (a) Only conclusion I follows.

   (b) Only conclusion II follows.

   (c) Both I and II follow.

   (d) Neither I nor II follows.

29. A compiler is a

   (a) Hardware

   (b) Software

   (c) Neither Hardware nor Software

   (d) Card

30. Bina is the daughter of Mohan who is the only son-in-law of Meena. Meena has only one child. Kiran is the granddaughter of Meena. How is Kiran related to Bina?

   (a) Sister (b) Daughter

   (c) Maternal aunt (d) Mother

31. A man covers 1 km in 10 minutes. What is his speed in kmph?

   (a) 1.33 (b) 1.25

   (c) 1.67 (d) 1.50

DIRECTIONS (Qs. 32-34): *Consider the following information and answer questions based on it.*

P, Q, R, S are four friends who pursue teaching, law, banking, cooking and own red, blue, white and yellow house, in a random order. An individual owns only one house and pursues only one profession.

1. P owns a red house and is not a banker.
2. The owner of blue house is a lawyer.
3. The colour of S's house is neither yellow nor white.
4. R is a teacher.

32. White house is owned by
- (a) Q
- (b) R
- (c) S
- (d) Cannot be determined

33. Q is a
- (a) Lawyer
- (b) Banker
- (c) Cook
- (d) Teacher

34. The owner of the blue house is
- (a) S
- (b) R
- (c) Q
- (d) Cannot be determined

35. Name the Chinese President who visited India in 2015.
- (a) Xi Jinping
- (b) Hu Jintao
- (c) Jiang Zemin
- (d) Li Xian Ning

36. Capital of Nagaland is
- (a) Dimapur
- (b) Kohima
- (c) Mokokchung
- (d) Tezpur

37. Consolation : Grief :: Sedative : __________
- (a) Chloroform
- (b) Anesthesia
- (c) Pain
- (d) Bum

38. Which ailment is not related to heart?
- (a) Aneurysm
- (b) Cardiomyopathy
- (c) Diphtheria
- (d) Myocardial rupture

39. If the arithmetic mean of 10 numbers is 35 and each number is increased by 2, find the mean of the new set of numbers.
- (a) 28
- (b) 34
- (c) 40
- (d) 37

40. Find the fourth proportional to 3.6, 6.9 and 11.4.
- (a) 20.3
- (b) 18.9
- (c) 19.6
- (d) 21.9

41. A statement followed by some conclusions are given below.

Statement: Based on his performance, Rajesh got a poor rating in his office. Conclusions:

I. Rajesh did not perform well.

II. The rating given to Rajesh was not up to the mark.

Find which of the given conclusions logically follow from the given statement.
- (a) Only conclusion I follows.
- (b) Only conclusion II follows.
- (c) Both I and II follow.
- (d) Neither I nor II follows.

42. If $a + 2b = 55$ and $a - 2b = -13$, find the value of b.
- (a) 21
- (b) 14
- (c) 17
- (d) 19

43. $2\cos(\theta - \pi/2) + 3\sin(\theta + \pi/2) - (3\sin\theta + 2\cos\theta) = ?$
- (a) $\cos\theta - \sin\theta$
- (b) $\sin\theta - \cos\theta$
- (c) $\sin\theta + \cos\theta$
- (d) $\cot\theta - \tan\theta$

44. The ______ Five Year Plan of the Government of India (2012–17) is under drafting,
- (a) 10th
- (b) 11th
- (c) 12th
- (d) 13th

45. E and F can do a work in 10 days. If E alone can do it in 30 days, F alone can do it in _____ days.
- (a) 15
- (b) 20
- (c) 25
- (d) 18

46. Gunpowder mainly contains
- (a) Calcium sulphate
- (b) Potassium nitrate
- (c) Lead sulfide
- (d) Zinc sulfide

47. Who was the founder of Swaraj Party?
- (a) C. Rajagopalachari
- (b) Motilal Nehru
- (c) Lala Lajpat Rai
- (d) Mahatma Gandhi

48. Select the alternative that has a different relationship as the given pair -

Inside : Outside

(a) Day : Night   (b) Sun : Star

(c) Light : Dark   (d) White : Black

49. The HCF of two numbers is 6 and their LCM is 108. If one of the numbers is 12, then the other is

(a) 27   (b) 54

(c) 48   (d) 36

50. Find the odd statement out in relation to a triangle.

(a) The longest side is opposite to the greatest angle.

(b) Exterior angle of a triangle = the sum of interior opposite angles.

(c) The sum of any 2 sides is greater than the 3rd side.

(d) The square of one side = the sum of the squares of other two sides

51. 82, 70, 76, 64, 70, 58, ?

(a) 52   (b) 76

(c) 64   (d) 48

52. Which one does not belong to the group?

(a) Panda Global   (b) Rabbit

(c) Avast   (d) Kaspersky

53. 'Euro' is the currency of

(a) UK   (b) Sweden

(c) Euro Zone   (d) Denmark

54. The difference between the length and breadth of a rectangle is 6 m. If its perimeter is 64 m, then its area is:

(a) 256 sq.m   (b) 247 sq.m

(c) 264 sq.m   (d) 238 sq.m

55. 9876 − ? + 5431 = 5553

(a) 9754   (b) 9765

(c) 8754   (d) 9854

DIRECTIONS (Qs. 56-58): *The following table represents the marks of four students in five subjects.*

	Physics	Chemistry	Maths	History	Geography
Shyam	45	50	49	51	65
Sunil	60	55	60	59	61
Jagdish	35	41	39	30	45
Rajesh	50	55	51	57	62

Consider the information and answer questions based on it.

56. The difference between the total marks scored by Sunil and Jagdish is

(a) 190   (b) 125

(c) 105   (d) 115

57. Who has the highest marks in History and Geography put together?

(a) Shyam   (b) Sunil

(c) Jagdish   (d) Rajesh

58. Who has the highest average marks?

(a) Shyam   (b) Sunil

(c) Jagdish   (d) Rajesh

59. If ARC is written as \$@* and HIT is #&% then CHAIR is

(a) #*&\$@   (b) #*\$&%

(c) *#\$&@   (d) *#\$&%

60. Infra-red rays are

(a) Longitudinal waves

(b) Transverse waves

(c) Mechanical waves

(d) Electromagnetic waves

61. The HCF of two numbers is 4 and the two other factors of LCM are 5 and 7. Find the smaller of the two numbers.

(a) 10   (b) 14

(c) 20   (d) 28

62. Statue of Liberty is situated in

(a) Paris   (b) Washington

(c) Geneva   (d) New York

63. Headquarters of NASA is at

(a) New York   (b) Washington

(c) Boston   (d) Texas

64. A trader bought a bag of 40 kg of basmati rice at ₹ 125 per kg and another bag of 60 kg at ₹150 per kg. He sold the entire stock at a profit of 20%. Find the selling price per kg.

(a) ₹ 152   (b) ₹ 158

(c) ₹ 168   (d) ₹ 172

65. Car X and Y start at the same time at speeds of 12 kmph and 16 kmph. Find the distance between them after 3 minutes.

(a) 200 m   (b) 150 m

(c) 180 m   (d) 120 m

66. A man deposits ₹500 at the beginning of each year for 2 years at 10% p.a. compound annually. Find the maturity value at the end of the 2nd year.

(a) ₹ 1,050   (b) ₹ 1,150

(c) ₹ 1,155   (d) ₹ 1,200

67. Which one is not a good conductor of electricity?

(a) Porcelain   (b) Aluminum

(c) Tungsten   (d) Nickel

DIRECTIONS (Qs. 68-70): *Consider the following information and answer the questions based on it.*

In a group of 75 students, 12 like only cabbage, 15 like only cauliflower, 21 like only carrot, 12 like both carrot a cabbage, 13 like only capsicum and 2 like both capsicum and cauliflower.

68. What is the percentage of students that do not like cabbage?

(a) 16   (b) 32

(c) 24   (d) 68

69. The difference between the people who like carrot and cauliflower is

(a) 6   (b) 18

(c) 16   (d) 4

70. How many students like only one vegetable?

(a) 60   (b) 61

(c) 65   (d) 71

71. A student scored 470 marks in 6 subjects. The maximum marks for each subject was 100. What was his score in percentage terms?

(a) 67.33 %   (b) 69.45 %

(c) 78.33 %   (d) 78.67%

72. Read the given statements carefully and answer the question.

Knowledge and wisdom go hand in hand. The deeper the knowledge, the greater is the wisdom. Knowledge is awareness. Wisdom is required to tackle complications.

Which of the following is true according to the given statement?

(a) Knowledge and wisdom are synonymous.

(b) Knowledge and wisdom are entirely different.

(c) Knowledge and wisdom are complementary to each other.

(d) Wisdom can supplant knowledge.

73. The ratio of two numbers is 3:1 and their sum is 72. Find the difference between the numbers.

(a) 24   (b) 36

(c) 32   (d) 28

74. If 'health care is wealth' is written as 1372, 'health needs care' is 417, 'he needs wealth' is 463, then 'he is wealth' is

(a) 326   (b) 764

(c) 624   (d) 246

75. The average ages of parents and two children are 30 years and 8 years respectively. The average age of the family is

(a) 16 years   (b) 19 years

(c) 18 years   (d) 17 years

76. S can finish 50% of a work in a day. T can do 25% of the work in a day. Both of them together will finish the work in days.

(a) 2.66   (b) 2.33

(c) 1.33   (d) 1.67

77. The most significant feature of Indus Valley civilization was

(a) Barter system

(b) Local transport system

(c) Buildings made of brick

(d) Administrative system

78. India covers _______ of earth's land area, (approximate)

(a) 2.8%

(b) 2.4%

(c) 2.0%

(d) 3.2%

79. Usually, colour blindness is

(a) A genetic disposition.

(b) A non-genetic condition.

(c) A lifestyle disease.

(d) Caused by exposure to light.

80. Find the mean of the values: **1, 9, 7, 3, 5, 5, 6, 4, 2, 8**

    (a) 3 (b) 4

    (c) 5 (d) 6

81. In 2012 Olympics, the maximum gold medals were won by

    (a) China (b) Great Britain

    (c) U. S. A. (d) Russia

82. Rearrange the jumbled letters to make meaningful words and then select the one which is different.

    (a) DOGL (b) TSEVO

    (c) ENZROB (d) LVREIS

83. An article was sold for ₹3,600 at a discount of 10%. Find the selling price if the discount was 15%.

    (a) ₹ 3,600 (b) ₹ 4,000

    (c) ₹ 3,800 (d) ₹ 3,400

84. Which country won the U-19 World Cup Cricket 2016?

    (a) India (b) Sri Lanka

    (c) West Indies (d) Bangladesh

85. Human respiration releases

    (a) Mixture of gases (b) Carbon monoxide

    (c) Oxygen (d) Carbon dioxide

86. Who was the first cricketer to score 4 successive centuries in World Cup Cricket?

    (a) Kumar Sangakkara

    (b) AB de Viliiers

    (c) Ross Taylor

    (d) Saeed Anwar

87. The technology developed to track enemy submarines in World War II was

    (a) RADAR (b) SONAR

    (c) Echolocatian (d) LIDAR

88. The mean of 25 values was 40. But one value was written as 25 instead of 50. The corrected mean is

    (a) 39 (b) 41

    (c) 40 (d) 42

89. Bangladesh has a land border with

    (a) only India (b) India and Myanmar

    (c) India and Bhutan (d) India and China

90. ICT is the common abbreviation of

    (a) International Communication Technology

    (b) Intelligent Communication Technology

    (c) Inter-state Communication Technology

    (d) Information and Communication Technology

91. Read the given statements carefully and answer the question.

    Statement:

    A leading tennis star who faced media after failing a dope test said, "I don't want to end my career this way. I hope I will be given another chance to play this game. I let the sport down."

    Which of the following is true according to the given statement?

    (a) He was challenging the outcome of the dope test.

    (b) He was confident that he was right and would continue to play.

    (c) He had admitted to testing positive in dope test.

    (d) The sport let him down.

92. CBDA, GFHE, KJLI, ?

    (a) NOPM (b) MNOP

    (c) PMNO (d) ONPM

93. 'Khajuraho' group of monuments can be found in

    (a) Maharashtra (b) Bihar

    (c) Madhya Pradesh (d) Gujarat

94. Which one of the following is not alkaline?

    (a) Sodium (b) Potassium

    (c) Lithium (d) Sulphur

95. If 'code' = **6241**, 'made' = **5346**, 'come' = **3124**' and 'to' = **27** then 'dome' =?

    (a) 6134 (b) 5214

    (c) 6124 (d) 2634

96. A statement followed by some conclusions are given below.

Statement:

After landing on the moon, Neil Armstrong said "One small step for a man, a giant leap for mankind."

Conclusions:

I.   Neil Armstrong calls himself as mankind.

II. Neil Armstrong only echoed the feeling of achievement by mankind.

Find which of the given conclusions logically follow from the given statement.

(a) Only conclusion I follows.

(b) Only conclusion II follows.

(c) Both I and II follow.

(d) Neither I nor II follows.

97. A human adult's entire digestive tract from mouth to anus is about _____ meters long.

(a) 8   (b) 7

(c) 10   (d) 9

98. The communication satellite launched by India in November 2015 is

(a) GSAT-6   (b) GSAT-15

(c) GSAT-16   (d) IRNSS-1E

99. An article was sold for ₹ 26,000 at a discount of 35%. Find the selling price if the discount was 15%.

(a) ₹ 36,000   (b) ₹ 40,000

(c) ₹ 38,000   (d) ₹ 34,000

100. Replace # sign with the mathematical operators '+', '÷', '–' and '=' to get a 0 balanced equation out of **(27 # 15 # 2) # 10 # 4**. Choose the right sequence from below.

(a) $+ \div = -$ (b) $- + = \div$

(c) $+ - \div =$ (d) $+ = \div -$

HINTS & EXPLANATIONS

1. **(b)** Tashkent Declaration followed Indo-Pak war of 1965.

2. **(d)**   3. **(c)**

4. **(b)** Grandfather (K)

   Daughter in law

   Father (P) ——— (X) wife

   Daughter (E)

   Here X is daughter in law of K and wife of P.
   Hence E is the granddaughter of K.

5. **(d)** After changing the values
   $25 + 18 - 3 \times 7 \div 3 = 25 - 18 \div 3 + 7 \times 3$
   $= 25 - 6 + 21$
   $= 40$

6. **(d)**

7. **(b)** $99 \times 99 = (100 - 1) \times (100 - 1)$
   $= (100 - 1)^2$
   $= 10000 - 200 + 1$
   $= 9801$

8. **(c)**   9. **(a)**

10. **(c)** Length = LCM and Breadth = BCM

    New dimension $= \dfrac{5L}{4}$ cm and Breadth

    $= \dfrac{5B}{4}$ cm [After 25% increase]

    Old area $= L \times B$ Sq. cm

    New area $= \dfrac{25LB}{16}$ Sq.cm

    Hence, difference $= \dfrac{25LB}{16} - LB = \dfrac{9LB}{16}$ Sq.cm

11. **(d)**   12. **(a)**

13. **(b)** Let x and y be the two numbers.
    ATQ $x \times y = 24$ ......(1)
    and $x^2 + y^2 = 52$ ......(2)
    Since $x^2 + y^2 = (x + y)^2 - 2xy$.
    Substituting value of $x^2 + y^2$ in eqn (2)
    $(x + y)^2 = 52 + 2xy \Rightarrow (x + y)^2 = 52 + 48$
    $x + y = \sqrt{100} = 10$

14. **(b)**

15. **(d)** god is great → cp an bo ......(1)
    great help done → er cp fs ......(2)
    he is great → bo cp dq ......(3)
    From (1) and (2)
    great = cp
    From (1) and (3)
    is = bo
    ∴ god = an and he = dq
    Hence he is god = dq bo an

16. **(c)** On dividing 1265 by 29 we get 18 as the remainder
    ∴ 18 should be deducted from 1265 to make it divisible by 29 perfectly.

17. **(c)**

18. **(c)** Let the age of youngest child be x, then the ages of other children will be 'x + 4', 'x+8' and 'x + 12' years.
    Now, ATQ
    $x + x + 4 + x + 8 + x + 12 = 48$
    $\Rightarrow 4x + 24 = 48$
    $\Rightarrow 4x = 24$
    $\Rightarrow x = 6$
    ∴ age of youngest child = 6 years.

19. **(b)** Pandit Madan Mohan Malaviya, a great educationist and politician is known for his role in the Independence movement. He found Benaras Hindu University in 1916. It is one of the best and largest universities in Asia.

20. **(d)** A = S.I + P

    ATQ $2P = \dfrac{P \times 10 \times T}{100} + P$

    $\Rightarrow P = \dfrac{PT}{10} \Rightarrow T = 10$ years

21. **(c)**

22. **(c)** Since the man had no brother or sister. Hence the boy in the photo is the man himself.

23. **(c)**

24. (d) 6 kg rice = 12 kg sugar

$\Rightarrow$ 1 kg rice = 2 kg sugar

ATQ 10 kg Sugar + 8 kg rice = ₹1040

$\Rightarrow$ 10 kg sugar + 16 kg sugar = ₹1040

$\Rightarrow$ 26 kg sugar = ₹1040

$\Rightarrow$ 1 kg sugar $= \dfrac{₹1040}{26} = ₹40$

25. (c) The 21st session of the conference of parties (COP 21), held in Paris, France in December 2015, was historic in its outcome. The international climate agreement, COP is a decision making body responsible for monitoring and reviewing the implementation of the United Nations Framework Convention.

26. (b) The INSA-3D, India's advanced weather satellite was launched on 26th July, 2013 from Kourou French Guiana.

27. (d) cot 52° = b

$\Rightarrow$ cot (90° – 38°) = b

$\Rightarrow$ tan 38° = b

28. (b) God has distributed time equally but not the money and also God has given commonsense to all.

So from the above statement we can conclude that, One has to use commonsense to manage money wisely

Hence only conclusion II follows.

29. (b)

30. (a)

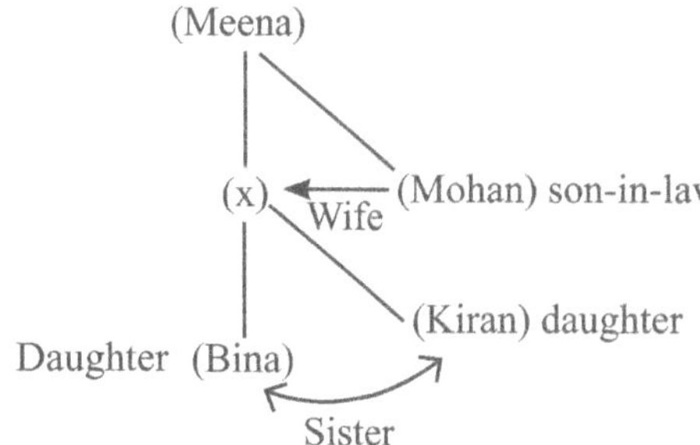

Here x is the daughter of meena. Mohan is son-in-law of meena means mohan and x are husband and wife.

$\therefore$ Bina and kiran are their daughter.

31. (*) Speed $= \dfrac{\text{distance}}{\text{time}} = \dfrac{1}{10}$ km/min

$= \dfrac{1}{10/60} = 6 \text{ km}/\text{h}$

answer not applicable.

Sol. (32-34):

Friends	Profession	House
P	Cooking	Red
S	Lawyer	Blue
R	Teacher	Yellow/ white
Q	Banker	White/ yellow

32. (d) While can be owned by either R or Q, hence cannot be determined

33. (b) Q is a Banker

34. (a) The owner of blue house is S.

35. (*)   36.   (b)   37.   (c)   38. (c)

39. (d) AM of 10 = 35

$\Rightarrow$ Sum = 350

Since each no. is increased by 2

$\therefore$ new sum = 350 + 10 × 2 = 370

Hence new mean $= \dfrac{370}{10} = 37$

40. (d) Let x be the fourth proportional

ATQ $= \dfrac{3.6}{6.9} = \dfrac{11.4}{x} \Rightarrow x = \dfrac{11.4 \times 6.9}{3.6}$

$\Rightarrow$ x = 21.85 $\approx$ 21.9

41. (c)

42. (c) a + 2b = 55   ... (1)

a – 2b = – 13   ...(2)

Subtracting eqn (2) from eqn (1)

a + 2b – a + 2b = 55 + 13

$\Rightarrow$ 4b = 68 $\Rightarrow$ b = 17.

43. (a) 2 cos (θ – π/2) + 3sin(θ + π/2)

$\quad$ – (3 sinθ + 2cosθ)

= 2 sin θ + 3 cos θ – (3sin θ + 2 cos θ)

= 2 sinθ + 3cosθ – 3sinθ – 2cosθ

= cosθ – sinθ

44. (*)

45. (a) Work done by E and F together = 10 days

$\Rightarrow$ 1 day's work of E and F $= \dfrac{1}{10}$

Also 1 day's work of E $= \dfrac{1}{30}$

$\therefore$ 1 day's work of F $= \dfrac{1}{10} - \dfrac{1}{30}$

$= \dfrac{3-1}{30} = \dfrac{2}{30} = \dfrac{1}{15}$

$\Rightarrow$ F alone can do it in 15 days

46. **(b)**

47. **(b)** The founder of Swaraj party was Motilal Nehru. The party was formed in India in January 1923 aftr the Gaya Annual Conference in December of the Indian National Congress. C.R. das was its president and Motilal Nehru was its secretary.

48. **(b)**

49. **(b)** Product of two numbers is equal to the product of their HCF and LCM

$\Rightarrow (6 \times 108) = 12 \times x$ {where x is the other number}

$$\Rightarrow x = \frac{648}{12} = 54$$

Hence the other number = 54.

50. **(d)** There is no such property of triangles that states, square of one side = sum of squares of other two sides

51. **(c)**

$$\underset{-12}{82} \quad \underset{+6}{70} \quad \underset{-12}{76} \quad \underset{+6}{64} \quad \underset{-12}{70} \quad \underset{+6}{58} \quad 64$$

52. **(b)**   **53.** **(c)**

54. **(b)** Let the length and breadth of rectangle be L and B respectively.

ATQ L – B = 6 m $\Rightarrow$ L = 6 + B

also 2 (L + B) = 64m

= 2(6 + B + B) = 64m $\Rightarrow$ B = 13 m

$\Rightarrow$ L = 19m

$\therefore$ area = 13 × 19 = 247 sq. m

55. **(a)** 9876–? + 5431 = 5553

9876 – ? = 5553 – 5431

? = 9876 – 122

? = 9754

56. **(c)** Total marks of sunil = 60 + 55 + 60 + 59 + 61 = 295

Total marks of Jagdish = 35 + 41 + 39 + 30 + 45 = 190

$\therefore$ Difference = 295 – 190 = 105

57. **(b)** Marks of : Shyam = 51 + 65 = 116

Sunil = 59 + 61 = 120

Jagdish = 30 + 45 = 75

Rajesh = 57 + 62 = 119

Hence highest marks are secured by sunil.

58. **(b)** Average marks of :

$$Shyam = \frac{45 + 50 + 49 + 51 + 65}{5} = 52$$

$$Sunil \quad = \frac{60 + 55 + 60 + 59 + 61}{5} = 59$$

$$Jagdish = \frac{35 + 41 + 39 + 30 + 45}{5} = 38$$

$$Rajesh = \frac{50 + 55 + 51 + 57 + 62}{5} = 55$$

Hence, Sunil has the highest average marks.

59. **(c)** A → \$ H → #

R → @   I → &

C → *   T → %

Comparing the values

C → *

H → #

A → \$

I → &

R → @

60. **(d)**

61. **(c)** Since HCF of the number = 4

The numbers are (4 × 5) and (4 × 7).

$\therefore$ Smaller number = 4 × 5 = 20

62. **(d)**   **63.** **(b)**

64. **(c)** CP of 100 kg of rice = ₹[(125 × 40) + (60 × 150)]

= ₹14000

Profit = 20%

$$SP \, of \, 100 \, kg \, of \, rice = \left[\left(\frac{100 + gain\%}{100}\right) \times CP\right]$$

$$= \left(\frac{100 + 20}{100}\right) \times 14000 = \frac{120}{100} \times 14000 = ₹16800$$

$$\therefore SP \, of \, 1 \, kg \, rice = ₹\frac{16800}{100} = ₹168$$

65. **(a)** Distance covered by car X in 1 hour = 12 km

Distance covered by car X in 3 mins $= \dfrac{12}{60} \times 3$

$$= \frac{12}{20} = \frac{3}{5} km$$

Distance covered by car Y in 3 mins

$$= \frac{16}{60} \times$$

$$= \frac{16}{20} = \frac{4}{5} km$$

$\therefore$ Distance between them after 3 mins

$$=\left(\frac{4}{5}-\frac{3}{5}\right)km=\frac{1}{5}km$$

$$=\left(\frac{1}{5}\times1000\right)m=200m$$

66. (c) 1st year $A=P\left(1+\dfrac{R}{100}\right)^{n}$

$$=500\left(1+\frac{10}{100}\right)^{1}=500\times\frac{110}{100}=₹550$$

2nd year
Now P = ₹ 550, R = 10% p.a.,
T = 1 year

$$\therefore\ A=P\left(1+\frac{R}{100}\right)^{n}=550\left(1+\frac{10}{100}\right)^{1}$$

$$=550\times\frac{110}{100}=₹605$$

Hence, maturity amount at the end of 2 year is ₹ 550 + ₹605
= ₹1155

67. (a)

68. (d) Percentage of Students that do not like cabbage $=\dfrac{15+21+13+2}{75}\times100$

$$=\left(\frac{51}{75}\times100\right)\%=68\%$$

69. (c) People like carrot = 21 + 12 = 33
People like cauliflower = 15 + 2 = 17
∴ Difference = 33 – 17 = 16

70. (b) Students like only one vegetable = 12 + 15 + 21 + 13 = 61

71. (c) Total maximum marks = 100 +100 + 100 + 100 + 100 + 100 = 600
∴ Percentage marks
$$=\left(\frac{470}{600}\times100\right)\%=78.33\%$$

72. (c)

73. (b) Let the two numbers be 3x and x.
Sum = 3x + x = 72

$$\Rightarrow 4x=72\Rightarrow x=\frac{72}{4}=18$$

∴ The numbers are 18 and 54.

Hence, Difference = 54 – 18 = 36

74. (a) health care is wealth → 1372 ...(1)
health needs care → 417 ...(2)
he needs wealth → 463 ...(3)
From 1 & 3 wealth = 3
From 1 & 2 care = 1
From 1 & 2 health = 7
⇒ is = 2
From 2 & 3 needs = 4
⇒ he = 6
Hence he is wealth → 326

75. (b) Average ages of parents = 30 yrs
Sum of parents' ages = (30 × 2) = 60 yrs.
Average ages of 2 children = 8 yrs.
Sum of children's age = (8 × 2) = 16 yrs.
∴ Average age of family
$$=\frac{60+16}{2+2}=\frac{76}{4}=19\,yrs$$

76. (c) S finishes work in 1 day $=\dfrac{1}{2}$

T finishes work is 1 day $=\dfrac{1}{4}$

Both finish work in 1 day
$$=\frac{1}{2}+\frac{1}{4}=\frac{2+1}{4}=\frac{3}{4}$$

∴ S and T both will finish work in $\dfrac{4}{3}$ days i.e. 1.33 days.

77. (c) The most significant feature of the Indus Valley Civilization was building made of bricks. Bricks used in the construction were built in the ratio of 4:2:1 having 11 inches length, 5.5 inches width and 2.75 inches depth.

78. (b)   **79. (a)**

80. (c) Mean
$$=\frac{1+9+7+3+5+5+6+4+2+8}{10}=\frac{50}{10}=5$$

81. (c) In 2012 Olympics, athletes from the United States won 46 gold medals.

82. (b)

83. (d) SP = ₹ 3600
Discount = 10%
Let MP = ₹ x
∴ SP = MP – Discount

$$\Rightarrow 3600=x-\frac{10}{100}x\ \Rightarrow 3600=\frac{90}{100}x$$

$\Rightarrow$ x = ₹4000

Now MP = ₹ 4000

Discount = 15% of MP

$$= \frac{15}{100} \times 4000 = ₹600$$

$\therefore$ SP = MP – discount

= ₹4000 – ₹600 = ₹3400

84. (d)   85. (d)   86. (a)   87. (b)

88. (b) Mean of 25 values = 40

Sum of 25 values = 40 × 25 = 1000

or Incorrect sum = 1000

Correct sum = 1000 – 25 + 50

= 1025

$$\therefore \text{ Correct mean } = \frac{1025}{25} = 41$$

89. (b)   90. (d)   91. (c)

92. (d) 3 2 4 1   3 2 4 1   3 2 4 1

C B D A   ,   G F H E   ,   K J L I

     3 2 4 1

$\Rightarrow$ O N P M

93. (c)   94. (d)

95. (d) code = 6241   ......(1)

made = 5346   ......(2)

come = 3124   ......(3)

to = 27   ......(4)

From 1, 2 and 3   e = 4

From 1, and 2   d = 6

From 1, 3 and 4   o = 2

From 2 and 3   m = 3

$\therefore$ dome = 2634.

96. (b) After landing on the moon, Neil Armstrong said, "one small step for a man, a giant leap for mankind".

In the above statement Neil Armstrong does not address himself as a mankind but rather echoes the feeling of achievement by mankind.

Hence, Only conclusion II follows.

97. (d)   98. (b)

99. (d) SP = ₹ 26000

Discount = 35% of MP

$\therefore$ SP = MP – discount

$$26000 = MP - \left(\frac{35}{100} \times MP\right)$$

$$= MP - \frac{7}{20}MP$$

$$= \frac{13}{20}MP$$

$$MP = 26000 \times \frac{20}{13} = 2000 \times 20 = 40000$$

again, discount = 15% of MP

$$= \frac{15}{100} \times 40000 = 6000$$

$\therefore$ SP = MP – discount

= ₹40000 – ₹6000

= ₹34000

100. (c) (27 + 15 –2)÷ 10 = 4

$\Rightarrow$ (27 + 15 – 2) ÷ 10 = (42 – 2) ÷ 10

= 40 ÷ 10

= 4

1. A recently discovered bird species named 'Himalayan Forest Thrush' was found in _______.
   - (a) Dehradun
   - (b) Northeast India
   - (c) Uttarakhand
   - (d) Ladakh Region

2. Leprosy is also known as
   - (a) Angina
   - (b) Hansen's disease
   - (c) Gaucher disease
   - (d) Hodgkin disease

3. Find the odd one out in relation world heritage sites.
   - (a) Rashtrapati Bhavan
   - (b) Chatrapati Shivaji Terminus
   - (c) Taj Mahal
   - (d) Sun Temple

4. One side of a rectangle is 12 m and its diagonal is 13 m. Find its area.
   - (a) 60 sq.m
   - (b) 55 sq.m
   - (c) 50 sq.m
   - (d) 45 sq.m

5. who was the coach for U-19 World Cup (2016) held in Bangladesh?
   - (a) Rahul Dravid
   - (b) Virendra Sehwag
   - (c) Sourav Ganguly
   - (d) Anil Kumble

6. Read the given statements carefully and answer the question. Statement:
   I. Domestic price of petrol has gone down.
   II. International price of crude oil has decreased.
   - (a) I is the cause and II is the effect.
   - (b) II is the cause and I is the effect.
   - (c) I and II are independent of each other.
   - (d) I and II are effects of independent causes.

7. In a map drawn to a scale of 1 cm = 18.5 km, the distance between places A and B = 22.25 cm. Find the actual distance in kilometer.
   - (a) 411.625
   - (b) 425.615
   - (c) 412.625
   - (d) 405.615

8. Find the odd one out.
   - (a) Silent valley
   - (b) Silicon valley
   - (c) Indus valley
   - (d) Damodar valley

9. Who was conferred the Arjuna Award for badminton in 2015?
   - (a) Kidambi Srikanth
   - (b) Saina Nehwal
   - (c) Chetan Anand
   - (d) Rohit Sharma

10. If 'you are john' is written as 'net let fat', 'who are you' is 'let wet net' and 'john is good' is 'get set fat', which represents 'is'?
    - (a) set
    - (b) get
    - (c) fat
    - (d) cannot be determined.

11. Till the end of 2015, India has established research stations in Antarctica.
    - (a) 2
    - (b) 3
    - (c) 4
    - (d) 5

12. A train running at 60 kmph crosses a pole in 30 seconds. What is the length of the train?
    - (a) 250 m
    - (b) 750 m
    - (c) 500 m
    - (d) 450 m

13. Jantar Mantar in Delhi was built by Maharaja __________.
    - (a) Jai Singh I of Jaipur
    - (b) Jai Singh II of Jaipur
    - (c) Ram Singh I
    - (d) Bishan Singh

14. A statement followed by some conclusions are given below.
    Statement: Customer service cannot be enforced. It has to come from within.
    Conclusions:
    I. Customer service should be voluntary.
    II. Employees do not serve customers.
    Find which of the given conclusions logically follow from the given statement.
    - (a) Only conclusion I follows.
    - (b) Only conclusion II follows.
    - (c) Both I and II follow.
    - (d) Neither I nor II follows.

15. As per the India State Forest Report 2015, _____________ has the largest forest cover in terms of its area.
    - (a) Assam
    - (b) Jammu and Kashmir
    - (c) Madhya Pradesh
    - (d) Arunachal Pradesh

16. $9876 + 34.567 - ? = 9908.221$
    (a) 23.45   (b) 234.6
    (c) 2.345   (d) 2.346

17. A's share is 2 times that of B whose share is 3 times that of C. ₹ 1800/- is to be given to them in that ratio. B's share is
    (a) ₹ 1080   (b) ₹ 540
    (c) ₹ 180   (d) ₹ 900

18. **Cell phone : Communication : : Cycle : ?**
    (a) Walking   (b) Gym
    (c) Mechanization   (d) Transportation

19. Name the security force which does not fall under Union Home ministry.
    (a) Sashastra Seema Bal
    (b) Border Security Force
    (c) Railway Protection Force
    (d) Indo-Tibetan Border Police Force

20. The greenhouse gas which is called laughing gas is
    (a) Methane   (b) Carbon dioxide
    (c) Nitrous oxide   (d) Sulphur dioxide

21. **If $(a + b + c) = 6$ and $a^2 + b^2 + c^2 = 14$, then $(ab + bc + ca) = ?$**
    (a) 22   (b) 11
    (c) 33   (d) 44

22. Which one is called the dwarf planet?
    (a) Venus   (b) Mercury
    (c) Moon   (d) Pluto

23. Major part of biogas is __________.
    (a) Hydrogen   (b) Nitrogen
    (c) Methane   (d) Carbon dioxide

24. Mac OS was introduced by
    (a) IBM   (b) Microsoft
    (c) Apple   (d) Micromax

25. Find the missing (?) in the series.
    BDACE, GIFHJ, ? , QSPRT..........
    (a) LMKNO   (b) NLKOM
    (c) LNKMO   (d) KLNOM

26. Find the least number required to be added to 3105 so that it is exactly divisible by 3, 4, 5 and 6.
    (a) 15   (b) 120
    (c) 115   (d) 125

27. Two vessels of equal volume contain milk and water in the ratio 1:3 and 2:1. If they are mixed together, what is the new ratio?
    (a) 11:13   (b) 13:11
    (c) 9:11   (d) 11:9

28. __________ extinguishes fire.
    (a) O_2 (b) CO_2
    (c) SO_2 (d) NO_2

29. Four pairs of words are given. Find the odd one out.
    (a) Saturn : Planet
    (b) Sun : Star
    (c) Milky Way : Constellation
    (d) Titan : Satellite

30. After entering Bangladesh, the main branch of the Ganges is known as
    (a) Hooghly river   (b) Jamuna river
    (c) Meghna river   (d) Padma river

31. The efficiency of work of P and Q are in the ratio 5 : 7. What will be the ratio of number of days taken by them to finish the work?
    (a) 7 : 5   (b) 3 : 4
    (c) 4 : 3   (d) 5 : 7

DIRECTIONS (Qs. 32-34): *Consider the following information and answer questions based on it.*

Among 60 students, 12 like only algebra, 13 like only geometry, 10 like only trigonometry, 5 like both algebra and trigonometry, 8 like only physics, 5 like both physics and geometry and the remaining like both algebra and physics.

32. The number of students who like physics but not geometry is
    (a) 8   (b) 13
    (c) 15   (d) 17

33. How many students like more than one subject?
    (a) 5   (b) 10
    (c) 12   (d) 17

34. The ratio of students who like algebra to those who like geometry is
    (a) 12 : 13   (b) 4 : 3
    (c) 17 : 18   (d) 17 : 13

35. Sagar has two daughters, Lata and Asha. Asha's only paternal aunt's son's grandfather is Aniket. How is Sagar related to Aniket's wife?
    (a) Father   (b) Son
    (c) Grandson   (d) Grandfather

36. If **OWL = 50** and **N = 14**, then **TIME** is
    (a) 45   (b) 47
    (c) 43   (d) 49

37. In a certain code, **'RIDE' = 3218, 'TALK' = 7564, 'DIRT' = 4213 and 'LIKE' = 8562.** Which digit represents 'A'?
    (a) 9   (b) 3
    (c) 5   (d) 7

38. Which of the following is not true in relation to the Global Positioning System?
    (a) It is a space-based navigation system.
    (b) It can predict cyclones.
    (c) It can be used to map vehicular traffic.
    (d) It can be used for in-car navigation

39. If the posts of the President and Vice-president fall vacant, who will act as the President of India?
    (a) Speaker of Lok Sabha
    (b) Prime Minister of India
    (c) Chief Justice of India
    (d) Union Council of Ministers

40. The average of first three out of four numbers is 18. The average of last three numbers is 14. The sum of first and last number is 16. The last number is
    (a) 17   (b) 13
    (c) 9   (d) 2

41. The difference between the ages of two sisters is 2 years when father's age was 52. Father is elder by 2 years to mother. Elder sister's age is half of mother's age. Find the age of younger sister.
    (a) 27   (b) 21
    (c) 25   (d) 23

42. The maturity value after three years, of a certain sum at 15% p.a. simple interest, is ₹ 8,700/-. Find the principal amount.
    (a) ₹ 5,000   (b) ₹ 6,000
    (c) ₹ 5,500   (d) ₹ 6,500

43. If **PIXIE** is **OHXHD** then **ELEANOR** is
    (a) DKDAMNQ   (b) DDKAMNR
    (c) DKDANMR   (d) DJDAMNQ

44. The marked prices of small and big note books are ₹ 10 and ₹ 15 respectively. A student bought 5 dozen small and 10 dozen big note books at a total discount of 5%. Find the total discount amount.
    (a) ₹ 100   (b) ₹ 110
    (c) ₹ 120   (d) ₹ 130

45. An event happening once in 4 years is described as
    (a) Biennial   (b) Quadrennial
    (c) Triennial   (d) Perennial

46. Read the following data carefully and answer the question based on it.
    (i) 'A + G' means 'A is mother of G'
    (ii) 'A ÷ G' means 'A is daughter of G'
    (iii) 'A – G' means 'A is husband of G'
    (iv) 'A × G' means 'A is maternal aunt of G'
    If L + M × N then how is L related to N?
    (a) Aunt   (b) Mother
    (c) Daughter   (d) Grandmother

47. Find the value of $[(525 + 252)^2 - (525 - 252)^2]/(525 \times 252)$.
    (a) 3   (b) 4
    (c) 5   (d) 6

48. If $2\cos\theta = \div3$, $\cos\theta \times \tan\theta =$?
    (a) 1   (b) $\sqrt{3}/3$
    (c) $\sqrt{3}/2$ (d) 1/2

49. A generator converts
    (a) mechanical energy into electrical energy.
    (b) electrical energy into chemical energy.
    (c) thermal energy into electrical energy.
    (d) electrical energy into light energy.

50. A man has equal number of five, ten and twenty rupee notes amounting to ₹ 385. Find the number of each notes?
    (a) 13   (b) 11
    (c) 15   (d) 21

51. Which key combination is used for pasting text in MS Word?
    (a) Ctrl + v   (b) Ctrl + z
    (c) Alt + r   (d) Alt + F4

52. Find the median of the data set:
    1.9, 8.4, 3.6, 5.8
    (a) 5.1   (b) 4.7
    (c) 5.2   (d) 5.6

53. In the following equation, if the mathematical operators '–' and '×' are interchanged then the value of $4 - 6 + 1 \times 15 \div 3$ will be
    (a) 24   (b) 20
    (c) –5   (d) –4

54. Which one is not a network protocol?
    (a) SSH   (b) HTML
    (c) PPP   (d) POP

55. The mean of first 11 natural numbers is
    (a) 5.5   (b) 6
    (c) 6.6   (d) 5

56. National Air Quality Index is determined on the basis of concentration of _______ pollutants.
    (a) 5   (b) 6
    (c) 7   (d) 8

57. Starting from her house a woman walks 15 km towards South. She turns right and walks 35 km. Again she turns right and walks 15 km. Then she turns left and walks 5 km. How far is her house now?
    (a) 35   (b) 40
    (c) 50   (d) 15

58. Motion of a spinning 'top' is an example of
  (a) Centripetal Force
  (b) Centrifugal Force
  (c) Gravitational Force
  (d) Frictional Force

59. Read the given statements carefully and answer the question. Statements:
  1. All teachers get angry.
  2. Some teachers are sad.
  3. Sad people may cry.
  Which of the following conclusion is true?
  (a) All sad people cry.
  (b) Some teachers may cry.
  (c) All angry people are teachers.
  (d) All sad people get angry.

60. If the mathematical operator '×' means by A, '+' means by R, '÷' means by E and '−'means by B, then the value of **24 B 6 E 2 A 9 R 17** is
  (a) 14   (b) −3
  (c) 17   (d) −10

61. Which one is anti-virus?
  (a) CodeRed   (b) Melissa
  (c) CryptoLocker   (d) Dr.Web

62. PM inaugurated the XII South Asian Games on 5th February 2016 at
  (a) Lucknow   (b) Guwahati
  (c) Kolkata   (d) Ahmadabad

63. Name the chess champion against whom Viswananthan Anand lost in 2014 World Chess Championship.
  (a) Vladimir Kramnik   (b) Veselin Topalov
  (c) Boris Gelfand   (d) Magnus Carlsen

64. Which one is different from the other three?
  (a) Spinach   (b) Lentil
  (c) Coriander   (d) Lettuce

65. Expand $(a - 4)^3$
  (a) $a^3 - 12a^2 + 48a + 64$
  (b) $a^3 - 48a^2 + 12a - 64$
  (c) $a^3 + 12a^2 - 48a - 64$
  (d) $a^3 - 12a^2 + 48a - 64$

66. B does 50% of a work in 20 days. C joins B and they together finish the remaining work in 4 days. C alone can do the whole work in _____ days.
  (a) 10   (b) 8
  (c) 12   (d) 9

67. Losoong festival is popular in
  (a) Himachal Pradesh   (b) Sikkim
  (c) Arunachal Pradesh (d) Tripura

68. The most popular folk dance of Tamil Nadu
  (a) Karagam   (b) Koodiyattam
  (c) Yakshagana   (d) Kathakali

69. The loss in selling an article for ₹ 1235 was 5%. At what price should it be sold to get a profit of 10%?
  (a) ₹ 1,335   (b) ₹ 1,380
  (c) ₹ 1,430   (d) ₹ 1,300

70. If $22x - 40 = 207 + 3x$, then x =?
  (a) 14   (b) 13
  (c) 12   (d) 11

71. The ratio of two numbers is 4 : 3 and their HCF is 8. Find their LCM.
  (a) 48   (b) 96
  (c) 64   (d) 84

72. The technique used for printing 'RESERVE BANK OF INDIA' appearing on the face of the Indian currency notes is
  (a) Intaglio printing   (b) Micro lettering
  (c) Latent printing   (d) Screen printing

73. The aim of the Civil Disobedience Movement of 1929 was
  (a) complete disobedience of the orders of the British Government.
  (b) to protest the Chauri Chaura incident.
  (c) partial disobedience of the orders of the British Government.
  (d) to ensure all civil rights of the citizens are granted by the Government.

74. The British Government agreed to grant independence to India in
  (a) 1944   (b) 1945
  (c) 1946   (d) 1947

75. Y is R's mother's mother-in-law's only daughter and Q's wife. How is Q related to R?
  (a) Paternal Uncle   (b) Nephew
  (c) Husband   (d) Father

76. Find the similarity in the following:
  Ginger, Turnip, Carrot, Radish
  (a) All are red in colour.
  (b) All are round in shape.
  (c) All of them grow above the soil.
  (d) All are roots.

77. Rearrange the jumbled letters to make a meaningful word and then select the one which is different.

(a) SUVNE　　　　(b) APTLE

(c) ARMS　　　　(d) RUJIIPE

78. The surface-to-air, Akash missile, was test fired from

(a) Sriharikota

(b) Abdul Kalam Island

(c) Thumba

(d) Pokhran

79. An article was sold at ₹ 920 at a profit of 15%. Find the selling price to get a profit of 20%,

(a) ₹ 1,000　　　　(b) ₹ 980

(c) ₹ 960　　　　(d) ₹ 940

80. Yeast used in making bread

(a) acts as a catalyst for fermentation.

(b) does not help the process of fermentation.

(c) makes it tasty.

(d) acts as a preservative.

81. The area of a triangle is 456 sq.cm and its height is 24 cm. The length of its base is

(a) 32　　　　(b) 36

(c) 34　　　　(d) 38

82. Louis Pasteur was known for discovery of

(a) Polio vaccine

(b) Chicken pox vaccine

(c) Small pox vaccine

(d) Rabies vaccine

83. Find the missing (?) in the series:

1, 1, 8, 4, 27, 9, ?, 16.....

(a) 32　　　　(b) 48

(c) 64　　　　(d) 72

DIRECTIONS (Qs. 84-86): *Consider the following information and answer questions based on it.*

Seven students J, K, L, M, N, O and P are standing in a row, in random order, from left to right, such that -

1. P, O, K and N do not stand on any of the extreme ends.

2. J is to the immediate left of P and immediate right of O.

3. M is not at the center.

4. K is to the immediate right of N and immediate left of L.

84. The student standing to the immediate left of O is

(a) L　　　　(b) J

(c) M　　　　(d) P

85. Who is at the center of the row?

(a) N　　　　(b) J

(c) P　　　　(d) K

86. Who stands fifth from the left of the row?

(a) K　　　　(b) P

(c) N　　　　(d) J

87. What is the difference between the maturity value of two deposits of ₹5,000 each invested for 2 years (i) at 5% simple interest and (ii) at the same interest compounded annually?

(a) ₹ 11.00　　　　(b) ₹ 11.50

(c) ₹ 12.00　　　　(d) ₹ 12.50

88. The area of a trapezium is 18 sq.cm. Its height and base are 3 cm and 5 cm respectively. Find the length of the side parallel to the base.

(a) 4 cm　　　　(b) 6 cm

(c) 8 cm　　　　(d) 7 cm

89. There are ____ zones in Indian Railways.

(a) 8　　　　(b) 18

(c) 16　　　　(d) 12

DIRECTIONS (Qs. 90-92): *The following table represents the category wise count of books in four local libraries.*

Category	ABL	GHL	MNL	PQL
Self-help	150	170	200	200
Nonfiction	500	600	550	600
Fiction	750	610	700	600
Management	100	130	100	110
Comics	175	100	100	75
Technical	115	100	150	200

Consider the table and answer questions based on it.

90. The self-help books in library GHL is how much less than its fictional books?

(a) 340　　　　(b) 430

(c) 440　　　　(d) 330

91. Which library has the highest total count of books?

(a) ABL　　　　(b) GHL

(c) MNL　　　　(d) PQL

92. The difference between the total number of nonfiction and management books of all four libraries is

(a) 1850　　　　(b) 1810

(c) 2250　　　　(d) 1800

93. Evaluate: (sinθ / cosθ) × (cotθ / cosecθ)

(a) cosθ　　　　(b) sinθ

(c) tanθ　　　　(d) secθ

94. A statement followed by some conclusions are given below.

Statement: Unlike Aryabhata, moon is a natural satellite of the Earth. Conclusions:

I.   Aryabhatta is not a satellite.

II. Moon is star and Aryabhatta is a satellite.

Find which of the given conclusions logically follow from the given statement.

(a) Only conclusion I follows.

(b) Only conclusion II follows.

(c) Both I and II follow.

(d) Neither I nor II follows.

95. The recently approved, LIGO-India project, is related to

(a) Research on use of solar energy

(b) Research on laser technologies

(c) Research on gravitational waves

(d) Research on relocation of lions

96. Statements followed by some conclusions are given below.

Statements:

1. Medical profession has become the most unethical.

2. People are afraid of falling sick.

Conclusions:

I.   Medical is the only unethical profession.

II. Unethical people fall sick.

Find which of the given conclusions logically follow from the given statements.

(a) Only conclusion I follows.

(b) Only conclusion II follows.

(c) Both I and II follow.

(d) Neither I nor II follows.

97. Name of the 8th UN Secretary General is

(a) B. Ghali

(b) Kofi A. Annan

(c) Ban Ki-moon

(d) Dr. Jim Yong Kim

98. K walked at 3 kmph for a certain distance with L and thereafter at 6 kmph with M to cover a total distance of 27 km in 7 hours. Find the distance travelled with M.

(a) 15 km   (b) 12 km

(c) 10 km   (d) 9 km

99. Who is considered to be the 'father of modem genetics'?

(a) Charles Darwin

(b) Gregor Mendel

(c) Alexander Fleming

(d) Otto Hahn

100. Name the country whose currency is not called 'Rupee'.

(a) Nepal   (b) Pakistan

(c) Sri Lanka   (d) Myanmar

HINTS & EXPLANATIONS

1. **(b)** Himalayan Forest Thrush-New Bird Species was found in Northeast India. It is the first Indian bird named after Dr. Salim Ali. Dr. Per Alstrom and Shashank Dalvi first discovered the Himalayan Forest Thrush in May-June 2009.

2. **(b)**

3. **(a)** Rashtrapati Bhavan is not included in the list of World Heritage Sites. The other three, i.e., Chhatrapati Shivaji Terminus was included in the UNESCO World Heritage in 2004. The Taj Mahal was designated as a UNESCO World Heritage Site in 1983 and Sun Temple was included in 1984.

4 **(a)** As given that
One side of a rectangle =12m
Diagonal (d) =13m

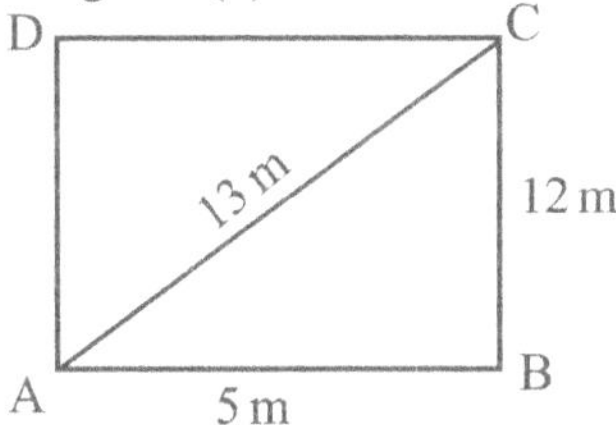

$(AB)^2 = (AC)^2 - (BC)^2$
$= (13)^2 - (12)^2$
$= 169 - 144$
$AB = \sqrt{25} = 5\,m$
So, area of rectangle $=$ length$\times$b
$= AB \times BC$
$= 5 \times 12$
$= 60$ sq. meter.

5. **(a)**   6. **(b)**

7 **(a)** If, 1 cm = 18.5 km
Then 22.25 cm = 18.5×22.25
$= 411.625$ km
Hence, the actual distance=411.625 kilometer.

8. **(b)** Silicon Valley is the centre for innovative technology companies. It is located in South of San Francisco. It is home to some of the world's largest technology corporations and thousands of technology related startup companies.

9. **(a)** Kidambi Srikanth, an Arjun awardee, was the first Indian male badminton player to win gold at the 2015 Swiss Open Grand Prix Gold.

10. **(d)**

| you   are | John | – | net let | fat |

| who | are   you | – | wet | net let |

| John | is   good | – | get set | fat |

Hence, code for 'is' may be 'get' or 'set'

11. **(b)**

12. **(c)** As given that
$$\text{Speed} = 60 \text{ kmph} \times \frac{5}{18} = \frac{50}{3} \text{ m/sec}$$
Length of train = (speed×time)
$$= \left[\frac{50}{3} \times 30\right]$$
$$= 500 \text{ meter.}$$

13. **(b)**   14. **(a)**   15. **(c)**

16. **(d)** $9876 + 34.567 - ? = 9908.221$
$? = 9910.567 - 9908.221$
$? = 2.346$

17. **(b)** Let, B's share is x
According to question,
A share $= 2x$
C's share $= x/3$
Now,
$$x + 2x + \frac{x}{3} = 1800 \qquad [\because \text{ given}]$$
$$\frac{6x + 3x + x}{3} = 1800$$
$$\frac{10x}{3} = 1800$$
$$x = ₹\ 540$$

18. **(d)** As we know that,
Just like, cellphone is used for communication, similarly cycle is used for transportation.

19. **(c)** Railway Protection Force is a security force established by Railway Protection Force Act, 1975 enacted by the Indian Parliament for the better protection and security of railway property. It comes under the control of Government of India, Ministry of Railways.

20. **(c)**

21. (b) As given that,
$(a + b + c) = 6$
$(a^2 + b^2 + c^2) = 14$
As we know that
$(a + b + c)^2 = (a^2 + b^2 + c^2) + 2(ab + bc + ca)$
$(6)^2 = 14 + 2(ab + bc + ca)$

So, $(ab + bc + ca) = \left[\dfrac{36 - 14}{2}\right] = \dfrac{22}{2} = 11$.

22. (d) Pluto, once considered the ninth and most distant planet from the Sun, is now the largest known dwarf planet in the Solar System.

23. (c)   24. (c)

25. (c)

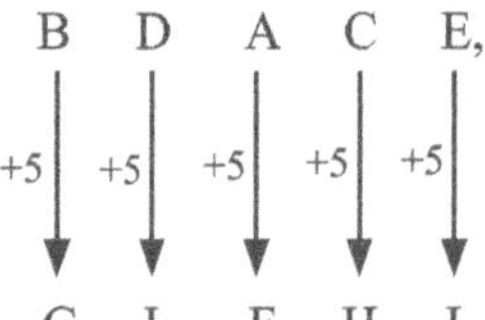

So,

Hence, option (c) is correct.

26. (a) Since the given number should be divisible by 3, 4, 5 and 6, so, it should be divisible by L.C.M. of 3, 4, 5 and 6 = 60.
Now, $60 \times 52 = 3120$
$3120 - 3105 = 15$
Hence, 15 is the least number required to be added to 3105, to exactly divisible by 3, 4, 5 and 6.

27. (a) As given that,
The ratio of milk and water = 1 : 3 & 2 : 1
So, $1 + 3 = 4$
$2 + 1 = 3$
By make quantities same.
$3 + 9 = 12$
$8 + 4 = 12$
So, $(3 + 8) = 11$
$(9 + 4) = 13$
Hence, the new ratio is 11:13

28. (b)   29.   (c)   30.   (d)

31. (a) More efficiency, less number of days required to finish the work.

Work efficiency and number of days are inversely proportional

So, ratio of number of days required = 7 : 5.

32. (c)

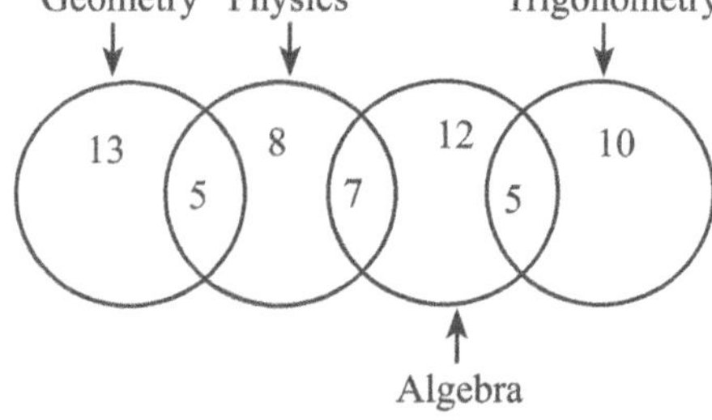

Total no. of student = 60
So, remaining like both algebra and physics
$= 60 - 53 = 7$
Hence, the number of student who like physics but not geometry $= 8 + 7 = 15$

33 (d) The number of students like more than one subject $= 5 + 7 + 5 = 17$

34. (b) The ratio of students who like algebra to those who like geometry is

$= \dfrac{[12 + 7 + 5]}{[13 + 5]} = \left[\dfrac{24}{18}\right] = 4 : 3$

35. (b)

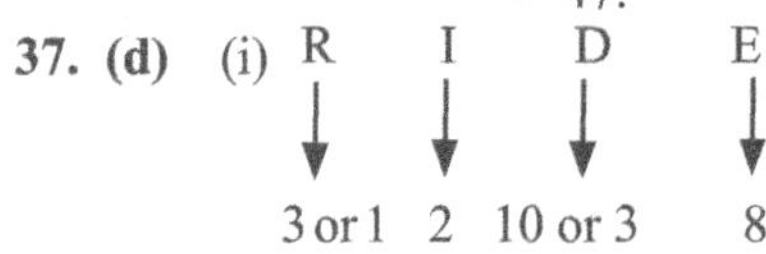

This above diagram shows the Aniket wife is the mother of Sagar
Hence, Sagar is a son of Aniket's wife.

36. (b) OWL = 50 , N = 14
OWL $= [15 + 23 + 12] = 50$
So, TIME $= [20 + 9 + 13 + 5]$
$= 47$.

37. (d) (i) R   I   D   E

3 or 1   2   10 or 3   8

(ii)   T   A   L   K
       ↓   ↓   ↓   ↓
       4   7   5   6

(iii) D   I   R   T
       ↓   ↓   ↓   ↓
       3/1   2   ⅓   4

(iv)   L   I   K   E
       ↓   ↓   ↓   ↓
       5   2   6   8

From, (i) or (iii)   RID   code = 3, 2, 1
So, E → 8   and   T → 4
From (i) or (iv)   I → 2
From (ii) or (iv)   L, K → 5, 6
Hence code of 'A' is 7

38. (b)

39. (c)   The Chief Justice of India will act as the President of India if the post of the President and Vice President falls vacant. For instance, when Zakir Hussain died suddenly on 3rd May, 1969, the then Vice President of India Mr. V.V. Giri became the acting President. Later, V.V. resigned from both offices as acting President and Vice President. Muhammad Hidayatullah, the Chief Justice of India then served as the President of India.

40. (d)   As given that,
$(A + B + C) = 18 \times 3 = 54$ ....(i)
$(B + C + D) = 14 \times 3 = 42$ ....(ii)
$(A + D) = 16$ ....(iii)
By subtracting the eq. (i) and (ii)
$A - D = 54 - 42 = 12$
$A = (12 + D)$
By putting the value of (A) into the equation (iii)
$12 + D + D = 16$
$2D = 4$
$D = 2$

41. (d)   As given that,
Father's age = 52
Mother's age = 50
Elder sister's age = 52/2 = 25
Difference of ages of two sister = 2
[Elder sister age – younger sister age] = 2
So, younger sister age = [elder sister age – 2]
= [25 – 2]
= 23 year.

42. (b)   As given that
Principle (p) + S.I = 8700

$$P + \frac{P \times R \times T}{100} = 8700$$

$$P + \frac{P \times 15 \times 3}{100} = 8700$$

$$\frac{145P}{100} = 8700$$

$$P = \frac{8700 \times 100}{145}$$

$$= ₹ 6000$$

43. (a)   As given that

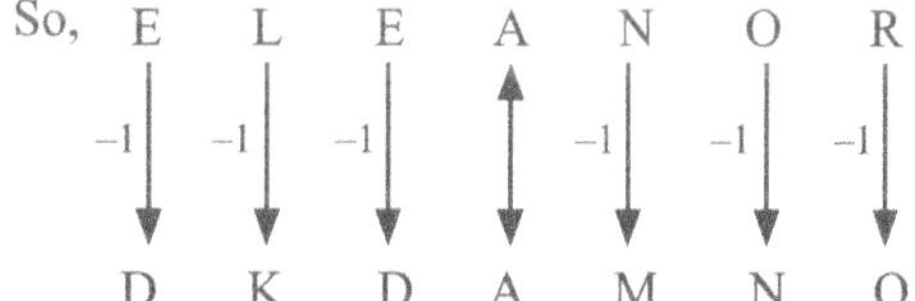

So,

D   K   D   A   M   N   Q

44. (c)   The price of five dozen small books
$= 5 \times 12 \times 10 = 600$
The price of ten dozen big books
$= 10 \times 12 \times 15 = 1800$
Total price of books $= 1800 + 600$
$= 2400$
(∵ Discount = 5%)
So total discount $= \dfrac{2400 \times 5}{100}$
$= ₹120$

45. (b)

46. (d)

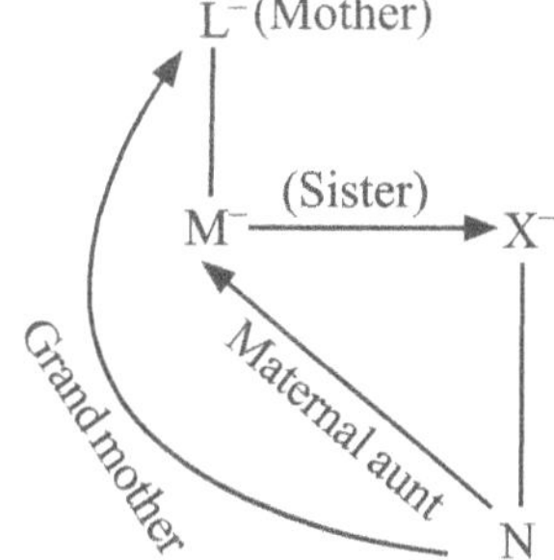

47. **(b)** $\Rightarrow \left[\dfrac{(a+b)^2 - (a-b)^2}{a.b}\right]$

$= \left[\dfrac{a^2 + b^2 + 2ab - [a^2 + b^2 - 2ab]}{ab}\right]$

$= \dfrac{4ab}{ab}$

Let, a = 525,   b = 252

$\Rightarrow \dfrac{\left[(525+252)^2 - (525-252)^2\right]}{[525 \times 252]}$

$= \dfrac{4 \times 525 \times 252}{525 \times 252} = 4$

48. **(d)** If $2\cos\theta = \sqrt{3}$, $\cos\theta = \sqrt{3}/2 \Rightarrow (\theta = 30°)$

So $\cos\theta \times \tan\theta = \cos\theta \times \dfrac{\sin\theta}{\cos\theta}$

$= \sin\theta$

$= \sin 30°$

$= \dfrac{1}{2}$

49. **(a)**

50. **(b)** Let x is the equal number of notes of five, ten and twenty rupees.

So, $5x + 10x + 20x = 385$

$35x = 385$

$\boxed{x = 11}$

51. **(a)**

52. **(b)** Arranging given data set in ascending order.

$\Rightarrow 1.9, 3.6, 5.8, 8.4$

Median of (3.6 and 5.8)

So, median $\Rightarrow \left[\dfrac{3.6+5.8}{2}\right] = \dfrac{9.4}{2} = 4.7$

53. **(b)** When mathematical operators '–' and '×' are interchanged then

Given expression

$= 4 - 6 + 1 \times 15 \div 3$

By interchanged the operator

$= (4 \times 6 + 1 - 15 \div 3)$

$= (24 + 1 - 5)$

$= 20$

54. **(b)**

55. **(b)** The mean of first 11 natural number is

$= \dfrac{1+2+3+4+5+6+7+8+9+10+11}{11}$

$= 66/11 = 6$

56. **(d)**

57. **(b)** According to given question

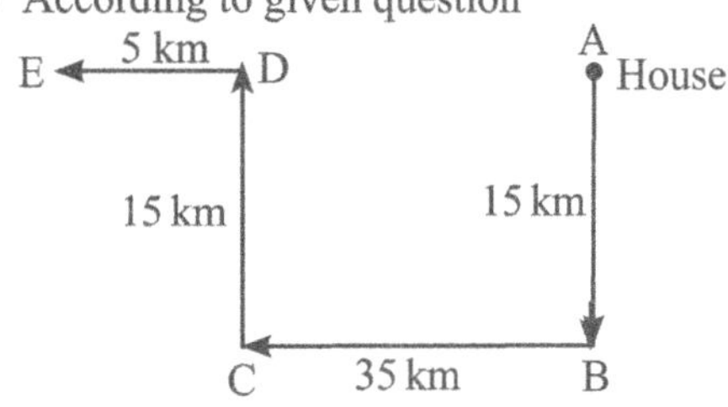

$\Rightarrow$ Total distance from her house $= BC + DE$

$= 35 + 5$

$= 40$ km.

58. **(a)**

59. **(b)** Conclusion:

(i) All sad people cry, it is not necessary but all sad people can cry or cannot cry.

(ii) Some teacher are sad, so some teacher may cry.

60. **(a)** As given that

'×'   means by A,

'+'   means by R

'÷'   means by E

'–'   means by B

Then, the value of given expression

$=$ 24B6E2A9R17

$=$ $(24 - 6 \div 2 \times 9 + 17)$

$=$ $(24 - 3 \times 9 + 17)$

$=$ $(24 - 27 + 17)$

$=$ 14.

61 **(d)** **62.** **(b)**   **63.** **(d)**   **64.** **(b)**

65. **(d)** As we know that

$(a-b)^3 = a^3 - b^3 - 3ab(a-b)$

So,

$(a-4)^3$

$= a^3 - 64 - 3a \times 4(a-4)$

$= a^3 - 12a^2 + 48a - 64$

Hence option (d) is correct.

66. **(a)** As given that,

B, does 50% of a work of 20 days

$\Rightarrow$ C join B and they together finish the remaining work in 4 days.

So, C alone can do the whole work

$\Rightarrow \dfrac{1}{40} \times 20 + \left(\dfrac{1}{40} + \dfrac{1}{C}\right) \times 4 = 1$

$\left(\dfrac{1}{2} + \dfrac{1}{10}\right) + \dfrac{4}{C} = 1 = 1$

$$\frac{6}{10}+\frac{4}{C}=1$$

$$\frac{4}{C}=\frac{4}{10}$$

C = 10 days.

67. (b) Losoong is one of the Sikkim's grand festivals. It is also called Namsoong by the Lepchas. The festival of Losoong is mostly celebrated in the month of December every year. Losoong is celebrated not only in India but also in Nepal and Bhutan.

68. (a)

69. (c) As given that,

S.P of article = ₹1235

The loss in selling an article = 5%

From formula,

$$\text{Cost price} = \left[\frac{100\times S.P}{(100-\text{Loss}\%)}\right]$$

$$= \left[\frac{100\times1235}{95}\right]=₹1300$$

$$S.P = \left[\frac{(100+\text{Profit }\%)\times \text{Cost price}}{100}\right]$$

Profit = 10%

$$=\left[\frac{(100+10)\times1300}{100}\right]= 13\times110=₹\,1430$$

70. (b) As given expression:

$22x-40 = 207+3x$

$\Rightarrow\quad 19x = 207+40 = 247$

$\qquad x = \mathbf{247/19}$

$\qquad\quad = 13$

71. (b) The ratio of two number $=\dfrac{4}{3}$

Let, first value = $4x$

Second value= $3x$

So, LCM= $4\times3\times x$

HCF $= x$ [x is common in both value]

So, $x = 8$

LCM = $4 \times 3 \times 8 = 96$

72. (a) The technique used for printing "Reserve Bank of India" appearing on the face of the Indian currency notes is Intaglio printing. The printing techniques often used in printing bank notes are intaglio and copperplate etching.

73. (a) Mahatma Gandhi led Civil Disobedience Movement that was launched in the Congress Session of December, 1929. The aim was a complete disobedience of the orders of British Government. During this movement it was decided that India would celebrate 26th January as Independence Day all over the country.

74. (c)

75. (a)

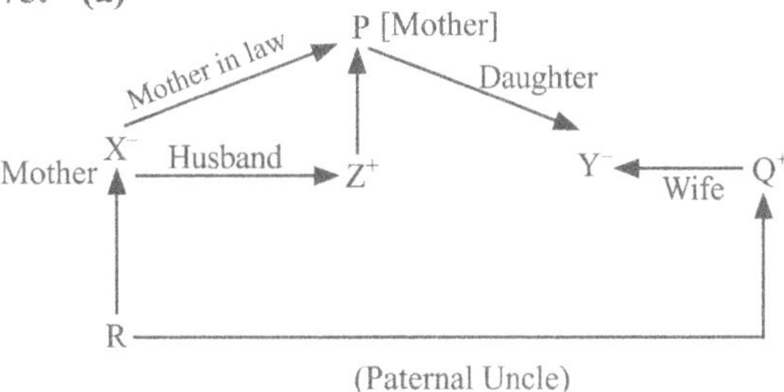

76. (d) 77. (b)   78. (b)

79. (c) As given that

S. P of article = 920

Profit = 15%

$$\text{Cost price} = \left[\frac{100\times S.P}{100+\text{Profit}}\right]$$

$$=\left[\frac{100\times920}{115}\right]= ₹800$$

$$\text{Now, S.P}= \left[\frac{(100+\text{Profit})\times \text{Cost price}}{100}\right]$$

$$=\left[\frac{(100+20)\times800}{100}\right]$$

$$= 120\times8$$

$$= ₹960$$

80. (a)

81. (d)

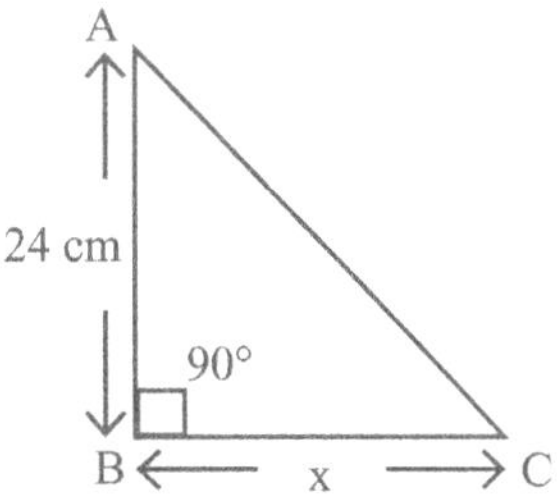

As we know that,

$$\text{Area} = \frac{1}{2}\times \text{Height}\times\text{Base}$$

$$456 = \frac{1}{2} \times AB \times BC = \frac{1}{2} \times 24 \times x$$

$$x = BC = \frac{456 \times 2}{24} = 38 \text{ cm}$$

82. (d)

83. (c)

1,	1,	8,	4,	27,	9,	64	16
↓	↓	↓	↓	↓	↓	↓	↓
$(1)^3$	$(1)^2$	$(2)^3$	$(2)^2$	$(3)^3$	$(3)^2$	$(4)^3$	$(4)^2$

Hence: $(4)^3 = 64$

Sol. (84-86):

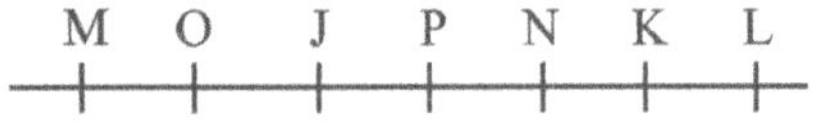

M   O   J   P   N   K   L

84. (c) The student standing to the immediate left of O is M.

85. (c) At the center of the row 'P' is standing

86. (c) From the left at fifth position 'M' is standing.

87. (d) For 2 year, the difference between the simple interest and compound interest for maturity value of two deposits is

$$= P \times \left(\frac{R}{100}\right)^2$$

Where p is Principle amount and r is interest rate

$$= 5000 \times \left(\frac{5}{100}\right)^2$$

$$= ₹12.50$$

88. (d) The area of a trapezium

$$= \frac{1}{2} \times Y \times (P + Z)$$

$$18 = \frac{1}{2} \times 3 \times (5 + Z)$$

$$(5 + Z) = \left[\frac{18 \times 2}{3}\right] = 12$$

$$Z = 12 - 5 = 7 \text{cm}$$

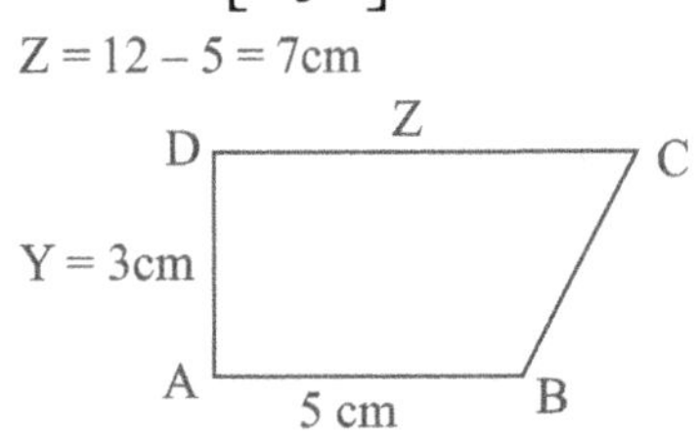

89. (*)

Sol. (90-92):

In, ABL libraries total no of books

$= 150 + 500 + 750 + 100 + 175 + 115 = 1790$

In, GHL libraries total no of books.

$= 170 + 600 + 610 + 130 + 100 + 100 = 1710$

In, MNL libraries total no of books.

$= 200 + 550 + 700 + 100 + 100 + 150 = 1800.$

In, PQL libraries total no of books.

$= 200 + 600 + 600 + 110 + 75 + 200 = 1485.$

90. (c) The self-half books in library GHL is: 170

The fiction books in library GHL is: 610

So, difference $= 610 - 170$

$= 440$

Hence, the self-half books in library GHL is 440 less than its fictional books.

91. (c) MNL library has the highest total count of books.

92. (b) The difference between total number of non-fiction and management books.

= Total No. of non-fiction book – Total No. of management book

$= [500 + 600 + 550 + 600] - (100 + 130 + 100 + 110)$

$= 2250 - 440 = 1810.$

93. (b) $\Rightarrow \dfrac{\sin\theta}{\cos\theta} \times \left[\dfrac{\cot\theta}{\mathrm{cosec}\,\theta}\right] \Rightarrow \dfrac{\sin\theta}{\cos\theta} \times \dfrac{\cos\theta}{\sin\theta} \times \sin\theta$

$\Rightarrow \sin\theta$

94. (d) Aryabhatta is a artificial satelite, hence neither (i) nor (ii) follows.

95. (c)   **96. (d)**   **97. (c)**

98 (b) Let, K walked at 3 kmph for a x km distance with L and K walked at 6 kmph for a certain distance with M is $= (27 - x)$ km.

$$\text{Speed} = \frac{\text{Distance}}{\text{Time}}$$

$$7 = \left(\frac{x}{3}\right) + \left(\frac{27 - x}{6}\right)$$

$$7 = \left[\frac{2x + 27 - x}{6}\right]$$

$$42 = x + 27$$

$$x = 42 - 27$$

$$= 15 \text{ km.}$$

99. (b)   **100. (d)**

1. Mahabharata war lasted for _____ days.
   (a) 17　　　　(b) 18
   (c) 19　　　　(d) 21

2. If $\sin x = \dfrac{4}{5}$ then $\dfrac{\sec x}{\sin x} = ?$

   (a) $\dfrac{23}{12}$　　　　(b) $\dfrac{25}{4}$

   (c) $\dfrac{4}{5}$　　　　(d) $\dfrac{25}{12}$

DIRECTIONS (Qs. 3-5): *Six students Lily. Mary, July, Daisy, Rosy and Fairy are sitting in a circle facing each other such that -*

1. Mary sits to the immediate right of July.
2. Lily does not sit near Fairy.
3. The student sitting on the immediate left of July, sits to the immediate right of Fairy.
4. Rosy does not sit to the immediate right of Mary.

3. If July leaves the circle, then who will be sitting to the immediate right of Lily?
   (a) Fairy
   (b) Rosy
   (c) Daisy
   (d) Cannot be determined

4. Who sits to the immediate right of Fairy?
   (a) Daisy
   (b) Rosy
   (c) Mary
   (d) Cannot be determined

5. _________ sits to the immediate left of Lily.
   (a) Daisy　　　　(b) Mary
   (c) Rosy　　　　(d) July

6. The variance of a set of data is 121. Then the standard deviation of the data is:
   (a) ±11　　　　(b) 11
   (c) 21　　　　(d) 60.5

7. Divide ₹ 221 in the ratio 1:3:6:7. The rupees in the respective ratios are
   (a) 13, 39, 77 & 92　　　(b) 13, 39, 79 & 90
   (c) 13, 39, 78 & 91　　　(d) 13, 40, 80 & 91

8. ITF Davis Cup is structured with a _____ nation World Group.
   (a) 8　　　　(b) 16
   (c) 20　　　　(d) 24

9. Mount Everest is located in
   (a) Tibet　　　　(b) India
   (c) Nepal　　　　(d) Bhutan

10. A telephone bill costs ₹13 for 19 minutes. What is the cost in rupees for 15 minutes 50 seconds? (Rounded to one decimal).
    (a) 10.8　　　　(b) 10.7
    (c) 10.6　　　　(d) 10.9

11. _________________ is not a chemical change.
    (a) Cooking an egg
    (b) Melting an ice cube
    (c) Baking a cake
    (d) Rotting bananas

12. Which of the following is not correct with reference to Bio-sand Water Filter?
    (a) It deactivates or kills pathogens.
    (b) Sedimentation removes larger particles.
    (c) Filtration removes smaller particles.
    (d) High quality water is always assured.

13. The length of a diagonal in cm of a rectangle of length 9 cm and width 5 cm is
    (a) $\sqrt{106}$　　　　(b) $\pm\sqrt{106}$
    (c) $2\sqrt{14}$　　　　(d) $\pm 2\sqrt{14}$

14. Physical Research Laboratory was founded by _________.
    (a) S. K. Mitra　　　(b) C. V. Raman
    (c) Homi Bhaba　　　(d) Vikram Sarabhai

15. If **O = 15** and **STAR = 58** then **CAMEL =?**
    (a) 35　　　　(b) 34
    (c) 33　　　　(d) 36

16. The mean of the data 2, 9, 9, 3, 6, 9, 4 is:

(a) $\dfrac{33}{7}$ (b) 6

(c) $\dfrac{43}{7}$ (d) 7

17. Nepal's first woman President is
(a) Rita Bhandary
(b) Vidya Devi Bhandari
(c) Aishwarya Rajya Laxmi
(d) Komal Rajya Laxmi

18. If **PQRST : SPTRQ** then **HIJKL : ?**
(a) KHJLI (b) KHLIJ
(c) KHLJI (d) KHELJ

19. 4 men can build a small house in 12 days. How long would it take for 6 men to build the same house?
(a) 9 days (b) 8 days
(c) 8.1 days (d) 8.2 days

20. The human spinal column is made up of _______ bones.
(a) 33 (b) 42
(c) 44 (d) 53

21. Simplify: $\dfrac{5}{28} \div \dfrac{28}{35} \div \dfrac{20}{112}$

(a) 4/5 (b) 5/4
(c) 4/7 (d) 7/4

22. A shopkeeper cheats to the extent of 8% while buying and selling fruits, by using tampered weights, his total gain in percentage is:
(a) 16.25 (b) 16.64
(c) 16.75 (d) 16.5

23. Select the alternative that shows a similar relationship as the given pair -

Impulsive : Impromptu
(a) Moderate : Increase
(b) Flawless : Impeccable
(c) Perpetual : Transitory
(d) Resistant : Receptive

24. Find the odd one out.

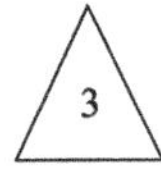 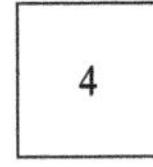 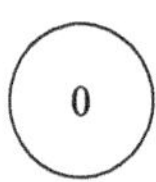 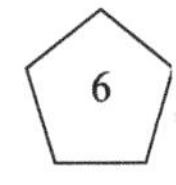

(i) (ii) (iii) (iv)

(a) iii (b) ii
(c) i (d) iv

25. If **Ammonia : Gas** then **Camphor : ?**
(a) Gas (b) Solid
(c) Liquid (d) Semi-solid

26. Which figure will replace the (?) in the given sequence?

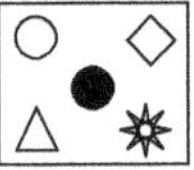 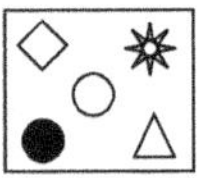 ? 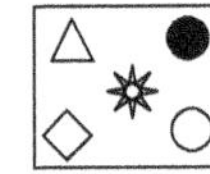 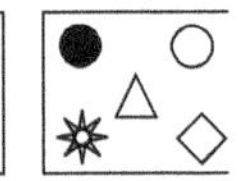

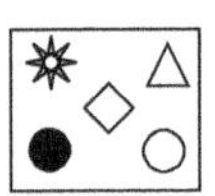  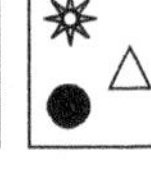 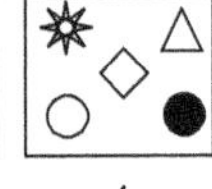

1 2 3 4

(a) 1 (b) 2
(c) 3 (d) 4

27. The cash difference between the selling price of an article at a profit of 2% and 12% is ₹3. The ratio of two selling prices is:
(a) 51:56 (b) 51:53
(c) 52:53 (d) 55:56

28. Which one does not relate to mobile phone touch panel sensing methods?
(a) Finger touch
(b) Voice recognition
(c) Gloved touch
(d) Light transmittance

29. Ms. Alina borrowed ₹ 650 at 6% per annum simple interest. What amount will she pay to clear her debt after 4 years?
(a) ₹ 165 (b) ₹ 860
(c) ₹ 806 (d) ₹ 156

30. Which is the correct ascending order of the given numbers?
(a) 1/3, 1/5, 2/5 (b) 1/3, 2/5, 1/5
(c) 1/5, 1/3, 2/5 (d) 1/5, 2/5, 1/3

31. _____ does not relate to measurement of memory capacity.
(a) GB (b) TB
(c) HB (d) ZB

32. Statements followed by some conclusions are given below.

Statements:
1. Some blues are violets whereas some are purples.

2. All oranges are reds and some reds are violets.

3. All purples are red.

Conclusions:

I. Some reds are blues.

II. Some oranges are violets.

Find which of the given conclusions logically follow from the given statements.

(a) Only conclusion I follows.

(b) Only conclusion II follows.

(c) Both I and II follow.

(d) Neither I nor II follows.

33. Ghoomar is the popular folk dance of

(a) Punjab

(b) Himachal Pradesh

(c) Rajasthan

(d) Jammu and Kashmir

34. Solve: $1000\,x - 5 = -6$

(a) $\dfrac{1}{1000}$

(b) $\dfrac{-1}{1000}$

(c) $\dfrac{-11}{1000}$

(d) $\dfrac{11}{1000}$

35. The order of rotational symmetry of a trapezium is:

(a) 2

(b) 0

(c) 1

(d) 3

36. Astronauts inside spaceship feel _____ weight.

(a) More

(b) Less

(c) Zero

(d) Depends on G force

37. Who awarded the Kaisar-i-Hind medal of the British to Mahatma Gandhi for his contribution to ambulance services in South Africa?

(a) Lord Dalhousie

(b) Lord Canning

(c) Lord Hardinge

(d) Lord Curzon

38. The median of the data –3, 4, 0, 4, –2, –5, 1, 7, 10, 5 is:

(a) 2

(b) 2.5

(c) 2.75

(d) 3

39. Correct expression of $0.0\overline{18}$ =?

(a) $\dfrac{1}{55}$

(b) $\dfrac{18}{100}$

(c) $\dfrac{18}{1000}$

(d) $\dfrac{1}{66}$

40. If $tan\,A = \dfrac{15}{8}$ and $tan\,B = \dfrac{7}{24}$, then $tan\,(A - B)$ = ?

(a) $\dfrac{304}{297}$

(b) $\dfrac{304}{425}$

(c) $\dfrac{416}{87}$

(d) $\dfrac{87}{416}$

41. Function key _____ in a Windows keyboard can perform several functions, and does not have an assigned Windows default.

(a) F1

(b) F6

(c) F8

(d) F9

DIRECTIONS (Qs. 42-44): *Out of the 100 nature lovers, 20 people wanted to see only bison, 30 wanted to see both bison and tiger, 15 wanted to see only leopard, 25 wanted to see only tiger, 5 wanted to see both bison and leopard and the remaining wanted to see only bear.*

42. The ratio of people to wanted to see tiger to those who wanted to see bear is

(a) 1/11

(b) 11/3

(c) 11/1

(d) 3/11

43. How many people who wanted to see bison did not want to see leopard?

(a) 5

(b) 15

(c) 50

(d) 55

44. How many people wanted to see only one animal?

(a) 35

(b) 65

(c) 60

(d) 50

45. Acid rain is caused by release of _______________ and ____________ into the air.

(a) Carbon dioxide and carbon monoxide

(b) Sulphur dioxide and nitrogen oxides

(c) Oxygen and water vapour

(d) Nitrous oxide and ozone

46. IF **JAGUAR = HCEWYT** then **ELEPHANT = ?**

   (a) CMCFRCLV   (b) CNCRFCLV

   (c) CNCFRCLV   (d) CNCRECLV

47. Given $w = 2$, $x = 3$, $y = 0$ & $z = \dfrac{1}{2}$. Find the value of $\dfrac{z}{w} + x$.

   (a) $3\dfrac{1}{4}$ (b) $-3\dfrac{1}{4}$

   (c) 3.2   (d) 3.5

48. Compute: $28854 \div 458 \div 9$

   (a) 70   (b) 567

   (c) 7   (d) 576

49. Who was elected as the Prime Minister of Nepal in 2015?

   (a) Khil Raj Regmi

   (b) Sushil Koirala

   (c) K. P. Sharma Oli

   (d) Baburam Bhattarai

50. Q is P's sister. R is P's mother, M is R's father. How is Q's father related to M?

   (a) Son

   (b) Grandson

   (c) Son-in-law

   (d) Brother

51. Chandan travelled equal distance with speed of 3 km/hr, 4 km/hr and 8 km/hr and takes a total time of 42.5 minutes. Find the total distance in km.

   (a) 4   (b) 2

   (c) 1   (d) 3

52. Which cricketer is not in the list of ICC Cricket Hall of Fame?

   (a) Anil Kumble

   (b) Bishen Singh Bedi

   (c) Kapil Dev

   (d) Ravi Shastri

53. Find the odd one out.

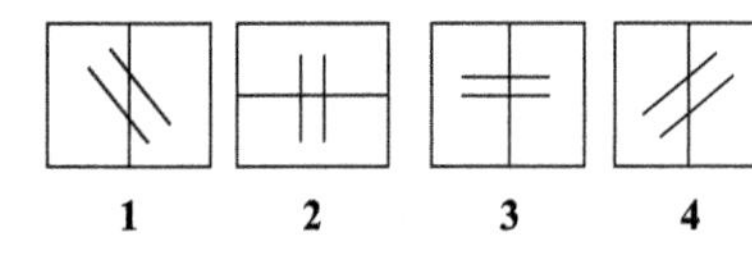

   (a) 1   (b) 2

   (c) 3   (d) 4

54. Borosilicate glass wear is used in microwave oven because

   (a) It is not brittle

   (b) It is highly heat resistant

   (c) It cooks faster than any other vessel

   (d) It is energy efficient

55. A junior college inducts students based on the following criteria —

1. Students who scored above 75% in Physics, 85% in Mathematics and 70% in Chemistry.

2. Students who scored at least 60% in English.

3. Students who are good in a sport or play a musical instrument or know a dance form.

Which student among the following will the college definitely take?

   (a) Shakti with 80% in Physics, 65% in Chemistry, 85% in Mathematics, 61% in English and plays Veena.

   (b) Megha secured 80% in Physics, 87% in Mathematics, 70% in English, 75% in Chemistry and is a singer.

   (c) Sheela secured 78% in Physics, 70% in Chemistry, 85% in Mathematics, 75% in English knows Manipuri folk dance.

   (d) Mallika secured 70% in Chemistry, 70% in Mathematics, 85% in Physics, 65% in English and plays basketball.

56. Manoj is twice as good a fisherman as Arunraj and together they finish a piece of work in 22 days. In how many days will Arunraj alone finish the work?

   (a) 44   (b) 66

   (c) 88   (d) 60

57. Mr. Devesh borrowed ₹ 4,500 at 4% per annum compound interest. The compound interest compounded annually for 2 years is:

   (a) ₹ 367.2   (b) ₹ 4,867.2

   (c) ₹ 4,876.2   (d) ₹ 376.2

58. Two numbers are in ratio 4:5 and their HCF is 13. Their LCM is:

   (a) 260   (b) 52

   (c) 65   (d) 265

59. In a certain code, 'book is big' is written as 756; 'big is story' is 764 and 'story book is interesting' is 4356. Which digit represents 'interesting'?

(a) 3   (b) 4

(c) 5   (d) 6

60. Transparency International (TI) has put India at rank _______ out of 168 countries in its Corruption Perception Index as on January 2016.

(a) 68   (b) 76

(c) 84   (d) 101

61. Simplify: $5x - 2x(x - 1)$

(a) $3x - 2$ (b) $3x + 2$

(c) $7x + 2x^2$ (d) $7x - 2x^2$

62. The number of sides of a regular polygon whose exterior angles are each $40°$ is.

(a) 7   (b) 10

(c) 9   (d) S

63. Western blot is the diagnostic test for

(a) Plague   (b) Leprosy

(c) HIV   (d) Typhoid

64. Kalindi is another name of the river

(a) Ganges   (b) Bhagirathi

(c) Yamuna   (d) Brahmaputra

65. Which of the following was described as the First Indian War of Independence?

(a) Partition of Bengal, 1905

(b) Uprising of 1857

(c) Civil Disobedience Movement, 1930 – 1931

(d) Quit India Movement, 1942

66. Mr. Akshar sold a bus for ₹ 20,400 with, a loss of 15%. At what price should the bus be sold to get a profit of 15%?

(a) ₹ 27,400   (b) ₹ 27,300

(c) ₹ 27,500   (d) ₹ 27,600

67. CMOS is a

(a) Battery-powered memory chip

(b) Basic input-output system

(c) Storage device

(d) Cache memory operating system

68. _____________ was India's first satellite launched from Indian-made launch vehicle.

(a) Aryabhata   (b) Rohini

(c) Bhasknra-1   (d) INSAT-1A

69. Which one of the following does not directly refer to cholesterol?

(a) Low density lipoprotein

(b) High density lipoprotein

(c) Rhesus factor

(d) Packaged protein coat

70. The nation-wide campaign 'Operation Smile' is related to

(a) Senior citizens   (b) War widow's

(c) Freedom fighters   (d) Missing children

71. The functioning of a very old

(a) Mechanical

(b) Mechanical and electrical

(c) Electrical

(d) Battery operated

72. Mughal Emperor Humayun's tomb is in

(a) Kabul   (b) Delhi

(c) Shahdara Bagh   (d) Khuldabad

73. _____________ won the FIFA Ballon d'Or award for the best player in the World in 2015.

(a) Cristiano Ronaldo   (b) Neymar

(c) Lionel Messi   (d) Luis Suarez

74. Air is a _____________.

(a) Pure compound.

(b) Mixture of only compounds.

(c) Mixture of only elements.

(d) Mixture of both elements and compounds.

75. Which one is not a football stadium in India?

(a) Bakshi Stadium. Srinagar

(b) Baichung Stadium, Sikkim

(c) Salt Lake Stadium, Kolkata

(d) Sardar Patel Stadium, Ahmedabad

76. **An assertion (A) and a reason (R) are given below.**

Assertion (A): Some land outside the forest area is not fertile.

Reason (R): Extensive cattle grazing leads to loss of soil fertility.

Choose the correct option.

(a) Both A and R are true and R is the correct explanation of A

(b) Both A and R are true, but R is not the correct explanation of A

(c) A is true, but R is false

(d) A is false, but R is true

77. If the product of two numbers is 2522 and their LCM is 97 then their HCF is:

(a) 28   (b) 29

(c) 27   (d) 26

78. Who was appointed as the Managing Director of International Monetary Fund for 5 years starting July 5, 2016?

(a) Strauss-Khan   (b) Christine Lagarde

(c) Jim Yong Kim   (d) Rodrigo de Rato

79. American astronaut Scott Joseph Kelly commanded the International Space Station consecutively for 340 days on __________.

(a) Expedition 24   (b) Expedition 25

(c) Expedition 26   (d) Expedition 27

80. Which article of the Constitution of India relates to Uniform Civil Code?

(a) 41   (b) 42

(c) 43   (d) 44

81. The value of $2.31 \times 0.34 = ?$

(a) 1.7854   (b) 0.7854

(c) 0.7845   (d) 0.7584

DIRECTIONS (Qs. 82-84): *The pie chart represents the favourite stars (Bollywood stars SRK, SK, AK, HR and VD) of the people of a family.*

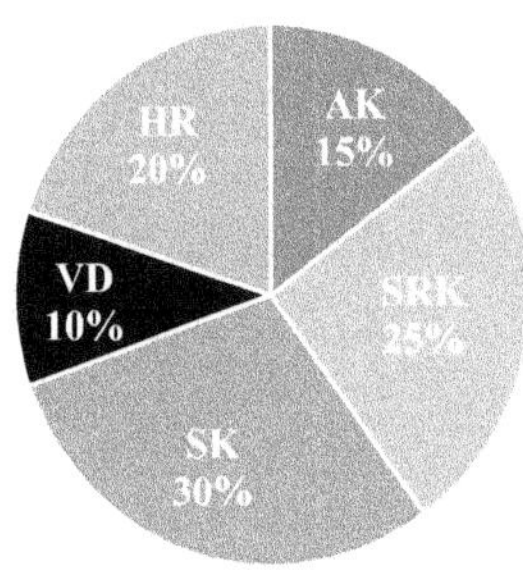

Consider the pie chart and answer questions based on it.

82. The ratio of people who like SRK to those who like SK is

(a) 6/5   (b) 5/6

(c) 1/2   (d) 2/1

83. The sector angle corresponding to the HR is

(a) 36°   (b) 72°

(c) 54°   (d) 108°

84. If there are 40 people in the family, what is the difference between those who like AK and those who like VD?

(a) 2   (b) 3

(c) 4   (d) 6

85. What is not true with CT Scan?

(a) Combines many X-ray images.

(b) Scanning is often painful.

(c) Generates 3-D cross-sectional views.

(d) Identifies normal and abnormal structures.

86. Find the odd one out.

(a) Cocaine   (b) Caffeine

(c) Nicotine   (d) Heroin

87. The number seats of Lok Sabha was increased from 525 to ________ in 1973.

(a) 560   (b) 555

(c) 550   (d) 545

88. Which of the following is not regarded as helpful to compost?

(a) Egg shells   (b) Sawdust

(c) Tea-bags   (d) Fish bones

89. Simplify: $(25)^{\frac{3}{2}}$

(a) 625   (b) 15625

(c) 125   (d) $\sqrt{125}$

90. Rearrange the jumbled letters to make a meaningful word and then select the one which is different

(a) GIANTLER   (b) NILE

(c) MUBORSH   (d) RASQUE

91. Aditya said, "I have two children and Anil is the father of my daughter's only niece". How is Anil related to Aditya?

(a) Father   (b) Son

(c) Grandfather   (d) Brother

92. Identify the positive impact of internet in life.
  (a) Cyber-crimes are on the increase.
  (b) Users suffer from internet addiction disorder.
  (c) Best source of knowledge through a click.
  (d) Leads to less physical activity and poor eye sight.

93. If the mathematical operator, '+' means '×', '÷' means '−', '−' means '+' and '×' means '÷', then the value of **11 + 14 × 7 − 5 ÷ 29** is
  (a) −5   (b) −12
  (c) −7   (d) −2

94. Statements followed by some conclusions are given below.
  Statements:
  (a) Ravi works more than Meera who works 8 hours every day.
  (b) Yuvi work for 9 hours a day which is lesser than Ravi's by 1 hour.
  Conclusions:
  I. Ravi works for 8 hour
  II. Ravi and Yuvi both work more than Meera every day.
  Find which of the given conclusions logically follow from the given statements.
  (a) Only conclusion I follows.
  (b) Only conclusion II follows.
  (c) Both I and II follow.
  (d) Neither I nor II follows.

95. Compute: 4082 ÷ 157 − 23
  (a) −3   (b) 3
  (c) 2041/67   (d) 2014/67

96. Keerthana takes 9 hrs 20 minutes in walking a distance and riding back to same place where she started. She could walk both ways in 11hrs 15minutes. The time taken by her to ride back both ways is:
  (a) 7 hrs 25 min   (b) 7 hrs 35 min
  (c) 7 hrs 45 min   (d) 7 hrs 15 min

97. If **BLACK = AMZDJ** then **BEAUTIFUL =**
  (a) AEZSUJEVK   (b) AFZVSJEVK
  (c) AEZSUJFVK   (d) AEZSSJEVK

98. The world heritage site Pashupatinath temple is located at
  (a) Peshawar   (b) Kabul
  (c) Kathmandu   (d) Multan

99. What is the next number in the series -
  4, 8, 8, 16, 12, 24, ____
  (a) 32   (b) 48
  (c) 28   (d) 16

100. Anand's mother is Chandra's father's son's sister. How is Anand related to Chandra's father?
  (a) Grandfather   (b) Father
  (c) Uncle   (d) Grandson

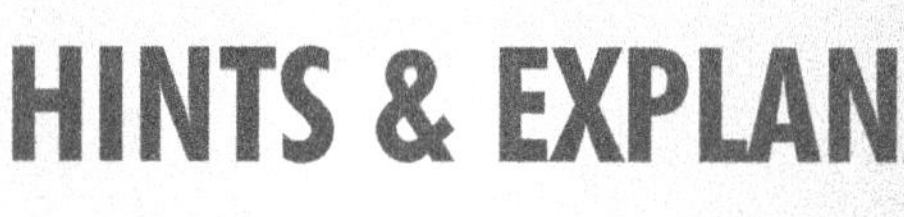

HINTS & EXPLANATIONS

1. (b)

2. (d) $\sin x = \dfrac{4}{5}$

$$\cos x = \sqrt{1 - \sin^2 x} = \sqrt{1 - \left(\dfrac{4}{5}\right)^2}$$

$$= \sqrt{\dfrac{25 - 16}{25}} = \dfrac{3}{5}$$

$$\therefore \quad \dfrac{\sec x}{\sin x} = \dfrac{\dfrac{5}{3}}{\dfrac{4}{5}} = \dfrac{5}{3} \times \dfrac{5}{4} = \dfrac{25}{12}$$

For Solution 3 to 5

Using the given information, we conclude

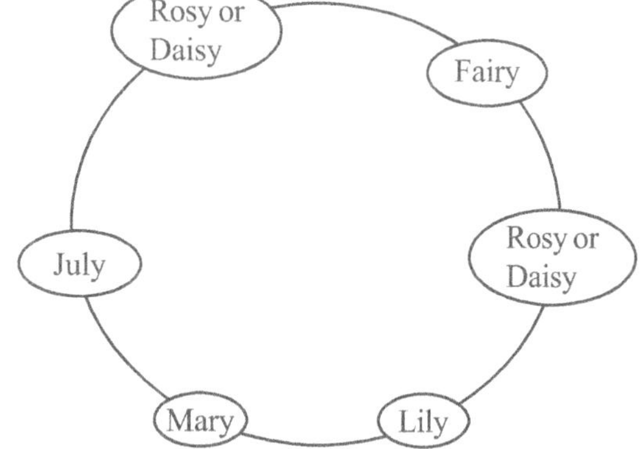

3. **(d)** Either Daisy or Rosy will be sitting to the right of Lily.

4. **(d)** Either Daisy or Rosy sits to the immediate right of Fairy.

5. **(b)** Mary sits to the immediate left of Lily.

6. **(b)** Variance = 121 (given)

∴ standard deviation $= \sqrt{\text{variance}}$

$$= \sqrt{121} = 11$$

7. **(c)** Let four parts of ₹ 221 are x, 3x, 6x and 7x.

∴ $x + 3x + 6x + 7x = ₹\ 221$

$\Rightarrow\ 17x = 221$

$$x = \frac{221}{17} = 13$$

Hence, the rupees in the respective ratios are ₹13, ₹ 39, ₹ 78 and ₹ 91.

8. **(b)** **9.** **(*)**

10. **(a)** Cost of bill for 19 mins = ₹ 13

Cost of bill for 1 min = ₹ $\dfrac{13}{19}$

Cost of bill for 15 mins 50 sec.

$$= ₹\left(\frac{13}{19} \times 15\frac{50}{60}\right)$$

$$= ₹\left(\frac{13}{19} \times \frac{95}{6}\right)$$

$$= ₹\ \frac{65}{6} = ₹\ 10.8$$

11. **(b)** **12.** **(d)**

13. **(a)** 5 cm

9 cm

length of diagonal $= \sqrt{l^2 + b^2}$

$$= \sqrt{9^2 + 5^2}$$

$$= \sqrt{81 + 25} = \sqrt{106}\ \text{cm}.$$

14. **(d)**

15. **(b)** O = 15 and STAR = 58

Here, each letter represents its position in alphabets.

STAR = 19 + 20 + 1 + 18 = 58

∴ CAMEL = 3 + 1 + 13 + 5 + 12 = 34

16. **(b)** Sum of observations

$$= 2 + 9 + 9 + 3 + 6 + 9 + 4 = 42$$

No. of observations = 7

∴ Mean $= \dfrac{42}{7} = 6$

17. **(b)**

18. **(c)** 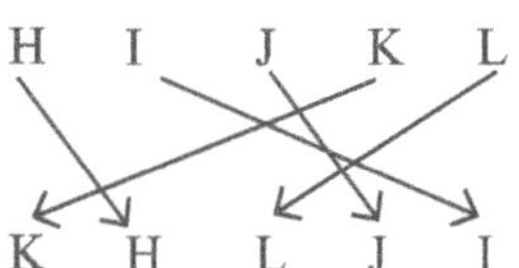

Changing the sequence of letters as per the first example.

19. **(b)**

No. of Men	4	6
No. of days	12	x

This is a case of increase relationship

∴ $4 \times 12 = 6 \times x$

$\Rightarrow\ x = \dfrac{4 \times 12}{6} = 8\ \text{days}$

20. **(a)**

21. **(b)** $\dfrac{5}{28} \div \dfrac{28}{35} \div \dfrac{20}{112}$

$$= \frac{5}{28} \times \frac{35}{28} \div \frac{20}{112}$$

$$= \frac{5}{28} \times \frac{35}{28} \times \frac{112}{20} = \frac{5}{4}$$

22. **(b)** Buying → 1 kg → 1.08 (8%) profit

Selling → 1kg → .92 kg (8%) profit

∴ percentage gain

$$= (1 - .92) + (1.08 - 1) + (.08 \times .08)$$

$$= 0.08 + 0.08 + 0.0064$$

$$= 0.1664\ \text{i.e.,}\ 16.64\%$$

23. **(b)**

24. **(d)** (i) 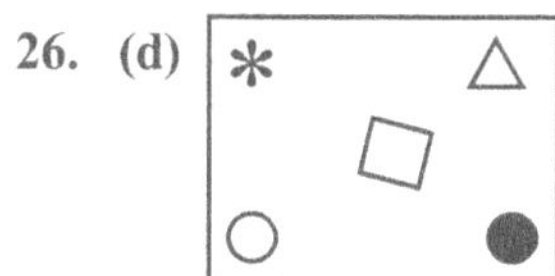 has 3 sides.

    (ii) $\boxed{4}$ has 4 sides.

    (iii) $\bigcirc\!0$ has no sides.

    (iv) 6 has 5 sides.

25. **(b)** Ammonia is a gas and camphor is a solid.

26. **(d)**

Fig. 4 is the missing figure.

27. **(a)** Let CP of the article = 100

    $\Rightarrow$ SP at 2% profit = 102

    and SP at 12% = 112

    $\therefore$ required ratio $=\dfrac{102}{112}$

    $=\dfrac{51}{56}$

28. **(b)**

29. **(c)** $SI = \dfrac{P \times R \times T}{100}$

    $=\dfrac{650 \times 6 \times 4}{100} = ₹\,156$

    $\therefore$ A = SI + P = ₹ (156 + 650) = ₹ 806

30. **(c)** $\dfrac{1}{3} = 0.33$; $\dfrac{1}{5} = 0.2$; $\dfrac{2}{5} = 0.4$

    $\therefore$ $\dfrac{1}{5} < \dfrac{1}{3} < \dfrac{2}{5}$

31. **(c)**

32. **(a)**

Thus, Conclusion I that some reds are blues is correct.

33. **(c)**

34. **(b)** $1000x - 5 = -6$

    $\Rightarrow$ $1000\,x = -6 + 5$

$\Rightarrow$ $x = \dfrac{-1}{1000}$

35. **(c)** The order of rotational symmetry of a trapezium is 1.

36. **(c)**

37. **(c)** Mahatma Gandhi was awarded Kaisar-i-Hind in 1915 by the Lord Harding of Penshurst for his contribution to ambulance services in South Africa. Gandhi returned the medal in 1920 as part of the national campaign protesting the Jallianwala Bagh massacre and in support of the Khilafat Movement.

38. **(b)** Arranging in ascending order

    $-5, -3, -2, 0, 1, 4, 4, 5, 7, 10$

    Here n = 10

    $\therefore$ Median $=\dfrac{\left(\dfrac{n}{2}\right)^{th}\text{ term}+\left(\dfrac{n}{2}+1\right)^{th}\text{ term}}{2}$

    $=\dfrac{5^{th}\text{ term}+6^{th}\text{ term}}{2}$

    $=\dfrac{1+4}{2} = 2.5$

39. **(a)** $x = 0.0\overline{18}$

    $10x = 0.1\overline{81}8...$ ...(i)

    $1000x = 18.\overline{18}...$ ...(ii)

    Subtract (i) from (ii),

    $1000x - 10x = 18$

    $990x = 18$

    $x = \dfrac{18}{990} = \dfrac{2}{110} = \dfrac{1}{55}$

40. **(a)** $\tan(A - B) = \dfrac{\tan A - \tan B}{1 + \tan A \tan B}$

    $\dfrac{\dfrac{15}{8} - \dfrac{7}{24}}{1 + \left(\dfrac{15}{8} \times \dfrac{7}{24}\right)} = \dfrac{\dfrac{45-7}{24}}{1 + \dfrac{35}{4}} = \dfrac{38}{24} \times \dfrac{64}{99}$

    $=\dfrac{19}{12} \times \dfrac{64}{99} = \dfrac{19}{3} \times \dfrac{16}{99} = \dfrac{304}{297}$

41. **(c)**

42. (c) People wanted to see bear only

$$= 100 - 20 - 30 - 15 - 25 - 5 = 5$$

$\therefore$ Required ratio $= \dfrac{30-25}{5} = \dfrac{55}{5} = \dfrac{11}{1} = 11:1$

43. (c) People wanted to see bison but not leopard

$$= 20 + 30 = 50$$

44. (b) 20 people wanted to see only bison.

15 wanted to see only leopard.

25 people wanted to see only tiger.

5 people wanted to see only bear.

$\therefore$ People wanted to see only one animal

$$= 20 + 15 + 25 + 5$$

$$= 65$$

45. (b)

46. (b)

$J \xrightarrow{-2} H$	$E \xrightarrow{-2} C$
$A \xrightarrow{+2} C$	$L \xrightarrow{+2} N$
$G \xrightarrow{-2} E$	$E \xrightarrow{-2} C$
$U \xrightarrow{+2} W$	$P \xrightarrow{+2} R$
$A \xrightarrow{-2} Y$	$H \xrightarrow{-2} F$
$R \xrightarrow{+2} T$	$A \xrightarrow{+2} C$
	$N \xrightarrow{-2} L$
	$T \xrightarrow{+2} V$

47. (a) $\dfrac{z}{w} + x = \dfrac{\frac{1}{2}}{2} + 3 = \dfrac{1}{2 \times 2} + 3$

$$= \dfrac{1}{4} + 3 = \dfrac{1+12}{4} = \dfrac{13}{4} = 3\dfrac{1}{4}$$

48. (c) $28854 \div 458 \div 9$

$$= 63 \div 9 = 7$$

49. (c) K.P. Sharma Oli was elected as the 38th Prime Minister of Nepal in 2015. He was the Chief of UML's International Department before being elected to the top position of the party. Oli served as the nation's Deputy Prime Minister and Minister for Foreign Affairs in Girija Prasad Koirala led interim government.

50. (c)

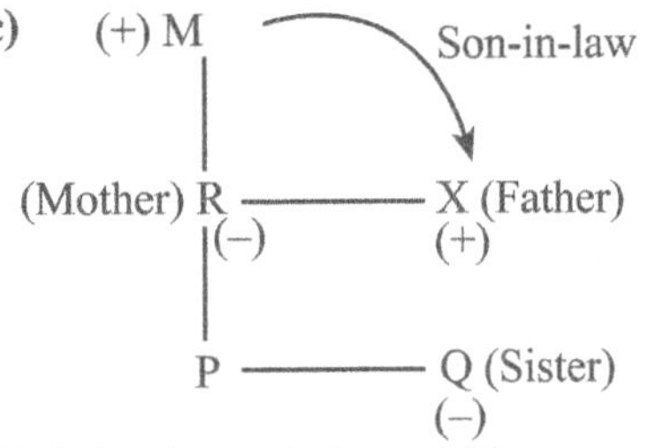

(+) M — Son-in-law → X (Father) (+)

(Mother) R ———— X (Father)

(−)

P ———— Q (Sister) (−)

Q's father is son-in-law of M.

51. (d) Let each of the distance travelled with speed of 3 km / hr, 4 km/hr and 8 km/hr be x km.

$\therefore$ Total time taken = 42.5 min

$\Rightarrow \dfrac{x}{3} + \dfrac{x}{4} + \dfrac{x}{8} = \dfrac{42.5}{60}$ hr

$\Rightarrow \dfrac{8x + 6x + 3x}{24} = \dfrac{42.5}{60}$

$\Rightarrow \dfrac{17x}{24} = \dfrac{425}{600} \Rightarrow x = \dfrac{425 \times 24}{600 \times 17} = 1$ km

Hence, total distance $= x + x + x$

$$= (1 + 1 + 1) \text{ km} = 3 \text{ km}$$

52. (d)

53. (b)

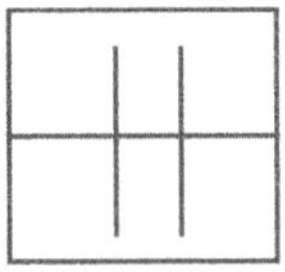

54. (b)

55. (c) Sheela got 78% in Physics, 70% in Chemistry, 85% in Mathematics, 75% in English and knows Manpuri folk dance, is eligible for the admission.

56. (b) Let work done by Manoj and Arunraj in a day be 2x and x respectively.

$\therefore$ Total work done in a day $= x + 2x = 3x$

Now, Manoj and Arunraj finish a work in 22 days.

Work done by Manoj and Arunraj in 1 day

$$= \dfrac{1}{22}$$

$\Rightarrow 3x = \dfrac{1}{22} \Rightarrow x = \dfrac{1}{66}$

Hence, Arunraj alone finishes the work in 66 days.

57. **(a)** $A = P\left(1 + \dfrac{R}{100}\right)^n = 4500\left(1 + \dfrac{4}{100}\right)^2$

$= 4500\left(1 + \dfrac{1}{25}\right)^2 = 4500\left(\dfrac{26}{25}\right)^2 = ₹\,4867.20$

$\therefore\quad CI = A - P$

$= ₹\,4867.20 - ₹\,4500 = ₹\,367.20$

58. **(a)** Let two numbers be 4x and 5x respectively.

HCF of 4x and 5x = x

$13 = x$ $\qquad\qquad$ ($\because$ HCF = 13)

$\therefore$ The two numbers are (4 × 13)

= 52 and (5 × 13) = 65

Hence, LCM of 52 and 65 = 260

59. **(a)** Book is big → 756 $\qquad\qquad$ ...(1)

Big is story → 764 $\qquad\qquad$ ...(2)

Story book is interesting → 4356 $\qquad$ ...(3)

From (1), (2) and (3),

is = 6, big = 7, book = 5, story = 4 and

interesting = 3

60. **(b)**

61. **(d)** $5x - 2x\,(x - 1)$

$= 5x - 2x^2 + 2x$

$= 7x - 2x^2$

62. **(c)** Exterior angle = 40°

$\therefore$ Number of sides

$= \dfrac{360°}{\text{Exterior angle}} = \dfrac{360°}{40°} = 9$

63. **(c) 64. (c)**

65. **(b)** India's first war of Independence, better known as the Indian Rebellion of 1857, began on 10th May, 1857. The rebellion of 1857 is considered the first blow that shattered the British the British rule in India.

66. **(d)** SP = ₹ 20400 and loss = 15%

$\therefore\quad CP = \dfrac{100}{(100 - \text{loss\%})} \times SP$

$= \dfrac{100}{(100 - 15)} \times 20400 = \dfrac{100}{85} \times 20400$

$= ₹\,24000$

Now Profit = 15%

$\therefore$ Required SP $= \left(\dfrac{100 + \text{gain\%}}{100}\right) \times CP$

$= \left(\dfrac{100 + 15}{100}\right) \times 24000$

$= \dfrac{115}{100} \times 24000 = ₹\,27600$

67. **(a) 68. (b) 69. (c)**

70. **(d)** The operation 'Smile' was first launched by Home Ministry in January 2015 to rescue and rehabilitate the missing children. Since then the programme has been continuing with the active help of state government.

71. **(a) 72. (b)**

73. **(c)** On February 19, 2016, the IMF Executive Board selected Christine Lagarde for a second five-year term which started on July 5, 2016. She was the first woman to hold the position as Managing Director.

74. **(d) 75. (d)**

76. **(b)** Some land outside the forest area is not fertile is true.

Extensive cattle grazing leads to loss of soil fertility is also true but is not the correct explanation of the first sentence.

77. **(d)** HCF $= \dfrac{\text{Product of two numbers}}{\text{LCM}}$

$= \dfrac{2522}{97} = 26$

78. **(b) 79. (c)**

80. **(d)** In Article 44, the Constitution of India clearly specifies the Uniform Civil Code that states " The state shall endeavour to secure the citizen a Uniform Civil Code throughout the territory of India."

81. **(b)** 2.31 × 0.34 = 0.7854

82. **(b)** Required ratio $= \dfrac{\text{People like SRK}}{\text{People like SK}}$

$= \dfrac{25}{30} = 5 : 6$

83. (b) Complete angle = 360°

∴ Sector angle corresponding to HR

= 20% of 360°

$$= \frac{20}{100} \times 360° = 72°$$

84. (a) Number of people like AK = 15% of 40

$$= \frac{15}{100} \times 40 = 6$$

Number of people like VD = 10% of 40

$$= \frac{10}{100} \times 40 = 4$$

∴ Difference = 6 – 4 = 2

85. (b) 86. (b)   87. (d)   88. (d)

89. (c) $(25)^{\frac{3}{2}} = \left(5^2\right)^{\frac{3}{2}} = (5)^{2 \times \frac{3}{2}} = (5)^3 = 125$

90. (b)

91. (b)

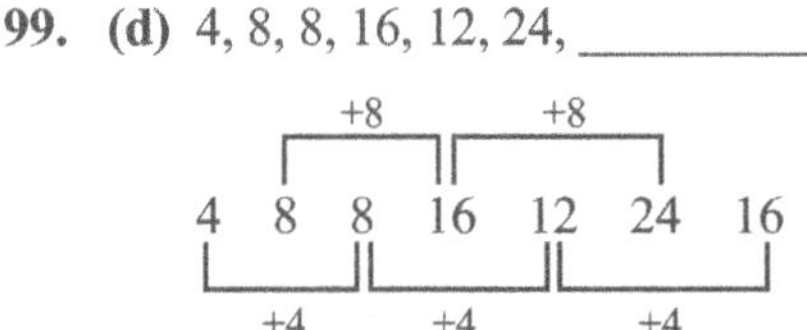

Anil is the son of Aditya.

92. (c)

93. (d) New expression

= 11 × 14 ÷ 7 + 5 – 29

= 11 × 2 + 5 – 29

= 22 + 5 – 29

= 27 – 29 = (–2)

94. (b) Ravi works more than Meera who works 8 hours every day ....(1)

Yuvi works for 9 hours a day which is lesser than Ravi's work by 1 hour ...(2)

from (1) and (2),

Ravi works for 10 hours

Hence only conclusion II follows

95. (b) 4082 ÷ 157 – 23

= 26 – 23 = 3

96. (a) Walk + walk = 11 hrs 15 mins

⇒ 2 walk = 11 hrs 15 mins

⇒ walk $= \dfrac{11 \, \text{hrs. } 15 \, \text{mins}}{2}$

Also, walk + riding = 9 h₹ 20 mins

⇒ riding $= 9 \, \text{hrs } 20 \, \text{mins} - \dfrac{11 \, \text{hrs } 15 \, \text{mins}}{2}$

⇒ riding = 7 hr 25 mins

97. (b)

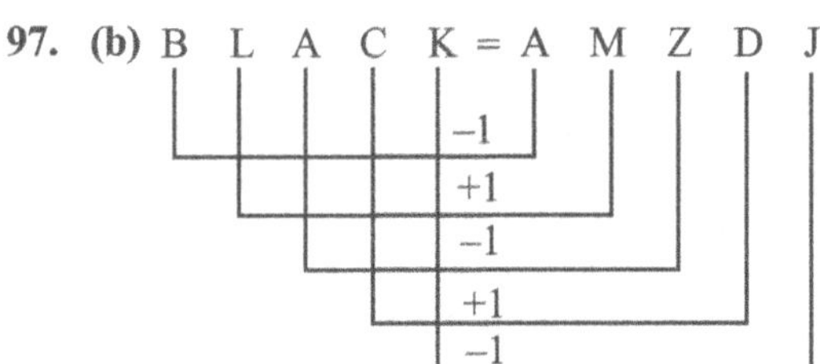

∴ BEAUTIFUL = AFZVSJEVK

98. (c) Pashupatinath temple is one of the 8 UNESCO Cultural Heritage Sites of the Kathmandu. Pashupatinath is one of the four most religious sites in Asia for devotees of Shiva. The temple has been on the heritage list since 1979.

99. (d) 4, 8, 8, 16, 12, 24, _______

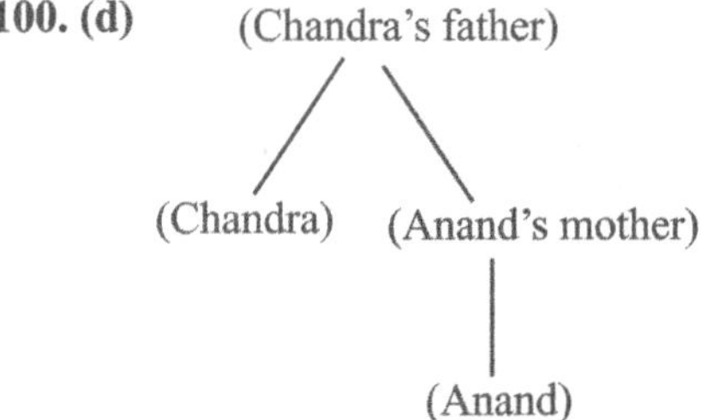

∴ 16 is next number.

100. (d)

Anand is the grandsons of Chandra's father.

RRB NTPC STAGE-I SOLVED PAPER-11
Held On 12ᵗʰ April 2016 (Shift-3)

1. Ritesh sold a pen for ₹ 36 with a profit of 20%. If it were sold for ₹ 33, then what could be the percentage of profit or loss?
   - (a) 10% Profit
   - (b) 15% Profit
   - (c) 12% Loss
   - (d) 18% Loss

2. Which sport has the highest rank of Yokozuna?
   - (a) Sumo wrestling
   - (b) Judo
   - (c) Jujitsu
   - (d) Kendo

3. Rearrange the jumbled up letters in their natural sequence and find the odd one out.
   - (a) SAMR
   - (b) MOETC
   - (c) USVNE
   - (d) PUJIERT

4. What does UFO stand for?
   - (a) Under Fire Object
   - (b) Unidentified Flying Object
   - (c) Unapproved Foreign Object
   - (d) Unidentified Free Object

5. The height of a light house is 20 meters above sea level. The angle of depression (from the top of the lighthouse) of a ship in the sea is 30°. What is the distance of the ship from the foot of the light house?
   - (a) 16 m
   - (b) $20\sqrt{3}$ m
   - (c) 20 m
   - (d) 30 m

6. Which queen of Ahmednagar opposed emperor Akbar?
   - (a) Rani Durgavati
   - (b) Zeenat Mahal
   - (c) Chand Bibi
   - (d) Razia Sultan

7. When is International day for Preservation of Ozone layer observed?
   - (a) September 16
   - (b) July 4
   - (c) January 23
   - (d) May 1

8. Who invented the bifocal glasses?
   - (a) Thomas Alva Edison
   - (b) Benjamin Franklin
   - (c) Evangelista
   - (d) Isaac Newton

9. Identify the odd one from the list below.
   - (a) Snake
   - (b) Lizard
   - (c) Reptiles
   - (d) Crocodile

10. What denotes learned and shared beliefs and behaviours?
    - (a) Culture
    - (b) Ethnicity
    - (c) Group
    - (d) Descent

11. Who invented the mobile phone?
    - (a) Joseph Wilson
    - (b) Edwin Land
    - (c) Martin Cooper
    - (d) John Lloyd Wright

12. What of the following refers to hypotheses which are confirmed by varied tests?
    - (a) Assumption
    - (b) Theory
    - (c) Answer
    - (d) Opinion

13. What does PDA stand for?
    - (a) Personal Data Assistant
    - (b) Personal Digital Assistant
    - (c) Prime Data Assistant
    - (d) Prime Digital Assistant

14. If the angles of a triangle are in the ratio of 1:4:7, then find the ratio of the greatest angle to the smallest angle.
    - (a) 7:2
    - (b) 2:3
    - (c) 7:1
    - (d) 3:5

15. Name the architect who designed New Delhi.
    - (a) Le Corbusier
    - (b) Sir Edwin Lutyens
    - (c) Andrew Paul
    - (d) George Baker

16. The mean of 10 observations is 17. One more observation is included and the new mean becomes 16. The 11th observation is

(a) 16   (b) 8

(c) 6   (d) 12

17. Battle of Plassey was fought by the British under the leadership of

(a) Robert Clive   (b) Lord Dalhousie

(c) Warren Hastings   (d) James Heartly

18. Arun and Amit can do a piece of work in 9 days and 12 days respectively. If they work for alternate days and Amit starts the work first, then in how many days 35/36 parts of whole work will be completed?

(a) 10 days   (b) 12 days

(c) 5 days   (d) 8 days

19. Aparna changes the marked price of an item to 50% above its C.P. What % of discount allowed (in approximately) to gain 10%?

(a) 27%   (b) 25%

(c) 35%   (d) 37%

20. A wholesaler purchased 7 hair clips for a rupee. How many for a rupee must he sell to get profit of 40%

(a) 6   (b) 5

(c) 4   (d) 3

21. If E = 5, GUN = 42 and ROSE = 57, then what is the value of GATE?

(a) 23   (b) 32

(c) 33   (d) 35

22. In which state is the Valley of Flowers National park situated?

(a) Uttarakhand

(b) Himachal Pradesh

(c) Jammu and Kashmir

(d) Assam

23. Three numbers are given in which the second is triple the first and is also double the third. If the average of the three numbers is 66. Find the first number.

(a) 36   (b) 54

(c) 108   (d) 72

24. Pihu and Aayu are running on a circular track of diameter 28 m. Speed of Pihu is 48 m/s and that of Aayu is 40 m/s. They start from the same point at the same time in the same direction. When will they meet again for the first time?

(a) 8 seconds   (b) 11 seconds

(c) 13 seconds   (d) 14 seconds

25. Who replaced B. S. Bassi as

(a) Alok Kumar Verma

(b) Rakesh Maria

(c) Dattatray Padsalgikar

(d) Neeraj Kumar

DIRECTIONS (Qs. 26-28): *In the following questions are to be based on the details given below:*

A salesman visits 274 houses in a town to find out the views about three products X, Y and Z. He found that 157 use X, 98 use only X, 22 use all the three, 14 use X and Z but not Y, 39 use Y and Z, 48 use only Y.

26. Which product is the most popular one?

(a) X   (b) Y

(c) Z   (d) Both X and Z

27. How many use product Z only?

(a) 10   (b) 50

(c) 52   (d) 25

28. What fraction used at least two products?

(a) 67/274   (b) 76/274

(c) 73/274   (d) 37/274

29. A superfast Duronto express running at 90 kmph overtakes a bike running at 36 kmph in 25 seconds. What is the length of the train in meters?

(a) 375 m   (b) 225 m

(c) 275 m   (d) 325 m

30. If EFMIJ means DELHI, then the last letter of the word got by decoding IQBOS is

(a) R   (b) T

(c) K   (d) M

31. An Assertion (A) and Reason (R) are given below.

Assertion (A): We prefer to wear white clothes in winter.

Reason (R): White clothes are good reflectors of heat.

Choose the correct option.

(a) A is true but R is false.

(b) A is false but R is true.

(c) Both A and R are true and R is the correct explanation of A.

(d) Both A and R are true and R is not the correct explanation of A.

32. Select the pair in which the numbers are similarly related as in the given pair:

$9 : 27 : : \_\_\_ : \_\_\_$

(a) $5 : 125$ (b) $8 : 64$

(c) $15 : 135$ (d) $81 : 729$

33. How many princely states were there in India at the time of Independence?

(a) 347   (b) 490

(c) 565   (d) 418

34. Given that $x + (1/x) = 15$, then find the value of $\dfrac{5x}{5x^2 - 20x + 5}$

(a) $1/3$ (b) $1/4$

(c) $1/5$ (d) $1/11$

35. Who is considered as the Father of Modern Indian Renaissance?

(a) Mahatma Gandhi

(b) Sardar Vallabhbhai Patel

(c) VinobaBhave

(d) Raja Ram Mohan Roy

36. Find the largest number of three digits exactly divisible by 15. 18, 27 and 30.

(a) 870   (b) 900

(c) 810   (d) 780

37. Who invented the Band-aid?

(a) Earle Dickson   (b) Alan Gant

(c) Louis Pasteur   (d) Frank Epperson

38. If $(x + 1/x) = 2$, then find the value of $(x^3 + 1/x^3) \div (x^{18} + 1/x^{18})$

(a) $2/9$ (b) 5

(c) 1   (d) $1/9$

39. Find the approximate simple interest on ₹2000 from March 9, 2010 to May 21, 2010 at 8.25% per annum.

(a) ₹ 43   (b) ₹ 37

(c) ₹ 33   (d) ₹ 40

40. The angle of elevation of the top of tower at a distance of 25 m from its foot is 60°. The approximate height of the tower is -

(a) 20.3 m   (b) 15.3 m

(c) 36.3 m   (d) 43.3 m

41. Which of the following refers to the number of pixels per inch, printed on a page?

(a) Print Margin   (b) Resolution

(c) Filter   (d) Colour mode

42. In which generation of computer was the mechanical language for programming used?

(a) First   (b) Second

(c) Third   (d) Fourth

43. Which is the fastest land animal in the World?

(a) Dog   (b) Cheetah

(c) Tiger   (d) Horse

44. If @ means +, # means − , \$ means × and * means ÷, then what is the value of 16 @ **4 \$ 5 # 72 * 8 =**

(a) 27   (b) 26

(c) 36   (d) 35

45. 4 years ago, the ratio of Vikah's to Rahul's age was 3 : 5. After 6 years, this ratio would become 4:5. Find present age of Rahul.

(a) 10   (b) 15

(c) 14   (d) 17

46. If in a certain code language, PROMOTION is written as 365458957, how will the word MONITOR be written in that code language?

(a) 4579856   (b) 4578956

(c) 4597866   (d) 4578596

47. If '+' means 'multiplication', '−' means 'division', 'x' means 'subtraction' and '÷' means 'addition', then $9 + 8 \div 8 − 4 \times 9$ is

(a) 65   (b) 11

(c) 26   (d) 56

48. Who was the American astronaut who returned to Earth after spending 340 days in International Space Station?

(a) Scott Kelly   (b) Mikhail Kornienko

(c) Eric Boe   (d) Douglas Hurley

49. Knife is an example for

    (a) Lever   (b) Wedge

    (c) Inclined plane   (d) Pulley

50. The famous tennis player Steffi Graf belongs to which among the following countries?

    (a) USA   (b) England

    (c) Germany   (d) Switzerland

51. When two liquids do not mix with each other to form a solution, what is it called?

    (a) Solvent   (b) Solute

    (c) Immiscible   (d) Decantation

DIRECTIONS (Qs. 52-54): *Study the following information carefully and answer the questions given below it.*

    (i) There are six members in a family in which there are two married couples.

    (ii) Sandhya, a lawyer, is married to the engineer and is mother of Charu and Suraj.

    (iii) Bhuvanesh, the teacher, is married Aruna.

    (iv) Aruna has one son and one grandson.

    (v) Of the two married ladies one is a housewife.

    (vi) There is also one student and one male doctor in the family

52. How is Aruna related to Charu?

    (a) Sister   (b) Mother

    (c) Grandfather   (d) Grandmother

53. Who among the following is the housewife?

    (a) Charu   (b) Aruna

    (c) Sandhiya   (d) None

54. Which of the following is true about the grand daughter in the family?

    (a) She is a Doctor   (b) She is a Teacher

    (c) She is a Student   (d) Data inadequate

55. Find the correct option which has a similar relationship.

    Produce : Waste : : Contrast : ?

    (a) Correct   (b) Match

    (c) Contradict   (d) Oppose

56. An Assertion (A) and a Reason (R) are given below.

    Assertion (A): Beriberi is a viral infection.

    Reason (R): Vitamin deficiency causes diseases.

Choose the correct option.

    (a) A is false but R is true.

    (b) A is true but R is false.

    (c) Both A and R are false

    (d) Both A and R are true and R is the correct explanation of A.

57. Glaciers are formed by

    (a) Melting snow

    (b) Accumulation of snow

    (c) Heavy hail fall

    (d) High rainfall

58. 12 men and 16 women together can complete a work in 4 days. It takes 80 days for one man alone to complete the same work, then how many days would be required for one woman alone to complete the same work?

    (a) 160   (b) 150

    (c) 130   (d) 175

59. Jalal, Amit and Feroz enter into partnership. Jalal invests 4 times as much as Amit and Amit invests three-fourth of what Feroz invests. At the end of the financial year, the total profit earned is ₹ 19,000. Find the share for Jalal.

    (a) ₹ 15,000   (b) ₹ 12,000

    (c) ₹ 13,000   (d) ₹ 10,000

60. How many astronauts have walked on the moon?

    (a) 2   (b) 5

    (c) 8   (d) 12

61. Identify the odd one from the list below.

    (a) Stream   (b) Bridge

    (c) Canal   (d) River

62. An Assertion (A) and Reason (R) are given below.

    Assertion (A): Leakages in household gas cylinders can be detected.

    Reason (R): LPG has a strong smell.

    Choose the correct option.

    (a) Both A and R are true and R is the correct explanation of A.

    (b) Both A and R are true and R is not the correct explanation of A.

    (c) Both A and R are false

    (d) A is true but R is false.

63. Who was sworn in as the Prime Minister of Nepal in 2015?
    (a) Sushil Koirala
    (b) Bidhya Devi Bhandari
    (c) Khadga Prasad Sharma Oli
    (d) Kul Bahadur Gurung

64. Who is the current FIFA president?
    (a) Sepp Blatter   (b) Gianni Infantino
    (c) Issa Hayatou   (d) Durgs

65. who won the 2015 Australian Grand Prix?
    (a) Louis Hamilton   (b) Kimi Raikkonen
    (c) Jenson Button   (d) Sebastian Vettel

66. What are the waves that are used to penetrate solids and are used by doctors and at airports?
    (a) Sound wave   (b) X-rays
    (c) Electro magnetic (d) Mechanical

67. If $(7x + 5)°$ and $(x + 5)°$ are complementary angles, then find value of x.
    (a) 10   (b) 20
    (c) 30   (d) 40

68. Rearrange the jumbled up letters in their natural sequence and find the odd one out.
    (a) EARSUQ   (b) ONGPOYL
    (c) NAEGRCELT   (d) RGETESNH

69. Choose the pair which is related in the same way as the words in the first pair from the given choices
    Savage : Civilized : _________ : _________
    (a) Brutal : Heroic   (b) Wild : Animal
    (c) Dark : Light   (d) Illiterate : Book

70. In a college, 25% of male faculties are same in number as 1/3rd of the female faculties. What is the ratio of male faculty to female faculty in that college?
    (a) 4:3   (b) 3:4
    (c) 2:3   (d) 3:2

71. If A denotes +, B denotes '–', C denotes '÷' D denotes '×' then the value of the expression 9 D 48 C 6 B 16 A 3 is
    (a) 53   (b) 35
    (c) 59   (d) 56

72. What is the process of slow cooling of hot glass called?
    (a) Annealing   (b) Humidifying
    (c) Condensation   (d) Decantation

73. Find the products : 0.5 x 0.05 x 0.005 x 500
    (a) 0.0625   (b) 0.00625
    (c) 0.06255   (d) 0.625

74. Boxing is related to Ring in the same way as Tennis is related to
    (a) Court   (b) Ground
    (c) Pool   (d) Arena

75. Find the degree of the polynomial $8x^4 + 2x^2y^3 + 4$
    (a) 4   (b) 5
    (c) 0   (d) 1

76. In which Schedule to the Constitution of India is the list of States and Union Territories given?
    (a) First Schedule   (b) Second Schedule
    (c) Fourth Schedule   (d) Sixth Schedule

77. In a certain code, TABLE is written as GZYOV, then CHAIR can be written as
    (a) XRZSI   (b) XZSRI
    (c) XSRZI   (d) XSZRI

78. Milk of Magnesia is used as a
    (a) Laxative   (b) Pain killer
    (c) Sedative   (d) Antibiotic

79. In a number system, on dividing 11509 by a certain number, Mukesh gets 71 as quotient and 7 as remainder. What is the divisor?
    (a) 132   (b) 172
    (c) 182   (d) 162

DIRECTIONS (Qs. 80-82): *The table below depicts the Number of Books Sold by 5 cities during 5 months. Study the following table and answer the questions:*

Months	City A	City B	City C	City D	City E
June	213	200	195	253	229
July	156	208	216	187	175
August	177	197	185	181	215
September	220	145	235	265	231
October	253	188	278	243	249

80. If 30% of the total number of books sold by City B, D and E together in July were academic books, how many non - academic books were sold by the same Cities together in the same month?

(a) 379   (b) 389

(c) 399   (d) 309

81. What is the respective ratio between the total number of books sold by City A in July and September together and total number of books sold by City E in August and October together?

(a) 57 : 49   (b) 49 : 57

(c) 58 : 47   (d) 47 : 58

82. What is the average number of books sold by City C in July. September and October together?

(a) 243   (b) 242

(c) 234   (d) 224

83. Find the missing value denoted by '?'

3 : 243 : : 5 : ?

(a) 625   (b) 465

(c) 3125   (d) 425

84. If the standard deviation of a population is 3, what would be the population variance?

(a) 9   (b) 6

(c) 8   (d) 15

85. Below are given statements followed by two conclusions I and II. You have to take the given statements to be true even if they seem to be at variance from commonly known facts.

Statements:

Some buds are flowers.

All flowers are trees.

All trees are leaves.

Conclusions:

I. Some leaves are buds.

II. All flowers are leaves.

Decide which of the below options logically follows the given conclusions.

(a) Only Conclusion I follows

(b) Only Conclusion II follows

(c) Both I and II follow

(d) Neither I nor II follows

86. Find the LCM of the following fractions: 2/3, 8/9, 16/27, 32/81

(a) 32/81   (b) 81/32

(c) 32/3   (d) 11/41

87. In which state is Koyna dam located?

(a) Madhya Pradesh   (b) Rajasthan

(c) Maharashtra   (d) Gujarat

88. Which planet is the nearest in size to Earth?

(a) Mercury   (b) Mars

(c) Venus   (d) Saturn

89. The mean of a distribution is 15 and the standard deviation is 5. What is the value of the coefficient variation?

(a) 16.66%   (b) 66.66%

(c) 33.33%   (d) 100%

90. If S is the midpoint of a straight line PQ and R is a point different from S, such that PR = RQ, then

(a) $\angle PRS = 90°$ (b) $\angle QRS = 90°$

(c) $\angle PSR = 90°$ (d) $\angle QSR < 90°$

91. Who constructed the Hawa Mahal?

(a) Maharaja Bhagvat Singh

(b) Maharaja Jagatjit Singh

(c) Maharaja Sawai Pratap Singh

(d) Maharajah Jaswant Singh

92. If '>' means 'minus', '<' means plus, '*' means multipled by and # means 'divided by', then what would be the value of

27 < 81 # 9 > 6 =

(a) 32   (b) 30

(c) 36   (d) 25

93. Which king's story is the subject of the play Mudrarakshasa?

(a) Jaychand

(b) Chandra Gupta II

(c) Chandrapeeda

(d) Chandragupta Maurya

94. The amount of alcohol in two different medicines is 1.5% and 2.5% respectively. In what ratio they should be mixed such that amount of alcohol in the new mixture is 3.5%?

(a) 1:2   (b) 2:1

(c) 3:2   (d) 2:3

95. who was responsible for building the Great wall of China?
    (a) Qin Shi Huang
    (b) Fa-Hien
    (c) Xuanzang or Hiuen Tsang
    (d) Yijing

96. Martin Crowe who passed away recently was the former cricket captain of which country?
    (a) Australia
    (b) England
    (c) New Zealand
    (d) South Africa

97. If 70% of 5/7th of a number is 90, find the number.
    (a) 150
    (b) 180
    (c) 160
    (d) 190

98. Which among the following is called quicksilver?
    (a) Titanium
    (b) Mercury
    (c) Platinum
    (d) Radium

99. which of the following is a vertebrate?
    (a) Kiwi
    (b) Sponges
    (c) Star fish
    (d) Threadworm

100. Find the total Simple Interest on ₹500 at 7% per annum on ₹ 700 at 10% per annum and on ₹ 1000 at 4% per annum for 3 years.
    (a) 435
    (b) 500
    (c) 700
    (d) 1000

HINTS & EXPLANATIONS

1. (a) Cost price of the pen

$$= \text{selling price} \times \frac{100}{(100 + \text{profit\%})}$$

$$= 36 \times \frac{100}{(100 + 20)}$$

$$= \frac{36 \times 100}{120} = ₹\ 30$$

When selling price = ₹ 33

Then profit % $= \dfrac{(33 - 30)}{30} \times 100$

$= 10\ \%$

2. (a)

3. (b)

SAMR → MARS ⎫
USVNE → VENUS ⎬ There are planets
PUJIERT → JUPITER ⎭

But MOETC → COMET

4. (b)

5. (b)

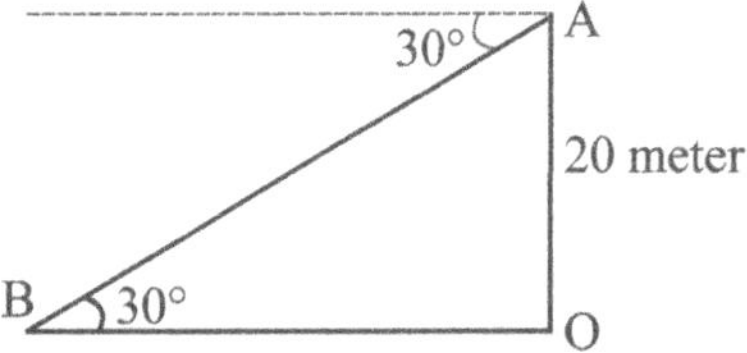

Let, OA is the hight of a light house. and OB is the distance of the ship from the foot of the light house.

So, $\tan \theta = \left[\dfrac{\text{OA}}{\text{OB}}\right]$

Where $\theta = 30°$, OA = 20 meter

$\tan 30° = \dfrac{20}{\text{OB}}$

Hence, Distance (OB) $= \dfrac{20}{\tan 30°}$

$= 20\sqrt{3}$ meter

6. (c) 7. (a)

8. (b) In 1770's or 1780's, Benjamin Franklin, an American polymath invented discovered bifocal glasses.

9. (c) 10. (a) 11. (c) 12. (b) 13. (b)

14. (c) The ratio of the angles are given in the question 1 : 4 : 7

So, ratio of grertest to smallest angle = 7 : 1

15. (b)

16. (c) The 11th observation = Sum of 11 observation – Sum of 10 observation

$= 11 \times 16 - 17 \times 10$

$= 176 - 170$

$= 6$

Hence, the 11th observation is 6.

17. (a)

18. (a) Work done by Arun and Amit in two days when they work alternately starting with Arun

$$= \frac{1}{9} + \frac{1}{12} = \frac{4 + 3}{36} = \frac{7}{36}$$

Work done by them in 10 days, when they works in same ways

$$= \frac{10}{2} \times \frac{7}{36} = \frac{35}{36} \text{ works}$$

Hence, required number of days = 10.

19. (a) Let the
Cost price is 100,
So, Mark Price is 150.
To, earns Profit of 10%
(Selling Price) = 110
Then, Discount = 150 – 110 = 40

Hence, Discount percentage $= \left[\dfrac{40 \times 100}{150}\right]$

$= 26.66 \simeq 27\%$

20. (b) Let the required number be x.

$$\Rightarrow 40 = \left[\frac{7 \times 1}{x \times 1} - 1\right] \times 100$$

$$\Rightarrow 40 = \left[\frac{7 - x}{x}\right] \times 100$$

$$\Rightarrow 40x = (7 - x) \times 100$$

$$\Rightarrow 40x = 700 - 100x$$

$$\Rightarrow 140x = 700$$

$$\Rightarrow x = \left[\frac{700}{140}\right] = 5$$

Hence; He has to sell of 5 pair of Clips for a rupee to get profit of 40%.

21. (c) Here, E = 5

$\Rightarrow$ GUN = 7 + 21 + 14 = 42

$\Rightarrow$ ROSE = 18 + 15 + 19 + 5 = 57

Hence, GATE = 7 + 1 + 20 + 5

$$= 33$$

22. (a)

23. (a) Let, first number is x,

So, second number is $(3x)$

And, third number is $(3x/2)$

Average of the these three number = 66 (given)

So, $$\dfrac{x + 3x + \left(\dfrac{3x}{2}\right)}{3} = 66$$

$$\dfrac{2x + 6x + 3x}{6} = 66$$

$11x = 66 \times 6$

$x = 6 \times 6$

$\quad = 36$

Hence, first number $x = 36$

24. (b) The length of the circular track (L) = $\pi \times$ d.

$$(L) = \pi \,.\, 28 \text{ m}$$

As we know that,

When two person A and B, running around a circular track of length L meters. with speed of P, Q m/s in the same direction, then they meet each other at any point on the track

= L / (P – Q) sec.

$$= \frac{\pi \times 28}{[48 - 40]} = \frac{22 \times 28}{7 \times 8} = 11 \text{ seconds.}$$

25. (a)

Sol. (26-28):

By using Venn diagram:

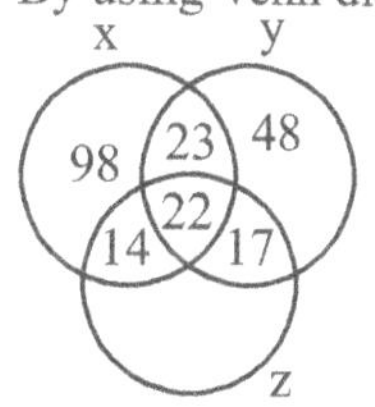

26. (a) This figure shows the x is the most popular one.

27. (c) Number of products only (z) = 274 – 157 – 48 –17 = 52

28. (b) Friction used at least two products

$$\frac{22 + 23 + 14 + 17}{274} = \frac{76}{274}$$

29. (a) As we know that,

The length of the train or distance traveled by the train while overtaking the bike

= Relative speed between the train and bike × time taken.

Where,

Relative speed between the train and bike

= Difference between their relative speeds.

= (90 – 36) = 54 kmph

So, Distance traveled by the train while overtaking the bike

= 54 kmph × 25 seconds

$$= 54 \times \frac{5}{18} \times 25$$

= 375 meter

30. (a) If EFMIJ means DELHI, It means each letter is moved one step backward.

So, the last letter of the word got by decoding IQBOS is R.

31. (b) White clothes are good reflectors of heat because light colours reflect maximum amount of heat and make us feel cool, and hence, they are worn in summers.

32. (d) The relationship between these two numbers is $x^2 : x^3$

Hence, the correct relation of second ratio is : 81 : 729.

33. (c)

34. (d) As given that

$$x + \frac{1}{x} = 15$$

Then, $x^2 + 1 = 15\,x$, By multiply by 5, then

$$5x^2 + 5 = 75x \quad ....(i)$$

$$\Rightarrow \frac{5x}{(5x^2 - 20x + 5)}$$

$$\Rightarrow \frac{5x}{(5x^2 + 5 - 20x)}$$

By Putting the value of $5x^2 + 5$ from equation (i) in above expression

$$\Rightarrow \left[\frac{5x}{75x - 20x}\right] = \frac{5}{55}$$

$$= \frac{1}{11}$$

35. (d)

36. (c) By taking the L.C.M of 15, 18, 27 and 30 is 270

The largest three digit number is 999.

Now, we will divide this number by LCM of 15, 18, 27, and 30, we will get,

$\Rightarrow$ 999/270 will get remainder 89

Now, 999 – 89 = 810

Now, we will check it out for the number we will get

$\Rightarrow$ 810/15 = 54

$\Rightarrow$ 810/18 = 45

$\Rightarrow$ 810/27 = 30

$\Rightarrow$ 810/30 = 27

Hence, the largest number of three digit that exactly divisible by 15, 18, 27 and 30 is 810.

37. (a)

38. (c) As given that,

$$x + \frac{1}{x} = 2$$

By taking cube

$$\Rightarrow \left(x + \frac{1}{x}\right)^3 = 2^3$$

$$\Rightarrow x^3 + \frac{1}{x^3} + 3\left[x + \frac{1}{x}\right] = 8$$

$$\Rightarrow x^3 + \frac{1}{x^3} + 3[2] = 8$$

$$\Rightarrow x^3 + \frac{1}{x^3} = 2 \qquad \qquad ...(i)$$

Now taking square both side

$$\left(x^3 + \frac{1}{x^3}\right)^2 = x^6 + \frac{1}{x^6} + 2$$

By equation (i)

$$x^6 + \frac{1}{x^6} = 4 - 2 = 2 \qquad ...(ii)$$

$$\Rightarrow \left(x^6 + \frac{1}{x^6}\right)^3 = (x^6)^3 + \frac{1}{(x^6)^3} + 3\left[x^6 + \frac{1}{x^6}\right]$$

$[\therefore$ By equation (2)]

$$x^{18} + \frac{1}{x^{18}} = 8 - 6 = 2$$

So, The value of $\left(x^3 + \frac{1}{x^3}\right) \Big/ \left(x^{18} + \frac{1}{x^{18}}\right)$

$\Rightarrow$ 2/2 = 1

39. (c) As given that

Principle = 2000,

Rate = 8.25%

Time = March 9, 2010 to May 21, 2010 = 73 days

$$= \left[\frac{73}{365}\right] \text{ years.}$$

So, simple Interest $= \dfrac{P \times R \times T}{100}$

$$= \left[\frac{2000 \times 8.25 \times 75}{365 \times 100}\right]$$

$$= ₹ 33$$

40. (d) Let the height of tower is AB.

As given that

The Distance of point C from the foot of tower is

So, BC = 25 m.

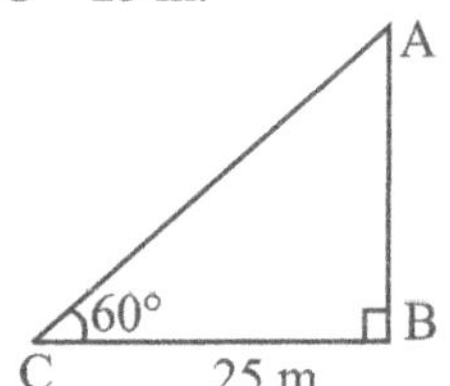

Angle of elevation = 60°

Since, tower is vertical so $\angle ABC = 90°$

So, In right angle triangle ABC,

$$\tan 60° = \frac{AB}{25}$$

AB = 25 × tan 60°

$$= 25\sqrt{3} \quad 43.3 \text{ meter.}$$

Hence, the Approximate height of the tower is 43.3 meters.

41. (b) **42. (a)** **43. (b)**

44. (a) As given that, @ means +, # means –,

$ means × and * means ÷, then

The value of given expression is:

$\Rightarrow$ 16 @ 4 $ 5 # 72 * 8

$\Rightarrow$ 16 + 4 × 5 – 72 ÷ 8

$\Rightarrow$ 16 + 20 – 9 = 27

45. (c) Let, present value of Vikah's is x,

Present value of Rahul is y,

4, year ago, $\dfrac{x-4}{y-4} = \dfrac{3}{5}$

$5x - 20 = 3y - 12$

$5x - 3y = -12 + 20$

$5x - 3y = 8 \qquad ...(i)$

Also After 6 year,

$\dfrac{x+6}{y+6} = \dfrac{4}{5} \Rightarrow 5x + 30 = 4y + 24$

$5x - 4y = -6 \qquad\qquad ...(ii)$

By substrating Equation (ii) from equation (i), we will get y = 14

46. (a)

P R O M O T I O N
↓ ↓ ↓ ↓ ↓ ↓ ↓ ↓ ↓
3 6 5 4 5 8 9 5 7
M O N Z   T O R
↓ ↓ ↓ ↓   ↓ ↓ ↓
4 5 7 9   8 5 6

47. (a) As given that,

'+' means × (multiplication)

'–' means ÷ (division)

'×' means – (Subtraction)

'÷' means + (Addition)

Then,

$\Rightarrow 9 + 8 \div 8 - 4 \times 9$

$\Rightarrow 9 \times 8 + 8 \div 4 - 9$

$\Rightarrow 74 - 9 = 65$

48. (a) NASA astronaut and Expedition 46 Commander Scott Kelly spent 340 days on the International Space Station (ISS) between 2015 and 2016.

49. (b) **50. (c)** **51. (c)**

52. (d) According to given question :

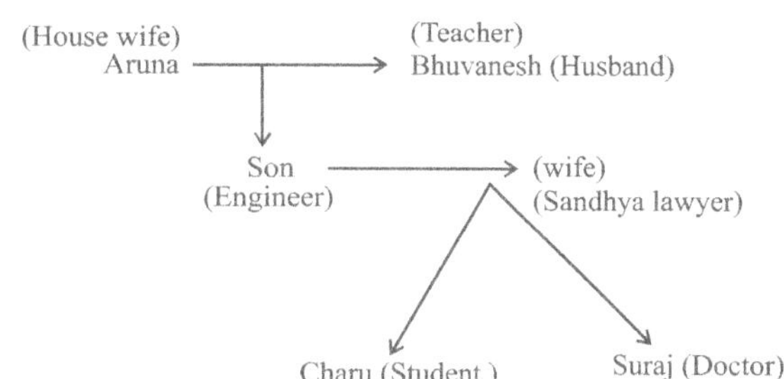

'According to above diagram, Aruna is a grandmother of Charu.

53. (b) According to above diagram of 52 Question. Aruna is a house wife.

54. (c) According to the above diagram of 52 Question Charu is a grand daughter in the family.

55. (*)

56. (a) Deficiency of the essential vitamins is usually a result of poor dietary habits like low intake of fruits and vegetables. Deficiency of vitamins can lead to various diseases such as rickets, scurvy, night blindness, beriberi, etc. Beriberi is a disease caused by the deficiency of vitamin B1.

57. (b)

58. (a) Work done by one man in 1 day = 1/80

Work done by 12 men in 1 day = 12/80

$= \dfrac{3}{20}$

Work done by 12 men and 16 women in 1 day $= \dfrac{1}{4}$

So, Work done by 16 woman in 1 day

$= \left[\dfrac{1}{4} - \dfrac{3}{20}\right]$

$= \left[\dfrac{5-3}{20}\right]$

$= \dfrac{1}{10}$

Work done, by 1 women in 1 day $= \dfrac{1}{10 \times 16}$

$= \dfrac{1}{160}$

Hence, one woman alone needs 160 days to complete the work.

59. (b) Let, feroz capital = ₹ x

Then Amit capital = ₹ $\left(\dfrac{3}{4}\right)x$

And Jalal capital = $4 \times \left(\dfrac{3}{4}\right)x = ₹3x$

Now, ratio of their capitals = $3x : \dfrac{3}{4}x : x$

$$= 12 : 3 : 4$$

Hence, Jalal share = $19000 \times 12/19 = ₹12000$

60. (d) In total 12 people have walked on the moon. These 12 people are Neil Armstrong, Buzz Aldrin, Pete Conrad, Alan Bean, Alan Shepard, Edgar Mitchell, David Scott, James Irwin, John Young, Charles Duke, Eugene Cernan, and Harrison Schmitt.

61. (b)

62. (d) Leakages in household gas cylinders can be detected because of the strong smell of ethyl merceptan mixed with L.P.G.

63. (c) 64. (b) 65. (a)

66. (d) Leakages in houshold gas cylinders can be detected because of the strong smell of Ethyl Mercaptan or Ethanethiol mixed with LPG.

67. (a) As given that,

$(7x + 5)°$ and $(x + 5)°$ are complementary angles

As we know that,

Complementary angles are those angles whose sum equals to 90°

So, $7x + 5 + x + 5 = 90°$

$8x + 10 = 90°$

$8x = 80°$

$x = 10°$

Hence, option (a) is correct.

68. (d) options (a) SQUARE (b) POLYGON (c) RECTANGLE all are the geometrical figure and option (d) GREENTS is not related to geometrical figure.

Hence option (d) is odd one out.

69. (c)

70. (d) Let x denote the number of males faculties and y denote the number of female faculties

Then, According to Question,

$$\frac{25x}{100} = \frac{y}{3}$$

$$\frac{x}{y} = \frac{100}{75} = \frac{4}{3}$$

Hence, required ratio is 4 : 3

71. (c) As, given that,
A denote '+'
B denote '−'
C denote '÷'
D denote ' ×'
Then,
The value of given expression

$$\begin{aligned}
&= \quad 9D48C6B16A3 \\
&= \quad 9×48 ÷ 6 - 16 + 3 \\
&= \quad 9 \times 8 - 16 + 3 \\
&= \quad 56 + 3 = 59
\end{aligned}$$

72. (a) Annealing is a process of slowly cooling hot glass objects after they have been manufactured to reduce the residual internal stress which is introduced during manufacturing. To anneal glass, it is necessary to heat it to its annealing temperature.

73. (a) The Required value of given expression

$$\begin{aligned}
&= 0.5 \times 0.05 \times 0.005 \times 500 \\
&= \quad 0.025 \times 0.005 \times 500 \\
&= 0.000125 \times 500 \\
&= 0.0625
\end{aligned}$$

74. (a)

75. (b) As given that,
The Polynomial equation is
$8x^4 + 2x^2 y^3 + 4$
As we know that,
The degree of a polynomial is equal to the highest degree of any individual term with in the polynomial.
So, the degree of a term is found by adding together the exponents of the variable's with in term
$8x^4$ has a degree = 4
$2x^2 y^3$ has degree = $(2 + 3) = 5$
Hence, the highest degree of any individual term within this polynomial is 5, so the degree of the polynomial is also 5.

76. (a)

77. (d) As given that
In a certain code, TABLE is written as GZYOV

In this code, a letter is the nth letter from the beginning of English alphabet then in that code the corresponding letter is the nth letter from the end.

Hence, CHAIR is written as XSZRI.

78. (a) Milk of Magnesia, also known as magnesium hydroxide, is used as a laxative to relieve occasional constipation. It is also used to treat symptoms caused by too much stomach acid such as heartburn or upset stomach.

79. (d) As given that N = 11509, q = 71, r = 7

As we know that,

Numbers = d × q + r

11509 = d × 71 + 7

So, $d = \left[\dfrac{(11507-7)}{71}\right] = \left[\dfrac{11502}{71}\right] = 162$

80. (c) As given that

Total number of books sold by city B, city D, City E in July is = 208 + 187 + 175

= 570

Number of academic book

$= \dfrac{570 \times 30}{100} = 171$

Hence, the number of non - academic book

= 570 – 171

= 399

81. (d) Number of books sold by city A in July & September = 156 + 220

= 376

So,

Number of books sold by city E in August and October = 215 + 249

= 464

Hence, required ratio $= \dfrac{376}{464} = \dfrac{47}{58}$

82. (a) Average number of books sold by city C in July, September and October is

$= \dfrac{216 + 235 + 278}{3}$

$= \dfrac{729}{3} = 243$

83. (a) The relationship between these two given numbers is $x : x^5$.

Hence, the correct relation of second ratio is 5 : 3125

84. (a) As we know that

The population variance = [standard deviation of a population]^2

So, Population variance = $(3)^2 = 9$

Hence option (a) is correct.

85. (c)

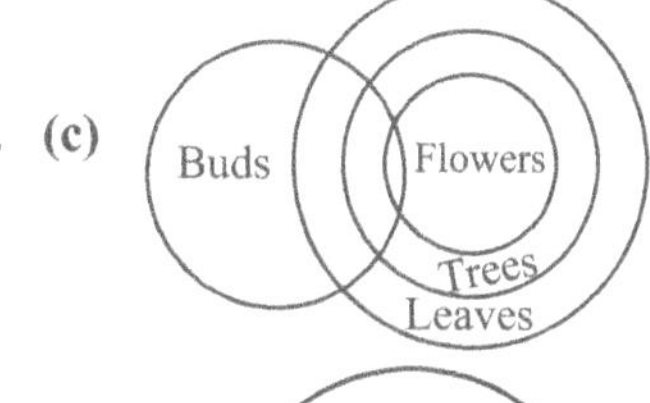

or

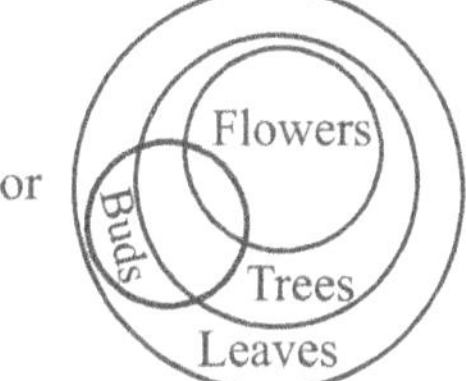

or

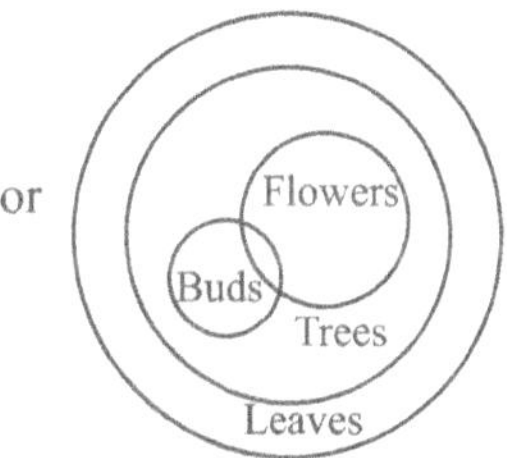

Hence option (c) is correct

86. (c) As we know that,

$LCM\,of\,fractions = \left[\dfrac{LCM\,of\,numerators}{HCF\,of\,denominators}\right]$

$= \left[\dfrac{LCM(2,8,16,32)}{HCF(3,9,27,81)}\right]$

$= \left[\dfrac{32}{3}\right]$

Hence option (c) is correct.

87. (c) 88. (c)

89. (c) As we know that,

The coefficient of variation of a sample or population is the standard deviation divided by the mean.

So, coefficient of variation $= \dfrac{5}{15} = \dfrac{1}{3}$

$= 0.3333$

% of coefficient of variation is 33.33%.

90. (c) According to the Question, If S is the mid point of straight line PQ, and R different from S.

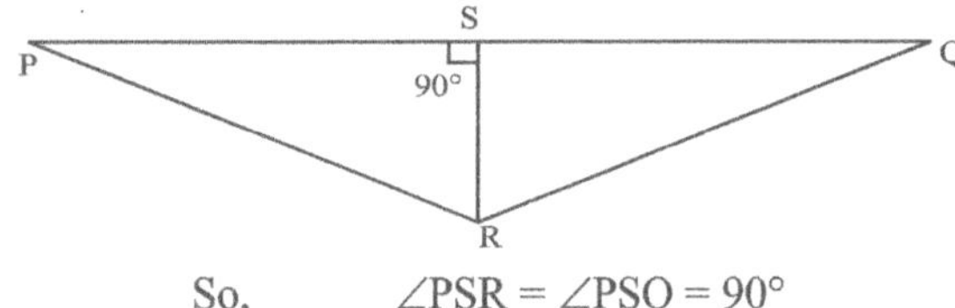

So, $\angle PSR = \angle PSQ = 90°$

Hence option (c) is correct

91. (c)

92. (b) After exchanging the values.

$$27 < 81 \# 9 > 6 = 27 + 81 \div 9 - 6$$
$$= 27 + 9 - 6$$
$$= 36 - 6$$
$$= 30.$$

93. (d)

94. (a) According to the given question:

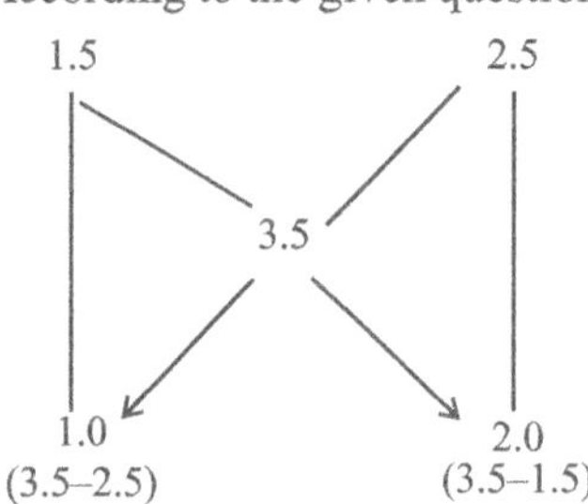

Hence the required ratio is 1 : 2

95. (a)   96. (c)

97. (b) $0.70 \times \dfrac{5}{7}x = 90$

$$\dfrac{5}{7}x = \dfrac{90}{0.70}$$

$$x = \dfrac{90 \times 7 \times 100}{70 \times 5}$$

$$= \dfrac{900}{5} = 180$$

98. (b)   99. (a)

100. (a) Total S.I

$$= \left[\dfrac{500 \times 7 \times 1}{100} + \dfrac{700 \times 10 \times 1}{100} + \dfrac{1000 \times 4 \times 1}{100}\right]$$

$$= 35 + 70 + 40$$
$$= 145 \text{ per annum}$$

$\therefore$ Total S.I for 3 year $= 145 \times 3 = 435$

RRB NTPC STAGE-I SOLVED PAPER-12
Held On 16ᵗʰ April 2016 (Shift 3)

1. Who founded Twitter?
   (a) Mark Zuckerberg
   (b) Tim Cook
   (c) Noah Ark
   (d) Evan Williams

2. An Assertion (A) and a Reason (R) are given below.
   Assertion (A): In India, females have higher life expectancy than the males.
   Reason (R): Females receive a better diet.
   Choose the correct option.
   (a) A is true but R is false.
   (b) A is false but R is true.
   (c) Both A and R are true
   (d) Both A and R are false.

3. Vikash purchased 5 bananas for Rs. 4 and sold 4 bananas for Rs. 5. Calculate his % profit?
   (a) 55.56%   (b) 53.25%
   (c) 45.50%   (d) 56.25%

4. Which State in India has the highest forest cover?
   (a) Kerala
   (b) Madhya Pradesh
   (c) Maharashtra
   (d) Bihar

5. Based on the analogy given, find the missing word from the given options.
   Butter : Milk : : Book : ________
   (a) Author   (b) Paper
   (c) Chapter   (d) Printing

6. ________________ is a unit of length, roughly the distance from Earth to the Sun.
   (a) Light years
   (b) Astronomical unit
   (c) Kelvin
   (d) Joule

7. What is the name of the process where gas is directly converted to solids called?
   (a) Sublimation   (b) Deposition
   (c) Condensation   (d) Evaporation

8. In which city is the newly proposed AIIMS to be setup in Maharashtra?
   (a) Nagpur   (b) Mumbai
   (c) Aurangabad   (d) Pune

9. Which vaccine is primarily used against tuberculosis?
   (a) BCG   (b) DPT
   (c) HiB   (d) Varicella

10. Based on the analogy given, find the missing pair from the given options. 5 : 35 : : ___ : ___
    (a) 11 : 55   (b) 7 : 49
    (c) 3 : 24   (d) 9 : 45

11. Consider the following statement and select the correct option:
    1. It is possible to draw at least 3 straight line from given 2 points.
    2. If angle of one side is parallel to angle of other side than both the angle is neither equal nor supplementary.
    (a) 1 and 2 both are not right.
    (b) 1 and 2 both are right
    (c) 1 is wrong and 2 is right.
    (d) 1 is right and 2 is wrong.

12. An Assertion (A) and a Reason (R) are given below.
    Assertion (A): Simla is colder than Delhi.
    Reason (R): Simla is at a higher altitude as compared to Delhi. Choose the correct option.
    (a) A is true but R is false.
    (b) A is false but R is true.
    (c) Both A and R are true and R is the correct explanation of A.
    (d) Both A and R are true but R is not the correct explanation of A.

DIRECTIONS (Qs. 13-15): *Study the following information carefully and answer the questions given below it.*

There are six persons in a family - three males and three females. Out of these, there are two married couples and two persons who are unmarried. Each one of them likes different colour, viz. Blue, Red, Pink, Green, Yellow and White.

Seema, who likes Red colour, is Anitha's mother-in-law and Anitha is Raja's wife. Dinesh is Rohan's father and he does not like the blue colour or White colour. Bavya likes the Yellow colour and is Rohan's sister, who likes Pink colour, Raja does not use white colour.

13. Which of the following is one of the married couples?
    (a) Rohan – Bavya
    (b) Dinesh – Bavya
    (c) Dinesh – Seema
    (d) Rohan – Seema

14. Which of the following colours is liked by Anitha?
    (a) White   (b) Yellow
    (c) Pink   (d) Green

15. How is Rohan related to Seema?
    (a) Brother   (b) Son
    (c) Father   (d) None of these

16. If DRIVER is coded as 5 and BELIEVED is
    (a) 9   (b) 7
    (c) 11   (d) 8

17. Anil can do a piece of work in 14 days which Rohit can do in 21 days. They worked together for few days after which Anil left. If Rohit worked alone for 3 days, find the total number of days it took to complete the whole work.
    (a) 31/5   (b) 51/5
    (c) 21/5   (d) 13/5

18. Rearrange the jumbled up letters to form a meaningful word and find the odd one out.
    (a) ESAEIDS   (b) EAHLTH
    (c) LISESNL   (d) CKSESNS

19. If A:B = 3:4 and B:C = 6:5 then A:(A+C) is:
    (a) 9:11   (b) 9:10
    (c) 9:19   (d) 6:7

20. If two complimentary angles are in the ratio of 11:7, find the smaller angle.
    (a) 35°   (b) 55°
    (c) 45°   (d) 25°

21. what does TCP stand for with respect to computer networks?
    (a) Transmission Control Protocol
    (b) Transfer Call Plan
    (c) Transfer Control Process
    (d) Transmission Call Protocol

22. 30 litres of salt solution contains 5% salt. How many litres of water must be added so as to get a resultant solution containing 3% salt?
    (a) 20 litres   (b) 25 litres
    (c) 30 litres   (d) 35 litres

23. If DI JOB means CHINA, then the last letter of the word got by decoding KBQBO is
    (a) I   (b) A
    (c) M   (d) N

24. Below are given statements followed by two conclusions I and II. You have to take the given statements to be true even if they seem to be at variance from commonly known facts.
    Statements: All birds are tall. Some tall are peacocks.
    Conclusions:
    I. Some birds are peacocks.
    II. Some peacocks are tall.
    Decide which of the below options logically follows the given Statement.
    (a) Both conclusions I and II follows
    (b) Neither conclusion I nor II follows
    (c) Only conclusion I follows
    (d) Only conclusion II follows

25. If the length of the shadow of a vertical pole on the horizontal ground is $\sqrt{3}$ times its height, then the angle of elevation
    (a) 40°   (b) 50°
    (c) 30°   (d) 45°

26. On which river is the city Madurai situated?
    (a) Cooum   (b) Kaveri
    (c) Vaigai   (d) Pennar

27. Engineer is related to Engineering in the same way as Doctor is related to
    (a) Medicine   (b) Hospital
    (c) Disease   (d) Body

28. Which of the following Prime Ministers was awarded Bharat Ratna?
    (a) V. P. Singh
    (b) Moraiji Desai
    (c) Charan Singh
    (d) Manmohan Singh

29. How much salt is present in our body?
    (a) 1%   (b) 2%
    (c) 0.4%   (d) 0.6%

30. What is the old name of Singapore?
    (a) Temasek   (b) Myanmar
    (c) Ceylon   (d) Bohemia

31. If the angles of a triangle are in the ratio of 2:5:8, then find the value of the largest angle.
    (a) 36°   (b) 96°
    (c) 84°   (d) 60°

32. What is the name of the moon of Pluto?
    (a) Charon   (b) Ganymede
    (c) Luna   (d) Triton

33. If GOAT can be written as KSEX, then WOLF can be written as _______
    (a) APJS   (b) AJSP
    (c) ASPJ   (d) ASSJ

34. Find the unit digit in the given product $(4211)^{102} \times (361)^{52}$
(a) 3   (b) 1
(c) 4   (d) 7

35. The traffic lights at four different road crossings change after every 15sec, 18sec, 27sec and 30 sec respectively. If they all change simultaneously at 6:10:00 hours, then at what time will they again change simultaneously?
(a) 6:14:30 hours
(b) 6:40:00 hours
(c) 6:14:00 hours
(d) 10:40:00 hours

36. The mean of a distribution is 21 and the standard deviation is 7. What is the value of the coefficient variation?
(a) 16.66%   (b) 66.66%
(c) 33.33%   (d) 100%

37. Michael Schumacher, a racing driver belongs to which country?
(a) USA   (b) Germany
(c) Canada   (d) Australia

38. Choose the one which is odd from the following options:
(a) Rupee   (b) Lira
(c) Coin   (d) Dinar

39. What was the element used in traditional thermometers which is highly toxic in nature?
(a) Carbon   (b) Mercury
(c) Arsenic   (d) Cadmium

40. Which of the following was built by the ancient Incas?
(a) City of Petra
(b) Hagia Sophia
(c) Machu Picchu
(d) Acropolis

41. In which year was the Aam Aadmi Party founded?
(a) 2010   (b) 2011
(c) 2012   (d) 2013

42. A spoon which looks bent is
(a) Reflection   (b) Refraction
(c) Retention   (d) Focus

43. Who discovered radioactivity?
(a) Max Planck
(b) James Clerk Maxwell
(c) Henri Becquerel
(d) Heinrich Hertz

44. What is special about a sword-billed hummingbird?
(a) It is the smallest bird in the world
(b) Its bill is longer than rest of its body
(c) It lives only in Antarctica
(d) It cannot fly

45. A boy running at 10/9th of his actual speed covers 39 km in 2 hours 20 minutes and 24 seconds. Find the actual speed of the boy (approx.).
(a) 15 km/hr.   (b) 50 km/hr.
(c) 39 km/hr.   (d) 150 km/hr.

46. who devised the policy of Doctrine of Lapse?
(a) Lord Curzon
(b) Lord Mountbatten
(c) Lord Dalhousie
(d) Robert Clive

47. Sonam's age after eight years will be half of her father's age. Eight years ago the ratio of their ages was 1: 3. Find the present age of Sonam's father.
(a) 48   (b) 56
(c) 36   (d) 65

48. Mohan earns a profit of 20% on selling a jean at 15% discount on printed price. The ratio of the cost price to printed price of the jean is
(a) 17:24   (b) 17:34
(c) 16:13   (d) 21:23

49. In accordance to the 18th Mercer Quality of Life study, which city in the World holds the first position as the best city to live in?
(a) Zurich   (b) Vienna
(c) Sydney   (d) Hyderabad

50. When was the battle of Chillianwala fought?
(a) 1865   (b) 1892
(c) 1849   (d) 1856

51. If 'W' means 'x', 'X' means '−', 'Y' means '+' and 'z' means '÷', then
28 Z 7 W 8 X 6 Y 4 = ?
(a) 30   (b) 3/2
(c) 32   (d) 34

52. If '<' stands for '−', '>' stands for '+', '+' stands for 'x' and '@' stands for '÷' then what will be the value of 27 > 81 @ 9 < 6
(a) 32   (b) 33
(c) 30   (d) 35

53. If 'x' means '−', '−' means 'x', '+' means '÷' and '÷' means '+', then what will be the value for 15 − 2 ÷ 900 + 90 x100?

(a) 60 (b) –60
(c) 0 (d) 1

54. A boy in a train notices that he can count 31 telephone posts in 60 seconds. The distance between two posts is 60 metres. Calculate the speed of the train?
(a) 90 km/hr (b) 108 km/hr
(c) 60 km/hr (d) 120 km/hr

55. Which of the following is a temple built out of marble by Vimal Shah?
(a) The Dilwara temple
(b) Brihadeeswarar temple
(c) Omkareswar temple
(d) Ranakpur Adinath temple

56. Who was the first Indian Badminton player to win the men's singles title at the All England Championship in 1980?
(a) Prakash Padukone
(b) Pullela Gopichand
(c) Syed Modi
(d) Chetan Anand

57. who won the Academy award for documentary 'Amy' in 2016?
(a) Duke Johnson (b) Asif Kapadia
(c) Steven Spielberg (d) Georae Miller

58. What is income available with a person after deducting for taxes called?
(a) Disposable Income
(b) Cash Income
(c) Salary
(d) General Income

59. Which of the following was the first super computer developed in 1976?
(a) Acom Atom (b) Cray-1
(c) PCW (d) PET

60. The average of five consecutive even numbers is 40. What is the value of smallest of these numbers?
(a) 35 (b) 36
(c) 44 (d) 48

61. Which series is India's First Supercomputer developed in Pune?
(a) Vigyan (b) Param
(c) Dhanush (d) Shakti

62. A sum of money (P) doubles in 10 years. How much would it be in 20 years at the same rate of simple interest? |
(a) P (b) 2P
(c) 3P (d) 4P

63. If $(a + c + 1) = 0$. then find the value of $(a^3 + c^3 + 1 - 3ac)$
(a) –1 (b) 1
(c) 2 (d) 0

64. Based on the analogy given, find the missing number from the given options.
49 : 81 : : 100 : ___
(a) 144 (b) 169
(c) 225 (d) 64

65. If $(x + y)^2 - xy = 0$, then find the value of $(x^3 - y^3)/(x - y)$.
(a) 2 (b) 3
(c) 0 (d) 5

66. One of four words is a class of which the other three belong. Identify the class.
(a) NOVELS (b) BOOKS
(c) POEMS (d) SHORT STORIES

67. A ladder is kept along a straight wall. The top of the ladder is at a distance of 9 m from the floor. When the bottom of the ladder is moved 3 m away then the two distances becomes equal. What is the length of the ladder?
(a) 16 m (b) 15 m
(c) 20 m (d) 30 m

68. Who propounded the homeopathic principle of 'like cures like'?
(a) Hippocrates (b) Samuel Hahnemann
(c) Samuel Cockburn (d) George Vithoulkas

DIRECTIONS Qs. (69-71): *Study the following table carefully and answer the questions based on it.*

The following table shows the domestic sales of cars of five manufacturers from 2005 to 2010.
(All the figures are in thousands)

Manufacturer	2005	2006	2007	2008	2009	2010
L	440	480	470	500	520	510
M	400	410	415	415	420	430
N	380	390	390	400	420	495
O	360	380	400	415	440	500
P	480	440	440	420	425	435

69. During 2006. what is the approximate share domestic sales of cars of the manufacturer M?
(a) 19.5% (b) 10.5%
(c) 20.5% (d) 25.5%

70. During 2010, the sales of which manufacturer has shown the maximum percentage increase over the previous year?
(a) L (b) M
(c) N (d) P

71. With respect to which of the following combinations, is the sales of cars the highest over the given period?
(a) L, 2009
(b) L, 2010
(c) L, 2008
(d) O, 2008

72. Which one of the following interchanges in signs and numbers would make the given equation correct?
$3 + 5 - 2 = 4$
(a) + and –, 2 and 5
(b) + and –, 3 and 4
(c) + and –, 2 and 4
(d) + and –, 3 and 5

73. Which dynasty had its capital at Chittorgarh?
(a) Chauhan
(b) Sisodia
(c) Hada
(d) Rathor

74. with which sport is the term 'Freestyle' connected with?
(a) Tennis
(b) Kho Kho
(c) Kabaddi
(d) Swimming

75. Atul and Binay together complete a piece of work in 5 days. If Binay alone can complete the same work in 8 days, how many days can Atul take to complete the same work alone?
(a) 40/3 days
(b) 20/3 days
(c) 9 days
(d) 10 days

76. Below, an assertion (A) and a reason (R) is given.
Assertion (A): In India, a rapid increase in the users of Smartphones is seen.
Reason (R): Best 3G and 4G services are available at low price.
Choose the right option.
(a) A is correct but R is wrong.
(b) A is wrong but R is correct.
(c) Both A and R are correct. R is the appropriate explanation of A .
(d) Both A and R are correct but – R is not the appropriate explanation of A.

77. Find the dividend if the divisor is $(x + 2)$. quotient is $(4x - 5)$ and the remainder is 12
(a) $4x^2 + 5x + 2$
(b) $4x^2 + 3x + 2$
(c) $4x^2 - 3x + 2$
(d) $4x^2 + 3x - 2$

78. Who is considered the greatest of the early Chola kings?
(a) Pulakeshi II
(b) Rajasimha
(c) Karikala
(d) Nandivarman

79. The mass per unit volume is called
(a) Force
(b) Work
(c) Density
(d) Pressure

80. The BRICS Development Bank is now called as
(a) Asia Development Bank
(b) World Bank
(c) New Development Bank
(d) New BRICS Bank

81. If MACHINE is coded as 19-7-9-14-15-20-11, how will you code DANGER?
(a) 10-7-20-13-11-24
(b) 13-7-20-11-10-25
(c) 11-7-20-16-11-24
(d) 13-7-20-9-11-25

82. What sum will produce the same interest in 9 years at the rate 8% simple interest as ₹ 800 produce in 3 years at 9/2% per annum?
(a) ₹ 100
(b) ₹ 125
(c) ₹ 150
(d) ₹ 110

83. Which among the following is not a qualification to become a Vice President of India?
(a) Citizen of India
(b) Above 35 years of age
(c) Possess the Membership of Lok Sabha
(d) Possess the Membership of Rajya Sabha

DIRECTIONS Qs. (84-86): *The following questions are based on the information given below:*

Out of a group of 60 students. 25 play Cricket, 30 play Football. 24 play Volleyball, 10 play Cricket and Football, 9 play Cricket and Volleyball, 12 play Volleyball and Football and 5 play all the three.

84. How many students play exactly two games?
(a) 7
(b) 13
(c) 5
(d) 16

85. How many students do not play any one of the games?
(a) 5
(b) 2
(c) 7
(d) 1

86. How many students play Cricket only?
(a) 11
(b) 13
(c) 8
(d) 5

87. Choose the pair which is related in the same way as the words in the first pair from the given choices Moon : Satellite : : Earth : _______
(a) Air
(b) Planet
(c) Sun
(d) Sea

88. Naveen purchased a gas cylinder and a stove for ₹4500. He sold the gas cylinder at a gain of 25% and the stove at a loss of 20%, still gaining 4% on the whole. Find the cost of the gas cylinder.

(a) ₹3600   (b) ₹2400
(c) ₹3000   (d) ₹2600

89. The name of our planet Earth originates from which language?
(a) Greek   (b) Roman
(c) English   (d) Sanskrit

90. Which of the following is a good source of Vitamin A?
(a) Cabbage   (b) Carrot
(c) Regular Potato   (d) Strawberry

91. In new government policy, the price of onion is raised by 35%. By what % should a person reduce onion consumption so that the expenditure on it does not increase?
(a) 25%   (b) 29%
(c) 26%   (d) 33%

92. The mean of 10 observations is 13. Two more observations are included and the new mean becomes 14. The mean of two new observations is
(a) 19   (b) 18
(c) 17   (d) 16

93. If the standard deviation of a population is 6.5, what would be the population variance?
(a) 40.25   (b) 42.25
(c) 18.25   (d) 13

94. Rearrange the jumbled up letters to form a meaningful word and find the odd one out.
(a) ROUWBR   (b) EDN
(c) OREO   (d) ETNS

95. How many natural numbers between 15 and 85 are divisible by 7?
(a) 9   (b) 10
(c) 8   (d) 7

96. Who proposed the Scientific Management School of thought as opposed to the Administrative Management School of thought?
(a) Henry Fayol
(b) Frederick Taylor
(c) Peter Drucker
(d) Max Weber

97. who discovered the ABO blood group system?
(a) Karl Roller
(b) Maurice Hilleman
(c) Karl Landsteiner
(d) Edward Jenner

98. Which value is closest to [5.168 x 4453 x 3.194 / 67.999 x 4224.017]
(a) 0.2   (b) 0.002
(c) 2   (d) 0.02

99. HCF of two numbers is 19 and their LCM is 665. If one of the number is 95, find the other.
(a) 19   (b) 133
(c) 190   (d) 77

100. Which of the following states in India has the highest area under mangroves?
(a) Gujarat   (b) Andhra Pradesh
(c) Maharashtra   (d) West Bengal

HINTS & EXPLANATIONS

1. (d)

2. (d) In India, due to high birth rate and due to neglect females have a lower life expectancy as compared to males and although females need a better diet, they do not receive.

3. (d) Vikash buy 5 bananas fof 4 rupees.

Vikas buy 1 bananas for $\dfrac{4}{5}$ rupees

Vikas sold, 4 bananas for 5 rupees.

Vikas sold, 1 bananas for $\dfrac{5}{4}$ rupees.

Gain = (S.P. – C.P.)

$$= \dfrac{5}{4} - \dfrac{4}{5}$$

$$= \dfrac{25-16}{20} = \dfrac{9}{20}$$

$$\text{Gain\%} = \left[\dfrac{\text{Gain} \times 100}{\text{C.P}}\right] = \left[\dfrac{\dfrac{9}{20} \times 100}{\dfrac{4}{5}}\right]$$

$$= \dfrac{45 \times 5}{4} = \dfrac{225}{4} = 56.25\%$$

4. (b)

5. (b) Just like, butter is made from milk, similarly Book is made from Paper.

6. (b) The Astronomical Unit (AU) is a unit of length which is used to measure the distance from Earth to the Sun. The AU has been defined as 149,597,870,700 meters (92,955,807 miles).

7. (b) The process of conversion of gas directly to solid state is called deposition. It is the reverse of sublimation, which is transition of a substance directly from solid to gaseous state

8. (a)

9. (a) BCG or bacille Calmette-Guerin vaccine is primarily used against tuberculosis (TB) disease. It was first used in 1921.

10. (b) $\dfrac{35}{5} = \dfrac{x}{7}$

$$= x = \dfrac{35 \times 7}{5} = 49$$

11. (a)

12. (c) The places at higher altitudes are colder because as you go up in the atmosphere, the pressure decreases. It is this lower pressure at higher altitudes that causes the temperature to be colder on top of a mountain. Shimla is at higher altitude as compared to Delhi, and hence, is colder than Delhi.

Sol. (13-15):

Family Member	Colour	Relationship
Seema	Red	Dinesh's wife
Dinesh	Green	
Bavya	Yellow	Rohan's sister
Anitha	White	Raja's wife
Raja	Blue	
Rohan	Pink	Dinesh's son

{Dinesh, Seema} and {Raja, Anitha} are married couple.
Rohan and Bavya are brother, sister and children of Dinesh.

13. (c) Dinesh-Seema is a married couple.

14. (a) Anita likes white colour.

15. (b) Rohan is a seema's son.

16. (b) As given that,
DRIVER is coded as 5.
Code of the given work = [number of letters in the world – 1]
So, BELIEVED is coded as = [8 – 1] = 7

17. (b) Anil can do $\dfrac{1}{14}$ of the work per day, and

Rohit can do $\dfrac{1}{21}$ of the work per day.

on each day that they work together, then they do, $\dfrac{1}{14}+\dfrac{1}{21}=\dfrac{5}{42}$ of the work.

As given that,

The last three days of the work Rohit will be working alone.

In those (3 days) he will do $= 3 \times \dfrac{1}{21}=\dfrac{1}{7}$ (of the job)

That means that the two of them working together must have done $\left(1-\dfrac{1}{7}\right)=\dfrac{6}{7}$ of the work before Anil left.

This would have taken them

$=\left[\dfrac{6/7}{5//42}\right]=\dfrac{6}{7}\times\dfrac{42}{5}=\dfrac{36}{5}$ days

Add that to 3 days that Rohit worked alone

So, that number of days it took to complete the whole work $= \left[\dfrac{36}{5}+3\right]=\left[\dfrac{51}{5}\right]$

18. (b)

19. (c) As given that,

A : B = 3 : 4 & B : C = 6 : 5

By multiplying both ratio:

$\Rightarrow \dfrac{A}{B}\times\dfrac{B}{C}=\dfrac{3}{4}\times\dfrac{6}{5}$

$\Rightarrow \dfrac{A}{C}=\dfrac{9}{10}$

A : B : C = 9 : 12 : 10

So, A : (A + C) = 9 : (9 + 10) = 9 : 19

20. (a) As given that,

The complimentary angles are in the ratio of 11 : 7.

Sum of the ratio = 11+7=18

So, 1st angle = 11/18 × 90° = 55°

IInd angle = 7/18 × 90°=35°

Hence, the smallest angle is 35°

21. (a)

22. (a) The salt in 30 litre = [30/100] × 5 = 1.5 litres

This 1.5 litres is 3% salt, so

Total content $= \dfrac{1.5}{3}\times100 = 50$

Hence, 50 – 30 = 20 litres of water must be added so as to get a resultant solution containing 3% salt.

23. (d) The given word, DIJOB code is CHINA

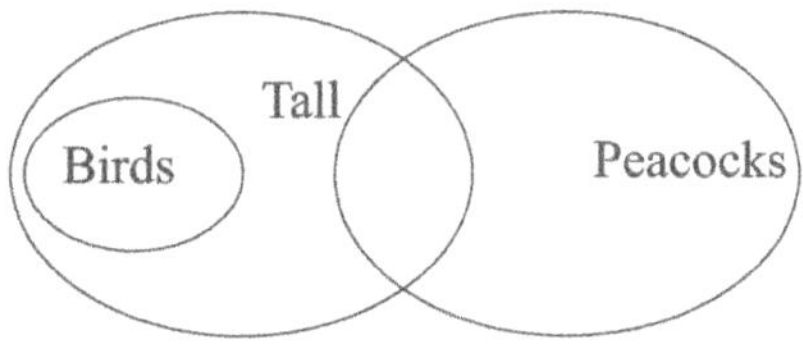

Hence the last letter of the word is N.

24. (d)

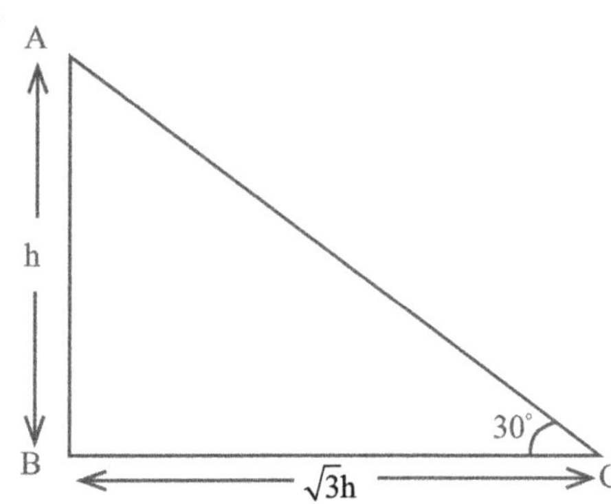

Some peacocks is tall is a possibility

So, conclusion II follows

25. (c)

Let the height of tower be h

∴   Length of shadow $= \sqrt{3}$h

In a triangle A B C

$\tan \angle ACB = h / \sqrt{3}\,h$

$\tan \angle ACB = \dfrac{1}{\sqrt{3}}$

$\angle ACB = 30°$

Hence, the angle of elevation is 30°

26. (c)   27. (a)   28. (b)

29. (c) Sodium chloride is the major salt present in the human body which makes up around 0.4% of human body weight. The adequate intake for sodium is 1.2 to 1.5 grams per day.

30. (a)

31. (b) As given that,

$\angle A:\angle B:\angle C=2:5:8$

$\angle A = 2x, \angle B = 5x, \angle c = 8x$

So, $2x + 5x + 8x = 180°$

$15x = 180°$

$x = \dfrac{180}{15}$

Hence the largest angle $= 8x$

$= 8 \times \dfrac{180}{15} = 96°$

32. (a)

33. (c) The given word 'GOAT' can be written as KSEX,

$$\begin{array}{cccc} G & O & A & T \\ +4 & +4 & +4 & +4 \\ \downarrow & \downarrow & \downarrow & \downarrow \\ K & S & E & X \end{array}$$

Similarly

$$\begin{array}{cccc} W & O & L & F \\ +4 & +4 & +4 & +4 \\ \downarrow & \downarrow & \downarrow & \downarrow \\ A & S & P & J \end{array}$$

Hence, WOLF word can be written as ASPJ.

34. (b) As given expression:

$\Rightarrow (4211)^{102} \times (361)^{52}$

for, $(4211)^{102}$, 1 will be unit digit $\{ \therefore (1)^n = 1,$ where n is an integer$\}$

also for $(361)^{52}$, 1 will be the unit digit

$\therefore$ The product of $(4211)^{102} \times (361)^{52}$ will have 1 as the unit digit.

35. (a) As given that,

The traffic lights at four different road crossing change after every 15 sec., 18 sec., 27 sec and 30 sec. respectively.

$15 = 3 \times 5$

$18 = 2 \times 3 \times 3$

$27 = 3 \times 3 \times 3$

$30 = 3 \times 2 \times 5$

LCM of 15, 18, 27, 30 is $(3 \times 3 \times 3 \times 2 \times 5) = 270$

That is after 270 seconds they will change Simultaneously 270 sec = 4 min 30 sec.

Hence, the traffic lights change simultaneously at 6 : 10 : 00 + 4 min 30 sec.

$\Rightarrow$ 6 : 14 : 30 hours.

36. (c) As given that, $\bar{x}$ 21, S.D. = 7

As we know that,

The coefficient of variation (C.V.)

$= \dfrac{\text{S.D.}}{\bar{x}} \times 100$

$(C.V) = \dfrac{7}{21} \times 100$

$(C.V) = 33.33\%$

37. (b)   38. (c)

39. (b) Mercury is a silvery-white poisonous metallic element. Commonly known as quicksilver, it is used in thermometers, barometers, mercury switches, fluorescent lamps, etc.

40. (c)   41. (c)   42. (b)

43. (c) Antoine Henri Becquerel was the first person to discover radioactivity in 1896. Though it was Marie Curie who coined the term, it was Henri Becquerel who discovered radioactivity. The SI unit for radioactivity (Bq) is named after him.

44. (b) The sword-billed hummingbird is a neotropical species of hummingbird from the Andean regions of South America. The species belongs to a monotypic genus, *Ensifera*, and is the only bird to have a beak longer than the rest of its body.

45. (a) As given that

Time taken = 2hr. 20 minutes 24 seconds.

$= 2 \text{ hr } 20\dfrac{2}{5} \text{ min} = 2\dfrac{51}{150} \text{ hrs.}$

$= 351 / 150$ hrs.

Let the actual speed be x km/hr.

Then, $\dfrac{10}{9} x \times \dfrac{351}{150} = 39$

$x = \left[\dfrac{39 \times 9 \times 150}{10 \times 351} \right]$

$= \left[\dfrac{52651}{3510} \right] = 15 \text{km / hr.}$

46. (c)

47. (b) Let, the present ages of the two be A and B. Eight year ago the ratio of their ages was 1 : 3

So, $\dfrac{A - 8}{B - 8} = \dfrac{1}{3}$

$3(A - 8) = B - 8$

$3A - B = 16 \qquad\qquad ...(i)$

After eight years sonam's age will be half of her father's age.

So, $(A+8) = \left(\dfrac{B+8}{2}\right)$

$2A + 16 = B + 8$

$2A - B = -8$ ...(ii)

By subtracting equation (i) and (ii)

$3A - B = 16$

$-2A - B = -8$

$\quad + \quad +$

$A = 24$

And $B = 2 \times 24 + 8$

$= 48 + 8 = 56$

Hence, the present age of sonam's father is 56 years.

48. (a) As given that,

Profit = 20% D

Selling a jean at discount = 15% P

$\dfrac{C.P}{M.P} = \dfrac{100-D}{100+P}$

$\dfrac{C.P}{M.P} = \dfrac{100-15}{100+20} = \dfrac{85}{120}$

$\dfrac{C.P}{C.P} = \dfrac{17}{24}$

49. (b)   50. (c)

51. (a) As given that

$\Rightarrow 28\ Z\ 7\ W\ 8\ X\ 6\ Y\ 4$

$\Rightarrow 28 \div 7 \times 8 - 6 + 4$

$\Rightarrow 4 \times 8 - 6 + 4$

$\Rightarrow 32 - 2 = 30$

52. (c) $\Rightarrow 27 > 81\ @\ 9 < 6$

$\Rightarrow 27 + 81 \div 9 - 6$

$= 27 + 9 - 6 = 30$

53. (b) $15 - 2 \div 900 + 90 \times 100$

$15 \times 2 + 900 \div 90 - 100$

$= 30 + 10 - 100 = -60$

54. (b) Number of gaps between 31 posts is 30 and adjacent post are 60 metres apart.

It means $= 30 \times 60 = 1800$ meters are covered in 1 minutes.

Distance $= 1800\ m = 1.8\ km$

Time $= 60$ sec. $= \dfrac{1}{60}$ hr.

Hence, Speed $= \left[\dfrac{1.8 \times 60}{1}\right] = 108\ km/hr$

55. (a)   56. (a)   57. (b)   58. (a)

59. (b)

60. (b) Smallest no. $= x$

$x + x + 2 + x + 4 + x + 6 + x + 8 = 40 \times 5$

$5x + 20 = 200$

$5x = 180$

$x = 36$

61. (b)

62. (c) As we know that

$A = \dfrac{P \times R \times T}{100} + P$

According to question,

$2P = \dfrac{P \times R \times 10}{100} + P$

$\Rightarrow P = \dfrac{P \times R}{10} \Rightarrow R = 10\%$

Now for 20 year at interest of 10% so, amount will be

$A = \dfrac{P \times 10 \times 20}{100} + P$

$= 2P + P = 3P.$

63. (d) As we know that,

$a^3 + b^3 + c^3 - 3abc = (a + b + c).[(a^2 + b^2 + c^2) - (ab + bc + ca)]$

So, $a^3 + c^3 + 1 - 3ac = [(a + c + 1)(a^2 + c^2 + 1) - (ac + c + a)]$

As given that,

$(a + c + 1) = 0$

Hence, $a^3 + c^3 + 1 - 3ac = 0$

64. (a) As given two number are related to $x^2 : (x+2)^2$

$49 : 81 :: 100 : 144$

Hence, the missing number is 144.

65. (c) As given that,

$(x + y)^2 - xy = 0$

So, $\left[\dfrac{x^3 - y^3}{x - y}\right] = \left[\dfrac{(x - y)(x^2 + xy + y^2)}{x - y}\right]$

$= (x^2 + xy + y^2) \Rightarrow x^2 + 2xy - xy + y^2$

$= (x + y)^2 - xy = 0\ [(x + y)^2 - xy = 0$ (given)$]$

66. (b)

67. (b)

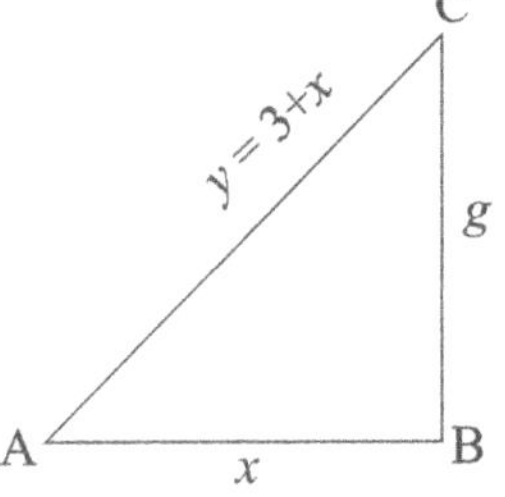

$AB^2 + BC^2 = AC^2$

$x^2 + 9^2 = (3 + x)^2$

$x^2 + 81 = x^2 + 9 + 6x$

$6x = 72$

$x = 12$

Length of Ladder $= x + 3 = 12 + 3$

$\qquad\qquad\qquad = 15$ m

68. (b)

Sol. (69-71):

Total number of car sales during 2006.

$= 480 + 410 + 390 + 380 + 440 = 2100$

69. (a) The approximate share domestic sales of cars of the manufacture M is

$= \dfrac{410}{2100} \times 100 = 19.52 \approx 19.5\%$

70. (c) From the given table its clear that the maximum percentage increase over the previous year during 2010, manufacturer is N.

71. (a) From the given table its clear that the sales of the cars the highest over the given period is L, 2009.

72. (d) As given equation $3 + 5 - 2 = 4$

and numbers '3' & '5' then the given equation is correct.

If we interchanges the '+' & '–' sign

$\Rightarrow 5 - 3 + 2 = 4$

Hence, option (d) is correct.

73. (b)   74. (d)

75. (a) Both Atul and Binay can do $\dfrac{1}{5}$ of the work per day.

Binay alone can do $\dfrac{1}{8}$ of the work per day.

Atul + Binay $= \dfrac{1}{5}$ [one day work]

Atul $+ \dfrac{1}{8} = \dfrac{1}{5}$

Atul one day work $= \dfrac{1}{5} - \dfrac{1}{8}$

$= \left[\dfrac{8-5}{40}\right] = \left[\dfrac{3}{40}\right]$

Hence, Atul take 40/3 days to complete the same work alone.

76. (c)

77. (b) As we know that

Dividend $=$ (divisor $\times$ Quotient) $+$ Remainder

$= (x + 2) \times (4x - 5) + 12$

$= 4x^2 - 5x + 8x - 10 + 12$

$= 4x^2 + 3x + 2$

78. (c)   79. (c)   80. (c)

81. (a) As given word 'MACHINE' is coded as 19–7–9–14–15–20–11, it means all letters position number added by 6.

Hence, DANGER is coded as

10–7–20–13–11–24.

$$
\begin{array}{cccccc}
\text{D} & \text{A} & \text{N} & \text{G} & \text{E} & \text{R} \\
4+6 & 1+6 & 14+6 & 7+6 & 5+6 & 18+6 \\
\downarrow & \downarrow & \downarrow & \downarrow & \downarrow & \downarrow \\
10 & 7 & 20 & 13 & 11 & 24
\end{array}
$$

82. (c) Firstly we need to calculate the S.I. with principal 800, time 3 years and rate 9/2%

$$\text{S.I} = \dfrac{\text{P.r.t.}}{100} = \dfrac{800 \times 4.5 \times 3}{100} = 108$$

So, we can get sum with the same interest rate in 9 year is:

$$= \left[\dfrac{100 \times \text{S.I}}{\text{T} \times \text{r}}\right]$$

$$= \left[\dfrac{100 \times 108}{9 \times 8}\right] = \dfrac{1200}{8} = ₹150$$

83. (c)

Sol. (84–86):

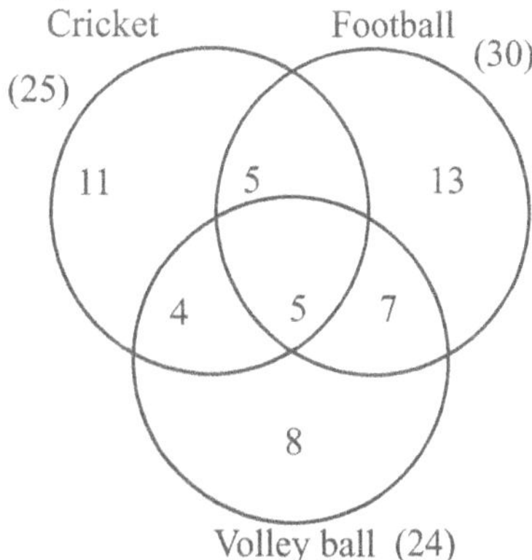

84. (d) From the above ven diagram,

The total number of students play exactly two games $= 5 + 4 + 7 = 16$

85. (c) Number of student which do not play any of the game $= 60 - [21 + 13 + 11 + 8] = 7$

86. (a) Total number of students play cricket only

$[25 - [5+5+4]] = 11$

87. (b)

88. (b) Let x be the price of gas cylinder and y be the price of store.

According to question:

$x + y = 4500$ ...(i)

So $\left[\dfrac{\frac{5x}{4}+\frac{4y}{5}\,y-(x+y)}{4500}\right]\times100=4$

$\left[\dfrac{25x+16y-20x-20y}{20\times45}\right]=4$

$5x-4y=3600$ ....(ii)

By solving equation (i) and (ii) x = 2400, y = 2100

Hence, the cost of the gas cylinder is ₹2400.

89. (c)　　90. (b)

91. (c) Let the original price of onion be x.

After raised price of Onion the price is

= x + 35 % of x = 1.35 x

So, expenditure is :

1.35 x = 100%

$x=\dfrac{100}{1.35}=74.07\%$

Hence, expenditure decrevased by

= 100 – 74.07 ≈ 26%

92. (a) ∴ The sum of 10 observation = 10 × 13 = 130

2 more observation are included to this addition = 12 × 14 = 168

New observation = 168 – 130 = 38

So, the mean of two new observation = 38/2 = 19.

93. (b) As we know that

Population variance = [Standard deviation]^2

= $(6.5)^2$ = 42.25

94. (c)

95. (b) As given that,

a = 21 [first number divisible by 7) in the sange]

d = 7 (As the number divisible by 7

T(n) = 84 (last number divisible by 7 in the range)

⇒ T(n) = a + (n – 1).d

⇒ 84 = 21 + (n – 1)×7

⇒ (n–1) = 9 ⇒ n = 10

96. (b)　　97. (c)

98. (a)

⇒ [5.168 × 4453 × 3.194 / 67.999 × 4224.017]

$=\left[\dfrac{73503.854176}{287228.931983}\right]=0.255\approx0.2$

99. (b) We know that, N_2(number)

$=\left[\dfrac{\text{HCF of two no.}\times\text{LCM of two no.}}{N_1\,(\text{Number})}\right]$

The other number $(N_2)=\dfrac{19\times665}{95}=133$

100. (d)

1. Which is India's first defience satellite?
   - (a) INSAT 2B
   - (b) GSAT-7
   - (c) GSAT 6
   - (d) IRS-1A

2. Below are given statements followed by two conclusions I and II. You have to take the given statements to be true even if they seem to be at variance from commonly known facts.

   Statements: A: All mothers are aunts.
   B: All aunts are ladies.

   Conclusions: I. All ladies are mothers.
   II. All ladies are aunts.

   Decide which of the below options logically follows the given Statement.
   - (a) Only conclusion I follows
   - (b) Only conclusion II follows
   - (c) Both conclusion I and II follow s
   - (d) Neither conclusion I nor II follows

3. Which of the following ratio is greatest?
   - (a) 7:15
   - (b) 15:23
   - (c) 17:25
   - (d) 21:29

4. Choose the one which is odd from the following options.
   - (a) Coffee
   - (b) Rice
   - (c) Tobacco
   - (d) Sugarcane

5. The passenger reservation system of the Indian Railways is designed by
   - (a) TCS
   - (b) CRIS
   - (c) Google
   - (d) CMS

6. What is the chemical name of chalk?
   - (a) Calcium Sulphate
   - (b) Calcium Nitrate
   - (c) Calcium Carbonate
   - (d) Calcium Phosphide

7. What is the name of the book in Harry Potter series written by Jack Thome to be published in mid-2016?
   - (a) Harry Potter and the Cursed Child
   - (b) Harry Potter and the Deathly Hallows.
   - (c) Fantastic Beasts and Where to Find Them
   - (d) The Tales of Beedle the Bard.

8. If $3.5x = 0.07y$, then find the result of $[y - x/y + x]$
   - (a) 51/49
   - (b) 49/53
   - (c) 49/51
   - (d) 53/57

9. Article 29 of the Constitution of India grants which of the following rights?
   - (a) Protection in respect of conviction for offences
   - (b) Traffic in human beings prohibited
   - (c) Protection of interests of minorities
   - (d) Prohibits taxes on religious grounds

10. Find 150% of X, if X is the least number which when divided by 6, 7, 8, 9 and 12 leaves remainders 2, 3, 4, 5 and 8 respectively.
    - (a) 750
    - (b) 500
    - (c) 1000
    - (d) 1200

11. For real a, b and c if $a^2 + b^2 + c^2 = ab + bc + ca$, then find the value of $(a + b + c)^2$
    - (a) $9a^2$
    - (b) $81a^2$
    - (c) $27a^2$
    - (d) $243a^2$

12. MATHEMATICS is related to NUMBERS in the same way HISTORY is related to
    - (a) EVENTS
    - (b) PEOPLE
    - (c) WARS
    - (d) DATES

13. In which year was Facebook started?
    - (a) 2002
    - (b) 2004
    - (c) 2008
    - (d) 2009

14. What is the chemical formula of Ozone?
    - (a) O
    - (b) O_2
    - (c) O_3
    - (d) O_4

15. An Assertion (A) and a Reason (R) are given below.

    Assertion (A): Earthworms are not good for agriculture.

    Reason (R): Earthworms break down the soil into fine particles and make it soft.

    Choose the correct option.
    - (a) A is true but R is false.
    - (b) A is false but R is true.
    - (c) Both A and R are true and R is the correct explanation of A.
    - (d) Both A and R are false

16. What is the sound made by seal called?
    - (a) Bark
    - (b) Moo
    - (c) Screech
    - (d) Growl

17. Based on the analogy given, find the missing number from the given options. 7528 : 5306 : : 4673 : ?
    (a) 2351   (b) 2541
    (c) 2451   (d) 2531

18. If STUDENT is coded as 103, what is the code for SCHOOL?
    (a) 72   (b) 27
    (c) 37   (d) 73

19. If 'P' means 'divided by', 'T' means 'add', 'M' means 'subtract' and 'D' means 'multiplied by', then what will be the value of the following expression?

    12 M 12 D 28 P 7 T 15
    (a) –21   (b) 15
    (c) 30   (d) –15

20. Who was the dentist who killed Cecil-the Lion in 2015?
    (a) John Walker   (b) Gary Crow
    (c) Walter Palmer   (d) Rupert Watson

21. The energy which we get from food is measured in
    (a) Calories   (b) Kelvin
    (c) Tat   (d) Amperes

22. How many litres of blood does an adult body have?
    (a) 3   (b) 4
    (c) 5   (d) 6

23. Who is known as the Father of video games?
    (a) Karl Benz   (b) Emile Berliner
    (c) Rudolf Diesel   (d) Ralph H. Baer

24. If Sunita earns 75/4% more than her boyfriend, find the approximate % her boyfriend earns less than Sunita.
    (a) 16%   (b) 14%
    (c) 25%   (d) 11%

25. If the angles of a triangle are in the ratio of 2:3:7. then find the ratio of the greatest angle to the smallest angle.
    (a) 7:2   (b) 2:3
    (c) 7:1   (d) 3:5

26. Which wood is used to make a cricket bat?
    (a) Teak   (b) Willow
    (c) Bamboo   (d) Rosewood

27. What of the given below devices converts chemical energy to electrical energy?
    (a) Transformer
    (b) Battery
    (c) Electric Generator
    (d) Wheel

28. An angle is 30 more than one half of its complement. Find difference between the greater and the smaller angles.
    (a) 10°   (b) 20°
    (c) 30°   (d) 25°

29. what are the components of $(x^6 – x^4 – x^5 – x^4 + x^2 – 4)$?
    (a) $(x – 1)$
    (b) $(x + 1)$
    (c) Both $(x – 1)$ and $(x + 1)$
    (d) Neither $(x – 1)$ or $(x + 1)$

30. Who fought Ahmad Shah Abdali at the third battle of Panipat?
    (a) Mughals   (b) Lodhis
    (c) Marathas   (d) Khiljis

31. Which of the following is not a greenhouse gas?
    (a) Carbon dioxide
    (b) Methane
    (c) Chlorofluorocarbons
    (d) Oxygen

32. What are stars primarily made of?
    (a) Oxygen and Hydrogen
    (b) Hydrogen and Carbon
    (c) Hydrogen and Helium
    (d) Oxygen and Helium

33. On which date was the partition of India announced?
    (a) 15th Aug 1947   (b) 3rd June 1947
    (c) 17th July 1947   (d) 1st July 1947

34. Find the simple interest on ₹ 50 for 6 months at the rate of 10 paise per rupee per month.
    (a) ₹ 35   (b) ₹ 40
    (c) ₹ 25   (d) ₹ 30

35. Two numbers are in the ratio 5:6. When 6 is added to each, the ratio becomes 7:8 then the numbers are
    (a) 10 & 12   (b) 20 & 24
    (c) 15 & 18   (d) 5 & 6

36. If the given interchanges namely: signs + and ÷ and numbers 2 and 4 are made in signs and numbers, which one of the following would be correct?
    (a) $4 + 2 ÷ 6 = 1.5$ (b) $2 + 4 ÷ 6 = 8$
    (c) $2 + 4 ÷ 3 = 3$ (d) $4 ÷ 2 + 3 = 4$

37. Stainless steel was invented by
    (a) William Howard Livens
    (b) Joseph Aspdin
    (c) Harry Breadey
    (d) James Dyson

38. If BORDER is coded as 579649, than ORDER can be coded as
(a) 79469
(b) 79649
(c) 76949
(d) 79667

39. The disease cirrhosis affects which organ in the body?
(a) Brain
(b) Liver
(c) Heart
(d) Kidney

40. The ratio between the speeds of two buses is 11:9. If the second bus runs 270 kms in 15 hours, then the speed of the first bus is?
(a) 23 km/hr
(b) 11 km/hr
(c) 2 km/hr
(d) 22 km/hr

41. Who presented the first Union Budget in 1947?
(a) Indira Gandhi
(b) Morarji Desai
(c) R. K. Shanmukham Chetty
(d) John Mathai

42. On which network was the first SMS sent?
(a) Airtel
(b) Vodafone
(c) Verizone
(d) Digicel

43. McAfee is a ___________________?
(a) Anti-virus software
(b) Programming language
(c) Output device
(d) Computer device

44. An Assertion (A) and a Reason (R) are given below.
Assertion (A): In India judiciary is independent of the executive.
Reason (R): Judiciary favors the government and helps in the implementation of its plans.
Choose the correct option.
(a) A is true but R is false.
(b) A is false but R is true.
(c) Both A and R are true and R is the correct explanation of A.
(d) Both A and R are false

45. The product of the ages of Swati and Aparna is 120. If thrice the age of Aparna is more than Swati's age by 2 years, find the age of Swati.
(a) 18
(b) 20
(c) 24
(d) 16

46. A wholesaler sold a water purifier at a loss of 40%. If the selling price has been increased by ₹ 125. then wholesaler will get the profit of 10%. What was the cost price of the purifier?
(a) ₹ 250
(b) ₹ 225
(c) ₹ 275
(d) ₹ 300

47. If IRON is written as GOKI, then KNIEF may be written as
(a) IKZEZ
(b) IEKZZ
(c) IKEZZ
(d) IZKEZ

48. Which tennis player has been awarded the Padma Bhushan award 2016?
(a) Sania Mirza
(b) Leander Paes
(c) Mahesh Bhupathi
(d) Rohan Bopanna

49. What does ATM stand for?
(a) Any Time Money
(b) Automated Teller Machine
(c) Automatic Talking Media
(d) Analog Time Machine

50. When Vijay sells 12 pens, he gains the selling price of 2 pens. Calculate his % profit?
(a) 15%
(b) 20%
(c) 18%
(d) 12%

51. To which dynasty did the famous patron of literature king Bhoja belong?
(a) Chalukya
(b) Chola
(c) Paramara
(d) Pala

52. Based on the analogy given, find the missing word from the given options.
Mother : Child : : Cloud : ?
(a) Rain
(b) Thunder
(c) Water
(d) Weather

53. If the standard deviation of a population is 7, what would be the population variance?
(a) 14
(b) 21
(c) 49
(d) 28

DIRECTIONS (Qs. 54-56): *Read the following Passage and answer the questions based on it.*

There are six members in a family. One couple has parents and their children in the family. Arjun is the son of Raju and Elamathi is the daughter of Arjun. Divya is the daughter of Rani who is the mother of Elamathi and Banu is the mother of Arjun.

54. How many female members in the family?
(a) 2
(b) 3
(c) 4
(d) Cannot be determined

55. Which of the following pairs is the parents of the children?
(a) Raju & Banu
(b) Arjun & Banu
(c) Raju & Rani
(d) Arjun & Rani

56. What relationship to Divya and Elamathi bear to each other respectively?
(a) Sisters
(b) Mother & Daughter
(c) Grandmother & Granddaughter
(d) Cannot be determined

57. A sum of ₹ 2000 at 40% per annum compounded annually. Calculate the interest for the third year at compound interest.
    (a) 1500   (b) 1600
    (c) 1568   (d) 1750

58. Who received the Man Booter Prize in 2015 for his novel 'A brief history of seven killings'?
    (a) Marlon James   (b) Richard Flanagan
    (c) Arvind Adiga   (d) E.O. Wilson

DIRECTIONS (Qs. 59-61): *The following questions are based on the information given below:*

An advertising agency finds that, of its 170 clients, 115 read Indian Express, 110 read The Hindu and 130 read Times of India. Also 85 read Indian Express and Times of India, 75 read Indian Express and The Hindu, 95 read The Hindu and Times of India and 70 read all the three.

59. How many read only The Hindu?
    (a) 5   (b) 10
    (c) 25   (d) 35

60. How many read Indian Express and Times of India but not The Hindu?
    (a) 10   (b) 20
    (c) 15   (d) 30

61. How many read only Indian Express?
    (a) 15   (b) 25
    (c) 5   (d) 10

62. For what value of C_2, the system of equation $6x + 2y = 2$ & $3x + y = C_2$ will be coincident?
    (a) 4   (b) 0
    (c) 2   (d) 1

63. What is the increase in the number of workdays under the rural job guarantee scheme (MNREGA) in drought-affected areas?
    (a) 10   (b) 25
    (c) 40   (d) 50

64. By dividing 14528 by a certain number, Suresh gets 83 as quotient and 3 as remainder. What is the divisor?
    (a) 165   (b) 185
    (c) 195   (d) 175

DIRECTIONS (Qs. 65-67): *Read the following table carefully and answer the questions given below:*

The percentage change in sales of six departmental stores from 2010 to 2012 is shown in the following table:

Store	Percentage Change	
	From 2010 to 2011	From 2011 to 2012
P	+20	−20
Q	−20	+9
R	+5	+12
S	−7	−15
T	+17	−8
U	+21	+9

65. Sales in store P amounted to ₹ 80 lakhs in 2010. What was the sales amount of the same store in 2012?
    (a) 76.8 lakhs   (b) 78.6 lakhs
    (c) 80 lakhs   (d) 74 lakhs

66. In store T the sales for 2011 amounted to about what percentage of the sales for 2012?
    (a) 113   (b) 109
    (c) 105   (d) 101

67. In 2012 which of the stores had greater sales than any other stores?
    (a) R   (b) P   (c) T   (d) Q

68. Sunil and Gopal are partners in a business. Sunil invests ₹ 20,000 for 9 months and Gopal invests ₹ 30.000 for 12 months. Find the share of Sunil from the total profit of ₹ 60,000.
    (a) ₹ 15000   (b) ₹ 18000
    (c) ₹ 25000   (d) ₹ 20000

69. The mean of a distribution is 11 and the standard deviation is 5. What is the value of the coefficient variation?
    (a) 45.45%   (b) 35.35%
    (c) 25.25%   (d) 55.55%

70. The mean of 14 observations is 11. One more observation is included and the new mean becomes 12. The 15th observation is
    (a) 20   (b) 24   (c) 26   (d) 28

71. Five women can do a work in thirty six days. If the ratio between the capacity of a man and a woman is 3:1, then find how many days it will take 5 men to complete the same work?
    (a) 12 days   (b) 15 days
    (c) 18 days   (d) 108 days

72. Who conferred the title of 'Gurudev' on Rabindranath Tagore?
    (a) Mahatma Gandhi
    (b) Pandit Nehru
    (c) Lala Lajpat Rai
    (d) Bal Gangadhar Tilak

73. If NCLAGJ stands for PENCIL, then AMJMSP stands for
(a) ERASER   (b) PAPERS
(c) KOLOUR   (d) COLOUR

74. If $(\sin A + \cos A)/(\sin A - \cos A) = 5/4$, the value of $(\tan^2 A + 1)/(\tan^2 A - 1) = ?$
(a) 41/40   (b) 12/13
(c) 40/41   (d) 3/5

75. If 15 persons can do a job in 30 days, then 30 persons with twice the efficiency can do the same job in how many days?
(a) 7   (b) 3.5
(c) 5   (d) 7.5

76. If two complementary angles are in the ratio of 2:3, find the ratio of square of smaller angle to square of greater angle.
(a) 3:2   (b) 9:11
(c) 4:5   (d) 4:9

77. What denotes offering several products for sale as one combined product?
(a) Advertisement   (b) Product mix
(c) Product bundling (d) Differentiation

78. Which was the capital of the first Sri Lankan kingdom?
(a) Jaffna   (b) Polonnaniwa
(c) Anuraclhapura   (d) Kandy

79. $\sin^6 A + \cos^6 A - 1$ is equal to
(a) $-3\sin^2 A\cos^2 A$ (b) $1 - 3\sin A\cos A$
(c) $1 + 3\sin^2 A\cos^2 A$ (d) 0

80. In the following expression 'α' stands for '>'; 'β' stands for '<'; 'γ' stands for 'not greater than'; 'δ' stands for 'not less than'; and 'μ' stands for '='.
If 3C δ 2A and B α C, then which of the following statement is true?
(a) 3B μ 2A   (b) B μ A
(c) 3B α 2A   (d) 2A α 3B

81. Which of the following is a bad conductor of heat?
(a) Wood   (b) Diamond
(c) Water   (d) Mica

82. Choose the pair which is related in the same way as the words in the first pair from the given choices
Mosquito : Malaria : : _________ : _________
(a) Housefly : Food (b) Road : Accident
(c) Soil : Erosion   (d) Tobacco : Cancer

83. where will the 2022 Commonwealth Games be played?
(a) Glasgow   (b) Durban
(c) Gold Coast   (d) New Delhi

84. Rearrange the jumbled up letters in their natural sequence and find the odd one out.
(a) LAFC   (b) UKCGIDLN
(c) RILNIGHE   (d) BCU

85. Sita starts to calculate sum of all odd natural numbers less than 72. What result does she get?
(a) 1196   (b) 1296
(c) 1331   (d) 1276

86. On an average how many times does lightning strike the Earth?
(a) 100 times per second
(b) 100 times per day
(c) 1000 times per day
(d) 100 times per hour

87. An Assertion (A) and a Reason (R) are given below.
Assertion (A): We feel comfortable in hot and humid climate.
Reason (R): Sweat evaporates faster in humid climate.
Choose the correct option.
(a) A is true but R is false.
(b) A is false but R is true.
(c) Both A and R are true and R is the correct explanation of A.
(d) Both A and R are false

88. Rearrange the jumbled up letters in their natural sequence and find the odd one out.
(a) UTNA   (b) EINEC
(c) OMEHRT   (d) ROBEHRT

89. Which is the form of market where there is lack of competition?
(a) Monopoly
(b) Oligopoly
(c) Perfect competition
(d) Marketisation

90. One of four words is a class to which the other three belong. Identify the class.
(a) Hawaii   (b) Cubav
(c) Island   (d) Greenland

91. Based on the analogy given, find the missing pair from the given options.
32 : 13 : : _____ : _____
(a) 51 : 36   (b) 83 : 121
(c) 71 : 81   (d) 47 : 65

92. Find the LCM of 0.36, 2.72, 0.12 and 1.44
(a) 24.48   (b) 2448
(c) 2.448   (d) 244.8

93. Which of the following is called 'The queen of Arabian sea'?
    (a) Mumbai
    (b) Thiruvananthapuram
    (c) Kochi
    (d) Surat

94. What is the name of the castle that was built in honour of world renowned composer Richard Wagner?
    (a) Balmoral Castle
    (b) Neuschwanstein Castle
    (c) Conwy castle
    (d) Rronborg

95. Select the correct set of symbols which will fit in the given equation?
    5   0   3   5 = 20
    (a) $+, -, +$ (b) $\times, +, \times$
    (c) $-, +, \times$ (d) $\times, \times, \times$

96. Evaporation of water from leaves of a plant is called
    (a) Transpiration   (b) Respiration
    (c) Perspiration   (d) Evaporation

97. How do you know Yarlung Tsangpo better?
    (a) Ganges   (b) Brahmaputra
    (c) Mahanadi   (d) Sutlej

98. The famous Sanchi Stupa was commissioned by
    (a) Bindusara
    (b) Ashoka
    (c) Chandragupta Maurya
    (d) Kanishka

99. How long will Ramesh take to run round a square park of edge 50 metres, if he runs at the rate of 18 km/hr?
    (a) 40 sec   (b) 20 sec
    (c) 80 sec   (d) 160 sec

100. Ramesh sold a phone at a loss of 5%. Had he sold it for ₹ 200 more, he would gave gained 15%. To gain 25%, he should sell it for :
    (a) ₹ 1175   (b) ₹ 1150
    (c) ₹ 1225   (d) ₹ 1250

HINTS & EXPLANATIONS

1. **(b)** GSAT 7, named Rukmini, is a multi-band military communications satellite developed by the Indian Space Research Organisation (ISRO). It is the first dedicated military communication satellite that will provide services to the Indian defence forces with the main user being the Indian Navy.

2. **(d)** From above diagram : some ladies are mothers Some ladies are aunts.

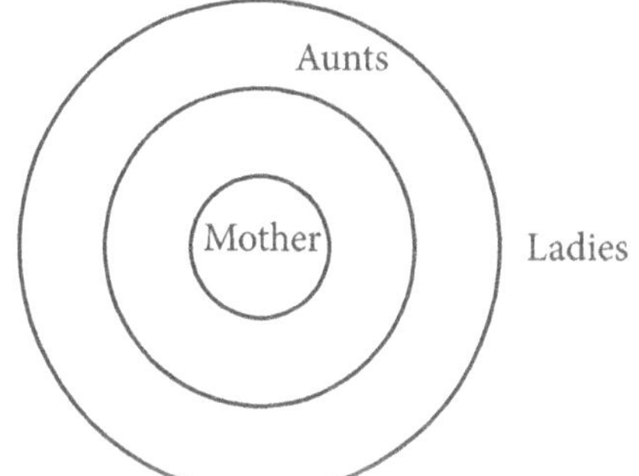

∴ neither conclusion I nor II follows.

3. **(d)** $\dfrac{7}{15} = 0.46$, $\dfrac{15}{23} = 0.652$,

$\dfrac{17}{25} = 0.68$, $\dfrac{21}{29} = 0.724$,

∴ $\dfrac{21}{29}$ is the greatest ratio.

4. **(b)** 5. **(b)**

6. **(c)** Calcium Carbonate is the chemical name of chalk with chemical formula $CaCO_3$. It is a common substance found as rock and is the main component of shells of marine organisms, snails, and eggshells.

7. **(a)**

8. **(c)** $3.5x = 0.07y \Rightarrow \dfrac{x}{y} = \dfrac{0.07}{3.5} = \dfrac{1}{50}$ (i)

$$\text{Now} = \frac{y-x}{y+x} = \frac{\dfrac{y}{y}-\dfrac{x}{y}}{\dfrac{y}{y}+\dfrac{x}{y}} = \frac{1-\dfrac{1}{50}}{1+\dfrac{1}{50}}$$

$$= \frac{\dfrac{50-1}{50}}{\dfrac{50+1}{50}} = \frac{\dfrac{49}{50}}{\dfrac{51}{50}} = \frac{49}{51}$$

9. **(c)**

10. **(a)** Since difference of each divisor and its remainder is same i.e. 4.

LCM of 6, 7, 8, 9 and 12 = 504

Now, least number, $x = 504 - 4 = 500$

∴ 150% of $x = \dfrac{150}{100} \times 500 = 750$

11. **(a)** $a^2 + b^2 + c^2 = ab + bc + ca$

$\Rightarrow (a^2 + b^2 + c^2 - ab - bc - ca) = 0$

$\Rightarrow 2(a^2 + b^2 + c^2 - ab - bc - ca) = 0$

$\Rightarrow 2a^2 + 2b^2 + 2c^2 - 2ab - 2bc - 2ca = 0$

$\Rightarrow (a^2 + b^2 - 2ab) + (b^2 + c^2 - 2bc) +$

$\quad (c^2 + a^2 - 2ac) = 0$

$\Rightarrow (a-b)^2 + (b-c)^2 + (c-a)^2 = 0$

$\Rightarrow (a-b)^2 = 0, (b-c)^2 = 0, (c-a)^2 = 0$

$\Rightarrow a = b, b = c, c = a$

$\Rightarrow a = b = c$

∴ $(a + b + c)^2 = (3a)^2 = 9a^2$

12. **(a)** MATHEMATICS is related to NUMBERS in the same way as HISTORY is related to EVENTS.

13. **(b)** 14. **(c)**

15. **(b)** Earthworms are one of the most important soil animals that have the capability to maintain the fertility of the soil. They help restore soil nutrients, improve soil structure, allow water and air to enter the soil more freely, conserve energy, and boost biodiversity.

16. **(a)** The sound made by the seal is a mixture of a bark and an eerie whaling sound, depending on the species of seal. Sea lions bark whenever they come out of the water as they snort to clear their nostrils.

17. **(c)** The relationship is $x : (x - 2222)$

Thus, 7528 : 5306 :: 4673 : 2451

18. (a) STUDENT = $(19 + 20 + 21 + 4 + 5 + 14 + 14 + 20) = 103$
Here each no. corresponds to the rank of letter in english alphabet series.
SCHOOL = $(19 + 3 + 8 + 15 + 15 + 12) = 72$

19. (a) 12 M 12 D 28 P 7 T 15 = $12 - 12 \times 28 \div 7 + 15$

$= 12 - 12 \times 4 + 15$

$= 12 - 48 + 15$

$= 27 - 48 = (-21)$

20. (c)   21. (a)   22. (c)   23. (d)

24. (a) Let Sunita's boy friend earns = ₹100.

Sunita's earnings = $₹\left(100 \times \dfrac{75}{400}\right) + ₹\ 100$

$= ₹\ \dfrac{475}{4} = ₹\ 118.75$

Now, difference between Sunita's and her boy friend's earnings = ₹118.75 − ₹ 100

$= ₹18.75$

$\therefore$ Required percentage = $\left(\dfrac{18.75}{118.75} \times 100\right)\%$

$= \dfrac{187500}{11875}\% = 15.78\%$

$= 16\%$ (approx)

25. (a) Let the angles be $2x$, $3x$ and $7x$.

Hence ratio $= \dfrac{Greatest\ angle}{Smallest\ angle} = \dfrac{7x^\circ}{2x^\circ} = 7:2$

26. (b)   27. (b)

28. (a) Let the angle be x° and its compliment be $(90^\circ - x)$

Now, angle $= 30 + \dfrac{1}{2} \times$ compliment

$\Rightarrow x = 30 + \dfrac{1}{2}\left(90^\circ - x\right)$

$\Rightarrow x = 30 + 45 - \dfrac{x}{2}$

$\Rightarrow x + \dfrac{x}{2} = 75^\circ \Rightarrow \dfrac{3}{2}x = 75^\circ \Rightarrow x = 50^\circ$

Hence, difference $= 50^\circ - (90^\circ - 50^\circ) = 50^\circ - 40^\circ = 10^\circ$

29. (d) $f(x) = x^6 - x^4 - x^5 - x^4 + x^2 - 4$

$f(1) = (1)^6 - (1)^4 - (1)^5 - (1)^4 + (1)^2 - 4$

$= 1 - 1 - 1 - 1 + 1 - 4 = (-5)$

$\therefore (x - 1)$ is not the component of $f(x)$.

Also, $f(-1) = (-1)^6 - (-1)^4 - (-1)^5 - (-1)^4 + (-1)^2 - 4$, $1 - 1 - (-1) - 1 + 1 - 4$

$= 1 - 1 + 1 - 1 + 1 - 4 = (-3)$

$\therefore (x + 1)$ is also not the component of $f(x)$.

30. (c)   31. (d)

32. (c) Stars are big exploding balls of gas. This gas is mostly hydrogen and helium which are the two lightest elements. Stars shine by burning hydrogen into helium in their cores.

33. (b)

34. (d) P = ₹50
T = 6 month
R = 10 paise per rupee per month

$= \left(\dfrac{10}{100} \times 100\right)\%\ p.m. = 10\%\ p.m.$

$\therefore$ SI $= \dfrac{P \times R \times T}{100} = \dfrac{50 \times 10 \times 6}{100} = ₹\ 30$

35. (c) Let the numbers be $5x$ and $6x$ respectively.

Now, $\dfrac{5x + 6}{6x + 6} = \dfrac{7}{8}$

$\Rightarrow 8(5x + 6) = 7(6x + 6) \Rightarrow 40x + 48 = 42x + 42$

$\Rightarrow 48 - 42 = 42x - 40x \Rightarrow x = \dfrac{6}{2} = 3$

Thus, the numbers 15 and 18.

36. (b) New expression $4 \div 2 + 6 = 2 + 6 = 8$

37. (c)

38. (b)

B → 5	O → 7
O → 7	R → 9
R → 9 $\Rightarrow$	D → 6
D → 6	E → 4
E → 4	R → 9
R → 9	

39. (b) Cirrhosis is a disease which occurs when healthy cells in the liver are damaged and replaced by scar tissue. It is usually caused as a result of alcohol abuse or chronic hepatitis.

40. (d) Let the ratios of speeds of buses be $11x$ km/hr and $9x$ km/hr.

Now, speed of 2nd bus $= \dfrac{\text{Distance}}{\text{time}}$

$$\Rightarrow 9x = \dfrac{270}{15}$$

$$\Rightarrow x = \dfrac{270}{15 \times 9} = 2$$

Hence, speed of first bus $= 11x = 22$ km/hr

41. (c)   42. (b)

43. (a)   44. (a)

45. (a) Let Swati's age $= x$ yrs.

$\therefore$ Aparna's age $= \dfrac{120}{x}$ yrs.

Now, $\left(3 \times \dfrac{120}{x}\right) - x = 2$

$$\Rightarrow \dfrac{360}{x} - x = 2$$

$$\Rightarrow \dfrac{360 - x^2}{x} = 2 \Rightarrow 360 - x^2 = 2x$$

$$\Rightarrow x^2 + 2x - 360 = 0$$
$$\Rightarrow (x + 20)(x - 18) = 0$$
$$x = 18$$

Hence Swati's age $= x = 18$ yrs.

46. (a) Let the cost price of water purifier is $₹x$

Loss % = 40%

Then,

$$\text{SP} = \dfrac{100 - \text{loss}\%}{100} \times \text{CP} = \left(\dfrac{100 - 40}{100}\right)x$$

$$= ₹\dfrac{60}{100}x = ₹\dfrac{3}{5}x$$

New S.P. $= ₹\left(\dfrac{3}{5}x + 125\right)$

Profit = 10%

$$\therefore \text{CP} = \dfrac{100}{100 + \text{gain}\%s} \times \text{SP}$$

$$x = \left(\dfrac{100}{100 + 10}\right)\left(\dfrac{3}{5}x + 125\right)$$

$$\Rightarrow \dfrac{110}{100}x = \dfrac{3}{5}x + 125 \Rightarrow \dfrac{11}{10}x - \dfrac{3}{5}x = 125$$

$$\Rightarrow \dfrac{11x - 6x}{10} = 125 \Rightarrow \dfrac{5x}{10} = 125 \Rightarrow x = ₹250$$

47. (c)

$$I \xrightarrow{-2} G \qquad\qquad K \xrightarrow{-2} I$$
$$R \xrightarrow{-3} O \qquad\qquad N \xrightarrow{-3} K$$
$$O \xrightarrow{-4} K \qquad\qquad I \xrightarrow{-4} E$$
$$N \xrightarrow{-5} I \qquad\qquad E \xrightarrow{-5} Z$$
$$\qquad\qquad\qquad\qquad\qquad F \xrightarrow{-6} Z$$

48. (a)   49. (b)

50. (b) Let SP of 1 pen $= ₹1$

SP of 12 pens $= ₹12$

Gain = SP of 2 pens $= ₹2$

$\therefore$ CP = SP profit

$= 12 - ₹2 = ₹10$

and profit % $= \left(\dfrac{2}{10} \times 100\right) = 20\%$

51. (c)   52. (a)

53. (c) Variance = (Standrad Deviation)^2

$$= (7)^2 = 49$$

Solution:- 54 - 56

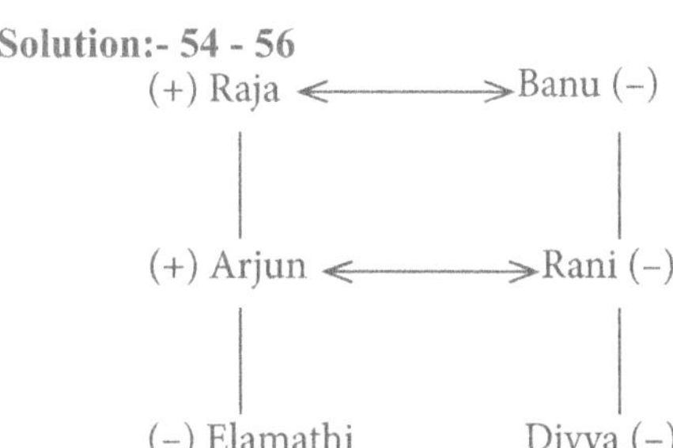

54. (c) These are 4 female members in the family Banu, Rani, Elamathi and Divya.

55. (d) Arjun and Rani is the pair who are parents of the children.

56. (a) Divya and Elamathi are sisters.

57. (c) CI for third year = CI for 3 years − CI for 2 yrs.

$$= \left[P\left(1 + \dfrac{R}{100}\right)^3 - P\right] - \left[P\left(1 + \dfrac{R}{100}\right)^2 - P\right]$$

$$= P\left(1 + \dfrac{R}{100}\right)^3 - P - P\left(1 + \dfrac{R}{100}\right)^2 + P$$

$$= P\left(1 + \dfrac{R}{100}\right)^3 - P\left(1 + \dfrac{R}{100}\right)^2$$

$$= P\left(1 + \dfrac{R}{100}\right)^2 \left[1 + \dfrac{R}{100} - 1\right]$$

$$= = \dfrac{81 + 1}{81 - 1} = \dfrac{82}{80} = \dfrac{41}{40}$$

$$= 2000\left(1+\frac{40}{100}\right)^2\left(\frac{40}{100}\right)$$

$$= 2000\left(\frac{7}{5}\right)\left(\frac{2}{5}\right) = 2000 \times \frac{49}{25} \times \frac{2}{5}$$

$$= ₹\, 1568$$

58. (a)

Sol. (59 - 61):

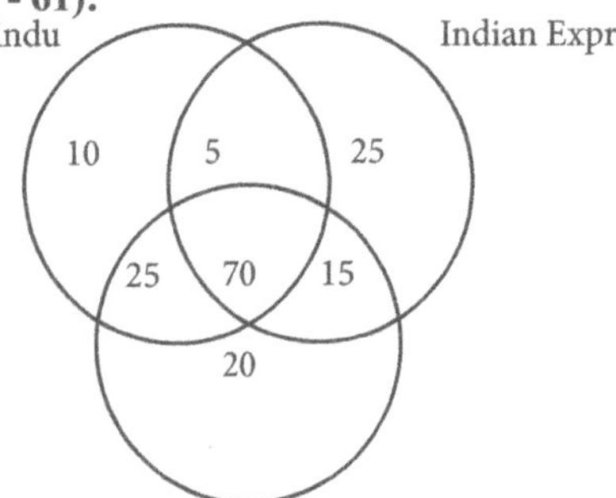

59. (b) There are 10 clients that read only The Hindu.

60. (c) These are 15 clients that read Indian Express and Times of India but not the Hindu.

61. (b) There are 25 clients that read only Indian Express.

62. (d) $6x + 2y = 2$ ...(i)

$3x + y = c_2$ ...(ii)

Multiply both sides of eq (ii) by 2,

$2(3x + y) = 2c_2$

$6x + 2y = 2c_2$ ...(iii)

On comparing the eqs. (i) and (iii) we get

$2 = 2c_2$

$c_2 = 1$

63. (d)

64. (d) Dividend $=$ Divisor $\times$ Quatient $+$ Remainder

$14528 =$ Divisor $\times 83 + 3$

$$\text{Divisor} = \frac{14528 - 3}{83} = \frac{14525}{83} = 175$$

65. (a) Sales in store P in 2010 $= ₹\, 80$ lakhs

Sales in store P in 2011

$$= ₹\left[80 + \left(80 \times \frac{20}{100}\right)\right] \text{lakhs}$$

$= ₹96$ lakhs

Sales in store P in 2012

$$= ₹\left[96 - \left(96 \times \frac{20}{100}\right)\right] \text{lakhs}$$

$$= ₹(96 - 19.2)\text{lakhs}$$

$$= ₹76.8 \text{ lakhs}$$

66. (b) Let sales in store T in 2011 $= ₹x$

$$\text{Sales in store T in 2012} = ₹\left[\left(x - \frac{8}{100} \times x\right)\right]$$

$$= ₹\left(x - \frac{8x}{100}\right)$$

$$= ₹\frac{92}{100}x$$

$\therefore$ Required percentage

$$= \left(\frac{x \times 100}{92x} \times 100\right)\%$$

$$= \frac{100 \times 100}{92}\% = 108.7\%$$

$$= 109\% \text{ (approx.)}$$

67. (d) Store Q had greater sales in 2012 than any other store.

68. (d) Based in the time period and the amount invested by Sunil and Gopal, the profit sharing ratio will be,

Sunil : Gopal

$₹\,(20000 \times 9) : ₹(30000 \times 12)$

$₹\, 180000 : 360000$

$18 : 36$

$= 1 : 2$

Thus, Sunil's share of profit

$$= ₹\left(\frac{1}{1+2} \times 60000\right)$$

$$= ₹\, 20000$$

69. (a) Coef. Variation

$$= \left(\frac{\text{Standard Deviation}}{\text{Mean}} \times 100\right)\%$$

$$= \left(\frac{5}{11} \times 100\right)\% = \frac{500}{11}\% = 45.45\%$$

70. (c) Mean of 14 observations $= 11$

Sum of 14 observations = $11 \times 14 = 154$
Since one more observation, x is added,
Sum of 15 observations = $154 + x$

$$\text{New mean} = \frac{\text{Sum of 15 observations}}{15}$$

$$\Rightarrow 12 = \frac{154 + x}{15}$$

$$\Rightarrow 12 \times 15 = 154 + x$$

$$180 - 154 = x \Rightarrow x = 26$$

71. (a) 5 women can do a work in 36 days.

$$\therefore \text{Work done in 1 day} = \frac{5}{36} \qquad ...(i)$$

5 men can do a work in x days

$$\therefore \text{Work done by men in 1 day} = \frac{5}{x} \quad ....(ii)$$

$$\text{Now, } \frac{\dfrac{5}{x}}{\dfrac{5}{36}} = \frac{3}{1} \Rightarrow \frac{36}{x} = 3 \Rightarrow x = 12 \text{ days}$$

72. (a)

73. (d)

$$N \xrightarrow{+2} P \qquad A \xrightarrow{+2} C$$
$$C \xrightarrow{+2} E \qquad M \xrightarrow{+2} O$$
$$L \xrightarrow{+2} N \qquad J \xrightarrow{+2} L$$
$$A \xrightarrow{+2} C \qquad M \xrightarrow{+2} O$$
$$G \xrightarrow{+2} I \qquad S \xrightarrow{+2} U$$
$$J \xrightarrow{+2} L \qquad P \xrightarrow{+2} R$$

74. (a) $\dfrac{\sin A + \cos A}{\sin A - \cos A} = \dfrac{5}{4}$

Applying componendo & Dividendo,

$$\frac{(\sin A + \cos A) + (\sin A - \cos A)}{(\sin A + \cos A) - (\sin A - \cos A)} = \frac{5 + 4}{5 - 4}$$

$$\frac{2 \sin A}{2 \cos A} = \frac{9}{1}$$

$$\tan A = 9$$

$$\text{Now, } \frac{\tan^2 A + 1}{\tan^2 A - 1} = \frac{(9)^2 + 1}{(9)^2 - 1}$$

$$= \frac{81 + 1}{81 - 1} = \frac{82}{80} = \frac{41}{40}$$

75. (d) By work equivalence method,
man $\times$ days $\times$ work = Man $\times$ Days $\times$ Work

$$\Rightarrow 15 \times 30 \times 1 = 30 \times x \times 2$$

$$\Rightarrow x = \frac{15 \times 30}{30 \times 2} = 7.5 \text{ days}$$

76. (d) Let the angles the $2x$ and $3x$

$$\therefore \text{Ratio} = \frac{(\text{Smaller angle})^2}{(\text{greater angle})^2} = \frac{(2x)^2}{(3x)^2}$$

$$= \frac{4x^2}{9x^2} = 4 : 9$$

77. (c) 78. (c)

79. (a) $\sin^6 A + \cos^6 A - 1$
$= (\sin^2 A)^3 + (\cos^2 A)^3 - 1$
$= [(\sin^2 A \cos^2 A)] (\sin^4 A + \cos^4 A - \sin^2 A \cos^2 A)] - 1$
$= (\sin^4 A + \cos^4 A - \sin^2 A \cos^2 A - 1)$
$\quad (\sin^2 A + \cos^2 A)^2 - 2 \sin^2 A \cos^2 A - \sin^2 A$
$\quad \cos^2 A - 1$
$= 1 - 3 \sin^2 A \cos^2 A - 1$
$= (-3 \sin^2 A \cos^2 A)$

80. (c)

Here
$$\begin{aligned} \alpha &\rightarrow & > \\ \beta &\rightarrow & < \\ \gamma &\rightarrow \ngtr &\rightarrow \leq \\ \delta &\rightarrow \nless &\rightarrow \geq \\ \mu &\rightarrow & = \end{aligned}$$

$\Rightarrow 3C \,\delta\, 2A = 3 C \geq 2A \quad ....(1)$
and $B \propto C = B > C \qquad ....(2)$
Eqn. (2) can allow be writen as
$\Rightarrow 3B > 2A = 3B \propto 2A$

81. (a) 82. (d)

83. (b) 84. (c)

85. (b) $1 + 3 + 5 + ... + 71$
$t_n = 71$
$\Rightarrow a + (n + 1) d = 71 \Rightarrow 1 + (n - 1)2 = 71$
$$\Rightarrow n = \left(\frac{71 - 1}{2}\right) + 1 = 35 + 1 = 36$$

$$\therefore \text{Sum} = \frac{n}{2}\big[2a + (n - 1)d\big]$$

$$= \frac{36}{2}\big[2(1) + (36 - 1)2\big]$$

$$= \frac{36}{2}(2 + 70) = \frac{36}{2} \times 72 = 1296$$

86. (a) Every second about 100 lightning bolts strike the earth's surface which is about 8 million per day and 3 billion each year.

87. (d)   88. (d)   89. (a)   90. (c)

91. (d) The relationship is :-

$$ab : a^2 + b^2 :: cd : c^2 + d^2$$
$$\therefore 32 : 3^2 + 2^2 :: 47 : 4^2 + 7^2$$

92. (a) 0.36, 2.72, 0.12, 1.44

or $\dfrac{36}{100}, \dfrac{272}{100}, \dfrac{12}{100}, \dfrac{144}{100}$

or $\dfrac{9}{25}, \dfrac{68}{25}, \dfrac{3}{25}, \dfrac{36}{25}$

$$\text{LCM of fractions} = \frac{\text{LCM of numerators}}{\text{HCF Denominators}}$$

$$= \frac{\text{LCM of } 9, 68, 3, \text{ and } 36}{\text{HCF of } 25, 25, 25 \text{ and } 25}$$

$$= \frac{612}{25} = 24.48$$

93. (c)   94. (b)

95. (c) $5 - 0 + 3 \times 5$
$$= 5 + 3 \times 5$$
$$= 5 + 15 = 20$$

96. (a) Transpiration is the process by which moisture is carried through plants and its evaporation from roots to small pores, where it changes to vapor and is released to the atmosphere. Water is necessary for plants but only a small amount of water taken up by the roots is used for growth and metabolism.

97. (b)   98. (b)

99. (a) Length of park = 50 m

Distance covered in 1 round of park = Perimeter of park

$$= 4 \times \text{side}$$
$$= 4 \times 50m = 200 \text{ m}$$

$$\text{Speed} = 18 \, \text{km/hr} = \frac{18 \times 1000}{3600} \, \text{m/s} = 5 \, \text{m/s}$$

$$\text{Time} = \frac{\text{distance}}{\text{speed}} = \frac{200}{5} \, \text{sec.} = 40 \, \text{sec.}$$

100. (d) Let CP = ₹$100x$

Loss = 5%

SP = ₹ $95x$

Now, Gain = 15%

new SP = ₹$(95x + 200)$

$$\therefore CP = \left(\frac{100}{100 + \text{gain}\%} \right) \times SP$$

$$\Rightarrow 100x = \frac{100}{100 + 15} \times (95x + 200)$$

$$\Rightarrow \frac{100x \times 115}{100} = 95x + 200$$

$$\Rightarrow 115x - 95x = 200 \Rightarrow x = 10$$

$$\therefore CP = ₹100x = ₹1000$$

Again Gain = 25%

CP = ₹1000

$$SP = ₹\left(1000 + \frac{25}{100} \times 1000 \right)$$

$$= (1000 + 250)$$

$$= ₹1250$$

1. If '**summer it hot**' it coded as '**de fe ba**' and '**come cold summer**' as '**ja ha ba**' and '**winter is cold**' as '**pa ja de**' then '**come hot winter**' is coded as __________.
   (a) de ba ja
   (b) fe ba pa
   (c) ba pa ha
   (d) pa ha fe

2. What is the minimum number to be subtracted from 6321, which makes it completely divisible by 14?
   (a) 8
   (b) 12
   (c) 7
   (d) 11

3. Jahangir was the _______ Mughal emperor of India.
   (a) 3rd
   (b) 4th
   (c) 5th
   (d) 6th

4. If P means '÷' R means '×', Q means '+' and S means '−', then
   48 P 8 Q 6 R 9 S 31 =?
   (a) 60
   (b) 29
   (c) 31
   (d) 54

5. ____________ granted charter to East India Company to establish trading posts in India in 1600.
   (a) Queen Elizabeth I
   (b) Queen Elizabeth II
   (c) King George V
   (d) King George VI

6. Ramdas invested Rs. 90000 in a cosmetic business. After few months. Shyamdas joined him with Rs. 30000. At the end of the year, the total profit was divided between them in ratio 4 : 1. After how many months did Shyamdas joined business?
   (a) 4
   (b) 3
   (c) 1
   (d) 6

7. Methane is known as ______________.
   (a) Laughing gas
   (b) Tear gas
   (c) Marsh gas
   (d) Non-greenhouse gas

8. Hawa Mahal in Jaipur is constructed using
   (a) White and green marble
   (b) Granite
   (c) Red and Pink sandstone
   (d) Normal rocks

9. If the angles of a triangle are in the ratio of 1:2:3, then find the value of the largest angle.
   (a) 30°
   (b) 60°
   (c) 90°
   (d) 120°

10. Read the given statements carefully and answer the question.
    Statement: Though the school bags policy has been announced, it is not clear how many schools arc following it. The state Government is also clueless whether schools have implemented the rules.
    Which of the following is true according to the given statement?
    (a) School bags policy has been implemented by the Government.
    (b) Schools are not interested in following the rules.
    (c) There is no monitoring system.
    (d) State Government is not interested in follow-up.

11. The concept of the game of ____________ is eliminating an opponent by touching.
    (a) Kho Kho
    (b) Kabaddi
    (c) Judo
    (d) Kalari

12. The mean of 22 observations is 10. Two more observations are included and the new mean becomes 11. The mean of two new observations is
    (a) 19
    (b) 20
    (c) 21
    (d) 22

13. An angle is 10° more than one third of its complement. Find the greater angle.
    (a) 30°
    (b) 60°
    (c) 45°
    (d) 75°

14. Neelam and Manisha starting from the same place run at a rate of 7 kmph and 9 kmph respectively. What time will they take to be 12 km apart. If they walk in the same direction?
    (a) 3 hours
    (b) 6 hours
    (c) 12 hours
    (d) 9 hours

15. Delhi metro covers a distance in 40 minutes, if it runs at a speed of 48 kmph on an average. Find the speed at which the train must run to reduce the time of journey to 32 minutes.
    (a) 60 kmph   (b) 50kmph
    (c) 70kmph   (d) 80kmph

16. The mean of a distribution is 13 and the standard deviation is 7. What is the value of the coefficient variation?
    (a) 50%   (b) 76.77%
    (c) 53.85%   (d) 38.88%

17. A car stops on applying brakes mainly due to __________ force.
    (a) Gravitational   (b) Centripetal
    (c) Frictional   (d) Centrifugal

18. Statements followed by some conclusions are given below.
    Statements:
    1. Knowledge is not a skill. It is learning and experience.
    2. The illiterate are not those who cannot read and write but those who cannot learn.
    Conclusions:
    I. Those who cannot read and write are literate.
    II. Knowledge and skill are two different things.
    Find which of the given conclusions logically follows from the given statements.
    (a) Only conclusion I follows.
    (b) Only conclusion II follows.
    (c) Both I and II follow.
    (d) Neither I nor II follows.

19. Statements followed by some conclusions are given below.
    Statements:
    1. Depleting natural resources is a major concern in our country.
    2. Unless we go for renewable energy sources in a big way, increase in population being a heavy burden on the energy resources, will reduce the quality of life.
    Conclusions:
    I. Depleting resources impacts quality of life.
    II. Use of renewable energy sources is a solution to counter increase in population.
    Find which of the given conclusions logically follows from the given statements.
    (a) Only conclusion I follows.

    (b) Only conclusion II follows.
    (c) Both I and 11 follow.
    (d) Neither I nor 11 follows.

20. Quartz used in clocks is __________ __________.
    (a) Nitrogen silicate   (b) Silicon dioxide
    (c) Sodium silicate   (d) Calcium silicate

21. The head of the state in India is the __________________.
    (a) Prime Minister
    (b) President
    (c) Parliament
    (d) Chief Justice of India

22. Name the type of government in Bangladesh.
    (a) Islamic Republic
    (b) Parliamentary Democracy
    (c) Federal Republic
    (d) Constitutional Monarchy

23. Which pair is not exactly similar to the other three pairs?
    (a) Principal : School
    (b) Pages : Note book
    (c) Letters : Word
    (d) Students : Class

24. Which Indian state shares its borders with the maximum number of other Indian states?
    (a) Manipur   (b) West Bengal
    (c) Assam   (d) Uttarakhand

25. __________________ does not refer to the game of playing card.
    (a) Bridge   (b) Blackjack
    (c) Squash   (d) Solitaire

26. __________________ was appointed as one of the Goodwill Ambassadors by UNDP in March 2016,
    (a) Ashley Judd   (b) Michelle Yeoh
    (c) Merrick Garland   (d) Hillary Clinton

27. __________ is the process of absorption of moisture from air.
    (a) Deliquescence   (b) Capillary action
    (c) Absorption   (d) Osmosis

28. The process of optimizing fat content in milk is called __________________.
    (a) Vitamin fortification
    (b) Pasteurization
    (c) Standardization
    (d) Homogenization

29. **Bird : Wings : : Fish : ?**
    (a) Gills   (b) Head
    (c) Fins   (d) Legs

30. An assertion (A) and a reason (R) are given below.

 Assertion (A): Perennial rivers mostly originate from the Himalayas.

 Reason (R): The fountains in the Himalayas feed the rivers.

 Choose the correct option.
 (a) Both A and R are true and R is the correct explanation of A
 (b) Both A and R are true, but R is not the correct explanation of A
 (c) A is true, but R is false
 (d) A is false, but R is true

31. Find the missing (?) in the series -
 3, 7, 13, 21, 31, ?
 (a) 41 (b) 42
 (c) 43 (d) 44

32. Which state has the second highest number of seats in the Lok Sabha?
 (a) Uttar Pradesh (b) Andhra Pradesh
 (c) West Bengal (d) Bihar

33. If **TABLE = RYZJC**, then **CHAIR = _______**
 _______.
 (a) AFZHQ (b) AFYGP
 (c) FAGYP (d) ZFAHQ

34. Find the odd pair out.
 (a) Nitrogen & oxygen : Air
 (b) Sulphur & Phosphorous : Match stick
 (c) Hydrogen & Oxygen : Water
 (d) Magnesium & Silver : Stainless steel

35. _____________ was the first Geographical Indication (GI) tagged product in India.
 (a) Darjeeling Tea (b) Solapuri Chaddar
 (c) Nagpur Orange (d) Orissa Ikat

36. Freezing point of water is _______.
 (a) 40° F (b) 42° F
 (c) 34° F (d) 32° F

37. **ADGJ, CFIL, EHKN, _____________.**
 (a) FILO (b) HKNQ
 (c) DGJM (d) GJMP

38. If the rate of interest is 8% per annum and Rs. 10000 lent at the compound interest half yearly then calculate the equivalent simple rate of interest for the first year?
 (a) 8.16% (b) 9%
 (c) 7% (d) 10%

39. '.docx' file is created with
 (a) Spreadsheet (b) Powerpoint
 (c) Word processor (d) Paint

40. Evaluate $(35/2)$% of 800 gm $- (45/2)$ % of 400 gm
 (a) 50 gm (b) 150 gm
 (c) 100 gm (d) 80 gm

41. 12 men finished 1/4 part of whole work in 6 days. Find the number of additional men required to complete the job in next 6 days.
 (a) 36 (b) 12
 (c) 18 (d) 24

42. B is the brother of C. D is the sister of B. F is the sister of E who is the son of C. K is the husband of C. How is D related to F?
 (a) Maternal Aunt (b) Mother
 (c) Sister (d) Niece

43. _____________ does not belong to the twelve zodiac signs.
 (a) Ophiuchus (b) Aquarius
 (c) Libra (d) Pisces

44. Rearrange the jumbled letters to make meaningful words and then select the one which is different.
 (a) ENIMSAJ (b) DLOGIRAM
 (c) TORRAC (d) REWOLFNUS

45. Taxonomy is basically related to _______ _____________.
 (a) Biodiversity
 (b) Tax structure
 (c) A branch of astronomy
 (d) Study of human behaviour

46. Ramesh purchased a memory card at a price of Rs. 625 including the sales tax. The rate of sales tax is 25%. If the seller has made a gain of 50%. then the cost price of the memory card is :
 (a) ₹ 333 (b) ₹ 310
 (c) ₹ 350 (d) ₹ 360

47. The shadow of a standing tower of height $25\sqrt{3}$ m is found to be 50 m longer when the sun's elevation changes from 60° to X°. Find the measure of X.
 (a) 45° (b) 30°
 (c) 75° (d) 90°

48. 30 person can finish a job in 20 days. After 6 days how many persons should leave the job, so that work is completed in a total of 26 days?
 (a) 9 (b) 12
 (c) 8 (d) 7

49. An investor invested 1/2 of his capital at 5%, 1/4 at 10% and rest at 8%. If his income after 2years is ₹2800, find the capital amount

(a) Rs. 10000   (b) Rs. 15000
(c) Rs. 20000   (d) Rs. 12000

50. The distance between the two poles of length 16 m and 9 m, is X m. If two angles of elevation of their respective top from the bottom of the other are complementary to each other then the value X is :
(a) 10m   (b) 15m
(c) 16m   (d) 12m

51. ___________________ is not a constituent of tooth paste.
(a) Abrasive   (b) Fluoride
(c) Lubricant   (d) Surfactant

DIRECTIONS (Qs. 52-54): *Consider the following information and answer questions based on it.*
Suresh is taller than Ramesh who is shorter than Rakesh. Jinesh is taller than the shortest person but shorter than Rakesh.
Pritesh is taller than Suresh but shorter than Jinesh.

---

52. Who is the shortest?
(a) Rakesh   (b) Ramesh
(c) Pritesh   (d) Suresh

53. If Jayesh who is taller taller Suresh joins the group, who will be fourth, if they are arranged in a descending order?
(a) Jayesh
(b) Jinesh
(c) Pritesh
(d) Cannot be determined

54. Which statement, among the following, is correct?
(a) Suresh is taller than Jinesh.
(b) Pritesh is shorter than Rakesh
(c) Jinesh is taller than Rakesh.
(d) Ramesh is taller than Pritesh.

55. If **VOTER = 41352, HEATER = 743654, TEASER = 645834**, which number represents S?
(a) 1   (b) 5
(c) 8   (d) 7

56. Pointing to a man, a woman said "he is the brother of the daughter of my husband's wife". What is the woman to the man?
(a) Son   (b) Mother
(c) Father   (d) Sister

57. Triangle PQR is such that PR=7.5 cm and triangle PQR is similar to triangle XYZ. If XY=18 and YZ=12 cm then find the ratio of PQ:QR

(a) 1:2   (b) 3:2
(c) 4:5   (d) 5:2

58. The planet Pluto was discovered in the year...
(a) 1925   (b) 1930
(c) 1935   (d) 1940

59. Two numbers are in the ratio 3:5. If each number is increased by 10, the ratio becomes 5:7. The smaller number is :
(a) 8   (b) 12
(c) 15   (d) 18

60. In 1955, ___________ was renamed as State Bank of India.
(a) Bank of Bengal
(b) Bank of Bombay
(c) Bank of Madras
(d) Imperial Bank of India

61. Two vessels contain milk and water in the ratio 2:3 and 7:5. Find the ratio in which the contents of the two vessels have to be mixed so that the ratio of milk and water in the new mixture is equal.
(a) 2:1   (b) 1:2
(c) 3:2   (d) 2:3

62. Find the value of 335 * 335 – 165 * 165?
(a) 20000   (b) 65000
(c) 85500   (d) 27500

63. Which one is not generally used as a fruit?
(a) Strawberry   (b) Grapes
(c) Pear   (d) Tomato

64. 'Make in India Week' was launched in ________________ from 13th to 18th February 2016.
(a) Bhubaneswar   (b) Udaipur
(c) Mysuru   (d) Mumbai

65. If **Chennai : Tamil Nadu**, the __________ : **Jharkhand**
(a) Raipur   (b) Ranchi
(c) Dhanbad   (d) Durgapur

66. **Read the given statements carefully and answer the question.**

Most people get their own cars to office. The number of vehicles on road is increasing day by day. It leads to traffic congestion and adds to the ever-increasing air pollution issues. As a result, respiratory problems are on a rise. People should, as far as possible, take public transport or do carpooling.

Which of the following situations better fits the above statement?

(a) People are becoming rich day by day and hence buying more cars.

   (b) People can go to the shopping malls in cars but not to office.

   (c) Respiratory problems doesn't affect the people who use public transport.

   (d) More number of vehicles on road leads to traffic congestion.

67. The famous forbidden city is in ____________.
(a) France
(b) Italy
(c) China
(d) USA

68. Rate of heat conduction in solids does not depend on ____________________.
(a) Density of the material
(b) Dimensions of the material
(c) Friction
(d) Electronic configuration

69. As per tiger census of 2014, tiger population in India was estimated at ____________.
(a) 1411
(b) 1706
(c) 2226
(d) 1906

70. ______________ was the theme for World Wetland Day in 2016.
(a) Sustainable Livelihoods
(b) Wetlands take care of water
(c) Wetlands for our future
(d) Wetlands and Agriculture

71. L is K's sister. M is the father of K. N and O are brothers. L is the mother of O. How is K related to N?
(a) Maternal Uncle
(b) Brother
(c) Nephew
(d) Cannot be determined

72. ______________ is used in refrigeration.
(a) Chlorofluorocarbon
(b) Carbon dioxide
(c) Nitrogen peroxide
(d) Ammonium oxide

73. If $(x^2 + 1/x^2)=6$, then find the value of $(10x - 10/x)$
(a) +/– 15
(b) +/– 20
(c) +/– 30
(d) +/– 40

74. Halley's comet is expected to return to the vicinity of earth in the year...
(a) 2086
(b) 2061
(c) 2041
(d) 2026

75. Asymmetric Digital Subscriber Line (ADSL) is ________ technology.
(a) a wireless data communication
(b) a wired data communication
(c) amateur radio communication
(d) satellite communication

76. Who was appointed as the Defense Minister when the 16th Lok Sabha was formed in 2014?
(a) Venkaiah Naidu
(b) Ravi Shankar Prasad
(c) Manohar Parikkar
(d) Suresh Prabhu

77. If '÷' means '+', '+' means '÷', and '–' means '×'. then
$$25 \div 25 + 5 \div 2 - 15 = ?$$
(a) 0
(b) –12
(c) 60
(d) 45

78. If **SMART = 31524, MARBLE = 428376** and **EAT = 537**, then **STABLE =?**
(a) 618537
(b) 253678
(c) 453678
(d) 243678

79. Choose the odd one out
(a) Optical disc
(b) Magnetic Storage
(c) Solid State Drive
(d) Petabyte

80. which one is not true with 'backup'?
(a) Exact copy of computer files.
(b) It is part of business continuity plan.
(c) PCs do not require regular back up.
(d) Offsite and on-site backup are more beneficial.

81. If the standard deviation of a population is 9.5, what would be the population variance?
(a) 19
(b) 90.25
(c) 81.25
(d) 93.25

82. Find the largest 6 digit number which is completely divided by 71.
(a) 999965
(b) 999954
(c) 999964
(d) 999974

83. The first, all women two wheeler public transportation service in India was started in
(a) Gurgaon
(b) Noida
(c) Chennai
(d) Bengaluru

84. If $(a - 1/a) = 3/4$, Find the value of $(a^3 - 1/a^3)$.
(a) 164/31
(b) 171/64
(c) 171/32
(d) 164/37

85. Find the greatest number which on dividing 3050 and 5200 leaves remainders 7 and 9 respectively.
(a) 149
(b) 111
(c) 153
(d) 179

DIRECTIONS (Qs. 86-88): *The following table represents the human resource profile of a global company.* Consider the table and answer questions based on it.

Country	No. of offices	Male		Female		Total
		Class I	Class II	Class I	Class II	
US	20	150	50	70	35	305
UK	15	115	40	65	20	240
India	10	125	25	45	90	285
Canada	10	80	30	50	10	170

86. The percentage of male employees in India to the total number of employees of the company is
   (a) 11%　　　　　(b) 15.5%
   (c) 15%　　　　　(d) 20%

87. Total number of employees in the company is
   (a) 950　　　　　(b) 960
   (c) 995　　　　　(d) 1000

88. The ratio of female employees of US to Canada is
   (a) 4 : 7　　　　　(b) 7 : 4
   (c) 21 : 17　　　　　(d) 21 : 29

89. The period of Dominion of India refers to
   (a) Pre-partition day
   (b) Pre-Independence day
   (c) Post Republic day
   (d) Independence day to Republic day

90. Who won the man of the match award in the 2016 Asia Cup T20 held in Bangladesh?
   (a) Bhuvaneshwar Kumar
   (b) Viral Kohli
   (c) Shikhar Dhawan
   (d) R Ashwin

91. What is the average of first 25 multiples of 11?
   (a) 152　　　　　(b) 147
   (c) 143　　　　　(d) 134

92. If $2x(x + y + z) = 250$, $2y(x + y + z) = 100$, $2z(x + y + z) = 100$. then find the value of $(3x + 6y + 15z)$.
   (a) 110　　　　　(b) 95
   (c) 85　　　　　(d) 69

93. Kakori train robbery took place in the year
   (a) 1923　　　　　(b) 1924
   (c) 1925　　　　　(d) 1926

94. By selling an article for Rs. 979, a shopkeeper bears a loss of 11%. If shopkeeper sells that article for Rs. 1232, then the profit % is:
   (a) 12%　　　　　(b) 21%
   (c) 11%　　　　　(d) 14%

95. The HCF and LCM of two numbers are 45 and 270 respectively. If the ratio of the two numbers is 2:3 and smaller of the two numbers is X. then find X^2.
   (a) 2025　　　　　(b) 4225
   (c) 8100　　　　　(d) 18225

96. Inflammation of the mucous membrane is called _________.
   (a) Bronchitis　　　　　(b) Hepatitis
   (c) Iritis　　　　　(d) Gastritis

DIRECTIONS (Qs. 97-99): *Consider the following information and answer the questions based on it.*

Out of 200 kids, 20 wanted to see only the galaxy, 25 wanted to see only stars, 30 wanted to see only planets, 50 wanted to see stars, planets and moon, 25 wanted to see both moon and galaxy, 25 wanted to see only moon and the remaining did not want to see anything.

97. In all, how many kids did not want to see only the galaxy?
   (a) 130　　　　　(b) 100
   (c) 155　　　　　(d) 125

98. In all, how many kids wanted to see the moon?
   (a) 50　　　　　(b) 75
   (c) 100　　　　　(d) 120

99. How many kids wanted to see at least 2 objects?
   (a) 50　　　　　(b) 25
   (c) 75　　　　　(d) 55

100. Manish purchased mobile phone and got 50% concession on the marked price of the phone and sold it for Rs. 8100 with 35% profit on the price he bought. What was the marked price?
   (a) ₹ 8000　　　　　(b) ₹ 12000
   (c) ₹ 10000　　　　　(d) ₹ 9000

HINTS & EXPLANATIONS

1. (d) Summer is hot $\longrightarrow$ de fe ba .....(1)

Come cold summer $\longrightarrow$ ja ha ba .....(2)

winter is cold $\longrightarrow$ pa ja de .....(3)

From (1) and (2) summer = ba

From (1) and (3) is = de

$\Rightarrow$ hot = fe

From (2) and (3) cold = ja

$\Rightarrow$ come = ha

$\Rightarrow$ winter = pa

$\therefore$ Come hot winter $\longrightarrow$ pa ha fe

2. (c)

$$14\overline{)6321}(451$$
$$\underline{-56}$$
$$72$$
$$\underline{70}$$
$$21$$
$$\underline{14}$$
$$\underline{7} \longleftarrow \text{Remainder}$$

$\therefore$ 7 must subtracted from 6321.

3. (b)

4. (b) 48 P 8 Q 6 R 9 S 31

= 48 ÷ 8 + 6 × 9 − 31

= 6 + 54 − 31

= 60 − 31 = 29

5. (a)

6. (b) Let Shyamdas joined for x months.

then $(90000 \times 12) : (30000 \times x) = 4 : 1$

$\Rightarrow$ 1080000 : 30000x = 4 : 1

$\Rightarrow \dfrac{1080000}{30000x} = \dfrac{4}{1}$

$\Rightarrow \dfrac{36}{x} = \dfrac{4}{1} \Rightarrow x = 9$

Hence, Shyamdas joined after (12 - 93) = 3 months.

7. (c) 8. (c)

9. (c) Let the angles be x, 2x and 3x respectively.

Now, sum of angles of a triangle = 180°

$\Rightarrow$ x + 2x + 3x = 180°

$\Rightarrow$ 6x = 180°

$\Rightarrow$ x = 30°

Hence, largest angle = 3x = 3 × 30° = 90°

10. (c) 11. (*)

12. (d) Mean of 22 observations = 10

Sum of 22 observations = 10 × 22 = 220

Mean of 24 observations = 11

Sum of 24 observations = 11 × 24 = 264

$\therefore$ Sum of 2 new observations = 264 − 220

= 44

mean of 2 new observations = $\dfrac{44}{2} = 22$

13. (b) Let the angle be $x°$.

its compliment = $(90° - x)$

Now, $x = 10° + \dfrac{1}{3}(90° - x)$

$\Rightarrow x - 10° = \dfrac{1}{3}(90° - x)$

$\Rightarrow 3(x - 10°) = 90° - x$

$\Rightarrow 3x - 30° = 90° - x$

$\Rightarrow 4x = 120° \Rightarrow x = 30°$

Hence, greater angle = $(90° - x) = (90° - 30)$

= 60°

14. (b) Both are running in the same direction,

So, relative speed = 9 − 7 = 2 kmph

Time required when they are aparted by 12 km

$= \dfrac{12}{2} = 6$ hours.

15. (a) Metro covers a distance in time = 40 minutes

Average speed = 48 kmph

$\therefore$ Distance = S × T

$= 48 \times \dfrac{40}{60} = 32\,\text{km}$

Now, new time = 32 minutes

$\therefore$ New speed = $\dfrac{\text{Distance}}{\text{time}} = \dfrac{32}{\dfrac{32}{60}}$

$= 32 \times \dfrac{60}{32} = 60\,\text{km/hr}$

16. (c) Coefficient variation

$= \left(\dfrac{\text{Standard Deviation}}{\text{Mean}} \times 100\right)$

$= \left(\dfrac{7}{13} \times 100\right) = 53.85\%$

17. (c) A car stops on applying brakes mainly due to frictional force because friction opposes the motion of an object, causing moving objects to lose energy, and hence, slows down.

18. (b) 19. (c)

20. (b) Silicon dioxide (SiO2), also known as silica, is a natural compound made of silicon (Si) and oxygen (O2). This compound has been known since ancient times, and in nature, silica is found as quartz.

21. (b) 22. (b) 23. (a) 24. (c) 25. (c) 26. (b)

27. (a) Deliquescence is the process by which a substance absorbs moisture from the atmosphere until it dissolves in the absorbed water and forms an aqueous solution. Most deliquescent materials are salts, including calcium chloride, magnesium chloride, zinc chloride, ferric chloride, potassium carbonate, etc.

28. (c) Standardization of milk is a process of rising or lowering of cream or fat in the milk. The cream is first removed, leaving skim milk and cream. The cream is then added back into the milk phase to 2.0% to give low fat milk. The standardization of milk is also done in the case of milk products, e.g., condensed milk, milk powder, ice-cream, cheese, etc.

29. (c) 30. (c)

31. (c)

$$\underset{+4}{3,}\ \underset{+6}{7,}\ \underset{+8}{13,}\ \underset{+10}{21,}\ \underset{+12}{31,}\ ?$$

$\therefore$ missing term $= 31 + 12 = 43$

32. (d)

33. (b)

$T \xrightarrow{-2} R$ $C \xrightarrow{-2} A$

$A \xrightarrow{-2} Y$ $H \xrightarrow{-2} F$

$B \xrightarrow{-2} Z \Rightarrow$ $A \xrightarrow{-2} Y$

$L \xrightarrow{-2} J$ $I \xrightarrow{-2} G$

$E \xrightarrow{-2} C$ $R \xrightarrow{-2} P$

34. (d) Stainless steel is a metal alloy, made up of steel mixed with elements such as chromium, nickel, molybdenum, silicon, aluminum, and carbon. Iron mixed with carbon to produce steel is the main component of stainless steel.

35. (a) 36. (d)

37. (d)

$$\underset{+3\ +3\ +3}{A\ D\ G\ J}\ ,\ \underset{+3\ +3\ +3}{C\ F\ I\ L}\ ,$$

$$\underset{+3\ +3\ +3}{E\ H\ K\ N}\ ,\ \underset{+3\ +3\ +3}{G\ J\ M\ P}$$

38. (a) ATQ

$$10000\left[1+\frac{8}{200}\right]^2 - 10000 = \frac{10000 \times r \times 1}{100}$$

$$\left[1+\frac{8}{200}\right]^2 - 1 = \frac{r}{100}$$

$$\left[\frac{26}{25}\right]^2 - 1 = \frac{r}{100}$$

$$\frac{26^2 - 25^2}{25^2} = \frac{r}{100} \quad \Rightarrow \quad \frac{51 \times 1}{625} = \frac{r}{100}$$

$\therefore$ r $= 8.16\%$

39. (c)

40. (a) $\dfrac{35}{2}$ % of 800 gm $- \dfrac{45}{2}$ % of 400 gm

$$= \left(\frac{35}{2 \times 100} \times 800\right) gm - \left(\frac{45}{2 \times 100} \times 400\right) gm$$

$$= \left[(35 \times 4) - (45 \times 2)\right] gm$$

$$= (140 - 90) gm$$

$$= 50 \ gm$$

41. (d) According to question

Total work

$= \quad 12 \times 6 \times 4$

Work left $= 1 - \dfrac{1}{4} = \dfrac{3}{4} \times (12 \times 6 \times 4)$, which

is equal to $\left[(12+x) \times 6\right]$; where x is the additional no. of men.

$\therefore \quad \dfrac{3}{4} \times (12 \times 6 \times 4) = (12 + x) \times 6$

$\Rightarrow \quad \dfrac{3 \times 12 \times 6}{6} = (12 + x)$

$\Rightarrow \quad 36 - 12 = x$

$\therefore \quad x = 24$

42. (a)

$$\overset{(-)}{D} \text{——} \overset{(+)}{B} \text{——} \overset{(-)}{C} \longleftrightarrow \overset{(+)}{K}$$

$$\overset{}{E} \text{——} \overset{}{F}$$
$$\underset{(+)}{} \quad \underset{(-)}{}$$

Here K and C are husband wife. E, F are childrens of C.

D, B and C are siblings

$\therefore$ D is the Maternal Aunt of F.

43. (a) 44. (c) 45. (a)

46. (a) Let CP of memory card $= ₹$ x

gain $= 50\%$

$\therefore$ SP for seller $= \dfrac{100 + \text{gain}\%}{100} \times CP$

$$= \frac{100+50}{100} \times x = \frac{150}{100}x = ₹\frac{3}{2}x$$

sale tax = 25%

now Ramesh paid for memory card = ₹625

$$\Rightarrow \quad \frac{3}{2}x + \left(\frac{3}{2}x \times 25\%\right) = 625$$

$$\Rightarrow \quad \frac{3}{2}x + \left(\frac{3}{2}x \times \frac{1}{4}\right) = 625$$

$$\Rightarrow \quad \frac{3}{2}x + \frac{3x}{8} = 625$$

$$\Rightarrow \quad \frac{15}{8}x = 625 \quad \Rightarrow \quad x = \frac{625 \times 8}{15}$$

$$= ₹\,333.33 \quad \Rightarrow ₹\,333 \text{ (approx)}$$

47. (b)

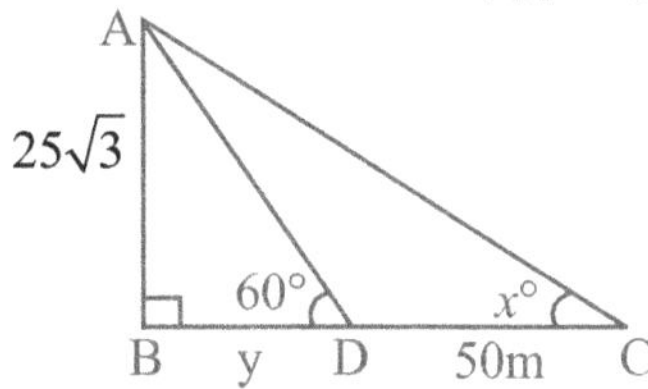

In $\triangle ABD$,

$$\tan 60° = \frac{\text{Perp.}}{\text{Base}} = \frac{AB}{BD} = \frac{25\sqrt{3}}{y}$$

$$\Rightarrow \quad \sqrt{3} = \frac{25\sqrt{3}}{y} \Rightarrow \quad y = 25$$

In $\triangle ABC$,

$$\tan x° = \frac{\text{Perp.}}{\text{Base}} = \frac{AB}{BC}$$

$$\Rightarrow \quad \tan x° = \frac{25\sqrt{3}}{y+50} = \frac{25\sqrt{3}}{25+50}$$

$$\Rightarrow \tan x° = \frac{25\sqrt{3}}{75} \quad \Rightarrow \tan x° = \frac{\sqrt{3}}{3} = \frac{1}{\sqrt{3}}$$

$$\Rightarrow \quad \tan x° = \tan 30° \quad \Rightarrow x° = 30°.$$

48. (a) Let x people left the job affter 6 days

Total work = 30 × 20

Work done in 6 days by 30 men = 30 × 6

∴ Remaining work = 30 × 14

This work,

∴ (30 − x) people will work in next 20

(= 26 − 6) days.

$$\Rightarrow \quad 30 \times 14 = (30 - x) \times 20$$

$$(30 - x) = \frac{30 \times 14}{20} = 21$$

$x = 30 - 21 = 9$ men

49. (c) Let the capital be ₹x

∴ Total income after 1 year $= ₹\dfrac{2800}{2}$

$$\Rightarrow \left(\frac{1}{2}x \times \frac{5}{100}\right) + \left(\frac{1}{4}x \times \frac{10}{100}\right) + \left(\frac{1}{4}x \times \frac{8}{100}\right) = 1400$$

$$\Rightarrow \quad \frac{x}{40} + \frac{x}{40} + \frac{x}{50} = 1400$$

$$\Rightarrow \quad \frac{5x+5x+4x}{200} = 1400 \quad \Rightarrow \quad x = \frac{1400 \times 200}{14}$$

$$\Rightarrow \quad x = 100 \times 200 = ₹20000$$

50. (d)

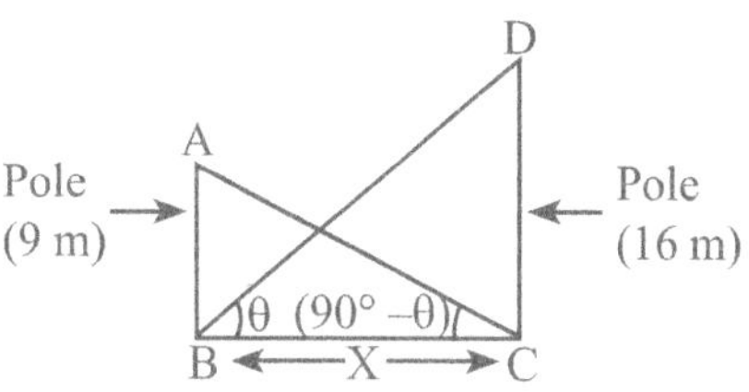

In $\triangle BCD$,

$$\tan\theta = \frac{CD}{BC} = \frac{16}{X} \qquad \dots (i)$$

In $\triangle ABC$,

$$\tan(90° - \theta) = \frac{AB}{BC} \Rightarrow \cot\theta = \frac{9}{X}$$

$$\Rightarrow \quad \frac{1}{\tan\theta} = \frac{9}{X} \quad \Rightarrow \frac{1}{\frac{16}{X}} = \frac{9}{X} \Rightarrow \frac{X}{16} = \frac{9}{X}$$

$$\Rightarrow \quad X^2 = 16 \times 9 \quad \Rightarrow \quad x = 4 \times 3 = 12m$$

51. (c)

Sol. (52-54)

Rakesh ← Tallest
Jinesh
Pritesh
Suresh
Ramesh ← Shortest

52. (b) Ramesh is the shortest

53. (d) If Jayesh tatter than Suresh joins the group. He can be at any place above Suresh so we are not sure who will be at 4th spot after arranging in descending order.

54. (b) Among the following statements, Pritesh is shorter than Rakesh is the correct one.

55. (c)

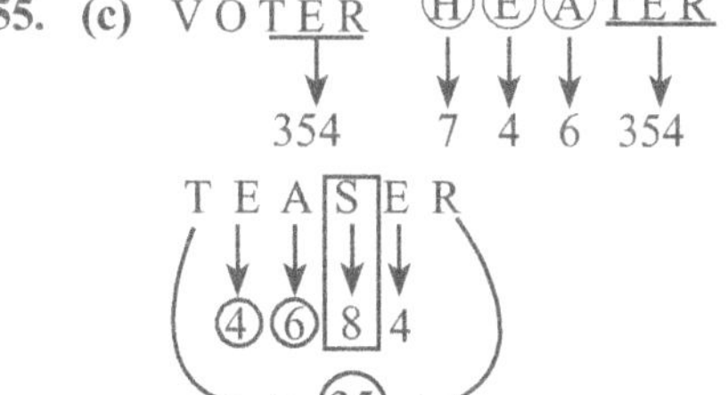

56. (b) Brother of the daughter of my husband's wife, means brother of my daughter, means by son And so, that women is mother of that man

57. (b) $\dfrac{PQ}{XY} = \dfrac{QR}{YZ}$ (by S - S - S)

$\Rightarrow \dfrac{PQ}{QR} = \dfrac{XY}{YZ} \Rightarrow \dfrac{18}{12} = \dfrac{PQ}{QR} \Rightarrow \dfrac{PQ}{QR} = \dfrac{3}{2}$

$\therefore$ PQ : QR = 3 : 2

58. (b)

59. (c) Let the numbers be 3x and 5x. Now,

$$\dfrac{3x+10}{5x+10} = \dfrac{5}{7}$$

$\Rightarrow$ 7(3x + 10) = 5 (5x + 10)

$\Rightarrow$ 21x + 70 = 25x + 50

$\Rightarrow$ 70 − 50 = 25x − 21x

$\Rightarrow$ 20 = 4x

$\Rightarrow$ x = $\dfrac{20}{4}$ = 5

Hence, smaller number = 3x = 3×5=15

60. (d)

61. (a) Let the quantity of milk in two vessels be 2x and 3x and quantity of water in two vessels be 7y and 5y respectively

$\therefore \quad \dfrac{2x+7y}{3x+5y} = \dfrac{1}{1}$

$\Rightarrow$ 2x + 7y = 3x + 5y

$\Rightarrow$ 7y − 5y = 3x − 2x

$\Rightarrow$ 2y = x

$\Rightarrow \dfrac{2}{1} = \dfrac{x}{y} \Rightarrow x : y = 2 : 1$

62. (c) $335 \times 335 - 165 \times 165 = (335)^2 - (165)^2$

= (335 + 165) (335 − 165)

= 500 × 170

= 85000

63. (d) 64. (d) 65. (b) 66. (d) 67. (c) 68. (c)

69. (c) 70. (a)

71. (d) M (+)

K ——— L (−)

(+) O ——— N(+)

Here K and L are children of M and L is the mother of O and N since we are not sure about the gender of K.

$\therefore$ K can either be maternal uncle or maternal aunt of N. Hence cannot be determined.

72. (a) Chlorofluorocarbons are compounds that were used as refrigerants in air conditioning systems and refrigerators. Since it was found that CFCs contribute to ozone depletion in the atmosphere, they were replaced with other products such as hydrofluorocarbons.

73. (b) $x^2 + \dfrac{1}{x^2} = 6$

$\Rightarrow \left(x^2 + \dfrac{1}{x^2} - 2\right) = 6 - 2$

$\Rightarrow \left(x - \dfrac{1}{x}\right)^2 = 4$

$\Rightarrow \left(x - \dfrac{1}{x}\right) = \pm 2$

Now, $10x - \dfrac{10}{x} = 10\left(x - \dfrac{1}{x}\right) = 10(2)$ or $10(-2)$

= 20 or (−20)

= ±20

74. (b) The next predicted perihelion of Halley's Comet is 28 July 2061. It is expected to be better positioned for observation as this time it will be on the same side of the Sun as Earth. The comet's periodicity was first determined in 1705 by English astronomer Edmond Halley after whom it is now named.

75. (b) 76. (c)

77. (c) $25 \div 25 + 5 \div 2 - 15 = 25 + 25 \div 5 + 2 \times 15$

= 25 + 5 + 2 × 15

= 25 + 5 + 30

= 60

78. (a) SMART = 31524 .....(1)

MARBLE = 428376 .....(2)

EAT = 537 .....(3)

From 1, 2 and 3, A = 3

From 1 and 3, T = 5 $\Rightarrow$ E = 7

From 1 and 2, S = 1 $\Rightarrow$ $\left.{}^{M_1}_{R}\right\} \to 2,4$

$\therefore$ STABLE = 153687 = 618537

$= \left.{}^{B}_{L}\right\} \to 6, 8$

79. (d) 80. (c)

81. (b) Variance = (Standard Deviation)^2

= (9.5)^2

= 90.25

82. (c) Largest 6 digit number = 999999

$$71\overline{)999999}\;(14084$$

$$\begin{array}{r} 71 \\ \hline 289 \\ 284 \\ \hline 599 \\ 568 \\ \hline 319 \\ 284 \\ \hline 35 \end{array}$$

Hence, required largest 6 digit no.
= 999999 – 35 = 999964

83. (a)

84. (b) $\left(a - \dfrac{1}{a}\right) = \dfrac{3}{4}$

$$\left(a - \frac{1}{a}\right)^3 = a^3 - \frac{1}{a^3} - 3a\left(\frac{1}{a}\right)\left(a - \frac{1}{a}\right)$$

$$\Rightarrow \left(\frac{3}{4}\right)^3 = a^3 - \frac{1}{a^3} - 3\left(\frac{3}{4}\right)$$

$$\Rightarrow a^3 - \frac{1}{a^3} = \frac{27}{64} + \frac{9}{4}$$

$$= \frac{27 + 144}{64} = \frac{171}{64}$$

85. (d) 3050 – 7 = 3043

5200 – 9 = 5191

HCF of 3043 and 5191 = 179

∴ 179 is the greatest number which on dividing 3050 and 5200 leaves remainders 7 and 9 respectively.

86. (c) Male employees in India = 125 + 25 = 150

Total employees of company = 305 + 240 + 285 + 170

= 1000

∴ % of male employees = $\left(\dfrac{150}{1000} \times 100\right)$ %

= 15%

87. (d) Total number of employees in the company

= 305 + 240 + 285 + 170

= 1000

88. (b) Female employees in US = 70 + 35 = 105

Female employees in Canada = 50 + 10 = 60

∴ Required ratio $= \dfrac{105}{60} = \dfrac{21}{12}$

$$= \frac{7}{4} = 7:4$$

89. (d) 90. (*)

91. (c) 11, 22, 23, ... 25 terms.

$n = 25$

$a = 11$

$d = 11$

Sum of 25 multiples $= \dfrac{n}{2}\left[2(a) + (n-1)d\right]$

Here n = 25

$$Sum = \frac{25}{2}[2(11) + (25-1)11]$$

$$= \frac{25}{2}[22 + 264] = 25 \times 143 = 3575$$

∴ Mean $= \dfrac{Sum}{25} = \dfrac{3575}{25} = 143$

92. (b)

2x (x + y + z) = 250	........(i)
2y (x + y + z) = 100	........(ii)
2z (x + y + z) = 100	........(iii)

Adding (i), (ii) and (iii), we get

(2x + 2y + 2z) (x + y + z) = 450

2 (x + y + z)² = 450

(x + y + z) = $\sqrt{225}$ = 15 ....(iv)

Putting (x + y + z) = 15 in

Eq. (i), (ii), (iii), we get

$x = \dfrac{25}{3}, y = \dfrac{10}{3}$ and $z = \dfrac{10}{3}$

∴ (3x + 6y + 15z)

$$= 3\left(\frac{25}{3}\right) + 6\left(\frac{10}{3}\right) + 15\left(\frac{10}{3}\right)$$

= 25 + 20 + 50

= 95

93. (c)

94. (a) SP = ₹ 979 and loss = 11%

$$\therefore CP = \left[\frac{100}{(100 - loss\%)} \times SP\right]$$

$$= \left[\frac{100}{(100 - 11)} \times 979\right]$$

$$= ₹\left(\frac{100}{89} \times 979\right) = ₹\ 1100$$

Again new S.P. = ₹ 1232

∴ Profit % $= \left[\left(\dfrac{SP - CP}{CP}\right) \times 100\right]\%$

$$= \left(\frac{1232 - 1100}{1100} \times 100\right)\% = \left(\frac{132}{1100} \times 100\right)\%$$

= 12%

95. (c) Let the numbers be $2x$ and $3x$.

$$X = 2x \text{ (given)} \qquad \text{.........(i)}$$

Now, HCF × LCM = Product of two numbers

$$\Rightarrow \quad 45 \times 270 = 2x \times 3x$$

$$\Rightarrow \quad x^2 = \frac{45 \times 270}{2 \times 3} = 2025$$

$$\Rightarrow \quad x = \sqrt{2025} = 45$$

$$\therefore X^2 = (2x)^2 = (2 \times 45)^2 = 8100$$

96. (a)

Sol. (97-99):

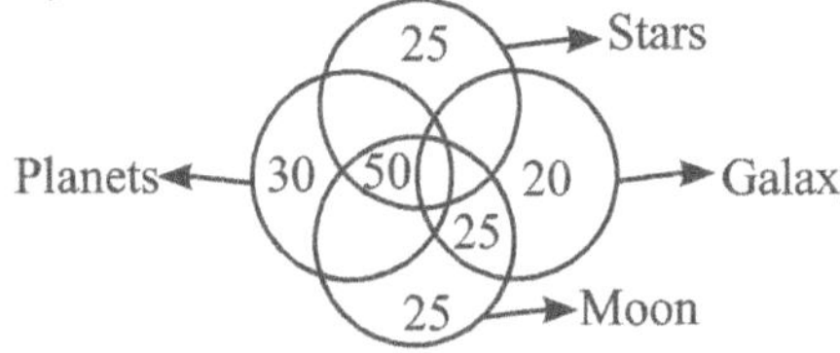

From the diagram : Total no. of Kids who wanted to see Stars or Planets or Galaxy or Moon
$$= 25 + 30 + 20 + 25 + 25 + 50 = 175$$

97. (c) No. of Kids who didn't want to see only Galaxy = $175 - 20 = 155$

98. (c) No. o f kids who wanted to see the moon
$$= 25 + 25 + 50 = 100$$

99. (c) No. of kids who wanted to see at least 2 objects
$$= 20 + 50 = 75$$

100. (b) SP of phone = ₹ 8100

Profit = 35%

$$\therefore CP = \left(\frac{100}{100+35}\right) \times 8100$$

$$= \left(\frac{100}{135} \times 8100\right)$$

$$= ₹ 6000$$

or Manish bought mobile phone for ₹ 6000 after 50% concession.

$$\therefore \qquad MP = ₹ 6000 + (50\% \text{ of } MP)$$

$$\Rightarrow \qquad MP = ₹ 6000 + \frac{1}{2}$$

$$\Rightarrow MP - \frac{1}{2} MP = ₹ 6000$$

$$\Rightarrow \qquad \frac{1}{2} MP = ₹ 6000$$

$$\Rightarrow \qquad MP = ₹ 6000 + 2 = ₹ 12000$$

1. If '**how are you**' is written as '**ne kl se**' and '**where are you**' as '**ne bl se**' and '**you were here**' as '**ke ne jo**', then '**how you here**' is written as
   (a) ke kl ne
   (b) se ne kl
   (c) ne bl ke
   (d) bl se ne

2. _______________ is not a type of heat transfer.
   (a) Diffusion
   (b) Reflection
   (c) Convection
   (d) Radiation

3. International Women's day is celebrated on _______ March every year.
   (a) 6th
   (b) 7th
   (c) 8th
   (d) 9th

4. Replace # sign with the mathematical operators '+', '÷', '–' or = to get balanced equation out of 186 #31 #36 #30
   (a) + ÷ =
   (b) – = +
   (c) – + ÷
   (d) ÷ = –

5. Triangle PQR is such that PQ = 9 cm, QR = 6 cm, PR = 7.5 cm and triangle PQR is similar to triangle XYZ. If XY = 18 cm, find the value of YZ.
   (a) 15cm
   (b) 18 cm
   (c) 12 cm
   (d) 9 cm

6. _______________ is used as a stabilizer in ice cream.
   (a) Gelatin
   (b) Sugar
   (c) Milk
   (d) Strawberry

7. The major ingredient of sweetened soft drink is
   (a) Carbonated water
   (b) Hydrochloric acid
   (c) Phosphoric acid
   (d) Caffeine

8. ₹10000 is being compounded at 20% per annum. Calculate the amount alter 2 years if rate of interest is charged half yearly.
   (a) ₹ 10041
   (b) ₹ 14641
   (c) ₹ 12000
   (d) ₹ 13660

9. Pakistani film industry is known as _______________.
   (a) Pollywood
   (b) Lollywood
   (c) Kollywood
   (d) Mollywood

10. The mean of a distribution is 18 and the standard deviation is 4.5. What is the value of the coefficient of variation?
    (a) 50%
    (b) 25%
    (c) 100%
    (d) 75%

11. If $a^3 + b^3 + c^3 - 3abc = 0$, then find the value of $(a^2/bc + b^2/ac - 3)$.
    (a) $-c^2/ab$
    (b) $-c^2/bc$
    (c) $-c^3/ba$
    (d) $-c/a$

12. Pointing to a woman, I said that her brother's only son is the brother of my wife. How is the woman related to me?
    (a) Father-in-law's sister
    (b) Mother-in-law
    (c) Sister-in-law
    (d) Sister

13. Which of the following states does not share a border with Myanmar?
    (a) Assam
    (b) Mizoram
    (c) Nagaland
    (d) Manipur

14. Geographical Indication (GI) is related to _______________ having unique geographic origin and evolution over centuries.
    (a) Hills
    (b) Mountain ranges
    (c) Plains
    (d) Products

15. In March 2016 Rlection Commission of India declared assembly elections in ____ states scheduled for April May 2016.
    (a) 3
    (b) 7
    (c) 5
    (d) 6

16. 10 persons can do a job in X days. If 20 persons with twice the efficiency can do the same job in 5 days, then find the value of X?
    (a) 40
    (b) 15
    (c) 20
    (d) 30

17. P can do a piece of work in 60 days & Q can do the same work in 50 days. Find the ratio of working efficiencies of P to Q.
    (a) 1/3
    (b) 6/5
    (c) 5/6
    (d) 4/5

18. A kite is flying at a height of 50m. If the length of string is 100m then the inclination of string to the horizontal ground in degree measures is:
    (a) 90
    (b) 45
    (c) 60
    (d) 30

19. Retinol is mainly related to ___________.
    (a) Vitamin A   (b) Vitamin B
    (c) Vitamin D   (d) Vitamin E
20. A lady said that father of Rahul's father is my father. How is the lady related to Rahul?
    (a) Mother   (b) Paternal aunt
    (c) Sister   (d) Niece
21. Bollywood actor _________ has been selected for the 47th Dadasaheb Phalke Award for 2015.
    (a) Dilip Kumar   (b) Manoj Kumar
    (c) Rajinikanth   (d) Anupam Kher
22. **Read the given statement carefully and answer the question.**

    A group of people getting together casually without prior planning and in a relaxed manner is called informal gathering.

    Which of the following situations better fits the above statement?
    (a) A group celebrates every month on salary day.
    (b) Invitees gather on the occasion of wedding reception.
    (c) Soon after the release of mark list, top 10 rankers gather to greet each other.
    (d) People gather to witness beating retreat at Wagah border in Amritsar.
23. Sleep apnea is related to ________ while sleeping.
    (a) walking   (b) talking
    (c) snoring   (d) smiling
24. Boiling point of water is _________.
    (a) 210°F   (b) 212°F
    (c) 214°F   (d) 208°F
25. **Circumvent : Bypass : : Comprehensible :**

    ____
    (a) Understandable   (b) Unclear
    (c) Grasping   (d) Apprehend
26. Find the sum of first 8 odd prime numbers.
    (a) 77   (b) 98
    (c) 75   (d) 100
27. If $a = 2b/3$, $b = 2c/3$, and $c = 2d/3$, then find the ratio of b and d :
    (a) 8/9   (b) 4/9
    (c) 4/3   (d) 5/27
28. Window's 10 is
    (a) an utility software.
    (b) a browser.
    (c) an application software.
    (d) an operating system.
29. One of the techniques used for desalination of sea water is
    (a) Filtration   (b) Distillation
    (c) Evaporation   (d) Condensation

DIRECTIONS (Qs. 30-32): *The following table represents the number of fans of stars MSD, VK, RD and SR in different areas of a town. Consider the information and answer the following questions based on it.*

	Area 1	Area 2	Area 3	Area 4
VK	2500	1700	2300	5000
MSD	3000	3000	4000	3100
RD	1500	3500	4500	5200
SR	1500	4000	3500	2500

30. What is the difference between the numbers of fans of Area 2 to that of Area 3?
    (a) Area 2 has 2200 more fans
    (b) Area 2 has 2100 less fans
    (c) Area 3 has 2200 more fans
    (d) Area 3 has 2200 less fans
31. What is the difference between the total number of fans of SR and MSD?
    (a) 1500   (b) 1600
    (c) 3000   (d) 3200
32. In all. who has the highest number of fans?
    (a) VK   (b) MSD
    (c) RD   (d) SR
33. Echocardiogram is more closely related to
    (a) Doppler effect
    (b) Zeeman effect
    (c) Photoelectric effect
    (d) Magnetic effect
34. Statements followed by some conclusions are given below.
    Statements:
    1. Compulsive online shopping has become a common behavior among youngsters.
    2. This is evident from most of those seeking counseling for de-addiction.
    Conclusions:
    I. All youngsters are addicted online shopping.
    II. All youngsters seek counseling for de-addiction.

Find which of the given conclusions logically follows from the given statements.
(a) Only conclusion I follows
(b) Only conclusion II follows
(c) Both I and II follow
(d) Neither I nor II follows

35. In a mixture 25 litres, the ratio of milk and water is 4:1. How many litres of milk must be added to make the ratio 16:1?
(a) 21   (b) 25
(c) 60   (d) 36

36. World Wetland day is celebrated every year on _______ February.
(a) 2nd (b) 3rd
(c) 4th (d) 5th

37. Night blindness : Sight : : ______ : speech
(a) Talk   (b) Stutter
(c) Speak   (d) Lecture

38. Davis Cup 2015 final was held in _________.
(a) UK   (b) Australia
(c) Belgium   (d) Argentina

39. Mohan starts to calculate sum of all odd natural number less than 83. What result does he get?
(a) 1456   (b) 1681
(c) 1437   (d) 1671

40. 'Start' menu in a standard personal computer is
(a) Part of the hardware
(b) A set of options and commands
(c) Nothing but the status bar
(d) Network related

41. If the mathematical operator '÷' means '×', '+' means '−', '×' means '+' and '−' means '÷', then
$24 + 48 − 12 × 4 ÷ 2 = ?$
(a) 6   (b) −6
(c) 16   (d) 28

42. Avalanche : Ice :: Volcano : _________
(a) Lava   (b) Sand
(c) Heat   (d) Earth

43. The process of reducing the milk fat globules size to allow them to stay evenly distributed in milk is called ________.
(a) Standardization   (b) Pasteurization
(c) Homogenization   (d) Fortification

44. _____________ was the 3rd Mughal Emperor of India.
(a) Humayun   (b) Akbar
(c) Aurangzeb   (d) Jahangir

45. Velocity of a car does not depend on
(a) Speedometer
(b) Change in direction
(c) Change in speed
(d) Change in acceleration

46. The Colosseum, known as the Flavran amphitheater, is located in ____.
(a) Venice   (b) Rome
(c) Milan   (d) Vatican City

47. Mukesh got series of discount 30%, 25%, 15% on his shirt. Find out the single equivalent discount.
(a) 52.34%   (b) 38.35%
(c) 55.38%   (d) 57.38%

48. In March 2016 National Green Tribunal imposed an initial compensation of Rs. 5 Crore on _______________ for tampering with the Yamuna river's flood plains.
(a) Kalki Avatar Foundation
(b) Art of Living Foundation
(c) Emissaries of Divine Light
(d) Sant Nirankari Mission

49. The ancient Indian legal document 'Manusmriti' was written in ___________.
(a) Tamil   (b) Hindi
(c) Sanskrit   (d) Bengali

50. Find the missing (?) in the series:
...., FHJ, KMO, PRT, ?
(a) UVZ   (b) UXZ
(c) UVW   (d) UWY

51. India won the 2016 Asia Cup T20 held in Bangladesh by ___________ wickets.
(a) 7   (b) 6
(c) 5   (d) 8

52. Kakori train robbery was organized by the _______________ in 1925.
(a) Swaraj Party
(b) Indian National Congress
(c) Anushilan Samiti
(d) Hindustan Republican Association

53. The mean of 20 observations is 19. One more observation is included and the new mean becomes 20. The 21th observation is:
(a) 20   (b) 30
(c) 40   (d) 42

54. Golconda Fort was built during ___________.
(a) Vijayanagara Empire
(b) Qutb Shahi dynasty
(c) Satavahana dynasty
(d) Hoysala Dynasty

55. Provincial Autonomy was provided by _______________.
(a) The Government of India Act 1935
(b) The Montague-Chelmsford Report
(c) The Government of India Act 1919
(d) The Indian Independence Act 1947

56. Who is number 1 in the Forbes 2016 ranking of World's billionaires?
(a) Warren Buffet (b) Amancio Ortega
(c) Bill Gates (d) Carlos Slim Helu

57. In a factory, 60 workers can stitch 120 m of clothes in 7 days, what length of clothes can be stitched by 70 workers in 5 days?
(a) 100 m (b) 90 m
(c) 85 m (d) 110 m

58. Which one reveals, more appropriately, functioning of the heart?
(a) Electrocardiogram (b) Echocardiogram
(c) Stethoscope (d) Lipid profile

59. Given that $(a^2 + b^2) = 60$, then find the value of $(a + b)^2 + (a - b)^2$.
(a) 90 (b) 120
(c) 140 (d) 150

60. Mother of K's father is the sister of G. S is the daughter of G. How is S related to K's father?
(a) Cousin sister
(b) Mother
(c) Paternal Aunt
(d) Cannot be determined.

61. A balloon is connected to a meteorological station by a cable of length 130 m. inclined at 60° to the horizontal. Find the height of the balloon from the ground. Assume that there is no slack in cable.
(a) 110.32 m (b) 173 m
(c) 163.25 m (d) 112.58 m

62. Orbital period of Halley's comet is _______ years.
(a) 25 (b) 50
(c) 75 (d) 100

63. Find the greatest number which on dividing 1580 and 3800 leaves remainders 8 and 1 respectively.
(a) 262 (b) 131
(c) 65.5 (d) 393

64. Which one is not the cause of kidney stone formation?
(a) Drinking more water
(b) Diabetic mellitus
(c) Taking nuts rich in oxalate
(d) Eating lot of stone forming foods

65. If the angles of a triangle are in the ratio of 2:3:5, then find the ratio of the greatest angle to the smallest angle.
(a) 7:2 (b) 5:2
(c) 5:3 (d) 3:5

66. The annual financial statement prepared under article 112 of the Indian Constitution is called _______________.
(a) Public account
(b) Consolidated account
(c) Budget
(d) Revenue account

67. Ram travels $4/9^{th}$ of the total journey by bus. $5/18^{th}$ by rail and the remaining 10 km on foot. Find the distance of total journey.
(a) 42 km (b) 90 km
(c) 36 km (d) 18 km

68. If $a = 5$, $b = 4$, $c = 8$ then find the value of $(a^3 + b^3 + c^3 - 3\,abc)/(ab + bc + ca - a^2 - b^2 - c^2)$.
(a) 15 (b) 17
(c) −17 (d) −15

69. The average age of a batch of 19 members is 24 years. If the age of the faculty be included, then the average increases by 4 months. What is the age of the faculty?
(a) 35 yean (b) 30 years 8 months
(c) 37 years 4 months (d) 32 yean 8 months

70. **Courtroom : Judge :: Stadium : _______ _______.**
(a) Landlord (b) Organizer
(c) Referee (d) Promoter

71. The tennis star, _________________ was provisionally suspended after testing positive for banned drugs during Australian open 2016.
(a) Maria Sharapova
(b) Serena Williams
(c) Ana Ivanovic
(d) Andy Murray

DIRECTIONS (Qs. 72-74): *Consider the following information and answer the questions based on it.*

Out of the 75 birders, 15 wanted to see only sunbird. 10 wanted to see only flycatcher, 12 wanted to see both sunbird and nuthatch, 15 wanted to see only bee-eater, 13 wanted to see both sunbird and bee-eater, 5 wanted to see both flycatcher and nuthatch and the remaining wanted to see only nuthatch.

72. The difference between the birders who want to see sunbird and those who want to see flycatcher is
(a) 12 (b) 25
(c) 30 (d) 15

73. How many birders wanted to see only one bird?
(a) 30 (b) 40
(c) 45 (d) 50

74. The ratio of birders who like nuthatch to those who like bee-eaters is
    (a) 11/14   (b) 10/7
    (c) 11/20   (d) 30/8

75. Find the missing (?) in the series:
    9, 4, 16, 6, 36, 9, 81, ?
    (a) 12   (b) 10
    (c) 11   (d) 13

76. Charles Wilkinson's English version of Bhagavad Gita was first published in the year
    (a) 1685   (b) 1725
    (c) 1785   (d) 1885

77. A sum of money of ₹1000 is lent out in two parts in such a way that the interest on one part at 10% per annum for 5 years is equal to another at 5% for 10 years. Calculate the sum lent out at 5%.
    (a) ₹ 500   (b) ₹ 800
    (c) ₹ 1000   (d) ₹ 1200

78. In a certain code, **329** means '**you are bad**', **419** means '**bad is good**' and 195 means 'nothing is bad:- represents 'good'.
    (a) 9   (b) 4
    (c) 1   (d) 3

79. Any online 'demo' is ______________
    ______________.
    (a) An interactive presentation
    (b) A non-interactive presentation
    (c) Not a sequential presentation
    (d) An active user interface

80. In a certain code, **324** means '**are you alright**'. **783** means '**you come home**' and **9271** means '**we are at home**'. Which digit represents 'come'?
    (a) 8   (b) 9
    (c) 7   (d) 3

81. The game of football is also referred to as ______________.
    (a) Rugby   (b) Poker
    (c) Soccer   (d) Ping-Pong

82. Rearrange the jumbled letters to make meaningful words and then select the one which is different.
    (a) OMESU   (b) ROTINOM
    (c) RETIAW   (d) RETNTRP

83. Find the odd pair out.
    (a) Nitrogen : Air
    (b) Hydrogen : Water
    (c) Uranium : Coins
    (d) Sulphur : Match stick

84. Neeraj purchased a few shirts for his shop at cost prices ranging from ₹ 400 to ₹ 550 and sold at prices ranging from ₹ 450 to ₹ 650. What is the maximum profit that might be made in selling 10 shifts?
    (a) ₹2800   (b) ₹2500
    (c) ₹2400   (d) ₹2000

85. As per historical astronomy there are ______________ zodiac divisions.
    (a) 9   (b) 10
    (c) 11   (d) 12

86. How much is the maximum % discount that Sheela can offer to her customer on her Marked Price so that she sells her product at no profit or loss, if she had already marked her product by 25% more than the cost price?
    (a) 25%   (b) 20%
    (c) 30%   (d) 40%

87. If the standard deviation of a population is 10, what would be the population variance?
    (a) 100   (b) 30
    (c) 5   (d) 20

88. An assertion (A) and a reason (R) are given below.
    Assertion (A): Electric wires are generally made of copper.
    Reason (R): Copper is a good conductor of electricity.
    Choose the correct option.
    (a) Both A and R are true and R is the correct explanation of A
    (b) Both A and R are true, but R is not the correct explanation of A
    (c) A is true, but R is false
    (d) A is false, but R is true

89. Ram is thrice as fast as Mohan and Mohan is twice as fast as Sohan. The distance covered by Sohan in 42 minutes will be covered by Mohan in:
    (a) 18 minutes
    (b) 21 minutes
    (c) 20 minutes
    (d) 22 minutes

90. An angle is 60° more than one fifth of its complement. Find the smaller angle in degrees.
    (a) 65°   (b) 35°
    (c) 25°   (d) 45°

DIRECTIONS (Qs. 91-93): *Consider the following information and answer questions based on it.*

Seven bottles colored – brown, blue, black, violet, white, indigo and purple are kept in a row, in random order, from left to right such that the —

1. White and purple bottles are not at either extremes.
2. Brown bottle is to the immediate right of violet bottle and to the immediate left of the white bottle.
3. White, violet and brown bottles are not at the center.
4. Black bottle is to the immediate left of purple bottle.
5. Blue bottle is neither second last nor at either extremes.

91. Bottles at the extreme right and left ends are
(a) Violet and purple   (b) Indigo and violet
(c) Black and indigo   (d) Black and violet

92. Which bottle is at the center of the row?
(a) Black bottle   (b) Indigo bottle
(c) Blue bottle   (d) Purple bottle

93. Which of the following statement is correct?
(a) Indigo bottle is to the immediate left of the purple bottle.
(b) Blue is to the immediate right of the purple bottle.
(c) There are at least five bottles between brown and black.
(d) Black bottle is to the immediate right of the blue bottle.

94. **Statements followed by some conclusions are given below.**
Statements:
1. Demand and supply determine the prices of goods and services.
2. When there are too many buyers, prices are pushed up and too many sellers push down prices.
Conclusions:
I. Buyers and sellers determine the prices.
II. Price discovery is market driven.
Find which of the given conclusions logically follows from the given statements.

(a) Only conclusion I follows
(b) Only conclusion II follows
(c) Both I and II follow
(d) Neither I nor II follows

95. Find the value of $6 + 11 + 16 + 21 + ... + 71$.
(a) 539   (b) 561
(c) 661   (d) 639

96. The astronomer who discovered planet Pluto was _______.
(a) Sylvain Arend   (b) Joseph Asbrook
(c) Edwin Hubble   (d) Clyde Tombaugh

97. Read the given statements carefully and answer the question.
Statement: the main reasons behind cyber criminals using international phone numbers to cheat the public, by asking their secured credit card details are
(i) it is easy to convince people and
(ii) it is difficult to trace the calls coming from foreign countries.
Which of the following is true according to the given statement?
(a) There are only two reasons behind such calls.
(b) People have full faith in foreign calls.
(c) It is not possible to trace foreign calls.
(d) Cyber criminals prefer international calls to cheat gullible people.

98. Three numbers are in the ratio of 3:5:10 and LCM is 630. Find their HCF.
(a) 21   (b) 42
(c) 63   (d) 36

99. 3 years ago, the ratio of Maya's and Shikha's age was 5:9 respectively. After 5 years, this ratio would become 3 : 5. Find present age of Maya?
(a) 40   (b) 45
(c) 43   (d) 53

100. If '**god is fair**' = '**ge se fa**', '**who is god**' = '**ge we fa**' and '**you are god**' = '**ne le fa**', which code does represent '**is**'?
(a) se   (b) ge
(c) fa   (d) we

HINTS & EXPLANATIONS

1. (a) How are you $\longrightarrow$ ne kl se ......(1)
Where are you $\longrightarrow$ ne bl se ......(2)
You were here $\longrightarrow$ ke ne go ......(3)
From (1), (2) and (3)
You = ne, are = se, where = bl, how = kl, were = go and here = ke
$\therefore$ how you here $\longrightarrow$ ke kl ne

2. (b) 3. (c)

4. (d) 186 # 31 # 36 # 30

replacing # with mathematical operator signs
$$186 \div 31 = 36 - 30$$
$$\Rightarrow \qquad 6 = 6$$

5. (c) Since the triangles are similar.

$\therefore$ taking the ratio of corresponding sides of these triangles.

$$\frac{PQ}{XY} = \frac{QR}{YZ} \qquad \Rightarrow \qquad \frac{9}{18} = \frac{6}{YZ}$$
$$\Rightarrow \qquad YZ = 12 \text{ cm}$$

6. (a) Gelatin is a common ingredient added in ice creams, puddings and several other recipes. It absorbs free water in the ice cream and prevents the formation of large crystals. It also gives the less watery taste to ice creams.

7. (a) 90% of carbonated water is present in sweetened soft drinks. There are no key ingredients of carbonated water and it is sweetened with either sugar or high-fructose corn syrup, which is a combination of fructose and dextrose.

8. (b) Amount $= P\left(1 + \dfrac{r}{n}\right)^{nt}$

here p = 10000
r = 20%
n = 2
t = 2

$$\therefore \quad A = 10000\left(1 + \frac{20}{200}\right)^{4}$$
$$= 10000\,(1.1)^4$$
$$= 10000\,(1.4641)$$
$$A = ₹14641$$

9. (b)

10. (b) Coefficient of variation $= \dfrac{\text{S.D}}{\text{Mean}} \times 100$

$$\Rightarrow \quad CV \quad = \frac{4.5}{18} \times 100$$
$$= 25\%$$

11. (a) $\dfrac{a^2}{bc} + \dfrac{b^2}{ac} - 3 = \dfrac{a^3}{abc} + \dfrac{b^3}{abc} - 3$

{Equalizing the denominutors}

$$= \frac{a^3 + b^3 - 3abc}{abc}$$
$$= \frac{3abc - c^3 - 3abc}{abc}$$

$[\therefore a + b + c = 0]$
$[\therefore a^3 + b^3 + c^3 = 3abc.]$

$$= \frac{-c^3}{abc} = \frac{-c^2}{ab}$$

12. (a) Woman's brother's only son is the brother of my wife $\Rightarrow$ Woman's brother is my Father-in Low

$\therefore$ woman is Father-in-law's sister.

13. (a) 14. (d) 15. (c)

16. (c) 10 persons can do a job in x days.

20 persons can do it in $\dfrac{x}{2}$ days.

So 20 persons with twice the efficiency can do job in $\dfrac{x}{4}$ days.

But since 20 persons can do it in 5 days [given]

$$\therefore \quad \frac{x}{4} = 5 \quad \Rightarrow x = 20$$

17. **(c)** Work efficiency of P = $\dfrac{1}{60}$

Work efficiency of Q = $\dfrac{1}{50}$

∴ required ratio = $\dfrac{\dfrac{1}{60}}{\dfrac{1}{50}} = \dfrac{50}{60} = \dfrac{5}{6}$

18. **(d)** Here AC is the length of string = 100 m and AB is the height of kite = 50 m

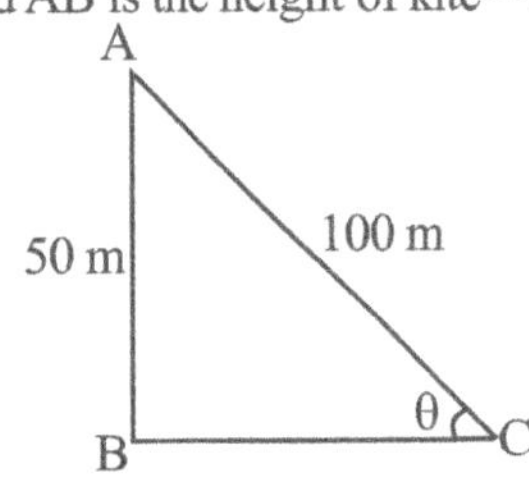

$\Rightarrow \sin\theta = \dfrac{AB}{AC} = \dfrac{50}{100}$

$\Rightarrow \sin\theta = \dfrac{1}{2}$

$\Rightarrow \sin\theta = \sin 30°$

$\Rightarrow \quad \theta = 30°$

19. **(a)** Retinol, also known as Vitamin A, is a yellow, fat-soluble substance. It is used to treat and prevent the deficiency of Vitamin A. According to the World Health Organization's List of Essential Medicines, it is the most effective and safe medicines needed in a health system.

20. **(b)**

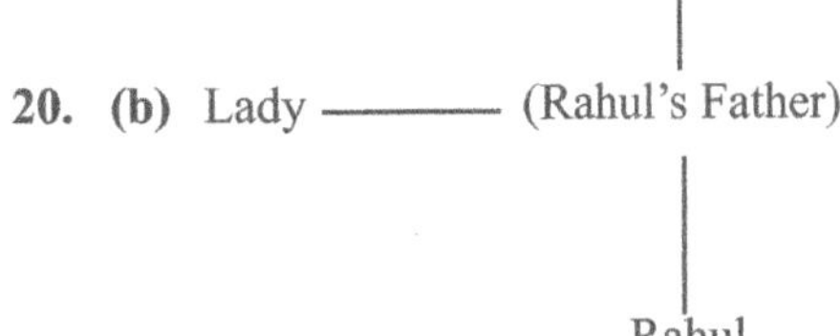

Lady is sister of Rahul's father and hence paternal aunt of Rahul.

21. **(b)** **22.** **(c)**

23. **(c)** Sleep apnea is sleep disorder that causes your breathing to become shallow or stop completely during sleep. Snoring, breathing pauses or choking noises during sleep are some of the symptoms of sleep apnea.

24. **(b)** **25.** **(a)**

26. **(b)** First 8 odd prime numbers are {3, 5, 7, 11, 13, 17, 19, 23}
Sum = 3 + 5 + 7 + 11 + 13 + 17 19 + 23 = 98

27. **(b)** a = 2b/3 , b = 2c/3 and c = 2d/3

$\Rightarrow b = \dfrac{2(2d/3)}{3} = \dfrac{4d}{9}$

$\Rightarrow 9b = 4d$

$\Rightarrow b/d = 4/9$

28. **(d)**

29. **(b)** Distillation is the most commonly used method for desalination of seawater. Distillation is a method whereby saline water is heated to produce water vapor, which is then condensed to produce freshwater. The boiling phase only evaporates the water while leaving other elements (including dissolved salts) behind.

30. **(b)** No. of fans of Area 2 = 12200
No. of fans of Area 3 = 14300
Difference = 14300 – 12200 = 2100
⇒ Area 2 has 2100 less fans.

31. **(b)** Total no. of fans of SR. = 11500
Total no. of fan of MSD = 13100
Difference = 13100 – 11500 = 1600

32. **(c)** No. of fans of VK   = 11500
No. of fans of MSD = 13100
No. of fans of RD   = 14700
No. of fans of SR   = 11500
The star with the highest no. of fans is RD.

33. **(a)** Echocardiogram is more closely related to Doppler's effect because echocardiogram uses high frequency of sound waves to create an image of the heart while Doppler Effect determines the speed and direction of blood flow.

34. **(d)**

35. **(c)** Total mixture = 25 litres

and ratio of milk to water = 4 : 1

$\Rightarrow$ $4x + x = 25 \Rightarrow x = 5$

$\therefore$ 20 litres of milk and 5 litres of water

Now ratio = 16 : 1

Let y litres of milk be added to the old mixture

$\therefore$ $\dfrac{20 + y}{5} = \dfrac{16}{1}$ $\Rightarrow 20 + y = 80$

$\Rightarrow y = 60$

36. **(a)**   **37.** **(b)**   **38.** **(c)**

39. **(b)** Required sum = 1 + 3 +.........+ 81

Let n be the total no. of term

Now $t_n = [a + (n-1)d]$

$\therefore$ $81 = [1 + (n-1)2]$

$81 = 2n - 1$ $\Rightarrow n = \dfrac{82}{2} = 41$

Also sum of n terms $= \dfrac{n}{2}[2a + (n-1)d]$

$= \dfrac{41}{2}[2 + (80)] = \dfrac{41 \times 82}{2}$

$= 1681$

40. **(b)**

41. **(d)** $24 + 48 - 12 \times 4 \div 2 = 24 - 48 \div 12 + 4 \times 2$

$= 24 - 4 + 8$

$= 28$

42. **(a)**

43. **(c)** The homogenization of milk is the process where the milk fat globules are reduced in size and dispersed uniformly through the rest of the milk. Homogenization breaks the fat into smaller sizes so that it no longer separates. Homogenization is achieved by a mechanical device called a homogenizer.

44. **(b)**   **45.** **(a)**   **46.** **(b)**

47. **(c)** Required single equivalent discount

$=$

$\left[1 - \left(1 - \dfrac{30}{100}\right)\left(1 - \dfrac{25}{100}\right)\left(1 - \dfrac{15}{100}\right)\right] \times 100\%$

$= \left[1 - \dfrac{70}{100} \times \dfrac{75}{100} \times \dfrac{85}{100}\right] \times 100\%$

$= [1 - 0.44625] \times 100\%$

$= 0.55375 \times 100\%$

$= 55.375\% \approx 55.38\%$

48. **(b)**   **49.** **(c)**

50. **(d)**

U   W   Y   F   H   J
$+2$ $+2$ $+2$ $+2$

K   M   O   P   R   T
$+2$ $+2$ $+2$ $+2$

51. **(d)**   **52.** **(d)**

53. **(c)** Means of 20 observation is 19

$\Rightarrow$ sum = 20 × 19 = 380

After 1 observation is added.

New mean = 20

$\Rightarrow$ New sum = 21 × 20 = 420

Hence 21st observation = 420 − 380

$= 40$

54. **(b)**   **55.** **(a)**   **56.** **(c)**

57. **(a)** 60 workers in 7 days stitch 120 m of cloth

$\Rightarrow$ 1 worker in 7 days stitches $\dfrac{120}{60}$m

$\Rightarrow$ 1 worker in 1 day stitches $\dfrac{120}{60 \times 7}$

$\therefore$ 70 workers in 5 day stitch

$\dfrac{120}{60 \times 7} \times 70 \times 5\text{m}$

$= \dfrac{120 \times 10 \times 5}{60}\text{m}$

$= 100\text{m}$

58. **(b)**

59. **(b)** $a^2 + b^2 = 60 \Rightarrow$ $(a+b)^2 - 2ab = 60$

$\Rightarrow (a+b)^2 + (a-b)^2 = (a+b)^2 + a^2 + b^2 - 2ab$

$= (a+b)^2 - 2ab + (a^2 + b^2)$

$= 60 + 60 = 120$

60. **(a)** Mother of k's father ———— G

K's father   S

K

Mother of K's father is the sister of G and S is daughter of G. $\Rightarrow$ S is the cousis sister of K's father.

61. **(d)**   **62.** **(c)**

63. **(b)** We first subtract 8 from 1580 and 1 from 3800 and then find the HCF of remaining numbers.

∴ HCF of 1572 and 3799

$3799 = 29 \times 131$

$1572 = 2 \times 2 \times 3 \times 131$

$HCF = 131$

∴ 131 is the required number.

64. **(a)**

65. **(b)** Since the ratio of angles is $2 : 3 : 5$

Hence ratio of greatest to smallest angle $= 5 : 2$

66. **(c)**

67. **(c)** Let total Journey $= x$ km

$$\Rightarrow \frac{4x}{9} + \frac{5x}{18} + 10 = x$$

$$\Rightarrow x - \left(\frac{4x}{9} + \frac{5x}{18}\right) = 10$$

$$\Rightarrow x - \frac{13x}{18} = 10 \qquad \Rightarrow 5x = 180$$

$$\Rightarrow x = 36 \text{ km}$$

68. **(c)**

$$\frac{(a^3 + b^3 + c^3 - 3abc)}{(ab + bc + ca - a^2 - b^2 - c^2)}$$

$$= \frac{(a + b + c)(a^2 + b^2 + c^2 - ab - bc - ca)}{-(a^2 + b^2 + c^2 - ab - bc - ca)}$$

$$= -(a + b + c) \qquad \qquad ...(1)$$

Substituting the values of a, b & c equation (1) becomes $\qquad -(5 + 4 + 8) = -17$

69. **(b)** Sum of ages of 19 members $= 19 \times 24 = 456$ Years

New average $= 24\dfrac{1}{3}$ years

New sum $= 24\dfrac{1}{3} \times 20$

$= 486\dfrac{2}{3}$ years

∴ age of faculty $= 486\dfrac{2}{3} - 456$

$= 30\dfrac{2}{3}$ years

$= 30$ years 8 months

70. **(c)**

71. **(a)**

Sol. (72–74):

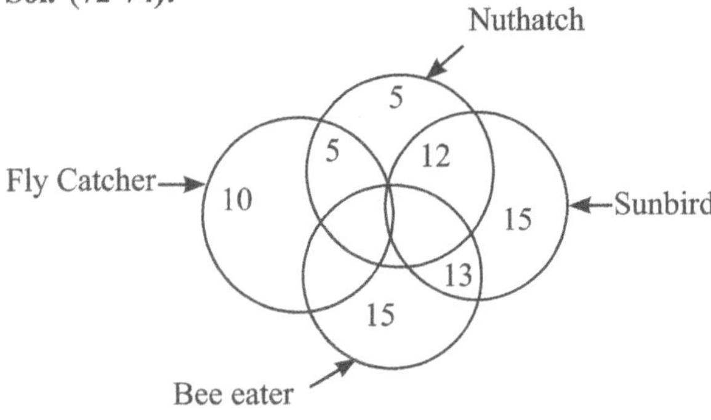

72. **(b)** No. of birders that wanted to see sunbird $= 15 + 12 + 13 = 40$

No. of birders that wanted to see fly catcher $= 10 + 5 = 15$

Difference $= 40 - 15 = 25$

73. **(c)** No. of birders that wanted to see only one bird $- 15 + 15 + 10 + 5 = 45$

74. **(a)** No. of birders who like nuthatch $= 5 + 5 + 12 = 22$

No. of birders who like bee-eaters $= 15 + 13 = 28$

∴ required ratio $= \dfrac{22}{28} = \dfrac{11}{14}$

75. **(c)**   **76.** **(c)**

77. **(a)** Let x be the sum lent out at 5%

Then, ATQ

$$\frac{x \times 10 \times 5}{100} = \frac{(1000 - x) \times 5 \times 10}{100}$$

$$\Rightarrow x = 1000 - x$$

$$\Rightarrow x = 500$$

78. **(b)** You are bad $\longrightarrow$ 329 $\qquad$ ...(1)

bad is good $\longrightarrow$ 419 $\qquad$ ...(2)

nothing is bad $\longrightarrow$ 195 $\qquad$ ...(3)

from (1) (2) and (3)

bad $= 9$, is $= 1$, good $= 4$, nothing $= 5$

∴ good $= 4$

79. **(b)**

80. **(a)** are you alright $\longrightarrow$ 324 $\qquad$ ...(1)

you come home $\longrightarrow$ 783 $\qquad$ ...(2)

we are at home $\longrightarrow$ 9271 $\qquad$ ...(3)

from (1), (2) and (3)

home $= 7$, you $= 3$, come $= 8$

∴ come $= 8$

81. (c)   82. (c)   83. (c)

84. (b) Cost price rangers from ₹ 400 – ₹ 550 and selling price rangers from ₹ 450 – ₹ 650

Now for maximum profit, cost price should be minimum and selling should be maximum.

$$\Rightarrow \qquad CP = ₹ \ 400 \ \& \ SP = ₹ \ 650$$

for 10 shirts $CP = 400 \times 10 = ₹ \ 4000$

$$SP = 650 \times 10 = ₹ \ 6500$$

∴   profit $= ₹6500 – ₹ \ 4000$

$$= ₹ \ 2500$$

85. (d)

86. (b) ATQ

Marked price $= \dfrac{125}{100} \times$ cost price $= \dfrac{5}{4}$ CP

For no profit no loss

$$SP = CP$$

$$SP = MP – discount$$

$$\Rightarrow \quad \frac{5}{4} CP \left(1 - \frac{x}{100}\right) = CP \Rightarrow 1 - \frac{x}{100} = \frac{4}{5}$$

$$\Rightarrow x = 20\%$$

87. (a) Here SD $\left(\sqrt{\sigma}\right) = 10$

$$\Rightarrow \quad \text{population variance } (\sigma) \ = \quad 10^2$$

$$= \quad 100$$

88. (a) As copper is a highly conductive metal, electric wires are generally made of copper. This is because copper can carry more electrical current per area of wire than any other non-precious metal. Moreover, the ductile properties of copper allow copper electrical wires to bend and flex and still transmit electric current to pass easily.

89. (b) Let speed of Mohan $= v_m$

and Time $= t_m$

also speed of Sohan $= v_s$

and Time $= t_s = 42$ minutes [given]

Now $v_m = 2v_s \Rightarrow \dfrac{v_m}{v_s} = 2$

Since $v \ \alpha \ \dfrac{1}{t} \ \Rightarrow \dfrac{v_m}{v_s} = \dfrac{t_s}{t_m}$

$$\Rightarrow \quad \frac{t_s}{t_m} = 2 \ \Rightarrow \ t_m = \frac{42}{2} = 21 \text{ minutes}$$

90. (c) Let θ be the smaller angle.

ATQ

$$\theta = \frac{1}{5}(90 - \theta) + 60°$$

$$\Rightarrow 5\theta = 90° – \theta + 300°$$

$$\Rightarrow 5\theta = 390° – \theta \Rightarrow 6\theta = 390°$$

$$\Rightarrow \quad \theta = 65°$$

∴   Smaller angle $= 90° – 65° = \quad 25°$

Sol. (91-93):

The correct order of bottles in the row will be as Violet, Brown, White, Blue, Black, purple, Indigo

91. (b) Indigo and Violet are at the extreme right and left ends of the row.

92. (c) Blue bottle is at the Centre of the row.

93. (d) Black bottle is to the immediate right of the blue bottle.

94. (c)

95. (a) $6 + 11 + 16 + ... + 71$

$t_n = 71$

$$\Rightarrow a + (n – 1)d = 71 \Rightarrow 6 + (n –1)5 = 71$$

$$\Rightarrow 6 + 5n – 5 = 71$$

$$\Rightarrow 5n = 71 – 1 = 70 \Rightarrow n = 14$$

∴ $S_{14} = \dfrac{14}{2}[2(6) + (14 – 1)(5)] = 7(12 + 65) = 7(77)$

$$= 539$$

96. (d)   97. (d)

98. (a) Let the there numbers be $3x$, $5x$, and $10x$

$\Rightarrow$ LCM of $(3x, 5x, 10x) = 30x$

But LCM = 360 (Given)

$\Rightarrow$ $30x = 360 \quad \Rightarrow x = 21$

∴   The number are $(3 \times 21, 5 \times 21$ and $10 \times 21)$

$\Rightarrow$ HCF of $3 \times 21, 5 \times 21$ and $10 \times 21 = 21$

Hence their HCF = 21

99. (c) Let the present age of Maya and Shikha be x and y respectively.

ATQ $\dfrac{x-3}{y-3} = \dfrac{5}{9}$ $\Rightarrow 9x - 27 = 5y - 15$

$\Rightarrow 9x - 5y - 12 = 0$ ...(1)

also $\dfrac{x+5}{y+5} = \dfrac{3}{5}$ $\Rightarrow 5x + 25 = 3y + 15$

$\Rightarrow 5x - 3y + 10 = 0$ ...(2)

Multiply equation (1) by 3 and equation (2) by 5

$27x - 15y - 36 = 0$ ...(3)

$25x - 15y + 50 = 0$ ...(4)

Subtracting equation (4) from equation (3)

$x = 43, y = 75$

Hence Maya's present age is 43 years.

100. (b) god is fair $\longrightarrow$ ge se fa   ...(1)

who is god $\longrightarrow$ ge we fa   ...(2)

you are god $\longrightarrow$ ne le fa   ...(3)

from (1), (2) and (3)

god = fa, is = ge

$\therefore$ is = ge

1. Which of the following is NOT a fundamental right of an Indian Citizen?
   - (a) Right to Equality
   - (b) Right to Privacy
   - (c) Right to Life
   - (d) Right against Exploitation

2. If **TRACTER = 14** and **TROLLEY = 14**, then **SCOOTER =**
   - (a) 24
   - (b) 14
   - (c) 28
   - (d) 30

3. If **TIGER** is coded as **REGIT**, how is **LEOPARD** coded?
   - (a) DRAOPLE
   - (b) DRAPLED
   - (c) DRAPOEL
   - (d) DRAOPEL

4. Correct expression of $0.02\overline{36}$ =?
   - (a) $\dfrac{13}{550}$
   - (b) $\dfrac{236}{1000}$
   - (c) $2\dfrac{30}{1000}$
   - (d) $\dfrac{15}{555}$

DIRECTIONS (Qs. 5-7): *Read the data given below and answer the questions based on it.*

There were 3 sections namely A, B, and C in a test. Out of three sections, 33 students passed in Section A, 34 students passed in Section B and 32 passed in Section C. 10 students passed in Section A and Section B, 9 passed in Section B and Section C, 8 passed in Section A and Section C. The number of students who passed each section alone was equal and was 21 for each section.

5. How many passed only one of the three sections?
   - (a) 21
   - (b) 42
   - (c) 63
   - (d) 52

6. How many passed all the three sections?
   - (a) 3
   - (b) 6
   - (c) 5
   - (d) 7

7. The ratio of the number of students passed in one or more of the sections to the number of students who passed in Section A alone is:
   - (a) 78/21
   - (b) 3
   - (c) 73/21
   - (d) $\dfrac{65}{21}$

8. If "÷" denotes "multiplication", "−" denotes "addition", "+" denotes "division" and "×" denotes "subtraction", then which of the following is the value of the expression
   $19 \div 9 \times 51 - 171 + 19$
   - (a) 143
   - (b) 129
   - (c) 179
   - (d) 131

9. Divide Rs.156 in the ratio 1:2:4:5. The rupees in the respective ratios are given by:
   - (a) 13, 26, 53 & 64
   - (b) 13, 26, 51 & 66
   - (c) 13, 26, 52 & 65
   - (d) 13, 25, 53 & 65

10. To prevent rancidity of oil (due to oxidation) in which potato chips are fried, the bags of chips are flushed with the gas -
   - (a) Oxygen
   - (b) Hydrogen
   - (c) Nitrogen
   - (d) Chlorine

11. The other term for genetic engineering is:
   - (a) DNA fingerprinting
   - (b) DNA editing
   - (c) Recombinant DNA technology
   - (d) Gene therapy

12. Which Hollywood star has been confirmed to act with Indian actor Rajnikanth in upcoming film Enthiran 2?
   - (a) Dwayne Johnson
   - (b) Vin Diesel
   - (c) Arnold Schwarzenegger
   - (d) Sylvester Stallone

13. Monica takes 9 hrs 15 minutes in walking a distance and riding back to same place where she started. She could walk both ways in 11 hrs 12 minutes. The time taken by her to ride back both ways is:

(a) 7 hrs 18 min   (b) 7 hrs 35 min

(c) 7 hrs 45 min   (d) 7 hrs 15 min

14. Choose the pair which is related in the same way as the words in the first pair from the given choices.

LUNG : MAN :: GILL : _______________

(a) FISH   (b) COW

(c) PEACOCK   (d) BIRD

15. Which one of the following insects **cannot** be called a 'social insect'?

(a) Bees   (b) Crickets

(c) Termites   (d) Ants

16. Mr. Yudish borrowed Rs.3500 at 4% per annum compound interest. The compound interest compounded annually for 2 years is:

(a) 285.6   (b) 3785.6

(c) 3758.6   (d) 258.6

17. Which is the correct ascending order of the given numbers?

(a) $\dfrac{3}{7}, 0.3, \dfrac{2}{7}$ (b) $0.3, \dfrac{2}{7}, \dfrac{3}{7}$

(c) $\dfrac{2}{7}, 0.3, \dfrac{3}{7}$ (d) $\dfrac{2}{7}, \dfrac{3}{7}, .3$

18. Out of the FIFA World Cup awards which one is awarded to the best goal keeper?

(a) Golden Boot   (b) GoLden Ball

(c) Golden Glove   (d) Golden Cap

19. Compute $35968 \div 562 \div 8 = ?$

(a) 80   (b) 512

(c) 8   (d) 521

20. Compute $7497 \div 147 - 8 = ?$

(a) −20   (b) 20

(c) $\dfrac{7497}{116}$ (d) $\dfrac{7479}{116}$

21. The most recently discovered link in human evolution is the discovery of fossils of:

(a) Lucy   (b) Homo naledi

(c) Homo sapiens   (d) Austiopithelines

22. Even before East India Company consolidated power, India was exporting find textiles made of :

(a) only cotton   (b) only silk

(c) only nylon   (d) cotton and silk

23. If **COUNTER** is coded as **NTERCOU**, then **ANALOGY** is coded as

(a) LOGYAAN   (b) LOGAYNA

(c) LOGYANA   (d) LGOYNAA

24. Ashok Pillar of Delhi has baffled scientists as it weathers all vagaries of weather and yet does not rust or corrode. Which is it made of?

(a) Iron   (b) Bronze

(c) Terracotta   (d) Single rock stone

25. Prior to independence, the first Indian jute mill was set up in _______________.

(a) Gujarat   (b) Bengal

(c) Odisha   (d) Maharashtra

26. Choose the pair which is related in the same way as the words in the first pair from the given choices.

EDITOR : MAGAZINE _________ : DRAMA.

(a) PLAY   (b) ARTISTS

(c) STAGE   (d) DIRECTOR

27. If the product of two numbers is 3192 and their HCF is 56 then their LCM is:

(a) 58   (b) 59

(c) 56   (d) 57

DIRECTIONS (Qs. 28–30): *The table below represents the distance (in km) travelled by six trucks on six different days of the week. Read the table and answer the questions based on it.*

Day	Truck					
	P	Q	R	S	T	U
Monday	240	250	320	325	330	300
Tuesday	320	264	308	314	318	314
Wednesday	324	294	330	312	310	325
Thursday	288	300	310	278	260	275
Friday	366	302	288	292	270	268
Saturday	292	284	260	274	280	242

28. What is the average distance travelled by Truck S on all the days together?

(a) 296 km   (b) 1795/6 km

(c) 198 km   (d) 199 km

29. What is the total distance travelled by all the trucks together on Saturday?

(a) 1623 km   (b) 1263 km

(c) 1362 km   (d) 1632 km

30. If to travel the given distance, the time taken by Truck Q on Friday was 8 hours, then what was its average speed on that day?

(a) 37.75km/hr   (b) 42.50 km/hr

(c) 28.25 km/hr   (d) 32.25 km/hr

31. Reema pointed towards a painting and said. "He is my son's paternal grandfather's only daughter-in-law's father's father". How is he related to Reema?

(a) Paternal Uncle

(b) Paternal Grandfather

(c) Maternal Grandfather

(d) Father

32. Mr. Piyush sold a bus for Rs.3400 with a loss of 15%. At what price should the bus be sold to get a profit of 15%?

(a) 4500   (b) 4300

(c) 4700   (d) 4600

33. An assertion and a reason are given below.

Assertion: India is a Sovereign country.

Reason: Its parliament is placed in Delhi.

Choose the answer.

(a) Both Assertion and Reason are true and Reason is the correct explanation of Assertion.

(b) Both Assertion and Reason are true but Reason is not the correct explanation of Assertion.

(c) Both Assertion and Reason are false.

(d) Assertion is true but Reason is false.

34. From the given series of jumbled letters separate the names of flower and tree and select from the given choices the first letter of the name of flower and tree "saltoteuk"

(a) SR   (b) RE

(c) LK   (d) LT

35. Which of the following is a **wrong** example of friction?

(a) Washing machine pushed along a floor

(b) Sled sliding across snow

(c) A person sliding down a slide

(d) A person lifting an heavy object

36. Sundarbans is the largest single block of tidal halophytic __________ forest in the world.

(a) Woody shrubs   (b) Papyrus

(c) Mangrove   (d) Marsh

37. Which of the following organizations were NOT formed outside India to help in the struggle for Indian independence?

(a) India Mouse

(b) Gadar Party

(c) Hindustan Socialist Republican Association

(d) Berlin Committee

38. The mode of the data –3, 4, 0, 4, –2, –5, 1, 7, 10, 5 is:

(a) 0   (b) 4

(c) –2   (d) 7

39. Given $w = -2$, $x = 3$, $y = 0$ & $z = \_\_$. Find the value of $2x(w - z)$.

(a) –9   (b) 9

(c) 8   (d) –8

40. Which unit is used to measure Noise?

(a) Decibel   (b) Hertz

(c) Ohm   (d) Volt

41. A shopkeeper cheats to the extent of 9% while buying and selling fruits, by using tampered weights. His total gain in percentage is:

(a) 18.25   (b) 18.81

(c) 18.75   (d) 18.5

42. The Hubble Space Telescope, which belongs to __________, captured the first-ever predicted supernova explosion,

(a) USA   (b) UK

(b) Canada   (c) Russia

43. If signs – and ×, and numbers 5 and 14 are interchanged, then the value of $5 + 4 \div 2 - 8 \times 14$ is

(a) 15   (b) 20

(c) 25   (d) 30

44. The first human to travel in space -

(a) Neil Armstrong

(b) Yuri Gagarin

(c) Edwin Aldrin

(d) Valentina Tereshkova

45. A mobile bill costs Rs 10 for 3 minutes 30 seconds. What is the cost in rupees for 4 minutes 10 seconds? (rounded to one decimal).

(a) 11.9   (b) 12

(c) 11.8   (d) 11.7

46. Which article of the India constitution guarantees rights to arrested persons.

(a) Article 22   (b) Article 35

(c) Article 20   (d) Article 42

47. Below are given statements followed by some conclusions. You have to take the given statements to be true even if they seem to be at variance with the commonly known facts and then decide which of the given conclusions logically follow(s) from the given statements

Statement:

Domestic demand has been increasing faster than the production of indigenous crude oil.

Conclusions:

I.   Crude oil must be imported.

II. Domestic demand must be reduced.

(a) Only conclusion I follows.

(b) Only conclusion II follows.

(c) Neither I nor II follows.

(d) Both I and II follow.

48. .css file extension usually refers to what kind of file?

(a) Image File

(b) System File

(c) Animation File

(d) Hypertext related File

49. Who is the current Minister of State for Commerce and Industry?

(a) Nirmala Sitharaman

(b) Vasundhara Raje Scindia

(c) Smriti Irani

(d) Sushma Swaraj

50. An assertion and a reason are given below.

Assertion: Water is essential for life.

Reason: It is formed using three parts of Hydrogen and one part of Oxygen.

Choose the answer.

(a) Both Assertion and Reason are true and Reason is the correct explanation of Assertion.

(b) Both Assertion and Reason are true but Reason is not the correct explanation of Assertion.

(c) Both Assertion and Reason are false.

(d) Assertion is true but Reason is false.

51. To which country does the 'MOST' (Microvariability and Oscillation of Stars) Space Telescope belong?

(a) India   (b) Canada

(c) Russia   (d) USA

52. Which one of the three rivers at Triveni Sangam, Allahabad, is an underground river?

(a) Ganges   (b) Yamuna

(c) Saraswati   (d) Kaveri

53. Which of the following rebellions was NOT against restrictions imposed by the British rulers?

(a) Faqir and Sanyasi Rebellion

(b) The Indigo rebellion

(c) Santhal Rebellion

(d) Naxalbari Rabellion

54. Solve: $-4 = -7 + 3x$.

(a) -1 (b) 1

(c) $\dfrac{11}{3}$ (d) $\dfrac{-11}{3}$

55. What is the chemical name of common salt that we eat?

(a) Sodium bicarbonate

(b) Sodium chloride

(c) Sodium salicylate

(d) Sodium hydroxide

56. If **39574** is Written as **XPLMD**, and **0826** as **TBNQ**, then **DBMTX** will be coded as

(a) 48730   (b) 48603

(c) 48703   (d) 48743

57. The cash difference between the selling price of an article at a profit of 2% and 14% is ₹3. The ratio of two selling prices is:

(a) 17:19   (b) 17:20

(c) 19:20   (d) 17:53

58 Simplify $7x + 3x(x - 4) = ?$

(a) $10x + 12$ (b) $10x - 12$

(c) $3x^2 + 5x$ (d) $3x^2 - 5x$

59. Satish Dhawan Space Centre is located in:

(a) Uttar Pradesh   (b) Madhya Pradesh

(c) Andhra Pradesh   (d) Tamil Nadu

60. The variance of a set of data is 144. Then the standard deviation of the data is:
(a) ±12
(b) 12
(c) 44
(d) 72

61. Choose the pair which is related in the same way as the words in the first pair from the given choices.

ROASTER : DUTY :: INVENTORY : ___________

(a) GOODS
(b) SALES
(c) EXPORT
(d) PRODUCTION

62. Compute of $54367 \times 9999 =$?
(a) 546315633
(b) 543655633
(c) 543651633
(d) 543615633

63. Mr. Yashwanth invested money in FD. How much will he get on maturity, if Rs. 10000 is invested at 20% per annum compound interest for 6 months, compounded quarterly?
(a) 11025.25
(b) 11025
(c) 11025.75
(d) 11025.5

64. HIV is passed from one person to another in all of the following ways except:
(a) Mosquito bite
(b) Breast Feeding
(c) Sharing Needles
(d) Sexual Contact

65. Bloodless surgery is done with ________ ___________
(a) Lasers
(b) Microneedles
(c) Scalpels
(d) Fine scissors

66. Yuvraj is Dipti's mother's father's only
(a) Nephew
(b) Son
(c) Maternal Uncle
(d) Grandson

67. Two numbers are in ratio 4:9 and their HCF is 11. Their LCM is:
(a) 396
(b) 44
(c) 99
(d) 400

68. Which one of the following countries' official language is Dari, a form of Persian?
(a) Pakistan
(b) Bangladesh
(c) Nepal
(d) Afghanistan

69. The order of rotational symmetry of a rhombus is:
(a) 1
(b) 4
(c) 2
(d) 0

70. The number of sides of a regular polygon whose exterior angles are each 45° is:
(a) 7
(b) 6
(c) 8
(d) 9

71. Which country does Roger Federer represent in Lawn Tennis competitions?
(a) Serbia
(b) US
(c) Switzerland
(d) UK

72. Choose the pair which is related in the same way as the words in the first pair from the given choices.

CLIMB : TREE :: ___________ : ___________
(a) ROW : SHIP
(b) RISE : TOP
(c) ASCEND : CLIFF
(d) FILE : FINGER

73. The gland in the human body which secretes both enzymes and hormones is:
(a) Liver
(b) Pancreas
(c) Salivary gland
(d) Pituitary

74. Which of the storage device of computers has now become obsolete?
(a) Floppy
(b) CD ROM
(c) Pen drive
(d) Hard disk

75. An assertion and a reason are given below.
Assertion: The phenomenon of nuclear fission generates great energy.
Reason: The process in which a nucleus is broken into two parts is called nuclear fission.
Choose the answer.
(a) Both Assertion and Reason are true and Reason is the correct explanation of Assertion.
(b) Both Assertion and Reason are true but Reason is not the correct explanation of Assertion.
(c) Both Assertion and Reason are false.
(d) Assertion is true but Reason is false.

76. Which instrument does Dr. L. Subramaniam play?
(a) Sitar
(b) Sarod
(c) Violin
(d) Guitar

77. What is galvanized iron?
(a) A form of steel
(b) Zinc coated iron
(c) Pig iron
(d) Iron ore

78. In November 2015. the Government of India announced an increase in FDI for 'News and current affairs channels' from 26% to ______ .

(a) 49%   (b) 51%

(c) 100%   (d) 75%

79. If "−" and "×" signs as well as "7" and "3" are interchanged, their which of the one following is correct?

(a) $20 \times 1 - 7 = 3$ (b) $1 \times 20 - 7 = 20$

(c) $3 - 7 \times 1 = 20$ (d) $20 - 3 \times 1 = 7$

80. Monal Kumar travelled equal distance with speed of 3 km/hr, 5 km hr and 8 km hr and takes a total time of 39.5 minutes. Find the total distance in km.

(a) 4   (b) 2

(c) 1   (d) 3

81. Which of the following is a branch of technology that deals with dimensions and tolerances of less than 100 nanometers, especially the manipulation of individual atoms and molecules?

(a) Biotechnology   (b) Femtotechnology

(c) Nanotechnology   (d) Microtechnology

82. The mean deviation of the data 2, 9, 9, 3, 6, 9, 4 from the mean is:

(a) $\dfrac{42}{7}$ (b) $\dfrac{18}{7}$

(c) 2.5   (d) $\dfrac{50}{7}$

83. The building up and movement of ships is based on:

(a) Archimedes' principle

(b) Faradays laws

(c) Fleming's right hand rule

(d) Newton's 2nd law of motion

84. Mouma Das and Soumyajit Ghosh represent India in:

(a) Table Tennis   (b) Badminton

(c) Tennis   (d) Carrom

85. Bhimbetka caves are located in:

(a) Uttar Pradesh

(b) Madhya Pradesh

(c) Andhra Pradesh

(d) Himachal Pradesh

86. The length of a diagonal in cm of a rectangle of length 9 cm and width 6 cm is:

(a) $3\sqrt{13}$ (b) $\pm 3\sqrt{13}$

(c) $3\sqrt{5}$ (d) $\pm 3\sqrt{5}$

87. Interchanging which two signs will make the following equation correct?

$$15 + 3 \times 9 - 4 \div 16 = 57$$

(a) − and +   (b) − and ÷

(c) − and ×   (d) + and ÷

88. Prashanth is twice as good a sportsman as Tarun and together they finish a piece of work in 21 days. In how many days will Tarun alone finish the work?

(a) 42   (b) 63

(c) 84   (d) 50

89. Aquarium is a container in which there are living fish and aquatic plants. Which statement about aquarium is correct?

(a) It is human made ecosystem

(b) It is a natural ecosystem

(c) It is not an ecosystem at all

(d) It can only be termed a community

90. If $Sin\ x = \dfrac{4}{5}$, then $\dfrac{Tan\ x}{Cot\ x} = ?$

(a) $\dfrac{13}{9}$ (b) $\dfrac{3}{4}$

(c) $\dfrac{9}{16}$ (d) $\dfrac{16}{9}$

91. Below are given statements followed by some conclusion they seem to be at variance with the commonly known facts and then decide which of the given conclusions logically follow(s) from the given statements

Statements:

(a) If all players play to their full potential, we will win the match.

(b) We have won the match.

Conclusions:

I. All players played to their full potential.

II. Some players did not play to their full potential.

(a) Only conclusion 11 follows.

(b) Only conclusion I follows.

(c) Neither I nor II follows.

(d) Both I and II follow.

DIRECTIONS (Qs. 92–94): *Read the following passage and answer the questions based on it.*

(i) Radha, Rekha, Rakhi, Ragini, Rashmi, Reema and Renu are sitting around a circle facing the center.

(ii) Reema is not an immediate neighbor of Rashmi.

(iii) Radha is to the immediate right of Ragini.

(iv) Rekha is second to the left of Reema.

(v) Radha is third to the left of Renu.

92. Which of the following pairs of persons has the first person sitting to the immediate left of second person?

(a) Radha-Reema   (b) Rakhi-Rekha

(c) Reema-Rakhi   (d) Ragini-Rashmi

93. Who is second to the left of Ragini?

(a) Reema   (b) Rakhi

(c) Radha   (d) Rashmi

94. Which of the following groups has the first person sitting between the other two?

(a) Reema-Rashmi-Radha

(b) Rakhi-Ragini-Reema

(c) Renu-Rekha-Ragini

(d) Renu-Rekha-Rakhi

95. Degradation of global environment has not resulted in one of the following.

(a) Biodiversity loss

(b) Increased Carbon-di-oxide concentration in the atmosphere

(c) Exposure to UV radiations

(d) Landfills

96. In India, most villages suffer due to one of the following and not the others:

(a) Air pollution

(b) Sound pollution

(c) Radiation pollution

(d) Water pollution

97. Sharad introduced Meena as his son's paternal grandfather's only sister. How is Meena related to Sharad?

(a) Mother   (b) Sister

(c) Paternal Aunt   (d) Daughter

98. A jug has two holes. The Ist hole alone makes the jug empty in 15 minutes and 2nd hole alone makes the jug empty in 20 minutes. If water leaks out at a constant rate, how long in minutes does it take if both the holes together empty the jug?

(a) $\dfrac{4}{7}$ (b) $7\dfrac{4}{7}$

(c) $8\dfrac{5}{7}$ (d) $8\dfrac{4}{7}$

99. If $Tan\ A = \dfrac{15}{8}$ and $Tan\ B = \dfrac{7}{24}$, then $Tan\ (A + B) = ?$

(a) $\dfrac{416}{87}$ (b) $\dfrac{87}{416}$

(c) $\dfrac{304}{297}$ (d) $\dfrac{297}{304}$

100. Simplify: $2^4 \div 2^{-1}$

(a) 1/32   (b) 16

(c) 32   (d) 8

HINTS & EXPLANATIONS

1. **(b)**

2. **(b)** TRACTOR = 14

   TROLLEY = 14

   Here, each letter has the value of 2

   ∴ SCOOTER = 2×7=14, as it has 7 letters of value of 2 units each.

3. **(c)** Since the code of 'TIGER' is just reverse of its alphabets.

   ∴ 'LEOPARD' is coded as 'DRAPOEL'

4. **(a)** $x = 0.02\overline{36}$

   $100x = 2.3\overline{636}$ ...(i)

   $10000x = 236.\overline{36}$ ...(ii)

   Subtract (ii) from (i)

   $9900x = 234$

   $$x = \frac{234}{9900} = \frac{13}{550}$$

Sol. (5-7):

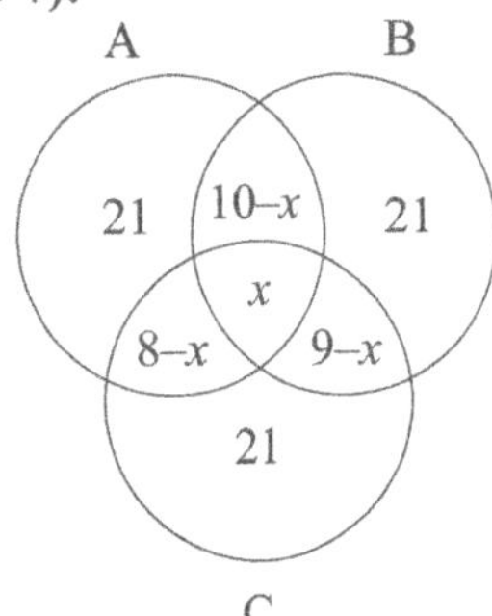

5. **(c)** Total numbers of students who passed only one of three sections = 21+21+21 = 63

6. **(b)** Students passed in section A = 33

   ⇒ $21 + (10 - x) + x + (8 - x) = 33$

   ⇒ $39 - x = 33 \Rightarrow x = 6$

   Hence, 6 students passed all the 3 sections

7. **(a)** Students passed in 1 or more sections

   $= 21 + 21 + 21 + (10 - x) + x + (8 - x) + (9 - x)$

   $= 73 + x + 17 - 3x = 90 - 2x = 90 - 2(6) = 78$

   ∴ Ratio $= \dfrac{78}{21}$

8. **(b)**

   $19 \div 9 \times 51 - 171 + 19 = 19 \times 9 - 51 + 171 \div 19$

   $= 171 - 51 + 9$

   $= 129$

9. **(c)** Let four Parts of ₹156 be ₹x, ₹$2x$, ₹$4x$ and ₹$5x$

   ∴ ₹x, + ₹$2x$ + ₹$4x$ + ₹$5x$= ₹156

   ⇒ $12x = 156$

   ⇒ $x = \dfrac{156}{12} = ₹13$

   Hence, the four parts are ₹13, ₹26, ₹52, and ₹65

10. **(c)** We know that potato chips contain oil. When they are left to the exposure of oxygen for a long time, they react with oxygen and become rancid. To avoid rancidity of fats and oils, the packets of chips are flushed or surrounded with nitrogen gas to prevent its contact with oxygen of air.

11. **(c)** Recombinant DNA Technology is a closely related term for Genetic Engineering. Genetic Engineering refers to a technique which is used to modify or manipulate the genotype of a particular organism. While, Recombinant DNA Technology refers to the methods used to modify, measure, manipulate and manufacture within the DNA molecule.

12. **(c)**

13. **(a)** According to the question

    walk + riding = 9 hrs. 15 mins ...(i)

    walk + walk = 11 hrs. 12 mins ...(ii)

    ⇒ 2 walk = 11 hrs. 12 mins.

    ⇒ walk = 5 hrs. 36 mins ...(iii)

    Put (iii) in eq. (i) we get

    walk + riding = 9 hrs. 15 mins.

    ⇒ 5 hrs. 36 mins + riding = 9 hrs. 15 mins

    ⇒ riding = 9 hrs. 15 mins – 5 hrs 36 mins.

    = 3 hrs. 39 mins.

    Hence, time taken by Monika to ride both ways

= 3 hrs. 39 mins. + 3 hrs. 39 mins.

= 6 hrs. 78 mins.

= 7 hrs. 18 mins.

14. (a)

15. (b) All termites, ants and some bees and wasps are social insects and comprise of about 75% of world's insect biomass. Crickets are generally classified as subsocial. They may live near each other in a suitable habitat, but that is by chance. This means they live mainly on their own.

16. (a) $A = P\left(1 + \dfrac{R}{100}\right)^n$

$= 3500\left(1 + \dfrac{4}{100}\right)^2$

$= 3500\left(1 + \dfrac{1}{25}\right)^2 = 3500\left(\dfrac{26}{25}\right)^2$

$= 3500 \times \dfrac{26}{25} \times \dfrac{26}{25} = ₹\,3785.60$

$\therefore$ CI $= A - P$

$= ₹\,3785.60 - ₹\,3500$

$= ₹\,285.60$

17. (c) $\dfrac{3}{7} = 0.428$, $\quad \dfrac{2}{7} = 0.285$

Hence, $\dfrac{2}{7} < 0.3 < \dfrac{3}{7}$

18. (c)

19. (c) $35968 \div 562 \div 8$

$= 64 \div 8$

$= 8$

20. (*) $7497 \div 147 - 8 = 51 - 8$

$\qquad\qquad\qquad = 43$

21. (b) 22. (d)

23. (c)   COU NTER   –   NTER COU

Similarly, ANA LOGY   –   LOGY ANA

24. (a) 25. (b) 26. (d)

27. (d) Product of two number = HCF × LCM

$\Rightarrow 3192 = 56 \times$ LCM

$\Rightarrow$ LCM $= \dfrac{3192}{56} = 57$

28. (b) Average distance by Truck S

$= \dfrac{325 + 314 + 312 + 278 + 292 + 274}{6}$

$= \dfrac{1795}{6}$ km

29. (d) Total distance travelled on Saturday

= (292+284+260+274+280+242) km.

= 1632 km.

30. (a) Distance covered by Truck Q on Friday

$\qquad\qquad = 302$ km

Time taken = 8 hrs.

$\therefore$ Speed $= \dfrac{\text{Distance}}{\text{Time}} = \dfrac{302}{8}$ km/hr

$\qquad\qquad = 37.75$ km/hr

31. (b) Reema's son's paternal grand father is Reema's father in law.

Paternal grandfather's daughter-in-law's is Reema herself.

Now, Reema's father's father is her paternal grandfather

32. (d) SP $= ₹3400$ and Loss $= 15\%$

CP $= \left(\dfrac{100}{100 - \text{loss}\%}\right) \times$ SP

$= \left(\dfrac{100}{100 - 15}\right) \times 3400 = \dfrac{100}{85} \times 3400$

$= ₹4000$

Profit $= 15\%$

$\therefore$ New SP $= \left(\dfrac{100 + \text{Gain}\,\%}{100}\right) \times$ CP

$= \dfrac{100 + 15}{100} \times 4000 = \dfrac{115}{100} \times 4000$

$= ₹4600$

33. (b) 34. (d) 35. (d) 36. (c) 37. (c)

38. (b) $-5, \quad -3 \quad -2 \quad 0, \quad 1, \quad 4, \quad 4, \quad 5, \quad 7, \quad 10$

$\therefore$ Mode $= 4$, as it occurs maximum times.

39. (a) $2x(w - z) = 2(3)\left[(-2) - \left(-\dfrac{1}{2}\right)\right]$

$= 6\left(-2 + \dfrac{1}{2}\right)$

$= 6\left(-1\dfrac{1}{2}\right) = 6\left(\dfrac{-3}{2}\right) = (-9)$

40. (a)

41. (b) According to question

Cheats while buying $(x) = 9\%$

Cheats while selling $(y) = 9\%$

$\therefore$ Total gain in percentage $= \left(x + y + \dfrac{xy}{100}\right)\%$

$$= \left(9 + 9 + \dfrac{9 \times 9}{100}\right)\%$$

$$= (18 + 0.81)\%$$

$$= 18.81\%$$

42. (a)

43. (c) $5 + 4 \div 2 - 8 \times 14 = 14 + 4 \div 2 \times 8 - 5$

$$= 14 + 2 \times 8 - 5$$

$$= 14 + 16 - 5$$

$$= 25$$

44. (b)

45. (a) 3 mins 30 secs $= (3 \times 60) + 30 = 210$ sees.

and 4 mins 10 sec $= (4 \times 60) + 10 = 250$ see

Now

Cost of bill for 210 sec $= ₹10$

Cost of bill for 250 sec $= \left(\dfrac{10}{210} \times 250\right)$

$$= ₹11.9$$

46. (a) 47. (c) 48. (d) 49. (a) 50. (d)

51. (b) 52. (c) 53. (d)

54. (b) $\quad -4 = -7 + 3x$

$\Rightarrow 3x = -4 + 7$

$\Rightarrow 3x = 3 \Rightarrow x = 1$

55. (b)

56. (c)

3	9	5	7	4		0	8	2	6
↓	↓	↓	↓	↓		↓	↓	↓	↓
X	P	L	M	D		T	B	N	Q

Here each letter is allotted an analogical coding with numerical value.

$\therefore$ DBMTX will be coded as 48703.

57. (a) Let the CP be ₹100.

Then, SP at a profit of 2% = CP + 2% of CP

$$= ₹(100 + 2) = ₹102$$

SP at a profit of 14% $= $ CP + (14% of CP)

$$= ₹(100 + 14)$$

$$= ₹114$$

$\therefore$ Ratio $= \dfrac{102}{114} = \dfrac{17}{19} = 17 : 19$

58. (d) $7x + 3x(x - 4) = 7x + 3x^2 - 12x$

$$= 3x^2 - 5x$$

59. (c)

60. (b) Standard Deviation $= \sqrt{\text{Variance}}$

$$= \sqrt{144} = 12$$

61. (a)

62. (d) $54367 \times 9999 = 54367 \times (10000 - 1)$

$$= (54367 \times 10000) - (54367 \times 1)$$

$$= 543670000 - 54367$$

$$= 543615633$$

63. (b) R $= 20\%$ P.a $= \dfrac{20}{4}\%$ quarterly

$$= 5\% \text{ quarterly}$$

T $= 6$ months $= 2$ quarters

$$A = P\left(1 + \dfrac{R}{100}\right)^n = 10000\left(1 + \dfrac{5}{100}\right)^2$$

$$= 10000\left(\dfrac{105}{100}\right)^2 = 10000 \times \left(\dfrac{21}{20}\right)^2$$

$$= ₹11025$$

64. (a) HIV can pass from one person to another through direct contact, i.e., breast feeding, sharing needles or sexual contact but HIV virus is not carried or spread by mosquitoes.

65. (a) Bloodless surgery is a non-invasive surgical method developed by an orthopaedic surgeon, Adolf Lorenz. It involves specialized techniques and instruments to minimize bloodless therapy, avoiding the need for blood transfusion. Some of these techniques are— Laser surgery, Cyberknife, Cryosurgery, etc.

66. (a)

67. (a) Let two numbers be $4x$ and $9x$ respectively.

HCF of $4x$ and $3x = x$

From question H.C.F. $= 11$

$\therefore \qquad\qquad x = 11$

Product of two numbers $= $ HCF $\times$ LCM

$\Rightarrow 4x \times 9x = 11 \times $ LCM

$$\Rightarrow \text{LCM} = \frac{4x \times 9x}{11}$$

$$= \frac{4 \times 11 \times 9 \times 11}{11}$$

$$= 396$$

68. (d)

69. (c) Order of rotational symmetry of rhombus = 2

70. (c) No. of sides $= \dfrac{360°}{\text{exterior angle}} = \dfrac{360°}{45} = 8$

71. (c) 72. (c)

73. (b) Pancreas, located in the abdomen, is both an endocrine and an exocrine gland. The pancreas contains exocrine glands that produce **enzymes** important to digestion, whereas the endocrine component of the pancreas consists of islet cells that create and release important **hormones** directly into the bloodstream.

74. (a) 75. (b) 76. (c)

77. (b) Galvanization is the process of applying a protective coating of zinc to iron or steel to prevent it from rusting. A galvanized iron, is thus, zinc coated iron. The zinc protects iron by corroding it first.

78. (a)

79. (c) $3 - 7 \times 1 = 7 \times 3 - 1$

$$= 21 - 1$$

$$= 20$$

80. (d) Let each of the distance travelled with speed of 3 km/hr, 5 km/hr and 8 km/hr be x km.

∴ Total time taken $= 39.5$ min

$$\Rightarrow \frac{x}{3} + \frac{x}{5} + \frac{x}{8} = \frac{39.5}{60} \text{ hr}$$

$$\Rightarrow \frac{40x + 24x + 15x}{120} = \frac{395}{600}$$

$$\Rightarrow \frac{79x}{120} = \frac{395}{600} \Rightarrow x = 1$$

Hence total distance travelled $= (x + x + x)$ km

$$= 1 + 1 + 1 = 3 \text{ km}$$

81. (c) Nanotechnology is the study and application of extremely small things and can be used across all the other science fields, such as chemistry, biology, physics, materials science, and engineering. It is defined as the study and use of structures between 1 nanometer and 100 nanometers in size.

82. (b) Mean $= \dfrac{2+9+9+3+6+9+4}{7}$

$$= \frac{42}{7} = 6$$

Observation	$(x_i - \bar{x})$	$|x_i - \bar{x}|$
2	−4	4
9	3	3
9	3	3
3	−3	3
6	0	0
9	3	3
4	−2	2
		$\Sigma|x_i - \bar{x}| = 18$

∴ Mean deviation $= \dfrac{\Sigma|x_i - \bar{x}|}{7}$

$$= \frac{18}{7}$$

83. (a) 84. (a) 85. (b)

86. (a) Length of diagonal $= \sqrt{l^2 + b^2}$

$$= \sqrt{9^2 + 6^2} = \sqrt{81 + 36}$$

$$= \sqrt{117} = 3\sqrt{13} \text{ cm}$$

87. (d) $15 + 3 \times 9 - 4 \div 16 = 15 \div 3 \times 9 - 4 + 16$

$$= 5 \times 9 - 4 + 16$$

$$= 45 - 4 + 16$$

$$= 61 - 4$$

$$= 57$$

88. (b) Let the work done by Prashanth and Tarun in 1 day be $2x$ and x respectively.

∴ Work done by them in 1− day $= \dfrac{1}{21}$

$$\Rightarrow x + 2x = \frac{1}{21} \Rightarrow 3x = \frac{1}{21} \Rightarrow x = \frac{1}{63}$$

Hence, Tarun alone can complete the work in 63 days

89. (a)

90. (d) $\sin x = \dfrac{4}{5}$

$$\cos x = \sqrt{1-\sin^2 x} = \sqrt{1-\left(\dfrac{4}{5}\right)^2} = \sqrt{\dfrac{9}{25}} = \dfrac{3}{5}$$

$$\therefore \quad \dfrac{\tan x}{\cot x} = \dfrac{\tan x}{\dfrac{1}{\tan x}} = \tan^2 x = \dfrac{\sin^2 x}{\cos^2 x}$$

$$= \dfrac{\left(\dfrac{4}{5}\right)^2}{\left(\dfrac{3}{5}\right)^2} = \dfrac{4^2}{3^2} = \dfrac{16}{9}$$

91. (b)

Sol.(92-94):

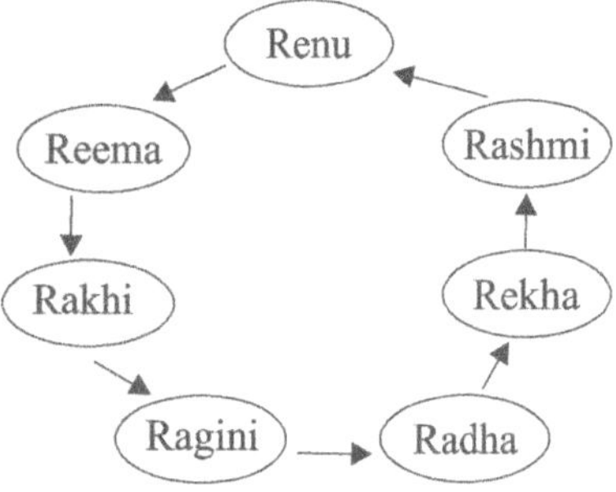

92. (c) Reema is sitting to the immediate left of Rakhi.

93. (a) Reema is second to the left of Ragini.

94. (b) Rakhi is sitting between Reema and Ragini.

95. (d) 96. (d)

97. (c) Sharad's Son's paternal grandfather is Sharad's father. Sharad's father's sister is Sharad's paternal aunt.

98. (d) Part emptied by 1st hole in 1 min $= \dfrac{1}{15}$

Similarly, Part emptied by 2nd hole in 1 min

$= \dfrac{1}{20}$

Total part emptied in 1 min by both holes

$$= \left(\dfrac{1}{15} + \dfrac{1}{20}\right)$$

$$= \dfrac{4+3}{60}$$

$$= \dfrac{7}{60}$$

$\therefore$ Both the Pipes empty the jug in $\dfrac{60}{7}$ i.e. $8\dfrac{4}{7}$ minutes

99. (a) $\tan(A+B) = \dfrac{\tan A + \tan B}{1 - \tan A \ \tan B}$

$$= \dfrac{\dfrac{15}{8} + \dfrac{7}{24}}{1 - \left(\dfrac{15}{8} \times \dfrac{7}{24}\right)} = \dfrac{\dfrac{45+7}{24}}{1 - \dfrac{35}{64}}$$

$$= \dfrac{52}{24} \times \dfrac{64}{29} = \dfrac{416}{87}$$

100. (c) $2^4 \div 2^{-1} = 2^{4-(-1)}$

$$= 2^{4+1}$$

$$= 2^5 = 32$$

1. In 2015, Chennai and a few areas in Tamil Nadu were affected by floods. The centre had declared this as a 'Calamity of severe nature'. Which of the following was NOT a part of the relief plan?
   (a) Sanitation drive
   (b) Vaccination drive
   (c) Measures for rehabilitation of those rendered homeless
   (d) Opening of new schools

2. Two numbers are in ratio 21:29 and their HCF is 8. Their LCM is:
   (a) 4872   (b) 168
   (c) 232   (d) 4782

3. Where in China is the Forbidden City located?
   (a) Guilin   (b) Beijing
   (c) Shanghai   (d) Guanzho

4. The number of sides of a regular polygon whose exterior angles are each 60° is:
   (a) 7   (b) 5
   (c) 6   (d) S

5. If **LOW** is coded as **468, BOW** as **768**. and **SOWS** as **3683**, then the code of **BOWLS** is
   (a) 76843   (b) 76890
   (c) 63387   (d) 36891

6. Below are given statements followed by some conclusions. You have to take the given statements to be true even if they seem to be at variance with the commonly known facts and then decide which of the given conclusions logically follow(s) from the given statements.

   Statement:

   Morning walks are good for health.

   Conclusions:

   I. All healthy people go for morning walks.

   II. Evening walks are harmful.

   Choose which of the given conclusions logically follow(s) from the given statements.

   (a) Only conclusion I follows.
   (b) Only conclusion II follows.
   (c) Both I and II follows.
   (d) Neither I nor II follow.

7. Which kind of cell division is used to repair an injury by the body?
   (a) Mitosis only
   (b) Meiosis only
   (c) Both Mitosis and Meiosis
   (d) Neither Mitosis nor Meiosis

8. Solve: $2x + 4 = x - 3$.
   (a) 7   (b) –7
   (c) –1   (d) 1

9. If **SON = 678** and **TEN = 948**, then **STONE =**
   (a) 69797   (b) 69784
   (c) 68784   (d) 69764

10. Mr. Sanjeev invested money in FD. How much will he get on maturity, if ₹11000 is invested at 20% per annum compound interest for 6 months, compounded quarterly?
    (a) 12127.25   (b) 12127.5
    (c) 12127.75   (d) 12127

11. If the product of two numbers is 2646 and their HCF is 42 then their LCM is:
    (a) 64   (b) 26
    (c) 46   (d) 63

DIRECTIONS (Qs. 12-14): Read the data and answer the questions.

(i) Vinay, Vinod, Vikas, Vasu, Vaibhav, Varun and Vishal are sitting around a circle facing at the center.

(ii) Vasu is the third to the right of Vikas.

(iii) Varun is second to the left of Vinay and second to the right of Vishal.

(iv) Vaibhav is third to the right of Vinod and is not an immediate neighbor of Varun.

12. Who is second to the right of Vinod?
  (a) Vaibhav   (b) Vasu
  (c) Vishal   (d) Vikas

13. Who is to the immediate right of Vikas?
  (a) Vinay   (b) Vishal
  (c) Vaibhav   (d) Varun

14. Who is third to the left of Varun?
  (a) Vaibhav   (b) Vasu
  (c) Vishal   (d) Vikas

15. Compute of $29292 \times 9999 = ?$
  (a) 222890708   (b) 298290708
  (c) 292809708   (d) 292890708

16. Which of the following is NOT based on principle of relationship between volume and pressure of air?
  (a) Fountain pen   (b) Bicycle pump
  (c) Hand pump   (d) Pulley

17. If **NOTEBOOK** is coded as **REGOLEEN**, and **SHIRT** as **XYZBG**, then **TORN** is coded as
  (a) GZBR   (b) GEBN
  (c) GEBR   (d) GOBR

18. If $Tan\ A = \dfrac{15}{8}$ and $Tan\ B = \dfrac{7}{24}$, then $Cos\ (A - B) = ?$
  (a) $\dfrac{297}{425}$ (b) $\dfrac{304}{425}$
  (c) $\dfrac{87}{425}$ (d) $\dfrac{416}{425}$

19. Simplify $4(x - 1) - 3x$
  (a) $7x - 4$ (b) $7x + 4$
  (b) $x + 4$ (c) $x - 4$

20. Simplify: $(27)^{\frac{-2}{3}}$
  (a) 1/18   (b) 9
  (c) 1/9   (d) 18

21. If **UPTO** is coded as **PTLO**, how is **CANT** coded?
  (a) NCTA   (b) ANCT
  (c) ANTC   (d) NTCA

22. If "+" and "×" signs as well as "3" and "2" are interchanged, which of the one following is correct?
  (a) $4 + 2 \times 3 = 14$ (b) $14 + 3 \times 2 = 4$
  (c) $4 + 2 \times 14 = 3$ (d) $2 + 3 \times 4 = 14$

23. Computers **cannot** work without:
  (a) Scanner   (b) Internet
  (c) Mouse   (d) CPU

24. If signs – and ×, and numbers 3 and 15 are intercnanged, what is the value of $3 + 12 \div 6 - 4 \times 15$ is
  (a) 20   (b) 30
  (c) 40   (d) 50

25. Which is the correct inverted sequence (last to first) of Mughal Emperors who ruled the Indian Subcontinent?
  (a) Akbar, Shah Jahan, Aurangzeb, Bahadur Shah II
  (b) Aurangzeb, Bahadur Shah II, Shah Jahan, Akbar
  (c) Bahadur Shah II, Aurangzeb, Shah Jahan, Akbar
  (d) Akbar, Aurangzeb, Shah Jahan and Bahadur Shah II

26. The median of the data $1\dfrac{1}{2}, \dfrac{1}{2}, \dfrac{3}{4}, \dfrac{1}{4}, 2\dfrac{1}{2}, \dfrac{1}{4}, \dfrac{2}{4}$ is :
  (a) $\dfrac{1}{4}$ (b) $\dfrac{1}{2}$
  (c) $\dfrac{1}{6}$ (d) $\dfrac{3}{4}$

27. Who among the following participated in the 'Chittagong' armoury raid as part of freedom movement?
  (a) Ganesh Joshi
  (b) Kalpana Chawla
  (c) Ananta Waddedar
  (d) Preetilata Waddedar

28. Which of the following is used to detect current in a circuit?
  (a) Galvanometer   (b) Anemometer
  (c) Barometer   (d) Lactometer

29. It has been possible to obtain potable (drinking) water from sewage water with the use of:
  (a) Ultrathin filter paper
  (b) Ultrathin sand paper
  (c) Polymer filter membranes with pores smaller than one millionth of a millimeter
  (d) Aerobic and anaerobic bacteria

30. Choose the pair which is related in the same way as the words in the first pair from the given choices.

    NESTS : BIRDS :: _________ : LION
    (a) DWELLING   (b) BUSH
    (c) FOREST   (d) DEN

31. If "÷" denotes "subtraction", "–" denotes "addition", "+" denotes "multiplication" and "×" denotes "division", which of the following is the value of the expression

    $182 \div 91 \times 7 + 3 - 1$
    (a) 16   (b) 24
    (c) 144   (d) 150

32. Divide ₹288 in the ratio 2:3:5:6. The rupees in the respective ratios are given by:
    (a) 36, 54, 91 & 107
    (b) 36, 54, 89 & 109
    (c) 36, 54, 90 & 108
    (d) 36, 55, 89 & 108

33. A shopkeeper cheats to the extent of 1% while buying and selling fruits, by using tampered weights. His total gain in percentage is:
    (a) 2.25   (b) 2.01
    (c) 2.75   (d) 2.5

34. Given $w = -2, x = 3, y = 0$ & $z = -\dfrac{1}{2}$. Find the value of $2(w^2 + x^2 + y^3)$.
    (a) 26   (b) –26
    (c) 25   (d) 28

35. Which of the following is NOT an application of Fiber optics?
    (a) Power Generation
    (b) Computer Networking
    (c) Sensors
    (d) Power Transmission

36. Among the pairs of rivers given below, which flow in the southern part of India?
    (a) Krislina and Ganges
    (b) Kaveri and Godavari
    (c) Narmada and Tapi
    (d) Brahmaputra and Yamuna

37. Tom Hanks is associated with which of the following?
    (a) Films   (b) Sports
    (c) Music   (d) Science

38. which is the smallest planet in our solar system?
    (a) Mercury   (b) Mars
    (c) Jupiter   (d) Saturn

39. In 1969, who among the following was a part of the crew of spaceflight Apollo-XI?
    (a) Yuri Gagarin   (b) Pete Conrad
    (c) Alan Shepard   (d) Neil Armstrong

40. The order of rotational symmetry of a parallelogram is:
    (a) 1   (b) 4
    (c) 2   (d) 0

41. Which of the following technique is used to know the age of a tree in years?
    (a) Counting the number of branches
    (b) Counting the number of tree rings
    (c) Measuring the size of the bark
    (d) Counting the seasons of its flowering

42. The village 'Lambasingi' is an upcoming tourist attraction where temperature drops to zero or below zero in December and January. Lambanisingi is in:
    (a) Maharashtra   (b) Uttarakhand
    (c) Andhra Pradesh   (d) Haryana

43. From the given series of jumbled letters separate the names of two parts of body and select from the given choices the first letters of the name of those parts of body.

    "duhelhesaord"
    (a) SH   (b) HL
    (c) EA   (d) AS

44. Compute of $1848 \div 231 - 10 =$?
    (a) 2   (b) –2
    (c) $\dfrac{1848}{221}$ (d) $\dfrac{1884}{221}$

45. A famous Shiva temple, Pashupatinath is in:
    (a) Burma   (b) Bangladesh
    (c) Nepal   (d) Tibet

46. Which of the following is at the second trophic level of a food chain?
    (a) Grass   (b) Rats
    (c) Snake   (d) Eagle

47. The mean of the data 3, 10, 10, 4, 7, 10, 5 is:
    (a) $\dfrac{18}{7}$ (b) 7
    (c) $\dfrac{39}{7}$ (d) 6

48. Interchanging which two signs will make the following equation correct?

$42 \div 4 + 2 - 3 \times 5 = 29$

(a) $+$ and $\times$ (b) $+$ and $-$

(c) $-$ and $\times$ (d) $\div$ and $+$

49. Which of the following is NOT expected of a Golf Caddy?

(a) Carrying the Golfer's Bag

(b) Clearing dried grass of the field

(c) Carrying the Golfer's Clubs

(d) Calculate the yardage to the pin

50. How is Anil related to Chetna if he introduced her as his mother's mother's only granddaughter's daughter?

(a) Father   (b) Maternal Uncle

(c) Cousin   (d) Grandfather

51. The Government of India in the Month of November 2015 decided to allow foreign portfolio investors (FPIs) to increase stakes in local defence units to 49%. What was the earlier permissible rate?

(a) 10%   (b) 16%

(c) 25%   (d) 24%

DIRECTIONS (Qs. 52-54): *The table below represents the number of Executives recruited by six different organization over the years. Read the table and answer the questions based on it.*

Organization	P	Q	R	S	T	U
2010	458	512	418	502	476	492
2011	522	536	472	500	482	523
2012	480	495	464	508	488	518
2013	506	506	428	444	490	534
2014	427	485	422	512	510	498
2015	492	488	444	499	512	510

52. What is the total number of Executives recruited by all the organizations together in the year 2012?

(a) 2864   (b) 2953

(c) 3042   (d) 2927

53. What is the average number of Executives recruited by organization S over all the years together (rounded off to the nearest integer)?

(a) 494   (b) 482

(c) 514   (d) 506

54. The number of Executives recruited by organization T in the year 2014 forms approximately, what percent of the total number of Executives recruited by all the organizations together in that year?

(a) 11%   (b) 18%

(c) 31%   (d) 26%

55. A newborn human baby is fed with the first secretion called colostrum from mammary gland. What does colostrum impart?

(a) Factors for growth

(b) Immunity

(c) Sleepiness

(d) Nutrition for development

56. Divya takes 4 hrs 45 minutes in walking a distance and riding back to same place where she started. She could walk both ways in 5 hrs 55 minutes. The time taken by her to ride back both ways is:

(a) 3 hrs 35 min   (b) 3 hrs 55 min

(c) 3 hrs 45 min   (d) 3 hrs 15 min

57. About 93% of Tribal women cannot contest for the post are the educational qualifications necessary?

(a) Minimum Qualification is Class 2

(b) Minimum Qualification is Class 5

(c) Minimum Qualification is Class 7

(d) Minimum Qualification is Class 10

58. Which is the correct ascending order of the given numbers?

(a) $\dfrac{1}{2}, \dfrac{2}{3}, \dfrac{7}{12}$ (b) $\dfrac{7}{12}, \dfrac{2}{3}, \dfrac{1}{2}$

(c) $\dfrac{1}{2}, \dfrac{7}{12}, \dfrac{2}{3}$ (d) $\dfrac{2}{3}, \dfrac{1}{2}, \dfrac{7}{12}$

59. In Jan 2016, who among the following was chosen as the new face for Incredible India Campaign?

(a) Aamir Khan   (b) Amitabh Bachchan

(c) Shah Rukh Khan   (d) Salman Khan

60. Compute of $15872 / 32 / 4 = ?$

(a) 142   (b) 1984

(c) 124   (d) 1948

61. Which of the following does NOT contribute to sparkling of Diamonds?

(a) Total Internal Reflection

(b) High Refractive Index of Diamonds

(c) Dispersion

(d) Low Refractive Index of Diamonds

62. In December 2015, which of the following was hailed as an important criteria for contesting Panchayat elections in Haryana?

(a) A functional toilet at home

(b) Minimum education qualification for women is Class 3 pass

(c) Exemption for Non-payment of arrears of electricity bill

(d) Exemption for Non-payment of arrears of cooperative banks

63. Urbanization and unsustainable development in India raised several environmental concerns but NOT one among the following:

(a) Deforestation

(b) Soil degradation

(c) Depletion of natural resources

(d) Erratic monsoon

64. Karteek is twice as good a foreman as Raju and together they finish a piece of work in 20 days. In how many days will Raju alone finish the work?

(a) 40   (b) 60

(c) 80   (d) 50

65. An assertion and a reason are given below.

Assertion: It has been observed that buffaloes like to remain in the water during the summer.

Reason: Contact with water cools the body in the summer.

Choose the answer.

(a) Both Assertion and Reason are true but Reason is not the correct explanation of Assertion.

(b) Both Assertion and Reason are true and Reason is the correct explanation of Assertion.

(c) Both Assertion and Reason are false.

(d) Assertion is true but Reason is false.

66. The variance of a set of data is 169. Then the standard deviation of the data is:

(a) ±13   (b) 13

(c) 69   (d) 84.5

67. Which acid is secreted by certain glandular cells in the stomach lining?

(a) Hydrochloric   (b) Ethanoic

(c) Formic   (d) Nitric

68. Smita is Aryan's maternal uncle's father's only daughter. How is Smita related to Aryan?

(a) Mother   (b) Sister

(c) Paternal Aunt   (d) Daughter

69. The cash difference between the selling price of an article at a profit of 2% and 16% is ₹3. The ratio of two selling prices is:

(a) 51:58   (b) 51:53

(c) 57:58   (d) 55:58

70. Which of the following organ does

(a) Kidneys   (b) Ureters

(c) Uterus   (d) Uretlira

71. To pinpoint a Criminal, Forensic Department uses the technique called?

(a) DNA Editing

(b) DNA Splicing

(c) DNA Fingerprinting

(d) DNA Amplification

72. Which among the following **cannot** be included among greenhouse gases?

(a) Nitrous Oxide   (b) Carbon Dioxide

(c) Methane   (d) Phosphine

73. Two vehicles start from a house with a speed of 25 km/hr at interval of 20 minutes. With how much more speed (km/hr) the woman coming from the opposite direction towards the house has to travel to meet the vehicles at an interval of 18 minutes?

(a) 2   (b) $2\frac{5}{9}$

(c) $2\frac{7}{9}$ (d) $2\frac{8}{9}$

74. What is the capital of Syria?

(a) Damascus   (b) Bahrein

(c) Adis Ababa   (d) Doha

75. Which of the following Newton's laws of motion can explain why a ball thrown at a wall rebounds?

(a) 1st law of motion

(b) 2nd law of motion

(c) 3rd law of motion

(d) Neither of the law's

76. Santosh Trophy is associated with which of the following sports?

    (a) Cricket   (b) Football

    (c) Hockey   (d) Basket ball

77. Which out of the following is not a launch vehicle of India for placing satellites in the orbit?

    (a) PSLV   (b) GSAT-8

    (c) GSLV   (d) Ariane SGS

78. An assertion and a reason are given below.

    Assertion: When velocity is kept constant and wavelength is halved, then the frequency is doubled.

    Reason: Velocity = Frequency × Wavelength.

    Choose the answer.

    (a) Both Assertion and Reason are true and Reason is the correct explanation of Assertion.

    (b) Both Assertion and Reason are true but Reason is not the correct explanation of Assertion.

    (c) Both Assertion and Reason are false.

    (d) Assertion is true but Reason is false.

79. Which among the following is a **mismatched** pair of religion practiced and its holy book?

    (a) Islam : Quran

    (b) Sikhism : Guru Granth Saheb

    (c) Jainism : Upanishad

    (d) Christianity : Bible

80. Which of the following awards is Sachin Tendulkar NOT awarded with?

    (a) Bharat Ratna

    (b) Dhyan Chand Award

    (c) Padma Vibhushan

    (d) Rajiv Gandhi Khel Ratna

DIRECTIONS (Qs. 81-83): *Read the data given below and answer the questions based on it.*

In the CBSE Board exams last year, 53% passed in Biology, 61% percent passed in English, 60% in Social Studies, 24% in Biology and English, 35% in English and Social Studies, 27% in Biology and Social Studies and 5% in none.

81. What is the ratio of percentage of students who passed in Biology and Social Studies but not English in relation to the percentage of students who passed in Social Studies and English but not Biology?

    (a) 5:7   (b) 7:5

    (c) 4:5   (d) 5:4

82. If the number of students in the class is 200, how many passed in only one subject?

    (a) 48   (b) 46

    (c) More than 50   (d) Less than 40

83. What is the percentage of students who passed in all subjects?

    (a) 8   (b) 12

    (c) 7   (d) 10

84. Mr. Joshi sold a bus for ₹5100 with a loss of 15%. At what price should the bus be sold to get a profit of 15%?

    (a) 6400   (b) 6800

    (c) 7000   (d) 6900

85. The length of a diagonal in Cms of a rectangle of length 5 Cm and width 6 Cm is:

    (a) $\sqrt{61}$ (b) $\pm\sqrt{61}$

    (c) $\sqrt{11}$ (d) $\pm\sqrt{11}$

86. How is Poonam related to Virat if he introduced her as his mother's father's only daughter's only daughter-in-law?

    (a) Wife   (b) Daughter

    (c) Maternal Aunt   (d) Paternal Aunt

87. A pile of book kept on the table will not be dislodged due to:

    (a) Inertia   (b) Momentum

    (c) Magnetism   (d) Gravity

88. An assertion and a reason are given below.

    Assertion: One should not take medicines without a prescription.

    Reason: Taking medicines without prescription is dangerous because only doctor knows the actual components in a medicine and the possible side effects of taking the medicine.

    Choose the answer.

    (a) Both Assertion and Reason are true and Reason is the correct explanation of Assertion.

    (b) Both Assertion and Reason are true but Reason is not the correct explanation of Assertion.

(c) Both Assertion and Reason are false.

(d) Assertion is true but Reason is false.

89. Correct expression of $0.126\overline{36}$ =?

(a) $\dfrac{139}{1100}$　　(b) $126\dfrac{36}{1000}$

(c) $\dfrac{139}{2200}$　　(d) $126\dfrac{36}{10000}$

90. One of the following is not among the revolutionaries of Freedom Movement hanged by the British.

(a) Bhagat Singh

(b) Rajguru

(c) Sukhdev

(d) Chandra Shekhar Azad

91. A water tank has two holes. The 1st hole alone makes the tank empty in 3 minutes and 2nd hole alone makes the tan empty in 5 minutes. If water leaks out at a constant rate, how long in minutes does it take if both the holes together empty the tank?

(a) $\dfrac{7}{8}$　　(b) $2\dfrac{7}{8}$

(c) $1\dfrac{5}{8}$　　(d) $1\dfrac{7}{8}$

92. Below are given statements followed by some conclusions. You have to take the given statements to be true even if they seem to be at variance with the commonly known facts and then decide which of the given conclusions logically follow(s) from the given statements.

Statements:

(a) Some businessmen are rich.

(b) Birla is rich.

Conclusions:

I.　Birla is a businessman.

II.　Birla has a big farm.

Choose which of the given conclusions logically follow(s) from the given statements.

(a) Only conclusion II follows.

(b) Only conclusion I follows.

(c) Neither I nor II follows.

(d) Both I and II follow.

93. A satellite airtime bill costs ₹8 for 5 minutes 40 seconds. What is the cost in rupees for 4 minutes 20 seconds? (Round upto one decimal).

(a) 6.1　　(b) 6

(c) 6.2　　(d) 6.3

94. If $Sin\ x = \dfrac{4}{5}$, then $1 + Tan^2\ x =$

(a) $\dfrac{9}{25}$　　(b) $\dfrac{25}{16}$

(c) $\dfrac{4}{25}$　　(d) $\dfrac{25}{9}$

95. To enlarge their hold over India, many wars were fought between British and Indians but NOT one of the following.

(a) Anglo-Maratha　(b) Anglo-Sikh

(c) Anglo-Mysore　(d) Anglo-Bangla

96. Which of the following is NOT a storage device?

(a) Hard Disk　　(b) CD ROM

(c) Flash Drive　　(d) Modem

97. Choose the pair which is related in the same way as the words in the first pair from the given choices.

PIGEON : PEACE :: WHITE FLAG : __________

(a) FRIENDSHIP　(b) VICTORY

(c) SURRENDER　(d) WAR

98. Ms. Sushmitha borrowed ₹900 at 6% per annum simple interest. What amount will she pay to clear her debt after 4 years?

(a) 261　　(b) 1161

(c) 1116　　(d) 216

99. Choose the pair which is related in the same way as the words in the first pair from the given choices.

HILL : MOUNTAIN :: STREAM : ________

(a) CANAL　　(b) GLACIER

(c) RIVER　　(d) DAM

100. Choose the pair which is related in the same way as the words in the first pair from the given choices.

BACTERIA : ILLNESS :: ________ : _____

(a) MEDICINE : GERMS

(b) CALCIUM : BONE

(c) KNIFE : LACERATION

(d) FLOOD : DAM

HINTS & EXPLANATIONS

1. (d)

2. (a) As given that two numbers ratio = 21 : 29.
Let, the numbers be 21x and 29x, their given,
H.C.F = 8, So, x = 8.
So, the number are 168, 232.
$168 = 2 \times 2 \times 2 \times 3 \times 7$
$232 = 2 \times 2 \times 2 \times 29$
Hence, their, L.C.M = $(2 \times 2 \times 2 \times 21 \times 29)$
= 4872.

3. (b)

4. (c) As we know that,
The exterior angles of any regular polygon must add up to 360°.
Since, the angle measure given is 60°.
So, it take, $\dfrac{360°}{60°} = 6°$,

Hence, there are 6 exterior angle and

therefore 6 sides to the polygon

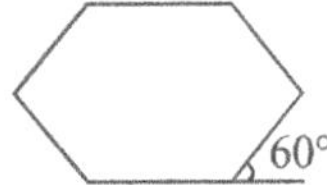

5. (a) As given that

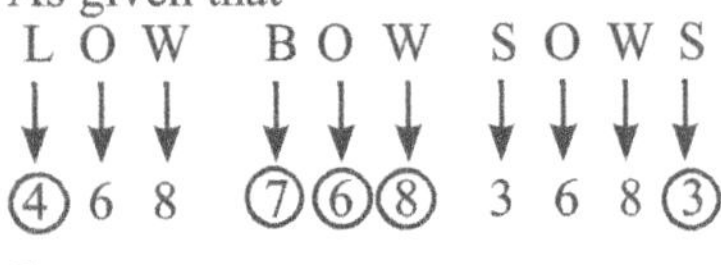

So,
B O W L S
↓ ↓ ↓ ↓ ↓
7 6 8 4 3
Hence, BOWLS is represented as 76843.

6. (d) In the given statements. Morning walks are good for health. But it does not means that all the healthy person go for morning walks. Hence, conclusion I does not follow. Also nothing is said about the evening walks in statement. Thus conclusion II also does not follow.

7. (a)

8. (b) $2x + 4 = x - 3$
$x = -3 - 4$
$x = -7$

9. (b) As given that,

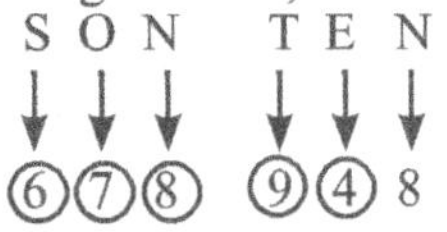

Then,
S T O N E
↓ ↓ ↓ ↓ ↓
6 9 7 8 4
Hence, 'STONE' word is represented as 69784.

10. (b) From formula

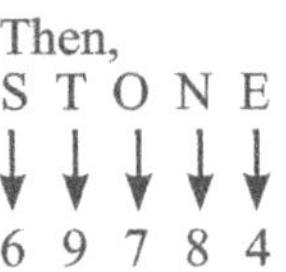

$$A = P\left[1 + \frac{r}{100}\right]^n = 11000\left[1 + \frac{5}{100}\right]^2$$
$= 11000\ [1.05]^2$
$= 12127.5$

11. (d) As we know that
Product of two Numbers $(N_1 \times N_2) = LCM \times HCF$
$2642 = L.C.M \times 42$
So, L.C.M $= \left[\dfrac{2642}{42}\right] = 63$

Sol. (12.-14):

Varun · Vinod · Vasu · Vinay · Vishal · Vikas · Vaibhav

12. (d) Vikas is second to the right of Vinod.

13. (c) Vaibhav is a immediate right of Vikas.

14. (a) Vaibhav is third to the left of Varun

15. (d) As given expression is:
$= 29292 \times 9999$
$= 29292 \times (10000 - 1)$
$= 292920000 - 29292$
$= 292890708$.

16. (d) The relationship between volume and pressure, known as Boyle's Law states that at constant temperature, the volume of a fixed amount of a gas is inversely proportional to its pressure. Fountain pen, Bicycle pump and hand pump functions similar to Boyle's Law, whereas a pulley is an example of simple machine. A pulley is a collection of one or more wheels which help you reverse the direction of your lifting force.

17. (c) As given that,

N O T E B O O K
↓ ↓ ↓ ↓ ↓ ↓ ↓ ↓
R E G O L E E N

and,

S H I R T
↓ ↓ ↓ ↓ ↓
X Y Z B G

So,

T O R N
↓ ↓ ↓ ↓
G E B R

Hence, TORN is represented as GEBR

18. (a) If Tan A $= \dfrac{15}{8}$, TanB $= \dfrac{7}{24}$

So, CosA $= \dfrac{8}{17}$, Cos B $= \dfrac{24}{25}$

Then

Cos $(A - B) = ($Cos A. Cos B $+$ Sin A. Sin B$)$

$=$ CosA.CosB$[1 +$ tanA. TanB$]$

$= \dfrac{8}{17} \times \dfrac{24}{25}\left[1 + \dfrac{15}{8} \times \dfrac{7}{24}\right]$

$= \dfrac{8 \times 24}{17 \times 25} + \dfrac{15 \times 7}{17 \times 25}$

$= \dfrac{192 + 105}{425} = \dfrac{297}{425}$

19. (d) Simplify

$\Rightarrow 4(x-1) - 3x$

$\Rightarrow 4x - 4 - 3x$

$\Rightarrow x - 4$

20. (c) As given exprassion

$\Rightarrow (27)^{-2/3}$

By simplify

$\Rightarrow [(3)^3]^{-2/3}$

$= [3]^{-2} = \dfrac{1}{9}$

21. (b) As given word is coddes as:

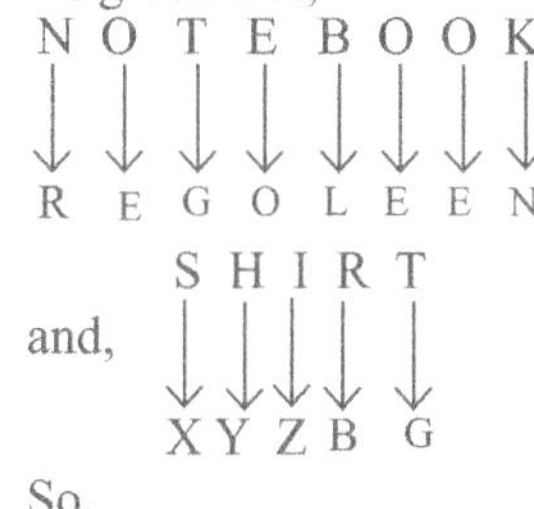

So,

Hence, 'CANT' word is represented as ANCT.

22. (a) As given that,
When, '+' and '×' signs as well as '3' and '2' are interchanged.
Then, By talking
option (a)
$4 + 2 \times 3 = 14$
By changing sign,
$\Rightarrow 4 \times 3 + 2 = 14$
Hence, option (a) is correct.

23. (d)

24. (a) As given that,
If signs '−' and '×' and numbers '3' and '15' are interchanged. Then,
the given expression:
$\Rightarrow 3 + 12 \div 6 - 4 \times 15$
By changing sign,,
$\Rightarrow 15 + 12 \div 6 \times 4 - 3$
$\Rightarrow 15 + 2 \times 4 - 3$
$\Rightarrow 20$

25. (c)

26. (b) As we know that
If the total number of data is odd then the median

$= \left(\dfrac{n+1}{2}\right)^{th}$ term

Here, n $= 7$

So, median $= \left(\dfrac{7+1}{2}\right)^{th}$ term

$= \dfrac{1}{2}$

27. (d) 28. (a)

29. (c) Polymer membranes act as a filter to desalinate and selectively remove contaminants from various water sources. Porous and polymeric membranes have a thin layer of semi-permeable material that is used for solute separation. Porous membranes are mainly used for microfiltration and ultrafiltration. The membrane contains pores ranging from

0.1 to 10 μm for microfiltration and 0.001 to 0.1μm for ultrafiltration.

30. (d)

31. (c) As given that

'÷' → Subtraction (–)

'–' → addition (+)

'+' → multiplication (×)

'×' → division (/)

$\Rightarrow 182 \div 91 \times 7 + 3 - 1$

$\Rightarrow 182 - 91/7 \times 3 + 1$

$\Rightarrow 182 - 13 \times 3 + 1$

$\Rightarrow 182 - 39 + 1 = 144$

32. (c) As given that

Divide, 288 into the ratio 2 : 3 : 5 : 6

So, Let A = 2x, B = 3x, C = 5x, D = 6x,

$2x + 3x + 5x + 6x = 288$

$16x = 288$

$x = 18.$

Then A = 36, B = 54, C= 90, D = 108

Hence, option (c) is correct.

33. (b) Let's say the market rate of that particular commodity is ₹per gm.

Cheating 1% by using false weight at the time of buying means:

He bought 1% extra quantity.

So, he had to pay ₹100 for 100 gm. but actually he got 101 gm for ₹100

Cost price of 101gm = ₹100

Cheating 1% by using false weight at the time for selling means.

He sold 1% 'less' quantity, So he sold saying that he was charging ₹100 for 100 gram (at the market rate ₹1 per gm).

to his customer but gave only 99 gm.

Selling price of 99 gram

$$= ₹100 \left[\text{Rate} = \frac{\text{Rs. } 100}{99} \text{ Per gm.} \right]$$

But he will sell all the quantity that he purchased i.e., 1010 gm to calculate his profit.

Selling price of 101 gm. $= \dfrac{100}{99} \times 101$

$= 102.02$

$$\text{Net profit} = \left[\frac{\text{S.P} - \text{C.P}}{\text{C.P}} \right] \times 100$$

$$= \left[\frac{102.02 - 100}{100} \right] \times 100$$

$= 2.02 \approx 2.01$

Hence, his total gain in percentage is 2.01.

34. (a) As given that

$w = -2, x = 3, y = 0, z = -\dfrac{1}{2}$

Then

The value of given expression is

$\Rightarrow 2 (w^2 + x^2 + y^3)$

$\Rightarrow 2[(-2)^2 + (3)^2 + (0)^3]$

$= 2(4 + 9 + 0) = 26$

35. (a) 36. (b) 37. (a) 38. (a)   39. (d)

40. (c)

41. (b) The branches and the trunks of trees have unique rings inside them. These rings appear as alternating rings of dark and light shaded wood. One can find out the age of a tree by counting the number of dark rings. Determining the age of tree by counting annual rings is called Dendrochronology.

42. (c) 43. (a)

44. (b) As given expression

$\Rightarrow 1848 \div 231 - 10$

$\Rightarrow 8 - 10 = -2$

Hence option (b) is correct.

45. (c)

46. (b) In an ecosystem, the plants which produce the grain are autotrophs or producers, and form the first trophic level. The rats which feed on the grain are primary consumers, and form the second trophic level.

47. (b) The mean of the given series 3, 10, 10, 4, 7, 10, 5

$$\overline{x} = \left[\frac{\text{Sum of the terms}}{\text{Number of terms}} \right]$$

$$= \left[\frac{\sum X_i}{n} \right] = \frac{3 + 10 + 10 + 4 + 7 + 10 + 5}{7}$$

$$= \frac{49}{7} = 7$$

48. (d) As given expression $42 \div 4 + 2 - 3 \times 5 = 29$

In this equation by interchanging the two sign '÷' and '+' then.

$\Rightarrow 42 + 4 \div 2 - 3 \times 5$

$\Rightarrow 44 - 15 = 29.$

49. (b) 50. (b) 51. (d)

52. (b) Total number of executives recruited by all the organizations together in the year 2012.

$= 480 + 495 + 464 + 508 + 488 + 518 = 2953$

53. (a) The average number of executevs recruited by organization over all the year together

$$\text{Avg} = \left[\frac{[502 + 500 + 508 + 444 + 512 + 499]}{6} \right]$$

$$= \frac{2965}{6} = 494.16 = 494$$

54. (b) The total number of executives recruited by all the organization together in 2014 is:
$$\Rightarrow \left(427 + 485 + 422 + 512 + 510 + 498\right)$$
$$\Rightarrow (2854).$$
No. of executives recruited by organization T in the year 2014 = 510
So,
$$\text{Required } \% = \frac{510}{2854} \times 100 = 17.86 \approx 18\%$$

55. (b)

56. (a) Let, the distance x km, then,
$\Rightarrow$ Time taken to walk x km + Time taken to ride x km.
$\Rightarrow$ 4 hrs. 45 min.
Time taken to walk 2x km = 5 hours 55 minutes
Time taken to ride 2x km
= 2 × [4 hrs. 45 minutes] – 5 hrs. 55 minutes]
= 3 hrs. 35 minutes.
Hence, option (a) is correct.

57. (b)

58. (c) The correct ascending order of the given numbers;
$$\Rightarrow \frac{1}{2}, \frac{7}{12}, \frac{2}{3}$$
$$\Rightarrow 0.5, 0.58, 0.66$$

59. (c)

60. (c) As given expression:
$\Rightarrow$ 15872/32/4 = 496/4 = 124

61. (d) 62. (a) 63. (d)

64. (b) Let Raju finish the work in x days.
Raju 1 day's work = 1/x
Karteek is twice as good as Raju.
So, Karteek 1 day's work = $\dfrac{2}{x}$
Since, Raju, and Karteek work together in 20 days.
So, 1 days work for both = 1/20
$$\Rightarrow \text{Hence } \frac{1}{x} + \frac{2}{x} = \frac{1}{20} \Rightarrow \frac{3}{x} = \frac{1}{20}$$
= 60 days
Hence, Rajui alone finish the work in 60 days

65. (b)

66. (b) As we know that,
Variance = [Standard deviation]²

So, standard deviation of the data
= (variance)$^{1/2}$
= $(169)^{1/2}$ = 13

67. (a) 68. (a)

69. (a) Let the cost price of article is ₹x.
Required ratio - (102% of x)/(116% of x)
$$= \frac{102}{116} = \frac{51}{58}$$

70. (c)

71. (c) DNA fingerprinting, also known as DNA profiling is a forensic technique used to determine an individual's DNA characteristics so as to assess the likelihood of their involvement in the crime. The DNA sample taken from a crime scene is compared with a DNA sample from a suspect. If the two DNA's match, then the evidence is supposed to have come from the suspect but if the two DNA profiles do not match, then the evidence cannot have come from the suspect.

72. (d)

73. (c) Let speed of the woman is x kmph,
Distance covered in 20 minutes of 25 kmph
= 25× 20/60
Now, distance covered by woman in 18 minutes = $\dfrac{25}{3}$ km
∴ speed of the women.
$$\frac{25/3}{18/60} = \frac{250}{9} \text{ kmph}$$
Hence difference in speed
$$= \frac{250}{9} - 25 = 2\frac{7}{9} \text{ meter}$$

74. (a)

75. (c) According to Newton's third law, "For every action, there is an equal and opposite reaction." When a ball is thrown onto a wall, the ball exerts a force onto the wall. According to Newton's Third Law, the wall will exert an equal and opposite force to the ball.

76. (b) 77. (b) 78. (a) 79. (c) 80. (b)

Sol. (81-83):

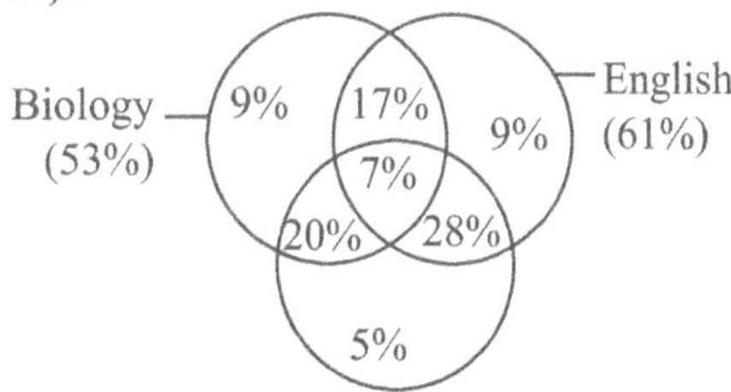

As we know that

n(E∪B∪ S.S) = n (E) + n (B) + n (S.S) – (E∩B)–n(B∩S.S)–n(S.S∩E)+n(E∩B∩S.S)

n (E∪B US.S) = 100 – 5 = 95

$95 = 61 + 53 + 60 - 24 - 27 - 35 +$ n[E∩B∩S.S]

n[E∩B∩S.S] = 95 + 24 + 27 + 35 – 61 – 60 – 53 = 7

81. (a) Required ratio $= \dfrac{20}{28} = \dfrac{5}{7}$

82. (b) Total No of students = 200.

So, The number of students passed in only one subject is $= \dfrac{200 \times 23}{100} = 46$

83. (c) The number of students passed in all subject = 7.

84. (d) S.P = ₹25100₹

Loss = 15%

Let C.P. = x

By condition

$$\Rightarrow \frac{-5100 + x}{x} = \frac{15}{100}$$

$- 20 \times 5100 + 20x = 3x$

$-102000 + 20x = 3x$

$17x = 102000$

$$x = \frac{102000}{17} = ₹6000$$

Then S.P $= 6000 \times \dfrac{15}{100} + 6000 = ₹6900$

Hence, Mr. Joshi sold his bus ₹6900

85. (a)

$AC^2 = AB^2 + BC^2$

$\quad\quad = (5)^2 + (6)^2$

$AC = \sqrt{25 + 36}$

$\quad\quad = \sqrt{61}$

86. (a)

87. (a) Inertia is a property of a body by virtue of which it cannot change its state of rest or uniform motion. That is why, a pile of book on the table will not be dislodged.

88. (a)

89. (a) Let, $0.12\overline{636} = r$

$$\therefore r = \frac{12636 - 126}{99000} = \frac{12510}{99000}$$

Hence, $r = \dfrac{139}{1100}$

90. (d)

91. (d) As given that,

A water tank has two holes, empty a tank in 3 & 5 minutes.

Time taken by both the hole to empty the tank $= \dfrac{xy}{x+y} = \dfrac{3 \times 5}{3+5} = \dfrac{15}{8} = 1\dfrac{7}{8}$

92. (c)

93. (a) A satellite airtime bill costs = ₹8

time = 5 minutes 40 seconds = 390 sec.

4 minutes 20 seconds = 260 seconds

So, the cost of airtime satellite in 260 seconds is

$$= \frac{8 \times 260}{340} = 6.1$$

94. (d) As given that,

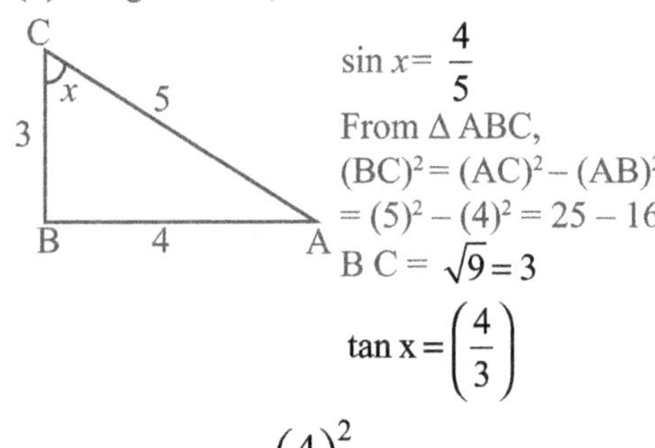

$\sin x = \dfrac{4}{5}$

From Δ ABC,

$(BC)^2 = (AC)^2 - (AB)^2$

$= (5)^2 - (4)^2 = 25 - 16$

$BC = \sqrt{9} = 3$

$\tan x = \left(\dfrac{4}{3}\right)$

$$1 + \tan^2 x = 1 + \left(\frac{4}{3}\right)^2$$

$$= 1 + \left(\frac{16}{9}\right) = \left(\frac{25}{9}\right)$$

95. (d)   96. (d)

97. (c) PIGEON is the symbol of PEACE, in the same way as the words WHITEFLAG is the symbol of SURRENDER.

98. (c) To calculate the total amount to be paid by him after 4 years, so it will be principal + simple interest.

Hence,

$$\Rightarrow \left[900 + \frac{900 \times 6 \times 4}{100}\right] \Rightarrow [900 + 216]$$

$= ₹1116$

99. (c) MOUNTAIN is buildup by the Hills and crage. In the same way as the words STREAM is build up by the RIVER.

100. (c)

1. The Crescograph, a device for measuring growth in plants, was invented by:
   (a) Hyder Ali
   (b) Satyendra Bose
   (c) Subrahmanyan Chandrasekhar
   (d) Jagadish Chandra Bose

2. The flag of Malaysia, comprises a field of ______________ alternating red and white stripes.
   (a) 20   (b) 18
   (c) 16   (d) 14

3. What is the median of the following distribution?
   42, 65, 18, 69, 29, 42, 48, 79, 25, 24, 98, 87, 63, 27, 17
   (a) 43.5   (b) 65
   (c) 42   (d) 69

4. If the cost price of 12 books is equal to the selling price of 8 books, what is the gain percent?
   (a) 12%   (b) 30%
   (c) 40%   (d) 50%

5. A shopkeeper buys an induction cooker for Rs. 2750 and sells it for Rs. 2860. Find his gain percentage.
   (a) 1%   (b) 2%
   (c) 3%   (d) 4%

6. Hiten introduced Mita as his son's maternal grandfather's only son's only sister's mother-in-law. How is Mita related to Hiten?
   (a) Mother
   (b) Mother-in-law
   (c) Wife
   (d) Maternal Aunt

7. What is the mean of the following distribution?
   54, 23, 66, 44, 79, 21, 54, 67, 29, 59
   (a) 51.4   (b) 49.6
   (c) 48.7   (d) 45.3

8. Which two signs should be interchanged to make the following equation correct?
   72 ÷ 9 + 5 × 3 − 2 = 41
   (a) ÷ and −   (b) × and +
   (c) ÷ and ×   (d) × and −

9. A Refrigerator works on which of the following principles?
   (a) Osmosis
   (b) Centrifugation
   (c) Dispersion
   (d) Evaporation

10. In which year did Indian Men
    (a) 1928   (b) 1956
    (c) 1975   (d) 1982

11. The company Interglobe Aviation, which recently came out with its IPO, controls which one of the following airlines?
    (a) Indigo   (b) Go Air
    (c) Spice Jet   (d) Air Asia

12. Which premier watchmaker has associated with Google to develop a smart luxury watch?
    (a) RADO   (b) Tag Heuer
    (c) Omega   (d) Titan

13. Who as per the Harvard Business Review was the top performing CEO in 2015?
    (a) Lars Rebien Sorensen, Novo Nordisk
    (b) Chuck Robbins. Cisco System
    (c) Pablo Isla, INDITEX
    (d) Howard Shultz, Starbucks

14. Adil and Biren together can complete a task in 20 days. Biren and Chirag together can complete the same task in 50 days. Adil and Chirag together can complete the same task in 40 days. If the same task was to be done by them alone, what would be the ratio of time taken by Adil alone to taken by Biren?
    (a) 11 : 9   (b) 11 : 3
    (c) 7 : 9   (d) 9 : 11

15. The Thousand Pillar Temple, a historic Hindu temple located in the town of Hanamakonda, was built by:
    (a) Rudra Deva   (b) Krishnadeva Raya
    (c) Jahangir   (d) Aurangazeb

16. Compute: 87654 × 99999
    (a) 8766624336   (b) 8765312346
    (c) 8857624336   (d) 8656624426

17. What is the value of the expression:
    (Tan0° Tan1° Tan2° Tan3° Tan4° ....
    Tan89°)
    (a) 0   (b) 1
    (c) 2   (d) 1/2

18. Based on the relationship between the first two
    words, find out the missing wor(d)
    BHARATANATYAM : TAMIL NADU ::
    KUCHIPUDI : ______________
    (a) ARUNACHAL PRADESH
    (b) ODISHA
    (c) ANDHRA PRADESH
    (d) KERALA

DIRECTIONS (Qs. 19-21): *Read the passage given*
below and answer the questions that follow:

In a club of 30 people, all of them belong to at least
one group - Chess, Drama and Art. 6 people belong
only to the Art group. 5 people belong to all the three
groups. 2 people have joined the Chess and the Art
group but not the Drama group. 15 people belong to
the Art group. 2 people have joined only the Chess
group. 3 people have joined only the Drama group.

19. How many people belong to exactly one group?
    (a) 11   (b) 10
    (c) 14   (d) 12

20. How many people have belong to the Chess
    group?
    (a) 21   (b) 13
    (c) 19   (d) 20

21. How many people have joined the Chess and
    the Drama group but not the Art group?
    (a) 12   (b) 10
    (c) 15   (d) 13

22. In which of the following states was the first
    passenger train stalled in India?
    (a) Maharashtra   (b) Tamil Nadu
    (c) Uttar Pradesh   (d) West Bengal

23. The Kyoto protocol was entered into force in
    the year:
    (a) 2005   (b) 1997
    (c) 2000   (d) 2002

24. Who is the real founder of the Gupta Empire?
    (a) Chandragupta II
    (b) Samudragupta
    (c) Sri Gupta
    (d) Ghatookacha

25. Which of the following is a philosophical
    system recognizing only that which can be
    scientifically verified or which is capable of
    logical or mathematical proof, and therefore
    rejecting metaphysics and theism?
    (a) Structural Functionalism
    (b) Symbolic Interaction
    (c) Conflicts
    (d) Positivism

26. Find the unit digit in
    $(1234)^{102} + (1234)^{103}$
    (a) 2   (b) 4
    (c) 0   (d) 1

27. Alassane Ouattara is:
    (a) The President of Ivory Coast
    (b) The President of Indonesia
    (c) The President of Malaysia
    (d) The Vice President of Maldives

28. In which year did archery have its official debut
    at the Summer Olympics?
    (a) 1896   (b) 1920
    (c) 1972   (d) 1900

29. Sumit scored 75% on a math test with 60
    questions. How many questions did he answer
    incorrectly?
    (a) 10   (b) 15
    (c) 17   (d) 20

30. The ratio of the speeds of two trains is 3 : 4. If
    the second train runs 300 km in 3 hours, then
    what would be the speed of the first train?
    (a) 100 km/hr   (b) 50 km/hr
    (c) 70 km/hr   (d) 75 km/hr

31. IPCC stands for:
    (a) Inter Parliamentary Panel for Climate
        Change
    (b) Intergovernmental Panel on Climate
        Change
    (c) Inter Government Parliamentary' Panel on
        Climate Change
    (d) International Panel on Climate Change

32. Which of the following is the first animal to go to
    into spatial orbit on board the Soviet Sputnik 2?
    (a) Laika, a dog
    (b) Albert, a mouse
    (c) Belka, a monkey
    (d) Baker, a rabbit

33. In the question given below, are given two
    statements followed by a few conclusions
    as options. You have to take the two given
    statements to be true even if they seem to be at

variance with commonly known facts. Read all the conclusions and then decide which of the given conclusions basically follows from the two given statements disregarding commonly known facts.

Statements:
1. All toys are books
2. All books are trains

Conclusions: ?
(a) All trains are books
(b) All books are toys
(c) Some trains are toys
(d) No train is a toy

34. Which of the following is the branch of physiology and medicine which deals with diseases and conditions specific to men?
(a) Andrology   (b) Astacology
(c) Bioecology   (d) Desmology

35. A purse contains ₹455 in the form of ₹1, ₹2, and ₹5 coins in the ratio of 2 : 4 : 5. What is the number of ₹2 coins in the purse?
(a) 26   (b) 52
(c) 65   (d) 13

36. Find the LCM of 18, 33 and 37.
(a) 2442   (b) 7326
(c) 814   (d) 1221

37. Who among the following was one of the founders of the Swaraj Party?
(a) Motilal Nehru
(b) Lala Lajpat Rai
(c) Subhas Chandra Bose
(d) Dadabhai Naoroji

38. If '+' means '×', '−' means '÷', '×' means '+' and '÷' means '−' then what is the value of:
$225 ÷ 5 + 96 − 3 × 31$
(a) 86   (b) 96
(c) 106   (d) 116

39. The classical dance of Kathakali belongs to which Indian state?
(a) Odisha   (b) Kerala
(c) Andhra Pradesh   (d) Assam

40. Which of the following Religious Communities has been granted the 'Minority' status by the Indian Government on 30th January 2014?
(a) Sikh   (b) Buddhist
(c) Jain   (d) Parsi

41. In order to help in the freedom struggle, which newspaper was started by Lokmanya Tilak?
(a) Kesari
(b) Amrit Bazar Patrika
(c) Ghadar
(d) Harijan

42. Which of the following space crafts was used by Rakesh Sharma to make his historic trip to space?
(a) Apollo 11   (b) Progress 1
(c) Soyuz T-11   (d) Salyut 7

43. Divya said, "That lady is my husband's sister's only sibling's son's paternal grandmother". How is that lady related to Divya?
(a) Mother
(b) Mother-in-law
(c) Maternal Aunt
(d) Maternal Grandmother

44. 7 men and 3 women complete the work together in 10 days. 8 men and 2 women complete the same work in 8 days. How much work can be done by 12 men in one day?
(a) 17.5%   (b) 20%
(c) 21%   (d) 23%

45. Thomas Clifford Allbutt is associated with the invention of:
(a) X Ray Machine
(b) Clinical Thermometer
(c) Stethoscope
(d) Microscope

46. If the Standard deviation of a distribution is 9, what is the value of variance?
(a) 18   (b) 27
(c) 81   (d) 36

47. Antonio Meucci is associated with the invention of:
(a) Telephone
(b) Automobile
(c) LED
(d) Industrial Robot

48. what is the correct ascending order for the given fractions?
(a) 22/7, 13/17, 11/19, 2/3
(b) 11/19, 2/3, 13/17, 22/7
(c) 2/3, 11/19, 13/17, 22/7
(d) 2/3, 13/17, 11/19, 22/7

49. Keeping voltage constant, if more lamps are put into a series circuit, the overall current in the circuit:
(a) Increases
(b) Decreases
(c) Remains the same
(d) Becomes infinite

DIRECTIONS (Qs. 50-52): *Read the passage given below and answer the questions that follow:*

Prema, Qutub, Rahul, Stalin, Tuhin, Ujala, Varun and Waheeda are sitting around a circle facing the center. Waheeda is to the immediate left of Prema but is not the neighbor of Tuhin or Stalin.
Ujala is to the immediate right of Qutub
Varun is sitting next to Tuhin.
Rahul is sitting between Tuhin and Ujala

50. Which of the following statements is TRUE?
    (a) Tuhin is sitting in between Ujala and Qutub
    (b) Ujala is sitting next to Varun
    (c) Varun is to the right of Tuhin and also to the left of Waheeda
    (d) Prema is second to the right of Stalin

51. In which of the following pairs, the second person is second to the right of the first person?
    (a) Rahul, Prema
    (b) Varun, Waheeda
    (c) Ujala, Tuhin
    (d) Stalin, Qutub

52. What is the position of Stalin?
    (a) On the immediate left of Qutub
    (b) Second to the right of Ujala
    (c) Between Varun and Waheeda
    (d) Exactly next to Rahul

53. Two Positive integers are in the ratio of 3 : 4. If the product of the two numbers is 1728, what is the value of the greater number?
    (a) 36   (b) 38
    (c) 48   (d) 72

54. In a right-angled triangle, the longest side is 1 cm longer than the middle side and the middle side is 49 cm longer than the shortest side. Calculate the length of the shortest side?
    (a) 11 cm   (b) 10 cm
    (c) 21 cm   (d) 60 cm

55. If a box contains 3 white cushions, 4 red cushions and 5 blue cushions, what is probability of selecting a white or blue cushions?
    (a) 2/3   (b) 3/4
    (c) 1/4   (d) 1/9

56. IRS series of Indian Satellites are used for:
    (a) Forestry
    (b) Communication
    (c) Remote Sensing
    (d) Astronomy

57. If **A = 26** and **TEA = 55**, then **SPATTER = ?**
    (a) 92   (b) 90
    (c) 91   (d) 95

58. Which element has the atomic number 3?
    (a) Boron   (b) Lithium
    (c) Beryllium   (d) Sodium

59. Compute: 4237.43 + 453.32 + 24.12 − 387.23
    (a) 4327.64   (b) 4646.64
    (c) 4676.64   (d) 4587.64

60. Which European country was the first to introduce bank notes and was recently in the news to soon become the first cashless country in the world?
    (a) UK   (b) Germany
    (c) Sweden   (d) Switzerland

61. Based on the relationship between the first two words, find out the missing wor(d)
    FISHES : AQUARIUM :: BIRDS : ______
    (a) AVIARY   (b) APIARY
    (c) BYRE   (d) DREY

62. When a natural number n is divided by 5 the remainder is 4. What is the remainder when 2n is divided by 5?
    (a) 2   (b) 3
    (c) 4   (d) 0

63. If **TEACHER** is coded as **UDBBIDS**, then **STUDENT** will be coded as:
    (a) RSTCDMS   (b) TUVEFOU
    (c) TSVCFMU   (d) RUTEDOS

64. In the Parliament of India, who was the first speaker of the Lok Sabha?
    (a) M. A. Ayyangar
    (b) Ganesh Mavalankar
    (c) Sardar Hukam Singh
    (d) Neelam Sanjeeva Reddy

65. Find the HCF of 315, 630 and 945.
    (a) 315   (b) 105
    (c) 210   (d) 140

66. Based on the statement(s) given below, choose the best possible conclusion(s) that follows:
    Statements:
    (a) Players who break records in a fair way are given a special rewar(d)
    (b) Player XYZ broke the world record but was found to be under the influence of a prohibited drug.
    Conclusions:
    I. The accusation on Player XYZ was false.
    II. Player XYZ will not get the special rewar(d)

(a) Only conclusion I follows
(b) Only conclusion II follows
(c) Both conclusion I and II follow
(d) Neither conclusion I nor II follows

67. Aparna said, "That man is my brother's wife's son's only paternal uncle's father". How is the man related to Aparna?
    (a) Paternal Grandfather   (b) Father
    (c) Uncle   (d) Son

68. Which of the following atoms has the largest diameter?
    (a) Iodine   (b) Fluorine
    (c) Chlorine   (d) Bromine

69. If the ratio of the angles of a triangle is 2 : 4 : 3, then what is the sum of the smallest angle of the triangle and the largest angle of the triangle?
    (a) 120 degrees   (b) 100 degrees
    (c) 140 degrees   (d) 110 degrees

DIRECTIONS (Qs. 70-72): *Read the information given below and answer the questions that follow:*

Information about the Number of Candidates who appeared, qualified and then were selected in a Competitive Examination from Delhi over the years 1997 to 2001 is given below.

Year	Appeared	Qualified	Selected
1997	8000	850	94
1998	4800	500	48
1999	7500	640	82
2000	9500	850	90
2001	9000	800	70

70. What is the average number of candidates selected over the given period (round it to the nearest integer)?
    (a) 79   (b) 77
    (c) 76   (d) 74

71. In which year is the lowest percentage of candidates selected over those qualified
    (a) 1998   (b) 2000
    (c) 2001   (d) 1999

72. For which year, is the ratio of number of candidates who were selected to the number of candidates who qualified the highest?
    (a) 1998   (b) 2000
    (c) 2001   (d) 1999

73. Rita invested a sum at 2.5% rate for 4 years. Sita invested the same amount at the same rate for 6 years. What is the ratio of the simple interest earned by Sita to that earned by Rita?
    (a) 3:2   (b) 2:3
    (c) 1:3   (d) 1:4

74. Which of the following is NOT a solution of the equation $3x - 4y = 8$?
    (a) (4, 1)   (b) (8, 4)
    (c) (1,4)   (d) (0,–2)

75. Based on the statement(s) given below, choose the best possible conclusion(s) that follows:
    Statements:
    (a) In a T20 match, the total runs made by a team was 210.
    (b) Out of these 147 runs were made by the spinners.
    Conclusions:
    I. 70% of the team consists of spinners.
    II. The opening batsmen were spinners.
    (a) Only conclusion I follows
    (b) Only conclusion II follows
    (c) Both conclusion I and II follow
    (d) Neither conclusion I nor II follows

76. if '+' means '×', '–' means '÷', '×' means '+' and '÷' means '–' then what is the value of:
    $208 - 4 + 3 \div 23 \times 57$
    (a) 190   (b) 195
    (c) 201   (d) 290

77. Which two signs should be interchanged to make the following equation correct?
    $5 \times 45 - 15 + 31 \div 41 = 5$
    (a) ÷ and –   (b) × and +
    (c) ÷ and ×   (d) × and –

78. If $\sin\theta - \cos\theta = 0$, then what is the value of the expression: $(\sin^6\theta + \cos^6\theta)$
    (a) 1   (b) 3/4
    (c) 1/2   (d) 1/4

79. Which of the following is the idea that new species are formed from the sudden and unexpected emergence of alterations in their defining traits?
    (a) Natural Selection
    (b) Mutation
    (c) Recombination
    (d) Non - Random Mating

80. Compute: $7/5 + 31/21 + 23/52$
    (a) 18339/5640   (b) 18119/5460
    (c) 18330/4780   (d) 18119/4780

81. Due to which of the below mentioned reasons, do clouds float in the sky?
(a) Low temperature   (b) Low speed
(c) Low pressure   (d) Low density

82. The river Godavari does NOT pass through which of the following states?
(a) Maharashtra
(b) Gujarat
(c) Chhattisgarh
(d) Andhra Pradesh

83. Given below are parts of a statement. Select the correct order of these parts to make a meaningful statement. P: the impact business management choices Q: the impact of climate change was R: would have on profitability S: not as significant as
(a) PQRS   (b) SRQP
(c) PRQS   (d) QSPR

84. An Integrated circuit, also referred as IC chip is a set of electronic circuit on a small plate is made of:
(a) Copper   (b) Silicon
(c) Silica   (d) Chromium

85. Which of the following is a waterborne disease causing acute gastrointestinal infection?
(a) Cholera   (b) Rabies
(c) Pneumonia   (d) Leprosy

86. Based on the statement(s) given below, choose the best possible conclusion(s) that follows:
Statements:
(a) In case of outstanding candidates, the condition of previous experience in HR may be waived by the admission committee for MBA (HR).
Conclusions:
I. Some of the students for MBA (HR) will have previous experience in HR.
II. Some of the students for MBA (HR) will not have previous experience in HR.
(a) Only conclusion I follows
(b) Only conclusion II follows
(c) Both conclusion I and II follow
(d) Neither conclusion I nor II follows

87. If **HOUSE** is coded as **10-13-23-17-7**. then how will you code **REHEARSE**?
(a) 20-7-10-7-3-20-21-7
(b) 16-3-6-3-25-16-17-3
(c) 20-3-10-3-3-16-21-3
(d) 18-5-8-5-1-18-19-5

88. Under a new scheme, a bank offers an interest of 30% per annum compounded annually. Suraj deposits₹10,000 under this new scheme and at the end of the tenure receives ₹28,561. What was the tenure of the scheme that Suraj had chosen?
(a) 2 years   (b) 3.5 years
(c) 4 years   (d) 4.5 years

89. If two supplementary angles are in the ratio of 4 : 5, find the ratio of the square of the first angle to the square of the second angle.
(a) 16 : 25   (b) 64 : 125
(c) 100 : 125   (d) 25 : 16

90. In the question given below, are given two statements followed by a few conclusions as options. You have to take the two given statements to be true even if they seem to be at variance with commonly known facts. Read all the conclusions and then decide which of the given conclusions basically follows from the two given statements disregarding commonly known facts.
Statements:
(a) All rivers are clouds
(b) Some animals are rivers
Conclusion:
1. Some rivers are animals
2. Some clouds are rivers
3. All clouds are rivers
4. All animals are clouds
(a) Conclusions 1 and 2 follow
(b) Conclusions 1, 2 and 3 follow
(c) Conclusions 1 and 3 follow
(d) Conclusions 2, 3 and 4 follow'

91. A fruit seller sells mangoes at the rate of ₹9 per kg and there by loses 10%. At what price per kg should he sell in order to earn a profit of 5%?
(a) ₹10   (b) ₹10.5
(c) ₹9.5   (d) ₹11.11

92. Which of the following statues is an icon of freedom designed by a French Sculptor?
(a) Statue of Unity
(b) Statue of Liberty
(c) Statue of Law
(d) Statue of Zeus

93. If **KINGS** is coded as **RFMHJ**, then how will you code **QUEEN**?
(a) RTDMD   (b) MDDTP
(c) VFFOT   (d) EUULG

94. Four words are given below out of which three are alike in some manner and one is different. Which one is different from the rest?
   (a) Titan
   (b) Triton
   (c) Titania
   (d) Taurus

95. The youngest Indian woman to achieve the title of Grandmaster in Chess is :
   (a) Tania Sachdev
   (b) Dronavalli Harika
   (c) Humpy Koneru
   (d) Eesha Karavade

96. Which of the following cell organelles is found in the plant cell but not in animal cell?
   (a) Chloroplast
   (b) Endoplasmic Reticulum
   (c) Mitochondrion
   (d) Ribosome

97. Sound waves cannot travel in :
   (a) Air
   (b) Water
   (c) Vacuum
   (d) Steel

98. Based on the relationship between the first two words, find out the missing wor(d)
   THE COLOSSEUM : ITALY :: PETRA : __________
   (a) MEXICO
   (b) JORDAN
   (c) GERMANY
   (d) BRAZIL

99. Arjun, travelling from Pune to Goa, covers a distance of 1000 km at 4 km/hr and the return journey at 3 km/hr. What was his average speed during his entire journey?
   (a) 3 km/hr
   (b) 3.43 km/hr
   (c) 3.5 km/hr
   (d) 5.4 km/hr

100. In MS Excel, what is function inside another function called?
   (a) Round function
   (b) Sandwich function
   (c) Switch function
   (d) Nested function

HINTS & EXPLANATIONS

1. (d)   **2.** (d)

3. (c) Arranging the numbers in ascending order
   17 18 24 25 27 29 42 42 48 63
   65 69 79 87 98
   No. of terms
   = 15 (odd)
   $$\therefore \text{median} = \left(\frac{n+1}{2}\right)^{th} \text{term}$$
   $$= \frac{15+1}{2} = 8^{th} \text{ term}$$
   $\therefore$ median = 42

4. (d) Let CP of 1 book = ₹ 1
   CP of 8 books = ₹ 8
   SP of 8 books = CP of 12 books = ₹ 12
   $\Rightarrow$ Gain = SP – CP
   = ₹12 – ₹8 = ₹ 4
   $$\therefore \text{ gain percent} = \frac{\text{gain}}{\text{CP}} \times 100$$
   $$= \frac{4}{8} \times 100 = 50\%$$

5. (d) Gain percentage $= \dfrac{2860 - 2750}{2750} \times 100$
   $$= \frac{110}{2750} \times 100 = 4\%$$

6. (a)

Hence, Mita is Hiten's Mother

7. (b)
$$\text{Mean} = \frac{54 + 23 + 66 + 44 + 79 + 21 + 54 + 67 + 29 + 59}{10}$$
$$= \frac{496}{10} = 49.6$$

8. (b) $72 \div 9 + 5 \times 3 - 2 = 41$
   After interchanging $\times$ and $+$ we have
   $72 \div 9 \times 5 + 3 - 2 = 41$
   $8 \times 5 + 3 - 2 = 41$
   $40 + 3 - 2 = 41$
   $43 - 2 = 41$
   $41 = 41$

9. (d) A refrigerator does not cool items by lowering their original temperatures; instead, an evaporating gas called a refrigerant draws heat away and leaves the surrounding area much colder. Refrigerators and air conditioners both work on the principle of cooling through evaporation.

10. (a) 11. (a) 12. (b) 13. (a)

14. (d) Let Adil, Biren and Chirag complete the whole work in A, B and C respectively

Then ATQ

$$\frac{1}{A} + \frac{1}{B} = \frac{1}{20} \qquad ...(1)$$

$$\frac{1}{B} + \frac{1}{C} = \frac{1}{50} \qquad ...(2)$$

$$\frac{1}{C} + \frac{1}{A} = \frac{1}{40} \qquad ...(3)$$

Adding (1), (2) & (3)

$$2\left[\frac{1}{A} + \frac{1}{B} = \frac{1}{C}\right] = \frac{19}{200}$$

$$\frac{1}{A} + \frac{1}{B} + \frac{1}{C} = \frac{19}{400} \qquad ...(4)$$

Subtracting (2) from (4) we get

$$\frac{1}{A} = \frac{19}{400} - \frac{1}{50} = \frac{11}{400}$$

Subtracting (3) from (4) we get

$$\frac{1}{B} = \frac{19}{400} - \frac{1}{40} = \frac{9}{400}$$

∴ required ratio

$$= \frac{A}{B} = \frac{1/B}{1/A} = \frac{9}{400} \times \frac{400}{11} = \frac{9}{11} = 9:11$$

15. (a)

16. (b) $87654 \times (100000 - 1)$

$$= 8765400000 - 87654$$

$$= 8765312346$$

17. (a) Tan 0° Tan 1° Tan 2° Tan 3° Tan 4°..... Tan 89°

Since Tan 0° = 0

∴ The whole expression will be equal to 0

18. (c)

Sol. (19 – 21):

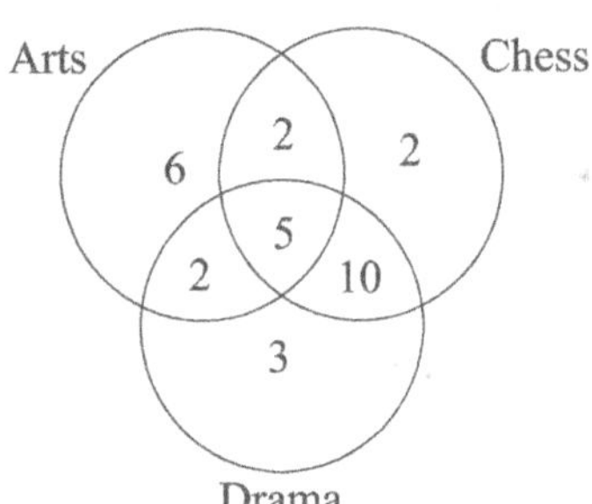

19. (a) No. of people that belong to one group
$$= 6 + 2 + 3$$
$$= 11$$

20. (c) No. of people belonging to Chess group
$$= 2 + 2 + 5 + 10$$
$$= 19$$

21. (b) No. of people who have joined Chess and drama but not Art group = 10

22. (a) 23. (a) 24. (c) 25. (d)

26. (c) Unit digit of $[(1234)^{102} + (1234)^{103}]$

= Unit digit of $[(4^2)^{51} + (4^2)^{51}.4]$

= Unit digit of $[(6)^{51} + (6)^{51}.4]$

= Unit digit of $6 + 6 \times 4$

= Unit digit of 30

= 0

27. (a) 28. (d)

29. (b) No. of questions answered correctly

$$= 60 \times \frac{75}{100} = 45$$

∴ No. of questions answered incorrectly

$$= 60 - 45$$

$$= 15$$

30. (d) Let the speed of first train $= x$ km/hr

ratio of speeds $= \frac{3}{4}$

also speed of second train $= \frac{300}{3} = 100\,\text{km/hr}$

$$\Rightarrow \frac{3}{4} = \frac{x}{100}$$

$$\Rightarrow 4x = 300$$

$$\Rightarrow x = \frac{300}{4} = 75 \text{ km/hr}$$

31. (b) 32. (a)

33. (c)

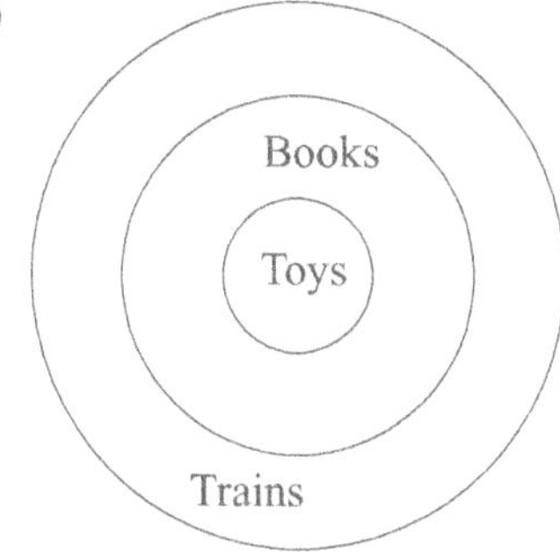

From the diagram conclusion (c) follows.
Some trains are toys.

34. (a) Andrology is the branch of physiology and medicine that deals with male health, particularly relating to the problems of the male reproductive system and urological problems that are unique to men.

35. (b) Let the ratio of the coins be $2x : 4x : 5x$
Then $(2x)\times1+(4x)\times2+(5x)\times5 = 455$
$2x + 8x + 25x = 455$
$\Rightarrow 35\,x = 455$
$\Rightarrow x = 13$
$\therefore$ No. of ₹ 2 coins $= 4x = 4\times13 = 52$

36. (b) $18 = 2\times3\times3$
$33 = 3\times11$
$37 = 37\times1$
$\therefore$ LCM $= 2\times3\times3\times11\times37$
$\qquad = 7326$

37. (a)

38. (b) $225 - 5 \times 96 \div 3 + 31 = 225 - 5 \times 32 + 31$
$= 225 - 160 + 31$
$= 96$

39. (b) 40. (c) 41. (a) 42. (c)

43. (b) Divya's husband's sister's only sibling's son means Divya's son. Now Divya's son's paternal grandmother is mother-in-law of Divya.

44. (c) $7m + 3w \to 1$ day $\to \dfrac{1}{10}$ part

$8m + 2w \to 1$ day $\to \dfrac{1}{8}$ part

Let 1 man complete the whole work in x days and 1 woman complete the whole work in y days

Now

$$\frac{7}{x}+\frac{3}{y}=\frac{1}{10} \qquad \text{...(1)}$$

$$\frac{8}{x}+\frac{2}{y}=\frac{1}{8} \qquad \text{...(2)}$$

Solving eqn. (1) and (2)
$\quad x = 57$
$\therefore$ work done by 12 men in one day

$= \dfrac{12}{57}\times100 \simeq 21\%$

45. (b)

46. (c) Variance $= (\text{S.D})^2$
Here S.D $= 9$
$\therefore$ Variance $= 9^2 = 81$

47. (a)

48. (b) $\dfrac{22}{7} = 3.14$

$\dfrac{13}{17} = .76$

$\dfrac{11}{9} = .57$

$\dfrac{2}{3} = .66$

$\therefore$ Correct ascending order for the given fraction

is $\dfrac{11}{9},\dfrac{2}{3},\dfrac{13}{17},\dfrac{22}{7}$

49. (b) In a series circuit, as more resistors are added, the overall current within the circuit decreases. This decrease in current is consistent with the conclusion that the overall resistance increases. As more and more lamps are added, the brightness of each bulb gradually decreases.

Sol. (50 – 52) :

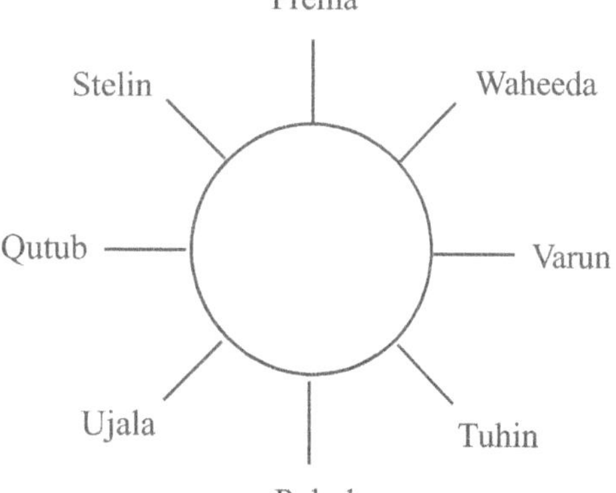

50. (c) Varun is to the right of Tuhin and also to the left of Waheeda

51. **(c)** Tuhin is second to the right of Ujala.

52. **(a)** Stelin is to the immediate left of Qutub.

53. **(c)** Let the two numbers be $3x$ and $4x$

$\Rightarrow$ $3x \times 4x = 1728$

$\Rightarrow$ $12x^2 = 1728$

$\Rightarrow$ $x^2 = 144$

$x = 12$

$\therefore$ Greater number is $4x = 4 \times 12 = 48$

54. **(a)**

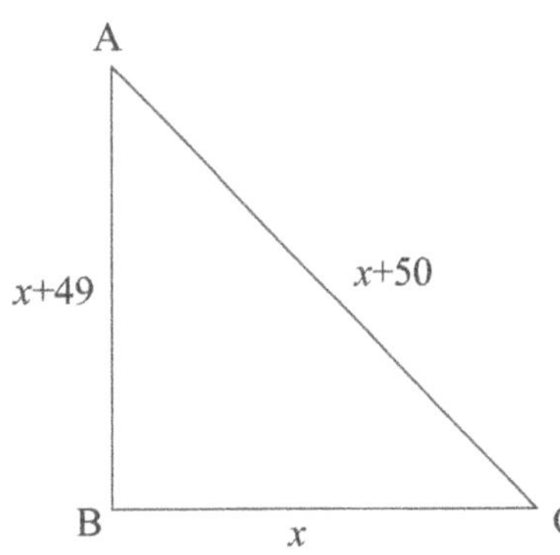

Let x be the shortest side

then middle side $= x + 49$

and longer side $= x + 50$

Now in rt. angled Δ ABC

$(AC)^2 = (AB)^2 + (BC)^2$

$\Rightarrow$ $(x + 50)^2 = (x + 49)^2 + x^2$

$\Rightarrow$ $x^2 + 100x + 2500 = x^2 + 98x + 2401 + x^2$

$\Rightarrow$ $x^2 - 2x - 99 = 0$

$x^2 - 11x + 9x - 99 = 0$

$x(x - 11) + 9(x - 11) = 0$

$(x + 9)(x - 11) = 0$

$\Rightarrow$ $x = -9, 11$

Discarding the negative value as length cannot be negative

$\therefore$ The shortest side $x = 11$ cm

55. **(a)** Let

P(W)   represent probability of white cushion.

P(R)   represent probability of red cushion.

P(B)   represent probability of blue cushion.

Then $P(W \cup B) = P(W) + P(B) - P(W \cap B)$

$= \dfrac{3}{12} + \dfrac{5}{12} - 0$

$= \dfrac{8}{12} = \dfrac{2}{3}$

56. **(c)**

57. **(b)** Here the rank of alphabetical series is given as A = 26, B = 25, C = 24 and so on.

$\Rightarrow$ A = 26

TEA = (7+22+26) = 55

$\therefore$ SPATTER $= (8+11+26+7+7+22+9)$

$= 90$

58. **(b)**

59. **(a)** (4237.43+453.32+24.12) – 387.23

$= 4714.87 - 387.23$

$= 4327.64$

60. **(c)** **61.** **(a)**

62. **(b)** When natural no. n is divided by 5, remainder is 4

Let n = 5K + 4   {where k is an integer}

Now for 2n we have

2n = 10k+8

$\Rightarrow$ 2n = 5 (2k + 1) + 3

Hence, remainder = 3

63. **(c)**

T	E	A	C	H	E	R
+1	–1	+1	–1	+1	–1	+1
U	D	B	B	I	D	S
S	T	U	D	E	N	T
+1	–1	+1	–1	+1	–1	+1
T	S	V	C	F	M	U

64. **(b)**

65. **(a)**

$315 = 3 \times 3 \times 5 \times 7$

$630 = 3 \times 3 \times 5 \times 7 \times 2$

$945 = 3 \times 3 \times 5 \times 7 \times 3$

$\therefore$ HCF $= 3 \times 3 \times 5 \times 7 = 315$

66. **(b)** Player XYZ broke the world record but was found to be under the influence of a prohibited drug.

From the above statement we can only conclude that player XYZ will not get the special reward.

Hence only conclusion II follows.

67. **(b)**

Brother's wife's son's only Paternal uncle → Aparna's brother →

Aparna's father ← Aparna's brother's father

Hence that man is Aparna's father.

68. (a)

69. (a) Let the angles be $2x$, $4x$, $3x$

Then $2x + 4x + 3x = 180° \Rightarrow 9x$

$= 180 \Rightarrow x = 20$

Smallest angle $= 2 \times 20 = 40°$

and largest angle $= 4 \times 20 = 80°$

Hence the sum of largest angle and smallest

angle $= 80° + 40° = 120°$

70. (b) Average no. of candidates selected over the given period

$$= \frac{94 + 48 + 82 + 90 + 70}{5} = \frac{384}{5} = 76.8 \approx 77$$

71. (c)

For 1997 required percentage $= \dfrac{94}{850} \times 100$

$= 11.05\%$

1998 required percentage $= \dfrac{48}{500} \times 100 = 9.6\%$

1999 required percentage $= \dfrac{82}{640} \times 100 = 12.8\%$

2000 required percentage $= \dfrac{90}{850} \times 100 = 10.5\%$

2001 required percentage $= \dfrac{70}{800} \times 100 = 8.7\%$

∴ In year 2001 the percentage of selected candidates is lowest.

72. (d) In year 1999 the ratio of selected candidates to qualified candidates is highest.

73. (a) Let x be the amount invested by Sita and Rita

Then S.I for Rita $= \dfrac{x \times 2.5 \times 4}{100}$ ...(i)

and S.I for Sita $= \dfrac{x \times 2.5 \times 6}{100}$ ...(ii)

∴ ratio of S.I earned by Sita to that by Rita

eqn (i) ÷ eqn (ii) $= \dfrac{x \times 2.5 \times 6}{100} \times \dfrac{100}{x \times 2.5 \times 4}$

$= \dfrac{6}{4} = \dfrac{3}{2} = 3 : 2$

74. (c) (4, 1) (8, 4) and (0, –2) satisfy the equation

$3x - 4y = 8$

(1,4) does not satisfy the equation.

Hence (1,4) is not a solution of the equation.

75. (d) From the given statements we are not sure enough to say 70% of the team consists of spinner and that the opening batsman were spinners.

Hence neither conclusion I nor II follows

76. (a) $208 - 4 + 3 \div 23 \times 57$

$= 208 \div 4 \times 3 - 23 + 57$

$= 52 \times 3 - 23 + 57$

$= 156 - 23 + 57$

$= 213 - 23$

$= 190$

77. (a) $5 \times 45 - 15 + 31 \div 41 = 5$

On interchanging $\div$ and $-$ the equation is correct

$5 \times 45 \div 15 + 31 - 41 = 5 \times 3 + 31 - 41$

$= 15 + 31 - 41$

$= 46 - 41$

$= 5$

78. (d) $\sin\theta - \cos\theta = 0 \Rightarrow \sin\theta = \cos\theta$

$\Rightarrow \mathrm{Tan}\theta = 1$

$\Rightarrow \theta = 45°$

Now $\sin^6\theta + \cos^6\theta = \left(\dfrac{1}{\sqrt{2}}\right)^6 + \left(\dfrac{1}{\sqrt{2}}\right)^6$

$= \left[\left(\dfrac{1}{\sqrt{2}}\right)^2\right]^3 + \left[\left(\dfrac{1}{\sqrt{2}}\right)^2\right]^3$

$= \dfrac{1}{8} + \dfrac{1}{8} = \dfrac{1}{4}$

79. (b) Mutation theory is the idea that new species are formed from the sudden and unexpected emergence of alterations in their defining traits. It was proposed by Prof Hugo Marie de Vries, a Dutch botanist and one of the first geneticists.

80. (b) $\dfrac{7}{5} + \dfrac{31}{21} + \dfrac{23}{52}$

$= \dfrac{1092 \times 7 + 260 \times 31 + 105 \times 23}{5460}$

$= \dfrac{7644 + 8060 + 2415}{5460} = \dfrac{18119}{5460}$

81. (c) Rising air expands as the pressure on it decreases, and that expansion into thinner, high-altitude air causes cooling. Enough cooling eventually makes water vapour condense, which contributes to the survival and growth of the clouds. Thus, from the ground clouds seem to float in the sky.

82. (b) 83. (d)

84. (b) An integrated circuit, also referred to an IC, a chip or a microchip, is a set of electronic circuits usually made of silicon, that can hold anywhere from hundreds to millions of transistors, resistors, and capacitors.

85. (a) Cholera is a bacterial disease that causes severe watery diarrhea which can lead to dehydration and even death, if untreated. It is caused by eating food or drinking water contaminated with a bacterium called Vibrio cholerae.

86. (c)

87. (c) HOUSE $\rightarrow$ [(8+2)(15–2)(21+2)(19–2)(5+2)]

$10 - 13 - 23 - 17 - 7$

For each alphabet we write down its rank and add/subtract 2 alternatively.

$\therefore$ REHEARSE $\rightarrow$ [(18+2) (5–2) (8+2)(5–2) (1+2) (18–2) (19+2) (5–2)]

$20 - 3 - 10 - 3 - 3 - 16 - 21 - 3$

88. (c) C.I $= P\left[1+\dfrac{r}{100}\right]^{T}$

Here C.I = 28561, P = 10000,

r = 30% and T = ?

$\Rightarrow 28561 = 10000\left[1+\dfrac{30}{100}\right]^{T}$

$2.8561 = (1.3)^{T}$

$(1.3)^{4} = (1.3)^{T}$

$\therefore$ T = 4 years

89. (a) Let the angles be $4x$ and $5x$

ATQ $4x + 5x = 180$ {Supplementary angles}

$\Rightarrow x = 20°$

$\therefore 4x = 80°$ & $5x = 100°$

Hence $\dfrac{(4x)^2}{(5x)^2} = \dfrac{6400}{10000} = \dfrac{16}{25} = 16:25$

90. (a)

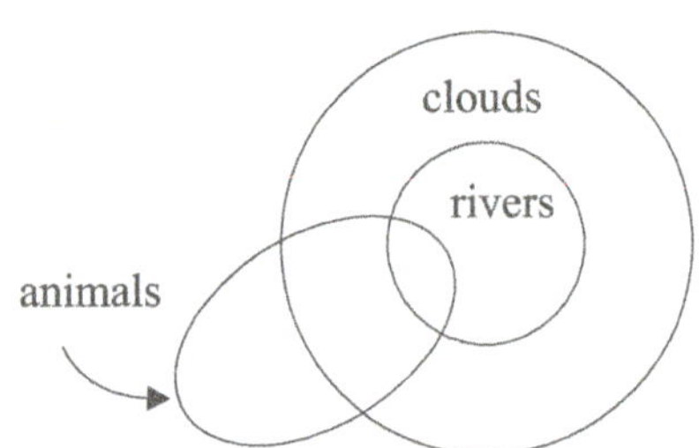

From the diagram only conclusion 1 and 2 follow

Some rivers are animals

Some clouds are rivers

91. (b) SP = ₹ 9 per kg

Loss w% = 10%

$\therefore$ CP $= \dfrac{9\times100}{90} = $ ₹10

To earn 5% profit SP will be $\dfrac{10\times105}{100}$

= ₹10.5

92. (b)

93. (b)

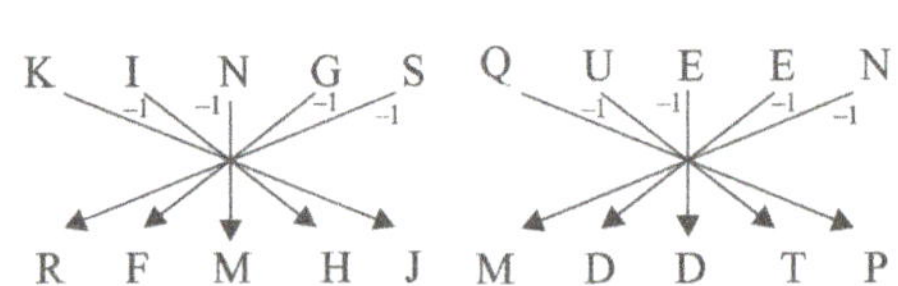

94. (d) 95. (c)

96. (a) Plant cells chloroplasts and other specialized plastids which are not found within animal cells. Chloroplasts are only present in plant cells because they trap energy of the sun for photosynthesis and the vacuoles keep the cell turgid.

97. (c) 98. (b)

99. (b) Time taken by Arun to go from Pune to Goa

$= \dfrac{1000}{4}$ hr

from Goa to Pune $= \dfrac{1000}{3}$ hr

Total distance = 1000 + 1000 = 2000

Average speed $= \dfrac{\text{Total distance}}{\text{Total time}}$

$= \dfrac{2000}{\dfrac{1000}{4}+\dfrac{1000}{3}} = \dfrac{2000}{250+334} = \dfrac{2000}{584} \approx 3.43\,\text{km/hr}$

100. (d)

1. Leukemia is a type of human disease which is
   (a) a cancer of the white blood cells
   (b) caused by deficiency of vitamins
   (c) a cancer in the brain
   (d) caused by an overdose of proteins

2. If $\sqrt{625} = 25$; then $\sqrt{(.00000625/25)}$ is:
   (a) 0.0025
   (b) 0.001
   (c) 0.0001
   (d) 0.0005

3. 30 pens and 75 pencils were purchased for ₹ 390. If the average price of a pencil is ₹ 2.00, then calculate the average price (in Rs.) of a pen.
   (a) 6
   (b) 4
   (c) 8
   (d) 12

DIRECTIONS (QS. 4-6): *Based on the diagram answer the following questions:*

The figure given below consists of three intersecting circles which represent sets of students who play Football, Cricket and Basket Ball. Each region in the figure is represented by a small letter.

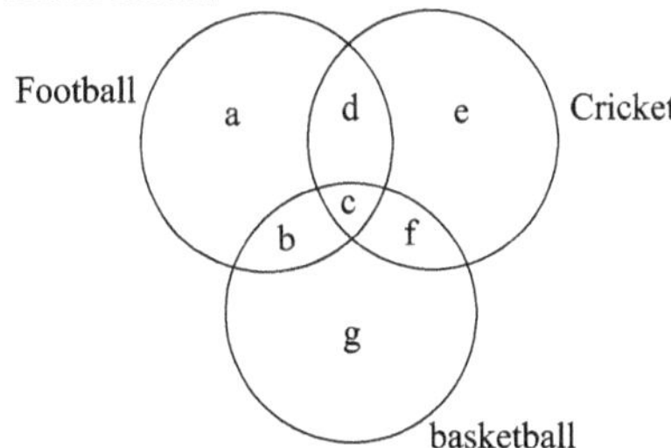

4. Which region represents the set of persons who play Football and Basket Ball but not Cricket?
   (a) Region g
   (b) Region e
   (c) Region c
   (d) Region b

5. Which region represents the set of persons who play Football but neither Cricket nor Basket Ball?
   (a) Region a
   (b) Region b
   (c) Region c
   (d) Region d

6. Which region represents the set of persons who play all the three games?
   (a) Region b
   (b) Region c
   (c) Region f
   (d) Region g

7. Hemant said to Naitik, "That boy playing with the football is the younger of the two brothers of the daughter of my father's wife." How is the boy playing football related to Hemant?
   (a) Son
   (b) Brother
   (c) Cousin
   (d) Nephew

8. Which of the following is not an output device?
   (a) Plotter
   (b) Speaker
   (c) Printer
   (d) Scanner

9. _________ was the first satellite launched by U.S in 1958.
   (a) Sputnik 1
   (b) Apollo 11
   (c) GSAT
   (d) Explorer 1

10. Two pipes, A & B can fill a tank in 12 & 16 minutes respectively. Both pipes are opened together, but 4 minutes before the tank is full, pipe A is closed. In how many minutes will the tank be full?
    (a) 9 minutes 8 seconds
    (b) 10 minutes 9 seconds
    (c) 11 minutes 19 seconds
    (d) 11 minutes 29 seconds

11. Name the monument which signifies the "seat of the holy Buddha" where it is believed that Lord Buddha delivered his first sermon.
    (a) Dhamekh Stupa, Sarnath
    (b) Sanchi Stupa, Sanchi
    (c) Shingardar Stupa, Swat valley
    (d) Dro-dul Chorten, Gangtok

12. Complete the Figure X from the given alternatives 1,2,3,4

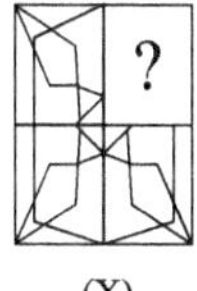 (X)    (1)   (2)    (3)    (4)

   (a) 1
   (b) 2
   (c) 3
   (d) 4

In an Exhibition, seven air conditioners of different companies - LG, Carrier, Samsung, Godrej, Whirlpool, Hitachi and Videocon are kept facing east in the following order :

LG is next to right of Videocon.

Videocon is fourth to the right of Samsung.

Godrej air conditioner is between air conditioner Carrier and Hitachi.

Samsung, which is third to the left of air conditioner Carrier, is at one end.

13. Which one of the following statements is correct?
    (a) Videocon air conditioner is in between air conditioner Carrier and Samsung.
    (b) LG is next left to Whirlpool air conditioner.
    (c) Videocon is next right of LG.
    (d) Godrej is fourth right of Whirlpool.

14. Which of the following groups of air conditioners is to the right of air conditioner Carrier?
    (a) LG, Videocon and Godrej
    (b) Whirlpool, LG and Videocon
    (c) Godrej, Hitachi and Samsung
    (d) Hitachi, LG and Videocon

15. Which of the following statements is correct?
    (a) Godrej is next left of air conditioner Carrier.
    (b) Hitachi is next left of Samsung.
    (c) Hitachi is at one end.
    (d) Samsung is next second to the right of Godrej.

16. Abdur Rahman and British Raj representative Mr. Mortimer signed an agreement establishing
    (a) Radcliffe Line (b) Durand Line
    (c) Mortimer Line (d) Macmohan Line

17. Four words are given below out of which three are alike in some manner and one is different. Which one is different from the rest?
    (a) Tower (b) Sea
    (c) Valley (d) Mountain

18. Name the committee, appointed to identify the creamy layer among the OBCs, which submitted its report in 1993 and was accepted?
    (a) Dr. K M Munshi Committee
    (b) G V Mavalankar Committee
    (c) Ram Nandan Committee
    (d) Swaran Singh Committee

19. What is the cause of biomagnification (or bio-accumulation)?
    (a) Ozone (b) Organochlorines
    (c) Lichens (d) Proteins

20. Which of the following power houses is/are associated with Damodar Valley Project?
    I. Durgapur II. Chandrapura
    III. Maithon IV. Hampi
    Choose the right option.
    (a) Only I and II (b) Only II and III
    (c) I, II and III (d) I, II, III and IV

21. Construction of the Qutub Minar, the world's tallest brick minaret commenced in 1193, under the orders of __________, the founder of the Delhi Sultanate.
    (a) Firoz Shah Tughlaq
    (b) Qutub-ud-din Aibak
    (c) Iltumish
    (d) Quali Qutub Shah

22. Krishnanattam is a famous dance of which of the following states?
    (a) Andhra Pradesh (b) Karnataka
    (c) Kerala (d) Tamilnadu

23. An example of conductor of heat is
    (a) paper
    (b) cloth
    (c) air
    (d) aluminum

24. Who among the following musicians who lived between 1253 and 1325 AD, was traditionally considered as the inventor of tabla and sitar?
    (a) Tansen (b) Amir Khusro
    (c) Swami Shastri (d) Baiju Bawra

25. A thief is 400m ahead of a policeman. The thief started running and the policeman started chasing simultaneously.
    Assuming the speed of thief be 10km/h & policeman be 15 km/h, calculate the distance (in metres) covered by thief before the policeman caught the thief?
    (a) 750 m (b) 800 m
    (c) 850 m (d) 900 m

26. Oil zapper technology to remove oil spills in ocean, is developed by?
    (a) IIT (b) TERI
    (c) CSE (d) ISRO

27. The Union Government has released a commemorative postage stamp to mark the Centenary year of _________, which is the apex institution on fauna taxonomy in India.
    (a) Zoological Survey of India.
    (b) Archaeological Survey of India
    (c) National Animal Species Survey of India
    (d) National Sample Survey Organization

28. Which Bank launched India's first contactless mobile payment solution?
    (a) AXIS   (b) SBI
    (c) ICICI   (d) HDFC

29. The presence of ozone in the ultra voilet light from passing to the Earth's surface.
    (a) troposphere   (b) mesosphere
    (c) stratosphere   (d) thermosphere

30. If $\sqrt{5} = 2.236$; then $\sqrt{5}/\sqrt{2}$ is:
    (a) 1.581   (b) 1.851
    (c) 2.236   (d) 1.782

31. The HCF of two numbers is 16 and their difference is 16. Find the numbers.
    (a) 80, 64   (b) 72, 88
    (c) 80, 100   (d) 96, 120

32. In 2001, the production of sugar is 1584 million kgs which is 20% more than that in 1991. Find the production (in million kgs) of sugar in 1991.
    (a) 1980   (b) 1280
    (c) 1300   (d) 1320

33. Who has been elected to the board of governors of the World Water Council (WWC) for 2016-18 in the 7th general assembly of WWC held at Marseille, France?
    (a) Chaudhary Birender Singh
    (b) Ram Kripal Yadav
    (c) Sanwar Lal Jat
    (d) Prithvi Raj Singh

34. There are over _________ capillaries in our lungs.
    (a) 100 million   (b) 200 million
    (c) 400 million   (d) 300 million

35. In a certain code language, if MOBILE is coded as 713694 and TABLET is coded as 253942, then BALLET will be coded as?
    (a) 329954   (b) 359942
    (c) 395942   (d) 359429

36. A & B can finish a work in 12 days, B & C in 15 days and A & C in 20 days. In how many days would A alone finish the work?
    (a) 20   (b) 30
    (c) 40   (d) 60

37. _________ is the first indigenous aircraft of India designed and built by HAL.
    (a) HF 25 MKI   (b) HT 2
    (c) HT 3 MKI   (d) HF 28

38. A tennis player, won 18 games out of 27 games played. Calculate the games won in terms of decimal.
    (a) 0.667   (b) 0.067
    (c) 0.50   (d) 0.333

39. The value of tan45° is:
    (a) $\sqrt{3}$ (b) $\sqrt{3}/2$
    (c) $1/\sqrt{3}$ (d) 1

40. The expenses of a person increases by ₹ 5000 for every month in February and March. If his expenses in January was ₹ 5000, Calculate his average expenditure (in Rs.) from January to March.
    (a) 10000   (b) 15000
    (c) 7500   (d) 5000

41. If Rahul walks at 4 km/h, he reaches office late by 10 minutes of the scheduled time. If he walks at 5 km/h he reaches office 5 minutes ahead of scheduled time. Calculate the distance of his office from his home.
    (a) 4 km   (b) 6 km
    (c) 5 km   (d) 8 km

42. Why it is remarked that "the pocket of the Indian President is bigger than that of the American President" in reference to   Pocket Veto Power of the President?
    (a) The power of the Indian President not to take any action (either positive or negative) on the bill for an indefinite period.
    (b) The President of USA has to return the bill for reconsideration within 10 days, as against 30 days for the Indian President.
    (c) The President of USA has to return the bill for reconsideration within 10 days, as against 20 days for the Indian President.
    (d) The President of USA can't return the bill for reconsideration, if he kept it for more than 10 days, while that is not the case with the Indian President.

43. A straight angle is equal to ?
    (a) 90°   (b) 180°
    (c) 270°   (d) 360°

44. Pointing to the lady in the metro, Twinkle said, "She is the sister of the father of my mother's son." Who is the lady to Twinkle?
(a) Mother   (b) Sister
(c) Aunt   (d) Niece

45. Read the statements and select a conclusion from the given alternatives:
Statements: Some doors are shelves.
All the shelves are windows.
Conclusions:
1. Some doors are windows.
2. No shelf is door
(a) Only (1) conclusion follows
(b) Only (2) conclusion follows
(c) Either (1) or (2) follows
(d) Neither (1) nor (2) follows

46. If the average age of 40 students in Class I is 10 years and the average age of 30 students in Class II is 12 years, find the average age (in years) for all students.
(a) 11   (b) 10.54
(c) 10.58   (d) 10.85

47. Pointing to a person, Arnav said to Preeti, "His mother is the only daughter of your father". How was Preeti related to that person?
(a) Aunt   (b) Mother
(c) Wife   (d) Daughter

48. Fill in the blanks with suitable option:
A/An _________ turns blue litmus red and a/an _________ turns _________ litmus blue.
(a) Base, acid, red
(b) Acid, base, green
(c) Base, acid, pink
(d) Acid, base, red

49. Which city hosted the first 'India International Science Festival. 2015'?
(a) Kolkata
(b) Bangalore
(c) New Delhi
(d) Chennai

50. In a fruit basket, the ratio of number of apples to bananas is A and the ratio of bananas to apples is B; then A+B is:
(a) exactly 1 (b) less than one
(c) more than one (d) zero

51. Insert the missing character in?

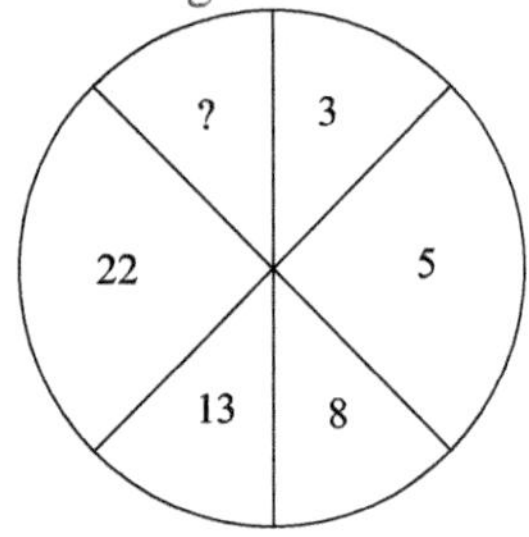

(a) 45   (b) 29
(c) 39   (d) 37

52. when was the GSLV used in India for the first time?
(a) 1980   (b) 1987
(c) 1994   (d) 2000

53. Insert the missing character in?

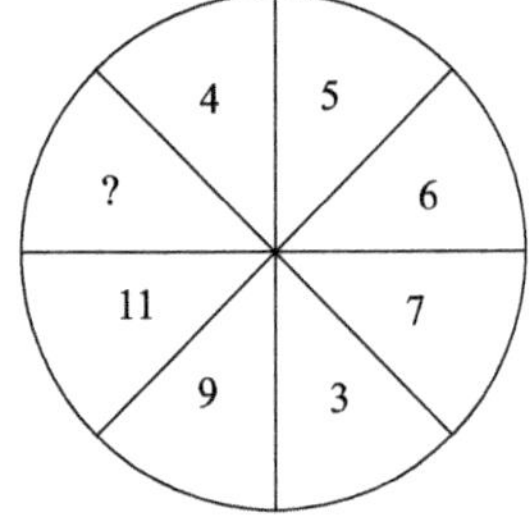

(a) 13   (b) 14
(c) 12   (d) 15

54. What fraction of 2 hours is 18 seconds?
(a) 1/200   (b) 1/300
(c) 1/400   (d) 1/600

55. Gitesh took a loan for 6 years at 5% Simple Interest. If the total interest paid was ₹ 615, calculate the principal.
(a) ₹ 2000   (b) ₹ 2050
(c) ₹ 2100   (d) ₹ 2150

56. Read the statements and select a conclusion from the given alternatives:
Statements: The national norm is 100 classrooms per thousand population, but in this state, 150 classrooms per thousand are available in the schools.
Conclusions:
I. Our national norm is appropriate.
II. This state's education system is taking adequate care in this regard.
Choose the right option.
(a) Only conclusion I follows
(b) Only conclusion II follows
(c) Either I or II follows
(d) Neither I nor II follows

57. If $40x^2 = 734^2 - 234^2$, then find the value of x.
(a) 110   (b) 121
(c) 11   (d) 144

58. **Consider the following statements & choose the correct option.**
1. Formation of blood cells in the bone marrow by a process called haemopoiesis.
2. Detoxification or removal of certain poisonous substances.
(a) Both 1 & 2 are functions of the skeleton.
(b) Both 1 & 2 are functions of the kidney
(c) 1 is the function of kidney and 2 of skeleton.
(d) 1 is the function of joints and 2 of skeleton

59. A blue, violet, or red flavonoid pigment found in plants is due to the presence of
(a) Carotene   (b) Anthocyanine
(c) Xanthophylls   (d) Chlorophyll

60. Which of the following chemical reactions is always endothermic in nature?
(a) Combustion reaction
(b) Decomposition reaction
(c) Displacement reaction
(d) Combination reaction

61. Who is the author of famous autobiography "Dreaming Big: My Journey to Connect India"?
(a) Abdul Kalam   (b) Sam Pitroda
(c) Nandan Nilekani (d) Azim Premji

62. If $4\sin\theta - 3\cos\theta = 0$, then $\sec\theta\cosec\theta$ is:
(a) 5/12   (b) 25/12
(c) 13/12   (d) 12/5

63. If in a certain language, STAR is coded as TSRA, how is MOON coded in that code?
(a) OMNO   (b) OOMN
(c) NMOO   (d) OMON

64. Who became the 1st player to win ATP (Association of Tennis Professionals) World Tour Finals for the 4th consecutive time?
(a) Novak Djokovic   (b) Rafael Nadal
(c) Serena Williams   (d) Roger Federer

65. Match the following correctly:

Invention/Discovery	**Inventor Scientist**
P) Dynamite	(a) J.J.Thomson
Q) Dynamo	(b) Michael Faraday
R) Electron	(c) Alfred Nobel
S) Proton	(d) Rutherford

(a) P-b. Q-c, R-a, S-d
(b) P-c, Q-b, R-d, S-a
(c) P-c, Q-b, R-a, S-d
(d) P-d, Q-c, R-b, S-a

66. Increase in carbon dioxide in atmosphere is caused by which of the following reasons?
1. Excessive use of fossil fuels
2. Deforestation
3. Increased number of vehicles
4. Excessive use of solar heaters
(a) 1 and 2
(b) 1, 2 and 4
(c) 1, 2 and 3
(d) 1, 2, 3 and 4

67. Calculate the amount if ₹ 400 is invested on compound interest at the rate of 5% per annum for 2 years.
(a) 440   (b) 441
(c) 445   (d) 480

68. Complete the Figure X from the 4 alternatives 1,2,3,4

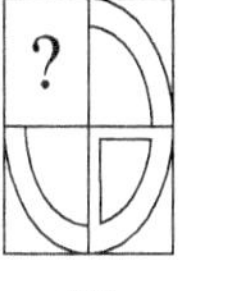    

(X)   (1)   (2)   (3)   (4)

(a) 1   (b) 2
(c) 3   (d) 4

69. Which among the following network topologies has the highest transmission speed?
(a) LAN
(b) WAN
(c) MAN
(d) Both LAN and WAN have equal transmission speeds.

70. On dividing $15y^3 - 30y^2 + 12y - 12$ by $3y - 6$, the remainder is:
(a) 6   (b) 36
(c) 30   (d) 12

71. Read the statements and select a conclusion from the given alternatives:
Statements: Some benches are autos.
All the boxes are autos.
All the pens are benches.
Conclusions:
(1) Some benches are boxes.
(2) No pen is auto.
(3) Some boxes are benches.
(a) None of three
(b) Only (1) and (2)
(c) Only (1) and (3)
(d) Only (2) and (3)

72. Indian has the largest area under _______________ crop in the World.
(a) Oil Seeds   (b) Sugarcane
(c) Wheat   (d) Apple

73. The longest chord in a circle is:
(a) Radius   (b) Diameter
(c) Segment   (d) Sector

74. Read the statements and select a conclusion from the given alternatives:
Statement: Good health is a luxury in country 'X' where rate of mortality due to hunger, malnutrition and unhygienic conditions is very high, as compared to other nations of that region.
Conclusions:
I. People in country 'X' can't afford to have many luxuries life.
II. Good health is a gift of nature.
Choose the right option
(a) only conclusion I follows.
(b) only conclusion II follows.
(c) either I or II follows.
(d) neither I nor II follows.

75. Which mirror is preferred as a rear-view (wing) mirrors in vehicles because of its wider field of view?
(a) Convex   (b) Plane
(c) Concave   (d) Concavo convex

76. The main objectives of Indian space programme are:
1. Mass Communication and education via satellite.
2. Survey and management of natural resources through remote sensing technology, environmental monitoring and meteorological forecasting.
3. Development of indigenous satellites and satellite launch vehicles.
(a) Only 1   (b) Only 2
(c) 1 & 3 both   (d) 1, 2 and 3

77. Four pair of words are given below out of which three are alike in some manner and one pair is different. Which is   different from the rest?
(a) Hard : Soft   (b) Long : High
(c) Sweet : Sour   (d) Pointed : Blunt

78. Read the statements and select a conclusion from the given alternatives:
Statements: All the wires are books.

All the plates are books.
Some wallets are plates.
Conclusions:
(1) Some wires are plates.
(2) Some books are wires.
(3) Some books are wallets.
(a) Only (1)   (b) Only (2) and (3)
(c) Only (1) and (2) (d) Only (1) and (3)

79. Four pair of words are given below out of which three are alike in some manner and one pair is different. Which is different from the rest?
(a) Student : Scholar
(b) Paddy : Husk
(c) Soldier : Warrior
(d) Politician : Leader

80. If Selling Price is ₹ 84 & Gain Percentage = 20%, Calculate the Cost Price.
(a) ₹ 70   (b) ₹ 68
(c) ₹ 71   (d) ₹ 69

DIRECTIONS (Qs. 81-83): *Based on the table below answer the following questions:*

The table given below shows the percentage distribution of the total expenditures of a company Zeta Interactive Services under various expense heads during 2003.

Infrastructure	**20**
Transport	**12.5**
Advertisement	**15**
Taxes	**10**
R&D	**5**
Salaries	**20**
Interest on Loans	**17.5**

81. If the interest on loans amounted to ₹2.45 crores, then the total amount of expenditure on advertisement, taxes and research and development of Zeta Interactive Services is
(a) ₹ 7 crores
(b) ₹ 5.4 crores
(c) ₹ 4.2 crores
(d) ₹ 3 crores

82. What is the ratio of the total expenditure on infrastructure and transport to the total expenditure on taxes and interest on loans of Zeta Interactive Services?
(a) 5:4   (b) 8:7
(c) 9:7   (d) 13:11

83. If the expenditure of Zeta Interactive Services on advertisement is 2.10 crores then the difference between the expenditure on transport and taxes is?
    (a) ₹ 1.25 crores   (b) ₹ 95 lakhs
    (c) ₹ 65 lakhs   (d) ₹ 35 lakhs

84. A shopkeeper purchased an article for ₹3500 and plays transport charge of ₹ 100. He incurred a loss of 12% in selling this. Find the selling price of the article
    (a) ₹ 3168   (b) ₹ 2168
    (c) ₹ 4168   (d) ₹ 1168

85. Who among the following is/was not associated with Cricket?
    (a) Farhaan Behardien (b) Aaron Phangiso
    (c) Vernon Philander   (d) Stan Wawrinka

86. Which of the following is the outermost part of human skin?
    (a) Epidermis   (b) Dermis
    (c) Hypodermis   (d) Nerve Fiber

87. Insert the missing character in?

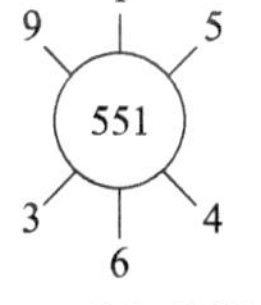

    (a) 262   (b) 622
    (c) 631   (d) 824

88. Indian National Army was formed by:
    (a) Mohan Singh
    (b) Subhash Chandra Bose
    (c) Chandrashekhar Azad
    (d) Ras Bihari

89. Factors of $x^2 - 6x + 8$ are:
    (a) $(x-4)(x-2)$ (b) $(x+4)(x+2)$
    (c) $(x+8)(x-2)$ (d) $(x-4)(x+2)$

90. Find the least number that must be subtracted from 87375, to get a number exactly divisible by 698.
    (a) 120   (b) 125
    (c) 250   (d) 375

91. Which company developed the Android OS, a mobile operating system Software in 2007?
    (a) Microsoft Corp.   (b) Google Corp.
    (c) Intel   (d) Apple Corp.

92. In a certain code language, if HISTORY is coded as 7326845 and CIVICS is coded as 135312, then VISITOR will be coded as?
    (a) 5323684   (b) 6843532
    (c) 8463352   (d) 5323648

93. A man buys 20 pencils for ₹ 6 and sells 16 pencils for ₹ 6. Calculate his gain or loss percentage.
    (a) 20   (b) 25
    (c) 27   (d) 30

94. What angle is formed between the minutes hand and second's hand of clock if they are 25 minutes apast?
    (a) 120°   (b) 150°
    (c) 180°   (d) 210°

95. If a/b = 1/3 ; b/c =1/2 and a=2 then the value of c is:
    (a) 8   (b) 10   (c) 12   (d) 16

96. If in a certain language, SINK is coded as ISKN, how is MINT coded in that code?
    (a) TMNI   (b) IMTN
    (c) EMMT   (d) TINM

97. To take the revenge for the Jallianwala Bagh Massacre, who killed General O'Dwyer in London?
    (a) Sardar Bhagat Singh
    (b) Sardar Udham Singh
    (c) Sardar Ajit Singh
    (d) Raj Guru

98. Read the statements and select a conclusion from the given alternatives:
    Statements: Our equity investments carry market risk. Consult your investment advisor or agent before investing.
    Conclusions:
    I.   One should not invest in equity.
    II. The investment advisor calculates the market risk with certainty.
    (a) Only conclusion I follows
    (b) Only conclusion II follows
    (c) Either I or II follows
    (d) Neither I nor II follows

99. In a right-angled triangle, the hypotenuse is 2cm longer than the perpendicular which is 2cm longer than the base. Calculate the length of the base.
    (a) 6 cm   (b) 9 cm   (c) 10 cm   (d) 8 cm

100. Who among the following is famously known as "The Haryana Hurricane"?
    (a) Mansoor All Khan Pataudi
    (b) Kapil Dev
    (c) Saina Nehwal
    (d) Vijender Singh

HINTS & EXPLANATIONS

1. **(a)**

2. **(d)** As given that,

$$\sqrt{625} = 25$$

Then

$$\Rightarrow \sqrt{0.00000625 / 25}$$

$$= \sqrt{0.00000025} = 0.0005$$

3. **(c)** As given that,
Average price of a pencil = '2'
The price of 30 pens and 75 pencils = 390
Let average price of a pen = P
$30 \times P + 75 \times 2 = 390$
$30\,P = 390 - 150$

$$P = \frac{240}{30} = 8$$

Hence, the average price of a pen is ₹ 8.

Sol. (4 – 6):
As given figure :

(Football)   (Cricket)

a   d   e

b   c   f

g

(Basketball)

4. **(d)** The set of persons who play Football and Basket ball but not cricket is (b) Region

5. **(a)** The set of persons who play football but neither cricket nor Basket ball is (a) region.

6. **(b)** The set of persons who play all the three games is (c) region.

7. **(b)** Younger brother of the daughter of my father's wife means my brother.

8. **(d)** **9. (d)**

10. **(a)** Let total time is x.
pipe A is closed 4 minutes before so time of pipe A is = (x – 4)
Total time will be required to full the tank.

$$\frac{(x-4)}{12} + \frac{x}{16} = 1$$

$4\,(x-4) + 3x = 48$

$\Rightarrow x = 64/7 = 9$ minutes 8 seconds.

11. **(a)**

12. **(c)** In given figure x, the remaining part of figure x match with option (c).

Sol. (13 to 15)

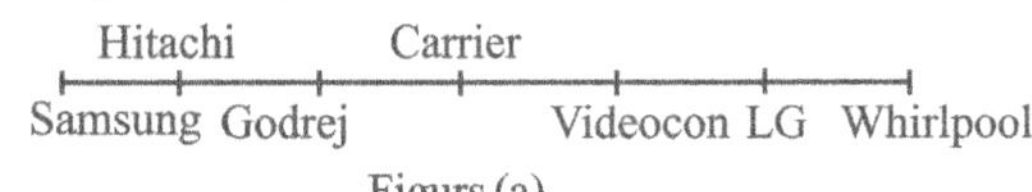

Figurs (a)

13. **(b)** LG is next left to whirlpool air conditioner.

14. **(b)** Videcon, LG, Whirlpool groups of air conditioners is to the right of air conditioner carrier.

15. **(a)** Godrej is next left of air conditioner carrier.

16. **(b) 17. (a) 18. (c)**

19. **(b)** Organochlorine (OC) pesticides are synthetic pesticides which are widely used all over the world. They belong to the group of chlorinated hydrocarbon derivatives. These compounds are known for their high toxicity, slow degradation and bioaccumulation.

20. **(c) 21. (b) 22. (c) 23. (*) 24. (b)**

25. **(b)** Let, Policeman caught thief at distance (x + 400 m)
And theif has traveled x meter.
As given that,
Speed of Policeman

$$= 15 \text{ km/h} = \left[\frac{15 \times 5}{18}\right] = \frac{25}{6} \text{ m/sec.}$$

Speed of theif = 10 km/h

$$= \left[\frac{10 \times 5}{18}\right] = \frac{25}{9} \text{ m / sec.}$$

In this case time is constant means Policeman covered (x + 400) meter, In same time thief covered x^m.
Thus,

$$\frac{\text{Speed of the thief}}{\text{Speed of policeman}} = \frac{x}{(400 + x)}$$

$$\frac{25/9}{25/6} = \frac{x}{(400 + x)} \Rightarrow \frac{2}{3} = \frac{x}{400 + x}$$

$800 + 2x = 3x$
$x = 800$ meter.

26. **(b)** The technique of using the bacteria to get rid of oil spill is called "Oil Zapping". The Energy and Resources Institute (TERI) had developed this technique over a period of seven years. The Oil Zapping project was supported by the Department of Biotechnology (Government of India) and the Ministry of Science and Technology.

27. **(a)** **28.** **(c)**

29. **(c)** The ozone layer is mainly found in the lower portion of the stratosphere. Ozone and oxygen molecules in the stratosphere absorb ultraviolet light from the Sun, providing a shield that prevents this radiation from passing to the Earth's surface.

30. **(a)** As given that,

$$\sqrt{5} = 2.236;$$

So, $\dfrac{\sqrt{5}}{\sqrt{2}} = \dfrac{2.236}{1.414} = 1.581$

31. **(a)** As given that,
HCF of two numbers is 16.
The difference of two number is 16.
Let the two number a and b.
So, $a - b = 16$ ....(i)
Since, HCF is 16, so two numbers must be multiply of 16.
So, Let a = 5, b = 4
By taking option (a), $80 = 16 \times 5$ and $64 = 16 \times 4$, Here HCF = 16
Hence, option (a) is correct.

32. **(d)** As given that the production of sugar in 2001 is 1584.
The production of sugar in 1991 is

$$1584 = x\left[1 + \frac{20}{100}\right]$$

$$x = \left[\frac{1584 \times 100}{120}\right] = ₹\,1320$$

33. **(d)** **34.** **(d)**

35. **(b)** As given that,

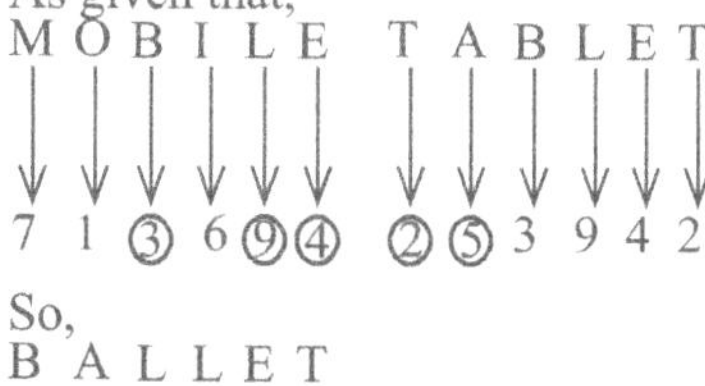

So,

Hence, 'BALLET' is coded as 359942.

36. **(b)** As given that,
$A + B = 1/12$ ...(i)
$B + C = 1/15$ ..(ii)
$A + C = 1/20$ ...(iii)
By subtracting equation (iii) from (ii)

$$B - A = \frac{1}{16}$$

From equation (i) and (iv)

$$2A = \left[\frac{1}{12} - \frac{1}{60}\right] = \left[\frac{5-1}{60}\right] = \frac{4}{60} = \frac{2}{30}$$

$$2A = \frac{2}{30} \Rightarrow A = 1/30$$

Hence, A alone finish the work in 30 days.

37. **(a)**

38. **(a)** The games won in teams of decimal is

$$= \frac{18}{27} = 0.667$$

39. **(d)** $\tan 45° = \dfrac{\sin 45°}{\cos 45°} = \dfrac{1/\sqrt{2}}{1/\sqrt{2}} = 1$

40. **(a)** The average expenditure

$$= \left[\frac{5000 + 10000 + 15000}{3}\right]$$

$$= \left[\frac{30000}{3}\right] = ₹\,10,000$$

41. **(c)** Let the distance of his office from his home is d km.
According to given question.
Then.

$$\frac{d}{4} = x + 10 \qquad ...(i)$$

and, $\dfrac{d}{5} = x - 5$ ...(ii)

By subtracting equation (ii) from equation (i)
We have,

$$\frac{d}{4} - \frac{d}{5} = 15$$

$$\frac{d}{20} = 15 \text{ minutes} = 15/60 \text{ sec.}$$

$$d = \frac{15 \times 20}{60} = 5km$$

42. **(a)**

43. **(b)** Straight angles are formed when the legs are pointing in exactly opposite directions. The two legs then form a single straight line through the vertex of the angle. Hence, the measure of a straight angle is thus always 180°.

44. (c) Twinkle mother's son $\rightarrow$ Twinkle brother
Twinkle brother's father $\rightarrow$ twinkle father
Father's sister is a twinkle's aunt.

45. (a)

46. (d) As given that,
Average age of 40 students in class I is 10 years.
So, total age of 40 students = $40 \times 10 = 400$ years.
Average age of 30 students in class II is 12 years.
So, total age of 30 students = $30 \times 12 = 360$ years.
So, Average age of all students

$$= \left[\frac{400 + 360}{70} \right] = 10.85 \text{ years}$$

47. (b) Preeti is the mother of that person in the photograph

48. (d) 49. (c) 50. (c)

51. (c) As given figure:

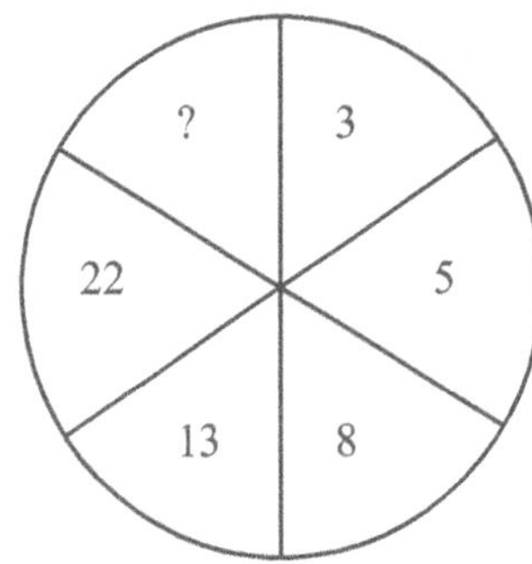

To find the missing term we can as follow!
$\Rightarrow 5 + (2 + 1) = 8$
$\Rightarrow 8 + (2 \times 2 + 1) = 13$
$\Rightarrow 13 + (2 \times 2 \times 2 + 1) = 22$
$\Rightarrow 22 + (2 \times 2 \times 2 \times 2 + 1) = 39$
Hence, 39 is a missing team in the given diagram.

52. (*) 53. (d)

54. (c) Required fraction

$$= \frac{18}{2 \text{ hours}} = \frac{18}{2 \times 60 \times 60}$$

$$= \left[\frac{9}{3600} \right] = \frac{1}{400}$$

Hence, Option (c) is correct.

55. (b) As given that,
S.I = ₹ 615

$t = 6$ year
$r = 5\%$, P = ?
From formula

$$P = \left[\frac{\text{S.I} \times 100}{r \times t} \right] = \left[\frac{615 \times 100}{5 \times 6} \right] = ₹\ 2050.$$

Hence, Principal is ₹ 2050.

56. (b) Whether the national norm is appropriate or not can not be said., So 1st does not follow, However, more number of school's per thousand population are available to adequate care in that state.
Hence IInd follows.

57. (a) As given that,
$40x^2 = (734)^2 - (234)^2$

$$x^2 = \left[\frac{(734)^2 - (234)^2}{40} \right]$$

$$= \frac{(734 + 234)(734 - 234)}{40}$$

$$= \left[\frac{968 \times 500}{40} \right] = \frac{484000}{40} = 12100$$

$$\therefore \quad x = 110$$

58. (*)

59. (b) Anthocyanin is a type of flavonoid which belongs to a class of compounds with antioxidant effects. Found naturally in a number of foods, anthocyanins are the pigments that give red, purple, and blue plants their rich colouring.

60. (b) 61. (b)

62. (b) As given that
$4 \sin\theta - 3 \cos\theta = 0$

$$= \quad \frac{\sin\theta}{\cos\theta} = \frac{3}{4} \Rightarrow \sin\theta = \frac{3}{5}$$

and $\cos\theta = \dfrac{4}{5}$

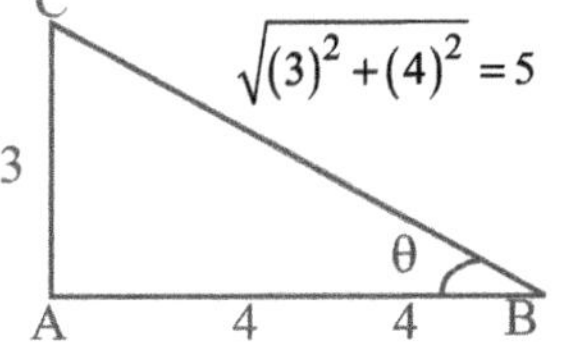

So, $\sec\theta \cdot \csc\theta = \dfrac{1}{\cos\theta \cdot \sin\theta}$

$$= \frac{1}{\left(\frac{4}{5} \times \frac{3}{5}\right)} = 25/12$$

Hence, Option (b) is correct.

63. (a) As given that

S   T   A   R

T   S   R   A

Similarly

M   O   O   N

O   M   N   O

Hence, 'MOON' is coded as 'OMNO'.

64. (a)   65. (c)   66. (c)

67. (b) From formula, compound interest

$$= \text{Principal}\left[1 + \frac{\text{Rate of Interest}}{100}\right]^{\text{time}}$$

$$= 400\left[1 + \frac{5}{100}\right]^2$$

$$= 400\left[1 + \frac{1}{20}\right]^2 = 400\left[\frac{21}{20}\right]^2$$

$$= ₹\ 441.$$

68. (d)   69. (a)

70. (d) $3y{-}6\,\overline{)15y^3{-}30y^2{+}12y{-}12}\,(5y^2{+}4$

$$\underline{-15y^3 \mp 30y^2}$$

$$0 \quad +12y - 12$$

$$\underline{-12y \mp 24}$$

$$12$$

Hence, the reminder is 12.

71. (a)   72. (b)   73. (b)

74. (a) Only 1st follows, A country where even good health is considered to be a luxury certainly can not affored luxuries IInd does not follow, Man may strive towards good health.

75. (a)   76. (d)   77. (b)

78. (b)

So, Some books are wires and wallets.
Hence option (b) is correct.

79. (b)

80. (a) Gain percentage

$$= \left(\frac{\text{selling price} - \text{cost price}}{\cos t\ \text{price}}\right) \times 100$$

$$20 = \left(\frac{84 - \text{CP}}{\text{CP}}\right) \times 100$$

$$6\ \text{CP} = 84 \times 5$$
$$\text{CP} = 14 \times 5$$
$$= ₹\ 70$$

Hence option (a) is correct.

Sol. (81–83):

81. (c) Then total amount of expenditure on advertisement , taxes and research.

$[15 + 10 + 5] = 30.$

So, According to question:

$$\Rightarrow \frac{17.5}{30} = \frac{2.45}{x}$$

$$x = \left[\frac{2.45 \times 30}{17.5}\right]$$

$$= \frac{73.5}{17.5} = 4.2\,\text{crores.}$$

82. (d) Required ratio $= \left[\dfrac{(20+12.5)}{(10+17.5)}\right]$

$$= \frac{32.5}{27.5} = \frac{13}{11}$$

83. (d) Difference between the expenditures on transport and taxes $= 12.5 - 10 = 2.5$

Now according to questions.

$$\Rightarrow \frac{15}{2.5} = \frac{2.10}{x}$$

$$x = \frac{2.10 \times 2.5}{15} = 0.35 = 35\,\text{lakhs}$$

84. (a) As given that

C.P. $= 3500 + 100 = 3600$

Loss $= 12\%$

$$\text{Loss \%} = \frac{(\text{CP} - \text{SP})}{\text{C.P}} \times 100$$

$$12 = \left[\frac{3600 - \text{S.P}}{3600}\right] \times 100$$

S.P. $= 3600 - 432 = ₹\ 3168.$

85. (a)   86. (a)

87. (b) As given figure.

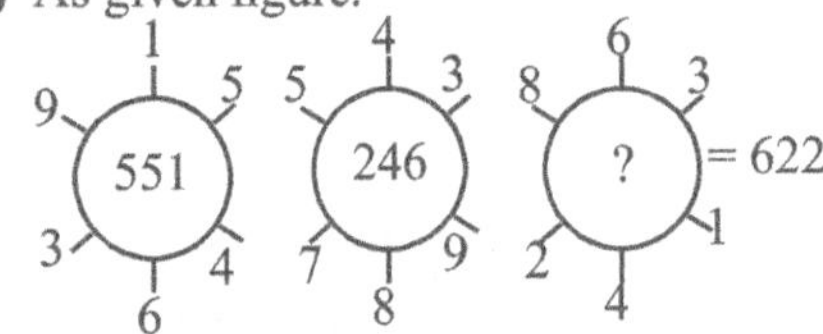

$915 - 364 = 551,$
$863 - 241$
$= 622$
$789 - 543$
$= 246$

88. (a)

89. (a) As given expression;
$\Rightarrow x^2 - 6x + 8$
$\Rightarrow x^2 - (4+2)x + 8$
$\Rightarrow x^2 - 4x - 2x + 8$
$\Rightarrow x(x-4) - 2(x-4)$
$\Rightarrow (x-2)(x-4)$
Hence, option (a) is correct.

90. (b) On dividing 87 375 by 698, we get 125 reminder, Hence, Required number to be subtracted is 125.

91. (b)

92. (a) As given that,

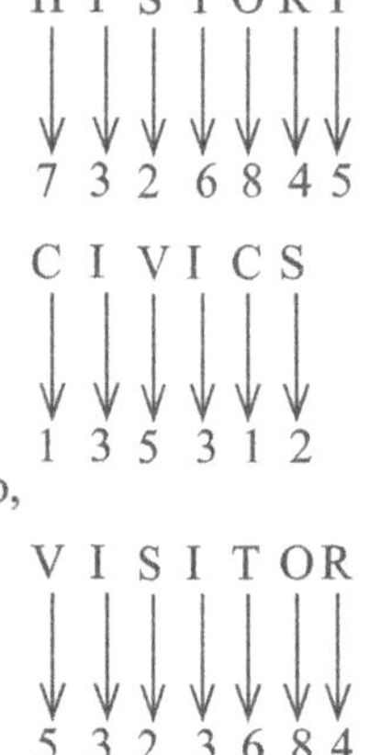

So,

Hence 'VISITOR' is coded as : 5323684

93. (b) A Man buys 20 Pencils price = ₹ 6.

1 Pencil price = ₹ $\dfrac{6}{20}$

Selling price of 16 Pencils = ₹ 6.

Selling price of 1 Pencil = ₹ $\dfrac{6}{16}$

Gain = Selling price – cost price

$= \left[\dfrac{6}{16} - \dfrac{6}{20}\right] = \left[\dfrac{30-24}{80}\right] = \dfrac{6}{80}$

Gain percentage

$= \left[\dfrac{\dfrac{6}{80} \times 100}{6/20}\right] = \dfrac{75 \times 20}{6} = 25\,\%$

94. (b) Angle rotated by minute hand in 1 minute

$= \dfrac{360°}{60°}$

$= 6°$

So, angle between two hands of the watch when they are 25 minutes apart.

$= 25 \times 6°$
$= 150°$

95. (c)

96. (b) 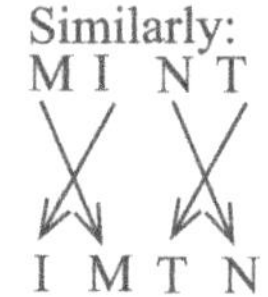

Similarly:

Hence, Option (b) is correct.

97. (b) 98. (b)

99. (a) Let the length of the base is x cm.
Then, perpendicular $= (x + 2)$
and hypotenuse $= (x + 2 + 2) = (x + 4)$.

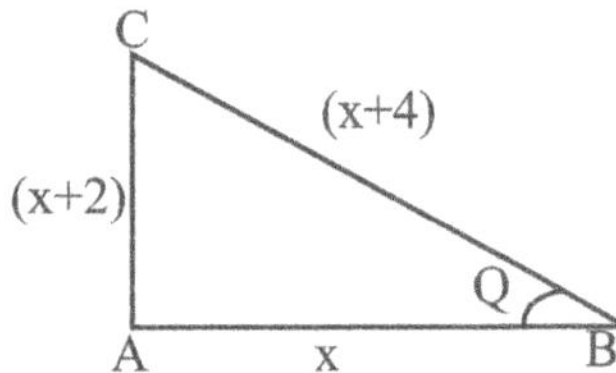

By Pythagorean theorem
$(CB)^2 = (AC)^2 + (AB)^2$
$(x + 4)^2 = (x + 2)^2 + x^2$
$x^2 + 16 + 8x = x^2 + 4 + 4x + x^2$
$x^2 - 4x - 12 = 0$
$(x - 6)(x + 2) = 0$
$\therefore x = 6$
Hence, Length of the base = 6 cm.

100. (b)

1. Introducing a man, Shamita said, "He is the only son of my mother's mother." How is Shamita related to the man?

   (a) Mother (b) Aunt

   (c) Sister (d) Niece

2. If $2x + 3 = 9$ then find the value of $3x + 2$

   (a) 12 (b) 16

   (c) 13 (d) 11

3. Radish is an example of:

   (a) bulb (b) root

   (c) tuber (d) fruit

4. Pointing to a man in a photograph, Gunjan said, "His mother's only daughter is my mother." How is Gunjan related to that man?

   (a) Nephew (b) Sister

   (c) Wife (d) Niece

5. One should use porcelain and not metal containers in a microwave oven because...

   (a) Charge may accumulate on the metal surface and there is danger of getting a shock.

   (b) Porcelain vessels are better conductors of heat and thus food gets cooked quickly.

   (c) Metal containers might undergo chemical reaction leading to spoilage of food.

   (d) Porcelain vessels are cheaper than the metal containers.

6. Thomas Cup is associated with which of the following sports?

   (a) Hockey (b) Badminton

   (c) Football (d) Cricket

7. When was the ASLV used in India for the first time?

   (a) 1980 (b) 1987

   (c) 1994 (d) 2000

8. Three clocks are designed to alarm in every hour, two hours and three hours respectively. If they all alarmed together three hours before, then after how many hours will they next alarm together?

   (a) 3 hours (b) 6 hours

   (c) 2 hours (d) 1 hours

9. Name the international independent agency whose key activities include scientific research, education, development & monitoring of anti-doping capacities and code in all sports and all countries.

   (a) International Body Against Doping

   (b) World Anti-Doping Agency

   (c) Play true, Play safe

   (d) International Body for Sports Ethics

10. Winner of Mixed doubles category in Wimbledon, 2015 is ______________________.

    (a) Sania Mirza & Leander Paes

    (b) Serena Williams & Roger Federer

    (c) Martina Hingis & Leander Paes

    (d) Serena Williams & Novak Djokovic

11. Insert the missing character depicted by

18	24	32
12	14	16
3	?	4
72	112	128

    (a) 2 (b) 3

    (c) 4 (d) 5

12. India has designed and developed pilotless target aircrafts named __________, and made successful test flights of its unmanned air vehicle (UAV).

    1. Nishant

    2. Lakshya

    3. Astra

    (a) Only 2 (b) Only 1

    (c) Only 2 and 3 (d) Only 1 and 2

13. Which of the following branch of medical science deals with the study and treatment of the liver?

(a) Helcology   (b) Hepatology

(c) Heterology   (d) Geriatrics

DIRECTIONS (Qs. 14-16): *Study the bar chart and answer the questions based on it.*

Production of Pesticides by Coromandal International Ltd. Company (in 1000 tonnes)

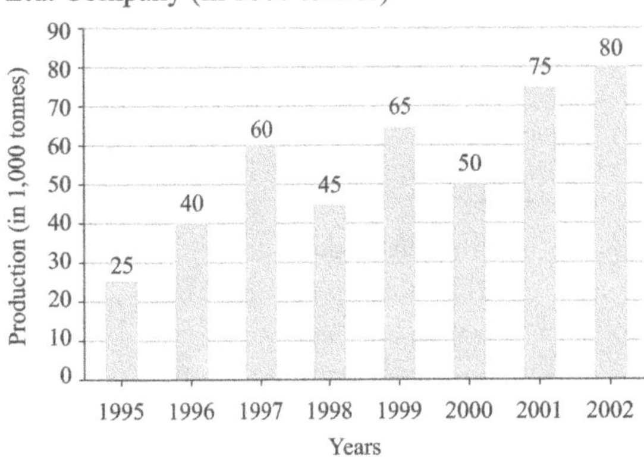

14. The average production of 1996 and 1997 was exactly equal to the average production of which of the following pairs of years?

(a) 2000 and 2001

(b) 1999 and 2000

(c) 1998 and 2000

(d) 1995 and 2001

15. In which year was the percentage increase in production as compared to the previous year the maximum?

(a) 2002   (b) 2001

(c) 1997   (d) 1996

16. What was the percentage increase in production of Pesticides in 2002 compared to that in 1995?

(a) 320%   (b) 300%

(c) 220%   (d) 200%

17. The President of India, Pranab Mukherjee presented the 24th Saraswati Sammaan for the year 2014 to:

(a) Govind Mishra

(b) Sugathakumari

(c) M Veerappa Moily

(d) Dilip Parulekar

18. ________________ is one of the states of matter obtained by cooling a gas of very low density to extremely low temperatures.

(a) Gas

(b) Plasma

(c) Bose-Einstein Condensate (BEC)

(d) Plasma Condensate

DIRECTIONS (Qs.19-21): *Study the following figure and answer the questions given below.*

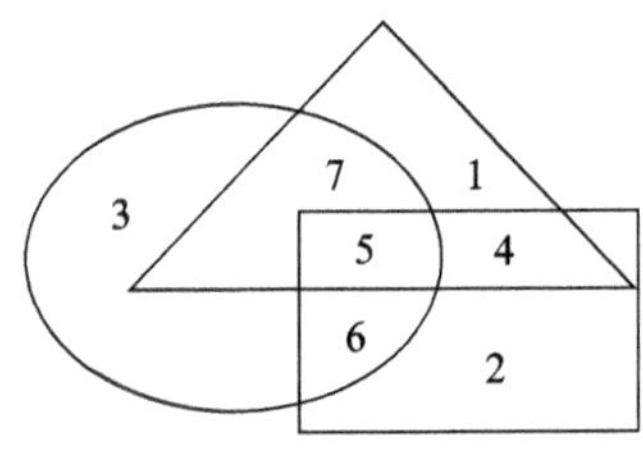

19. By which number, the trained unmarried lecturers in the college are represented?

(a) 6   (b) 5

(c) 7   (d) 4

20. If Ravenshaw College management requires only married trained lecturers for teaching, What is represented by the number 7?

(a) Married lecturers in the college

(b) Trained lecturers

(c) Unmarried trained lecturers

(d) Married trained lecturers

21. By which number, the trained married lecturers in the college are represented?

(a) 7   (b) 6

(c) 5   (d) 4

22. Four pairs of words are given below out of which three are alike in some manner and one is different. Which is different from the rest?

(a) Steel : Utensils

(b) Bronze : Statue

(c) Duralumin : Aircraft

(d) Wood : Rails

23. Find the least number that must be subtracted from 98534, to get a number exactly divisible by 824.

(a) 484   (b) 478

(c) 422   (d) 375

24. 20 pens and 46 pencils were purchased for Rs. 235. If the average price of a pencil is Rs. 2.50 then calculate the average price (in Rs.) of a pen.

(a) 6   (b) 4

(c) 8   (d) 12

25. Belur Math is located an

(a) West Bengal   (b) Maharashtra

(c) Uttar Pradesh   (d) Tamil Nadu

26. Galvanization a process to prevent rusting involves use of _______________ coating to steel or iron.

(a) Nickel   (b) Magnesium

(c) Copper   (d) Zinc

27. Direction:

There are three statements which are followed by three conclusions. Choose the conclusions which logically follow from the given statements.

Statements:

All the doors are keys.

All the keys are bats.

Some clocks are bats.

Conclusions:

(1) Some bats are doors.

(2) Some clocks are keys.

(3) All the keys are doors.

(a) Only (1) and (2)   (b) Only (1)

(c) Only (2)   (d) Only (1) and (3)

28. Insert the missing character depicted by '?'

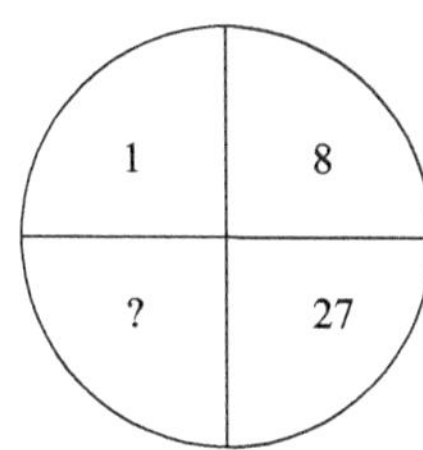

(a) 41   (b) 64

(c) 35   (d) 61

29. If $\sqrt{5} = 2.236$; then $\sqrt{5}/2$ is

(a) 1.851   (b) 1.118

(c) 2.236   (d) 1.782

30. which state of India produces the highest quantity of Jute?

(a) Bihar   (b) Odisha

(c) West Bengal   (d) Jharkhand

31. Which of the following languages was not included in the 8th schedule of Indian Constitution through 92nd amendment act?

(a) Maithili   (b) Bodo

(c) Santhali   (d) Kannada

32. A table tennis player, lost 12 games out of 18 games playe(d) Calculate the games won in terms of decimal.

(a) 0.667   (b) 0.067

(c) 0.50   (d) 0.333

33. What is the simplified value of $\sqrt{\dfrac{\sec A - 1}{\sec A + 1}}$?

(a) cosec A – cot A

(b) sec A – tan A

(c) $\sec^2 A$

(d) sec A cosec A

34. If in a certain language, MANURE is coded as EMRNUA, now is LIVELY coded in that code.

(a) YLLEVI   (b) YLVLEI

(c) YLLVEI   (d) YLVLIE

35. The value of (0.00000729/0.00000027) is

(a) 0.27   (b) 0.027

(c) 2.7   (d) 27

36. If $a/b = 1/4$; $b/c = 1/8$ and $a=2$ then the value of c is

(a) 8   (b) 16

(c) 32   (d) 64

37. The value of $\cos 0°$ is

(a) 0   (b) Infinite

(c) not defined   (d) 1

38. Read the statement and select a conclusion from the given alternatives:

Statement:

Company 'X' had asked its employees to declare income and assets but it has been strongly opposed by the employees' his/her union and no employee is going to declare his/her income.

Conclusions:

I. The employees of the company 'X' do

not seem to have any additional income besides their salary.

II. The employees' union want all the senior officer to declare their income first.

(a) only conclusion I follows.

(b) only conclusion II follows.

(c) either I or II follows.

(d) neither I nor II follows.

39. Prime Minister Narendra Modi has released two commemorative coins of denominations Rs. 125 & Rs. 10 as a mark of tribute to whom?

(a) Abdul Kalam

(b) Mahatma Gandhi

(c) Dr. Rajendra Prasad

(d) B. R.Ambedkar

40. If in an investment, Ramesh gains 50% more profit than Hemant, then by what percentage profit of Hemant is less than the profit of Ramesh.

(a) 50%　　　　　　　　(b) 25%

(c) $33\frac{1}{3}\%$　　　　　(d) $66\frac{2}{3}\%$

41. ___________ soils are red in color and not suitable for agriculture found along the Tamil Nadu, Odisha and small part of Chhotanagpur and Meghalaya.

(a) Alluvial Soil　　　　(b) Red Soil

(c) Laterite Soil　　　　(d) Regur Soil

42. Complete the Figure X from the given alternatives 1, 2, 3, 4

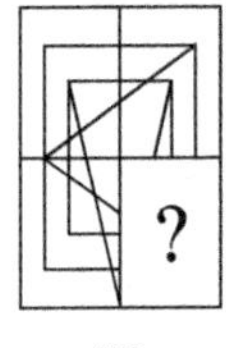 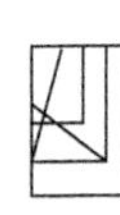  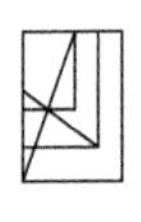 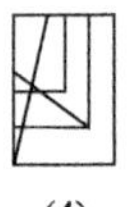

(X)　　　　(1)　　　　(2)　　　　(3)　　　　(4)

(a) 1　　　　　　　　　(b) 2

(c) 3　　　　　　　　　(d) 4

43. If on a marked price, the difference of selling prices with a discount of 30% and two successive discounts of 20% and 10% is ₹ 72, then the marked price (in rupees) is

(a) 3,600　　　　　　　(b) 3,000

(c) 2,500　　　　　　　(d) 2,400

44. Name the device used to connect computers for communication via telephone lines.

(a) HUB　　　　　　　(b) Switch

(c) Repeater　　　　　(d) MODEM

45. Factors of $x^2 + 7x + 10$ are

(a) $(x - 5)(x - 2)$　　(b) $(x + 5)(x + 2)$

(c) $(x - 5)(x + 2)$　　(d) $(x - 4)(x + 2)$

46. Who among the following is known as the Father of Civil Services in India?

(a) Lord Cornwallis

(b) Warren Hastings

(c) Lord Wellesley

(d) Lord William Bentinck

47. In terms of environmental studies, CER refers to:

(a) Certified Emission Reductions

(b) Capped Emission Repository

(c) Certified Emission Repository

(d) Capped Emission Reductions

48. World climate conference popularly known as COP-21 (2015) was held in ___________.

(a) New York　　　　　(b) London

(c) Paris　　　　　　　(d) Berlin

49. Gitesh took a loan for 4 years at 5% Compound Interest. If the total interest paid was Rs. 431.01, Calculate the principal.

(a) Rs. 2000　　　　　(b) Rs. 2050

(c) Rs. 2100　　　　　(d) Rs. 2150

50. A, B and C can complete the work in 4, 5 and 6 hours respectively. If they all work together and receive Rs. 777 as wages, then find the share of a

(a) Rs. 300　　　　　　(b) Rs. 315

(c) Rs. 326　　　　　　(d) Rs. 175

51. A shopkeeper purchased a pen drive of marked price Rs. 1000 at successive discounts of 10% & 15% respectively. He spent Rs. 35 on packaging and sold it on Rs. 1000. Calculate the Gain percent.

(a) No Gain　　　　　　(b) 25%

(c) 30%　　　　　　　(d) 35%

52. In a certain code language, if EXECUTE is coded as 5351695 and SCRIPT is coded as 714279, then EXIST will be coded as?

(a) 23579　　　　　　(b) 97532

(c) 23597　　　　　　(d) 53279

53. Complete the Figure X from the given alternatives 1, 2, 3, 4

(X)　　　(1)　　　(2)　　　(3)　　　(4)

(a) 1   (b) 2

(c) 3   (d) 4

54. Rampal told Arjun, 'Yesterday I defeated the only brother of the daughter of my grandmother.' Whom did Rampal defeat?

(a) Son   (b) Father

(c) Brother   (d) Father-in-law

55. Battle of Gulnabad was led by Mahmud Hotaki and fought in the year __________ .

(a) 1770   (b) 1722

(c) 1712   (d) 1702

56. Apollo 11, the first artificial satellite that landed humans on moon, was launched in which year?

(a) 1975   (b) 1968

(c) 1969   (d) 1958

57. The smallest number that is completely divisibly by 6, 8, 12 and 16 is

(a) 48   (b) 24

(c) 64   (d) 80

58. Name the committee appointed in 1986 by Rajiv Gandhi on "Revitalisation of Panchayati Raj Institution for Democracy & Development".

(a) Ashok Mehta Committee

(b) L M Singhvi Committee

(c) G.V.K Rao Committee

(d) Balwant Rai Mehta Committee.

59. ________________ are a mountain range that runs almost parallel to the western coast of the Indian peninsula, and is one of the eight "hottest hotspots" of biological diversity in the world sometimes called the "Great Escarpment of India".

(a) Eastern Ghats

(b) Western Ghats

(c) Himalayas

(d) Satpura Range

60. A man, rowing a boat, covers a distance of 16 km in two hours downstream. He covers half the distance in same amount of time when rowing upstream. Calculate the speed of the stream.

(a) 4 km/hr   (b) 2 km/hr

(c) 3 km/hr   (d) 1 km/hr

61. Match the Correct Memory Units.

(a) 4 bit   (p) 1 MB

(b) 1024 KB   (q) 1 byte

(c) 1024 TB   (r) 1 nibble

(d) 8 bit   (s) 1 PB

(a) a-r, b-p, c-s, d-q

(b) a-p, b-s, c-q, d-r

(c) a-r, b-s, c-q, d-p

(d) a-r, b-q, c-s, d-p

62. Read the statement and select a conclusion from the given alternatives:

Statement:

The Official Secret Act (OSA) enacted by the 'ABC' Government in the year 1930 seems to be one of the major sources of corruption in the country 'X'.

Conclusions:

I.   The Official Secret Act has to be abolished immediately to put an end to the corruption in the country 'X'.

II. The 'ABC' Government had an intention of encouraging corruption in the Government offices.

(a) only conclusion I follows.

(b) only conclusion II follows

(c) either I or II follows.

(d) neither I nor II follows

63. After whom is the Amrut Yojana scheme named? (initiative to meet the nutrition needs of pregnant, lactating women in the tribal areas)

(a) Mahatma Gandhi   (b) Abdul Kalam

(c) B R Ambedkar   (d) Indira Gandhi

64. Find the maximum area of a rectangular field which is surrounded by a rope of 400 m.

(a) 5000 m^2 (b) 6250 m^2

(c) 4000 m^2 (d) 10000 m^2

65. Read the statements and select a conclusion from the given alternatives:

Statement:

The minimum qualification for this job is MTECH.

However, candidates who have appeared for the final year of MTECH can also apply.

Conclusions:

I. All candidates who have yet to post graduate will be there in the list of selected candidates.

II. All candidates having MTECH as their minimum qualification will be there in the list of selected candidates.

(a) only conclusion I follows.

(b) only conclusion II follows.

(c) either I or II follows.

(d) neither I nor II follows

66. If $19x^2 = 100^2 - 90^2$, then find the value of x

(a) 10   (b) 9

(c) 11   (d) 12

67. ______________ a professional Tennis player, became the new goodwill ambassador for the UN Fund for Children.

(a) Sania Mirza

(b) Serena Williams

(c) Roger Federer

(d) Novak Djokovic

68. Rahul and Raghav are 110 km apart from each other and they started horse-riding towards each other at same time at a speed of 20 km/hr. and 24 km/hr. After how many hours of riding will they be a distance of 22 km?

(a) 1 hour   (b) 1 hour 30 min

(c) 2 hours   (d) 2 hours 30 min

69. The lady who played an important role in the awakening of Indian women to right for independence and who is also known as Nightingale of India is -

(a) Vijaya Lakshmi Pandit

(b) Durga Bai Deshmukh

(c) Sarojini Naidu

(d) Madam Bhikaiji Cama

70. A man buys 10 oranges for Rs. 3 and sells 8 for Rs, 3. Calculate his gain percent.

(a) 20 %   (b) 25 %

(c) 27 %   (d) 30 %

71. A motorist knows four different routes from Jaipur to Bhangarh. From Bhangarh to Alwar he knows three different routes and from Alwar to Carlisle he knows two different routes. How many routes does he know from Jaipur to Carlisle?

(a) 12   (b) 24

(c) 48   (d) 60

72. The expenses of a person increases by Rs. 50000 for every month in February and March. If his expenses in January was Rs. 50000, Calculate his average expenditure (in Rs.) from January to March.

(a) 100000   (b) 150000

(c) 75000   (d) 50000

73. An example of Full Duplex communication channel.

(a) Radio Broadcasting

(b) Television Broadcasting

(c) Walkie-Talkie

(d) Telephone conversation

74. Ravi, Rohan and Rajesh alone can complete a work in 10, 12 and 15 days respectively. In how many days can the work be completed, if all three work together?

(a) 4 days   (b) 5 days

(c) 3 days   (d) 8 days

75. In an examination, student gets on average 76 marks. The total marks for five subjects is 500. His marks in 4 subjects are mentioned; calculate the marks obtained by the student in Mathematics marked as "x" in the table below.

Subject	Maths	English	Sanskrit	Science	Social Science
Marks Obtained	X	87	83	78	57

(a) 80   (b) 83

(c) 72   (d) 75

76. If Selling Price is Rs. 72 & Gain Percentage = 20%, calculate the Cost Price.
(a) Rs. 60   (b) Rs. 58
(c) Rs. 61   (d) Rs. 59

77. Complete the given series
15, 155, 1545, 15455 ....
(a) 154545   (b) 15555
(c) 154555   (d) 155454

78. What fraction of 2 hours is 12 seconds?
(a) 1/200   (b) 1/300
(c) 1/400   (d) 1/600

79. Who has been appointed as first-ever Ombudsman (Ethics officer) of BCCI?
(a) Justice A. P. Shah
(b) Justice Anil R. Dave
(c) Justice Dipak Misra
(d) Justice Jagdish Singh Khehai

80. Insert the missing character depicted by '?'

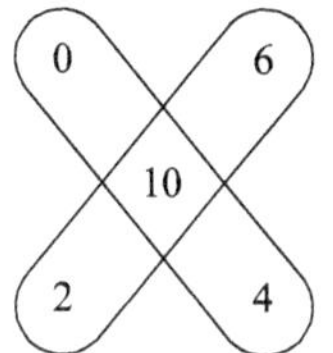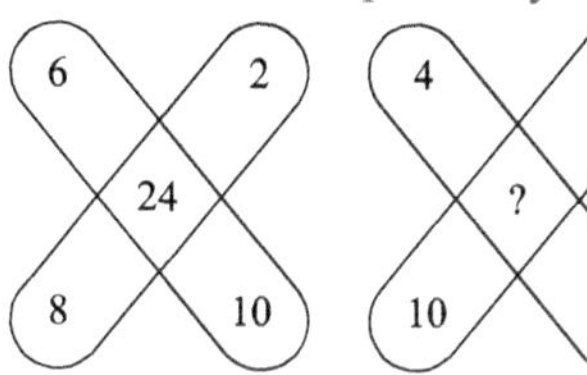

(a) 36   (b) 48
(c) 38   (d) 30

81. If the average age of 20 students in Class I is 10 years and average age of 25 students in Class II is 12 years, find the average age (in years) of all students.
(a) 11   (b) 11.111
(c) 10.50   (d) 10.85

82. Which part of the human brain is the centre for intelligence, memory and emotions?
(a) Hypothalamus   (b) Cerebrum
(c) Corpus Callosum   (d) Mid Brain

83. Two numbers are in ratio 3:4. When 3 is subtracted from both the numbers, the ratio becomes 2:3. Find the sum of the numbers.
(a) 16   (b) 20
(c) 21   (d) 22

84. If @ stands for +
$ stands for −
% stands for ×
> stands for ÷
Then what is the value of 48 > 4 $ 8 % 2@8
(a) 12   (b) −8
(c) −4   (d) 4

85. Calculate the principal if an amount of Rs. 441 is received on compound interest at the rate of 5% per annum after 2 years.
(a) Rs. 400   (b) Rs. 390
(c) Rs. 380   (d) Rs. 350

DIRECTIONS (Qs. 86-88): *Answer the questions based on the following information:*

Six colleagues are sitting in a circle and are facing the center of the circle. Diana is between Puskar and Padma Priyanka is between Mahesh and Lucky. Puskar and Mahesh are opposite to each other.

86. Who are the neighbours of Mahesh?
(a) Puskar and Diana
(b) Diana and Priyanka
(c) Priyanka and Padma
(d) Lucky and Priyanka

87. Who is just right to Padma?
(a) Diana   (b) Lucky
(c) Puskar   (d) Priyanka

88. Who is sitting opposite to Priyanka?
(a) Puskar   (b) Diana
(c) Padma   (d) Lucky

89. **Directions:**
There are three statements which are followed by four conclusions. Choose the conclusions which logically follow from the given statements
Statements:
Some cups are pins.
Some pins are covers.
All the covers are pens.
Conclusions:
(1) Some pens are pins.
(2) Some covers are cups.
(3) No cup is pin.
(4) Some pins are cups.
(a) Only (1) and (2)
(b) Only (2) and (4)
(c) Only (2) and (3)
(d) Only (1) and (4)

90. A man is 3 years older than his wife and four times as old as his son. If the son becomes 15 years old after 3 years, what is the present age of the wife ?
(a) 60 years   (b) 51 years
(c) 48 years   (d) 45 years

91. If $\sin\theta = 40/41$, then $\cot\theta$ is

   (a) 40/9   (b) 9/40

   (c) 9/41   (d) 41/9

92. If the sum of LCM and HCF of two numbers is 60 and their LCM is 30 more than their HCF, then the product of two numbers will be.

   (a) 625   (b) 675

   (c) 525   (d) 575

93. If in a certain language, SCARCE is coded as CSRAEC, how is STABLE coded in that code?

   (a) TBSAEL   (b) BTSAEL

   (c) BTELSA   (d) TSBAEL

94. **Direction:**

There are three statements which are followed by four conclusions. Choose the conclusions which logically follow from the given statements

Statements:

Some images are answers.

Some answers are videos.

All the videos are poems.

Conclusions:

(1) Some videos are answers.

(2) Some poems are images.

(3) All the images are poems.

(4) Some poems are answers.

   (a) Only (1) and (2)

   (b) Only (1) and (4)

   (c) Only (1) and (3)

   (d) Only (2) and (4)

95. In a certain code language, if CHECK is coded as 97294 and QUERY is coded as 51238, then CHERRY will be coded as?

   (a) 729833   (b) 792338

   (c) 972338   (d) 338972

96. Human blood platelets releases __________ which helps in clotting of bloo(d)

   (a) prothrombin   (b) fibrin

   (c) fructose   (d) sucrose

97. Light can travel __________ km in a year.

   (a) 5 billion   (b) 10 billion

   (c) 5 trillion   (d) 10 trillion

98. What was the major decision that took place in 1987 Montreal Conference?

   (a) Developed countries will completely ban CFC production by 2000

   (b) Developed countries will completely ban CFC production by 2010

   (c) Developing countries will completely ban CFC production by 2000

   (d) Developing countries will completely ban CFC production by 2020

99. The major objective of INSAT series satellites is to facilitate.

   (a) TV relay to remote areas

   (b) mobile network in remote areas

   (c) internet services

   (d) mapping locations through GPS

100. A good cricket fielder while catching a fast moving ball moves his hand along with the ball because __________.

   (a) He decreases the time of contact therefore increasing the force of contact.

   (b) He increases the time of contact thereby reducing the force of contact.

   (c) He is afraid to take the ball and thus takes his hand out.

   (d) He decreases the time of contact therefore reducing the force of contact

HINTS & EXPLANATIONS

1. **(d)** Son of Mother's mother means Maternal uncle.
   Hence, Shamita is Niece of that man.

2. **(d)** $2x + 3 = 9$
   $\Rightarrow 2x = 6$
   $\Rightarrow x = 3$
   Hence $3x + 2 = 3(3) + 2 = 9 + 2$
   $= 11$

3. **(b)**

4. **(d)** His Mother's only daughter is my mother means, Gunjan is the Niece of that man.

5. **(a)**

6. **(b)**

7. **(b)**

8. **(a)** Since the three clock alarm in every 1 hour, 2 hour and 3 hour respectively.
   ∴ the time after which they will alarm together = LCM of $(1, 2, 3) = 6$ hours
   The clocks have already alarmed three hours ago.
   So the next alarm will be in $(6 - 3)$ hours
   $= 3$ hours.

9. **(b)**

10. **(c)**

11. **(b)**

18	24	32
12	14	16
3	3	4
72	112	128

$\longrightarrow (32 \div 4) \times 16 = 128$

$(18 \div 3) \times 12 = 72 \longleftarrow$

$(24 \div 3) \times 14 = 112 \longleftarrow$

12. **(d)**

13. **(b)** Hepatology is a branch of medicine concerned with the study, prevention, diagnosis and management of diseases that affect the liver, gallbladder, biliary tree and pancreas. The term hepatology is derived from the Greek words "hepatikos" which mean liver and "logia" and which mean study, hence the study of liver.

14. **(d)** Average production of 1996 and 1997
   $= \dfrac{40 + 60}{2} = 50$
   From the graph it is quite clear the average production of 1995 and 2001 is 50 from the given options.

15. **(d)** From the given options:
   Percentage increase in production for year
   $2002 = \dfrac{80 - 75}{75} \times 100 = 6.6\%$
   $2001 = \dfrac{75 - 50}{50} \times 100 = 50\%$
   $1997 = \dfrac{60 - 40}{40} \times 100 = 50\%$
   $1996 = \dfrac{40 - 25}{25} \times 100 = 60\%$
   ∴ For year 1996 the percentage increase in production was maximum as compared to previous year.

16. **(c)** Percentage increase in production of pesticides in 2002 compared to that in 1995
   $= \dfrac{80 - 25}{25} \times 100 = 220\%$

17. **(c)**

18. **(c)** BEC (Bose-Einstein Condensate) is a state of matter of a dilute gas of bosons cooled to near absolute zero (0 K or -273.15 °C). A BEC is formed by cooling a gas of extremely low density, about one-hundred-thousandth the density of normal air, to ultra-low temperatures.

19. **(d)** Trained unmarried lecturers is represented by the number 4 in the common area between square and triangle (outside the circle).

20. **(a)** From the diagram No. 7 represents Married lecturers in the college.

21. (c) The common area between square, circle and triangle represents trained married lecturers in the college which corresponds to number 5.

22. (d)

23. (b) On dividing 98534 by 824 we get 478 as the remainder.

Hence we subtract 478 from 98534 to make it exactly divisible by 824.

24. (a) Price of (20 pens + 46 pencils) = ₹ 235

Average price of pencil = ₹ 2.5

Price of 46 pencils $= 46 \times 2.5 = ₹\ 115$

$\Rightarrow$ Price of 20 pens $= ₹\ 235 - ₹\ 115$

$= ₹\ 120$

$\therefore$ Average price of pen $= \dfrac{120}{20} = ₹\ 6$

25. (a)

26. (d) Galvanization is the process of applying a protective zinc coating to steel or iron to prevent rusting. Zinc may be applied by two methods that are hot dipping and electrolytic deposition.

27. (b)

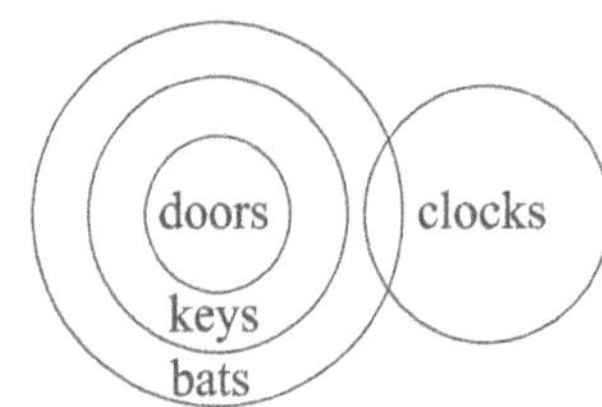

From the diagram only conclusion 1 "Some bats are doors" follows.

28. (b)

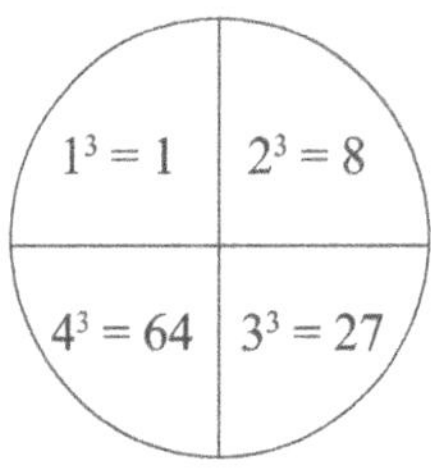

Missing number = 64

29. (b) $\sqrt{5} = 2.236$

$\therefore \dfrac{\sqrt{5}}{2} = \dfrac{2.236}{2} = 1.118$

30. (c) 31. (d)

32. (d) No. of games won = 18 − 12 = 6

In terms of decimal no. of games won

$= \dfrac{6}{18} = .333$

33. (a) $\sqrt{\dfrac{\sec A - 1}{\sec A + 1} \times \dfrac{\sec A - 1}{\sec A - 1}} \Rightarrow \dfrac{\sec A - 1}{\sqrt{\sec^2 A - 1}}$

$= \dfrac{\sec A - 1}{\sqrt{\tan^2 A}}$

$\Rightarrow \dfrac{\sec A - 1}{\tan A} \Rightarrow \dfrac{\sec A}{\tan A} - \dfrac{1}{\tan A}$

$= \operatorname{cosec} A - \cot A.$

34. (c)

35. (d) $\dfrac{0.00000729}{0.00000027} = \dfrac{729}{100000000} \times \dfrac{100000000}{27}$

$= \dfrac{729}{27} = 27$

36. (d) $\dfrac{a}{b} = \dfrac{1}{4}$

$a = 2$

$\Rightarrow \dfrac{2}{b} = \dfrac{1}{4} \Rightarrow b = 8$

Again $\dfrac{b}{c} = \dfrac{1}{8} \Rightarrow \dfrac{8}{c} = \dfrac{1}{8}$

$c = 64.$

37. (d) We know that Cos 0° = 1.

38. (d) None of the conclusions given in the question follows the statement.

39. (d)

40. (c) Let profit of Ramesh = R

and profit of Hemant = H

ATQ $R = H\left(1 + \dfrac{50}{100}\right)$

$\Rightarrow R = H\left(\dfrac{3}{2}\right)$

$\Rightarrow H = \dfrac{2}{3}R$

$H = \left(1 - \dfrac{1}{3}\right)R$

$H = \left(1 - \dfrac{100}{3}\%\right)R = \left(1 - 33\dfrac{1}{3}\%\right)R$

$\therefore$ The percentage profit of Hemant that is less than the profit of Ramesh is $33\dfrac{1}{3}\%$

41. **(c)** Laterite soil is of rusty-red colouration with a lower content of nitrogen, phosphorus, potassium, lime, and magnesia. Found in the southern parts of Maharashtra, parts of Karnataka, Andhra Pradesh, West Bengal Orissa, Jharkhand, Kerala, Assam, and Meghalaya, the laterite soil is formed under conditions of high temperature and heavy rainfall. It lacks fertility due to a lower base-exchanging capacity, and hence, is not suitable for cultivation.

42. **(d)** 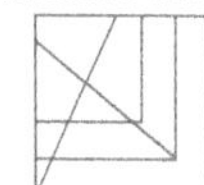

43. **(a)** Let the marked price be ₹ x.

∴ In case I, SP $= ₹\dfrac{70x}{100}$

Single discount equivalent to successive discounts of 20% and 10%.

$$= \left(20 + 10 - \dfrac{20 \times 10}{100}\right)\% = 28\%$$

∴ S.P. in this case $= ₹\dfrac{70x}{100}$

∴ $\dfrac{72x}{100} - \dfrac{70x}{100} = ₹\,72$

$$\Rightarrow \dfrac{2x}{100} = 72$$

∴ $x = \dfrac{72 \times 100}{2} = ₹\,3600$

44. **(d)**

45. **(b)** $x^2 + 7x + 10 = 0$

$x^2 + 5x + 2x + 10 = 0$

$\Rightarrow\quad x(x + 5) + 2(x + 5) = 0$

∴ $(x + 2)(x + 5)$ are the required factors.

46. **(a)**

47. **(a)** **48.** **(c)**

49. **(a)** C.I. $= ₹\,431.01$, T $= 4$ years and $r = 5\%$

Then ATQ

$$431.01 = P\left[\left(1 + \dfrac{5}{100}\right)^4 - 1\right]$$

$$431.01 = P\left[(1.05)^4 - 1\right]$$

$$431.01 = P\left[1.216 - 1\right]$$

$$\Rightarrow\quad P = \dfrac{431.01}{.216} \approx ₹\,2000.$$

50. **(b)** Share of A : Share of B : Share of C

$$= \dfrac{1}{4} : \dfrac{1}{5} : \dfrac{1}{6}$$

$$= \dfrac{60}{4} : \dfrac{60}{5} : \dfrac{60}{6}$$

$$= 15 : 12 : 10$$

∴ Share of A $= \dfrac{15}{15 + 12 + 10} \times (777)$

$$= \dfrac{15}{37} \times (777) = ₹\,315.$$

51. **(b)** MP $= ₹\,1000$

Total discount $= 10 + 15 - \dfrac{10 \times 15}{100}$

$$= 25 - \dfrac{150}{100}$$

$$= 23.5\%$$

CP $= 1000 \times \dfrac{76.5}{100}$ + Packaging cost

$= ₹\,765$ packaging cost

Packaging cost $= ₹\,35$

$\Rightarrow$ CP $= ₹\,765 + ₹\,35$

$= ₹\,800$

Since SP $= ₹\,1000$

∴ Gain % $= \dfrac{1000 - 800}{800} \times 100$

$= 25\%$

52. **(d)**

E	X	E	C	U	T	E		S	C	R	I	P	T
↓	↓	↓	↓	↓	↓	↓		↓	↓	↓	↓	↓	↓
5	3	5	1	6	9	5		7	1	4	2	7	9

Observing the above values

E X I S T $\longrightarrow$ 5 3 2 7 9

53. **(d)**

54. **(b)** Only brother of the daughter of grandmother means father.

Hence, Rampal defeated his father.

55. (b) 56. (c)

57. (a) Smallest number divisible by 6, 8, 12 and 16 is the LCM of 6, 8, 12 and 16.

$$6 = 2 \times 3$$
$$8 = 2 \times 2 \times 2$$
$$12 = 2 \times 2 \times 3$$
$$16 = 2 \times 2 \times 2 \times 2$$

LCM $= 2 \times 2 \times 2 \times 2 \times 3 = 48$

$\therefore$ 48 is the required smallest number.

58. (b) 59. (b)

60. (b) Let the speed of boat $= x$ km/hr
and speed of stream $= y$ km/hr
Then ATQ

$$x + y = \frac{16}{2} \Rightarrow x + y = 8 \text{ km/hr} \quad ...(1)$$

also $x - y = \frac{8}{2} \Rightarrow x - y = 4 \text{ km/hr} \quad ...(2)$

Solving (1) and (2)
$x = 6$ km/hr & $y = 2$ km/hr
$\therefore$ Speed of stream $= 2$ km/hr.

61. (a) 62. (a) 63. (b)

64. (d) Length of rope $= 400$ m
For maximum area of rectangular field parameter of rectangular field
= Length of rope
$\Rightarrow \quad 2 (L + B) = 400$ m
$\quad\quad\quad L + B = 200$ m
For maximum area L will be equal to B
$\Rightarrow \quad\quad L = B = 100$ m
$\therefore$ area $= 100 \times 100 = 10000$ m^2

65. (d) The criteria given in statement is for the eligibility of the job and not the criteria to select a candidate.
$\therefore$ neither conclusion I nor II follows

66. (a)
$$19x^2 = 100^2 - 90^2$$
$$= (100 - 90)(100 + 90)$$
$$= 10 \times 190$$
$$\Rightarrow \quad 19x^2 = 1900 \Rightarrow x^2 = 100 \Rightarrow x = 10.$$

67. (d)

68. (c) Initial distance $= 110$ km

Final distance $= 22$ km

Distance to be travelled $= 88$ km

Total speed $= 20 + 24 = 44$ km/hr

$\therefore$ Required time $= \dfrac{88}{44} = 2$ hours.

69. (c)

70. (b) CP of 10 oranges $= ₹\ 3$

CP of 1 orange $= ₹\ \dfrac{3}{10}$

$\Rightarrow$ CP of 8 oranges $= ₹\ \dfrac{24}{10} = ₹\ 2.4$

SP of 8 oranges $= ₹\ 3$

$\therefore$ Gain percent $= \dfrac{3 - 2.4}{2.4} \times 100 = 25\%.$

71. (b) No. of routes from:
Jaipur to Bhangarh $= 4$
Bhangarh to Alwar $= 3$
Alwar to Carbisle $= 2$

$\therefore$ No. of routes from Jaipur to Carbisle
$= 4 \times 3 \times 2 = 24$

72. (a) Expenses in January $= ₹\ 50000$

Expenses in February $= ₹\ 50000 + ₹\ 50000 = ₹\ 100000$

Expenses in March $= ₹\ 150000$

$\therefore$ Average expenditure =

$$\frac{150000 + 100000 + 50000}{3}$$

$$= \frac{300000}{3} = ₹\ 100000.$$

73. (d)

74. (a) Ravi's 1 day work $= \dfrac{1}{10}$

Rohan's 1 day's work $= \dfrac{1}{12}$

Rajesh's 1 day's work $= \dfrac{1}{15}$

Ravi, Rohan and Rajesh 1 day's work

$$= \frac{1}{10} + \frac{1}{12} + \frac{1}{15} = \frac{15}{60}$$

$$= \frac{1}{4}$$

$\therefore$ No. of day required to complete the work by all three of them together $= 4$ days.

75. (d) Average marks $= \dfrac{x + 87 + 83 + 78 + 57}{5} = 76$

$\Rightarrow \quad 305 + x = 76 \times 5$

$\Rightarrow \quad x = 380 - 305$

$\quad\quad = 75$

Hence marks obtained in Math $= 75$

76. (a) We know that Gain% $= \dfrac{SP - CP}{CP} \times 100$

$\Rightarrow 20\% = \dfrac{72 - CP}{CP} \times 100$

$\Rightarrow 20\,CP = 7200 - 100\,CP$

$\Rightarrow 120\,CP = 7200$

$CP = \dfrac{7200}{120} = ₹60$

77. (a) 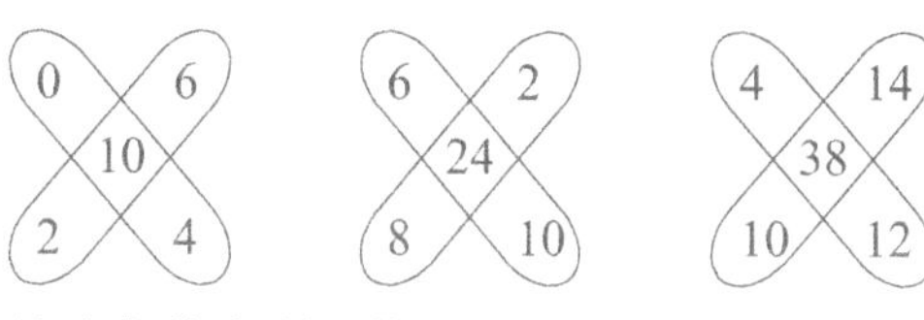

78. (d) $\dfrac{12}{2 \times 60 \times 60} = \dfrac{12}{7200} = \dfrac{1}{600}$

79. (a)

80. (c)

(6+4+2+0)−2=10   (2+10+8+6)−2=24
(14+12+10+4)−2=38.

81. (b) Average age of class I = 10 years

Total age $= 20 \times 10 = 200$ years

Average age of class II = 12 years

Total age $= 12 \times 25$

$= 300$ years

$\therefore$ Average of all students $= \dfrac{300 + 200}{20 + 25}$

$= \dfrac{500}{45}$

$= 11.111$ years

82. (b) The cerebrum is the largest and most highly developed part of the human brain. It encompasses about two-thirds of the brain mass and is responsible for all the high functions, including all voluntary functions, controlling emotions, hearing, vision, personality and much more.

83. (c) Let the number be x & y

Then ATQ $\dfrac{x}{y} = \dfrac{3}{4}$ $\Rightarrow 4x = 3y \Rightarrow x = \dfrac{3}{4}y$

also $\dfrac{x-3}{y-3} = \dfrac{2}{3}$ $\Rightarrow 3x - 9 = 2y - 6$

$\Rightarrow 3x - 2y = 3 \ .....(1)$

Substitute value of x in eqn (1)

$3 \times \dfrac{3}{4}y - 2y = 3$

$\Rightarrow 9y - 8y = 12$

$\Rightarrow y = 12$

$\therefore x = \dfrac{3}{4} \times 12 = 9$

Hence the sum $= 12 + 9 = 21$

84 (d) $48 > 4 \ \$ \ 8\% \ 2 \ @ \ 8 = 48 \div 4 - 8 \times 2 + 8$

$= 12 - 16 + 8$

$= 20 - 16$

$= 4$

85. (a) Amount $= P\left[1 + \dfrac{r}{100}\right]$

$\Rightarrow 441 = P\left(1 \ \dfrac{}{100}\right)$ $\Rightarrow 441 = P(1.05)^2$

$\Rightarrow 441 = P(1.1025)$

$\Rightarrow P = \dfrac{441}{1.1025}$

$= ₹400$

Sol. (86 – 88):

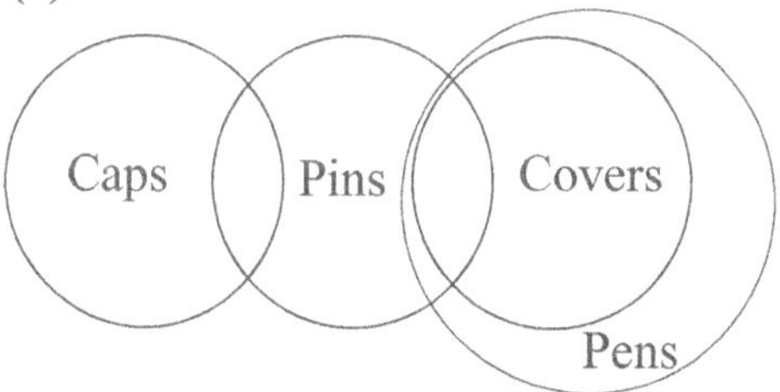

86. (c) Priyanka and padma are neighbour of Mahesh.

87. (a) Diana is to the immediate right of Padma.

88. (b) Diana is sitting just opposite to Priyanka.

89. (d)

Only Conclusion 1 & 4 follows

90. (d) Suppose the present age of son is x years.

Therefore, present age of the father = 4x years

According to question,

x + 3 = 15

∴ x = 15 – 3 = 12 years

The present age of father

= 4x = 4 × 12 = 48 years

∴ The present age of man's wife

= 48 – 3 = 45 years

91. (b) $\sin\theta = \dfrac{40}{41}$, then $\cot\theta$

we know that

$$\cos\theta = \sqrt{1-\sin^2\theta} = \sqrt{1-\left(\dfrac{40}{41}\right)^2}$$

$$= \sqrt{1-\dfrac{1600}{1681}} = \sqrt{\dfrac{81}{1681}} = \dfrac{9}{41}$$

$$\therefore \cot\theta = \dfrac{\cos\theta}{\sin\theta} = \dfrac{9}{41}\times\dfrac{41}{40} = \dfrac{9}{40}$$

$$\therefore \cot\theta = \dfrac{9}{40}$$

92. (b) Let LCM and HCF be x and y respectively

ATQ $x + y = 60$ (1)

$x = y + 30 \Rightarrow x - y = 30$ (2)

Squaring eqn. (1) and (2)

$(x+y)^2 = 60^2 \Rightarrow x^2+y^2+2xy = 3600$ (3)

$(x-y)^2 = 30^2 \Rightarrow x^2+y^2-2xy = 900$ (4)

Subtracting eqn (4) from (3)

$4xy = 2700 \Rightarrow xy = 675$

⇒ Product of LCM & HCF = 675

∴ Product of two numbers will be 675 as the product of LCM & HCF of two no.'s is equal to the product of the numbers.

93. (d)

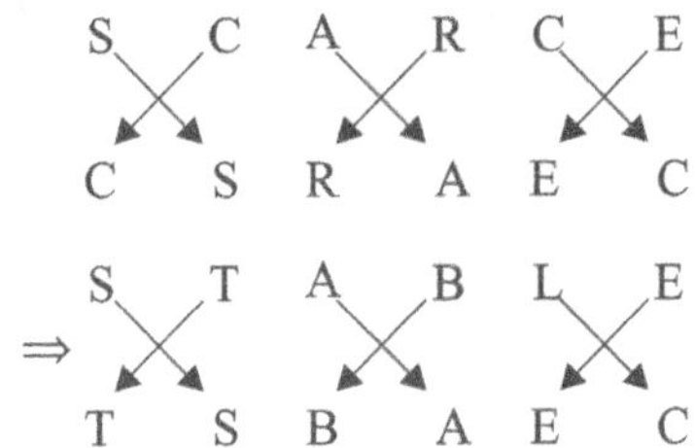

94. (b)

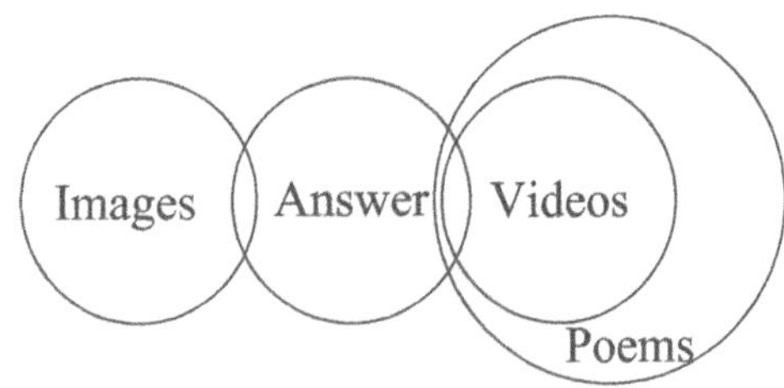

Only conclusion 1 &4 follows.

95. (c)

C	H	E	C	K		Q	U	E	R	Y
↓	↓	↓	↓	↓		↓	↓	↓	↓	↓
9	7	2	9	4		5	1	2	3	8

⇒ CHERRY → 972338

96. (a)

97. (d) Light moves at a velocity of about 300,000 kilometers (km) each second. So in one year, it can travel about 10 trillion km.

98. (a)

99. (a) Insat (Indian National Satellite System) is a multipurpose satellite system launched by ISRO for telecommunications, broadcasting, meteorology and search and rescue operations. Commissioned in 1983, it serves the television and communication needs of India.

100. (b)

RRB NTPC STAGE-II SOLVED PAPER-1
Held On 18th Jan 2017 (Shift-1)

1. Hubble's Law is related to______.
   - (a) Air Pressure
   - (b) Sound
   - (c) Heat
   - (d) Astronomy

2. Which of the following group of rulers was NOT called 'Sultans'?
   - (a) Mughals
   - (b) Lodis
   - (c) Tughlaqs
   - (d) Khiljis

3. The total amount of interest received on two deposits of ₹ 5,000 for 4 years and ₹4,000 for 5 years made at the simple rate of interest per annum was ₹ 2,400. Find the rate of interest per annum.
   - (a) 8%
   - (b) 4%
   - (c) 6%
   - (d) 7%

4. Select the correct combination of mathematical signs from the options given to replace # signs in order to get a balance equation :
   14 # 9 # 3 # 19 # 6
   - (a) $+ = + -$
   - (b) $+ \times = +$
   - (c) $= \times - +$
   - (d) $- \div + =$

5. The cost price of a set of 2 pants + 4 shirts or 1 pant + 6 shirts is ₹5,600. A shopkeeper decided to sell them separately. He sold 10 shirts for ₹6,000. Find the amount of profit or loss per shirt.
   - (a) Loss ₹ 100
   - (b) Profit ₹ 100
   - (c) Loss ₹ 1000
   - (d) Profit ₹ 1000

6. The escape velocity on the Earth's surface is about______.
   - (a) 11.2 km/sec
   - (b) 21.3 km/sec
   - (b) 13.8 km/sec
   - (d) 4.3 km/sec

7. ______, an Assamese wildlife biologist won the Royal Bank of Scotland (RBS) Earth Heroes Award 2016.
   - (a) Subrata Sharma
   - (b) Angoorlata Deka
   - (c) Purnima Devi Barman
   - (d) Aparajita Borkotoki

8. The difference between the selling prices of an item at a profit of 9% and 7% was ₹190. Find the cost price of the item.
   - (a) ₹ 9,500
   - (b) ₹ 9,200
   - (c) ₹ 9000
   - (d) ₹ 8,700

9. Train P starts from A at 10 am and runs at a constant speed of 60 kmph on a straight track and reaches B covering a distance of 360 km. Train Q starts from B at 11 am and runs towards A at a constant speed. It crosses train P at a distance of 120 km from B. What is the speed of train Q?
   - (a) 50 kmph
   - (b) 30 kmph
   - (c) 40 kmph
   - (d) 60 kmph

10. In a class of 135 students, the number of boys is twice that of girls. One-sixth of the boys and one-third of the girls failed in the final examination. Find the percentage of students who passed the examination.
   - (a) 75%
   - (b) 71.45%
   - (c) 77.78%
   - (d) 81.23%

11. Find the discount in percentage, if a book whose marked price is ₹ 90 is sold for ₹ 76.
   - (a) 14.75 %
   - (b) 13.45%
   - (c) 15.56%
   - (d) 14.65%

12. A Statement followed by some conclusions is given below.
   Statement : Adversity is the best teacher.
   Conclusions:
   I. Poor people are learned.
   II. Adversity provides opportunities to learn.
   Find which of the given conclusions logically follows from the given statement.
   - (a) Both I and II follow
   - (b) Only conclusion I follows
   - (c) Neither I nor II follows
   - (d) Only conclusion II follows

13. In which of the following countries did United Kingdom's rule formally end in the year 1986?
   - (a) Australia
   - (b) Sir Lanka
   - (c) Canada
   - (d) Maldives

14. The Nobel Peace Prize 2016 was awarded to :
   - (a) David J. Thouless
   - (b) Bob Dylan
   - (c) Bernard L. Feringa
   - (d) Juan Manuel Santos

15. Choose the one which is not similar to the others in the group given below:

Lizard, Crocodile, Reptile, Snake

(a) Lizard   (b) Crocodile

(c) Snake   (d) Reptile

16. RMSK : SLUI :: KMFZ : ?

(a) HKIB   (b) LIHB

(c) LHKX   (d) LLHX

17. Which of the following Vedas contains treatment for diseases?

(a) Sama   (b) Atharva

(c) Yajur   (d) Rig

18. The Home Rule Leagues set up in 1915-16 worked as auxiliary units of the ______.

(a) Indian National Congress

(b) Extremists

(c) Muslim League

(d) British Raj

19. How is X related to Y ?

Statement:

I. Y says. " I have only one brother

II. X say. "I have only one sister

(a) Only statements I sufficient.

(b) Only statements II sufficient.

(c) Either statements I or II

(d) Neither statements I, nor II

20. Find the increase in circumference of a circle of radius 14 cm, if the radius is increased by 7 cm $(\pi = \frac{22}{7})$

(a) 22 cm   (b) 66 cm

(c) 44 cm   (d) 88 cm

21. Which of the following sites was added to the list of UNESCO's World heritage sites in July 2016?

(a) Kaziranga Wildlife Sanctuary

(b) Khangchendzonga National Park, Sikkim

(c) Mahabodhi Temple Complex at Bodh Gaya

(d) Keibul Lamjao National Park, Manipur

22. Complete the analogy

Admiral : Indian Navy : : ? : Indian Air Force

(a) Flight Lieutenant

(b) Air Vice Marshal

(c) Air Chief Marshal

(d) Air Marshal

23. Antimatter particles corresponding to electrons are called ______.

(a) Protons   (b) Neutrons

(c) Positrons   (d) Antielectron

24. The sum of two positive integers is 42 and their difference is 4. Find their product.

(a) 376   (b) 402

(c) 416   (d) 437

25. 'RailWire' is related to :

(a) Railway broadband service

(b) Fencing of railway stations

(c) Brand name of a cable

(d) Railway electrification

DIRECTIONS (Qs. 26-29): *Read the following information and answer the following questions.*

The table contains the total number of students hired by IT companies I, II, III and the respective percentages of such hiring from colleges P, Q, R and S.

IT Company	No. of students hired	P (%)	Q (%)	R (%)	S (%)
I	1800	24	32	28	16
II	2400	27	30	25	18
III	1500	32	20	25	23

26. How many more students did all the three companies together hire from College P in comparison with College S?

(a) 510   (b) 495

(c) 535   (d) 480

27. What is the difference between the number of students hired by Company III from College P and that hired by Company I from College Q?

(a) 118   (b) 132

(c) 96   (d) 124

28. Find the difference between the number of students hired by Companies II and III from College R.

(a) 200   (b) 225

(c) 220   (d) 210

29. What is the total number of students hired by Company II from Colleges P, R and S?

(a) 1752   (b) 1968

(c) 1680   (d) 1800

30. What will be the next number in the series?

6, 25, 62, 123, 214, ?

(a) 334   (b) 292

(c) 317   (d) 341

31. Statements followed by some conclusions are given below:
 Statements :
 A. All men are mechanics.
 B. All mechanics are engineers.
 Conclusions:
 I. Some mechanics are men
 II. Some engineers are mechanics.
 Find which one of the given conclusions logically follows from the given statement.
 (a) Only conclusion I follows
 (b) Only conclusion II follows
 (c) Neither I nor II follows
 (d) Both I and II follow

32. Identify the professional Indian shooter from the following options.
 (a) Shivani Katariya   (b) Sudha Singh
 (c) Anjali Bhagwat   (d) Lalita Babar

33. A pre-independence era bunker was discovered in August 2016 at the Raj Bhavan in__________.
 (a) Tamil Nadu   (b) Arunachal Pradesh
 (c) Maharashtra   (d) Gujarat

34. The peripheral devices of a basic computer system does NOT include the:
 (a) Monitor   (b) CPU
 (c) Printer   (d) Keyboard

35. Which of the following international football stars belongs to Brazil?
 (a) Gabriel Batistuta   (b) Marcos Rojo
 (c) Neymar   (d) Lionel Messi

36. Find the area of a triangle whose sides are 5 cm, 12 cm and 13 cm.
 (a) 38 sq. cm   (b) 30 sq. cm
 (c) 42 sq. cm   (d) 46 sq. cm

37. GSAT-18 launched by India in October 2016, was essentially a________ satellite.
 (a) Earth observation   (b) Meteorological
 (c) Remote sensing   (d) Communication

38. **Fill up the blank with the most appropriate option below.**

 As mobile banking has come to stay, future financial transactions would be based on______
 (a) Wireless   (b) Graphics
 (c) Point of Sale   (d) Robotics

39. A is Q's sister. C is Q's mother. P is C's father, E is P's mother. How is Q related to P?
 (a) Grandson
 (b) Cannot be determined
 (c) Daughter
 (d) Granddaughter

40. ________ clicking on mouse selects the entire paragraph by default, while working with text document in Ms Word.
 (a) Triple   (b) Alt + Single
 (c) Single   (d) Double

41. If two-third of three-fifth of a number is 42, find one-third of that number.
 (a) 35   (b) 40
 (c) 45   (d) 30

42. 'Absolute zero' refers to__________.
 (a) minus 273°C   (b) minus 255°C
 (c) minus 295°C   (d) minus 300° C

43. The principle of gyroscope is NOT used in a __________.
 (a) Computer mouse   (b) Racing car
 (c) Inkjet printers   (d) Smart Phone

44. Pointing to a photograph a lady said, "he is the son of my grandfather's only son". How is the person in the photo related to the lady?
 (a) Father   (b) Son
 (c) Brother   (d) Grandfather

45. WWF stands for:
 (a) World Wildlife Fund
 (b) World Wildlife Federation
 (c) Web World Federation
 (d) World Web Federation

46. How many players are there in one Kho Kho team ?
 (a) 8   (b) 7
 (c) 9   (d) 11

47. Interchange two mathematical operators and balance the incorrect equation given below:
 $16 - 24 \times 2 \div 10 + 104 = 0$
 (a) + and ×   (b) − and +
 (c) ÷ and −   (d) ÷ and ×

48. Find out which of the following sets form co-prime numbers.
 (a) (12, 7)   (b) (21, 42)
 (c) (43, 129)   (d) (3, 9)

49. 8 boxes of a fruit were purchased for ₹ 9,600. 5 boxes were sold at a profit of 10% and 3 boxes were sold at a loss of 10%. What is the net gain in percentage?
 (a) 2.5%   (b) 2%
 (c) 2.75%   (d) 2.25%

50. If fire is called ice, ice is called sky, sky is called fire and water is called rain, then where do birds fly?

(a) Sky   (b) Air

(c) Water   (d) Fire

51. Human hypothalamus gland________.

(a) lies in the lower part of neck

(b) is attached to the wind pipe

(c) is present in the brain

(d) lies just below the stomach

52. Which of the following piece of literature was NOT written in Sanskrit?

(a) Meghdoot   (b) Ratnavali

(c) Rajatarangini   (d) Thirukkural

53. High tide : Sea :: ? : River

(a) Undercurrent   (b) Dam

(c) Bank   (d) Hydroelectricity

54. Which team won the Copa America 2016 Football Championship?

(a) Colombia   (b) Chile

(c) Argentina   (d) USA

55. Speed of a boat in still water is 12 kmph and that of the current is 3 kmph. A man rows a boat upstream up to 135 km and returns downstream to the starting point. Find the total time taken for the entire journey in hours.

(a) 24   (b) 48

(c) 36   (d) 30

56. Which of the following is the most appropriate description of INS Arihant?

(a) Indian Navy base   (b) Frigate

(c) Aircraft Carrier   (d) Submarine

57. ______ assumed charge as the Governor of the Reserve Bank of India in September 2016.

(a) Dr. A. Panagariya

(b) Dr. Rakesh Mohan

(c) Dr. Urjit R. Patel

(d) Dr. Raghuram Rajan

58. 10 men and 5 women can do a work in 60 days. If one man can do the work of two women, how long will 5 men and 20 women take to complete half of the work?

(a) 36   (b) 42

(c) 50   (d) 25

59. Rearrange the jumbled letters to make a meaningful English word and then select the word which is different from the rest.

(a) MIUNC   (b) LCIYHL

(c) HLTCO   (d) EVCOL

60. K and L can do a work in 15 and 20 days respectively. They work together for 5 days and leave. Calculate the unfinished portion of the work.

(a) $\dfrac{5}{12}$ (b) $\dfrac{1}{13}$

(c) $\dfrac{7}{12}$ (d) $\dfrac{1}{4}$

61. A person pays ₹ 8960 per month towards loan repayment which is 28% of his monthly salary. Calculate his monthly salary.

(a) ₹ 34,000   (b) ₹ 28,000

(c) ₹ 30, 000   (d) ₹ 32,000

62. The Rowlatt Act was passed in the year______.

(a) 1917   (b) 1915

(c) 1921   (d) 1919

DIRECTIONS (Qs. 63-64):

Yogesh is taller than Alpesh but shorter than Dharmesh. Suresh is shorter than Rajesh. Harish is not as tall as Alpesh. Ramesh is taller than Dharmesh but shorter than Suresh.

63. Height-wise, who is in the middle?

(a) Ramesh   (b) Dharmesh

(c) Yogesh   (d) Suresh

64. Who is the shortest of all?

(a) Ramesh   (b) Yogesh

(c) Harish   (d) Alpesh

65. Which of the following is NOT a characteristic of the 'wave'?

(a) Amplitude   (b) Wavelength

(c) Medium   (d) Frequency

66. 'Tropism' mostly refers to the:

(a) Longevity of animal species

(b) Directional growth of a plant

(c) Behavioural pattern of humans

(d) Bird migration

67. A question and three statements labeled (I), (II) and (III) are given. You have to decide which statement(s) is/are sufficient to answer the question.

Question : Find out the minimum number of nurses needed by the hospital

Statements:

I. There are three shifts round the clock.

II. There are thirteen wards requiring two nurses per shift.

III. The town needs at least three nurses per thousand population.

(a) Both statements I and II are sufficient.

(b) Both statements I and III are sufficient.

(c) Both statements II and III are sufficient.

(d) Only statement I is sufficient.

68. 'RailTel Corporation' is a__________ .

(a) Private Sector Enterprise

(b) Public Sector Undertaking

(c) Joint Sector Enterprise

(d) Partnership Firm

69. In April 2016, the National Green Tribunal suspended the environmental clearance given to the proposed hydropower project in Arunachal Pradesh to save the________ .

(a) Black-necked Cranes (b) Gayals

(c) Great Hornbills   (d) Medicinal Plants

70. 15 persons can complete a work in 60 days. If the number of persons is increased by 5, how many days earlier will the work get completed?

(a) 15 days   (b) 10 days

(c) 45 days   (d) 20 days

71. 'Leader of the House' in the context of Lok Sabha refers to______ .

(a) Leader of the Opposition

(b) Either the Prime minister or a Minister who is nominated by the Prime Minister

(c) The President of India

(d) Any designated member of the ruling party or coalition

72. Indian Railways network connects about______ stations.

(a) 10,000   (b) 8,000

(c) 12,000   (d) 14,000

73. __________lake is one of the largest fresh water lakes in Asia.

(a) Sambhar   (b) Vembanad

(c) Wular   (d) Chilika

74. Indra Nooyi, an Indian origin leader, is associated with___ .

(a) CocaCola   (b) Microsoft

(c) IBM   (d) PepsiCo

75. The amount of a simple interest on a deposit of ₹ 8,500 for 3 years is ₹ 2,040. Find the rate of interest per annum.

(a) 8.5%   (b) 9%

(c) 8%   (d) 7.5%

76. If & means '+', \$ means '−', # means '÷' and % means '×', then the value of 9 % 3 & 22 \$ 52 & 85 # 17.

(a) 5   (b) 8

(c) 2   (d) −3

77. HORSE : SERHO : : CURSE :

(a) SERCU   (b) ERCUS

(b) SECRU   (d) RCUES

78. **Statements:**

I. All the dogs are black.

II. All the cats are white.

Study the above statements and select the appropriate answer option based on them.

(a) No animal is black and white.

(b) No animal is brown.

(c) All the animals are either black or white.

(d) Some animals are black and some are white.

79. The speed of Car M is twice that of car W. If car M covers 120 km in 2 hrs & 30 mins, what is the speed of car W?

(a) 36 kmph   (b) 24 kmph

(c) 42 kmph   (d) 48 kmph

80. Which of the following activity is NOT allowed for Payment banks in India?

(a) Accepting deposit

(b) Offering remittance facility

(c) Distributing simple insurance products

(d) Lending money

81. Find the mode of the following data:

100, 120, 110, 90, 120, 140, 130, 120, 110, 100, 90, 140, 120, 100

(a) 100   (b) 140

(c) 120   (d) 90

82. On July 25, 2012, Shri Pranab Mukherjee assumed office as the________ th President of India.

(a) 13   (b) 11

(c) 12   (d) 14

83. Find the least number which should be added to 1456 so that is divisible by 6, 5 and 4 without leaving a remainder.

    (a) 61   (b) 6

    (c) 16   (d) 44

84. The famous Brihadeeswara Temple is located in_____.

    (a) Karnataka   (b) Kerala

    (c) Telangana   (d) Tamil Nadu

85. The minimum age limit prescribed for appointment as Governor of a State in India is—— years.

    (a) 30   (b) 40

    (c) 25   (d) 35

86. Total solar eclipse occurs when_______.

    (a) The Moon enters the Earth's shadow

    (b) The Sun Moon and Earth are in a direct line

    (c) The Sun, Moon and Earth are not exactly lined up

    (d) The moon is farthest from Earth

87. Find the value of k in $\dfrac{26}{21} : \dfrac{24}{9} :: k : \dfrac{14}{13}$

    (a) $\dfrac{1}{2}$ (b) 3

    (b) 2   (d) $\dfrac{1}{3}$

88. Which of the following Indian States does NOT share an international border?

    (a) Haryana   (b) Punjab

    (c) West Bengal   (d) Himachal Pradesh

DIRECTIONS (Qs. 89-90): *In a group of 85 persons, 45 read novels and 37 read poems and 8 do not read either novels or poems.*

89. Find the number of persons who read either novels or poems.

    (a) 53   (b) 82

    (c) 77   (d) 45

90. Find the number of persons who read both novels and poems.

    (a) 8   (b) 6

    (c) 5   (d) 7

91. Which one of the following islands does NOT belong to Lakshadweep?

    (a) Kavaratti   (b) Amini

    (c) Minicoy   (d) Neil

92. What is the cost price of a product, if the gain in selling it for ₹ 27,120 is 13%?

    (a) ₹ 24,000   (b) ₹ 24,600

    (c) ₹ 25,300   (d) ₹ 22,800

93. In July 2016, a Russian priest set a new record of flying solo in an air balloon around the World, in just over______ days.

    (a) 17   (b) 11

    (c) 15   (d) 13

94. The length of a rectangular board is 4 times that of its breadth. If the area of the board is 256 sq meters find its length.

    (a) 32 m   (b) 16 m

    (c) 8 m   (d) 24 m

95. _______is NOT a common bitmap-based file type extension.

    (a) PNG   (b) PCX

    (c) ODT   (d) TIFF

96. Arrange the numbers in descending order:

    $2\sqrt{11}, 4\sqrt{3}, 3\sqrt{5}, 5\sqrt{2}$

    (a) $4\sqrt{3}, 3\sqrt{5}, 2\sqrt{11}, 5\sqrt{2}$

    (b) $5\sqrt{2}, 4\sqrt{3}, 3\sqrt{5}, 2\sqrt{11}$

    (c) $2\sqrt{11}, 4\sqrt{3}, 3\sqrt{5}, 3\sqrt{2}$

    (d) $3\sqrt{5}, 4\sqrt{3}, 5\sqrt{2}, 5\sqrt{11}$

97. The monthly salaries of P and Q are in the ratio 4 : 3 If P and Q get an increase of 10% and 5% of their existing salaries respectively, what will be the new ratio?

    (a) 63 : 88   (b) 60 : 45

    (c) 45 : 60   (d) 87 : 63

98. Who was the Speaker of the first Lok Sabha?

    (a) Sardar Hukam Singh   (b) G. V. Mavalankar

    (c) M. N. Kaul   (d) M. A. Ayyangar

99. The river island Majuli which became "India's first and only island district" is located in_____.

    (a) Himachal Pradesh   (b) Jammu and Kashmir

    (c) Karnataka   (d) Assam

100. Complete the analogy with the most suitable option:
Rice : Carbohydrate :: Sprouts : ?
(a) Protein
(b) Water
(c) Fat
(d) Heat

101. Select the number which is different from the other numbers given below:
157, 571, 599, 387
(a) 571
(b) 157
(c) 387
(d) 599

102. K borrowed ₹ P at a compound interest of 20% p.a. for 2 years. Interest amount payable was ₹5,280. What was the value of P?
(a) ₹ 12,000
(b) ₹ 11,000
(c) ₹ 12,500
(d) ₹ 11,750

103. The value of which one of the following fractions falls in between $\dfrac{3}{5}$ and $\dfrac{7}{8}$?
(a) $\dfrac{6}{7}$
(b) $\dfrac{4}{7}$
(c) $\dfrac{8}{9}$
(d) $\dfrac{12}{13}$

104. 'Ponzi' scheme refers to the______ scam.
(a) Food grain
(b) Coal allocation
(c) Fodder
(d) Investment

105. Evaluate : $\dfrac{\sin 30}{\cos 45} \times \dfrac{\sin 45}{\cos 30}$
(a) $\dfrac{\sqrt{2}}{\sqrt{3}}$
(b) $\dfrac{1}{\sqrt{3}}$
(c) $\dfrac{2}{\sqrt{3}}$
(d) $\dfrac{1}{\sqrt{2}}$

106. Which of the following is NOT true with reference to a real number?
(a) A real number is unique
(b) All irrational numbers are real numbers
(c) All rational numbers are real numbers
(d) A real number need not necessarily be a point on the number line

107. Which one of the following is NOT a correct description of median?
(a) It is not affected by extreme values.
(b) It can be determined graphically.
(c) For odd number of values (n), median is (n+1)/2.
(d) It is based on all observations of data.

108. **Statement :**
Srinivas is a mathematician and hence, he cannot be a musician.
Which of the following would justify the above statement?
(a) Music and mathematics do not go together.
(b) No musician can become a mathematician.
(c) Majority of the mathematicians are not good musicians.
(d) Those who cannot appreciate music become mathematicians.

109. Sam is the husband of Rosy. Geni is the mother of Rita and Rosy. Vaz is the father of Rita. What is the relation of Vaz to Sam?
(a) Father-in-law
(b) Son
(c) Father
(d) Brother

110. Which of the following species is also called the 'Kashmir Deer'?
(a) Sangai
(b) Cheetal
(c) Hangul
(d) Barasingha

111. 111 Russian, 407 Chinese and 259 Japanese tourists have assembled at a place. Identical batches containing the same number of persons from each nationality has to be formed without leaving out anybody. Find the total number of persons in each batch.
(a) 21
(b) 14
(c) 10
(d) 18

112. According to experts, raging forest fires that took place in Uttarakhand recently have caused the formation of______.
(a) Black Carbon
(b) Sulphur
(c) Phosphorous
(d) Carbon Nanotubes

113. Indian Space Research Organization was formed in______.
(a) 1975
(b) 1962
(c) 1971
(d) 1969

114. If $(2a/m + b/n) = 2$ and $(a/m - b/n) = 4$, find the values of 'a' and 'b' respectively.
(a) $2m, -2n$
(b) $-2n, 2m$
(c) $2m, 2n$
(d) $-2m, 2n$

115. If p and q are in the ratio 4 : 3 and their LCM is 36, p + q = ?

(a) 21   (b) 18

(c) 24   (d) 12

116. If EAR = 24 and EYE = 35, then LEG = ?

(a) 25   (b) 23

(d) 24   (d) 22

117. The simple interest at 10% p.a. on a deposit for 2 years is ₹4,000. If the interest is compounded on an annual basis, how much more will be the amount of interest?

(a) ₹ 200   (b) ₹ 190

(c) ₹ 240   (d) ₹ 220

118. EIMQUY : CGKOSW :: BFJNRV: ?

(a) ZDHLPT   (b) CGKOSW

(c) DHLPTX   (d) AEIMQU

119. If TEACHER is coded as 8412745, CHEATER will be coded as:

(a) 2741845   (b) 2748145

(c) 2714845   (d) 2741485

120. Find the value of '?' in the following series.

6 : 30 :: 7 : ?

(a) 56   (b) 49

(c) 35   (d) 42

HINTS & EXPLANATIONS

1. (d) 2. (a)

3. (c) SI total $= SI_1 + SI_2$

$$= \frac{P_1 \times R \times T_1}{100} + \frac{P_2 \times R \times T_2}{100}$$

$$2400 = \frac{5000 \times R \times 4}{100} + \frac{4000 \times R \times 5}{100}$$

$2400 = 200R + 200R$

$2400 = 400R$

$R = \dfrac{2400}{400}$

$R = 6\%$

Option (c) is correct

4. (c) $14 = 9 \times 3 - 19 + 6$

$14 = 14$

Option (c) (is correct

5. (a) C.P. of 2 Pants + 4 Shirts $= 5600$ ...(1)

C.P. of 1 Pant + 6 Shirts $= 5600$ ...(2)

S P of 10 Shirt $= 6000$ ...(3)

In Equation (1)

2 Pants + 4 Shirts $= 5600$

So, 1 Pants + 2 Shirts $= \dfrac{5600}{2} = 2800$ ...(4)

Eqn.   (2) – Eqn. (4)

1 Pant + 6 Shirts $= 5600$

1 Pant + 2 Shirts $= 2800$

——————————————

C.P. of   4 Shirts $= 2800$

C.P. of   1 Shirt $= 700$

Then C.P. of 10 Shirts $= 7000$

and from Eqn. (3)

S.P. of 10 Shirts $= 6000$

Loss $=$ C.P – S.P.

$= 7000 - 6000$

$= ₹1000$

Loss for Shirts $= \dfrac{1000}{10}$

$= ₹100$

6. (a) 7. (c)

8. (a) Suppose C.P. $= x$

Than S.P. at 9% Profit $= x \times \dfrac{(100+9)}{100} = \dfrac{109x}{100}$ ...(1)

and

S.P. at 7% Profit $= x \times \dfrac{(100+7)}{100} = \dfrac{107x}{100}$ ...(2)

Eqn (1) – Eqn (2)

$$\frac{109x}{100} - \frac{107x}{100} = 190$$

$$\frac{2x}{100} = 190$$

$$x = \frac{190 \times 100}{2} = 9500$$

C.P. $= ₹\ 9500$

Option (a) is correct

9. (c) From 10 A.M. to 11 A.M.

For 1 Hour only

P travel

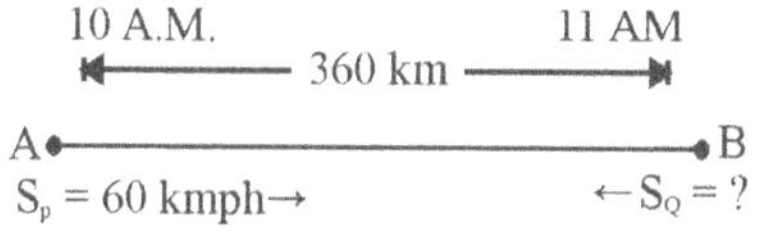

10 A.M.   11 AM
— 360 km —
A ————————————— B
S_p = 60 kmph→   ←S_Q = ?

After 1 Hour

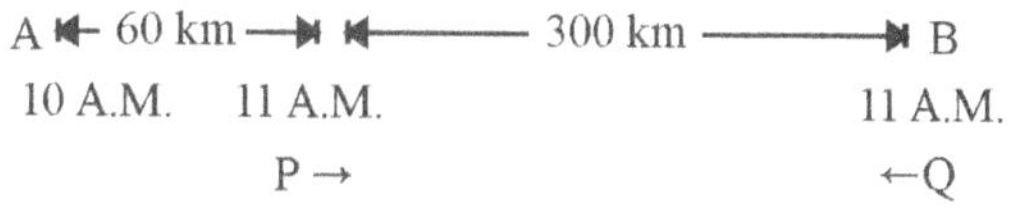

A ← 60 km → ← 300 km → B
10 A.M.   11 A.M.   11 A.M.
     P →   ←Q

So distance travel by
P in 1 Hour is
D $=$ S $\times$ T
$= 60 \times 1 = 60$ km

at 11 A.M. both P and Q start travelling in opposite direction. So relative speed

$$= S_P + S_Q = 60 + S_Q$$

The time at which both P & Q meets with each other is

$$T = \frac{300}{60 + S_Q}$$

Distance travel by Q in T hours is 120

Then,

$$\frac{300}{60 + S_Q} \times S_Q = 120$$

$$300\, S_Q = 120\,(60 + S_Q)$$

$$5S_Q = 2(60 + S_Q)$$

$$5S_Q = 120 + 2\, S_Q$$

$$3S_Q = 120$$

$$S_Q = 40 \text{ kmph.}$$

Speed of train Q is 40 kmph.

10. (c) Suppose number of boys $= B$

Number of girls $= a$

$$B + a = 135$$
$$B = 2a$$
$$\text{So } = B = 90$$
$$a = 45$$

Failed Student $= B \times \dfrac{1}{6} + a \times \dfrac{1}{3}$

$$= 90 \times \frac{1}{6} + 45 \times \frac{1}{3}$$

$$= 15 + 15$$

$$= 30$$

Passed students $= 135 - 30 = 105$

% of passed student $= \dfrac{105}{135} \times 100 = 77.78\%$

11. (c) % Discount $= \dfrac{M.P. - S.P.}{M.P.} \times 100$

$$= \frac{90 - 76}{90} \times 100$$

$$= \frac{14}{90} \times 100$$

$$= 15.56\%$$

12. (d) 13. (a) 14. (d) 15. (d)

16. (d)

R   M   S   K
$+1\downarrow$ $-1\downarrow$ $+2\downarrow$ $-2\downarrow$
S   L   U   I

K   M   F   Z
$+1\downarrow$ $-1\downarrow$ $+2\downarrow$ $-2\downarrow$
L   L   H   X

Option (d) is correct

17. (b) 18. (a)

19. (d) Neither I, nor II is sufficient. The statements in I and II do not provide any information regarding relation between x and y.

20. (c) Increased circumference

$$= 2\pi\,(14+7) - 2\pi 14$$

$$= 2\pi 7$$

$$= 2 \times \frac{22}{7} \times 7$$

$$= 44 \text{ cm.}$$

21. (b)

22. (c) Admiral is chief of Indian Navy same, as Air chief Marshal is the chief of Indian Air force

23. (c)

24. (d) Positive integers are X and Y

$$X + Y = 42 \qquad \ldots(1)$$

$$X - Y = 4 \qquad \ldots(2)$$

From Eqn. (1) & Eqn. (2)

$$X = 23$$

$$Y = 19$$

$$X\,.Y = 23 \times 19$$

25. (a) $\qquad = 437$

26. (b) Company (1) Hire From college P & S

$$P = \frac{1800 \times 24}{100} = 432$$

$$S = \frac{1800 \times 16}{100} = 288$$

Company (II) Hire From college P & S

$$P = \frac{2400 \times 27}{100} = 648$$

$$S = \frac{2400 \times 18}{100} = 432$$

Company (III)   Hire From college P &S

$$P = \frac{1500 \times 32}{100} = 480$$

$$S = \frac{1500 \times 23}{100} = 345$$

Number of Students Hire by all the Companies together from college P

$$432 + 648 + 480 = 1560$$

Number of Students Hire by all the Companies together from college S

$$= 288 + 432 + 345 = 1065$$

Than

Total 'P' – Total 'S'

$$= 1560 - 1065$$

$$= 495$$

27. (c) Difference between number of Students hired by Company III from college P and hired by Company I from college Q is

$$= \frac{1800 \times 32}{100} - \frac{1500 \times 32}{100}$$

$$= 3 \times 32$$

$$= 96$$

28. (b) Difference between the number of Students hired by Companies II and III from college R

$$\frac{2400 \times 25}{100} - \frac{1500 \times 25}{100}$$

$$= 24 \times 25 - 15 \times 25$$

$$= 9 \times 25$$

$$= 225.$$

29. (c) Total number of Students hired by company II from college P, R & S

$$= \frac{2400 \times 27}{100} + \frac{2400 \times 25}{100} + \frac{2400 \times 18}{100}$$

$$= 24 \times 27 + 24 \times 25 + 24 \times 18$$

$$= 24 \times 70 = 1680$$

30. (d)

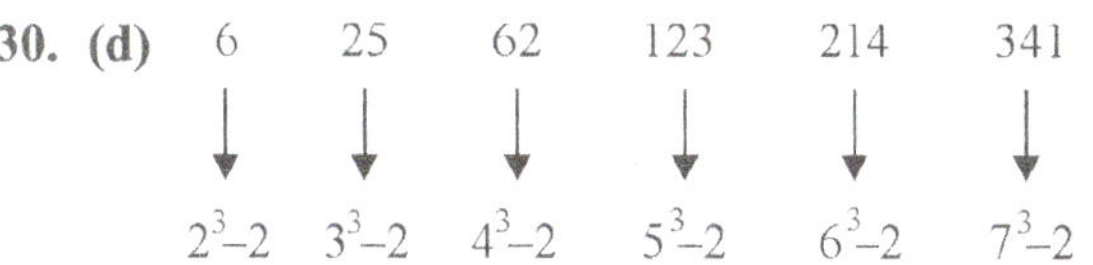

31. (d)

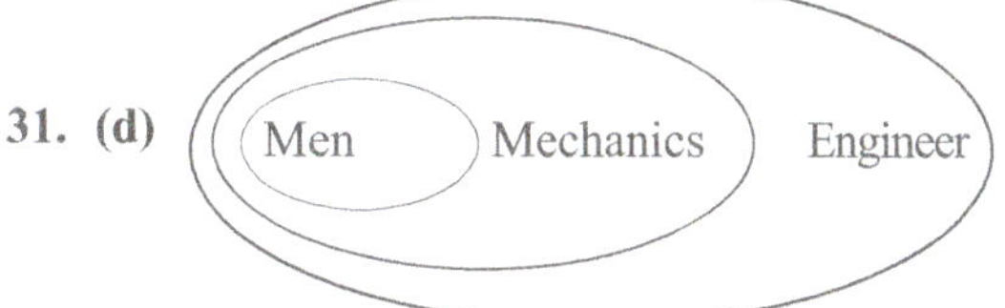

So some Mechanics are Men and Some engineer are Mechanics. Both follow.

32. (c) 33. (c)   34. (b) 35. (c)

36. (b)

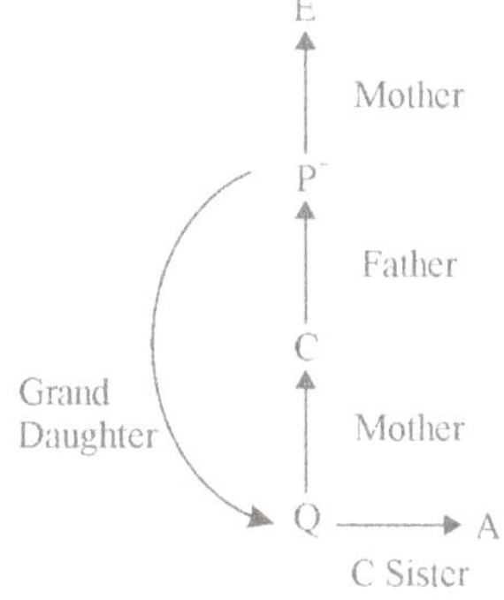

Area of $\Delta = \dfrac{1}{2} \times$ Base $\times$ Hight

$$= \frac{1}{2} \times 12 \times 5$$

$$= 30 \text{ Sq. cm.}$$

37. (d) 38. (a)

39. (b)

The gender of Q is unknown so we can not determine the relation between P and Q.

40. (a)

41. (a) Suppose the number is P
Than

$$\frac{2}{3} \times \frac{3}{5} \times P = 42$$

$$P= \frac{42 \times 15}{6}$$

$$P= 105$$

Than $\frac{1}{3} \times P$

$$= \frac{1}{3} \times 105$$

$$= 35$$

42. (a) 43. (c)

44. (c)

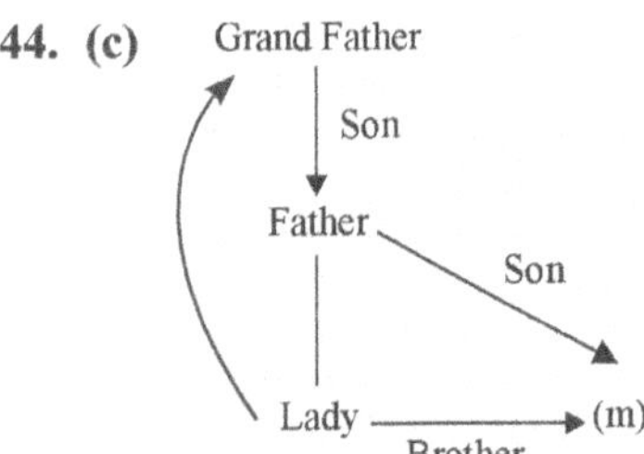

The person in the photograph is lady's Brother

45. (a) 46. (c)

47. (d) (After interchanging $\div$ and $\times$) $16 - 24 \div 2 \times 10 + 104$

$$= 16 - 12 \times 10 + 104$$

$$= 120 - 120$$

$$= 0$$

48. (a) Two Natural numbers are said to be co-primes if their HCF is 1.

(12, 7) are coprimes

49. (a) C.P. of 8 boxes of a fruit $=9600$

C.P. of 1 box of fruit $= \dfrac{9600}{8} = 1200$

S.P.. of 5 boxes of fruit with 10% of Profit

$$= 5 \times 1200 \times \frac{110}{100}$$

$$= 6600$$

S.P. of 3 boxes of fruit with 10% of losses

$$= \frac{3 \times 1200 \times 90}{100} = 3240$$

Total S.P. $= 6600 + 3240 = 9840$

$$\text{Profit \%} = \frac{9840 - 9600}{9600} \times 100$$

$$= 2.5\%$$

50. (d) Fire $\to$ Ice $\to$ Sky $\to$ **Fire** & water $\to$ Rain

Birds Fly in the Sky and Sky is fire so birds fly in the fire.

51. (c) 52. (d) 53. (a) 54. (b)

55. (a) Speed of boat in still water $S_B = 12$ kmph

Speed of current $\quad\quad S_C = 3$ kmph

Upstream speed $\quad = S_B - S_C = 12 - 3 = 9$ kmph

Down Stream speed $= S_B + S_C = 12 + 3 = 15$ kmph

Total time taken by the boat

$$= \frac{135}{9} + \frac{135}{15}$$

$$= 15 + 9$$

$$= 24 \text{ Hour}$$

56. (d) 57. (c)

58. (d)

$$\frac{P_1 \, T_1}{W_1} = \frac{P_2 \, T_2}{W_2}$$

$$\frac{(10m + 5w) \times 60}{W} = \frac{(5m + 20w) \times T}{W/2}$$

and $1m = 2w$

$$(10 \times 2w + 5w) \times 60 = \frac{(5 \times 2w + 20w) \times T}{1/2}$$

$$25w \times 60 = 30w \times T \times 2$$

$$T = \frac{25w \times 60}{30w \times 2}$$

$$T = \frac{50}{2} \text{ Days}$$

$$= 25 \text{ Days.}$$

59. (c)
$$\text{M I U N C} \quad \to \quad \text{C U M I N}$$
$$\text{L C I Y H L} \to \quad \text{C H I L L Y}$$
$$\text{H L T C O} \quad \to \quad \text{C L O T H}$$
$$\text{E V C O L} \quad \to \quad \text{C L O V E}$$

All are eatable except CLOTH.

60. (a)

	Total work	Efficiency
K $\to$ 15		$\dfrac{60}{15}$ = 4 Unit / Day
	60 (LCM)	
L $\to$ 20		$\dfrac{60}{20}$ = 3 Unit / Day

Work done by both in 5 days

$= (4+3) \times 5 = 35$ Unit

left work $60 - 35 = 25$ Units

Unfinished Portion $= \dfrac{25}{60}$

$= \dfrac{5}{12}$

61. (d) Monthly Salary $\times \dfrac{28}{100} = 8960$

Monthly Salary $= \dfrac{8960 \times 100}{28}$

$= ₹32,000$

62. (d)

Sol. (63-64):

Rajesh > Suresh > Ramesh > Dharmesh

1   2   3   4

> Yogesh > Alpesh > Harish

5   6   7

63 (b) Dharmesh is in the Middle

64. (c) Harish is Shortest of all

65. (c)   **66. (b)**

67. (a) Shift= 3

13 wards , 2 nurses per word per shift

Total nurses= $13 \times 2 \times 3$

$= 78$

Statement (I) and (II) are Sufficient.

68. (b)   **69. (a)**

70. (a) $P_1 T_1 = P_2 T_2$

$15 \times 60 = (15+5) \times T_2$

$T_2 = \dfrac{15 \times 60}{20}$

$T_2 = 45$ days

So the work complete in $(60 - 45) = 15$ days before

71. (b)   **72. (b)**   **73. (c)**   **74. (d)**

75. (c) $\text{SI} = \dfrac{R \times R \times T}{100}$

$2040 = \dfrac{8500 \times R \times 3}{100}$

$R = \dfrac{2040}{85 \times 3}$

$= 8\%$

76. (c) $9 \times 3 + 22 - 52 + 85 \div 17$

$= 27 - 30 + 5$

$= 2$

77. (a)

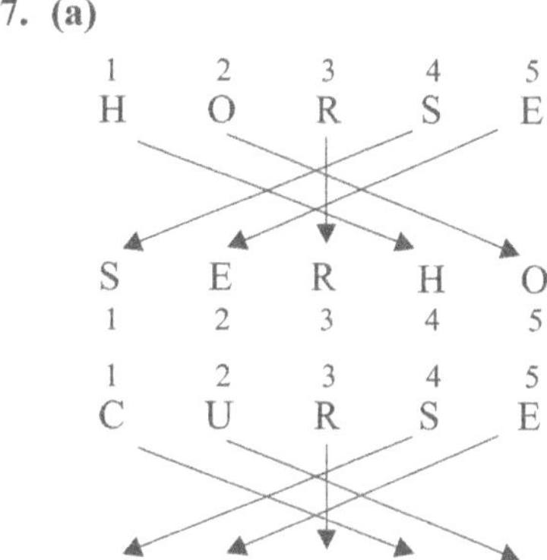

78. (d) Some animals are black and some are white follows

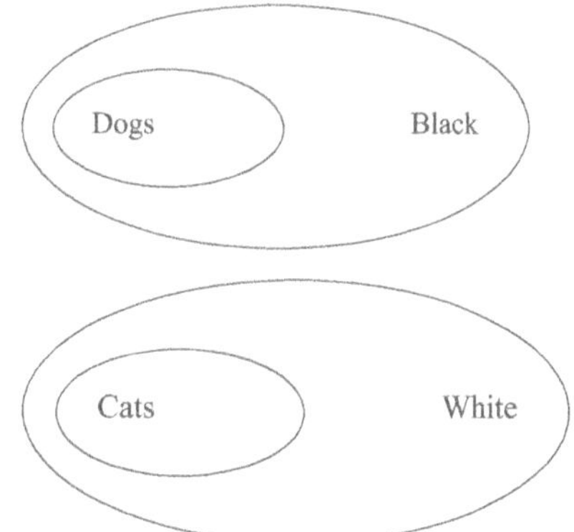

79. (b) Speed $= \dfrac{\text{Distance}}{\text{Time}}$

$\Rightarrow S_m = 2S_w$

$S_w = \dfrac{S_m}{2}$

$S_m = \dfrac{120}{2.5}$

$= 48$ kmph

$S_w = \dfrac{S_m}{2} = \dfrac{48}{2} = 24$

$S_w = 24$ kmph

Speed of w is 24 kmph.

80. (d)

81. (c) 90, 90, 100, 100, 100, 110, 110, 120, 120, 120, 120, 130, 140, 140

Mode is the most repetitive number so Mode is 120

82. (c)

83. (d) LCM of (6, 5, 4) = 60

$$60 \overline{)1456}(24$$
$$\underline{120}$$
$$256$$
$$\underline{240}$$
$$16$$

Number to be added $= (60 - 16) = 44$

84. (d)   **85. (d)**   **86. (b)**

87. (a) $\dfrac{26/21}{24/9} = \dfrac{k}{14/13}$

$$\frac{26}{21} \times \frac{9}{24} = k \times \frac{13}{14}$$

$$k = \frac{26}{21} \times \frac{9}{24} \times \frac{14}{13} = \frac{1}{2}$$

$$k = \frac{2}{3} \times \frac{9}{24} \times \frac{2}{1}$$

$$k = \frac{1}{2}$$

88. (a)

Sol. (89-90):

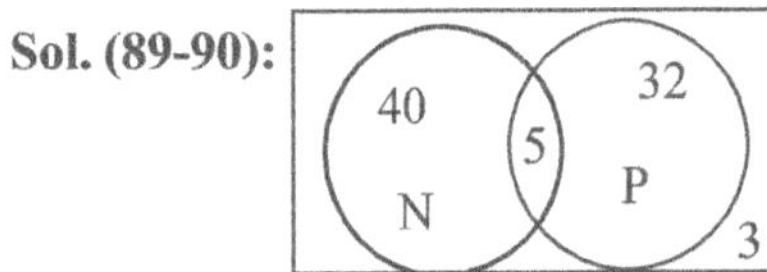

89. (c) Person who read either novel or poems
$= 40 + 32 = 77$

90. (c) Number of person who read both is x

Then, $45 + 37 + 8 - x = 85$

Then,

$x = 90 - 85$

$x = 5$

91. (d)

92. (a) $\text{S.P.} = \text{C.P.} \times \dfrac{113}{100}$

$$\text{C.P.} = \frac{100}{113} \times \text{S.P}$$

$$= \frac{100}{113} \times 27{,}120$$

$$= ₹24000$$

93. (b)

94. (a) Length $= L$

Breadth $= B$

given $L = 4B$

Area of Rectangular board

$= L \times B = 256$ Sq. meter.

$4B \times B = 256$

$$B^2 = \frac{256}{4} = 64$$

$B = 8m$, $L = 32m$

95. (c)

96. (b) $2\sqrt{11} = 6.633$

$4\sqrt{3} \quad = 6.928$

$3\sqrt{5} \quad = 6.708$

$5\sqrt{2} \quad = 7.071$

$$5\sqrt{2} > 4\sqrt{3} > 3\sqrt{5} > 2\sqrt{11}$$

97. (d) $\qquad\qquad$ P : Q

$\qquad\qquad\qquad$ 4 : 3

After increase $= \dfrac{4 \times 110}{100} : \dfrac{3 \times 105}{100}$

$\qquad\qquad = 440 \ : \ 315$

$\qquad\qquad\quad\; 88 \ : \ 63$

98. (b)   **99. (d)**   **100. (a)**

101. (c) All are prime number except 387.

387 is devisible by '3'

102. (a) $P + \text{C.I.} = P\left(1 + \dfrac{R}{100}\right)^2$

$$P + 5280 = P\left(1+\frac{20}{100}\right)^2$$

$$P + 5280 + 1 = P\left(\frac{120}{100}\right)^2$$

$$P + 5280 = \frac{144P}{100}$$

$$1.44P - P = 5280$$

$$0.44P = 5280$$

$$P = \frac{5280}{0.44}$$

$$= ₹12000$$

103.(a) $\frac{3}{5} = 0.6, \frac{7}{8} = 0.875$

$0.6 < x < 0.875$

(a) $\frac{6}{7} = 0.857$ (b) $\frac{8}{9} = 0.880$

(c) $\frac{4}{7} = 0.571$ (d) $\frac{12}{13} = 0.923$

Option (a) is lies between 0.6 and 0.875 correct.

104.(d)

105. (b) $\dfrac{\sin 30}{\cos 45} \times \dfrac{\sin 45}{\cos 30}$

$\tan 30° \tan 45°$

$= \dfrac{1}{\sqrt{3}} \times 1 = \dfrac{1}{\sqrt{3}}$

106. (d) 107. (d) 108. (a)

109. (a)

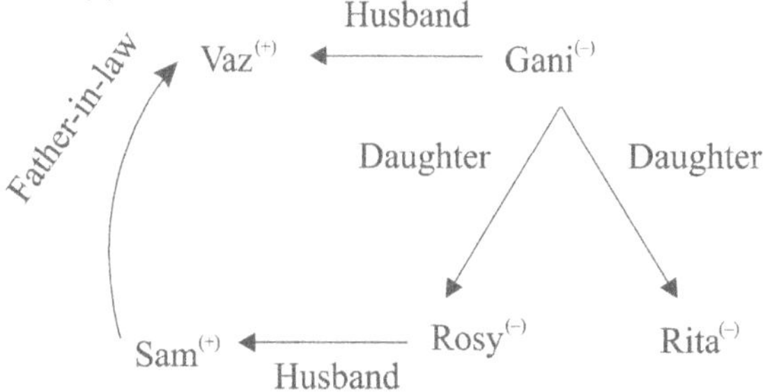

Vaz is Father-in-law of same

110.(a) Carbohydrate is found in Rice

Same as

Protein is found in Sprouts.

111.(a) Russian $\rightarrow$ $111 = 3 \times 37$

Chinese $\rightarrow$ $407 = 11 \times 37$

Japanese $\rightarrow$ $259 = 7 \times 37$

H C F $= 37$

37 batches

Total no. of Person in each batches

$= 3 + 11 + 7 = 21$

112.(a) 113.(d)

114.(a) $\dfrac{2a}{m} + \dfrac{b}{n} = 2$ ...(1)

$\dfrac{a}{m} - \dfrac{b}{n} = 4$ ...(4)

Equation (1) + Equation (2)

$\dfrac{3a}{m} = 6$

$a = 2m$

Putting the value of 'a' in equation (1)

$\dfrac{2 \times 2m}{m} + \dfrac{b}{n} = 2$

$4 + \dfrac{b}{n} = 6$

$b = n(2 - 4)$

$b = -2n$

Option 1. is correct.

$a = 2m$

$b = -2n$

115.(a) $p : q = 4 : 3$

$p = 4x$

$q = 3x$

$1 = LCM = 4 \times 3 \times x = 12x$

$12x = 36$

$x = 3$

$p + q = (4x + 3x)$

$= (4+3)\,x$

$= 7x$

$= 7 \times 3 = 21$

116. (c) E A R   E YE

$5 + 1 + 18 = 24$ $5 + 25 + 5 = 35$

L E G

$12 + 5 + 7 = 24$

117. (a) For 2 Jear

Short-trick

$$C1 \sim S1 = \frac{SI \times 2}{200}$$

$$C1 \sim S1 = \frac{4000 \times 10}{200}$$

$$= 200$$

C1 is 200 more than S1.

118. (a)

E	I	M	Q	U	Y
$-2\downarrow$	$-2\downarrow$	$-2\downarrow$	$-2\downarrow$	$-2\downarrow$	$-2\downarrow$
C	G	K	O	S	W

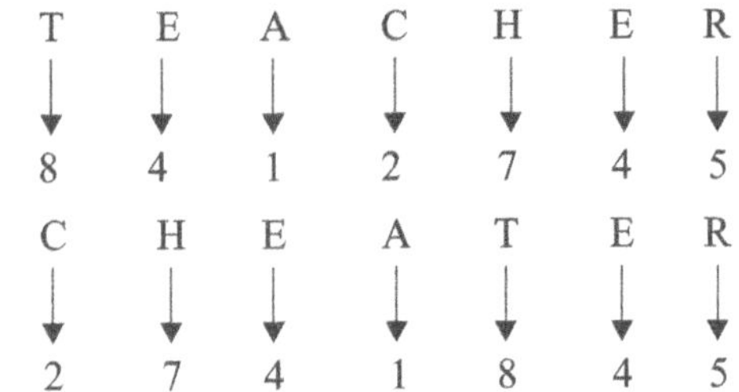

B	F	J	N	R	V
$-2\downarrow$	$-2\downarrow$	$-2\downarrow$	$-2\downarrow$	$-2\downarrow$	$-2\downarrow$
Z	D	H	L	P	T

119. (a)

T	E	A	C	H	E	R
↓	↓	↓	↓	↓	↓	↓
8	4	1	2	7	4	5
C	H	E	A	T	E	R
↓	↓	↓	↓	↓	↓	↓
2	7	4	1	8	4	5

Option (a) is correct

120. (d) $6 : 30 : : 7 : ?$

$6^2 - 6 = 36 - 6 = 30$

$7^2 - 7 = 49 - 7 = 42$

Option (d) is correct.

1. Find the mean of the distribution:
130, 90, 25, 77, 250, 100
   (a) 100   (b) 112
   (c) 25   (d) 77

2. B and C are husband and wife respectively. M is the father of K and C. How is B related to M?
   (a) Son-in-law   (b) Brother
   (c) Son   (d) Uncle

3. Who was sworn in as the Governor of Odisha on the 21st of March 2013?
   (a) Shri Ram Nath Kovind
   (b) Shri Keshari Nath Tripathi
   (c) Dr. S. C. Jamir
   (d) Shri Ram Naik

4. A father gives money to three of his sons, Ramu, Shamu and Dhamu, in the ratio 7 : 5 : 9 respectively. If Dhamu gets 120 more than Shamu, how much does Ramu get?
   (a) 210   (b) 420
   (c) 300   (d) 150

5. Which of the following contains the World's largest area of mangrove forests?
   (a) Rann of Kutch
   (b) Sundarbans
   (c) Balphakram National Park
   (d) Namdapha National Park

6. While editing a text document in MS Word, the combination keys used for copying and pasting text are respectively.
   (a) Ctrl + c, Ctrl + z   (b) Ctrl + c, Ctrl + v
   (c) Ctrl + v, Ctrl + c   (d) Ctrl + x, Ctrl + v

7. Find the mode of the following data:
110, 80, 70, 90, 120, 90, 80, 70, 60, 80
   (a) 120   (b) 110
   (c) 80   (d) 90

8. The maturity values of an amount in 5 and 6 years at 8% simple interest p.a. are ₹ 1120 and ₹1184 respectively. Find the amount.
   (a) 160   (b) 600
   (c) 560   (d) 800

9. The 'Kud dance' is a famous dance form of:
   (a) Rajasthan
   (b) Jammu & Kashmir
   (c) Odisha
   (d) Madhya Pradesh

10. The Buddhist shrine 'Temple of Tooth' is located in:
   (a) China   (b) Nepal
   (c) Malaysia   (d) Sri Lanka

11. X is the son of Z. Y is not a son of Z. K is Z's wife. X is the brother of Y. How is Y related to K?
   (a) Grandson   (b) Niece
   (c) Son   (d) Daughter

12. Tyndall effect is related to the_________of light.
   (a) Scattering   (b) Refraction
   (c) Dispersion   (d) Reflection

13. Prasar Bharati is an autonomous body that comprises:
   (a) Doordarshan only
   (b) AIR, Doordarshan and BSNL
   (c) AIR (All India Radio) only
   (d) Both AIR and Doordarshan

14. ? : Clock :: Temperature : Thermometer
   (a) Pendulum   (b) Wall
   (c) Analog   (d) Time

15. Find next two letters that follow in the series:
(A B B D E E E H I I I _ _ ......)
   (a) I I   (b) I J
   (c) J J   (d) I M

16. $30 \times 0.3 \times 0.03 \times 0.003 = ?$
   (a) 81×10^{-7} (b) 81×10^{-4}
   (c) 81×10^{-5} (d) 81×10^{-6}

17. 15 men can do a work in 20 days. How many days will 10 men take to do double the same work?

(a) 30   (b) 50

(c) 40   (d) 60

18. Car P covers certain distance in 11 hours at a speed of 66 kmph. Car Q covers 242 km more than car P in the same time. Find the average speed of car Q.

(a) 83 kmph\   (b) 88 kmph

(c) 718 kmph   (d) 77 kmph

19. _______________ soils are also known as 'regur'.

(a) Desert   (b) Alluvial

(c) Black   (d) Mountain

20. A worker's salary was increased by 30% so that his salary became Rs. 910. How much did he earn before the increase?

(a) 880   (b) 700

(c) 1300   (d) 810

21. Rearrange the jumbled letters to make a meaningful English word

(a) HISCYPS   (b) OLYGBOI

(c) AEVLTR   (d) YCEIHRTSM

22. Kabaddi is NOT the State game of _______________.

(a) Punjab   (b) Tamil Nadu

(c) Rajasthan   (d) Telangana

23. The idea of non-cooperation movement during freedom struggle did not envisage.

(a) the boycott of civil services

(b) the surrender of British titles

(c) popular violence

(d) the boycott of foreign goods

24. A chemical reaction is called _______ reaction when heat is given out.

(a) exothermic   (b) combination

(c) decomposition   (d) endothermic

25. A question and three statements labeled (I), (II) and (III) are given. You have to decide which statement(s) is/are sufficient to answer the question.

Question: Who is the shortest among P, Q, R, S and T?

Statements

I.   P is taller than T but shorter than S.

II.   Q is shorter than R but taller than T.

III.   S is taller than R and P is taller than Q.

Select the right option from the following.

(a) Only statement I is sufficient.

(b) Statement II and either I or III are sufficient.

(c) Only statement III is sufficient.

(d) Both I and III are sufficient.

26. The headquarters of the Indian Council of Agricultural Research (ICAR) is located at:

(a) New Delhi   (b) Bengaluru

(c) Dehradun   (d) Mumbai

27. Under the Railways dynamic fare pricing the fare component may _______ with the subsequent.

(a) decrease

(b) increase

(c) nay increase or decrease

(d) be scrapped

28. From the given options, find the rational number between the range $\frac{2}{4}$ and 0.6.

(a) $\frac{11}{4}$ (b) $\frac{3}{4}$

(c) $\frac{21}{40}$ (d) $\frac{11}{25}$

29. The Netaji Subhash National Institute of Sports is located in _______________

(a) New Delhi   (b) Dehradun

(c) Kolkata   (d) Patiala

30. 12 men or 24 boys can do a work in 20 days. In how many days, will 24 men and 12 boys together complete the same work?

(a) 8   (b) 10

(c) 15   (d) 12

31. _______________ is the "work done in moving a unit charge between two points in an electric circuit"

(a) Current

(b) Potential difference

(c) Power   (d) Resistance

DIRECTIONS (Qs. 32-35):

The following table represents the number of items sold by four divisions of a consumer goods dealer during 2010 to 2013.

Year	Division			
	W	X	Y	Z
2010	100	96	110	136
2011	130	134	114	108
2012	140	144	164	96
2013	86	112	76	80

32. During 2011which division performed better comparatively?
    (a) W   (b) Z
    (c) Y   (d) X

33. The combined sales figures in 2011 and 2013 of which division was the lowest?
    (a) X   (b) W
    (c) Z   (d) Y

34. What is the average number of items sold by division W during the four years?
    (a) 116.5   (b) 121.5
    (c) 114   (d) 118

35. What is the ratio of total number of items sold by Y in 2012 and 2013 to that of Z in the same period?
    (a) 11 : 16   (b) 11 : 15
    (c) 15 : 11   (d) 16 : 11

36. If TEMPORARY is written as RPMOAETRY then PERMANENT is
    (a) MNREAEPNT   (b) REANMEPNT
    (c) AMRNEEPNT   (d) NMRAEEPNT

37. Which of the following is NOT a threat to the tiger population in India?
    (a) Habitat Fragmentation
    (b) Reduction in available prey
    (c) Connecting Wildlife Corridors
    (d) Cattle Grazing

38. The name of the famous tigress of Ranthambore National Park, Rajasthan that died in August 2016, was______.
    (a) Sita   (b) Machali
    (c) Sundari   (d) Jhumroo

39. In the context of information technology, the process of examining large, pre-existing databases in order to generate new useful information is referred to as___________.
    (a) mining   (b) simulating
    (c) hewing   (d) resourcing

40. Classification of Public or Private sector is based on the :
    (a) Nature of activity
    (b) Service conditions of employees
    (c) Number of persons employed
    (d) Ownership

41. In economics, a very deep, long and painful recession is called_______________.
    (a) Depreciation   (b) Inflation
    (c) Deflation   (d) Depression

42. An assertion (A) and a reason (R) are given below.

    Assertion (A): Urban India is sicker than rural India in spite of better healthcare facilities.

    Reason (R): Urban life is facing the problems of increasing pollution levels, unhygienic garbage dumping, and a fast food culture

    Choose the correct option.
    (a) Both A and R are true and R is the correct explanation of A
    (b) A is false, but R is true
    (c) A is true, but R is false
    (d) Both A and R are true, but R is not the correct explanation of A

43. What is the fourth proportional to 15, 12, and 20.
    (a) 14   (b) 12
    (c) 16   (d) 18

44. The quorum to constitute a sitting of the Lok Sabha is____of the total number of members of the house.
    (a) One-sixth   (b) Two-thirds
    (c) One-tenth   (d) One-half

45. Complete the analogy.
    If D = 17, F = ?
    (a) 23   (b) 27
    (c) 37   (d) 33

46. Solve for 'a' : $\dfrac{7}{a-2} = \dfrac{5}{a+4}$

   (a) –38   (b) 19

   (c) –19   (d) 38

47. ____________ is the highest legislative body of India.

   (a) The Parliament

   (b) The Election Commission

   (c) The Supreme Court

   (d) The Cabinet of Ministers

48. International Tourist Bureau facility of Indian Railways is not available at________________.

   (a) Thiruvananthapuram

   (b) Secunderabad

   (c) Chennai

   (d) Bengaluru

49. Choose the most appropriate option from the following.

   GDP is the total value of________during a specific period.

   (a)   All the finished goods and services produced within a country

   (b)   All intermediate goods and services produced or sold

   (c)   Both intermediate and final goods and services produced within a country

   (d)   All goods and services produced or sold

50. Find the next term of the series:

   BDCA, FHGE, JLKI, ?

   (a) ONMP   (b) MNPO

   (c) NPOM   (d) MONP

51. The LCM of two numbers is 114 times their HCF. If the sum of LCM and HCF is 2300 and one of the numbers is 380, find the other number.

   (a) 190   (b) 140

   (c) 120   (d) 160

52. 'Biosphere Reserves' are most appropriately described as:

   (a) Learning sites for sustainable development

   (b) Sites affected by deforestation

   (c) Bio-gas production sites

   (d) Mineral deficient reserves

53. Which alphabet will replace the (*)?

   A, D, I, * , Y

   (a) T   (b) N

   (c) P   (d) L

54. If the mathematical operators –, +, × and ÷ are represented by G, P, U and S respectively, then find the value of

   48 S 8 P 7 U 2 G 21.

   (a) –1   (b) 20

   (c) –21   (d) 0

55. The Supreme Court of India came into being on

   (a) 15th of August, 1949

   (b) 26th of November, 1949

   (c) 28th of January, 1950

   (d) 26th of January, 1950

56. If cost price is 35% of the selling price, what is the profit margin in percentage?

   (a) 183.35%   (b) 187.51%

   (c) 181.75%   (d) 185.71%

57. What will be the next number in the following series?

   0, 7, 26, 63, 124, ?

   (a) 199   (b) 215

   (c) 187   (d) 147

58. 'Sahitya Akademi' is mainly dedicated to the promotion of:

   (a) Music   (b) Dance forms

   (c) Drama   (d) Literature

59. ___________ is an irrational number.

   (a) $\sqrt{9}$ (b) $\dfrac{11}{8}$

   (c) $\dfrac{2}{3}$ (d) $\sqrt{(2 \times 3)}$

60. Who among the following is NOT an international golfer?

   (a) Michael Bevan   (b) Jason Day

   (c) Anirban Lahiri   (d) ShivChawrasia

61. Silicon is a commonly used___________.

   (a) Insulator

   (b) Semi-conductor

   (c) Conductor

   (d) Amplifier

62. Two varieties of salt, T and S, costing Rs. 25 and Rs. 35 per kg respectively are mixed in the ratio of 4:6. The mixed variety is sold at Rs. 37 per kg. What is the approximate profit percentage?
(a) 25% (b) 38%
(c) 20% (d) 33%

DIRECTIONS (Qs.62-63): *Consider the following information and answer the questions based on it.*

In a building, 30 people drink only coffee, 40 drink only tea, 25 drink both tea and coffee, 20 drink both tea and milk and 15 drink all the three – tea, coffee and milk.

63. What is the difference between the number of people who drink tea and those who drink coffee?
(a) 30 (b) 10
(c) 70 (d) 40

64. The number of people who drink only coffee is________ than those who drink all the three (milk, tea and coffee).
(a) 15 more (b) 15 less
(c) 20 less (d) 5 more

65. ICR stands for
(a) Intelligent Character Recognition
(b) Institute for Cyber Research
(c) Information and Communication Reader
(d) Integrated Computer Research

66. Which of the following is NOT a cause of air pollution?
(a) Agricultural activities
(b) Burning of fossil fuels
(c) Acid rain
(d) Mining operations

67. Two buses X and Y leave from the same place and go in the same direction at speeds of 20 kmph and 50 kmph respectively. But Y leaves 6 hours after X has left. How far from the starting place will the buses meet?
(a) 100 km (b) 200 km
(c) 300 km (d) 150 km

68. After how many years, will Rs. 1,728 become Rs. 2,197 at $8\frac{1}{2}$% p.a. compound interest?
(a) 3 years (b) 2½ years
(c) 2 years (d) 1½ years

69. What will be the value of the expression if the signs '−' and '÷' are interchanged?
$38 - 2 + 1 \times 6 \div 6$
(a) 19 (b) 37
(c) 0 (d) 20

70. __________is the name of an Indian Light Combat Aircraft.
(a) Rudra (b) Chetak
(c) Tejas (d) Dhruv

71. The 'Rann Utsav' is a festival celebrated in:
(a) Gujarat
(b) Rajasthan
(c) Madhya Pradesh
(d) Himachal Pradesh

72. Workbook, in a computer application, is basically related to:
(a) MS Word
(b) MS PowerPoint
(c) Adobe Reader
(d) MS Excel

73. If $\dfrac{1}{43.21} = 0.02314$ then $\dfrac{1}{0.0004321} = ?$
(a) 23.14 (b) 231.14
(c) 0.0002314 (d) 2314

74. An article was purchased in a fluctuating market on different dates at a unit price of (i) Rs. 11, (ii) Rs. 9, (iii) Rs. 8 and (iv) Rs. 10. It was sold at Rs. 2 above the purchase price. Which article was the most profitable in percentage terms?
(a) (iv) (b) (i)
(c) (ii) (d) (iii)

75. 5, 20, 95, 470 ?
(a) 2245 (b) 2345
(c) 1860 (d) 2840

76. 'YouthSat' refers to a_________.
(a) Youth website (b) Satellite
(c) Motion picture (d) Weekend party

77. The number of boys in a bus at the starting point is twice the number of girls. On the way, when 15 boys got down and 10 girls entered the bus, the number of boys and girls became equal. How many boys were there at the start of the journey?
(a) 40 (b) 55
(c) 50 (d) 45

78. If HIJACK is coded as UVWNPX, then what is SPOON coded as:
(a) FCBBA   (b) GQPPO
(c) PSNNO   (d) EONNM

79. _________ is NOT a mode of heterotrophic nutrition.
(a) Saprotrophic   (b) Holozoic
(c) Automatic   (d) Parasitic

80. How much will Sangita get, if she deposits Rs. 37,000 at a simple rate of interest of 4.5% p.a. after two years?
(a) ₹ 3330   (b) ₹ 39960
(c) ₹ 40330   (d) ₹ 2960

81. The Government conferred Dronacharya Award 2016 for Gymnastics to:
(a) Raj Kumar Sharma
(b) Bishweshwar Nandi
(c) Sagar Mal Dhayal
(d) Nagapuri Ramesh

82. The process of splitting water molecule by light energy is called_________.
(a) Radiolysis   (b) Electrolysis
(c) Photolysis   (d) Thermolysis

83. The areas of two similar triangles are 121 sq. m and 64 sq. m. If the median of the 1st triangle $=12.1$ m, then the median of the 2nd triangle will be
(a) 6.4 m   (b) 8.4 m
(c) 8.8 m   (d) 9.2 m

84. Meera is the wife of Sachin. Sachin's sister is Sarda and she is the wife of Arjun. Arun is the son of Sarda. Arjun is the brother of Meera. Sonali is the daughter of Arjun. How is Arun related to Sonali?
(a) Brother   (b) Father
(c) Paternal uncle   (d) Cannot be determined

DIRECTIONS (Qs. 85-87): *Consider the following information and answer the questions based on it.*

Y is a housewife and her husband is an Inspector. Their sons J, a teacher and K, a banker are married to a nurse and teacher respectively. J's son P, an Inspector is married and has 2 sons. K's daughter Q, a software engineer is married and has two sons. All of them live in a joint family.

85. Q's grandmother is a_________.
(a) Nurse   (b) Housewife
(c) Teacher   (d) Banker

86. What is the male : female ratio?
(a) 4 : 8   (b) 8 : 4
(c) 9 : 5   (d) 1 : 1

87. Which of the following combinations is a couple, from the given information?
(a) Housewife – Banker
(b) Teacher – Teacher
(c) Teacher – Inspector
(d) Nurse – Teacher

88. Book : Author : : Movie :
(a) Editor   (b) Producer
(c) Director   (d) Master

89. Which one of the following names is NOT related to economic theory?
(a) John Maynard Keynes
(b) Niels Henrik David Bohr
(c) Thomas Robert Malthus
(d) David Ricardo

90. The 'Fountain of Wealth' is located in:
(a) Singapore   (b) Thailand
(c) Saudi Arabia   (d) London

91. A statement followed by some conclusions is given below.
Statement: Eating nutritious food is the only way to keep the doctor away.
Conclusions:
I. Doctors will be out of job soon.
II. Junk food is a main source of employment of doctors.
Find which of the given conclusions logically follows from the given statement.
(a) Only conclusion I follows
(b) Neither I nor II follows
(c) Only conclusion II follows
(d) Both I and II follow

92. A question and three statements labelled (I), (II) and (III) are given. You have to decide which statement(s) is/are sufficient to answer the question.

Question: What is 40% of a number?

Statements:

I. 25% of the number is 60 less than the number

II. 20% of the number is an even number.

III. 5% of twice the number is $\dfrac{1}{10^{th}}$ of the numbers.

Select the right option from the following:

(a) Statement II and either I or III are sufficient.

(b) Only III is sufficient.

(c) Only I is sufficient.

(d) Both II and III are sufficient.

93. Amjad Ali Khan is an Indian classical musician who plays the:

(a) Mandolin   (b) Tabla

(c) Sitar   (d) Sarod

94. Which one of the following options most appropriately describes ObamaCare?

(a) Cost of hospitalization

(b) Abolition of medical insurance

(c) Free medical care

(d) Affordable medical care

95. An article was sold for Rs. 2500 at a profit of 25%. What was the amount of profit?

(a) 250   (b) 2000

(c) 500   (d) 1000

96. Which of the following is different from the other three?

(a) Frog   (b) Crocodile

(c) Turtle   (d) Sea Horse

97. Which one of the following belongs to India's inter-planetary mission?

(a) Jugnu   (b) SARAL

(c) ANUSAT   (d) Mangalyaan

98. The ozone molecule is made up of________ atoms of oxygen.

(a) Six   (b) Three

(c) Four   (d) Five

99. A car covers a certain distance in 8 hours at a speed of 50 kmph. What should be the increase in speed to cover the same distance in 5 hours?

(a) 50 kmph   (b) 30 kmph

(c) 40 kmph   (d) 80 kmph

100. In the famous book, Hind Swaraj (1909), Mahatma Gandhi declared that the British rule in India was established:

(a) by using force

(b) by other foreign powers

(c) without the co-operation of Indians

(d) with the co-operation of Indians

101. In a certain code, if rat is called cat, cat is called bird, bird is called elephant, elephant is called fish and fish is called rat, then who can fly in the sky?

(a) Elephant   (b) Fish

(c) Cat   (d) Rat

102. The LCM of two numbers is 48. The numbers are in the ratio 1 : $\dfrac{2}{3}$. The sum of the numbers is________ .

(a) 40   (b) 60

(c) 20   (d) 45

103. Which one of the following operations will result in 26?

(a) $18 \times 16 \div 12 - 11 + 13$

(b) $18 \div 16 + 12 - 11 \times 13$

(c) $18 + 16 - 12 \times 11 \div 13$

(d) $18 - 16 \times 12 \div 11 + 13$

104. Find the area of a square whose diagonal is half of 12 cm.

(a) 64 sq. cm.   (b) 18 sq. cm.

(c) 72 sq. cm.   (d) 36 sq. cm.

105. An amount was invested at a simple rate of interest p.a. for 5 years. It would have fetched Rs. 300 more had it been invested at 2% higher rate. What was the amount invested?

(a) Rs. 2300   (b) Rs. 2000

(c) Rs. 3300   (d) Rs. 3000

106. What is $\dfrac{7}{8}$ th of 60% of 80?

(a) 48   (b) 28

(c) 56   (d) 42

107. Japan's 'Fukuoka prize-2016' for outstanding contribution towards South Asian traditional fusion music was:

(a) Shankar Mahadevan

(b) Yasmeen Lari

(c) A.R. Rahman

(d) Amit Trivedi

108. If $\cos\theta = \dfrac{4}{5}$, $\sec\theta + \tan\theta = ?$
   (a) 2   (b) 4
   (c) 3   (d) 1

109. World Sparrow Day is observed every year, on March 20 to:
   (a) Commemorate the birthday of Dr. Salim Ali
   (b) Increase awareness for conservation of sparrows
   (c) Celebrate the increasing number of sparrows
   (d) Show superiority of sparrows over other birds

110. What will be the least number which when doubled, will be exactly divisible by 4, 6, 9, 12 and 14?
   (a) 504   (b) 63
   (c) 126   (d) 252

111. A wheel has a diameter of 84 cm. How many revolutions should it make to cover a distance of 792 m? $(\pi = \dfrac{22}{7})$
   (a) 312   (b) 298
   (c) 256   (d) 300

112. Rekha reads 15 pages in 25 minutes. How many pages will she complete in 45 minutes?
   (a) 35   (b) 27
   (c) 30   (d) 25

113. A person is called *computer literate* if he/she is just able to:
   (a) Hack other computers
   (b) Write programs
   (c) Create anti-virus software
   (d) Run need-based applications

114. P is 4 times faster than Q in doing a job. Q takes 27 more days than P to finish the job. If they work together, in how many days will the work be finished?
   (a) $7\dfrac{1}{5}$ days   (b) $7\dfrac{2}{5}$ days
   (c) $7\dfrac{3}{5}$ days   (d) $6\dfrac{4}{5}$ days

115. A statement followed by some conclusions is given below

Statement: ABC Tuitions promise excellent teaching by excellent teachers for sure success.

Conclusions:

I. Their promise downgrades other tuition classes.

II. No candidate has been unsuccessful so far.

Find which of the given conclusions logically follows from the given statement
   (a) Only conclusion II follows
   (b) Only conclusion I follows
   (c) Neither I nor II follows
   (d) Both I and II follow

116. The contraction and expansion of the walls of food pipe is called________movement.
   (a) Peristaltic   (b) Oscillatory
   (c) Gastric   (d) Diastolic

117. ______________is a semi-luxury tourist train.
   (a) Golden Chariot
   (b) Royal Rajasthan on Wheels
   (c) Desert Circuit
   (d) Deccan Odyssey

118. 250 grams of a sweet has 20 grams of cashew and 30 grams of almonds. How many grams of cashew and almonds, respectively, will be there in 350 grams of the same sweet?
   (a) 40 and 60   (b) 25 and 45
   (c) 21 and 28   (d) 28 and 42

119. An Assertion (A) and a reason (R) are given below.

Assertion (A): The sale of mobile phones has increased manifold in recent times.

Reason (R): The craze for e-commerce drives mobile sales.

Choose the correct option.
   (a) Both A and R are true and R is the correct explanation of A
   (b) A is true, but R is false
   (c) A is false, but R is true
   (d) Both A and R are true, but R is not the correct explanation of A

120. Which number will replace (?) in the following series?
   4, 5, 8, 10, 12, 15, 16, 20, ?, 25, ...
   (a) 20   (b) 24
   (c) 21   (d) 22

HINTS & EXPLANATIONS

1. (b) Mean of distribution $= \dfrac{\text{Sum of all terms}}{\text{no. of terms}}$

$$= \dfrac{130 + 90 + 25 + 77 + 250 + 100}{6} = 112$$

2. (a)

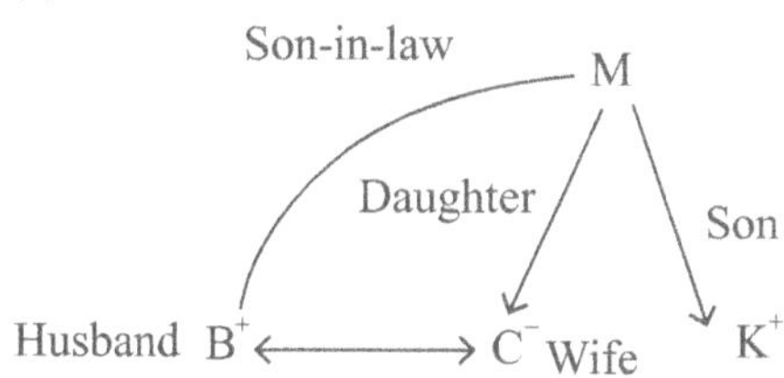

3. (c)

4. (a) Ramu : Shamu : Dhamu

$\quad\quad$ 7 $\quad$: $\quad$ 5 $\quad$: $\quad$ 9

$9x - 5x = 120$

$4x = 120$

$x = 30$

Ramu $= 7x = 7 \times 30 = 210$

5. (b) 6. (b)

7. (c) 60, 70, 70, 80, 80, 80, 90, 90, 110, 120

The Mode is the number that is repeated more often than any other so

Mode $= 80$

8. (d) For 5 years

$$1120 = P + \dfrac{P \times 8 \times 5}{100} \quad \dots(1)$$

For 6 years

$$1184 = P + \dfrac{P \times 8 \times 6}{100} \quad \dots(2)$$

Equation (2) $-$ Equation (1)

$$64 = \dfrac{P \times 8 \times 1}{100}$$

$$P = \dfrac{64 \times 100}{8}$$

$P = ₹\ 800$ Rs.

9. (b) 10. (d)

11. (d)

Husband $\quad\quad$ Wife

$Z^+ \longleftrightarrow K^-$

Daughter

$x^+ \longleftrightarrow y^-$

(Brother) $\quad\quad$ (Sister)

J is daughter of K

12. (a) 13. (d)

14. (d) 'Clock' Shows 'Time' same as 'Thermometer' Shows 'Temperature'.

15. (d) $A B B \underset{x}{\underline{C}} D E E E \underset{x}{\underline{FG}} H I I I I \underset{x}{\underline{JKL}} \underline{M}$

16. (d) $3.0 \times 3.0 \times 10^{-1} \times 3.0 \times 10^{-2} \times 3.0 \times 10^{-3}$

81×10^{-6}

17. (d) $\dfrac{P_1 T_1}{w_1} = \dfrac{P_2 T_2}{w_2}$

$$= \dfrac{15 \times 20}{w} = \dfrac{10 \times T_2}{2w}$$

$$= T_2 = \dfrac{15 \times 20 \times 2}{10} = 60 \text{ Days}$$

18. (b) Distance = Speed × Time

$= 66 \times 11$

$= 726$ km

For car Q

Distance $= 726 + 242 = 968$

Spread of car Q $= \dfrac{\text{Distance}}{\text{Time}}$

$$= \dfrac{968}{11} = 88 \text{ kmph}$$

19. (c)

20. (b) Suppose worker earn before is increas $= P$

$$P \times \dfrac{(100 + 30)}{100} = 910$$

$$P = \dfrac{910 \times 100}{130}$$

$P = ₹700$

21. **(c)** HISCYPS → PHYSICS → Subject

OLYGBOI → BIOLOGY → Subject

AEVLTR → TRAVEL

YCHEIHRTSM→CHEMISTRY→ Subject

All are subject except TRAVEL

22. **(c)**   **23.** **(c)**   **24.** **(a)**

25. **(b)** From statement (I) & (II)

$S > P > R > Q > T$

From statement (II) & (III)

$S > R > P > Q > T$

26. **(a)**   **27.** **(b)**

28. **(c)** $\dfrac{2}{4} < x < 0.6$

$0.5 < x < 0.6$

$\dfrac{11}{4} = 2.75$

$\dfrac{3}{4} = 0.75$

$\dfrac{21}{40} = 0.525$ $x = 0.525$

$\dfrac{11}{25} = 0.44$

29. **(d)**

30. **(a)** Short- Tricks
AND- OR Relation
For such type a problem we can use a short-
Trick i.e

$\dfrac{AND}{OR} \Rightarrow$ AND term is in Numerator OR

terms in Denominator

$= \left(\dfrac{24\,Men}{12\,Men} + \dfrac{12\,Boys}{24\,Boys} \right) \times \dfrac{1}{20\,days}$

$= \left(2 + \dfrac{1}{2} \right) \times \dfrac{1}{20} = \dfrac{5}{2} \times \dfrac{1}{20} = \dfrac{1}{8}$

= 8 Days

31. **(b)**

Sol. **(32.- 35):**

32. **(d)** Performance of w in all 4 years is
w = 100 + 130 + 140 + 86 = 456

Similarly

x = 96 + 134 + 144 + 112 = 486

y = 110 + 114 + 164 + 76 = 464

z = 136 + 108 + 96 + 80 + 420

Performance of x is highest among all.

33. **(c)** Combination of sale in 2011 and 2013 For
w = 130 + 86 = 216]

x = 134 + 112 = 246

y = 114 + 76 = 190

z = 108 + 80 = 188

z has lowest value.

34. **(c)** Average number of items sold by division
w during the four years:

$= \dfrac{100+130+140+86}{4} = \dfrac{456}{4} = 114$

35. **(c)** Items sold by y in 2012 & 2013
y = 164 + 76 = 240

Items sold by z in 2012 & 2013   ______

z = 96 + 80 = 176

Ratio $= \dfrac{y}{z} = \dfrac{240}{176} = \dfrac{15}{11} = 15 : 11$

36. **(d)**

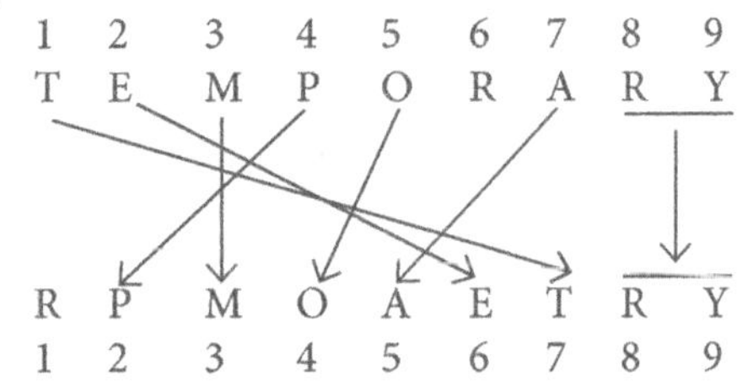

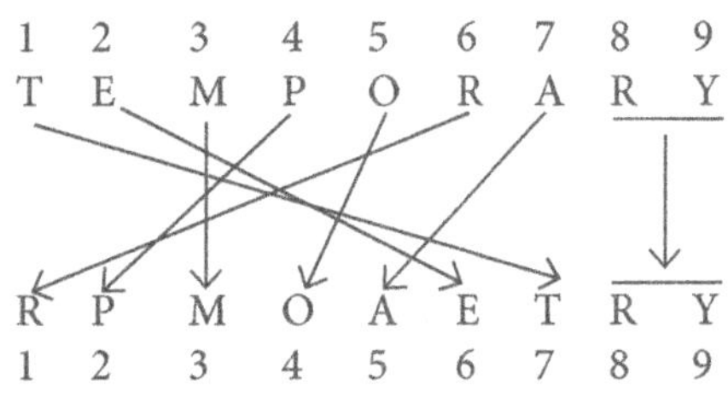

37. **(c)** **38.** **(b)** **39.** **(a)** **40.** **(d)** **41.** **(d)**

42. (a)

43. (c) $\dfrac{15}{12} = \dfrac{20}{x} =$

$x = \dfrac{20 \times 12}{15}$

$x = 16$

44. (c)

45. (c) $D = (4)^2 + 1 = 16 + 1 = 17$

$F = (6)^2 + 1 = 36 + 1 = 37$

46. (c) $\dfrac{7}{a-2} = \dfrac{5}{a+4}$

$\Rightarrow \quad 7(a + 4) = 5(a - 2)$

$\Rightarrow \quad 7a + 28 = 5a - 10$

$\Rightarrow \quad 7a - 5a = -28 - 10$

$2a = -38$

$a = \dfrac{-38}{2}$

$a = -19$

47. (a) 48. (a) 49. (a)

50. (c)

$$
\begin{array}{cccc}
B & D & C & A \\
+4\downarrow & +4\downarrow & +4\downarrow & +4\downarrow \\
F & H & G & E \\
+4\downarrow & +4\downarrow & +4\downarrow & +4\downarrow \\
J & L & K & I \\
+4\downarrow & +4\downarrow & +4\downarrow & +4\downarrow \\
N & P & O & M
\end{array}
$$

51. (c) Suppose HCF = x

LCM = 114x

LCM + HCF = 2300

114x + x = 2300

115x = 2300

$x = \dfrac{2300}{115}$

x = 20

LCM = 114 × 20 = 2280

Multiplications of numbers = LCM × HCF

$N_1 \times N_2 = $ LCM × HCF

$380 \, N_2 = 2280 \times 20$

$N_2 = \dfrac{2280 \times 20}{380}$

$N_2 = 120$

52. (a)

53. (c) A + 3 = D

D + 5 = I

I + 7 = P

P + 9 = y

54. (a) G → –

P → +

U → ×

S → ÷

$48 \div 8 + 7 \times 2 - 21$

$= 6 + 14 - 21$

$= -1$

55. (c)

56. (d) $C.P = \dfrac{35}{100} S.P$

$P\% = \dfrac{S.P - C.P}{C.P} \times 100$

$= \dfrac{S.P - \dfrac{35}{100} S.P}{\dfrac{35}{100} S.P} \times 100 = \dfrac{\dfrac{65}{100} S.P}{\dfrac{35}{100} S.P} \times 100$

$= \dfrac{65}{35} \times 100 = 185.71 \, \%$

57. (b) $1^3 - 1 = 0$

$2^3 - 1 = 8 - 1 = 7$

$3^3 - 1 = 27 - 1 = 26$

$4^3 - 1 = 64 - 1 = 63$

$5^3 - 1 = 125 - 1 = 124$

$6^3 - 1 = 216 - 1 = 215$

58. (d)

59. (d) $\sqrt{9} = 3$ Fixed No. $\rightarrow$ Rational Number

$\dfrac{11}{8} = 1.375$ Fixed no. $\rightarrow$ Rational Number

$\dfrac{2}{3} = 0.6667$ Fixed Repetitive number $\rightarrow$ Rational Number

$\sqrt{2 \times 3} = 4.89897948 \rightarrow$ non-Repetitive number after Decimal $\rightarrow$ Irrational Number

60. (a)   61. (b)

62. (c) $T : S = 4 : 6$

$T = 4x, \; S = 6x$

$C.P = 4x \times 25 + 6x \times 35 = 310x$

$S.P = (4x + 6x) \times 37 = 370x$

$$P\% = \dfrac{S.P - C.P}{C.P} \times 100$$

$$= \dfrac{370x - 310x}{310x} \times 100 = \dfrac{60}{310} \times 100$$

$$= 19.35 \simeq 20\%$$

63. (a) Only coffee = 30

only Tea = 40

Tea + Coffee = 25

Tea + Milk = 20

Tea + Coffee + Milk = 15

The number of people who drink tea

= 40 + 25 + 20 + 15

= 100

The number of people who drink coffee

= 30 + 25 + 15 = 70

Difference between the people those who drink tea and who drink coffee

= 100 – 70 = 30

64. (a) Number of people who drink only coffee than those who drink all three

= 30 – 15 = 15 More.

65. (a)   66. (c)

67. (b) $S_x = 20$ kmph

$S_y = 50$ kmph

In 6 hours distance travelled by x

= 20 × 6 = 120 km

After 6 hours bus y also start travelling, so there is a relative speed i.c.

$S_y - S_x = 50 - 20 = 30$ kmph

Time taken to cover the relative distance

$$= \dfrac{120}{30} = 4 \text{ Hour.}$$

Distance travel by x in these 4 hours

= 20 × 4 = 80

Total Distance = 120 + 80 = 200 km.

68. (a) $8\dfrac{1}{3} \Rightarrow \dfrac{25}{3}$

$$C.I. = P\left(1 + \dfrac{R}{100}\right)^n$$

$$2197 = 1728\left(1 + \dfrac{25/3}{100}\right)^n$$

$$\dfrac{2197}{1728} = \left(\dfrac{325}{300}\right)^n$$

$$\dfrac{2197}{1728} = \left(\dfrac{13}{12}\right)^n$$

$$\left(\dfrac{13}{12}\right)^3 = \left(\dfrac{13}{14}\right)^n = n = 3 \text{ years}$$

69. (a) $38 \div 2 + 1 \times 6 - 6$

= 19 + 6 – 6

= 19

70. (c)   71. (a)   72. (d)

73. (d) $\dfrac{1}{43.21} = 0.02314$

Multiple 10^5 in Both side

$$\dfrac{10^5}{43.21} = 0.02314 \times 10^5$$

$$\dfrac{1}{43.21 / 100000} = 2314$$

$$= \frac{1}{0.0004321} = 2314$$

74. (d) (i)   C.P. = 11, S.P = 13

$$P\% = \frac{S.P - C.P}{C.P} \times 100$$

$$\%P = \frac{2}{11} \times 100 = 18.18\%$$

(ii)   C.P = 9, S.P = 11, $\%P = \frac{2}{9} \times 10 = 22.22\%$

(iii)   C.P = 8, S.P = 10, $\%P = \frac{2}{8} \times 100 = 25\%$

(iv)   C.P = 10, S.P = 12, $\%P = \frac{2}{10} \times 100 = 20\%$

(iii)   Is most profitable.

75. (b)   5, 20, 95, 470, $\boxed{2345}$
      ×5–5 ×5–5 ×5–5 ×5–5

76. (b)

77. (c)   At starting Point Boys = 2 × Girls × I.C.
B = 2G on the way
Boys = B – 15
Girls = G + 10
B – 15 = G + 10
2G – 15 = G + 10
G = 25
B = 2G = 2 × 25 = 50

78. (a)

H	I	J	A	C	K
+13	+13	+13	+13	+13	+13
U	V	W	N	P	X

S	P	O	O	N
+13	+13	+13	+13	+13
F	C	B	B	A

79. (c)

80. (c) $SI = \dfrac{P \times R \times T}{100}$

$$= \frac{37000 \times 4.5 \times 2}{100} = 3330$$

Sangeeta get = 37000 + 3330 = 40330 Rs.

81. (b)   82. (c)

83. (c) $\dfrac{\text{Area of } \Delta 1}{\text{Area of } \Delta 2} = \dfrac{(\text{Median of } \Delta_1)^2}{(\text{Median of } \Delta_2)^2}$

$$\frac{121}{64} = \frac{(12.1)^2}{x^2}$$

$$x^2 = \frac{(12.1)^2 \times 64}{121}$$

$$x^2 = 77.44$$

$$x^2 = 8.8m$$

84. (a)

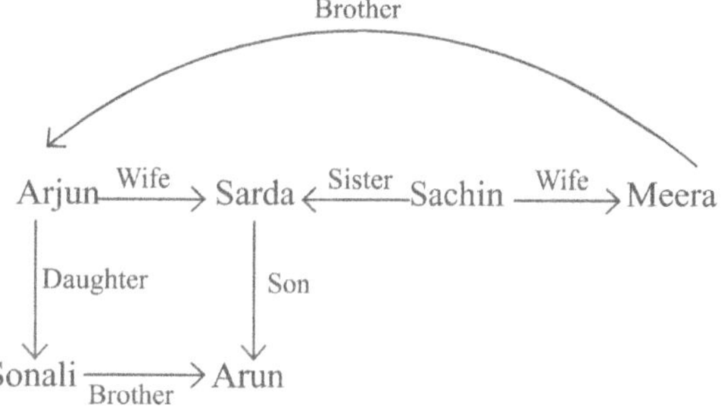

Arun is brother of Sonali

Sol. (85-87):

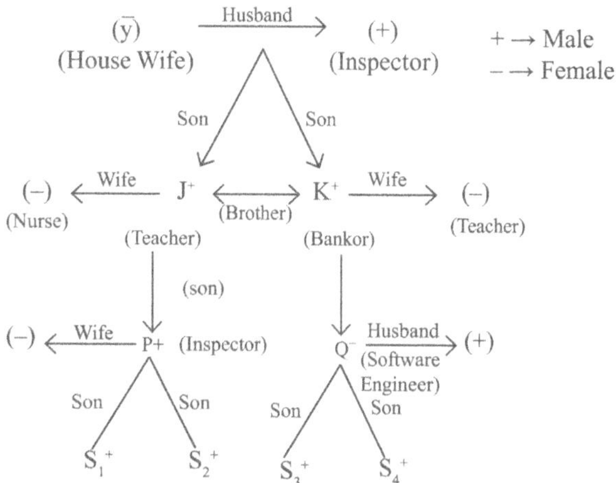

85. (b)   Q's grandmother is Y and she is a House wife.

86. (c)   Total number of Male = 9
Total number of Female = 5

Ratio $= 9 : 5$

87. (d) Nurse – Teacher

$(-) \xleftarrow{\text{Wife}} (\text{J})$

88. (c)   89. (b)   90. (a)   91. (b)

92. (d) $\dfrac{25 \times P}{100} + 60 = P$

$P - \dfrac{P}{4} = 4$

$P = 80$

93. (d)   94. (d)

95. (c) $S.P = C.P \times \left(\dfrac{100+25}{100}\right)$

$2500 = C.P \times \dfrac{125}{100}$

$C.P = \dfrac{2500 \times 100}{125}$

$C.P = 2000$

Profit $= S.P - C.P$

$= 2500 - 2000 = ₹500$

96. (d)   97. (d)   98. (b)

99. (b) $Speed = \dfrac{Distance}{Time}$

Initially $50 = \dfrac{D}{8}$

$D = 400$ km

To cover the same distance in 5 hours speed

required $S = \dfrac{400}{5} = 80$ kmph

increased speed $= 80 - 50 = 30$ kmph.

100. (d)

101. (a) Rat→ Cat→ Bird →(Elephant)→ Fish→ Rat

Bird can fly in the sky and it is called elephant So elephant is the answer.

102. (a) Number are in Ratio $= 1 : \dfrac{2}{3} = 3 : 2$

Suppose first number $N_1 = 3x$

Second number $N_2 = 2x$

LCM $= 3 \times 2 \times x$

and is

LCM $= 48$

$6x = 48$

$x = 8$

$N_1 = 3 \times 8 = 24$

$N_2 = 2 \times 8 = 16$

Sum of the number $= 24 + 16 = 40$

103. (a)
(a) $18 \times 16 \div 12 - 11 + 13 = 26$

(b) $18 \div 16 + 12 - 11 \times 13 = -129.875$

(c) $18 + 16 - 12 \times 11 \div 13 = 23.846$

(d) $18 - 16 \times 12 \div 11 + 13 = 13.545$

Option (a) is correct

104. (b) Digonal $d = \dfrac{12}{2} = 6$ cm

$AC^2 = AB^2 + BC^2$

$6^2 = a^2 + a^2$

$36 = 2a^2$

$a^2 = 18$

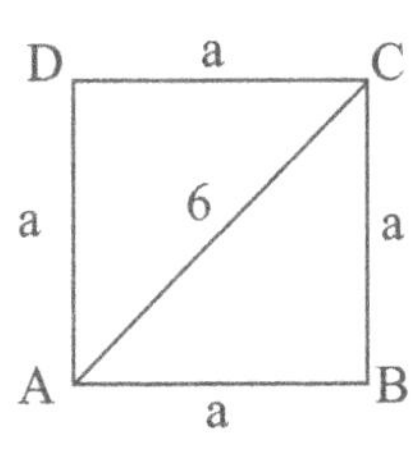

Area of square $= (Side)^2 = a^2 = 18$ sq. cm.

105. (d) When amount P is invested at R% for 5 years than

$SI_1 = \dfrac{P \times R \times 5}{100}$ ...(1)

When amount P is invested at 2% high rate than

$SI_2 = \dfrac{P \times (R+2) \times 5}{100}$ ...(2)

$SI_2 - SI_1 = 300 = \dfrac{P \times (R+2) \times 5}{100} - \dfrac{P \times R \times 5}{100}$

$$300 = \frac{P \times 2 \times 5}{100}$$

$$P = \frac{300 \times 100}{10}$$

$$P = ₹3000$$

106. (d) $\dfrac{7}{8} \times \dfrac{60}{100} \times 80$

$$= \frac{7}{8} \times \frac{60}{10} \times 8$$

$$= 42$$

107. (c)

108. (a) $\cos\theta = \dfrac{4}{5}$

$AC^2 = AB^2 + BD^2$

See

$AB^2 = AC^2 - BC^2$

$AB^2 = 5^2 - 4^2$

$AB^2 = 25 - 16$

$AB^2 = = 9$

$AB = 3$

$\sec\theta = \dfrac{5}{4}$

$\tan\theta = \dfrac{3}{4}$

$\sec\theta + \tan\theta = \dfrac{5}{4} + \dfrac{3}{4} = \dfrac{8}{4} = 2$

109. (b)

110. (c) LCM of $(4, 6, 9, 12, 14) = (2 \times 2 \times 3 \times 3 \times 7)$

$$= 252$$

$$\text{than} = \frac{252}{2} = 126$$

111. (d) Distance $= 792$ m $= 792 \times 100 = 79200$ cm

Diameter $= 2R = 84$ cm

Radious $= R = 42$

Distance cover By wheel in one revaluation

$= 2\pi R$

Number of Revaluation $= \dfrac{79200}{2\pi R}$

$$= \frac{79200 \times 7}{2 \times 22 \times 42}$$

$$= 300$$

112. (b) $\dfrac{P_1 T_1}{w_1} = \dfrac{P_2 T_2}{w_2}$

$P_1 = P_2 = $ Rekha.

$$\frac{T_1}{w_1} = \frac{T_2}{w_2}$$

$$= \frac{25}{15} = \frac{45}{w_2}$$

$$w_2 = \frac{45 \times 15}{25}$$

$w_2 = 27$

Rekha can read 27 pages

113. (d)

	P	:	Q
Efficiency	4	:	1

114. (a) Time   1 : 4

difference $= 4x - x = 27$

$3x = 27$

$x = 9$

P takes $= 9$ days

Q takes $= 9 \times 4 = 36$ day.

Time taken by both to complete the won

$$= \frac{P \times Q}{P + Q}$$

$$= \frac{9 \times 36}{9 + 36}$$

$$= \frac{9 \times 36}{45}$$

$$= \frac{36}{5}$$

$$= 7\frac{1}{5} \text{ days.}$$

115. (c)   **116. (a)**   **117. (c)**

118. (d) Sweet   Cashew Almond   Initially

250   20   30   (in grams)

Now   350

%   increase in sweet $= \dfrac{350-250}{250} \times 100$

$\dfrac{100}{250} \times 100 = 40\%$

With same % Cashew and Almonds also increase to make the Sweet 350 gm

cashew $= 20 \times \dfrac{(100+40)}{100}$

$= 20 \times \dfrac{140}{100}$

$= 28$ grams

Almonds, $= \dfrac{30 \times 140}{100} = 42$ grams

119. (b)

120. (a)

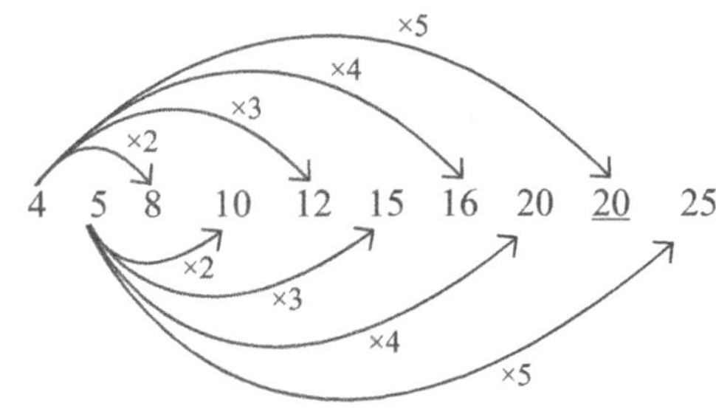

Answer is 20.

RRB NTPC STAGE-II SOLVED PAPER-3

Held On - 19th January 2017 (Shift-1)

1. Who among the following players was conferred the '2015 ICC Emerging Player of the Year' Award?
   - (a) Josh Hazlewood
   - (b) Joe Root
   - (c) Mohammed Shami
   - (d) Steve Smith

2. In which of the following states is the 'Losoong Festival' annually held?
   - (a) Nagaland
   - (b) Uttar Pradesh
   - (c) Uttarakhand
   - (d) Sikkim

3. Which of the following States hosted the 35th National Games in 2015?
   - (a) Kerala
   - (b) Andhra Pradesh
   - (c) Delhi
   - (d) Goa

4. Complete the Analogy :
   _____ : Foot :: Hand : Wrist
   - (a) Shoe
   - (b) Leg
   - (c) Ankle
   - (d) Length

5. Which of the following is NOT a Fundamental Duty as par the Constitution of India?
   - (a) to cherish and follow the noble ideals which inspired our national struggle for freedom
   - (b) to safeguard public property and to abjure violence
   - (c) to vote in public elections
   - (d) to value and preserve the rich heritage of our composite culture

6. Complete the Analogy :
   Speaker : Listener : : Film : _____
   - (a) Critic
   - (b) Viewer
   - (c) Broadcaster
   - (d) Actor

7. The Organisation for the Prohibition of Chemical Weapons (OPCW) is headquartered in _____
   - (a) Denmark
   - (b) Netherlands
   - (c) Sweden
   - (d) Switzerland

8. The order of the layers of the atmosphere from the earth's surface (moving away from the surface) is.
   - (a) Troposphere - Stratosphere - Mesosphere - Thermosphere
   - (b) Stratosphere - Troposphere - Mesosphere - Thermosphere
   - (c) Mesosphere - Troposphere - Stratosphere - Thermosphere
   - (d) Mesosphere - Stratosphere - Troposphere - Thermosphere

9. Simon Commission of 1927 was boycotted -
   - (a) to protest the arrest of Mahatma Gandhi
   - (b) an Indians were excluded from the Commission
   - (c) to protest the inclusion of Sir John Simon in the Commission
   - (d) to protest against the Jallianwala baug massacre

10. Elephants, Bears and Rhinos are examples of -
    - (a) Mammals
    - (b) Birds
    - (c) Reptiles
    - (d) Amphibians

11. Arun is the father of Chithra and Dinesh is the son of Bavana. Manish is Arun's brother. If Chithra is Dinesh's sister, how is Bavana related to Manish?
    - (a) sister-in-law
    - (b) mother-in-law
    - (c) daughter
    - (d) sister

12. The number of sides of a regular polygon whose exterior angles are each 10° is:
    - (a) 46
    - (b) 36
    - (c) 63
    - (d) 38

13. Dinesh is brother of Rakesh. Renu is sister of Ajith. Rakesh is son of Renu. How is Dinesh related to Renu?
    - (a) Father
    - (b) Brother
    - (c) Uncle
    - (d) Son

14. The Geneva II Conference was a United Nations-backed International peace conference on the future of _____
    - (a) Pakistan
    - (b) Iran
    - (c) Iraq
    - (d) Syria

15. In March 2016, which of the following biosphere reserve was included in UNESCO's World Network of Biosphere Reserves?
    (a) Nanda Devi Biosphere Reserve
    (b) Nilgiri Biosphere Reserve
    (c) Simlipal Biosphere Reserve
    (d) Agasthyamala Biosphere Reserve

16. How many gigabytes make a terabyte?
    (a) 128   (b) 16
    (c) 256   (d) 1024

17. What does UNHCR stand for?
    (a) United Nations Human Capital Research
    (b) United Nations Humanity Committee for Refugees
    (c) United Nations High Commissioner for Refugees
    (d) United Nations Humanity Commission for Refugees

18. If G = 7, EXCEL = 49, then ACCEPT = ——
    (a) 343   (b) 58
    (c) 49   (d) 48

19. As per the Railway Budget 2016, SMART coaches were proposed for more comfortable journeys. What does SMART stand for?
    (a) Specially Modified Aesthetic Refreshing Travel
    (b) Scientifically Modified Automatic Refreshing Travel
    (c) Scientifically Modified Aesthetic Refreshing Travel
    (d) Specially Modified Automatic Refreshing Travel

20. Find the fourth proportional to 12, 18, 20.
    (a) 30   (b) 40
    (c) 50   (d) 35

21. Find the similarity among the following dance forms.
    Kathak, Kathakali, Bharathanatyam, Madhubani
    (a) All these originated in North India
    (b) There is no similarity at all
    (c) All are South Indian dance forms
    (d) All are practiced by female artists only

22. The value of $\dfrac{3.24 \times 4}{0.2} = ?$
    (a) $\dfrac{324}{25}$ (b) $\dfrac{162}{5}$
    (c) $\dfrac{162}{25}$ (d) $\dfrac{324}{5}$

23. If the product of two numbers is 3360 and their LCM is 96, then their HCF is
    (a) 33   (b) 35
    (c) 34   (d) 29

24. Which of the following is true for a Car running at a constant acceleration on a uniform straight road?
    (a) Acceleration of the car is zero
    (b) Velocity of the car is constantly changing
    (c) Acceleration of the car is continuously changing
    (d) Velocity of the car is zero

25. In which of the following cases can Total Internal Reflection (when angle of incidence is greater than the critical angle) take place? When light travels from:
    (a) Glass to Diamond   (b) Air to Water
    (c) Air to Glass   (d) Diamond to Air

26. All irrational number are ______ numbers.
    (a) imaginary   (b) integers
    (c) real   (d) whole

27. In a class test, a student scored 21 marks out of 25 marks. The student's marks in percentage terms is:
    (a) 85   (b) 83
    (c) 84   (d) 86

28. The Meenakshi Temple is located in-
    (a) Tamil Nadu   (b) Rajasthan
    (c) Maharashtra   (d) Punjab

29. The *median* of the data 3, 3, 5, 7, 8, 8, 8, 9, 11, 12, 12 is:
    (a) 7   (b) 9
    (c) 12   (d) 8

30. Which of the following gases is also known as a 'Stranger' gas?
    (a) Argon   (b) Krypton
    (c) Xenon   (d) Neon

31. Arrange the given English words in alphabetical order and choose the one that comes first.
    (a) Quarter   (b) Quarry
    (c) Quarrel   (d) Qualify

32. A water tank has two holes. The 1st hole alone empties the tank in 8 minutes and 2nd hole alone empties the tank in 12 minutes. If water leaks out at a constant rate, how many minutes will it take, if both the holes together empty the tank?

(a) $\dfrac{4}{5}$ (b) $4\dfrac{4}{5}$

(c) $4\dfrac{3}{5}$ (d) $4\dfrac{2}{5}$

33. A telephone bill costs ₹35.50 for 3 minutes 20 seconds. What is the cost, in rupees, for 5 minutes 30 seconds? (Round up to one decimal).
   (a) 58.8   (b) 58.5
   (c) 58.7   (d) 58.6

34. Which of the following countries passed its first Anti-Terrorism law in December 2015?
   (a) Australia   (b) India
   (c) Syria   (d) China

35. A _____ is a piece of software code that can be applied after the software program has been installed, to correct an issue with that program.
   (a) Tutorial   (b) Version
   (c) Patch   (d) FAQ

36. Two numbers are in ratio 1 : 2 and their HCF is 16. Their LCM is:
   (a) 16   (b) 32
   (c) 60   (d) 23

37. In 1930, the first phase of the Civil Disobedience Movement, viz. The Salt Satyagraha, began with Mahatma Gandhi's marathon march from _____ .
   (a) Dandi   (b) Sabarmati
   (c) Bombay   (d) Delhi

Comprehension:
Study the following information carefully and answer the question given below it:
In a certain town, there are 5000 people. Out of them, 1200 do not subscribe for any newspaper, 2700 subscribe to 'The Indian Express' and 1800 subscribe to 'The Hindu'.

38. How many subscribe to 'The Indian Express' only?
   (a) 1800   (b) 1100
   (c) 2500   (d) 2000

Comprehension:
Study the following information carefully and answer the question given below it:
In a certain town, there are 5000 people. Out of them, 1200 do not subscribe for any newspaper, 2700 subscribe to 'The Indian Express' and 1800 subscribe to 'The Hindu'.

39. How many subscribe to both the newspapers?
   (a) 1000   (b) 500
   (c) 3800   (d) 700

40. In the Railway Budget 2016, which of the following was NOT mentioned as the pillars of strategy for Indian Railways?
   (a) Nav Sanrachna   (b) Nav Arjan
   (c) Nav Nirman   (d) Nav Manak

41. What is the highest denomination note ever printed by the RBI?
   (a) ₹ 1,00,000   (b) ₹ 10,000
   (c) ₹ 1,000   (d) ₹ 5,000

42. Mr. Prasad travelled equal distances at speeds of 2 km/hr., 4 km/hr., and 6 km/hr., and took a total of 55 minutes to complete. Find the total distance he travelled, in km.
   (a) 1   (b) 2
   (c) 3   (d) 4

43. The mean of the data 8, 0, 3, 3, 1, 7, 4, 1, 4, 4 is:
   (a) 3.5   (b) 3
   (c) 3.25   (d) 3.75

44. If $+$ means $\times$, $\div$ means $+$, $-$ means $\div$, $\times$ means $-$, then

$$\dfrac{(36 \times 4) - 8 \times 4}{4 + 8 \times 2 + 16 \div 1} = ?$$

   (a) 8   (b) 1
   (c) 4   (d) 0

45. A question and two statements labeled (I), (II) are given. You have to decide which statement(s) is/are sufficient to answer the question.
   In a code 'lee pin tee' means 'Always keep smiling'. What is the code for smiling?
   I. In the same code, 'tee lut lee' means 'Always keep left'.
   II. In the same code, 'dee pin' means 'Rose smiling'.
   (a) Both the statements together are needed.
   (b) Either I or II alone is sufficient.
   (c) Statement II alone is sufficient.
   (d) Statement I alone is sufficient.

46. By rearranging TUOONRD, what do you get?
   (a) Name of a train
   (b) Name of an animal
   (c) Name of a flower
   (d) Name of a river

47. Which one of the following has the largest population in a food chain?
    (a) Producers
    (b) Primary Consumers
    (c) Decomposers
    (d) Secondary Consumers

48. Pointing to an old man, Malini said, "His son is my son's maternal uncle". How is the old man related to Malini?
    (a) Grandfather   (b) Nephew
    (c) Brother   (d) Father

49. What is 15% of 75?
    (a) 11.75   (b) 11
    (c) 11.25   (d) 11.5

50. Mr. Rajesh is twice as good a worker as Mr. Vishal and together they finish a piece of work in 28 days. In how many days will Vishal alone finish the work?
    (a) 80   (b) 56
    (c) 112   (d) 84

51. The '2016 ExoMars Trace Gas Orbiter' is the first in a series of Mars missions to be undertaken jointly by the two space agencies. European Space Agency (ESA) and _____.
    (a) Roscosmos, Russia (b) ISRO, India
    (c) NASA, USA   (d) JAXA, Japan

52. In January 2016, _____ took charge as the India's ambassador to Thailand.
    (a) Pinak Ranjan Chakravarty
    (b) Anil Wadhwa
    (c) Bhagwant Singh Bishnoi
    (d) Harsh Vardhan Shringla

53. Given below is a statement followed by some conclusions. Decide which of the given conclusions logically follow(s) from the given statements.
    Statement:
    The best evidence of India's glorious past is the growing popularity of Ayurvedic medicines in the West.
    Conclusions:
    I. Ayurvedic medicines are not popular in India.
    II. Allopathic medicines are more popular in India.
    (a) Only conclusion II follows
    (b) Either I or II follows
    (c) Neither I nor II follow
    (d) Only conclusion I follows

54. Find the HCF of 1048 and 1441.
    (a) 131   (b) 113
    (c) 11   (d) 311

55. A question and two statements labeled (I), (II) are given. You have to decide which statement(s) is/are sufficient to answer the question.
    What is Rashmi's rank in the class?
    I. There are 25 students in the class.
    II. There are 8 students who have scored less than Rashmi.
    (a) Statement II alone is sufficient.
    (b) Both the statements together are needed.
    (c) Statement I alone is sufficient.
    (d) Either I or II alone is sufficient.

56. If PALE is coded as 5293, EARTH is coded as 32681, how is PEARL coded in that code?
    (a) 53269   (b) 53629
    (c) 53829   (d) 53289

57. In December 2015, who among the following was appointed as the new Chief Operating Officer (COO) of Apple Inc.?
    (a) Philip Schiller   (b) Tim Cook
    (c) Johny Srouji   (d) Jeff Williams

58. Kyoto Climate Change Conference took place in _____.
    (a) December 2000
    (b) December 2004
    (c) December 1994
    (d) December 1997

59. Complete the Analogy :
    When : Where : : Time :_____
    (a) Place   (b) Day
    (c) Money   (d) Watch

60. Fill in the blank:
    0, 2, 6, _____, 20, 30, 42
    (a) 10   (b) 6
    (c) 12   (d) 8

61. If > denotes +, < denotes −, + denotes ÷, # denotes ×, − denotes =, × denotes > and = denotes <, choose the correct statement from the following.
    (a) $9 < 7 + 7 = 6$
    (b) $7 \# 7 > 7 + 7 = 7 \# 7 > 1$
    (c) $7 > 7 < 7 + 7 = 14$
    (d) $9 + 9 > 9 = 9$

62. Which is the correct ascending order of the given numbers?

   (a) $\dfrac{2}{7}, \dfrac{4}{9}, 0.3$

   (b) $0.3, \dfrac{4}{9}, \dfrac{2}{7}$

   (c) $\dfrac{4}{9}, 0.3, \dfrac{2}{7}$

   (d) $\dfrac{2}{7}, 0.3, \dfrac{4}{9}$

63. The Andamans and Nicobars are separated by the _____, which is 150 km wide.
   (a) Ten Degree Channel
   (b) Kardiva Channel
   (c) Mozambique Channel
   (d) Nine Degree Channel

64. Anwesha Scheme which aims at providing quality education to SC and ST students was launched by the _____ government.
   (a) Uttar Pradesh   (b) Bihar
   (c) Maharashtra   (d) Odisha

65. Mohiniyattam is a classical dance form of _____.
   (a) Kerala   (b) Tamil Nadu
   (c) Maharashtra   (d) Rajasthan

66. Below are given statements followed by some conclusions. You have to take the given statements to be true even if they seem to be at variance with the commonly known facts and then decide which of the given conclusions logically follow(s) from the given statements.
   Statement:
   All caps are books. All books are pens.
   Conclusions:
   I.   Some caps are not pens.
   II. Some pens are caps.
   (a) Neither I nor II follows
   (b) Only conclusion I follows
   (c) Either I or II follows
   (d) Only conclusion II follows

67. A shopkeeper cheats to the extent of 15% while buying and selling fruits, by using tampered weights. His total gain, in percentage, is:
   (a) 32.25   (b) 32
   (c) 32.75   (d) 32.5

68. The volume (in cu.cm) of a right circular cylinder with radius 2 cm and height 2 cm is:

   (take $\pi = \dfrac{22}{7}$)

   (a) 176/7   (b) 176/21
   (c) 175/7   (d) 176

69. Compute: $10584 \div 168 - 63$

   (a) 0   (b) $\dfrac{540}{5}$

   (c) $\dfrac{504}{5}$ (d) 1

70. Below are given statements followed by some conclusions. You have to take the given statements to be true even if they seem to be at variance with the commonly known facts and then decide which of the given conclusions logically follow(s) from the given statements.
   Statement:
   Some ducks are birds. Some birds are cows.
   Conclusions:
   I.   Some ducks are cows.
   II. Some cows are ducks.
   (a) Neither I nor II follows
   (b) Only conclusion II follows
   (c) Either I or II follows
   (d) Only conclusion I follows

71. The surface area (in sq. cm) of a sphere with radius 2 cm is: (Take $\pi = \dfrac{22}{7}$)
   (a) 350/21   (b) 352/21
   (c) 350/7   (d) 352/7

72. 18 men built a ship model in 7 days. How many days would it take for 15 men?

   (a) 8.4   (b) $\dfrac{43}{5}$

   (c) 8.7   (d) 8.5

73. Jawahar Rozgar Yojana (JRY) was started with effect from _____.
   (a) April 1, 1977   (b) April 1, 1998
   (c) April 1, 1989   (d) April 1, 2012

74. INSAT-2E was launched from
   (a) French Guiana   (b) Peru
   (c) India   (d) Mayotte

75. Find the next term of the series:
   3F, 6G, 11I , 18L, _____.
   (a) 27N   (b) 27P
   (c) 25N   (d) 25P

76. Right to Education became a fundamental right in:
   (a) April 2010   (b) April 2004
   (c) April 2012   (d) April 2008

77. Ms. Revathi borrowed ₹ 600 at 6% per annum simple interest. What amount (in rupees) will she pay to clear her debt after 4 years?
   (a) 700   (b) 144
   (c) 150   (d) 744

78. Mr. Mahesh buys a toy for ₹ 25 and sells it for ₹ 30. Find the gain percentage.
   (a) 20%   (b) 25%
   (c) 21%   (d) 22%

79. Which of the following sports is Korada Ramana related to?
   (a) Archery   (b) Swimming
   (c) Football   (d) Weightlifting

80. Justice A P Shah Committee was setup to work on the dispute regarding Oil and Gas blocks in KG Basin between ONGC and _____ .
   (a) Hindustan Oil Exploration Company Ltd
   (b) Bharat Petroleum Corporation Ltd
   (c) Essar Oil
   (d) Reliance Industries Ltd

81. Almatti Dam is a hydroelectric project on the _____ river.
   (a) Krishna   (b) Yamuna
   (c) Godavari   (d) Kaveri

82. According to data from NASA's Cassini mission, a 'global ocean' lies beneath the icy crust of Saturn's moon named _____ .
   (a) Tethys   (b) Mimas
   (c) Enceladus   (d) Rhea

Comprehension:

Read the following information carefully and answer the questions given below it:

(i) Govind is shorter than Ashish but taller than Kamal.

(ii) Naren is shorter than Kamal.

(iii) Jeyanth is taller than Naren.

(iv) Ashish is taller than Jeyanth.

83. Who among them is the tallest?
   (a) Ashish   (b) Govind
   (c) Naren   (d) Jeyanth

84. Who among them is the shortest?
   (a) Naren   (b) Kamal
   (c) Ashish   (d) Govind

85. Which can be definitely deduced from the data?
   (a) Govind and Jeyanth are of same height.
   (b) Jeyanth is the 2nd tallest among the five.
   (c) Kamal and Jeyanth are of same height.
   (d) Kamal is shorter than Govind.

86. If Diamond is called Gold, Gold is called Silver, Silver is called Emerald and Emerald is called Ruby, which is the hardest substance?
   (a) Gold   (b) Silver
   (c) Emerald   (d) Ruby

87. Pranhita is the largest tributary of Godavari river conveying the combined waters of the Penganga river,__ river and the Wainganga river
   (a) Ulhas   (b) Wardha
   (c) Koyna   (d) Tapti

88. To determine the health of a water body, what is measured?
   (a) Dissolved Calcium
   (b) Dissolved Flourine
   (c) Dissolved Oxygen
   (d) Dissolved Methane

89. Given below is a statement followed by some conclusions. Decide which of the given conclusions logically follow(s) from the given statements.

Statement:

Industrial Revolution, which started in Europe first, has brought about the modern age.

Conclusions:

I. Disparity between rich and poor results in a revolution.

II. Revolution overhauls society.

   (a) Only conclusion II follows
   (b) Neither I nor II follow
   (c) Only conclusion I follows
   (d) Either I or II follows

90. Two buses start from a house at an interval of 5 minutes and move with a speed of 10 km/hr in the same direction. With how much speed

(km/hr) should a woman coming from the opposite direction towards the house travel, to meet the buses at an interval of 3 minutes?

(a) $6\frac{1}{3}$ (b) 6.5

(c) 6   (d) $6\frac{2}{3}$

91. Which of the following was India's first Lunar Mission?
(a) AVATAR   (b) ASTROSAT
(c) Aditya   (d) Chandrayaan-1

92. What will be the next number in the following series?

0, 2, 9, 28, 65, _____
(a) 126   (b) 125
(c) 81   (d) 256

93. Simplify: $(3y)^2 + x^2 - (2y)^2$
(a) $x^2 + y^2$ (b) $x^2 - y^2$
(c) $x^2 - 5y^2$ (d) $x^2 + 5y^2$

94. If $\sin x = \frac{4}{5}$, then $\sec x + \tan x = ?$

(a) 1/3   (b) 31/12
(c) 37/20   (d) 3

95. In December 2015, who among the following was appointed as the new CEO of Food Safety and Standards Authority of India (FSSAI)?
(a) Yudhvir Singh Malik
(b) Anil Kumar
(c) Pawan Kumar Agarwal
(d) Ashish Bahuguna

96. In 2014, the Reserve Bank of India (RBI) adopted the new _____ as the key measure of inflation.
(a) WPI (Wholesale Price Index)
(b) IPI (Import Price Index)
(c) PPI (Producer Price Index)
(d) CPI (Consumer Price Index, rural and urban, combined)

97. Saha Institute of Nuclear Physics is located in-
(a) Tamil Nadu   (b) Delhi
(c) West Bengal   (d) Maharashtra

98. If A denotes $\div$, B denotes $\times$, C denotes $+$ and D denotes $-$, then 18 B 12 A 4 C 5 D 6 = ——
(a) 53   (b) 63
(c) 56   (d) 36

99. There are total 200 students in a school, of which $\frac{2}{5}^{th}$ are boys. Find the number of girls in the school.
(a) 60   (b) 100
(c) 80   (d) 120

100. Mrs. Vijaya takes a total of 9 hours 50 minutes in walking a distance and running back to same place where she started. She could walk both ways in 12 hrs 20 minutes. The time taken by her to run both ways is:
(a) 7 hours 20 min   (b) 7 hours 35 min
(c) 7 hours 45 min   (d) 7 hours 15 min

101. Mr. Arun borrowed ₹ 6500 at 4% per annum compound interest. The compound interest compounded annually for 2 years is:
(a) ₹ 530.4   (b) ₹ 7300.4
(c) ₹ 7030.4   (d) ₹ 503.4

102. Find the odd one out:
(a) Goldsmith   (b) Carpenter
(c) Teacher   (d) Tailor

103. For a Computer, BIT stands for-
(a) Binary Integer Transfer
(b) Binary Task
(c) Built-in Integer
(d) Binary Digit

104. Divide ₹ 169 in the ratio 2 : 5 : 6. The rupees in the respective ratios are given by:
(a) 25, 67 & 78   (b) 26, 66 & 77
(c) 26, 65 & 78   (d) 26, 70 & 73

105. Correct expression of $2.\overline{56}$ = ? (the bar indicates repeating decimal)

(a) $2\frac{56}{100}$ (b) $2\frac{56}{1000}$

(c) $2\frac{56}{99}$ (d) $2\frac{560}{90}$

106. Which of the following is the first mammal species to be wiped out by human-induced climate change?
    (a) Bramble Cay melomys
    (b) Ursus maritimus
    (c) Panthera tigris
    (d) Panthera uncia

107. Which of the following is considered to be the largest volcano on Earth (in terms of its mass and footprint)?
    (a) Mauna Kea   (b) Ojos del Salado
    (c) Mount Vesuvius   (d) Tamu Massif

108. A woman invests ₹ 4000 at the start of each year at 5% compound interest per annum. How much will her investment be at the end of the 2nd year?
    (a) ₹ 8600   (b) ₹ 8615
    (c) ₹ 8610   (d) ₹ 8601

109. The House of the People (Lok Sabha) consists of not more than _____ members chosen by direct election only from territorial constituencies in the States.
    (a) 518   (b) 525
    (c) 530   (d) 550

110. A DVD is an example of-
    (a) Output device   (b) Hard disk
    (c) Optical disk   (d) Solid-state storage device

111. Mr. Manju sold a bus for ₹ 17,000 at a loss of 15%. At what price should the bus be sold to get a profit of 15%?
    (a) ₹ 23,500   (b) ₹ 24,500
    (c) ₹ 24,000   (d) ₹ 23,000

112. As envisaged in the Constitution of India, the Vice-President of India is elected by:
    (a) The President of India
    (b) The Prime Minister of India
    (c) The members of Rajya Sabha
    (d) The elected members of both Houses of the Parliament

Comprehension:

Following is a record of the performance of a football team for the seven tournaments played in a year.

Tournament	Matches Won	Matches Lost	Total matches played
First	5	3	8
Second	4	4	8
Third	5	2	7
Fourth	6	3	9
Fifth	4	2	6
Sixth	3	3	6
Seventh	2	4	6

113. Which tournament was the best for the team?
    (a) First   (b) Third
    (c) Fourth   (d) Fifth

Comprehension: Following is a record of the performance of a football team for the seven tournaments played in a year.

Tournament	Matches Won	Matches Lost	Total matches played
First	5	3	8
Second	4	4	8
Third	5	2	7
Fourth	6	3	9
Fifth	4	2	6
Sixth	3	3	6
Seventh	2	4	6

114. Which tournament was the worst for the team?
    (a) Seventh   (b) Second
    (c) Fifth   (d) Sixth

Following is a record of the performance of a football team for the seven tournaments played in a year.

Tournament	Matches Won	Matches Lost	Total matches played
First	5	3	8
Second	4	4	8
Third	5	2	7
Fourth	6	3	9
Fifth	4	2	6
Sixth	3	3	6
Seventh	2	4	6

115. What percent of the matches did the team win overall?

    (a) 58% (b) 75%
    (c) 52% (d) 80%

Comperhension : Following is a record of the performance of a football team for the seven tournaments played in a year.

Tournament	Matches Won	Matches Lost	Total matches played
First	5	3	8
Second	4	4	8
Third	5	2	7
Fourth	6	3	9
Fifth	4	2	6
Sixth	3	3	6
Seventh	2	4	6

116. How many matches did the team win during the year?

    (a) 21 (b) 50
    (c) 29 (d) 25

117. To avoid train accidents in the future, Minister of Railways, Suresh Prabhu launched which of the following?

    (a) Mission 'Rail Safety'
    (b) Mission 'Rail Efficiency'
    (c) Mission 'Unmanned Crossings'
    (d) Mission Zero Accident.

118. The cash difference between the selling price of an article at a profit of 4% and 8% is ₹ 3. The ratio of two selling prices is:

    (a) 26 : 27 (b) 25 : 27
    (c) 26 : 31 (d) 26 : 29

119. Find the next term of the series:

    (a) GEI (b) EIG
    (c) DBF (d) EGI

120. Mr. Sriram invested ₹ 14,000 in FD. How much will be get on maturity, if he invested it at 20% per annum compounded interest for 6 months, compounded quarterly?

    (a) 15,437 (b) 15,434
    (c) 15,435 (d) 15,436

HINTS & EXPLANATIONS

1. (a)
2. (d)
3. (a)
4. (b) Wrist is a part of hand. Similarly, foot is a part of leg.
5. (c)
6. (b) Listener listens to speaker. Similarly, viewer sees the film.
7. (b)
8. (a)
9. (b)
10. (a)
11. (a)

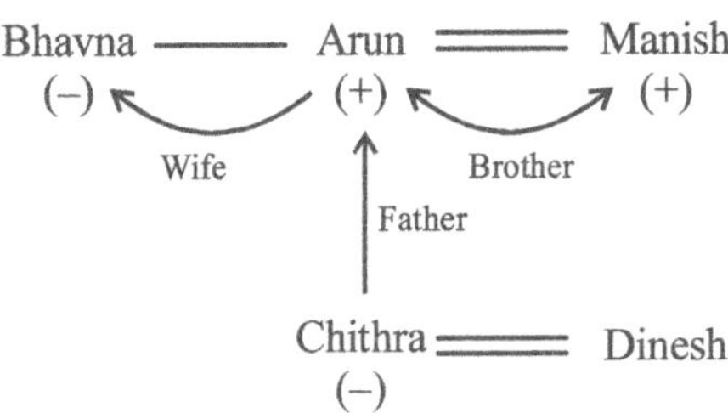

So, Bhavna is sister-in-law of Manish.

12. (b) Here,
exterior angle $= 10°$
$\therefore$ Number of sides of regular polygon
$= \dfrac{360°}{10°} = 36°$

13. (d)

So, Dinesh is son of Renu.

14. (d)
15. (d)
16. (d)
17. (c)
18. (d) Here, $G = 7$.
EXCEL $= 5 + 24 + 3 + 5 + 12 = 49$
Similarly, ACCEPT $= 1 + 3 + 3 + 5 + 16 + 20 = 48$.

19. (a)
20. (a) **Let fourth proportional is** x.
Then,
$12 : 18 :: 20 : x$

$\Rightarrow \dfrac{12}{18} = \dfrac{20}{x} \Rightarrow x = \dfrac{18 \times 20}{12} = 30$.

21. (b)
22. (d) $\dfrac{3.24 \times 4}{0.2} = \dfrac{324 \times 4}{20} = \dfrac{324}{5}$

23. (b) $\because$ Product of two numbers = Product of their HCF and LCM.

$\Rightarrow 3360 = 96 \times$ HCF

$\therefore$ HCF $= \dfrac{3360}{96} = 35$.

24. (b)
25. (d)
26. (c) All irrational numbers are real numbers.
27. (c) Required percentage $= \dfrac{21}{25} \times 100 = 84\%$.
28. (a)
29. (d) Median = the middle value of a set of ordered data.
Middle value $= 8$.
So, Median of the data $= 8$.

30. (c)
31. (d)
32. (b) First hole can empty a tank in 8 minutes.
Second hole can empty a tank in 12 minutes.

If both holes together empty the tank.

$$\Rightarrow \frac{1}{8} + \frac{1}{12} = \frac{3+2}{24} = \frac{5}{24}$$

$$\Rightarrow \frac{24}{5} \text{ min.} = 4\frac{4}{5} \text{ minutes.}$$

33. (d) 3 minutes 20 seconds = 200 seconds

∵ A telephone bill costs of 200 seconds = 35.50

∴ Costs of 5 minutes 30 seconds (5 minutes 30 seconds = 330 seconds)

$$= \frac{35.50}{200} \times 330 = 58.575 \approx 58.6.$$

34. (d)

35. (c)

36. (b) Let the numbers be 1 K and 2 K.

HCF of 1 and 2 = 1

Hence HCF of 1 K and 2 K = K

Given that HCF of 1 K and 2 K = 16

$$\Rightarrow K = 16$$

Hence the numbers are (1 × 16) and (2 × 16) = 16 and 32

∴ LCM of 16 and 32 = 32.

37. (b)

38. (d) Total subscribe to 'The Indian Express' only

$$= 3800 - 1800 = 2000.$$

39. (d) ∵ Total subscribe to 'The Indian Express' = 2700

Total subscribe to 'The Indian Express' only = 2000

∴ Total subscribe to both the news papers

$$= (2700 - 2000) = 700.$$

40. (c)

41. (b)

42. (c) Let distance = d

Speed = 2 km/hr, 4 km/hr, 6 km/hr

∴ Time $= \dfrac{\text{Distance}}{\text{Speed}}$

Time = 55 minute

According to question,

$$\frac{55}{60} = \frac{d}{2} + \frac{d}{4} + \frac{d}{6}$$

$$\Rightarrow \frac{55}{60} = \frac{6d + 3d + 2d}{12}$$

$$\Rightarrow \frac{55}{60} = \frac{11d}{12} \Rightarrow d = \frac{55}{60} \times \frac{12}{11} = 1 \text{ km}$$

∴ Total distance travelled by him = $3d$ = $3 \times 1 = 3$ km.

43. (a) Required mean value

$$= \frac{(8+0+3+3+1+7+4+1+4+4)}{10} = \frac{35}{10} = 3.5$$

44. (d) Here, $+ = \times, \div = +, - = \div, \times = -$

Then,

$$\frac{(36 - 4) + 8 - 4}{4 \times 8 - 2 \times 16 + 1} = \frac{\dfrac{32}{8} - 4}{32 - 31} = \frac{0}{1} = 0$$

45. (b) Statement-I :

$$\text{(lee)} \boxed{\text{Pin}} \text{(tee)} \rightarrow \text{(Always)} \boxed{\text{keep}} \boxed{\text{smiling}}$$

$$\boxed{\text{tee}} \text{ lut } \text{(lee)} \rightarrow \text{(Always)} \boxed{\text{keep}} \text{ left}$$

So, I statement is sufficient.

Statement-II :

$$\text{lee} \boxed{\text{Pin}} \text{ tee } \rightarrow \text{Always} \quad \text{keep} \boxed{\text{smiling}}$$

$$\text{tee} \boxed{\text{Pin}} \rightarrow \text{Rose} \boxed{\text{smiling}}$$

II statement is also sufficient.

So, either I or either II is sufficient.

46. (a)

$$\text{TUOONRD} \xrightarrow{\text{By rearranging}} \text{DURONTO}$$

DURONTO is a name of train.

47. (a)

48. (d)

49. (c) 15% of 75 = ?

$$\frac{75 \times 15}{100} = 11.25$$

50. (d) Mr. Rajesh can do in x days.

Vishal can do in $2x$ days.

According to question,

$$\Rightarrow \quad \frac{1}{x} + \frac{1}{2x} = \frac{1}{28}$$

$$\Rightarrow \quad \frac{2+1}{2x} = \frac{1}{28} \Rightarrow \frac{3}{2x} = \frac{1}{28}$$

$$\therefore \quad x = \frac{28 \times 3}{2} = 42 \text{ days}$$

$\therefore$ Vishal can finish in $2x = 2 \times 42 = 84$ days.

51. (a)

52. (c)

53. (c)

54. (a) Prime factorisation of $1048 = 2^3 \times 131$

Prime factorisation of $1441 = 11 \times 131$

So, HCF of 1048 and 1441 is 131.

55. (b) I. Total students in the class = 25

II. Total students who have scored less than Rashmi = 8

By I and II statements together,

Rashmi's rank = 25 – 8 = 17th

So, both the statements together are needed.

56. (a) P A L E and E A R T H

 ↓ ↓ ↓ ↓   ↓ ↓ ↓ ↓ ↓

 5 2 9 3   3 2 6 8 1

So,

P E A R L

↓ ↓ ↓ ↓ ↓

5 3 2 6 9

57. (d)

58. (d)

59. (a) When is related to where.

Similarly, Time is related to Place.

60. (c) The pattern is as follows :

0, 2, 6, **12,** 20, 30, 42

+2 +4 +6 +8 +10 +12

61. (c) If > = +, < = −, + = ÷, # = ×, − = =, × = >, = = <

Then,

I. $9 - 7 \div 7 < 6$ $8 < 6$ (Wrong)

II. $7 \times 7 + 7 \div 7 < 7 \times 7 + 1$ $50 < 50$ (Wrong)

III. $7 + 7 - 7 \div 7 < 14$ $13 < 14$ (True)

IV. $9 \div 9 + 9 < 9$ $10 < 9$ (Wrong)

So, only III is correct.

62. (d) $\dfrac{2}{7} < 0.3 < \dfrac{4}{9}$

63. (a)

64. (d)

65. (a)

66. (d)

So, only Conclusion II follows.

67. (a) Required gain in percentage

$$= \left(15 + 15 + \frac{15 \times 15}{100}\right) = 30 + 2.25 \Rightarrow 32.25\%$$

68. (a) Here, $r = 2$ cm, $h = 2$ cm.

$\therefore$ Volume of cylinder $= \pi r^2 h$

$$= \frac{22}{7} \times 2 \times 2 \times 2 = \frac{176}{7} \text{ cm}^3$$

69. (a) $10584 \div 168 - 63$

$$\Rightarrow \frac{10584}{168} - 63 \Rightarrow 63 - 63 = 0$$

70. (a)

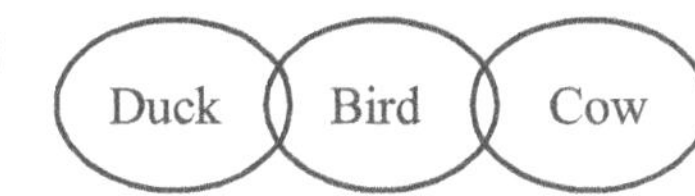

So, Neither I nor II follows.

71. (d) Here, $r = 2$ cm

Surface area of sphere

$$= 4_\pi r^2 = 4 \times \frac{22}{7} \times 2 \times 2 = \frac{352}{7} \text{ cm}^2$$

72. (a) $\therefore M_1 D_1 = M_2 D_2$

$$\Rightarrow 18 \times 7 = 15 \times D_2$$

$$\therefore D_2 = \frac{18 \times 7}{15} = 8.4 \text{ days}$$

73. (c)

74. (a)

75. (b) The pattern is as follows :

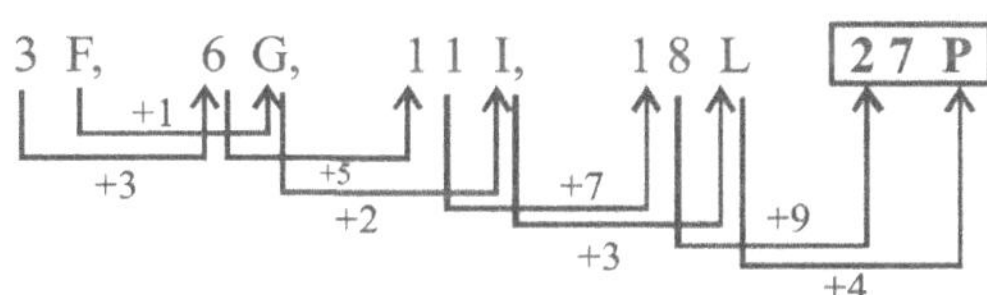

76. (a)

77. (d) Here,

$P = ₹600, r = 6\%, T = 4$ years, $A = ?$

$$\therefore \text{S.I.} = \frac{600 \times 6 \times 4}{100} = 144$$

$\therefore$ Amount $= 600 + 144 = ₹744.$

78. (a) CP $= 25$, SP $= 30$

$\therefore$ Profit $= 30 - 25 = 5$

$\therefore$ Gain percentage $= \dfrac{5}{25} \times 100 = 20\%.$

79. (d)

80. (d)

81. (a)

82. (c)

Sol. (83-85): Ashish > Govind > Kamal > Naren

Jayanth > Naren

83. (a) Ashish is the tallest.

84. (a) Naren is the shortest.

85. (d) Kamal is shorter than Govind →
Definitely true.

86. (a) Diamond is the hardest substance.
Diamond is called Gold. So, answer is
Gold.

87. (b)

88. (c)

89. (a) The cause of revolution cannot be
deduced from the given statement. So, I
does not follow.

However, the statement mentions that
industrial revolution brought about
modern age. This means that revolution
overhauls society. So, II follows.

90. (d) Distance between the buses

$$= 10 \times \frac{5}{60} = \frac{5}{6} \text{ Km}$$

Let the speed of the woman be x Kmph.

For the woman, $\dfrac{5}{6}$ Km is covered in 3

minutes with a relative speed of $(10 + x)$
Km/hr.

$$\frac{5}{6} = (10 + x)\frac{3}{60}$$

$$30 + 3x = 50$$

$$3x = 20$$

$$\therefore x = \frac{20}{3} = 6\frac{2}{3}$$

$\therefore$ Speed of woman $= 6\dfrac{2}{3}$ Kmph.

91. (d)

92. (a) The pattern is as follows.

$\Rightarrow n^3 + 1$ where n is a positive whole
number.

So, The next term will be

$(5^3 + 1) = (125 + 1) = 126.$

93. (d) Simplify :

$$(3y)^2 + x^2 - (2y)^2$$

$$\Rightarrow 9y^2 + x^2 - 4y^2$$

$$\Rightarrow 5y^2 + x^2 \text{ or } x^2 + 5y^2$$

94. (d) $\sin x = \dfrac{4}{5}$, then, $\sec x + \tan x = ?$

$$\because \sin\theta = \dfrac{p}{h} = \dfrac{4}{5}$$

$$\therefore b = \sqrt{h^2 - p^2} = \sqrt{(5)^2 - (4)^2} = \sqrt{25 - 16} \Rightarrow \sqrt{9} = 3$$

$$\therefore \sec x + \tan x = \dfrac{h}{b} + \dfrac{p}{b}$$

$$\Rightarrow \dfrac{5}{3} + \dfrac{4}{3} \Rightarrow \dfrac{5+4}{3} = \dfrac{9}{3} = 3.$$

95. (c)

96. (d)

97. (c)

98. (a) If, $A = \div, B = \times, C = +, D = -$

Then,

$$\Rightarrow 18 \times 12 \div 4 + 5 - 6 \Rightarrow 54 + 5 - 6 \Rightarrow 53$$

99. (d) Total students in a School $= 200$

$$\text{Total number of boy} = \dfrac{2}{5} \times 200 = 80$$

$\therefore$ Total number of girls $= (200 - 80) = 120.$

100. (a) Time taken in walking both the ways

$= 12$ hours 20 minutes   ...(i)

Time taken in walking one way and riding back

$= 9$ hours 50 minutes   ...(ii)

By the equation, (ii) $\times 2 - $ (i)

We get,

Time taken by her in riding both ways,

$\Rightarrow 19$ hours 40 minutes $- 12$ hours 20 minutes

$\Rightarrow 7$ hours 20 minutes

101. (a) $P = ₹6500$

$r = 4\%$

$T = 2$ years

C.I. $= ?$

$$\therefore \text{C.I.} = \left\{ P\left(1 + \dfrac{r}{100}\right)^t - 1 \right\}$$

$$\Rightarrow \left(6500\left(1 + \dfrac{4}{100}\right)^2 - 1 \right)$$

$$\Rightarrow \left[\left(6500 \times \dfrac{26}{25} \times \dfrac{26}{25}\right) - 1 \right]$$

$$= (7030.4 - 6500) = 530.4.$$

102. (c)

103. (d)

104. (c) Required ratio

$$= 169 \times \dfrac{2}{13} : 169 \times \dfrac{5}{13} : 169 \times \dfrac{6}{13}$$

$$= 26 : 65 : 78.$$

105. (c) $2.\overline{56} = 2 + \dfrac{56}{99} = 2\dfrac{56}{99}$

106. (a)

107. (d)

108. (c) Total amount after 1 year

$$= 4000 + \dfrac{4000 \times 1 \times 5}{100} \Rightarrow 4200$$

Total Principal for second year $= 4200 + 4000 = 8200$

$\therefore$ Total Amount after two years

$$= 8200 + \dfrac{8200 \times 5 \times 1}{100} \Rightarrow 8200 + 410 \Rightarrow 8610$$

109. (c)   110. (c)

111. (d) Here,

SP $= 17,000$

Loss $= 15\%$

So, CP

$$= \dfrac{100 \times 17,000}{(100 - 15)} = \dfrac{100 \times 17,000}{85} = 20,000$$

Now, CP = 20,000

Profit = 15%

So, SP $= \dfrac{20000 \times 115}{100} = 23,000$

∴ Selling Price of the bus = ₹23,000.

112. (d)

113. (b) According to given data,

Third tournament was the best for the team.

114. (a) According to given data,

Seventh tournament was the worst for the team.

115. (a) Total number of matches played = 50

Total number of matches won = 29

∴ Required percentage

$= \dfrac{29}{50} \times 100 = 58\%$

116. (c) Total number of matches did the team win during the year = 29 matches.

117. (d)

118. (a) Let the cost price of article is ₹ x.

∴ Required ratio $= \dfrac{104\% \text{ of } x}{108\% \text{ of } x}$

$= \dfrac{104}{108} = \dfrac{26}{27} = 26 : 27.$

119. (d) The pattern is as follows :

$$M\ O\ Q,\quad S\ U\ W,\quad Y\ A\ C,\quad \boxed{E\ G\ I}$$

$$+2\ +2\qquad +2\ +2\qquad +2\ +2\qquad +2\ +2$$

120. (c) $P = 14,000$

$r = 20\%$

$t = 6$ months

$A = ?$

When compounded quarterly,

then,

$P = 14,000$

$r = \dfrac{20}{4}\%$

$t = 6 \times 4 = 24$ months $= 2$ years

∴ $A = 14000\left(1 + \dfrac{20}{400}\right)^2$

$= 14000 \times \dfrac{21}{20} \times \dfrac{21}{20} = 15435.$

∴ After molarity, he will get ₹15,435.

www.ingramcontent.com/pod-product-compliance
Lightning Source LLC
Chambersburg PA
CBHW081405011025
33428CB00040B/1333